FEMINIST MANIFESTOS

FEMINIST MANIFESTOS

A Global Documentary Reader

Edited by
Penny A. Weiss
with Megan Brueske

NEW YORK UNIVERSITY PRESS
New York

NEW YORK UNIVERSITY PRESS
New York
www.nyupress.org

References to Internet websites (URLs) were accurate at the time of writing. Neither the author nor New York University Press is responsible for URLs that may have expired or changed since the manuscript was prepared.

ISBN: 978-1-4798-7180-3 (hardback)
ISBN: 978-1-4798-3730-4 (paperback)

For Library of Congress Cataloging-in-Publication data, please contact the Library of Congress.

New York University Press books are printed on acid-free paper, and their binding materials are chosen for strength and durability. We strive to use environmentally responsible suppliers and materials to the greatest extent possible in publishing our books.

Manufactured in the United States of America

10 9 8 7 6 5 4 3 2 1

Also available as an ebook

To every reader, *this feminism's for you:*

"ALL WOMEN married or not with or without children with or without a second job native or immigrant lesbian or straight" (New York 1975); "of different nations, classes, creeds and parties" (Netherlands 1915); "mothers, grandmothers, daughters, sisters, wives, and girlfriends" (Bulgaria 2010); "all women with disabilities, including aboriginal women, black women, Asian women, South Asian women, women of color, immigrant women, lesbians, older women, women in institutions and single mothers" (Ontario 1987); those "who have to send [their] daughters and sons to the soup kitchens because [they] have nothing to give them to eat, and those who still have something but don't know for how long" (Argentina 2002); those who are "midwives, spiritual leaders, healers, herbalists, botanists and pharmacists" (Malaysia 2004); "women activists, policy-makers, and scholars" (Japan 1997); "survivors of prostitution and trafficking" (Online 2005); those "born without wealth; [whose] education is very neglected" (Paris 1789); and those who "work in the halls of power, the halls of faith and the halls of [their] homes" (New York 2013).

And for the men who "promote the fight to eradicate gender violence" (Peru 2010) and "affirm that engaging men and boys to promote gender justice is possible and is already happening" (Brazil 2009), many of you "share the problems and anxieties" experienced by women "and join hands with them to remove social evils and obstacles to progress" (Johannesburg 1954).

And for the "Trans, Two Spirit, and Gender Non Conforming" (Brooklyn 2016), who are "particularly vulnerable to police brutality and criminalization" (California 2001) and who yearn for a world "where all people are valued equally irrespective of their gender identity and gender expression" (Malta 2009).

"[W]e cannot be indifferent on any occasion that appears nearly to affect the peace and happiness of our country" (North Carolina 1774). "[I]t has never been the case in history that any oppressed group has been emancipated without carrying out their own struggle" (Spain 1976). To start, "[W]e withdraw our consent from the institutions and practices that have put the world in peril" (Utah 2012). Next, we assert, "all rights are *human* rights" (Ohio 1850). Further, "We pledge ourselves to protect and promote women's rights, irrespective of individual political convictions, affiliations or religious belief" (Philippines 1958).

"We hope finally to free the word 'feminist' from the misunderstanding and uninformed prejudices under which it currently labours" (Hungary 1990). We are working "for a world where difference does not mean inequality, oppression or exclusion, as we struggle against all causes of oppression and discrimination" (Israel 2005).

"We women have been marching a long time" (Rwanda 2004).

"This time we are going all the way" (New York 1969).

* * *

Additionally, Penny dedicates this book to her friends and family, who for years listened to her with gracious indulgence about the latest declaration she had found. Megan dedicates this book to the strong women who shaped her: her Mom, who taught her everything and still models an endless thirst for knowledge; her Grandma Karen, who taught her love for books; and her Grandma Rita, who taught her love of education.

CONTENTS

PART III: 1900–1949

PART VI: THE TWENTY-FIRST CENTURY

PREFACE AND ACKNOWLEDGMENTS

I started collecting manifestos well over ten years ago. At first, I was looking for a way to introduce students to the range of issues that inform feminist inquiry and practice, and by using half a dozen or so manifestos I was able to provide a pretty good picture of the depth and range of feminist agendas. My feminist curiosity stayed piqued, however, and I continued to collect, truly unsure how many or what kind of documents were out there or even how to find them. The only ready-made lists were primarily of U.S. documents, and even those were problematic, as they included little from diverse identity groups or political traditions, and tended to focus on a few periods of unusually heavy activism and theorizing. I found the vast majority collected here by endless searching through the histories of individual countries and various population groups, on one hand, and studies of specific issues and feminist organizations, on the other. I used every search term (and combination thereof) I could think of, and chased down records of all sorts of conventions hoping for resolutions they might have passed. There are some documents I tried hard to track down but was ultimately unsuccessful at obtaining, such as the demands from the Egyptian Feminist Union in 1923, or the Brazilian Black Feminist Manifesto from 1975. Those I excluded, when choices had to be made, were primarily from a time or place or viewpoint already well represented. The United States dominates the early years, but after 1900, clearly does not. I hope readers who know of other manifestos will contact me at paw.fem@gmail.com. Perhaps we'll need another volume, or at least a way for people to learn what else is out there. Either way, having now read some three hundred documents, I can say that while reading some particular one, or a group of them on a specific issue or from a certain place or time, is exciting, reading them together is an entirely different experience. And I am certain more documents have yet to surface, documents that will continue to reshape our understanding of feminisms globally and historically.

This collection of documents from feminist groups, organizations, and meetings in over fifty countries (with representatives from most others present at international gatherings), spanning three centuries (with two earlier outliers), offers a powerful demonstration of how generations of advocates have understood, through constructive conversation and collective deliberation, the character of oppression and the possibilities for social justice. It is not so easy to envision feminism anew—but this set of documents invites us to rethink what feminism stands for and against and how it uses and creates processes of social change.

Because this assemblage of documents is unparalleled, and because most of the manifestos have not been read or used outside of the locales in which they were written, I put the individual documents themselves at the center of the enterprise. Each gets an introduction and, with the fewest possible exceptions, is reproduced in full. The individual introductions contextualize the declarations, providing information about the place and the organization or the meeting, as well as outlining some main points. I am thrilled to be able to include some photos and the graphics used to represent various groups; in fact, I chose NYU Press on the basis of their willingness—even their excitement—to publish so many documents and images.

I want to call attention to the agendas these documents establish. It is necessary to take back the phrase "feminist agenda" from opponents who infer that it is something hidden and nefarious. In reality, the priorities and principles shaping feminist agendas are broad, inspired, hopeful, and just, and we should proudly proclaim them. Too, it is worth emphasizing both that there is not *one* unchanging feminist agenda and that substantial common ground and traditions do exist amidst the diversity and evolution of multiple agendas. Differences point to the specifics of time and location (especially local history and politics), and the consequent multiplicity of approaches and creative combinations of ideologies; common ground points to adaptable but core political commitments.

I hope that feminist theorists will wrestle with the radical challenges these texts pose to common understandings of feminist schools of thought. I hope that transnational feminist scholars, and those interested in fuller representation of a more multicultural United States, will find the focus on collective yet unheralded international and "minority" voices novel and inspiring. I hope that readers from around the world will find their locations, cultures, and perspectives included in this retelling of feminist history and of contemporary feminist movements. Finally, as terms such as "post-protest culture" circulate, I hope that these declarations, agreed upon by people from countless social, economic, and cultural backgrounds, suggest ways to reinvigorate social activism and enhance the success of important contemporary movements.

I have chosen to organize this collection chronologically. The other obvious options were by issue or location. Structuring the book by issues would not work because, since most documents address multiple topics, it would require dividing single documents into multiple pieces, losing the important threads that connect them. Organization by region would definitely capture some distinctiveness that emerges from more local history, religion, politics, and culture. Geographical categories, however, cannot easily accommodate the multinational gatherings that gave rise to so many of the documents, or the similarities across geography. That left me with chronology, which is not only convenient but useful for watching development and influence. I have opted, however, not to organize by familiar historical eras since, as I say in the opening of the introduction, things like historical periods (the Enlightenment, etc.) are too often named and determined by what has happened to the more privileged, and we do not yet have a new, more inclusive set of markers. Centuries and parts thereof will have to do for now.

Writing this book allowed me to learn more than I have in any other academic venture (I learn the very most in my nonacademic ventures: parenting, first of all, and then gardening and tai chi). I have been privileged to have the time and assistance to do the fairly enormous amount of research this text required. I sincerely thank the Saint Louis University College of Arts and Sciences for a spring 2015 sabbatical semester, and the Dean's Office for another half-semester research leave in spring 2016 that allowed me to make great progress on this book. I owe a large debt of gratitude to several graduate research assistants over the last few years, also provided by Saint Louis University, who have played a part in this massive creation, including Heather Bozant Witcher and Emily Tuttle in the early years, and Stephanie Wallace and Amanda Hagedorn most recently. Lauren Kersey and Megan Brueske worked with me for two busy years in the middle, and we went through the process together of writing a prospectus. They pursued every lead to find documents I had heard of and then worked to get them organized. Lauren, our computer expert, made charts of where and when our documents came from, enabling me to check for the broad representation I wanted. Megan gets credit on the cover of having written this book "with" me, for she is quite simply an organizational wizard (something I am about as likely to be called as I am to be touted a computer maven). Without her, the large assortment of documents I collected in boxes over the years might never have been formatted and managed online. She and Lauren Kersey wrote several introductions to documents, too, though I finalized all of them and wrote the vast majority.

Somewhat surprisingly, nearly all of the declarations were available in English, though not always in the most grammatical English, and I made minor adjustments on a few. Here I should note that it is difficult to know sometimes what counts as the "original text" of these manifestos. Some of the documents were written in relatively remote locations, hastily transcribed or typed, finally posted and perhaps translated, well or poorly. My goal is to put their best faces forward, so to minimize attention to minor errors and typos, I preferred they be silently corrected, in general, or in some cases, made more readable through the use of brackets and ellipses. I thank my wonderful daughter Brennin Weiswerda for help with the final set of edits.

For the manifestos that did not come to me in English, I relied on my Saint Louis University connections for those translations that were necessary. I thank Ina Seethaler for a translation of the 1848 French manifesto, and Alexander Ocasio and Ana Heredero Garcia for their thoughtful work on the Spanish 2013 "Deciding Makes Us Free." Two translators, Madeleine Brink and Violeta Martinez Morones, now of Ardilla Translations, most ably tackled multiple documents originally in Spanish, some from convention notes: Argentina 1910, Mexico 1916, Spain 1936, Honduras 2013, and Spain 2016. All of the folks at NYU worked so hard editing and shepherding this beast of a manuscript. Thanks to Ilene Kalish, Alexia Traganas, and Emily Wright.

I thank Wynne Moskop for being the best writing buddy ever, the person with whom I have visited endless coffee shops and shared both my findings and my questions. I am grateful to my partner Robert for the way he has always celebrated my scholarship, and for his ridiculous ability to explain the political history behind every manifesto I asked him about. I owe much to the Saint Louis University Women's and Gender Studies Department, which both makes me crazy and keeps me sane (I trust most readers know exactly what I mean.). I wish for my children, Linden, Brennin, and Avian Weiswerda, now young adults, that you might continue to carry on in your own ways some of the inspired thinking and activism captured in these documents.

Introduction
Feminist Manifestos and Feminist Traditions

We know that we do not know about women's lives to the extent we know about men's. The sexes are not social equals, and all hierarchies of power require more attention to and celebration of those on the top, and anything associated with them.

> Men's physiology defines most sports, their needs define auto and health insurance, their socially designed biographies define workplace expectations and successful career patterns, their perspectives and concerns define quality in scholarship, their experiences and obsessions define merit, their objectification of life defines art, their military service defines citizenship, their presence defines family, their inability to get along with each other—their wars and rulerships—defines history, their image defines god, and their genitals sex. (MacKinnon 1988, 36)

What most affects their lives distinguishes one historical period from another, and the arenas in which they act (industrial, military, legal, etc.) are those in which the vital deeds worth recording are said to happen. Four things (at least) are usually left out of our histories that get the attention they are due in this book: the impact of these familiar events (wars, elections, globalization, etc.) on various groups of women, and the stories of diverse women acting within these familiar boundaries (i.e., at work, in political office), beyond them (in their communities, as victims of gender-based violence, as caregivers, raising crops, etc.), and in opposition to them (participating in protests, for example, and as members of feminist organizations). This collection thus adds to our growing understanding of what has heretofore been omitted, minimized, or misrepresented. In telling how women in widely different contexts understood and challenged the inequalities that colored so much of their existence, these declarations portray the realities of their daily lives, reveal their dreams, and testify to their practical political wisdom. They are incredible sources of information and inspiration.

It is curious, isn't it, that while feminism is a collective political movement, feminist scholars have not paid much attention to collectively written or ratified documents? Perhaps we remain convinced that great ideas come from individual geniuses laboring alone in dimly lit libraries. Perhaps, like academic institutions, we "count" coauthored pieces as worth less (for a faculty member coming up for promotion, say) than the essay penned by just one. Perhaps, too, the fact that the documents collected here are overwhelmingly written by groups of women, and often by marginalized women from less powerful countries, to boot, adds to their fragile hold on our attention. The common representation of collectively authored manifestos as "applied" or "activist" pieces, rather than more highly esteemed "theoretical" pieces, also contributes to our neglect of them. While all of these factors make our disinterest in feminist declarations more understandable, the neglect is ultimately unjustified and unfortunate. It results in a loss of knowledge of the continuous tradition of feminist praxis around the world, and renders invisible the theory embedded in most manifestos. That loss of knowledge reflects and feeds disrespect for women and feminism, and allows ridiculous myths about both to thrive.

The inattention to collectively authored documents also misses the fact that something important happens in the process of collective deliberation and writing that explains why the practice is so popular among feminists and what these documents contribute. First, collective authorship means that feminist manifestos not only *inspire* political action but also are the *outcome* of, or *reflect* feminist action—a diversity of voices, informed by experience and reflection and dialogue, together confronting enormous practical and theoretical problems. These documents are clearly collaborations—"cooperative endeavor[s] involving two or more people that result in a rhetorical product" that is "constructed and completed through the direct and indirect contributions of" many (Buchanan 2003, 43), each negotiating a variety of opinions in a context requiring a high degree of consensus. Communications scholar Lindal Buchanan insightfully argues that historically, "collaboration permitted women not only to negotiate gender norms but also to challenge and reshape them through the assumption of new discursive roles in the public forum" (45). Collectively written manifestos help create feminist space and actors.

Next, manifestos bring life to the realization that "[t]o let the 'other' speak requires the invention of multiple methods that subvert racist, heterosexist, and imperializing language" (Hurtado 2003, 217). Manifestos differ dramatically in form, one resembling an indictment, another an oath; one an essay, another a letter; one a set of demands, another a set of principles. This suppleness both allows different voices to find expression and permits the document to reflect its "embeddedness in a particular time and place" (Weeks 2013, 217). Flexibility in form means that we hear from the unflinchingly angry, the necessarily dogged, and the unapologetically passionate; from historical, political, and cultural viewpoints; and in analytical, statistical, rhetorical, and narrative tones. Form can fit the needs of equality.

Another admirable aspect of collective feminist declarations is their tendency to contain elements of both theory and practice, and still to be written in ways that prioritize accessibility. As cultural theorist Gloria Anzaldúa wrote, "High theory does not translate well when one's intention is to communicate to masses of people made up of different audiences. We need to give up the notion that there is a 'correct' way to write theory" (1990, xxv). Ideally, feminists desire an ongoing conversation between experience and theory, allowing each to inform the other as both continue to develop. In feminist manifestos, the critiques and the visions focus on the concrete, daily consequences of ongoing and possible practices as well as the ideologies behind them. Deep understandings of the dynamics of social change and stability emerge in the documents, as do clear conceptions of the relationships among various economic, political, religious, and social structures and systems.

Finally, feminists repeatedly claim that "theory should . . . come . . . from the collective experience of the oppressed—especially that of women of Color" (Hurtado 2003, 215). That edict speaks to the importance, even the centrality, of the feminist manifesto as a tool and as data—a site where a diversity of women's experiences, knowledge, concerns, and demands never fades into invisibility. In all eras, collaboration has been "crucial in bringing marginalized women to public voice" (Buchanan 2003, 45). Thus, manifestos allow us to hear from the professional and the educated, the more privileged and the politically experienced, and also from the battered, the prostituted, and the illiterate, and from the poor, the peasant, the indigenous, and the "untouchable," often while attending the same meeting.

Generally speaking, the manifesto, which "has played so decisive a role in the history of radical democracy and dissent" (Lyon 1991, 101), is "a subversive, marginal writing" (Yanoshevsky 2009b, 257). Collective feminist manifestos are a distinctive subgroup. The manifestos included here are assertions of agency that function to establish working groups, build community, and direct joint actions and relationships. They are critical, oppositional pieces that make the marginalized more central and visible, suggest new ways of interpreting the familiar, and propose alternatives to it (Yanoshevsky 2009a). They are creative, strategic, and theoretical political acts. They assume the validity and power of political discourse even while they critique the existing forms and content of it. They hope to be factors in emancipation and social transformation. Untapped feminist declarations fill in gaps we have not even always recognized.

Criteria for Inclusion

As just discussed, my first criterion for inclusion was that a document be collectively authored, even though that meant omitting many important and lovely ones written by individuals.[1] Still, authorship is not always easy to pinpoint when one is dealing with usually unsigned manifestos, and I would not be surprised to find that something slipped in here that was singly authored, though even that would have gone through some collaborative discussion and ratification at a convention or other gathering. Short political treatises written and/or ratified by feminist groups and communities working together to critique inequality and envision equality constitute a fascinating subgenre that surely merits its own study.

Next, in terms simply of genre, the "ideal" document for this collection

- reveals and criticizes an unjust status quo;
- offers visions of more egalitarian, respectful, democratic communities; and
- addresses strategies for bringing about change.

Not all the entries in this volume were overly accommodating with regard to these criteria, for rarely do they come with such tidy subtitles as "grievances," "alternatives," and "tactics." But every manifesto, more or less explicitly, surely contains one or more of these items. They offer critiques of a practice, a policy, an institution, a society, an ideology, or all of the above. Some focus their gaze on a particular issue (prostitution, political participation, education) or cluster of them (working conditions, war and peace, reproduction), while others tackle an even broader range. Both the specific and the general are important, as together they provide that perfect complement of breadth and depth.

While I remain convinced that one consequence of domination is an impoverishment of the imagination, these documents amply demonstrate that cracks necessarily develop in every situation and institution through which we can indeed glimpse and envisage something better. We learn from them about alternative ways of structuring our families and our communities, of describing citizens and supporting workers, of distributing resources and sharing burdens. In this aspect, manifestos are "exercises in thinking collective life and imagining futurity, . . . a species of utopianism" (Weeks 2013, 217). The visions of alternatives in the manifestos incorporate every arena in which we move: where we *should* find ourselves in legal systems and workplaces, how we *should* be represented in the media and in schoolbooks, what sorts of families and communities we might actually *choose* to be a part of, etc. It is often astonishing, really, just how much people are able to generate, together, while living in the midst of oppressive and even downright dystopian conditions, for every document reveals that what we are up against is deeply ingrained in social structures and practices, internalized in every individual to some extent or another, naturalized by religions and science, and enforced by governments and public opinion. Part of the explanation for this generative energy is the power of the collective process itself, the commitment and ideas created within a group that make change seem truly possible. In the positive resolutions we perhaps come the closest to finding self-described feminist agendas, a *history* of *global feminist agendas*, that the reader can watch evolve and adapt to particular circumstances. Many know more about what feminism supposedly stands for as told by antifeminists than as told by feminists. Here are the other stories.

The next ground for inclusion was that these be *feminist* declarations. Rather than prejudging, I used the contents of the documents themselves to create the following criteria, not as a checklist but for a general sense of what fit together:

- They are based on listening to previously silenced stories; as the documents repeatedly assert, they base their analyses especially (though not exclusively) on women's experiences and viewpoints and visions, and they understand that the failure to do so is a measure of the problem.
- They openly characterize the wrongs women and other marginalized groups suffer as injustices that are injurious to them, their families, and their communities, and advocate equal treatment and opportunity, equal dignity and respect.
- They grasp the problem of and the solutions to oppression as political, and the struggle for change as necessarily collective—an endeavor through which people learn together and devise actions through negotiation for common goods and individual possibility.
- They usually include consciousness of at least some forms of diversity among women, and at least some common ground or shared fate with certain men. Groups often strive both to work across these differences and to discover commonalities.
- They holistically address the multiple roles that women fulfill and perform, some chosen and some decided for them, sometimes enacted simultaneously, sometimes serially, usually varying over the lifespan (worker, citizen, activist, community member, family member, etc.), and consider what the demands of equality say about how these roles might be reconceived and reconstructed.
- With a focus set on the local as well as beyond it, they reflect a flexibility in and accommodation to resources and situations through their almost endless variety of strategies.
- They both recommend and use structures and strategies that are overwhelmingly and broadly democratic. They seek ever more social justice, individual flourishing, and peaceful, inclusive, and participatory communities.

Finally, and perhaps most controversially, I gave preference to the grassroots documents and thus, the groups who wrote the treatises I have chosen are not affiliated with governments or with the United Nations, though they may be in conversation with them. You will not find here even the most familiar: the UN's 1979 Convention on the Elimination of All Forms of Discrimination Against Women (CEDAW) or the 1995 Beijing Platform for Action. Why not?

First, documents written by independent (especially grassroots) groups seem likeliest to offer the clearest, least inhibited expressions of women's needs and desires, and are most apt to capture pictures of women's daily experiences as they see them. The authors of these documents decide for themselves whose lives to represent, what issues to highlight, what practices to criticize, what risks to take, and what language to express themselves in to what audiences, without over-whelming concern about the receptivity or hostility of the state or of funding agencies. The term "grassroots" has many meanings:

> [It] suggests being outside the control of any state, church, union, or political party. . . . being free from any constraining political affiliations and being responsible to no authority except their own group, . . . mainly concerned with local issues, with what affects ordinary people every day. The media and public opinion are preoc-cupied with the spectacular, with the activities of celebrities. What's more, the par-ticipants in grassroots movements are ordinary women attempting to accomplish necessary tasks, to provide services rather than to build power bases . . . [and] to transform politics in far more democratic directions than ever seemed possible. (Kaplan 1997, 6–7)

As I will discuss in a moment, these manifestos are not free from all traditional political affiliation, in that working within a union or talking to a party was often deemed constructive. But they all do have a great degree of autonomy and even challenge the organizations with which they are affiliated.

Second, the authors of these documents, even absent outside "officials" or "experts," clearly possess expertise sufficient for their task. Feminism in all its va-rieties and manifestations over time has increasingly sought to reclaim and le-gitimize the voices of the silenced and the marginalized, those deemed irrational or incredible, those written off as being without virtue, merit, or respectability. These writings only occasionally contain the "whereas" and "affirming that" rife in state documents. They do not spend pages defining terms and listing account-able bodies and similar treaties and legal norms in anticipation of lawsuits and parliamentary debates. Instead, their style varies widely, the texts are accessible, the audiences numerous. Legalese does not mute the passion or the sense of cri-sis. Focusing on independent groups, all this is to say, gives us the best shot at contributing to that project of reclaiming and legitimizing silenced and marginal-ized voices.

Third, to the extent that *any* declarations are taken seriously, used as resources to help us understand movements and groups and eras, those I leave out are most likely to be the recipients of attention, even though these tend to be the longest, most formal and legalistic of the genre. Thus, I follow a feminist trend of bringing light to the least studied and most marginalized, even among texts, and privilege accessibility (Weiss 2009).

Finally, the selected documents include a story about the complicity of gov-ernments in sustaining inequality and the limits of the UN and some NGOs (they call it "NGO-ization") in bringing about social transformation. I take this critique seriously. The Feminist Collective of Istanbul writes,

> Everyday three women are killed in Turkey. The murderers and the rapists receive no punishments. The state is not trying to stop the violence against women, but [is] try[ing] to stop the divorces. AKP (Justice and Development Party, which is the gov-ernment) . . . has taken our right of abortion. . . . [and limited] contraceptive methods. The government doesn't hesitate to step forward in order to control the women's

body. They are preparing the laws which are going to condemn us to [a] flexible and insecure work life. (Istanbul 2014)[2]

Even when states are not so actively complicit, these declarations show, the promise of inclusion in a constitution or the signing of a UN document turns out to leave the status quo remarkably unchanged, and so we need at least to look elsewhere.

In general, intergovernmental, UN, and even some transnational feminist documents tend to be more reformist than radical, more policy oriented than multifaceted, more professional than lay. Feminism (as an ideology and a practice) simply cannot be defined or limited by governments, and governmental action is not going to bring about feminist revolution. We need to hear the conversations of ground-level feminists coming to consensus on what is wrong with the status quo and how to change it toward what ends. Working with and/or within the machinery of the state or the UN is often useful, often included as a strategy, and understood as a necessity or benefit in certain circumstances, but that is always only part of the story. The Managua Declaration of 2006 offers three criticisms: "the United Nations system is presently in a debilitated state"; "[s]tates do not respond adequately to the human rights discourse" (especially as opposed to "the market"); and UN documents such as "the objectives of the Development of the Millennium will not be effective unless they incorporate" more fully racial, ethnic, and gender perspectives. Via Campesina contrasts the recommendations it offers with the neoliberal, capitalist ones "of the FAO and the governments" (Jakarta 2013).[3]

A small minority of declarations included here do mention or appeal to UN and intergovernmental documents. They do so because those documents offer legitimacy and cover, and can be used to call governments to account by their own standards as signatories to treaties, bodies obligated to follow their constitution, etc. Less cynically, the Beijing Platform inspired many of those who are active today to build and continue feminist movements locally and in coalition, and CEDAW remains the high-water mark of international documents opposing sex-based discrimination. Still, these international documents are easily available and, given their great length, I opt to save space for less heralded but nonetheless informative, distinctive, and inspiring others.

Two similar types of documents fell between those I clearly wanted and those I wanted to exclude: the state charter and the national manifesto. These, too, tend to be lengthy, reformist, policy-oriented documents heavily influenced by major NGOs, though they generally arise from a more collaborative process committed to feminist goals. They are often written in response to mainstream political events such as elections and the writing of new constitutions. There are a great number of them, as is evident in the appendix, and in the end I decided to include three as samples of the genre. Most charters were written within ten years of each other, and follow very similar patterns. They have the definite advantage of dealing with numerous aspects of the role of the state in social change, and should neither be ignored nor equated with the more wide-ranging history of feminist manifestos.[4]

Learning from the Manifestos

It is a daunting task to summarize what I have learned from compiling and researching these documents. The lessons are so numerous, the links among documents almost endless. Below I use multiple resolutions and manifestos to support each of the following points: while (1) there is no feminist utopia, (2) feminist activism has arisen in almost every conceivable setting, (3) usually involving coalition building and (4) demonstrating a determination to be heard, (5) not always in the most "agreeable" language, but (6) with a broad commitment to democracy and (7) touching on most social issues.

No Feminist Utopia

"Nowhere in the world . . . have women received their rightful share of their country's wealth or been fully represented in the political process; nor have they benefited equally from the education and health systems" (Tolunay 2014). Simply put, there is no feminist utopia to which you somehow failed to receive an invitation. Among the documents in this collection, some emanate from countries listed as among the "best" on international rankings of gender equality, others from countries listed among the "worst."[5] Patriarchy is alive and all too well, mingling ubiquitously with a large cohort of friends, including racism, classism, colonialism, heterosexism, and ableism.

As mentioned above, virtually every document in this collection contains some extractable list of complaints, grievances, or problems. The political ventures that are recommended begin—it makes perfect sense—with a collective sense of material, social, intellectual, and spiritual exclusion, suffering, violence, dissatisfaction, despair, and/or outrage. Many of the problems could not seem more obviously troubling; nonetheless, the societies from which the documents emerge ignore the issues or fail to prioritize them (or, worse, sometimes call them social goods, or individual virtues), and so the rethinking involved is a deep, difficult, and ongoing project that encounters multiple tides of resistance.

To be sure, then, sometimes these declarations induce despair. The lists of grievances are lengthy, varied, specific, evolving, and, like systems of domination, touch every area of life.

- Documents from the United States in the mid-nineteenth century list problems including the lack of suffrage and ineligibility for office; unequal property rights; unequal educational and employment opportunities; the enslavement of millions; double moral and sexual standards; and lack of choice regarding marriage and absence of remedies for marital rape.
- The list of wrongs in the 1954 South African Women's Charter a century later includes laws and conventions that deny women the right to own, inherit, or alienate property and that treat women as minors subject to husbands; anxieties imposed by poverty; and a society divided into poor and rich, non-European and European, the harshly treated many and the privileged few.
- The list from NOW in 1966 mentions tokenism and the underrepresentation of women in high-level positions in industry and government; sex segregation in the labor force and unequal pay for equal work; extra burdens on women of color; feminism as a dirty word; unequal marriages; lack of access to childcare; images of women in the media that perpetuate contempt for them; and political party disinterest in sexual equality.
- The New Zealand Working Women's Charter of 1977 laments the continued existence of discrimination based on sex, race, marital and parental status, sexuality, and age; unequal pay for equal work; unequal educational opportunities, including

vocational training; a long, inflexible work week; unsafe working conditions; inadequate attention to the needs of ethnic women; limited childcare; unpaid parental leave with no job security; limited sex education, costly birth control, and poor access to abortion services.

- The document from the 1997 Okinawan conference on militarism raises the effects of U.S. military bases on the social environment; lack of firm environmental guidelines for the cleanup of toxic military contamination; violence against women perpetrated by U.S. military personnel; money being spent on the U.S. military by taxpayers that could be devoted to socially useful programs benefiting women and children; land devoted to military use that could be developed to benefit local people rather than investors and transnational corporations; and media that refuse to investigate and report on all these issues.
- The 2007 Women's Declaration of Food Sovereignty claims that as a result of neoliberal and sexist policies, we suffer poverty, inadequate access to resources, patents on living organisms, rural exodus and forced migration, war, and all forms of physical and sexual violence. It states that monocultures and the widespread use of chemicals and genetically modified organisms harm the environment and human health, particularly reproductive health. The industrial model and transnationals, it continues, threaten the very existence of peasant agriculture, small-scale fishing, and herding, all sectors where women play a major role.
- The 2014 Indian Women's Charter contains a long catalogue of grievances that includes increasing violence against women; crimes in the name of honor; piecemeal legislation that does not fully address gender-based issues; a conservative backlash; inadequate enforcement of laws demanding equal treatment; unrelenting rise in food prices; and privatization of public services.

Just these few lists of wrongs show that what are readily referred to or identified as "women's issues"—for example, reproduction, sexual violence, childcare, employment and educational opportunity, and so on—do, in fact, form a set of core concerns across time and place. But there is definitely more to the story. In the documents, we will see these "traditional" feminist issues associated with rather than separated from political life generally, challenging the boundaries often used to justify their irrelevance or consignment to "special interest" politics. Employment opportunity is linked to issues from trade unionism to globalization, for example, just as reproductive freedom is variously related to religious fundamentalism, war, and definitions of work. Consequently, there is an insistence that we treat things like "gender-based violence as a community's responsibility instead of making it a 'women's issue'" (Kampala 2003), just as we do other issues of such magnitude and significance to the entire social fabric. The 1994 Women's Declaration on Population Policies asserts,

> [A] wide range of conditions . . . affect[s] the reproductive health and rights of women and men. These include unequal distribution of material and social resources among individuals and groups; . . . changing patterns of sexual and family relationships; political and economic policies that restrict girls' and women's access to health services and methods of fertility regulation; and ideologies, laws and practices that deny women's basic human rights.

Public and private are bridged, as the economic touches the personal, which influences the social, and so on. Feminist issues are not somehow cordoned off from general community issues, and are most successfully addressed if they are deemed relevant to the general welfare.

A second point about scope is that supposedly gender-neutral or nongendered political questions contain gendered dimensions. The fact that issues from immigration and genetic engineering to war and poverty appear repeatedly in feminist manifestos might astonish those with a contracted conception of feminism's agendas over time. The 2008 Women's Declaration to the G8 on the global food crisis points out that

> support for small farmers must include a focus on women, who produce most of the world's food, [but whose] capacity . . . is badly undermined by laws and customs that discriminate against women. In many countries, women . . . are not even recognized as farmers. They are denied the right to own land and excluded from government programs that facilitate access to credit, seeds, tools, and training.

The failure to perceive and attend to this gendered dimension of agriculture contributes to the failure to resolve the food crisis and women's oppression. In the recorded history we know, it seems every question at least has gendered dimensions.

While many of the grievances refer to well-known events, the focus on women and gender brings less familiar, less visible aspects of those events directly to center stage. We read, for example, about the effects of nuclear testing on fertile women and their children, the impact of genetic engineering on Indigenous communities, and the consequences of religious fundamentalism for relationships between the sexes. These neglected declarations thus offer essential information, voices, and ideas that fill out and redirect political conversations that regularly disregard or marginalize certain lives. Some form of marginalization is a sad universal in this collection: "The history of our country the past hundred years, has been a series of assumptions and usurpations of power over woman, in direct opposition to the principles of just government" (1876 Declaration of Rights).

Importantly, these documents insist that the various crises they address "demonstrate that this [patriarchal capitalist global] system is not viable. Financial, food, climate and energetic crises are not isolated phenomena, but represent a crisis of the model itself, driven by the super exploitation of work and the environment. . . . We [feminists] need to advance in the construction of alternatives" (Brazil 2009). The lists of grievances, so many of which are repeated across time and place despite containing different emphases and forms, constitute a broad indictment of patriarchal culture, politics, institutions, and relationships, as well as of racism, colonialism, and ableism.

On the subject of that which induces despair, the most disheartening element in the documents, even those of the last twenty years, may be the extent to which they believe that women's status has not improved much, even as it has altered. The Abuja Declaration (1989), for example, says that "several studies on women in development suggest that the condition of women has worsened: they are poorer, live in increasingly hazardous environments and have lost the supportive mechanisms of the past." It also notes how "little progress has been achieved in [the] elimination [of] hazardous traditional practices, such as early marriage and pregnancy, female circumcision, nutritional taboos, [and] inadequate child spacing and unprotected delivery." The 2008 declaration from the First Asian Rural Women's Conference in India claims that "the process of neo-liberal globalization . . . [has] exacerbated human and labour rights violation[s] and economic injustices." The pan-Canadian young feminist gathering (2008) points out that "[i]n reality, many of the demands of our feminist mothers and grandmothers remain unmet. . . . Violence is normalized, sexual abuse eroticized. Our sexual health education is inadequate and our reproductive rights are disrespected. Our needs are not being met." Finally, the 2011 Kuwait Declaration on Gender Equality starkly contrasts "the winds of democratic change which have strongly swept the Arab world [with] the increase in attempts to exclude and discriminate against women, as well as the development of violations of women's rights by certain extremist groups." Even when women have made gains in education, obstacles still prevent them from making full use of their training; where laws have changed, their "implementation is very poor and disappointing" (Nepal 2011), the laws proving impotent against sexist culture and religious practices. Even where women have entered the halls of power, they are not always heard. Where progress has been made, new forces arise that threaten it. Incremental change is slow and uncertain.

Further, many gains are in fact fragile. Dating back at least to the 1876 Declaration of Rights of the Women of the United States, victories are understood as only partial, tenuous, and ever-threatened holds on sexual equality:

> But the privileges already granted in the several states are by no means secure. The right of suffrage once exercised by women in certain States and Territories, has been denied by subsequent legislation. . . . Laws passed after years of untiring effort, guaranteeing married women certain rights of property, and mothers the custody of their children, have been repealed in States where we supposed all was safe. Thus have our most sacred rights been made the football of legislative caprice, proving that a power which grants, as a privilege, what by nature is a right, may withhold the same as a penalty, when deeming it necessary for its own perpetuation.

Spain liberalized abortion laws in 2010 and then tried to roll them back in 2013. The rising forces of extremism today are rolling back women's gains in the areas of marriage, employment, and education, in multiple nations (Tajikistan 2000). As wastefully frustrating and time-consuming as reinventing the wheel, repeatedly waging the same battles generation after generation, in one location and then another, depletes and demoralizes, and requires vigilant watch over past victories while new issues are continuously tackled.

Even women's sense of self is still an issue. In the 1848 Declaration of Sentiments, one complaint was that man "has endeavored, in every way that he could, to destroy her confidence in her own power, to lessen her self-respect, and to make her willing to lead a dependent and abject life." A century and a half later, the 1990 Serbian Women's Party Charter of Intentions observes a need to "promote women's self-confidence and their faith in their own abilities, strength and maturity to fight independently for legal rights and genuine interests of their own." The 1990 Independent Women's Democratic Initiative includes a call for "assertiveness-training courses," speaking yet again to a lack of confidence in one's own voice. In the 1991 Riot Grrrl Manifesto, there is still talk of a desire "and need to encourage and be encouraged in the face of all our own insecurities." At the Black Women in Europe 1991 conference, there was a call "that EC training programmes . . . encompass assertiveness and confidence-building."

The recurrence of this theme is startling, and related to the long-denigrated status of feminism. Regarding feminism, supporters of the Declaration of Sentiments

(1848) foresee encountering "no small amount of misconception, misrepresentation, and ridicule [as they] enter . . . upon the great work before us." One hundred and sixty years later, the Guatemalan Feminist Declaration describes a system that "responds to any challenge with the use of violence against our bodies, criminalization, smear campaigns, and repression against our movements." Sigh.

There Has Always Been Feminist Movement

What this repeated telling of injustices and injuries amounts to is that around the world, under every sort of political regime, in every era and possible set of circumstances, there has been feminist resistance—still mostly but never exclusively consisting of women, working together to create a world in which wealth *is* more equally distributed, in which more voices *are* represented in the political process, in which the media responsibly tackle important issues, in which concern for the environment is prioritized, where social priorities are more humane, and in which every citizen does benefit equally from the education and health systems, among others. Feminists protest, rewrite policies, boycott, organize, lobby, speak out, educate, and set up alternative institutions as they challenge, to cite just one cluster of issues, child sex abuse; child labor; child soldiers; child marriage; child custody; children living in poverty; discrimination against children based on disability, ethnicity, race, and class; inaccessible and culturally insensitive public childcare; and poor education, especially of girls.

- In 1789 Paris, working women of the Third Estate (who were often mistaken for prostitutes because they, too, sold their labor publicly) did not have the right to meet, to petition the king, or to vote in elections, yet they did indeed meet, and draft a written document to the king, and, "in a gesture of revolutionary hopefulness," described their present lives and their hopes for the future (Moore, Brooks, and Wigginton 2012, 222).
- Young factory women in Lowell, Massachusetts—girls, really, whose meager wages were reduced in 1836—organized one of the first labor strikes in the United States. In their Constitution they argued "firmly and fearlessly" that they should be able to both develop and keep a good moral character while they worked in the mills, which they could only do if given due recompense for their work. They were seen but did not see themselves as easily seduced. They claimed the right to unionize and vowed to stand together as a united front.
- At the Second Annual Anti-Slavery Convention of American Women in 1838, Black and White women spoke over rocks crashing in and shouts from outside. They exited arm-in-arm and moved to another site when opponents actually burned down their convention hall. They resolved "[t]hat the Anti-Slavery enterprise presents one of the most appropriate fields for the exertion of the influence of woman, and that we pledge ourselves, with divine assistance, never to desert the work, while an American slave groans in bondage."
- In 2005, women from fourteen Canadian Inuit communities, perhaps 50 percent of them the victims of forced or attempted sexual violence as minors, shared stories in icy northern Quebec and then "demand[ed] that violence directed against women and children must stop. [It] is absolutely intolerable and must end," they wrote, and they painfully acknowledged, "Inaction perpetuates the cycles of violence."
- The Dalit women of Nepal, who endure a poverty rate of 90 percent, a life span of fifty-one years, an illiteracy rate of 80 percent, and a domestic violence rate of 75 percent, formed the Feminist Dalit Organization and wrote the 2007 Dalit Women's

Charter to "motiv[at]e destitute, oppressed and downtrodden Dalit women to live their lives with self-respect and social dignity" and because "[w]e believe that Nepal can be transformed into a fully democratic republic state . . . by ensuring the representation of Dalit women . . . in all aspects of state restructuring."

As mentioned, these documents indicate an ongoing concern about women's low sense of self and the resistance and backlash that follow feminist gains. But just as persistent is the belief in the potential power of women and of feminism. The Kigali Declaration (1997) affirms women's "resourcefulness in organizing for peace, stability, security and sustainable development." The Khatmandu Declaration of Indigenous Women (2011) treats as unquestionable "the will and determination of indigenous women to change the existing social relation based on domination, exclusion, exploitation and discrimination to a new order based on justice[,] equality and respect for human dignity." And the Combahee River Collective (1977) states, "Our politics evolve from a healthy love for ourselves, our sisters, and our community which allows us to continue our struggle and work." Such collective self-worth is a necessary condition of feminist social action fighting against the elements denigrating the marginalized and their movements.

One source of strength is the recovery of the history of women's activism that these documents (and this book, too) contribute to and use to justify and inspire continued resistance. The Gabriela Women's Party (Philippines 2007) is named for Gabriela Silang, an eighteenth-century Filipino revolutionary in the battle for independence from Spain. The African Feminist Forum (Ghana 2006) "acknowledge[s] the historical and significant gains that have been made by the African Women's Movement over the past forty years," and notes that "African Feminists led the way, from the grassroots level and up; they strategised, organized, networked, went on strike and marched in protest, and did the research, analysis, lobbying, institution building and all that it took for States, employers and institutions to acknowledge women's personhood." AMES, the Association of Salvadoran Women (Costa Rica 1981), lists the many groups of women who agitated in the 1970s, from peasant women to street vendors.

Another source of power is feminism, for these manifestos reveal that their authors find in feminism a sound explanation of major ills from which we suffer, a dynamic account of the internalization of domination, an accurate description of intersecting systems of oppression, a pragmatic understanding of the forces that resist equality, and a hopeful, profound vision of how else we might organize flourishing communities, from romantic partnerships and friendship groups to political organizations and nation-states. These feminist clarifications and illuminations keep making sense, especially but not only to the oppressed, generation after generation, keeping hope alive and activism growing.

Building Coalitions and Bridges

Feminists have long worked and continue to work within and with not only a broad diversity of progressive social and political organizations and movements but also nearly every political, ethnic, cultural, and religious tradition, in the name of sexual equality and social justice. Limits to this exist, of course, to the extent that some bodies define themselves in outright opposition to feminism; otherwise, coalitions exist either to inch along the more conventional or to challenge the more revolutionary, even when feminism is not at the center of the mission of some in the coalition.

- The 1649 petition to the British parliament, which is estimated to have contained as many as ten thousand signatures, is from women in the antimonarchical Leveller movement, who use the group's democratic tactics and principles to argue for their own political rights.
- The 1846 Petition for Women's Rights works within the framework of liberal democracy, arguing that if "all governments must derive their just powers from the consent of the governed," then "the present government of this state has widely departed from the true democratic principles upon which all just governments must be based by denying to the female portion of community the right of suffrage and any participation in forming the government and laws under which they live."
- The 1909 Resolutions from the Women's Trade Union League work to expand to females, who were excluded from all-male unions, the principles of the American Federation of Labor.
- The 1972 document "Jewish Women Call for Change" is written by committed Conservative Jews urging the convention of the Conservative Rabbinical Assembly to forsake past discriminatory practices in favor of women's right to participate in their groups' religious observances.
- Similarly, Musawah argues in 2009 that while "[m]any laws and practices in Muslim countries are unjust," the group can still work within their tradition and claim that "Qur'anic teachings encompass the principles of justice, equality, equity, human dignity, love and compassion, . . . values [that] can guide further development of family laws and practices in line with the contemporary notion of justice, which includes equality between the sexes and before the law."

Really, the list is endless. The 1973 Statement of Purpose of the National Black Feminist Organization says that their autonomous organizing will "strengthen the current efforts of the Black Liberation struggle." The 2014 Feminist Principles of the Internet emerges from a conference that worked "to bridge the gap between feminist movements and internet rights movements and look at intersections and strategic opportunities to work together as allies and partners." The 2014 Rural Women's Manifesto in Northern Ireland brings feminists together with folks working in rural development.

Four points about alliances are worth emphasizing. First, while virtually all feminist groups build coalitions, those with whom they connect vary, depending upon their politics. One feminist group is more likely to link with the Communist Party, another with the Christian Democrats, another with the Greens, yet another with a Women's Party. In most places, few responsive political parties even exist. Still, both common ground and differences exist among feminists, and those differences can be revealed in whether one's links are with the mainstream or the margins; the female-only or the all-genders groups; the state or civil society organizations; local collectives, regional groups, international coalitions, or all of the above.

Second, given what I said above about belief in the power and passion of feminism, something like an eternal hopefulness often exists in coalition building, a yearning that liberal-leaning groups will be at least modestly receptive to at least some feminist demands, so that cooperative efforts seem worth it. Such work does reap rewards, as numerous party platforms incorporate gender issues, for example, and groups oblivious to women's subordination commit themselves to ending some aspects of it. Coalitions also help in situations where funding of feminist organizations is low or reduced, and money difficult to raise. Such successes help sustain feminist groups and causes, can add to their legitimacy, and contribute to the strength of civil society and the stability of democracy, to which feminism is fundamentally committed.

The explanation for the consistent efforts toward coalition is pragmatic, but also philosophical. The 1976 Women's Liberation Front in Spain says, "[F]eminist struggle is linked to the combined action of all oppressed sectors to achieve democratic freedoms," while the more recent but similarly named California Women's Liberation Front (2014) adds, "We are enmeshed in overlapping systems of sadistic power built on misogyny, white privilege, stolen wealth, and human supremacism. As individuals, it is our responsibility to acknowledge those systems, overcome our entitlement, and make alliances with the dispossessed. Collectively, it is our task to bring those systems down." A commitment to certain coalitions is a commitment to an inclusive, intersectional feminism.

There are frequent mentions of sympathy and solidarity with oppressed groups across national boundaries, too. The Young Lords' Position Paper on Women (New York 1970) ends with a section on "Revolutionary Women" that includes the stories of five Puerto Rican women (Mariana Bracetti, Lola Rodriguez de Tio, Antonia Martinez, Blanca Canales, and Lolita Lebron) and two Vietnamese women (La Thi Tham and Kan Lich) resisting colonialism. The 2008 Guatemalan Feminist Declaration mentions resistance in Nicaragua, Mexico, and Haiti, as well as activism by indigenous women and labor leaders. Overall, then, feminists have accrued a great deal of experience with and knowledge about both oppressive and liberatory political processes. Further, an intersectional understanding of the different effects of domination on various populations is apparent across the globe. The only limit, as the Revolutionary Association of the Women of Afghanistan (2004) cautions, is that we "should never make cease-fires or deal with this or that faction of fundamentalists."

Long and short term, single and multi-issued, coalitions and alliances of overlapping groups build a movement. The commitment to coalition is a commitment to difficult work, to conversation about contentious issues, usually in the presence of unequal privilege and disadvantage (Reagon 1983). Some degree of common purpose does not entail easy agreement and should not allow conflict to be buried, especially in the longer run. "Building coalitions across significant differences between women is a hallmark of feminist activism" (Gilmore 2008, 7).

Getting Heard

Feminists, probably few are surprised to hear, generally do not have overwhelming social power or a surfeit of epistemic credibility, critics of "political correctness" notwithstanding. We have to fight for air space, for authority, for believability, for our right to protest, even for the basic legitimacy of our assessments and agendas. And that description of the status quo across the globe does not even reckon with the staunch opponents, who rally their forces precisely against demonized feminist stands on issues from reproductive justice to environmentalism to pacifism. In the face of both indifference and opposition, feminists take advantage of every opportunity to make their voices heard, just as they take advantage of openings in political movements and religious traditions. Coalitions, then, provide only part of the story of getting heard.

Some of the opportunities are in fact crises that either permit or require new voices. The crisis may be the taking of Native lands, as it was for the Cherokee Women's Council in the early 1800s, or the possible loss of land due to climate change, as it is for feminists in Fiji today (2014). The opportunity may be due to rare, widespread public outrage over civilian rape (India 2014), or to infuriation over rape in war (England 2004). Feminists speak out and get some press in the face of a growing conflict, as the International Conference of Women at the Hague (1915) and Australia Women's Peace Army (1916) did, or because of a new approach to or angle on a seemingly irreconcilable conflict, as both Israeli (2006) and Kurdish feminists (Turkey 2013) do. The opportunity may be presented by a political event on which a group hopes to exert influence, such as an upcoming international meeting (New York 2013), an election (South Sudan 2009), or the fall of a government (Hungary 1990). Feminist groups piggyback on events from the World's Fair (France 1878) to gatherings of the World's Social Forum (Brazil 2009). They announce their manifestos, and thus garner more publicity for them, on commemorative days, such as the Fourth of July (Philadelphia 1876), International Woman's Day (Palestine 2015, Honduras 2013), and International Day for the Elimination of Violence Against Women (Peru 2010). They write declarations in response to obnoxious speeches (Utah 2007 and 2012, and Washington D.C. 1896), and at regularly held gatherings and conferences, such as of the U.S. National Women's Party (1922) or the International Socialist Women's Conference (1907). They organize in answer to exclusion from all-male or male-dominated organizations, as did the Female Anti-Slavery Society (Massachusetts 1832), to neglect of their issues in organizations of which they are a part, as the anarcha-feminists (Norway 1982) and women of the Young Lords (New York 1970) did, or to the virtual invisibility or misrepresentation of their issues in general (Canada 2014).

These documents, all of these examples show, emerge from master strategists possessing practical wisdom, learning together about what is possible, and deeply involved in the politics and social world around them. Further, their documents and actions testify to great imagination (see the tactics employed by Sweden's Feminist Initiative, or Spain's Deciding Makes Us Free, for example), group perseverance, and a deep desire for justice. Speaking out is a chance not only to succeed on a particular issue but also to build or sustain feminist movement and to hear more marginalized voices in the process (Northern Ireland 2015). As detailed in the introductions to each manifesto, the process of collective writing often brings in quite large numbers of people and groups. The priority given to democratic process is high, based on knowledge about the effects of participation.

Democracy

There is much critique in these manifestos of standard political processes, workplace practices, and family dynamics and, in their place, advocacy of democratization at virtually every level. Some of the earliest and most persistent demands are for political rights and participation. The Zapatista Women's Revolutionary Law (1994) supports the right of all "women, regardless of their race, creed, colour or political affiliation . . . to participate in the revolutionary struggle in any way that their desire and capacity determine." Going a step beyond participation, the Riot Grrrl Manifesto (1991) speaks of interest "in creating non-hierarchical ways of being AND making music, friends, and scenes based on communication + understanding, instead of competition + good/bad categorizations." The European Charter for Women in the City (1994), too, insists on "egalitarian participatory processes," which "favour renewed ties of solidarity," and the Declaration of Sentiments (1848) focuses as much on democratic culture and society as on democratic government (Weiss 2009). The Women's Caucus Declaration (Seattle 1999) asks for transparency, open participation, inclusiveness, the consensus process, equal access to information, dialogue, democratization of dispute settlements, and gender and regional balance in all decision-making bodies. I could go on.

Feminists work to recognize and remove context-specific barriers to democracy. The Working Women's Charter (1974), for instance, criticizes and aims to remove "all legal and bureaucratic impediments to equality," wisely citing a long list of practices used antidemocratically, including "tenancies, mortgages, pension schemes, taxation, passports, control over children, social security payments, [and] hire purchase agreements." The Comilla Declaration (1989) opposes genetic engineering as linked to an antidemocratic view of some humans as superior to others, while many others speak and struggle against poverty and illiteracy as limiting democracy.

Democracy seems relevant everywhere, too, as the Australian group Women's Liberation (1971) advocates for "democratisation of the existing family institution," and the Women in Prison Manifesto (1985) calls for both "democratic control of the criminal justice and penal systems" and "prisoner participation in the organization of the prison."

Both democratic ideas and practices are widely endorsed in this collection, marking a connection that should, perhaps, be more celebrated. What is the nature of the connection?

Democratic concerns include who is at the table, what is on the agenda, the manner in which items will be discussed, who will be listened to, and how decisions will be made and implemented. The insistence on attention to inclusive processes clearly emerges from experiences of silencing, invisibility, tokenism, marginalization, and disillusionment; but it also arises, on the other hand, from an understanding of the democratic process as both educational and empowering for participants and linked to greater voice and sounder policy.

The women's movement itself is linked to democratic progress. There is recognition "that the process of social renewal cannot be truly democratic without an active, independent women's movement" (Russia 1990). The New Zealand Working Women's Charter (1977) states, "[F]eminist struggle is linked to the combined action of all oppressed sectors to achieve democratic freedoms." Hungary's Declaration of Intent (1991) also asserts, "The feminist movement is an organic part of Western democracy." Moreover, the 2011 Kuwait Declaration on Gender Equality notes that "equal participation of women and men is an essential element of democracy of peoples and societies," and one that feminism thus contributes to mightily.

Not only is feminism important to democracy, but democracy is also crucial to the women's movement. As the Chicago Women's Liberation Union said (1972), "We believe in democracy. . . . We are trying to act on our ideas." The importance of democracy to feminism is apparent in these documents in the attention paid to their own processes. (Democratization, I should note, is contrasted, as in the 1990 Yugoslavian Charter of Intentions, with "authoritarian consciousness and behaviour, . . . lust for power and dictatorship over human needs.") Briefly, regarding democracy in their internal politics, the pan-Canadian feminists (2008) declared themselves "committed to an ongoing process of critical self-reflection to inform and transform our movement." The Combahee River Collective (1977) states, "We believe in collective process and a nonhierarchical distribution of power within our own group and in our vision of a revolutionary society." The Sudanese Women's Declaration on Darfur (2008) calls for "regular dialogue between women constituencies in Darfur, between Darfuri women and the other Sudanese sisters, as well as between Sudanese women and the African Women Peace Networks." Like critical self-reflection and flattening of unnecessary hierarchies, dialogue is an enduring democratic value and practice, and a conscious commitment to difficult dialogue comes up repeatedly in these documents, whether between women and men, NGOs and states, citizens and repressive governments, or women of different cultures, races, and ethnicities.

Refusing to "Moderate" Feminist Voices

Perhaps the authors of these documents already knew how far being "nice" really gets women, all the advice about the womanly virtues of being accommodating, long-suffering, understanding, self-sacrificing, and gentle notwithstanding. Their advice to us seems to be to tell the truth and push for change. Abiding by rules of femininity in action does little more than doing nothing—preserving the status quo.

Thus, in 1836, the Lowell Factory Girls tell us the truth about the "danger and inconvenience" to which they are subjected by "ungenerous, illiberal, and avaricious capitalists." The Woman's Rights Convention Resolutions (Ohio 1851) call institutional and customary gender inequalities "criminal injustice," and chastise women for "reprehensible submissiveness" in their "unresisting toleration of them." In 1870, the Daughters of St. Crispin straightforwardly call the unequal pay women receive a "usurpation and fraud." The Colored Women's Congress in 1896 forthrightly condemns "all tendency toward mob rule, lynching, burning, and midnight marauding" as "a menace to every department of justice and the well-being of posterity." In 1909, the National Women's Trade Union League boldly asserts that "[a]ll wars in our day are wars for the extension of markets" and that "the industrial and social conditions" of women workers "are in time of peace disastrously influenced by the enormous expenditure of civilized nations upon battleships and other preparations for war, and in time of war by the depredations, cruelties, and horrors of war." The 1915 Resolutions from the International Congress of Women call such war "madness" and "horror . . . involving as it does a reckless sacrifice of human life and the destruction of so much that humanity has labored through centuries to build up." The 1969 Redstockings Manifesto does not mince words, either. "Women," it declares, "are an oppressed class. Our oppression is total, affecting every facet of our lives. Our humanity is denied. Our prescribed behavior is enforced by the threat of physical violence. . . . All men receive economic, sexual, and psychological benefits from male supremacy." In 1970, the Women's Caucus of the Young Lords Party challenges machismo, which it describes as "sexual fascism, men putting themselves at the head of everything without considering women," and concludes frankly, "[M]achismo means physical abuse, punishment and torture." In 1973 the National Black Feminist Organization openly charged "the distorted male-dominated media image" of feminism with "cloud[ing] the vital and revolutionary importance of this movement to Third World women, especially black women," and the Combahee River Collective in 1977 stated directly that "eliminating racism in the white women's movement is by definition work for white women to do," and promised, "[W]e will continue to speak to and demand accountability on this issue." Finally, the Norwegian Anarchafeminist Manifesto of 1982 reminds us that, quite simply, "female power and female prime ministers will neither lead the majority of women to their ends nor abolish oppression." These forceful messages cross borders of time and place, politics and race, and inspire continued truth telling over covering up and making nice.

I do not underestimate the work it takes for women to overcome socialization and the pressure put on them to be nice. I do not underestimate the interpersonal value of niceness, either. But when only certain types of civility are behavioral norms, when those norms are imposed disproportionately on women and marginalized others, and when they are imposed especially when such groups defend themselves or work for equality, then what we have is not really a valuing of civility, which feminists advocate, but a defense of inequality and a practice of silencing. Nothing uncivil or impolite is inherent in challenging gender-based violence, or demanding fair media representation of people of color, or asserting that women's rights are human rights; more regularly, both incivility and false politeness are used to maintain inequality, which in turn supports incivility toward some.

Education

Taken together, the manifestos offer comprehensive, feminist treatment of numerous issues. Education is one of many specific recurring concerns in this set of documents, and I use it here as an example of the sophistication, continuity, and expansiveness of feminist analyses. (So many other topics are also worth a comparative, thematic treatment, both across time and place and within certain eras and regions, from childhood and religion to men and care work.) The problem was put in effective and blunt terms by the Women's National Coalition of the African National Congress (1994): education "has been male oriented, inaccessible, inappropriate and racially discriminatory."

The most basic complaint regarding education relates to girls' and women's lack of or unequal access to educational opportunities: The charge that "[h]e has denied her the facilities for obtaining a thorough education—all colleges being closed against her" (New York 1848) precedes consequent calls for girls to receive "institutional education in all the intellectual and physical disciplines" (Tajikistan 2000), to have "equal access to education, equal opportunities for higher education, and . . . free[dom] to choose [one's] subject of study" (New York 1997), and to climb "higher up the diploma ladder" (Abuja 1989). The broadest basis of the demand for equal educational opportunity is "that men and women are born equally free and independent members of the human race, equally endowed with intelligence and ability, and equally entitled to the free exercise of their individual rights and liberty" (Germany 1904).

Two additional reasons "that all institutions of learning and of professional instruction, including schools of theology, law, and medicine, should . . . be as freely opened to women as to men" are that having a broadly educated populace is "in the interests of humanity" (Washington, D.C., 1888) and that education supplies the means of avoiding limited and dire alternatives for women, on the one hand, and of having opportunities and fostering social change, on the other. Negatively, the lack of education leads to poverty (Hungary 2012) and invisibility (Thailand 2004), and has "ensured both that [women] remain unpaid household servants, and that they do not have an equal chance with men in the world of paid work" (Hungary 1990). On the positive side, a broadly educated population is necessary as a way to control government abuse and neglect (Nicaragua 2002), a topic near to the democratic heart of feminism, and to put more power in the hands of everyone. Knowledge about sexuality, health, and birth control, for example, needs to be disseminated not only to medical and social workers but to everyone and anyone (New York 1921).

The effects of education are essentially boundless. As the Chiang Mai Declaration (2004) states, "Just as education of women is today understood to be critical in transforming the world, so providing women with religious education is critical in transforming religion." The Statement of Conscience: A Feminist Vision for Peace (2002) adds, "We demand immediate response to the pleas of women . . . for immediate assistance with literacy programs to ensure their full participation in brokering peace, in decision-making, and in post-conflict reconstruction." Education is consistently seen as among the most powerful tools; its denial or limitation carves a well-trodden path to subordination.

But to be truly liberatory, education must go beyond mere access to what already exists. To be sure, no document simply applauds an existing educational system. The 1789 Petition of Women of the Third Estate protests the "very neglected or very defective" education the petitioners receive, "the impediments which are forever being placed on our education." "We ask," they continue, "to be enlightened," and so they request free schools that teach more subjects in greater depth. History lessons, for example, should give "special preference" to "those things that reveal the various progressive aspects of communities and societies, more than to the narration of wars and battles" (Argentina 1910).

One long-standing concern revolves around the biased tools of education, from particular texts to general curricula. "Sex-stereotyping in education, media and at the place of work must be abolished" (Norway 1982). This task requires vigilance: "The books and activities of nurseries and schools must be examined critically in order to prevent the continued propagation of obsolete and destructive prejudices regarding gender roles" (Hungary 1990). New material must be introduced: The Canadian young feminists (2008) "envision communities committed to . . . learning and teaching true herstory and histories of our victories and struggles, especially those of women of colour and Aboriginal women," just as Black Lives Matter urges inclusion of Black history (2015). Professional programs must be included in curriculum change. For example, the Victoria Falls Declaration (1994) emphasizes teaching about human rights in law schools, while the European Charter for Women in the City (1994) notes that "gender issues in cities must be taught in . . . institutes for architecture and town planning." Humans are not born racist or sexist, but we imbibe social prejudices at very young ages, and thus have an active need, as the InterAmerican Convention in Brazil (1994) puts it, for "educational programs appropriate to every level of the educational process, to counteract prejudices, customs and all other practices which are based on the idea of the inferiority or superiority of either of the sexes or on the stereotyped roles for men and women which legitimize or exacerbate violence against women."

Attention in many documents is given to particular groups of people who are treated especially unjustly in educational systems, and/or whose education needs special attention and resources. Education is thus again related to more inclusive democratic politics. The 1848 Manifesto of the Parisian Society for the Emancipation of Women asks first of all for schools for the women of the working classes. The 1910 Second International Conference of Socialist Women recommends "establishment of school homes where unprovided children are looked after," as well as free meals for all schoolchildren, "even in holidays and vacancies." The All India Women's Conference (1927) urges educational facilities for girls in purdah and schools for those with disabilities. The Committee on the

Status of Women in India (1974) mentions the need for "an alternative system [that] has to be designed to provide basic education to adult women, particularly in the 15–25 age." The Women in Prison Manifesto (1985) calls for "improved, non-discriminatory and non-paternalistic education [and] job training" behind bars, while the National Alliance of Black Feminists (1977) speaks to prison diversion programs. The First World Whores' Congress (1985) notes the need for "re-training programs for prostitutes wishing to leave the life," the Feminist Peace Network (2002) addresses the education of children in postconflict zones, and the International Feminist Congress of Argentina (1910) reminds us that for everyone, "educational methods should adapt to the student and not the student to the method."

There is concern over low enrollment of girls/women in particular areas, such as "science-based training programmes and professions" (Abuja 1989) and political leadership (Soviet Union 1990). Such focused attention in all these examples has to start from a clear-eyed view of every particular status quo, so that we do not settle on generalities and miss the fact that, for example, Roma children are often segregated in schools and placed in special needs classrooms, and consequently drop out at a much higher rate than others (Greece 2010). Yet several documents cite a lack of such accurate information or of studies still needed to do more educational justice to more people.

Women are not only portrayed on the receiving end of education. Feminist manifestos speak about the importance of women's knowledge being recognized, preserved, passed on, and expanded upon. There is attention to how "commercialization and monopoly control are destroying the traditional knowledge and practices that have kept indigenous women self-sufficient," and therefore "call[s] for . . . reclaim[ing] rural women's knowledge and skills" (India 2008). The 2011 Rights of Indigenous Women in Nepal speaks to the need "to preserve and promote the traditional indigenous know how and [also] to increase [Indigenous women's] capacity to access and use the modern information, communication and technology."

An interesting extension of basic educational concerns addresses political education broadly understood, and especially education for liberation. There has long been concern that women "ought to be enlightened with regard to the laws under which they live, that they may no longer publish their degradation by declaring themselves satisfied with their present position, nor their ignorance by asserting they have all the rights they want" (New York 1848). The Victoria Falls Declaration (1994) mentions the need for governments "to translate the international human rights instruments and the African Charter of Human and Peoples' Rights into local languages, in a form accessible to the people [and to] mount extensive awareness campaigns through diverse means to disseminate and impart human rights education." The South African Women's Charter and Aims (1954) declares an "intention to carry out a nation-wide programme of education that will bring home to the men and women of all national groups the realization that freedom cannot be won for any one section or for the people as a whole as long as we women are kept in bondage." In their 1899 Constitution and By-Laws, the National Consumers League suggest that consumers be educated so that they purchase only goods that "promote better conditions among the workers." In addition to traditional educational issues, Turkey's Panlyurfa Declaration on Violence against Women (2003) focuses more on "introduc[ing] education projects in schools addressing the risk of children being exposed to sexual abuse. In addition, education should be provided on the subject of gender in high schools. The education of women on the subject of struggle against violence against women is crucially important." That Declaration also mentions educating sexual partners, together, about family planning, and using women's organizations to develop educational units in schools. Altogether, declarations of sexual equality highlight the importance and complexities of establishing forms and methods of education that will actively serve as a means toward equality.

This political education is not reserved for adults. Indeed, the presence of children in feminist declarations is noteworthy. Concern begins with the availability of culturally competent childcare (Houston 1971). It extends to education for peace and equality. Feminists advocate "educat[ing] children in the principles of peace, and special abhorrence of that warfare, which gives aid to the oppressor against the oppressed" (New York 1837). It was expressed thus at the following year's antislavery gathering: "[E]very mother [and involved adult] is bound by imperative obligations, to instruct her children in the principles of genuine abolition, by teaching them the nature and sanctity of human rights, and the claims of the great law of love, as binding alike on every member of the human family" (1838). Children should be politically educated, against racial discrimination and for universal human rights. Similarly, among the political tasks laid out by the First Viennese Democratic Women's Association in 1848 was "to inspire the love of freedom in a child's heart from the very beginning of a child's upbringing."

Concluding Thoughts and Questions

In closing, I want to raise some of the questions for both feminist theory and feminist activism that I believe these documents bring to the fore, questions that require more sustained attention than I can give them here. I also want to confront one final stereotype of feminism that the manifestos demolish.

What does it mean that even in the partial reconstruction of it in this volume, feminist activism and theory have been around in just about every decade for the last two centuries? How, for example, does this unbroken global thread sit with the (mostly) Western notion of three or more distinct feminist waves? Where are the ripples and swells in this metaphor? Might we think, instead, of high and low tides on different shores in always churning waters, waters that meet and merge in various ways around the world, and whose impact is determined most by local factors? Can we incorporate the fact that the "stages" these waves are usually thought to represent are neither as linear nor as universal as the metaphor implies, or must the image be replaced? What does it mean, both about the role of women in resisting fascism and the presence of underground or nascent feminism, that as soon as there is even semi-safe space for feminist activism, as in post-Franco Spain (1976) and post-Khomeni Iran (2008), it simply explodes in books, journals, organizations, policies, and public protests? What turmoil was there before the wave broke? Are we safer assuming that such tumult is always present, that it has been present in every age? Will that require being somewhat less accepting of those we now say could not have known better, should not be expected to have been ahead of their time?

What are the implications of the fact that while some documents neatly fit into textbook categories of feminist theories (El Salvador's "We Cannot Wait" [1981] with socialist feminism, for example), most do not? Do we even have names for the various feminisms certain manifestos develop (such as the anticolonial, environmentalist feminist, or the antiracist, communitarian, pacifist feminist), or are we still trying to fit feminism into categories that were made for something else? Dramatically, the development of varieties of feminism based more on feminist manifestos—on feminists in dialogue and in action with each other and in coalitions—than on (mostly male) philosophies made for other purposes would be welcome and inspiring.

For liberal feminism in particular, what do we think about the fact that we see attention to legal changes not only in "liberal feminist" NOW's Statement of Purpose (1966) but almost everywhere (with varying degrees of faith in the power of such changes)—that, on the other hand, the relatively liberal 1850 Resolutions radically wonder "whether the monopoly of capital, or in other words, the control of the means of living, is not the cause of the wrongs woman suffers in regard to compensation for labor"? Does NOW's 1966 Statement remain the paradigmatic liberal feminist document even when the organization has evolved, as evidenced, for example, in its 2014 resolutions?[6] And despite its seemingly permanent and prominent presence in popular presses, and however widely spread the myth, what do we conclude from the fact that something perhaps identifiable as "white middle-class liberal feminism" is a minor presence in this collection, the exception rather than the norm, and that this is true dating to the earliest declarations, which come from working-class women, widows, democratic groups, and multiracial groups of abolitionists? If but a handful of the piles of documents do no more than ask for relatively privileged women to be treated as more privileged men have been treated in homes, workplaces, and politics, is liberal feminism a straw theory without a theorist, or at least in need of broader definition? Might liberal feminism simply be a "building out from where we are" philosophy inspired by more radical visions?

The strongest connection between a document and a "feminist school of thought" far and away is between the Combahee River Collective's Black Feminist Statement and Black feminism. The Statement has played an important role in the very defining of Black feminism, appearing unabridged in anthologies spanning three decades.[7] It is exciting to see any declaration playing such an important role, but where did the productions by other groups concerned with race, gender, and sexuality go, by comparison? Many documents with and without "Black Women" in the title confront issues of race; many more address multiple forms of oppression in various cultures and contexts; and "Black feminism" has a deep history in manifestos, with a variety of political strains, arising in a number of locales (at least two from Brazil alone)[8] and in conversation with a wide range of issues: "We need to demand the history, variety, and breadth in our theories that match our action on the ground and enable us to learn from each other."

Challenges to other familiar feminisms also arise from these documents. Postmodern feminism is virtually invisible in this collection. Does that fact support the critique that postmodernism is not very helpful for directing action, as educational scholar Aida Hurtado suggests? "Postmodernism is a helpful plank from which to question all discourse and social categories. However, it becomes much less helpful as a framework to propose political action to change material conditions" (2003, 21). "Socialist feminism," often represented by both the Black Feminist Statement (oh, how these categories overlap, without sufficient comment) and the Berkeley-Oakland Women's Union Statement, too often is portrayed without the history of socialist feminism dating from the First (1907) and Second (1910) International Conferences of Socialist Women to "We Cannot Wait," written by the Association of Women of El Salvador (1981). Histories are distorted and imaginations impoverished when we too readily confine ourselves to the familiar and already discovered, and to narrow readings even of those. New and/or reimagined feminisms might emerge from this collection, and might include a greater emphasis on common ground and local context.

While it can be incredibly challenging to see feminists historically and globally as parts of some broad tradition, some ongoing conversation, this book is asking readers to consider such a possibility. Many issues are truly timeless, including peace and poverty, equal rights and equal opportunity, domestic work and domestic violence, institutionalized domination and internalized oppression, and citizenship and education. Some of the early analyses of these issues are as powerful as more recent ones, and should not be overlooked. To discover patterns, threads, and traditions is neither to advocate for some ill-conceived universalized version of feminism, nor to wipe out the local diversity that we are still discovering and that has so much more to teach. Instead, naming traditions and themes is a call to pay as much attention to connections as to distinctions, an opportunity to put the disparate into potentially fruitful conversation, a demand to hear each other into existence by recognizing the full range of both questions and answers that constitute feminism.

What might the consequences be of seeing feminism as an ongoing conversation—full of arguments, laughter, tough questions, mutual learning, affection, compromises, joint victories, steaming silences, excited interruptions, joyful consensus, and painful partings of the way? Would we better understand and be less threatened by the different tones and tenors? Could we be inspired to listen harder? Would we feel it easier to join in? Might we wonder what got said before we entered the room? Could we talk more comfortably across generations, in different tongues, hesitantly and humbly, congenially and confidently?

In speaking of threads, connections, and traditions, I do not deny, either, that differences of opinion exist within feminism. One document in this collection advocates the decriminalization of prostitution while two others consider prostitution the essence of oppression and think decriminalizing it makes as much sense as unionizing battered women. Some documents speak for the value of only women working together, while others claim that liberation requires collaboration with men in the struggle for gender justice and against other forms of oppression. Two documents argue for compensating women for private care work, others talk about degendering such work, and still others for changing paid workplaces to make them more compatible with all participating in care work. Do these varied stances reflect rigid differences in understanding the nature of oppression and liberation, are they attempts to alleviate the situation in notoriously different locations, or are they even much-needed experiments in how to reallocate, revalue, and liberate? (How enormous a task it can be newly to give voice and grant credibility to the subordinated, not just on an individual level but through practices, policies, symbols, and institutions.) Manifestos show that feminists do in fact find some common ground and develop complementary projects, and they display creativity and openness when it comes to strategizing. Some shared values, priorities, or strategies exist between (some of) the differences, we build coalitions on that, and we create room for efforts to evolve. Every document in this volume is evidence of some degree of coming to consensus, amidst groups large and small, more and less heterogeneous. Collaborative, political, feminist work is getting done every day.

Perhaps the weightiest accusation ever levied against feminism, one still cited with almost mystifying regularity and granted way more plausibility than it merits, suggests that feminism is an overwhelmingly white, middle-class, and Western movement. The charge is often made by those who do not identify as feminists, and who challenge feminism's legitimacy in a certain place or among a certain group; however, it is also a charge made from within about who and what is centered and marginalized. Much to our loss, the accusation contributes to rendering invisible feminists of color from around the world, in addition to those from the poor and working classes, with diverse abilities and disabilities, of all sexes and genders, who, across the centuries, have committed themselves to greater gender justice and equality. What we see in these manifestos is an incredibly rich history of feminism in every global region, touching on a wealth of issues, written by every imaginable population group. When made too broadly, the allegation also leaves out all the difficult dialogues that *have* taken place, and "forgets" the ways feminist praxis has always involved bridging some divides that can be used to further expand feminist knowledge, commitments, and agendas. These documents testify to feminism's commitment, long-standing yet still growing, to investigate, understand, and change multiple systems of oppression that have been operating in diverse structures, systems, and ideologies—an imperfect effort, to be sure, but no small achievement, either.

Recognition of differences among women, and of multiple systems of oppression, has a history in collective feminist documents, whose authors often start by describing the diversity in the setting where they are meeting. True, in neither Canada nor India, neither Turkey nor Israel, did inclusion of LGBT issues appear before some sixty years ago, and we only recently have access to the language of intersectionality and matrices of oppression, but awareness is present from the earliest documents that women are far from identically impacted by patriarchy. Similarly, while recent documents confront a plethora of seemingly new issues, including religious extremism and the war on terror, sustainability and climate change, and what the Declaration of the Central American Meeting of Women (2014) calls "the fierce alliance between patriarchy and neoliberalism," in fact our historical documents have much to say about the forces that oppose us and the ways our well-being is repeatedly sacrificed for other supposedly more important social goals; too, the fight against fascism, and concern about how we relate to the land and each other appeared in these documents long ago and repeatedly (the World Committee of Women against War and Fascism dates to 1935, while the Cherokee documents came from the early 1800s). As feminists, we owe it to ourselves to keep in mind, from the present and the past, our bold statements of principles, our status-quo-challenging accomplishments, our deep and broad understandings of oppression, our continuous political commitments, and our diverse collectives.

The most sustained critique of feminism has always been that it is a white, middle-class movement. This is not true. Women from all backgrounds stand up to the social forces around them and are engaged in feminist activism. The feminist story belongs to all women everywhere but that is not the impression you would receive from the mainstream media. (Nagarajan and Okolosie 2012)

Accordingly, a critique of "the mainstream media" has understandably been part of feminism since coverage of the earliest conventions and continues today

(India 2006 and Czech Republic 2015). May "a capacious definition of feminism" (Gilmore 2008, 5) help us "shatter the stereotype of a white, middle-class, politically rigid movement" (Evans 2008, vii), and inspire us to continue contributing to a movement this collection shows is still growing, vibrant, and urgently needed.

Notes

1 Among those written by individuals and thus not included here: Olympe de Gouges, "Declaration of the Rights of Woman the Female Citizen" (1791); Emma Goldman, "A New Declaration of Independence" (1909); Yamakawa Kikue, "Manifesto" (1921); Ghada Samman, "Our Constitution—We the Liberated Women" (1961); Frances M. Beal, "Double Jeopardy: To Be Black and Female" (1969); Leslie Weisman, "Women's Environmental Rights: A Manifesto" (1971); Robert Avakian, "A Declaration: For Women's Liberation and the Emancipation of all Humanity" (2009); Shek, "The Black Girl's Manifesto: The Basic Rights of Femininity" (2010); Melissa W. Wright, "A Manifesto against Femicide" (2001); and Lindsey German, "A Feminist Manifesto for the 21st Century" (2010).

2 Documents referenced in this introduction that are not in the book are listed in the appendix.

3 The FAO is the Food and Agricultural Organization of the UN, dealing with hunger.

4 A handbook on feminist charters was recently published. See Rashida Manjoo, *Feminist Charters and Declarations* (Women Living Under Muslim Laws, 2012).

5 Two recent survey examples: Lydia Smith, "Equal Rights: 10 Best and Worst Countries for Attitudes towards Gender Equality." *International Business Times,* Nov. 12, 2015, www.ibtimes .co.uk; and "The Best and Worst Places for Women." *Daily Beast,* Sept. 20, 2011, www.the dailybeast.com.

6 2014 National NOW Conference Resolutions, June 29, 2014. National Organization of Women website, www.now.org.

7 *This Bridge Called My Back: Writings by Radical Women of Color* (Cherrí Moraga and Gloria Anzaldúa 1981); *Home Girls: A Black Feminist Anthology* (Barbara Smith 1983); *Words of Fire: An Anthology of African-American Feminist Thought* (Beverly Guy-Sheftall 1995); and *Still Brave: The Evolution of Black Women's Studies* (Stanlie James, Francis Foster, and Beverly Guy-Sheftall 2009).

8 Included are the Black Women's Manifesto (1975) and the Mulata Globeleza: A Manifesto (2016).

References

Anzaldúa, Gloria. *Haciendo Caras/Making Face, Making Soul: Creative and Critical Perspectives by Women of Color.* San Francisco: Aunt Lute Press, 1990.

Anderson, Bonnie. 2000. *Joyous Greetings: The First International Women's Movement, 1830–1860.* Oxford: Oxford University Press.

Buchanan, Lindal. 2003. "Forging and Firing Thunderbolts: Collaboration and Women's Rhetoric." *Rhetoric Society Quarterly* 33.4 (Autumn): 43–63.

Coalition Against Trafficking in Women. Trafficking and Sexual Exploitation: Who Represents Women in Prostitution? NOMAS. European Parliament, October 17, 2005. Original URL no longer active; full text can be found through NOMAS.

Dallery, Arleen. 1989. "The Politics of Writing (the) Body: *Ecriture Feminine.*" In *Gender/Body/Knowledge: Feminist Reconstructions of Being and Knowing,* ed. Alison Jaggar and Susan Bordo. New Brunswick, NJ: Rutgers University Press, pp. 52–67.

Eisenstein, Zillah. 1978. *Capitalist Patriarchy and the Case for Socialist Feminism.* New York: Monthly Review Press.

Evans, Sara. 2008. Foreword to *Feminist Coalitions: Historical Perspectives on Second-Wave Feminism in the United States,* ed. Stephanie Gilmore. Urbana: University of Illinois Press.

Gilmore, Stephanie, ed. 2008. *Feminist Coalitions: Historical Perspectives on Second-Wave Feminism in the United States.* Urbana: University of Illinois Press.

Hurtado, Aida. 2003. "Theory in the Flesh: Toward an Endarkened Epistemology." *International Journal of Qualitative Studies in Education* (March): 216–25.

Kaplan, Jemma. 1997. *Crazy for Democracy: Women in Grassroots Movements.* New York: Routledge.

Lyon, Janet. 1991. "Transforming Manifestoes: A Second-Wave Problematic." *Yale Journal of Criticism* 5.1: 101–27.

MacKinnon, Catherine. 1988. *Feminism Unmodified: Discourses on Life and Law.* Cambridge, MA: Harvard University Press.

Moore, Lisa, Joanna Brooks, and Caroline Wigginton, eds. 2012. *Transatlantic Feminisms in the Age of Revolutions.* Oxford: Oxford University Press.

Moynagh, Maureen, and Nancy Forestell. 2015. *Documenting First Wave Feminisms.* Volume 1, *Transnational Collaborations and Crosscurrents.* Toronto, Canada: University of Toronto Press.

Nagarajan, Chitra, and Lola Okolosie. 2012. "You Don't Need an MA in Gender Studies to Know That Race Matters to Feminism." *Guardian*, October 23, www.theguardian.com.

Reagon, Berenice Johnson. 1983. "Coalition Politics: Turning the Century." In *Home Girls: A Black Feminist Anthology*, ed. Barbara Smith. New York: Kitchen Table Press, pp. 356–68.

Rhodes, Jacqueline. 2002. "Substantive and Feminist Girlie Action: Women Online." *College Composition and Communication* 54.1 (September): 116–42.

Tolunay, Özlem İlyas. 2014. "Women in Erdoğan's Turkey." *New Politics* 14.4 (Winter). www.newpol.org.

Weeks, Kathi. 2013. "The Critical Manifesto: Marx and Engels, Haraway, and Utopian Politics." *Utopian Studies* 24.2: 216–31.

Weiss, Penny. 2009. *Canon Fodder: Historical Women Political Thinkers.* University Park: Pennsylvania State University Press.

Yanoshevsky, Galia. 2009a. "The Literary Manifesto and Related Notions: A Selected Annotated Bibliography." *Poetics Today* 30.2 (Summer): 287–315.

Yanoshevsky, Galia. 2009b. "Three Decades of Writing on Manifesto: The Making of a Genre." *Poetics Today* 30.2 (Summer): 257–86.

Part I

Seventeenth and Eighteenth Centuries

Petition of the Gentlewomen and Tradesmen's Wives
London, England
February 4, 1642

In the free enjoying of Christ in his own laws, and flourishing estate of
the church and commonwealth, consisteth the happiness of women as
well as men.[1]

The oldest collective document found so far, this pamphlet had three parts: a
petition, a justification for it, and an account of its reception. It is a stretch to
call this "feminist," for the document states that the petitioners are not "seeking
to equal ourselves with men, either in authority or wisdom." Nonetheless, this
early selection both speaks to certain fears of women in their traditional roles and
presents a list of reasons for women speaking out in public that does not appeal
to such roles. It is an early instance, of which many more will be seen, of recalling
political and biblical examples of women acting publicly and on principle that the
petitioners then follow.

> The women who petitioned Parliament in early 1642 articulated new arguments
> about their rights as women. They point out that they are equal to men in God's
> eyes and that they have suffered for their religious beliefs in the same ways that men
> have, making a kind of translation from the realm of the spirit to the temporal world
> of Newgate and Smithfield. Second, these women are claiming the right to speak in
> public. . . . It is difficult for us to recover just how shocking these women's public ac-
> tions were to their contemporaries. Silence was a virtue closely associated with the
> female sex in early modern England. . . . From fiction to embroidery patterns, from
> sermons to household guides, women were everywhere reminded that silence was
> to be their adornment.[2]

Indeed, the official response to the petition testifies to what women were up
against. These are the words attributed to Mr. Pym, at the door of the Commons:

> Good women, your petition and the reasons have been read in the house; and is very
> thankfully accepted of, and is come in a seasonable time: You shall (God willing)
> receive from us all the satisfaction which we can possibly give to your just and lawful
> desires. We entreat you to repair to your houses, and turn your petition which you
> have delivered here into prayers at home for us; for we have been, are and shall be (to
> our utmost power) ready to relieve you, your husbands, and children, and to perform
> the trust committed unto us towards God, our King and country, as becometh faith-
> ful Christians and loyal subjects.

This would hardly be the last time it would be suggested that women "repair
to your houses" and leave these matters to men. Nor would it be the last time
women ignored the suggestion. It is important to see how Pym's

> authoritative remark strives to reinforce a gendered segregation of social space and
> discursive activity across class hierarchies and to translate the register of women's
> political engagement into the (patriarchally oriented and endorsed) language of

devotion. It is no accident, therefore, that the vast majority of women's printed petitions from the period spend some considerable time interrogating the assumptions that it is "strange and unbeseeming of our sex to shew ourselves by way of petition."[3]

Petition of the Gentlewomen and Tradesmen's Wives

The most humble Petition of the Gentlewomen, Tradesmen's Wives,[4] and many others of the female sex, all inhabitants of the city of London, and the suburbs thereto.

With lowest submission showing,

That we also with all thankful humility acknowledging the unwearied pains, care and great charge, besides hazard of health and life, which you the noble worthies of the honorable and renowned assembly have undergone, for the safety both of church and commonwealth, for a long time already past; for which not only we your humble petitioners, and all well affected in this kingdom, but also all other good Christians are bound now and at all times to acknowledge; yet notwithstanding that many worthy deeds have been done by you, great danger and fear do still attend us, and will, as long as Popish Lords and superstitious bishops are suffered to have their voice in the House of Peers, and that accursed and abominable Idol of the Mass suffered in the kingdom, and that archenemy of our prosperity and reformation lyeth in the Tower [Archbishop Laud], yet not receiving his deserved punishment.

All these under correction, gives us great cause to suspect, that God is angry with us, and to be the chief causes why your pious endeavors for a further reformation proceedeth not with that success as you desire, and is most earnestly prayed for of all that wish well to true religion, and the flourishing estate both of king and kingdom; the insolencies of the papists and their abbettors, raiseth a just fear and suspicion of sowing sedition, and breaking out into bloody persecution in this kingdom, as they have done in Ireland, the thoughts of which sad and barbarous events, maketh our tender hearts to melt within us, forcing us humbly to Petition to this honorable Assembly, to make safe provision for yourselves and us, before it be too late.

And whereas we, whose hearts have joined cheerfully with all those petitions which have been exhibited unto you in the behalf of the purity of religion, and the liberty of our husbands persons and estates, recounting our selves to have an interest in the common privileges with them, do with the same confidence assure ourselves to find the same gracious acceptance with you, for easing of those grievances, which in regard of our frail condition, do more nearly concern us, and do deeply terrify our souls: our domestical dangers with which this kingdom is so much distracted, especially growing on us from those treacherous and wicked attempts already are such, as we find ourselves to have as deep a share as any other.

We cannot but tremble at the very thoughts of the horrid and hideous facts which modesty forbids us now to name, occasioned by the bloody wars in Germany, his

Majesty's late Northern Army, how often did it affright our hearts, whilst their violence began to break out so furiously upon the persons of those, whose husbands or parents were not able to rescue: we wish we had no cause to speak of those insolencies, and savage usage and unheard of rapes, exercised upon our sex in Ireland, and have we not just cause to fear they will prove the forerunners of our ruin, except Almighty God by the wisdom and care of this Parliament be pleased to succor us, our husbands and children, which are as dear and tender unto us, as the lives and blood of our hearts, to see them murdered and mangled and cut in pieces before our eyes, to see our children dashed against the stones, and the mother's milk mingled with the infants' blood, running down the streets; to see our houses on flaming fire over our heads: oh how dreadful would this be! We thought it misery enough (though nothing to that we have just cause to fear) but few years since for some of our sex, by unjust divisions from their bosom comforts, to be rendered in a manner widows, and the children fatherless, husbands were imprisoned from the society of their wives, even against the laws of God and nature; and little Infants suffered in their fathers' banishments: thousands of our dearest friends have been compelled to fly from Episcopal persecutions into desert places amongst wild Beasts, there finding more favor than in their native soil, and in the midst of all their sorrows, such hath the pity of the Prelates been, that our cries could never enter into their ears or hearts, nor yet through multitudes of obstructions could never have access or come nigh to those royal mercies of our most gracious Sovereign, which we confidently hope, would have relieved us: but after all these pressures ended, we humbly signify, that our present fears are, that unless the blood-thirsty faction of the Papists and Prelates be hindered in their designs, ourselves here in England as well as they in Ireland, shall be exposed to that misery which is more intolerable than that which is already past, as namely to the rage not of men alone, but of devils incarnate, (as we may so say) besides the thralldom of our souls and consciences in matters concerning God, which of all things are most dear unto us.

Now the remembrance of all these fearful accidents aforementioned, do strongly move us from the example of the woman of Tekoa (II Samuel 14.2–20) to fall submissively at the feet of his Majesty, our dread sovereign, and cry Help, oh King, help oh ye the noble Worthies now sitting in Parliament: And we humbly beseech you, that you will be a means to his Majesty and the House of Peers, that they will be pleased to take our heartbreaking grievances into timely consideration, and to add strength and encouragement to your noble endeavors, and further that you would move his Majesty with our humble requests, that he would be graciously pleased according to the example of the good King Asa, to purge both the court and kingdom of that great idolatrous service of the Mass, which is tolerated in the Queen's court, this sin (as we conceive) is able to draw down a greater curse upon the whole kingdom than all your noble and pious endeavors can prevent, which was the cause that the good and pious King Asa would not suffer idolatry in his own mother, whose example if it shall please his Majesty's gracious goodness to follow, in putting down Popery and Idolatry both in great and small, in court and in the kingdom throughout, to subdue the Papists and their abettors, and by taking away the power of the Prelates, whose government by long and woeful experience we have found to be against the liberty of our conscience and the freedom of the Gospel, and the sincere profession and practice thereof, then shall our fears be removed, and we may expect that God will pour down his blessings in abundance both upon his Majesty, and upon this Honorable Assembly, and upon the whole land.

For which your new petitioners shall pray affectionately.

The Reasons follow.

It may be thought strange, and unbeseeming our sex to show ourselves by way of petition to this Honorable Assembly: but the matter being rightly considered, of the right and interest we have in the common and public cause of the Church, it will, as we conceive (under correction) be found a duty commanded and required.

First, because Christ hath purchased us at as dear a rate as he hath done men, and therefore requireth the like obedience for the same mercy as of men.

Secondly, because in the free enjoying of Christ in his own laws, and a flourishing estate of the church and commonwealth, consisteth the happiness of women as well as men.

Thirdly, because women are sharers in the common calamities that accompany both church and commonwealth when oppression is exercised over the church or kingdom wherein they live; and an unlimited power have been given to Prelates to exercise authority over the consciences of women, as well as men, witness Newgate, Smithfield, and other places of persecution, wherein women as well as men have felt the smart of their fury.

Neither are we left without example in scripture, for when the state of the church, in the time of King Ahasuerus, was by the bloody enemies thereof sought to be utterly destroyed, we find that Esther the Queen and her maids fasted and prayed, and that Esther petitioned to the King in the behalf of the church: and though she enterprised this duty with the hazard of her own life, being contrary to the law to appear before the King before she were sent for, yet her love to the church carried her through all difficulties, to the performance of that duty.

On which grounds we are emboldened to present our humble petition unto this Honorable Assembly, not weighing the reproaches which may and are by many cast upon us, who (not well weighing the premises) scoff and deride our good intent. We do it not out of any self-conceit, or pride of heart, as seeking to equal ourselves with men, either in authority or wisdom: But according to our places to discharge that duty we owne to God, and the cause of the church, as far as lieth in us, following herein the example of the men which have gone in this duty before us.

Notes

1 Epigraphs without citations are from the document being discussed.
2 Mary Elizabeth Fissell, *Vernacular Bodies: The Politics of Reproduction in Early Modern England* (Oxford: Oxford University Press, 2004), pp. 99–101.
3 Marcus Nevitt, *Women and the Pamphlet Culture of Revolutionary England, 1640–1660* (Farnham, UK: Ashgate, 2006), p. 166.
4 *English Women's Voices, 1540–1700*, ed. Charlotte F. Otten (Gainesville: University of Florida Press, 1992), pp. 95–99.

2

The Humble Petition of Divers Well-Affected Women
England
May 5, 1649

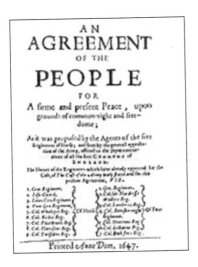

The Petition.

Have we not an equal interest with the men of this nation in those liberties and securities contained in the Petition of Right, and other the good laws of the land?

History and for that matter historians have not been kind to women who took part in political activity on both sides of the English Civil War. There is a dearth of material on women's struggle at this time. As far as I can ascertain no major biography exists of two of the most important Leveller women Katherine Chidley and Elizabeth Lilburne.[1]

Women have long worked together to contest their unequal treatment in the household and their limited roles in public life, and to demand respect for their full humanity and their social contributions. As we will see, they have done so in every era, from within every political, religious, ethnic, and economic setting, group, or tradition. This remarkable seventeenth-century petition, whose authorship is uncertain (as is that of many by men), may have had as many as ten thousand women's signatures. It was written during a time when women were frequently engaging in direct political action, and its authors and signatories, as Leveller women, were especially fortunate because "they had access to printing materials and presses."[2]

The Parliamentarians and Royalists did battle in the English Civil War over whether the people or the king should rule. The Levellers were one of many political groups in the conflict supporting democracy and the end of monarchy. The Levellers produced a manifesto, "Agreement of the People," which proposed a written constitution that would limit government authority and guarantee such rights as those now-familiar ones for suffrage, freedom of religion and press, legal equality, and conscientious objection, and against self-incrimination, monopolies, and debtors prisons.

Despite the obvious democratic (even revolutionary) tendencies of the Levellers evident in this list of guarantees, they only urged that suffrage be extended to more men. Laws that kept females legally and financially dependent upon men, and focused on their duties as wives and mothers alone, were generally unchallenged—except, perhaps, by Leveller women, who readily adopted the Levellers' popular political techniques and strategies on their own behalf, including mass demonstrations, petitioning, and lobbying members of Parliament. The contradiction between the group's general principles and its repressive treatment of women is, as we will see, common in all eras and diverse ideologies. As Ann Hughes argues, "[F]eminist scholarship has been a major means by which linear notions of progressive change have been challenged in recent decades. The assumption of equality has been replaced by a darker stress on the contradictory relationships between women and radical movements."[3]

The petition defends women's equal political voice and right to engage in political agitation. And agitate they did! As Helena Wojtczak describes it,

> [F]or the first time, a group of women became involved in direct political action. They mounted large scale public demonstrations and petitions, but were often dragged away by soldiers after trying to thrust petitions into the hands of MPs entering parliament. Hundreds even tried to storm the gates of parliament. As a result, common women were thrown into prison, mental institutions or workhouses. Middle class women were simply escorted away by soldiers and told to "go back to women's work."[4]

The petition asserts women's spiritual equality, and their equal interest and stake in political reforms. They protest the unjust imprisonment of Leveller men. They oppose "force and arbitrary power" and object to demands for women's domesticity in the face of "abominable cruelty and injustice." Like their political movement in general, they present themselves as embedded in familial and political communities. As was the case in the Cherokee Women's Council petitions of the early nineteenth century, included in this volume, the women here seem to argue that the situation they confront is so dire that they must take the exceptional step of making their voices heard in political affairs.

On April 23, 1649, women tried unsuccessfully to present their petitions to a House of Commons "too busy" to receive them. They made it into the lobby on April 25, but Parliament declined to accept the women's petitions. They were, instead, answered "through the Serjeant by 'word of mouth.'"[5] The answer:

> Mr Speaker (by the direction of the House) hath commanded me to tell you, that the matter you petition about, is of an higher concernment then you understand, that the House gave an answer to your Husbands, and therefore that you are desired to go home, and look after your owne businesse, and meddle with your housewifery.

They did not oblige.

The Humble Petition of Divers Well-Affected Women

Since we are assured of our creation in the image of God, and of an interest in Christ equal unto men, as also of a proportionable share in the freedoms of this commonwealth, we cannot but wonder and grieve that we should appear so despicable in your eyes as to be thought unworthy to petition or represent our grievances to this honorable House. Have we not an equal interest with the men of this nation in those liberties and securities contained in the Petition of Right, and other the good laws of the land? Are any of our lives, limbs, liberties, or goods to be taken from us more than from men, but by due process of law and conviction of twelve sworn men of the neighborhood? And can you imagine us to be so sottish or stupid as not to perceive, or not to be sensible when daily those strong defenses of our peace and welfare are broken down and trod underfoot by force and arbitrary power?

Would you have us keep at home in our houses, when men of such faithfulness and integrity as the four prisoners, our friends, in the Tower, are fetched out of their beds and forced from their houses by soldiers, to the affrighting and undoing of themselves, their wives, children, and families? Are not our husbands, our selves, our children and families, by the same rule as liable to the like unjust cruelties as they? And are we Christians, and shall we sit still and keep at home, while such men as have borne continual testimony against the injustice of all times and unrighteousness of men, be picked out and be delivered up to the slaughter? And yet must we show no sense of their sufferings, no tenderness of affections, no bowels of compassion, nor bear any testimony against so abominable cruelty and injustice?

Have such men as these continually hazarded their lives, spent their estates and time, lost their liberties, and thought nothing too precious for defense of us, our lives and liberties, been as a guard by day and as a watch by night; and when for this they are in trouble and greatest danger, persecuted and hated even to the death, should we be so basely ungrateful as to neglect them in the day of their affliction? No, far be it from us. Let it be accounted folly, presumption, madness, or whatsoever in us, whilst we have life and breath we will never leave them nor forsake them, nor ever cease to importune you, having yet so much hopes of you as of the unjust judge (mentioned, Luke 18), to obtain justice, if not for justice's sake, yet for importunity, or to use any other means for the enlargement and reparation of those of them that live, and for justice against such as have been the cause of Mr Lockyer's death.[6]

And therefore again we entreat you to review our last petition in behalf of our friends above mentioned, and not to slight the things therein contained because they are presented unto you by the weak hand of women, it being a usual thing with God, by weak means to work mighty effects.

Notes

1 Alison Stuart, "Leveller Women and the English Revolution." *Hoydens and Firebrands* blog, May 6, 2012. hoydensandfirebrands.blogspot.com.

2 Ibid.

3 Ann Hughes, "Gender and Politics in Leveller Literature," in *Political Culture and Cultural Politics in Early Modern England*, ed. Susan Amussen and Mark Kishlansky (Manchester, UK: Manchester University Press, 1993), p. 162.

4 Helena Wojtczak, "British Women's Emancipation since the Renaissance." Accessed Sept. 2017, historyofwomen.org.

5 This is reported in Hughes, p. 163.

6 Robert Lockyer was a Leveller agitator who was hanged.

3

Petition to *Journal* Editor John Peter Zenger

New York

1733

The *New York Weekly Journal*.

This brief petition, addressed to *New York Weekly Journal* editor John Peter Zenger, is fascinating for several reasons. First, again a particular group of women come together, but in this case they do so as widows, not members of an existing political movement. They are a population group that continues to struggle in certain places even today, as evidenced by the group Widows for Peace through Democracy, found in this volume. Second, these women "have had a meeting." They come together to discuss their common situation—"something Deplorable"—and determine how to act publicly on it as a group. Thus they are participants in an autonomous democratic process. Third, they declare themselves industrious Americans, since they trade, pay taxes, and thus "contribute to the Support of Government." Some, probably mostly white women, were able at the time to contribute to their family's coffers by owning businesses (taverns and lodges, for example), helping to run a family business, or selling goods such as seeds or produce. Many, as today, simply *had* to support themselves. Nancy Cott considers this document evidence "that at least *some* urban women were aware of their importance to the local economy—and that they were beginning to chafe against the second-class status accorded to female workers."[1] Finally, they feel, on these grounds, "Intitled to some of the Sweets" of government. This latter is an argument about citizenship that will reappear regularly over the next two centuries.

How seriously to take the second part of the petition is unclear. It is reminiscent of Elizabeth King's comment, included in the next (1774) document, favorably comparing women's bravery to that of men. Cott's interpretation is again noteworthy.

We do not know what the *Journal*'s readers made of this striking request. They may have found these protestations of bravery in the face of an invasion outlandish. No foreign invasion or domestic insurrection was then visible on the horizon. Within a generation, however, the ability of women like New York's "she Merchants" to conduct themselves as loyal and prosperous Americans would become essential to the colonies' claims to stand as a nation.[2]

Petition

Mr. Zenger,

We, the widdows of this city, have had a Meeting, and as our case is something Deplorable, we beg you will give [our petition a] Place in your Weekly Journal. . . . it is as follows:

We are House keepers, Pay our Taxes, carry on Trade, and most of us are she Merchants, and as we in some measure contribute to the Support of Government, we ought to be Intitled to some of the Sweets of it; but we find ourselves entirely neglected, while the Husbands that live in our Neighborhood are daily invited to Dine at Court; we have the Vanity to think we can be full[y] as Entertaining, and make as brave a Defence in Case of an Invasion and perhaps not turn Tail so soon as some of them.

Notes

1   Nancy Cote, ed., *No Small Courage: A History of Women in the United States.* (Oxford: Oxford University Press, 2007), p. 107.

2   Ibid., p. 108.

Declaration *and* Resolution
Edenton, North Carolina
October 25, 1774

"A Society of Patriotic Ladies," a British cartoon mocking the Edenton Ladies gathering.

Penelope Barker, a woman with both great wealth and responsibilities, organized this group of fifty-one White women, many from slave-owning families. White colonial women certainly had political opinions before this, and surely took part in discussions about them; still, this all-female group gathered at the home of Elizabeth King *in order* to talk politics and, in particular, to discuss their possible political roles *as women*, on at least one set of issues.

The Edenton petition bears witness to the fact that in endless relatively informal settings, women discuss a broad range of topics, not necessarily confining themselves to what others deem appropriate. It is, in fact, out of informal conversations that larger ones often emerge, ones that occasionally develop into organized efforts—for a day, as in this case, or for decades, in instances we will soon encounter. Even those that are short-lived, it bears emphasizing, often have ripple effects, as the authors and actors usually hope for and intend.

"Nonconsumption" and "nonimportation" of British goods (like boycotting goods made with slave labor and continuing forms of "conscious consumption" today) was an act of resistance—in this case, to taxes on the colonists, both because of their direct and often dire impact and because of acts of the British king that the taxes indirectly supported. The stance taken in the Edenton petition was not new—except that it was taken by an organized group of women in an act of civil disobedience.

This infamous cartoon, "A Society of Patriotic Ladies, at Edenton in North Carolina," was drawn by Philip Dawes and published in a London newspaper on March 25, 1775. His satirization of what is usually called the "Edenton Ladies Tea Party" comes complete with a neglected baby under the table being pulled by a dog, ridiculously "high-fashioned" hairdos on "masculinized" women, public flirtation, and alcohol flasks. It most obviously derides the important role that women had to have played in any effective boycott of English household goods; given the antagonistic responses to the letter that was sent by the actual gathering of women in Edenton and published in British newspapers, what is being lampooned is the very idea of women as political actors.

And these were to some extent *audacious*, political, late-eighteenth-century feminists, both single and married, talking and writing in the Kings' home. The group clearly was writing as women citizens, their legal and social status notwithstanding, bringing themselves uninvited into a conversation about politics. Despite the caricature of promiscuous, ridiculous women neglecting their duties, they portray themselves in the document as simultaneously honorable, determined, patriotic, faithful, and reasonable. They declare that women are not

Penelope Barker.

simply self-interested, and not interested only in their families, but have duties to the well-being of larger communities. In the Declaration, which serves as a sort of "preamble" to the Resolution, they practically redefine a "strong union" as requiring women's participation in it. The signatories were coming to understand themselves not only as affected by but also as capable of influencing politics.

> Maybe it has only been men who have protested the king up to now. That only means we women have taken too long to let our voices be heard. We are signing our names to a document, not hiding ourselves behind costumes like the men at Boston did at their tea party. The British will know who we are (Penelope Barker).

The reasons we have record of this petition are revealing. First, it was published in three newspapers in England. It survived, that is, through British accounts. Second, it provoked responses in England, public and private, serious and sarcastic, that kept the document alive. But even that would not have been enough had not women's historians, beginning in the 1970s, set out in search of records of women's roles in the politics of the era, and continued to discuss and reprint it.

Many feminist ideas and forms of feminist activism are ridiculed still today, and feminists around the world continue to encounter scorn, disapproval, and danger (see, for example, Guatemala 2008). This petition, ignored by most and remembered primarily due to a famous cartoon satirizing the gathering, still shows women beginning to come to terms with their own political voices and collective power.[1]

Edenton Declaration *and* Resolution
Letter from North Carolina, October 27, 1774.

The Provincial Deputies of North Carolina having resolved not to drink any more tea, nor wear any more British cloth, &c. many ladies of this Province have determined to give a memorable proof of their patriotism, and have accordingly entered into the following honourable and spirited association. I send it to you, to shew your fair countrywomen, how zealously and faithfully American ladies follow the laudable example of their husbands, and what opposition your Ministers may expect to receive from a people thus firmly united against them.

Edenton, North Carolina, Oct. 25, 1774.

As we cannot be indifferent on any occasion that appears nearly to affect the peace and happiness of our country, and as it has been thought necessary, for the public good, to enter into several particular resolves by a meeting of Members deputed from the whole Province, it is a duty which we owe, not only to our near and dear connections who have concurred in them, but to ourselves who are essentially interested in their welfare, to do every thing as far as lies in our power to testify our sincere adherence to the same; and we do therefore accordingly subscribe this paper, as a witness of our fixed intention and solemn determination to do so.

Note
1 A group of women in Wilmington, North Carolina, apparently burned tea in protest before the Edenton gathering, but left no written document. The Women's War of 1929, in which Igbo market women in Nigeria protested British taxation, is a later example of women using their traditional power against colonial rulers.

5

Petition of Women of the Third Estate

Paris, France
January 1, 1789

In the period leading up to the Revolution, women did not have the right to meet as a group, draft grievances, or vote in the elections of estate representatives, yet these women met and put their concerns on paper in a gesture of revolutionary hopefulness.[1]

Like the women who wrote the earlier documents, the group that penned this petition to King Louis XVI of France wrote during a time of general political ferment. Women did not have basic political rights in either case, but could use cracks in the status quo created by reforms and revolutions to find their voices and dare to express themselves publicly.

A bankrupted and frustrated King Louis XVI reconvened the Estates-General, the French parliament that had not met since the 1500s. As a companion strategy, French subjects were invited to create for their representatives "*cahiers de doleance*" (ledgers of complaints) that listed their grievances and their desires. The Estates-General were then to present the various concerns to the king. People met as guilds and parishes, for example, to draw up their specific documents. As the petition below says, "At a time when the different orders of the state are occupied with their interests . . . could [women] not also make their voices heard midst this general agitation?" This group of working-class women declined to go through the parliamentary body, however, a move they saw as futile; instead, they chose a direct appeal to the king's "heart."

Three classes were recognized at the time: the clergy (first estate), the nobility (second estate), and the commoners (third estate).

Peasants in the countryside, though excluded from wealth by the . . . system of land tenure, could sometimes hope to grow their own food, but the urban working poor depended on affordable bread to survive. Poor crops led to widespread hunger during the revolutionary years, and women were especially vulnerable. Because their work as seamstresses, embroiderers, and clothing sellers took women of the third estate into the marketplace, they were regarded in the same light as prostitutes, as women who sold their labor publicly for subsistence. Indeed, during times of hardship many women were forced into prostitution to obtain food for themselves and their children.[2]

There is a deferential tone to sections of the petition, and a seeming determination on the part of the anonymous writers to make their demands modest by carefully stating what they are *not* asking for as well as what they want. When the document is "minimized" as more conservative, the emphasis is on the assurance that the women complainants aim not "to usurp men's authority" or to enter "male" professions, and their assertion that they aspire only to embody female virtues: "gentleness, modesty, patience, charity" and, later, "sensibility." But this is arguably a stronger feminist declaration, for several reasons.

First, especially given what passed (and continues to pass) for "virtue" among other groups, the list of "female virtues" that were not contested is perhaps worth some consideration as a list of decent social guides for behavior. Too, one reads in the document about desirable social changes that complement these personal goods and make it "safe" to practice them without become self-sacrificing or vulnerable. Next, the authors explain in moving detail what the everyday lives of working-class girls and women of modest means look like at various stages of life. Nearly half of the petition, in fact, is spent describing their limited life options and the challenges and dangers they confront. They bared their fears regarding sexual and economic vulnerability. In laying the legal, political, educational, social, religious, economic, and familial causes of their condition next to each other, they offer an early understanding of the intertwined structures and practices that simultaneously determined their classed and gendered fate. Finally, they set the stage for a contrast with what their lives *could* be like, and what they *could* contribute to their families and communities, were certain reforms to take place. The power that systems of domination wield can be seen in the impoverishment of imagination itself. Nonetheless, these representatives of the third estate *do* ask that their options be broadened beyond the limited opportunities of the nunnery, prostitution, or undesirable marriages. What would this require? Guaranteed employment in fields reserved for them; a free, "sound and reasonable education" for themselves and their children, rather than a perfunctory religious education; and the respect of men, which would be based on women's education, morality, and employment. They invite us to continue to consider the quest at the heart of this book: starting wherever we are, in whatever set of circumstances, to envision something better.

Petition of Women of the Third Estate

Sire,[3]

At a time when the different orders of the state are occupied with their interests; when everyone seeks to make the most of his titles and rights; when some anxiously recall the centuries of servitude and anarchy, while others make every effort to shake off the last links that still bind them to the imperious remains of feudalism; women—continual objects of the admiration and scorn of men—could they not also make their voices heard midst this general agitation?

Excluded from the national assemblies by laws so well consolidated that they allow no hope of infringement, they do not ask, Sire, for your permission to send their deputies to the Estates General; they know too well how much favor will play a part in the election, and how easy it would be for those elected to impede the freedom of voting.

We prefer, Sire, to place our cause at your feet; not wishing to obtain anything except from your heart, it is to it that we address our complaints and confide our miseries.

The women of the Third Estate are almost all born without wealth; their education is very neglected or very defective: it consists in their being sent to school with a teacher who himself does not know the first word of the language he teaches. They continue to go there until they can read the service of the Mass in

French and Vespers in Latin. Having fulfilled the first duties of religion, they are taught to work; having reached the age of fifteen or sixteen, they can earn five or six *sous* a day. If nature has refused them beauty they get married, without a dowry, to unfortunate artisans; lead aimless, difficult lives stuck in the provinces; and give birth to children they are incapable of raising. If, on the contrary, they are born pretty, without breeding, without principles, with no idea of morals, they become the prey of the first seducer, commit a first sin, come to Paris to bury their shame, end by losing it altogether, and die victims of dissolute ways.

Today, when the difficulty of subsisting forces thousands of them to put themselves up for auction, when men find it easier to buy them for a short time than to win them over forever, those whom a fortunate penchant inclines to virtue, who are consumed by the desire to learn, who feel themselves carried along by a natural taste, who have overcome the deficiencies of their education and know a little of everything without having learned anything, those, finally, whom a lofty soul, a noble heart, and a pride of sentiment cause to be called prudes, are obliged to throw themselves into cloisters where only a modest dowry is required, or forced to become servants if they do not have enough courage, enough heroism, to share the generous devotion of the girls of Vincent de Paul.

Also, many, solely because they are born girls, are disdained by their parents, who refuse to set them up, preferring to concentrate their fortune in the hands of a son whom they designate to carry on their name in the capital; for Your Majesty should know that we too have names to keep up. Or, if old age finds them spinsters, they spend it in tears and see themselves the object of the scorn of their nearest relatives.

To prevent so many ills, Sire, we ask that men not be allowed, under any pretext, to exercise trades that are the prerogative of women—whether as seamstress, embroiderer, millinery shopkeeper, etc., etc.; if we are left at least with the needle and the spindle, we promise never to handle the compass or the square.

We ask, Sire, that your benevolence provide us with the means of making the most of the talents with which nature will have endowed us, notwithstanding the impediments which are forever being placed on our education.

May you assign us positions, which we alone will be able to fill, which we will occupy only after having passed a strict examination, following trustworthy inquiries concerning the purity of our morals.

We ask to be enlightened, to have work, not in order to usurp men's authority, but in order to be better esteemed by them, so that we might have the means of living safe from misfortune and so that poverty does not force the weakest among us, who are blinded by luxury and swept along by example, to join the crowd of unfortunate women who overpopulate the streets and whose debauched audacity disgraces our sex and the men who keep them company.

We would wish this class of women might wear a mark of identification. Today, when they adopt even the modesty of our dress, when they mingle everywhere in all kinds of clothing, we often find ourselves confused with them; some men make mistakes and make us blush because of their scorn. They should never be able to take off the identification under pain of working in public workshops for the benefit of the poor (it is known that work is the greatest punishment that can be inflicted on them). . . . [ellipses in text] However, it occurs to us that the empire of fashion would be destroyed and one would run the risk of seeing many too many women dressed in the same color.

We implore you, Sire, to set up free schools where we might learn our language on the basis of principles, religion and ethics. May one and the other be offered to us in all their grandeur, entirely stripped of the petty applications which attenuate their majesty; may our hearts be formed there; may we be taught above all to practice the virtues of our sex: gentleness, modesty, patience, charity. As for the arts that please, women learn them without teachers. Sciences? . . . [in text] they serve only to inspire us with a stupid pride, lead us to pedantry, go against the wishes of nature, make of us mixed beings who are rarely faithful wives and still more rarely good mothers of families.

We ask to take leave of ignorance, to give our children a sound and reasonable education so as to make of them subjects worthy of serving you. We will teach them to cherish the beautiful name of Frenchmen; we will transmit to them the love we have for Your Majesty. For we are certainly willing to leave valor and genius to men, but we will always challenge them over the dangerous and precious gift of sensibility; we defy them to love you better than we do. They run to Versailles, most of them for their interests, while we, Sire, go to see you there, and when with difficulty and with pounding hearts, we can gaze for an instance upon your August Person, tears flow from our eyes. The idea of Majesty, of the Sovereign, vanishes, and we see in you only a tender Father, for whom we would give our lives a thousand times.

Notes

1 Lisa Moore, et al., *Transatlantic Feminisms in the Age of Revolutions* (Oxford: Oxford University Press, 2012), p. 222.

2 Ibid., p. 221.

3 "Petition of Women of the Third Estate to the King," in *The French Revolution and Human Rights*, ed. Lynn Hunt (Boston: Bedford/St. Martin's, 1996), pp. 60–63.

Part II

The Nineteenth Century

6

Petitions to the Cherokee National Council
Cherokee Women's Councils
Cherokee Lands
May 2, 1817, June 30, 1818, and October 17, 1821

Cherokees numbered around twenty-five thousand at the time of these petitions, and lived in central Georgia, northeastern Alabama, eastern Tennessee, and western North Carolina, lands respected as essential to their spirituality and identity. The United States and Georgia first encouraged, then ultimately forced their relocation west, despite the 1785 Treaty of Hopewell, which defined their territorial boundaries. By the 1820s about a third of the nation had moved west, while many of the rest

> set themselves upon a deliberate program of "civilization" on the white man's terms. Accepting the Jeffersonian ideal of the individual farmer, the Cherokees established successful farms, multiplied their livestock, began educating their children in missionary schools, and eventually, in 1827, developed a full-scale republican political organization with institutions patterned directly upon those of the United States. They adopted a written Constitution, and were soon to develop their own written language and alphabet and establish their own press. Every step toward "civilization" intensified their interest in retaining their homeland. News from the Cherokees in the West was discouraging about prospects there. . . . Cherokee "progress" was interpreted, unsympathetically, by land-hungry Georgians as "permanence."[1]

Native American women at this time probably had more authority and autonomy than their European counterparts; though there was a gendered division of labor, it established balance rather than hierarchy. Gender equality declined due to colonialism since, for example, Euro-American men preferred to negotiate and trade with Native men, and the new Christian religion being spread came complete with its own form of patriarchy. Nonetheless, matrilineal inheritance and matrilocal culture remained the norm in many Native communities and, as the documents below attest, women "continued to use their maternal authority to influence political decisions within and outside of their own nations."[2] In particular, "The Indian removal crisis provided an opportunity for Cherokee women to voice their dissent in various petitions to the Cherokee National Council. They expressed their distaste for land cession and allotment using both moral and kin-based arguments."[3] They were successful, for a time.

Speaking to multiple audiences, the documents below show women using tribal-based maternal defenses and more Anglo-influenced defenses of their "civilization," as well as early environmental arguments. As with much of their culture, understandings of motherhood and womanhood were in flux. In general, "[T]he language prioritizes community survival rather than individualistic achievement, and it seeks to retain common landownership. Both the first and second petitions invoke the rhetoric of motherhood, but . . . the second assumes a more supplicant tone. In addition, the second petition differs substantially by pointing to 'Christian authority in the fight against removal' instead of basing its authority on 'indigenous motherhood.'"[4] The third, like every document in this collection, insists that women have the right to speak on any matter "where our interest is as much at stake as any other part of the community." The petitions were presented orally to the very council whose actions were being questioned.

After the Indian Removal Act of 1830, some one hundred thousand members of the Cherokee, Creek, Chickasaw, Choctaw, and Seminole tribes were forced west of the Mississippi, and thousands died along the way. Women endured extra threats of rape by soldiers, as migrants do still today, and extra risks from childbirth and childcare while marching.

Petition of May 2, 1817

The Cherokee ladys now being present at the meeting of the chiefs and warriors in council have thought it their duty as mothers to address their beloved chiefs and warriors now assembled.[5]

Our beloved children and head men of the Cherokee Nation, we address you warriors in council. We have raised all of you on the land which we now have, which God gave us to inhabit and raise provisions. We know that our country has once been extensive but by repeated sales has become circumscribed to a small track, and [we] never have thought it our duty to interfere in the disposition of it till now. If a father or mother was to sell all their lands which they had to depend on, which their children had to raise their living on, which would be indeed bad & to be removed to another country. We do not wish to go to an unknown country [to] which we have understood some of our children wish to go over the Mississippi, but this act of our children would be like destroying your mothers.

Your mothers, your sisters ask and beg of you not to part with any more of our land. We say ours. You are our descendants; take pity on our request. But keep it for our growing children, for it was the good will of our creator to place us here, and you know our father, the great president, will not allow his white children to take our country away. Only keep your hands off of paper talks for its [sic] our own country. For [if] it was not, they would not ask you to put your hands to paper, for it would be impossible to remove us all. For as soon as one child is raised, we have others in our arms, for such is our situation & will consider our circumstances.

Therefore, children, don't part with any more of our lands but continue on it & enlarge your farms. Cultivate and raise corn & cotton and your mothers and sisters will make clothing for you which our father the president has recommended to us all. We don't charge any body for selling any lands, but we have heard such intentions of our children. But your talks become true at last; it was our desire to forwarn you all not to part with our lands.

Petition of June 30, 1818

Beloved Children,[6]

We have called a meeting among ourselves to consult on the different points now before the council, relating to our national affairs. We have heard with painful feelings that the bounds of the land we now possess are to be drawn into very narrow limits. The land was given to us by the Great Spirit above as our common right, to raise our children upon, & to make support for our rising generations. We therefore humbly petition our beloved children, the head men & warriors, to hold out to the last in support of our common rights, as the Cherokee nation have been the first settlers of this land; we therefore claim the right of the soil.

We well remember that our country was formerly very extensive, but by repeated sales it has become circumscribed to the very narrow limits we have at present. Our Father the President advised us to become farmers, to manufacture our own clothes, & to have our children instructed. To this advice we have attended in every thing as far as we were able. Now the thought of being compelled to remove the other side of the Mississippi is dreadful to us, because it appears to us that we, by this removal, shall be brought to a savage state again, for we have, by the endeavor of our Father the President, become too much enlightened to throw aside the privileges of a civilized life.

We therefore unanimously join in our meeting to hold our country in common as hitherto.

Some of our children have become Christians. We have missionary schools among us. We have heard the gospel in our nation. We have become civilized & enlightened, & are in hopes that in a few years our nation will be prepared for instruction in other branches of sciences & arts, which are both useful & necessary in civilized society.

There are some white men among us who have been raised in this country from their youth, are connected with us by marriage, & have considerable families, who are very active in encouraging the emigration of our nation. These ought to be our truest friends but prove our worst enemies. They seem to be only concerned how to increase their riches, but do not care what becomes of our Nation, nor even of their own wives and children.

Petition of October 17, 1821

To the Committee and Council,[7]

We the females, residing in Salequoree and Pine Log, believing that the present difficulties and embarrassments under which this nation is placed demands a full expression of the mind of every individual, on the subject of emigrating to Arkansas, would take upon ourselves to address you. Although it is not common for our sex to take part in public measures, we nevertheless feel justified in expressing our sentiments on any subject where our interest is as much at stake as any other part of the community.

We believe the present plan of the General Government to effect our removal West of the Mississippi, and thus obtain our lands for the use of the State of Georgia, to be highly oppressive, cruel and unjust. And we sincerely hope there is no consideration which can induce our citizens to forsake the land of our fathers of which they have been in possession from time immemorial, and thus compel us, against our will, to undergo the toils and difficulties of removing with our helpless families hundreds of miles to unhealthy and unproductive country. We hope therefore the Committee and Council will take into deep consideration our deplorable situation, and do everything in their power to avert such a state of things. And we trust by a prudent course their transactions with the General government will enlist in our behalf the sympathies of the good people of the United States.

Notes

1 *UC Davis History Project*, accessed Sept. 2017, historyproject.ucdavis.edu.
2 Ellen Holmes Pearson, "American Indian Women." *TeachingHistory.Org*, accessed Sept. 2017, www.teachinghistory.org.
3 Katherine Osburn, "American History to 1900." Accessed 2014, iweb.tntech.edu.
4 Karen Kilcup, *Fallen Forests: Emotion, Embodiment, and Ethics in American Women's Environmental Writing, 1781–1924* (Athens: University of Georgia Press, 2013), p. 37.
5 Qtd. from Theda Perdue, *The Cherokee Removal: A Brief History with Documents* (Boston: Bedford, 1995), pp. 125–29.
6 Ibid.
7 Ibid.

7

Constitution

Female Anti-Slavery Society of Salem, Massachusetts

Salem, Massachusetts

February 1832

Advertisement for a fund-raising sale held by the *first* Female Anti-Slavery Society in the United States, and signed by "females of color, of the Commonwealth of Massachusetts." From Salem Female Anti-Slavery Society, sarahparkerremond.wordpress.com.

Female antislavery societies are given credit for developing and employing women's political skills, for defying "gender conventions of submissiveness and domesticity," and for moving "toward a new ideology of equal rights."[1] Some authors refer to the participants as "feminist abolitionists."[2] Nonetheless, virtually all scholars still insist on naming the 1848 meeting at Seneca Falls *the first* women's rights convention, though this collection obviously does not.

The numerous organizations feminist abolitionists built, the meetings and conventions they held, and the documents they wrote together show an understanding of how reflections on experience and the practice of dialogue can lead to knowledge and democratic citizenship. The simultaneous gender, race, and class analysis in them is unmistakable. The members tried to break down racial divisions by working together in antislavery groups and appearing together in public, not only by having the more privileged speak for the less. They spoke as women, and were in fact the only collective voices consistently devoted to revealing and representing the realities of enslaved women's lives; they used the tools and strategies for change most "appropriate" to women but, simultaneously, expanded them.

Finding themselves excluded from all-male abolitionist associations, women immediately organized on their own. Some female antislavery organizations were all White, others were composed entirely of free Black women (many still at risk of being captured and sold), while the rest were, to different degrees, racially integrated. The Female Anti-Slavery Society of Salem, originally all Black, admitted White women in 1834 (when it changed its name slightly to the Salem Female Anti-Slavery Society). This first female antislavery society did not disband until 1866, after the Emancipation Proclamation.

The founding document provides us with a very early reference to "racial uplift"—a term evoking both spiritual and social solidarity and struggle—as the association devoted itself "to promote the welfare of our color." ("Lifting as we climb" became the motto of the National Association of Colored Women's Clubs in 1896.) Like the authors of the previous documents, these free Black women were a far cry from being recognized as citizens in 1832; they nonetheless simply worked as citizens should—but generally do not—to alleviate injustices within their own classes and among the more oppressed.

This, like all antislavery associations, most obviously worked to end the political and economic institution that kept millions of Americans in bondage. Although it is not obvious in the contents of the Constitution, the Salem society used a range of strategies and worked on a number of issues related but not identical to abolition, including segregation in the North. This broad approach allowed them to appeal to and engage more people in their cause; to use the skills, resources, and maneuvering room they had as women of different classes and races; and to confront the many-sided problem of racial discrimination.

The notice above, for example, advertises a typical fund-raising bazaar, to which "all who are disposed to aid the cause, are respectfully invited to attend." Money raised was used for numerous purposes, including supporting antislavery publications and organizing lecture series. The Salem Female Anti-Slavery Society also "supported secular and Sabbath schools for free blacks, [and] assisted newly freed or runaway slaves. . . . The SFASS established a sewing school for young black women and girls and raised funds to help sustain a local black church."[3]

Like the famous Enlightenment-era philosophers, the authors of this Constitution speak of "improvement," seeing things in their "true light," and "enlightenment" from "prejudice." The ideas here, however, confront forms of "the monster prejudice" that most of the aforementioned philosophers left untouched, deeply compromised as they were by their sexism and racism.

As noted in the introduction to this volume, attention to democratic values and practices, and recognition of the value of coalition building, is visible in multiple feminist documents across time and place. This early Constitution, for example, supports "all anti-slavery publications," and requires the practice of allowing "any member who wishes to speak" the "privilege" of doing so—without interruption.

SFASS member Sarah Remond, pictured in figure 7.2, was a famous Black abolitionist speaker who traveled without a male escort and spoke to inte-

Sarah Parker Remond.

grated audiences. The connections between and overlaps among abolitionist and women's rights activities are obvious just from looking at the Salem group: the society brought in Lucy Stone to speak, and the Grimke sisters also gave talks in Salem. Members of the lecture team at times included Abby Kelly Foster and Susan B. Anthony. In 1858 Remond appeared at the National Woman's Rights Convention in New York City.

Constitution

We the undersigned, females of color, of the Commonwealth of Massachusetts, being duly convinced of the importance of union and morality, have associated ourselves together for our natural improvement, and to promote the welfare of our color, as far as is consistent with the means of this Society; therefore we adopt the following resolutions.[4]

Resolved, that as we believe the *Boston Liberator* to be the means of enlightening the minds of many, in regard to the ungenerous scheme of African colonization, and also removing the monster prejudice from the minds of many, in regard to the free people of color, by representing things in their true light, we are determined to support it and all anti-slavery publications.

Resolved, that this Society be supported by voluntary contributions, a part to be appropriated for the purchasing of books, etc.: the other to be reserved until a significant sum be accumulated, which shall then be deposited in a bank for the relief of the needy.

Resolved, that the meetings of this society shall commence with prayer and singing. Any member who wishes to speak is allowed the privilege: when any member speaks, there shall be no interruption.

Resolved, that this Society shall be governed by a President, Vice President, Corresponding Secretary, Recording Secretary, Treasurer, and Librarian who are hereafter to be instructed in the duties of their offices.

Resolved that persons not conforming to the rules of the Society shall be expelled, by receiving a note or card bearing the names of the President and Vice President, and signed by the Corresponding Secretary.

Notes

1 Ruth Bogin and Jean Fagan Yellin, "Introduction," in *The Abolitionist Sisterhood: Women's Political Culture in Antebellum America*, ed. Jean Fagan Yellin and John C. Van Horne (Ithaca, NY: Cornell University Press, 1994), p. 6.

2 See, for example, Blanche Glassman Hersh and Clare Midgley, "Women, Anti-Slavery, and Internationalism," in *Women and Social Movements, International, 1840 to Present*, ed. Thomas Dublin and Kathryn Kish Sklar (Alexandria, VA: Alexander Street Press, 1980), wasi.alexanderstreet.com.

3 Shirley Yee, "Female Anti-Slavery Society, Salem, Massachusetts (1832–1866)," n.d. *BlackPast.org*, accessed Feb. 7, 2016, www.blackpast.org.

4 Female Anti-Slavery Society of Salem, "Constitution of the Female Anti-Slavery Society of Salem," 1832. *BlackPast.org*, accessed Feb. 7, 2016, www.blackpast.org.

8

Constitution
Lowell Factory Girls Association
Lowell, Massachusetts
October 1836

Image of the turnout for the Lowell Factory Girls Association's strike in February 1834. *"As our fathers resisted unto blood the lordly avarice of the British Ministry, so we, their daughters, never will wear the yoke which has been prepared for us."*[1]

The textile industry was booming in Lowell, Massachusetts, during the 1830s, and mill owners recruited mostly young women from around the New England area to work in their factories. The young women were lured by promises of good wages and housing. In 1836, however, the mill owners cut wages and added fees, reducing the wages by about a dollar a week—a significant enough portion that those who had previously been economically independent were now reduced to the position of indentured servants to the mill owners. This drastic change, and the increasingly severe conditions of work in the factories (long hours, poor facilities, and maltreatment by male overseers), led women workers to organize one of the first labor strikes in the United States. The "factory girls" decided to "turn out" of work in both 1834 and 1836; in 1836 they organized the Lowell Factory Girls Association and wrote a constitution to help them fight against the avaricious and unfair changes the mill owners made.

In the Preamble and Constitution below, the young women argue "firmly and fearlessly" that they should be able to develop and keep a good moral character while they work in the mills, which they are only able to do if they are given due recompense for their work. They were seen but did not see themselves as easily seduced, and instead insist upon their right to and "love of moral and intellectual culture." They forcefully claim the right to unionize against the "avaricious capitalists" to maintain their dignity, and they vow to stand together as a united front. One noteworthy part of the Constitution that might be overlooked is the second article, which asserts, "Any female of good moral character, and who works in any one of the Mills in this city, may become a member of the Association, by subscribing to the Constitution." This conflation of a woman of good moral character with a working woman—and the implication that such a woman would be allowed to speak publicly—was a revolutionary idea that would be taken up by women's groups advocating for labor rights as well as women's suffrage in the years to come.

Harriet Hanson Robinson, who documented the Lowell "turn outs" in her book *Loom and Spindle*, remembers, "One of the girls stood on a pump, and gave vent to the feelings of her companions in a neat speech, declaring that it was their duty to resist all attempts at cutting down the wages. This was the first time a woman had spoken in public in Lowell, and the event caused surprise and consternation among her audience."[2] These young women had the courage to speak out for justice and respect as participants in Republican America, and they established a precedent for labor strikes and organizations, especially when the labor force was mostly composed of women (see Stoneham 1870 and Chicago 1909 for examples).

Although the mill owners refused to meet the factory girls' demands, and the organization would protest again in 1845, this organization and "turn out" became part of the women's arsenal against unfair labor practices throughout the Industrial Revolution and echo even today in women's declarations that advocate for economic justice.

Constitution of the Lowell Factory Girls Association

PREAMBLE[3]

Whereas we, the undersigned, residents of Lowell, moved by a love of honest industry and the expectation of a fair and liberal recompence, have left our homes, our relatives and youthful associates, and come hither, and subjected ourselves to all the danger and inconvenience, which necessarily attend young and unprotected females, when among strangers, and in a strange land; and however humble the condition of Factory Girls, (as we are termed,) may seem, we firmly and fearlessly (though we trust with a modesty becoming our sex,) claim for ourselves, that love of moral and intellectual culture, that admiration of, and desire to attain and preserve pure, elevated and refined characters, a true reverence for the divine principle which bids us render to every one his due; a due appreciation of those great and cardinal principles of our government, of justice and humanity, which enjoins on us "to live and let live"—that chivalrous and honorable feeling, which with equal force, forbids us to invade others rights, or suffer others, upon any consideration, to invade ours; and at the same time, that utter abhorrence and detestation of whatever is mean, sordid, dishonorable or unjust—all of which, can alone, in our estimation, entitle us to be called the daughters of freemen, or of Republican America.

And, whereas, we believe that those who have preceded us have been, we know that ourselves are, and that our successors are liable to be, assailed in various ways by the wicked and unprincipled, and cheated out of just, legal and constitutional dues, by ungenerous, illiberal and avaricious capitalists,—and convinced that "union is power," and that as the unprincipled consult and advise, that they may the more easily decoy and seduce—we (being the weaker,) claim it to be our undeniable right, to associate and concentrate our power, that we may the more successfully repel their equally base and iniquitous aggressions.

And, whereas, impressed with this belief, and conscious that our cause is a common one, and our conditions similar, we feel it our imperative duty to stand by each other through weal and woe: to administer to each others wants, to prevent each others back-sliding—to comfort each other in sickness, and advise each other in health, to incite each other to the love and attainment of those excellences, which can alone constitute the perfection of female character—unsullied virtue, refined tastes and cultivated intellects—and in a word, do all that in us lies, to make each other worthy of ourselves, our country and Creator.

Therefore, for the better attainment of those objects, we associate ourselves together, and mutually pledge to each other, a females irrefragable vow, to stand by, abide by, and be governed by the following PROVISIONS.

Article 1st. It shall be denominated the LOWELL FACTORY GIRLS ASSOCIATION.

Art. 2d. Any female of good moral character, and who works in any one of the Mills in this city, may become a member of the Association, by subscribing to the Constitution.

Art. 3d. The officers of the Association shall be, a President, Vice President, a Recording Secretary, a Corresponding Secretary, a Treasurer, a Collector, and a Prudential Committee, two of whom shall be selected from each Corporation in this city.

Notes

1 Factory Girls Association, Article in *National Laborer*, 1836. PBU Builder, accessed Feb. 7, 2016, www.pbubuilder.org. Italics in original.

2 Harriet Hanson Robinson, *Loom and Spindle; or, Life among the Early Mill Girls* (New York: Crowell, 1898), pp. 83–86.

3 Lowell Factory Girls Association, "Constitution of the Lowell Factory Girls Association," 1836. University of Massachusetts, Lowell, accessed Feb. 7, 2016, http://library.uml.edu/clh/all/doc01.htm.

9

Resolutions
First Anti-Slavery Convention of American Women
New York, New York
May 9–12, 1837

Image of an antislavery medallion.

We doubly owe to the slave this convention, the first general one of
women ever held in our country, if not in the world.
—Maria Weston Chapman[1]

Sarah Grimke, who learned about the cruelties of both patriarchy and slavery
in her childhood home in the South, made the first comment at this meeting.
The minutes note that she "stated that the object of the Convention was to interest women in the subject of anti-slavery, and establish a system of operations
throughout every town and village in the free States, that would exert a powerful influence in the abolition of American slavery" (3–4). Grimke's statement
is a claim about the potential political power of women—an understanding of
how women's increased recognition of and attention to the wrongs of slavery,
combined with systematic organization, could bring about such deep political
change as the abolition of slavery. Women were urged to work "with the faith
of an Esther, and the untiring perseverance of the importunate widow" (8), and
"to do all that she can by her voice, and her pen, and her purse, and the influence of her example, to overthrow the horrible system of American slavery" (9).
What powerful claims and images in 1837, and what a way to begin the first-ever
national convention of women.

As local and state female antislavery associations proliferated, the need arose
for a national convention to coordinate their work, and for groups to educate
and inspire one another—still today a common motive for organizing beyond
the local level. The seventy-one delegates from seven states included Black and
White women, consistent with the resolutions urging women to integrate various
institutions and gatherings. (Only once is the color of the attendees mentioned
in the minutes; in response to the resolution condemning the American Colo-

nization Society, the minutes note, "This resolution elicited much expression of opinion, and some touching appeals from the colored members of the Convention" [13].)

Some in attendance already were or soon would be prominent organizers, including Lucretia Mott, Sarah and Angelina Grimke, and Lydia Maria Child, who together introduced the bulk of the resolutions throughout the gathering. The meeting was organized by a "Committee of Arrangements," and Mary Parker served as president; she was praised at the end for having "performed the duties of the chair" with "dignity and impartiality" (18). Committees were appointed to prepare pamphlets, including "Appeal to Women of the *Nominally* Free States," "Address to Free Colored Americans," "Letter to the Women of Great Britain," and "Letter to Juvenile Anti-Slavery Societies."

Three international links appear at this convention, showing how early the women's rights movement linked women across place, as well as race, and how informed they were about international events. One is a letter in the appendix from a women's antislavery association in England, the "Committee of the Newcastle on Tyne Ladies' Emancipation Society" (23), which mentions previous letters from the states; the second is the mention above of a pamphlet to the women of Great Britain; and the third is a reference in the Resolutions to the antislavery petition from the slaveholders of Martinique to the French Chamber of Deputies (17), which was held up as a model for the U.S. slaveholders of their power, too, to bring down the institution of slavery.

Also interesting and likely to escape notice is the political stance taken toward marriage and family. The document castigates those who would marry into slavery, refusing to treat marriage as separate from politics, and holds the corruption of marriage among the enslaved as one argument against slavery. Too, quite a bit is said about the role of women as mothers in ending racial prejudice. Finally, there is a short moment at the convention when there is confusion about what names the attendees will use for themselves. They resolve to follow each person's wishes, but seem aware that whether one refers to oneself as Jane Smith or as Mrs. Tom Jones reflects sexual politics.

We already know that female antislavery societies employed a wide range of strategies for change. The ones emphasized in this phenomenal national document—proposed, debated, and approved by women from local and state associations—are numerous and profound. They show the connections between women's rights and abolition as they urge women, as wives, sisters, daughters, and mothers, to petition their legislators; "to send up memorials to the different ecclesiastical bodies to which they belong, praying them to declare slavery a sin"; "fully to discuss the subject of slavery"; to make sacrifices in their personal and family lives so as to contribute more money to antislavery work (13); to refuse to purchase goods produced without remuneration, and to urge others to do the same; to think of and work for the freedom of the enslaved mother, who either watches her children be turned into slaves or sees them sold off; to refuse to marry southern slaveholders; to integrate the "nominally free states" by associating with free people of color (17) "as though the color of the skin was of no more consequence than the color of the hair, or the eyes" (13); and "to do all they can to establish and sustain day, evening, and Sabbath schools irrespective of color" (14).

The list of resolutions from this national gathering is quite lengthy. Only a few caused controversy at the gathering. Several additional themes are worth noting, in their strength, and in both their similarities and differences from those at the earlier meetings:

- Emphasis was placed on understanding the antislavery cause as godly and, flowing from that, recognition of the duty of all human beings to restore and preserve freedom, even in the face of "the unprincipled and violent efforts" against them.
- Resolutions were made specifically targeting and forcefully condemning fugitive slave laws, and refusing to discuss "better" and "worse" treatment of the enslaved, since dehumanization is common to all "ownership."
- The word "freedom" appears numerous times, directed very politically to those who see themselves as good American citizens. The references point out the inconsistency between enslavement and talk of the United States as a free nation; contrast the divine right and constitutional freedom to petition the government with congressional attempts to abridge such activity in the case of abolition; and contrast starkly external restrictions on women's freedom of speech and their recommended circumscribed sphere of action with their self-described right and duty "to overthrow the horrible system of American slavery."
- Numerous institutions, as well, are seen not as bulwarks of democracy but as corrupted by slaveholders and the political and economic system of slavery, including marriage, the legal system, virtually every political office, and religious societies. Congress comes in for the greatest condemnation, since it has as much power to abolish slavery as it has exercised "to create and sustain it." But colleges, shopkeepers, schools, and individuals are held to account, as well, for the diverse and unprincipled tactics they used to maintain the institution of slavery.

Following in the footsteps of the Philadelphia Female Anti-Slavery Association, which declared at its 1833 meeting that "[t]hey shall keep a record of their proceedings, which shall be laid before the Society, at each meeting," this document also includes a resolution that the minutes and "other documents, be published." These groups understood their important role and were creating for themselves a place in history.

Resolutions

Resolved,[2] That a thorough investigation of the anti-slavery cause, in all its various aspects and tendencies, has confirmed us in the belief that it is the cause of God, who created mankind free, and of Christ, who died to redeem them from every yoke. Consequently it is the duty of every human being to labor to preserve, and to restore to all who are deprived of it, God's gift of freedom; thus showing love and gratitude to the Great Redeemer by treading in his steps.

Resolved, That while we rejoice in any mitigation of cruelty in the treatment of our brethren and sisters held as slaves, we will bear in mind that the great question is not one of treatment, but of *principle*; hence, that no compromise can be made on the score of kind usage, while man is held as the property of man.

Resolved, That we regard the combination of interest which exists between the North and the South, in their political, commercial, and domestic relations, as the true, but hidden cause of the unprincipled and violent efforts which have been made, (at the North, but made in vain,) to smother free discussion, impugn the motives, and traduce the characters of abolitionists.

Resolved, That we regard the legalized practice of surrendering fugitive slaves to their southern task-masters, as utterly at variance with the principles of liberty *professed* by us "the freest nation in the world;" and a daring infringement of the divine commands, "Thou shalt *not* deliver unto his master, the servant that is escaped from his master unto thee."—"Hide the outcast, bewray [sic] not him that wandereth. Let my outcast dwell with thee, be thou a covert to them from the face of the spoiler."

Resolved, That the right of petition is natural and inalienable, derived immediately from God, and guaranteed by the Constitution of the United States, and that we regard every effort in Congress to abridge this sacred right, whether it be exercised by man or woman, the bond or the free, as a high-handed usurpation of power, and an attempt to strike a death-blow at the freedom of the people. And therefore that it is the duty of every woman in the United States, whether northerner or southerner, annually to petition Congress with the faith of an Esther, and the untiring perseverance of the importunate widow, for the immediate abolition of slavery in the District of Columbia and the Territory of Florida, and the extermination of the inter-state slave-trade.

Resolved, That we regard those northern men and women, who marry southern slaveholders, either at the South or the North, as identifying themselves with a system which desecrates the marriage relation among a large portion of the white inhabitants of the southern states, and utterly destroys it among the victims of their oppression.

Resolved, That we recommend to the women of those states where laws exist recognizing the legal right of the master to retain his slave within their jurisdiction, for a term of time, earnestly to petition their respective legislatures for the repeal of such laws; and that the right of trial by jury may be granted to all persons claimed as slaves.

Resolved, That whereas God has commanded us to "prove all things and hold fast that which is good,"—therefore, to yield the right, or exercise of free discussion to the demands of avarice, ambition, or worldly policy, would involve us in disobedience to the laws of Jehovah, and that as moral and responsible beings, the women of America are solemnly called upon by the spirit of the age and the signs of the times, fully to discuss the subject of slavery, that they may be prepared to meet the approaching exigency, and be qualified to act as women, and as Christians on this all-important subject.

Resolved, That as certain rights and duties are common to all moral beings, the time has come for woman to move in that sphere which Providence has assigned her, and no longer remain satisfied in the circumscribed limits with which corrupt custom and a perverted application of Scripture have encircled her; therefore that it is the duty of woman, and the province of woman, to plead the cause of the oppressed in our land, and to do all that she can by her voice, and her pen, and her purse, and the influence of her example, to overthrow the horrible system of American slavery.[3]

Resolved, That this Convention, with the deepest solicitude, offer to the Boards of the American Bible Society, the American and Foreign Bible Society, and kindred associations, the following suggestion and inquiry: It is our fear, respected fathers and brethren, that the Lord's treasury in this land has been hitherto polluted with the price of blood; and therefore the expected blessing has not rested upon our efforts to christianize the world. When Judas was stricken with remorse, the *Jewish* chief priests refused to receive his silver, because it was "the price of blood." And now we solemnly ask you, as stewards of the mysteries of God, can you continue to receive the contributions of those who sustain by their example, a system full of cruelty and crime—a system that denies to two millions of benighted souls the written Word of the living God.

Resolved, That our love to the perishing heathen—our gratitude to Christ for his last command—and our fervent desire for its speedy fulfillment, incite us to compare with the Word and Spirit of the sacred oracles, the present measures of the American church for evangelizing the world; and to declare that with the inconsistency of some of those measures we are grieved and distressed, and against them are constrained faithfully to remonstrate.

Resolved, That we earnestly recommend to all the followers of Christ in this land, to ascertain with fervent prayer, what God will have them to do in the matter; and through what channels their benevolence may flow to the heathen world, without mingling with the streams that arise from traffic "in *slaves,* and the *souls of men.*"

Resolved, That we must regard slavery in this country as a national sin, so long as it exists in the District of Columbia and the territory of Florida; as long as the northern states surrender the fugitive to his master, refuse to repeal those laws which recognize and secure the usurpation of the master over his slave, and continue pledged to put down servile insurrection at the South; as long as the inter-state slave trade is carried on, and there are governors in our free states, who pronounce the free discussion of the subject of slavery to be "a misdemeanor at common law," and that we regard slavery to be a national sin, because Congress has the power to abolish it, just so far as it has exercised that power to create and sustain it in our land.

Resolved, That there is no class of women to whom the anti-slavery cause makes so direct and powerful an appeal as to *mothers*; and that they are solemnly urged by all the blessings of their own and their children's freedom, and by all the contrasted bitterness of the slave-mother's condition, to lift up their hearts to God on behalf of the captive, as often as they pour them out over their own children in a joy with which "no stranger may intermeddle;" and that they are equally bound to guard with jealous care the minds of their children from the ruining influences of the spirit of pro-slavery and prejudice, let those influences come in what name, or through what connexions [sic] they may.

Resolved, That, Whereas we believe that the pure and Christian principles of PEACE commend themselves with peculiar power to the hearts of abolitionists; and

Whereas we feel that by publicly professing these principles, and engaging actively in their dissemination, we may give our friends at the South the best possible security that in all our measures for the relief of the oppressed slave, and for his restoration to freedom, we shall be governed by the forbearance and forgiving spirit of our Saviour;

Therefore, We recommend to mothers to educate their children in the principles of peace, and special abhorrence of that warfare, which gives aid to the oppressor against the oppressed.

Resolved, That as most of the merchants and editors of our large cities have done every thing they could, to close the door of access at the South against abolition doctrines, by villifying [sic] the characters and misrepresenting the motives of abolitionists, who have stood forth as the advocates of the oppressed American, whether bond or free; so we as their wives, mothers, sisters, and daughters, are resolved to do all that we can to open that door, by vindicating their characters from the aspersions which have been cast upon them, and to stand side by side with them in the great struggle between right and wrong, freedom and despotism, justice and oppression, Christian equality and American prejudice.

Resolved, That as northern churches are united to the southern slaveholding churches by the bonds of church government, or Christian fellowship, they are solemnly called upon to rebuke their brethren and not suffer sin upon them: And that it is the duty of women to send up memorials to the different ecclesiastical bodies to which they belong, praying them to declare slavery a sin which ought to be immediately repented of lest the curse of Almighty God fall upon their churches for refusing, as Meroz did, to come up "to the help of the Lord against the mighty."

Resolved, That we feel bound solemnly to protest against the principles of the American Colonization Society, as anti-republican and anti-christian, that we believe them to have had a most sorrowful influence in riveting the chains of the slave by recognizing him as the property of his master, and in strengthening the unreasonable and unholy prejudice against our brethren and sisters, by declaring them "almost too debased to be reached by the heavenly light," that to the slave, the Society offers exile or bondage; to the freeman, persecution or banishment, and that we view it as an expatriation Society.

Resolved, That this Convention do firmly believe that the existence of an unnatural prejudice against our colored population, is one of the chief pillars of American slavery—therefore, that the more we mingle with our oppressed brethren and sisters, the more deeply are we convinced of the sinfulness of that anti-christian prejudice which is crushing them to the earth in our nominally free states—sealing up the fountains of knowledge from their panting spirits, and driving them into infidelity, and that we deem it a solemn duty for every woman to pray to be delivered from such an unholy feeling, and to act out the principles of Christian equality by associating with them as though the color of the skin was of no more consequence than the color of the hair, or the eyes.

Resolved, That the support of the iniquitous system of slavery at the South is dependent on the co-operation of the North, by commerce and manufactures, as well as by the consumption of its products—therefore that, despising the gain of oppression we recommend to our friends, by a candid and prayerful examination of the subject, to ascertain if it be not a duty to cleanse our hands from this unrighteous participation, by no longer indulging in the luxuries which come through this polluted channel; and in the supply of the necessary articles of food and clothing, &c., that we "provide things honest in the sight of all men," by giving the preference to goods which come through requited labor.

Resolved, That we hail with high approbation the increasing number of those institutions of learning which, like Onedia [sic] Institute, Western Reserve College, and other seminaries, have practically reprobated the anti-republican prejudice that has so long excluded oppressed Americans from the advantages of a collegiate education in the United States; and we earnestly hope the time may soon arrive when all our academical institutions will inscribe over their portals, "Let him that is athirst for knowledge come, and whosoever will, of every clime and every creed, let him come and drink freely of the fountain of science and literature."

Resolved, That it is the duty of abolitionists to do all they can to establish and sustain day, evening, and Sabbath schools irrespective of color; and likewise to visit the schools in which colored pupils are taught, to encourage them in the acquisition of knowledge, and strengthen the teachers in their labor of love.

Resolved, That we view with heartfelt commendation the noble stand which Oberlin Collegiate Institute has taken with regard to prejudice; and it is with peculiar satisfaction we have learned that our oppressed sisters may find at least one seminary in our republican despotism, where they may enjoy the benefits of a liberal education.

Resolved, That we regard anti-slavery prints as powerful auxiliaries in the cause of emancipation, and recommend that these "pictorial representations" be multiplied an hundred fold; so that the speechless agony of the fettered slave may unceasingly appeal to the heart of the patriot, the philanthropist, and the christian.

Resolved, That as large funds are required in order to [facilitate] the rapid advancement of this cause, we consider it an imperious duty to make retrenchments from our own personal expenses, whenever in our power, that we may be the better able to contribute to such funds.

Resolved, That the members be designated according to their individual wishes.

Resolved, That the minutes of this Convention, with the other documents, be published.

Resolved, That a Convention of Anti-Slavery Women be held annually (with the permission of Providence) in Boston, New-York, Philadelphia, or elsewhere, until slavery is abolished.

Resolved, That when this Convention adjourns it be adjourned to meet in Philadelphia, on the third week in May, 1838.

Resolved, That we believe it to be the duty of abolitionists to encourage our oppressed brethren and sisters in their different trades and callings, by employing them whenever opportunities offer for so doing.

Resolved, That we, as abolitionists, use all our influence in having our colored friends seated promiscuously in all our congregations; and that as long as our churches are disgraced with side-seats and corners set apart for them, we will, as much as possible, take our seats with them.

Resolved, That the contribution of means for the purchase of men from their claimants, is an acknowledgment of a right of property in man, which is inconsistent with our principles, and not sanctioned by true humanity, unless it be accompanied by an absolute denial of the right of property, and a declaration that we contribute in the same spirit as we would do to redeem a fellow-creature from Algerine captivity.

Resolved, That we hail with heartfelt gratitude to God, and high approbation of man, the noble example with which the colored slaveholders in Martinique have set the slaveholders of the United States, in sending up a petition to the French Chamber of Deputies for the immediate abolition of slavery in that island, it being the first instance which slaveholders have themselves petitioned for the breaking of the yoke of the enslaved; and we earnestly recommend it to the prayerful consideration and speedy imitation of our southern brethren and sisters.

Resolved, That we recommend to the wives and daughters of clergymen, throughout the land, to strengthen their husbands and fathers to declare the whole counsel of God on the subject of slavery, fearing no danger, or prejudice, or privation, being willing "to suffer persecution with them for Christ's sake."

Resolved, That we have beheld with grief and amazement the death-like apathy of some northern churches on the subject of American slavery and the unchristian opposition of others to the efforts of the Anti-Slavery Society; and that as long as northern pulpits are closed against the advocates of the oppressed, whilst they are freely open to their oppressors, the northern churches have their own garments stained with the blood of slavery, and are awfully guilty in the sight of God.

Resolved, That we recommend to all whose consciences approve of appointed seasons for prayer, a punctual attendance upon the monthly concert of prayer for the slaves; and that around the family altar, and in their secret supplications before God, they earnestly commend to his mercy the suffering slave and the guilty master.

Resolved, That laying aside sectarian views, and private opinions, respecting certain parts of the preceding resolutions, we stand pledged to each other and the world, to *unite* our efforts for the accomplishment of the holy object of our association, that herein seeking to be directed by divine wisdom, we may be qualified to wield the sword of the spirit in this warfare; praying that it may never return to its sheath, until liberty is proclaimed to the captive, and the opening of the prison doors to those that are bound.

Notes

1 Appendix to the "Proceedings of the Anti-Slavery Convention of American Women: Held in the City of New-York, May 9th, 10th, 11th, and 12th, 1837," p. 19. All citations are to the *Samuel J. May Anti-Slavery Collection* edition, found at ebooks.library.cornell.edu.

2 Resolutions were made throughout the meeting (pp. 7–18). The only resolutions not recorded here concern who was on specific committees.

3 This proved to be among the most divisive resolutions. The Proceedings report that two amendments were offered, "which called forth an animated and interesting debate respecting the rights and duties of women." While the original resolution was "finally" adopted, "among those who voted against the adoption," a full twelve "wished to have their names recorded in the minutes, as disapproving of some parts of it" (p. 9). These words will reappear in the Declaration of Sentiments.

10

Preamble *and* Constitution
Lowell Female Labor Reform Association
Lowell, Massachusetts
January 1845

In January of 1845, twelve workers organized the first union of female factory workers in America, the Lowell Female Labor Reform Association. Within just six months, membership reached five hundred. Like the female antislavery associations, this group relied heavily on petitions, a favored tool of the disenfranchised; in this case they urged the state legislature to limit the workday to ten hours.

At stake was the need for leisure time to develop oneself physically, intellectually, spiritually, and morally. One could not be fully human without such development, and the claim of the association was that the worker should "hold that place in the social, moral and intellectual world, which a bountiful Creator designed him to occupy," rather than an inferior one of "ignorance and servitude." There is no "deferential" language here: "No! to us all has he given minds capable of eternal progression and improvement!" Today's language of "the 99 percent" has a foremother here in reference to "the favored few and the unfortunate many." Again, the intertwining of class and sex is at the heart of the document.

Like most documents in this collection, this 1845 association's Preamble and Constitution already had history behind them and foreshadow trends that remain visible over the decades. Beginning in the 1830s, early years of industrialization, women and girls from the Lowell mills went on strike over wages, hours, and conditions. Leading up to the formation of this association, earlier organizers employed numerous tactics over many years, in addition to the strike, including petitioning Congress for changes in labor laws; handing out pamphlets detailing labor conditions in first-person accounts; coordinating their actions with females at other nearby mills; holding rallies; starting up chapters in nearby towns; and, in 1843, setting up a monthly newspaper with the potential to keep its constituency informed and determined.

Under the guidance of the young labor leader Sarah Bagley, and with the *Voice of Industry* as its herald, the association tirelessly campaigned to convince the public of the need for reform in the mills. It published a series of widely distributed articles called "Factory Tracts," which documented the deteriorating conditions in the mills, and provided "a true exposition of the Factory system and its effects upon the health and happiness of the operatives." The associa-

Emblem of *The Voice of Industry*, a pro-worker publication.

tion would go on to become a leading organizing force in the Ten-Hour Movement in Lowell.

According to commentary about the Voice of Industry on the Industrial Revolution website, conditions

> gave rise to considerable discontent. Writing anonymously in the *Voice* as "one of the vast army of sufferers," an operative protested that while workers now tended "three or four looms, where they used to tend but two," and produced twice as much cloth, "the pay is not increased to them, while the increase to the owners is very great. Is this just?" Another, writing in 1845, observed that while the profits of 11 Lowell mills had doubled from the year before, the workers were being paid 12.5% less. "This is the natural result of the state of things in New England," she concluded, "the more wealth becomes concentrated in a few hands, and the poorer the great mass becomes."[1]

Addressing class and sex, the *Voice* featured articles on "woman's weakness," the rights of women, the rights of married women, and women's sphere of influence.

The society, which affiliated with the New England Workingmen's Association, renamed itself the Lowell Female Industrial Reform and Mutual Aid Society in 1847, and disbanded in 1850. Its place in history is as the first organization of working women to organize and bargain collectively for a variety of improved working conditions, including shorter hours and higher pay. The ten-hour workday became state law in 1874.

"Preamble" and "Constitution" of the Lowell Female Labor Reform Association

Whereas we, the Operatives of Lowell, believing that in the present age of improvement nothing can escape the searching glance of reform; and when men begin to inquire why the Laborer does not hold that place in the social, moral and intellectual world, which a bountiful Creator designed him to occupy the reason is obvious. He is a slave to a false and debasing state of society. Our Merciful Father in his infinite wisdom surely, has not bestowed all his blessings, both mental and moral on a favored few, on whom also he has showered all of [his] pecuniary gifts. No! to us all has he given minds capable of eternal progression and improvement!

It now only remains for us to throw off the shackles which are binding us in ignorance and servitude and which prevent us from rising to that scale of being for which God designed us. But how shall this be done? How shall the mass become educated? With the present system of labor it is impossible. There must be reasonable hours for manual labor, and a just portion of time allowed for the cultivation of the mental and moral faculties and no other way can the great work be accomplished.

We know no employment is respectable only as long as those employed are such and no farther than they are intelligent and moral can they merit the companionship and esteem of their fellow beings. It is evident, that with the present system of labor, the minds of the mass must remain uncultivated, their morals unimproved and our country be flooded with vice and misery!

Shall we, Operatives of America, the land where Democracy claims to be the principle by which we live and by which we are governed, see the evil daily increasing which separates more widely and more effectually the favored few and the unfortunate many, without one exertion to stay the progress? God forbid! Let the daughters of New England kindle the spark of philanthropy on every heart till its brightness shall fill the whole earth!

In consideration of which we adopt the following Constitution:

Art. 1st. This Association shall be called the Lowell Female Labor Reform Association.

[Articles 2–7 briefly and straightforwardly lay out the duties of the officers: a president, two vice-presidents, a secretary, a treasurer, and an eight-member board of directors.]

Art. 8th. Any person signing this Constitution, shall literally pledge herself to labor actively for Reform in the present system of labor.

Art. 9th. The members of this Association disapprove of all hostile measures, strikes and turn outs until all pacific measures prove abortive and then that it is the imperious duty of every one to assert and maintain that Independence which our brave ancestors bequeathed us, and sealed with their blood.

[Article 10 describes the process for amending the Constitution.]

Note

1 "Political Economy." *Voice of Industry.* Accessed Sept. 2017, www.industrialrevolution.org.

11

Petition for Women's Rights
Albany, New York
August 15, 1846

[T]he present government of this state has widely departed from the true democratic principles upon which all just governments must be based by denying to the female portion of [the] community the right of suffrage and any participation in forming the government and laws under which they live.

This petition[1] was submitted by Alpheus S. Greene to the state Constitutional Convention, which worked on revising the New York State Constitution from June 1 to October 9 of 1846. It is one of the earliest and most direct group petitions in United States history for women's political rights—especially suffrage—for which we have a record. Both the timing and some of the phrasing are reminiscent of Abigail Adams's now relatively famous letter to John Adams, her husband, calling for the legislators to "remember the ladies" as they wrote the U.S. Constitution; both accuse those who deny women their rights of being "ungenerous"—which then meant something akin to "irrational."

The six signatories (Eleanor Vincent, Susan Ormsby, Lydia A. Williams, Amy Ormsby, Lydia Osborn, and Anna Bishop) boldly remind the convention's participants of the principles and requirements of a just democratic government. While the basic argument of the petition is based on what were then the well-known principles of the Declaration of Independence, it would be a mistake to read it only as an extension of those concepts to women. First, employing the arguments of liberalism that lay behind the Declaration but were not expressed in it, the authors show themselves broadly educated, in the same way the authors were of the documents advocating for better working conditions and for an end to racial discrimination. This evidence of their intellect also stands as at least indirect support for their description of both their demands and themselves—despite their sex—as "reasonable," still a quite contested assertion at the time. Next, the petition asks for recognition of women's "civil" as well as "political rights," perhaps marking a beginning to the move from sole concern with democratic government to a broader focus on democratic society, which, increasingly, will be the focus of later documents in this collection. Relatedly, its distinction between "suffrage and any participation in forming the government and laws under which they live" is an intriguing but not entirely clear reference to greater participation in government—as elected and appointed officials, for example—beyond suffrage alone.

This petition is somewhat surprisingly unknown since it preceded the relatively celebrated Seneca Falls Convention by only two years. Both Lori Ginzberg, in *Untidy Origins: A Story of Woman's Rights in Antebellum New York* (2005), and Judith Wellman, in "Women's Rights, Republicanism, and Revolutionary Rhetoric in Antebellum New York State" (2000) suggest that Seneca Falls attendees such as Stanton and Anthony were very likely aware of the petition.[2] But most important, in Ginzberg's book, which is largely responsible for the rediscovery and analysis of this petition, she writes,

> The petition itself is stunning. [It] . . . is not the deferential and tentative plea that is often associated with petitioning by the disenfranchised. These women did not adopt the stance of supplicants or quasi-citizens, or, for that matter, "ladies." . . . Nor did they fortify their plea for full citizenship with the rhetorical arsenal of motherhood, as those familiar with the language of antebellum activism might expect. They did not use the honorifics "Mrs." or "Miss," as was customary for non-Quakers. On the contrary, they simply confronted their exclusion as full citizens and objected to it.[3]

Perhaps, given how few "deferential" pleas we have seen so far, and how women regularly assume the voice of citizens, legalities notwithstanding, these stereotypes should be dismantled, or the exception become the rule. The petition, like the letters of Adams, did not bring about immediate success, but became an influential part of the longer conversation over citizenship and democracy.

To the Constitutional Convention of the State of New-York

Your Memorialists inhabitants of Jefferson county, believing that civil government has its foundation in the laws of our existence, as moral and social beings, that the specific object and end of civil government is to protect all in the exercise of all their natural rights, by combining the strength of society for the defence of the individual—believing that the province of civil government is not to create new rights, but to declare and enforce those which originally existed. Believing likewise that all governments must derive their just powers from the consent of the governed "from the great body of society, and not from a favored class, although that favored class may be even a majority of the inhabitants," therefore respectfully represent: That the present government of this state has widely departed from the true democratic principles upon which all just governments must be based by denying to the female portion of [the] community the right of suffrage and any participation in forming the government and laws under which they live, and to which they are amenable, and by imposing upon them burdens of taxation, both directly and indirectly, without admitting them the right of representation, thereby striking down the only safeguards of their individual and personal liberties. Your Memorialists therefore ask your honorable body, to remove this just cause of complaint, by modifying the present Constitution of this State, so as to extend to women equal civil and political rights with men. In proposing this change, your petitioners ask you to confer upon them no new right but only to declare and enforce those which they originally inherited, but which have ungenerously been withheld from them, rights, which they as citizens of the state of New York may reasonably and rightfully claim. We might adduce arguments both numerous and decisive in support of our position, but believing that a self evident truth is sufficiently plain without argument, and in view of our necessarily limited space, we forbear offering any and respectfully submit it for consideration.

Notes

1 Jacob Katz Cogan and Lori Ginzberg, "1846 Petition for Woman's Suffrage," Aug. 8, 1846, Appendix, "1846 Petition for Woman's Suffrage, New York State Constitutional Convention." *Signs* 22.2 (Winter 1997): 427–39.

2 Lori Ginzberg, *Untidy Origins: A Study of Woman's Rights in Antebellum New York* (Chapel Hill: University of North Carolina Press, 2005), p. 9; Judith Wellman, "Women's Rights, Republicanism, and Revolutionary Rhetoric in Antebellum New York State." *New York History* 69.3 (1988): 354–55.

3 Ginzberg, p. 9.

12

Manifesto
Society for the Emancipation of Women
Paris, France
March 16, 1848

The first issue of *La Femme Libre*, August 15, 1832.

We have seen (1789 Petition) that the feminist movement in France dates back at least to the French Revolution. It became a major and complex force in the 1848 Revolution and the proclamation of the Second Republic, as well, which lasted until 1851 and adopted the familiar slogan, "Liberté, Égalité, Fraternité." Feminist activism is visible in the number of feminist organizations (the Fraternal Association of Both Sexes, the Union of Women, Society for the Emancipation of Women) and publications at the time (*La Femme Libre, La Voix des Femmes, La Politique des Femmes, L'Opinion des Femmes*); the range of feminist issues that became subjects of political debate (among them divorce, political rights, and education); and feminist involvement with democratic and socialist movements. Feminists were drawn to the Saint-Simonians, for example, who wanted the economic ties of marriage replaced with sexual and emotional connections. When the French Republic established universal male suffrage, a call for women's suffrage predictably followed. The government, after all, had announced, "Le suffrage sera direct et universel."

This Manifesto argues for women's rights not on the basis of the sameness of the sexes but on the unique and important social contributions made by women, primarily as mothers. Now seen as being like a loving mother, the new Republic in the Manifesto provides its female children as well as its male offspring with a good education. Actual mothers must be free in order to raise free children and create a peaceful society. Further, in addition to and to complement men's intelligence, woman's heart is indispensable to the accomplishment of those great French goals of liberty, equality, and fraternity. The 1848 Manifesto may appeal to traditional gendered characteristics, but it claims for them an expanded and critical role in the Republic. Women's influence could prove transformative. Although the language is often unfamiliar, many early references appear in this document to subjects that will be of lasting concern, such as domestic tyranny, political rights, economic independence, and the connections among them.

Tension appears as a result of this strategy, however, as when the Manifesto asks how "the principle of liberty can be introduced into the family without its harmony and hierarchy being disturbed." Change was imagined in politics, in education, and in the family, but the use of traditional gender norms that made change sound "safer" also put limits on it. As Susan Foley explains the difficult situation,

> [A]ppeals to women's special nature were historically produced, in a situation in which male definitions of "universalism" were masculine rather than gender-free. To see the feminist case as regressive for focusing on the particularity of women . . . ignores the fact that women also argued the individualist case more strongly and more logically than Republican men. Women were not immune from pervasive cultural assumptions of sexual difference. But men's refusal to acknowledge that women and men shared a common humanity made alternative arguments for female suffrage essential.[1]

Importantly, accepting gender differentiation does not mean accepting inequality or women's confinement to the domestic sphere; similarly, formal legal equality (that manifests, for example, as a universal right to own property or to have equal opportunity to an education) is not understood as necessarily based on a claim of sameness, and so was seen by the authors of this document as compatible with women claiming their rights "*as* women, as human beings who happened to be female."[2]

Jeanne Deroin, pictured in figure 12.2, was one of the most well-known feminist writers and activists of the revolutionary period. She was one of the publishers of *La Femme Libre*, the first French newspaper for women, and helped start (with Pauline Roland and others) the newspaper and the club *Voix des Femmes*. With Desirée Gay she founded the Association Mutuelle des Femmes and *Politique des Femmes*. She advised feminist groups in the United States.[3]

Jeanne Deroin, publisher of *La Femme Libre*.

Manifesto

Liberty, Equality, Fraternity,[4]

That is to say, truth, justice, morality. Everything ensues from these three principles, holy trinity from which one cannot remove one term without the other two, at the same time, losing much of their value.

Let us begin by clarifying how we understand these three words that are so magical that when hearing them, the heart already jumps for joy; these three words which are inscribed in the frontispiece of all our monuments!

LIBERTY, is material, intellectual, and moral independence; it is the exercise of every creature's right to the satisfaction of all the needs that God has given him, it is the respect for the other that one wants to see respected in oneself. In a word, freedom is the complete development of the three powers of being, blooming with the fertile breath of equality and fraternity.

EQUALITY, is the standard of justice and truth over all people; it is the essential culture of all relations, it is the exercise of the right to work for everyone in the measure and line of their faculties; it is the proportional distribution of all work in the general richness.

FRATERNITY, is the bond of love which must tie up again, one to another, all the members of the big human family; it is the purest vehicle for the passion of liberty and equality. Fraternity is the opposite of egotism, it is dedication, it is the expansion of one of the most adored reflections of the divine spirit in the human soul. The sight of all this injustice hurts fraternity; the spectacle of all this suffering rips it apart; its happiness is the happiness of all.

Women demand their emancipation. They want the inauguration of the real reign of true liberty, true fraternity. The coming of liberty and equality is an appeal made to their moral dignity; the coming of fraternity addresses their heart.

They want what they deserve, perhaps even less due to the legitimate need to finally see themselves raised from the secular debasement in which they have, more or less, until now, always been kept, than due to the conviction of the impossibility for all of humankind ever to arrive, without their active assistance, at the accomplishment of its happy fate.

The creator of the two halves of humankind, which he shaped in his image, God, all intelligence and all love, cannot have wanted one of them to be inferior to the other. He made them different, but equal, and so that they must mutually complement each other. If this one was endowed with a higher intelligence, that one received a bigger heart. Hence, in everything that demands as much heart as intelligence, the help of the woman is indispensable. But, like the realization that fraternity is essentially a work completely of the heart and that without fraternity there is no lasting equality or possible liberty; modern societies have inevitably arrived at this critical moment where they cannot but degrade if the people do not hasten to call for help the women in whom alone still resides, in their primitive purity, the greatest powers of the heart.

This, more clearly explained, but already irrefutable, will respond victoriously to those who oppose our nearing emancipation under the pretext that it would not facilitate but curb progress.

What do we mean by the fulfillment of our rights? First, independence of our persons, assured through the largest equal, obligatory, and free primary education system for both sexes.

This independence also guarantees on a more elevated level the diverse kinds of higher education, through similar institutions parallel to those that the Republic, as a good mother, will multiply, respond to all the vocations of her sons.

Assured and organized work prevents any exploitation of the weak for the strong and must guarantee to the last of the female workers, like the last of the male workers, her right to live, her place in the sun, her part of the goods which God has created for all.

The raising of moral standards in marriage, which is today most often only legal prostitution.

Divorce, poor amends for the troubles suffered in a poorly-matched union. The state of the children, devised in a way so that they do not have to suffer from the separation of their father and their mother.

The liberty to remarry for separated spouses.

Repeal, reworking of all the articles of the Civil Code that impair personal liberty, moral dignity, the fortune of all women who must see the hindrances that weigh on their property fall, like those that hold their intelligence in perpetual childhood and confine their person. Lastly, for the key to the edifice of their emancipation, their political rights.

How to pay the tax that one has not voted on oneself or through representatives of one's choosing? How to accept laws about which one was not consulted?

The decemvirs told the Romans:

"May you yourselves be the authors of the laws which create your happiness." The women must compete, with the men, for the making of the laws destined to realize the common good.

Here is the goal which we want to attain. Now, by which means can we achieve it?

That is what we need to research well, examine well, and debate well. As many laws as are put into practice, as many problems as there are to resolve for our present society.

First of all, we must work out how the principle of liberty can be introduced into the family without its harmony and hierarchy being disturbed. How can the liberty of the wife be made compatible with that of the husband? How to make it converge under all its faces, social, civil, political, religious? How to establish it in a way so that despotism can never again find entry, whether from one side or the other?

We must touch the organization of labor, the very basis on which everything depends. Were we granted today all our rights, they would remain sterile without the organization of labor.

What is particularly pressing in this moment is to prepare well for the holy baptism of emancipation those of our sisters whom the past has particularly deprived. Let us start by cultivating the field of intelligence. Moral freedom has to precede material freedom so that the latter does not become a good for which, every instant, one must worry one will see removed.

One preliminary instruction may be given to women of the working classes; let us open or obtain a government that will, as soon as possible, in all quarters of Paris, install schools where young girls and young women will come to educate themselves every day for an hour or two.

We only call on Paris, yet our thought goes much further! It must embrace all of France, even more still, all the latitudes where beings of our species capable of understanding and imitating us live. But Paris, the oracle and pilot of the century on the ocean of progress, naturally has the duty of the most generous initiatives.

Reading, writing, grammar, math; notions of geography, of cosmography, of universal history and, particularly, national history, of insights into the natural sciences, etc. will form the curriculum of our courses.

Who could say now that the spreading of the lights that science gathered is not as much the need of our sex as of the other? Do we not know, of the rest, the practical utility of certain parts of physics and chemistry? Is it not recognized that through ignorance one often risks compromising not only one's own existence, but also that of the beings by whom one is surrounded? Know thyself, so rightfully recommended for all (male and female), must it not understand itself as moral? Can the being advance integrally, when it does not also know its physiological constitution? Do not many mothers transmit to their children the germs of illnesses of which they would not have become victims if they had been less ignorant?

And also, through science one cuts into the root of the tree of all the superstitions which obscure intelligence and distort the purest and truest feelings of the heart; through science, one moralizes grandly, one exalts religious feeling.

The natural sciences prove God much better than the treaties of theology. "Every leave of a tree," Confucius said, "is a book written about divinity."

Music, as one already teaches to the workers, must also have a place in our courses.

One knows all its worth. It is, among the fine arts, the one that copies itself most noticeably onto the high divine harmonies. To apply it to education is to guide the good on the route of the beautiful.

The instruction which we demand for woman must be presented to her in the most attractive forms.

Altogether, few words, much substance. In universal and national history, attach oneself to showing the misfortunes of people, comment that they have always found themselves exploited. The history of the past is that of error. Error, too, has its torch that helps in finding the truth, like the one from this last one helps to depart from the path of the first.

All moral truth is deduced from the eternal, divine truth, written in the laws of universal attraction.

The preaching of rights happens parallel to instruction. Religious feeling is, naturally, our domain, because fraternity is one of the greatest manifestations of this feeling; but we must not occupy ourselves with cults. Every form is good when the feeling is true, when one does not take the letter for the spirit. In the case of the cult, everyone has complete liberty to choose the form that pleases them most.

The content of tenderness is superior in woman to her self-esteem, generally, but this will be less so when we address the dignity of our sisters as human beings rather than talking to their motherly heart, so that we will see prompt success crowning our work.

In the name of the happiness of her children, which we will show her is impossible without her assistance, one will have everything of the woman who today is the most remote from the thought of freedom. In seizing, with so much unction as with truth, this almighty leverage, motherly love, one will lead her, one will fill her with enthusiasm, one will transform her as through enchantment.

But, until the blessed day that will see her gain possession of the rights that she will have conquered with dignity, we also have the task to relieve her in her present state.

We must strive to procure work for those who do not have any. Preventing, with all the means of action that are within our range, the misery of destroying the good seeds which we have sown, must be our first duty. From the bare attic to the golden sitting room, and from there to the workshop, our brotherly speech must elevate defeated courage, excite the feeling of justice. We must position ourselves between richness and poverty, not only so that the one will open their wallet in favor of the other in the name of alms. Alms are no longer of this time! This pretended generosity of the rich, which only for a moment allayed the misery of the poor, soiled him with inferiority. The rich person has the duty to make the poor work; without this duty, he is nothing but an inequitable robber, he calls upon him all the misfortunes. It is, thus, work that we will demand from the latter first. No more ladies that one will call of charity; but ladies of equality, of fraternity. The nurseries, the asylum rooms, etc., all that touches the weak, young and old, will still be within our competence.

It is up to us to find the best ways of developing and instructing in the early childhood phase of both sexes, whose education is our prize, divine right.

We must, as well, occupy ourselves actively with the present state of those of our sisters whose education, knowledge, and talents seem to have placed them far from misery, but yet consume them!

The circle of intellectual and moral labor must be considerably enlarged for women.

Only one part of the medical art is accessible to them today; they must be allowed to go further if they can.

In the judicial order, they certainly do not think to fight with the present judiciary the places which it occupies, but it is for them to create: the institution, for example, of justices of the peace will not be complete, will not have all its conciliatory function, unless a certain number of women also be called to give wise advice to their lost sisters. Women understand women, they sense better what brings them back, what leads them.

Many places also in the administrative order, notably in hospitals, nurseries, asylums, etc., could be, if not better, at least as well filled with them as with men.

The establishment of *honor courts*, where women would intervene between men as judges of quarrels and divisions that do not resolve themselves today in a duel, would do more against the cruel rest of the institutions of a barbaric past than all the defenses of the law and all the precepts of philosophy.

We will content ourselves for the moment with these summary instructions. Whatever the needs of the future will further demand from us, we will always find what we have to be, active and devoted.

What do we still need to add, now that we have exposed our principles, enumerated our rights, and recommended the first means to realization? Nothing, if none of us wants to miss the work; nothing, if we all know what we owe all; nothing, if we are not mistaken about the difficulties of the task, about all the obstacles to overcome before reaching the goal. But the grandeur of that goal will be our strength.

It is a new Promised Land to be conquered by labor, perseverance and virtue; it is the kingdom of God to be fulfilled on earth! Daughters of this generous France which we love with all the power of our souls, daughters of this France so noble and grand, of this France at the sparkling forefront of art, of science, of genius, in the heart so burning with enthusiasm, we are inspired by your mother; in the hours of our roughest labors, she will be there to support us! She will tell us: Courage, my daughters, and we will march, we will always march.—Eternal love for this dear France; eternal love also for the Republic that she proclaims as the model and for the happiness of the world!

The Members of the Action Committee

Paris, 16 March 1848

Notes

1 Susan K. Foley, *Women in France since 1789: The Meanings of Difference* (New York: Palgrave Macmillan, 2004), p. 87.
2 Karen Offen, *European Feminisms, 1700–1950: A Political History* (Stanford, CA: Stanford University Press, 2000), pp. 112–13.
3 "Jeanne Deroin." *Wikipedia*, accessed Feb. 10, 2017, www.wikipedia.org.
4 French version: www.persee.fr/doc/genes_1155-3219_1992_num_7_1_1115. Translated for this collection by Ina Seethaler.

13

Declaration of Sentiments
Women's Rights Convention
Seneca Falls, New York
July 19–20, 1848

Women's Rights Convention.

A Convention to discuss the social, civil and religious condition and rights of Woman, will be held in the Wesleyan Chapel, at Seneca Falls, N. Y., on Wednesday and Thursday the 19th and 20th of July current, commencing at 10 o'clock A. M.

During the first day, the meeting will be exclusively for Women, which all are earnestly invited to attend. The public generally are invited to be present on the second day, when LUCRETIA MOTT, of Philadelphia, and others both ladies and gentlemen, will address the Convention.

An open call to the Women's Rights Convention. *Seneca County Courier*, July 14, 1848.

The convention held in Seneca Falls, and the document ratified there, mark for most historians the beginning of the women's rights movement. The language used, the issues delineated, the political framing employed, and the very tone of "Sentiments" were imitated, expanded upon, and revised in a flurry of subsequent conventions, and they remain influential.

In some respects this status as the distinctive "first" is surprising, given that many attendees at Seneca Falls knew of earlier gatherings—some were even present at female antislavery association meetings, for example, where issues of gender clearly were raised; and also because the Declaration of Sentiments is usually (though unjustifiably) denigrated as but an unoriginal amendment to the Declaration of Independence. More reflectively, the convention and its declaration are grand and influential parts of a movement with numerous precedents and endless successors. Keeping with the metaphor of conversation, this was perhaps an "aha!" moment that generated deeper thinking, but it did not come from nowhere or move forward unchanged.

Several features of the meeting recall earlier gatherings. First, women again worked with men, who helped them draft their unfamiliar document before the meeting, and participated in discussions at the meeting. Second, there was consciousness about how difficult public speaking could be for women and how to help women overcome this difficulty. In this instance, the record from the first session notes, "[R]emarks were made by Lucretia Mott, urging the women present to throw aside the trammels of education, and not allow their new position to prevent them from joining in the debates of the meeting."[1]

Too, while it is not undisputed, there is also an already familiar "origin story" of exclusion that traces the Seneca Falls convention back to Lucretia Mott and Elizabeth Cady Stanton being barred from speaking at the World Anti-Slavery Association Convention in London, England, in 1840. Stanton and Mott apparently discussed the need for a convention dedicated to discussion of the rights and wrongs of women. The idea and the indignation simmered for eight busy years before the right moment arrived: Martha Wright, Mary Ann McClintock, and Jane Hunt joined Mott and Stanton at Stanton's home and put the announcement reproduced in figure 13.1 in the *Seneca County Courier*. Although the event was advertised a mere five days before the meeting was to convene, three hundred people showed up at the Wesleyan Methodist Church Chapel, about a third of them men.

The main body of "Sentiments" was written before the meeting, with much debate, collaboration, and research of legal texts. Stanton is usually accorded greatest authorship. It was read in full at the convention several times, "freely discussed," with "much consideration" given to every paragraph, and "some changes were suggested and adopted."[2] In the end it was unanimously adopted, despite the controversy provoked by its support of women's suffrage.

While earlier manifestos borrowed phrases and principles from the 1776 Declaration of Independence, "Sentiments" borrows from its form, too, and even uses the original Preamble with only minor (if impactful) alterations, before taking off into much more novel terrain in the list of grievances and in the Resolutions. In changing the Preamble's phrase "all men are created equal" to "all men and women are created equal," the authors and the signatories asserted a different "self-evident truth": that women, too, have "inalienable rights," rights that governments are established to protect—those same governments that are only legitimate if consented to *by all*.

In using as a model a document written to provide a basis for the independence of the American colonies from Great Britain, the authors make an argument—symbolically powerful, newly explicit, and still broadly accepted today—for understanding the oppression of women as political and systematic, and for grasping "patriarchy" as an unjust form of government, akin to that of England's rule over the colonies. As the sentence linking the Preamble and the Grievances says, "The history of mankind is a history of repeated injuries and usurpations on the part of man toward woman, having in direct object the establishment of an absolute tyranny over her." Contending that it was not "the first," then, does not mean the meeting of three hundred people or the document signed by one hundred was not path-breaking.

The document from Seneca Falls shows how women are consigned, in one institution after another, from church to courtroom, to "a subordinate position."

At perhaps its political peak, "Sentiments" talks not only of individual laws and policies but also of their joint operations and shared general assumptions, and of the interaction among the political, the civil, and the personal. This is how "patriarchy" was theorized in this early collective document.

But "Sentiments" had to leave the political context of equal national sovereignty behind and move to a deeper understanding of social equality, found in many of the grievances and Resolutions. As in earlier declarations, there are arguments for understanding gender equality as *both* an individual and a social good: "the highest good of the race demands that she should be recognized as" man's equal, as does her own true happiness. Too, "Sentiments" asserts that "equality of human rights results" not only "from the fact of the identity of the race in capabilities" but also from the identity of "responsibilities." Its wording—less familiar than "all men [and women] are created equal"—not only makes possession of abilities important but emphasizes exercise of them, use of them, in an individually self-aware and socially responsible manner. A world in which both sexes cannot *use* their capacities is one in which people cannot act responsibly or morally—that is, a world in which everyone cannot use his or her capacities is itself unjust.[3]

Other elements of "Sentiments" seem like ancient accomplishments to many today. But the idea of there being distinct places or roles or arenas for women only, with boundaries drawn and defended by men, has not vanished from the face of the earth, as every recent declaration demonstrates. As the authors and signatories noted, the idea plays itself out not only in political rights, where perhaps most victories have been won, but also in employment practices (largely sex-segregated jobs remain the norm), interpretations of religious doctrines, social norms (including dress, language, and sexual double standards), familial institutions and practices (domestic violence; divisions of care-work and housework) and educational opportunities (who may study what, how, for what ends). The tasks and locations of "women's work" vary across time and geography; the feminists at Seneca Falls suggest we problematize any such demarcation.

In the end, perhaps the main difference between the Declaration of Independence and the Declaration of Sentiments is that the former deals primarily with relationships among states, while the latter pays most attention to relationships among citizens—to social democracy. The main differences between this declaration and earlier ones is its greater breadth—its attention to more aspects of sexual inequality—and its failure to represent issues either of class or of race as fully. And given that we call this meeting and manifesto "firsts," we unfortunately often miss the attention to race and class that goes back to feminism's earlier days.

Declaration of Sentiments

When, in the course of human events, it becomes necessary for one portion of the family of man to assume among the people of the earth a position different from that which they have hitherto occupied, but one to which the laws of nature and of nature's God entitle them, a decent respect to the opinions of mankind requires that they should declare the causes that impel them to such a course.[4]

We hold these truths to be self-evident: that all men and women are created equal; that they are endowed by their Creator with certain inalienable rights; that among these are life, liberty, and the pursuit of happiness; that to secure these rights governments are instituted, deriving their just powers from the consent of the governed. Whenever any form of Government becomes destructive of these ends, it is the right of those who suffer from it to refuse allegiance to it, and to insist upon the institution of a new government, laying its foundation on such principles, and organizing its powers in such form as to them shall seem most likely to effect their safety and happiness. Prudence, indeed, will dictate that governments long established should not be changed for light and transient causes; and accordingly, all experience hath shown that mankind are more disposed to suffer, while evils are sufferable, than to right themselves by abolishing the forms to which they are accustomed. But when a long train of abuses and usurpations, pursuing invariably the same object, evinces a design to reduce them under absolute despotism, it is their duty to throw off such government, and to provide new guards for their future security. Such has been the patient sufferance of the women under this government, and such is now the necessity which constrains them to demand the equal station to which they are entitled.

The history of mankind is a history of repeated injuries and usurpations on the part of man toward woman, having in direct object the establishment of an absolute tyranny over her. To prove this, let facts be submitted to a candid world.

He has never permitted her to exercise her inalienable right to the elective franchise.

He has compelled her to submit to laws, in the formation of which she had no voice.

He has withheld from her rights which are given to the most ignorant and degraded men—both natives and foreigners.

Having deprived her of this first right of a citizen, the elective franchise, thereby leaving her without representation in the halls of legislation, he has oppressed her on all sides.

He has made her, if married, in the eye of the law, civilly dead.

He has taken from her all right in property, even to the wages she earns.

He has made her, morally, an irresponsible being, as she can commit many crimes with impunity, provided they be done in the presence of her husband. In the covenant of marriage, she is compelled to promise obedience to her husband, he becoming, to all intents and purposes, her master—the law giving him power to deprive her of her liberty, and to administer chastisement.

He has so framed the laws of divorce, as to what shall be the proper causes of divorce; in case of separation, to whom the guardianship of the children shall be given; as to be wholly regardless of the happiness of women—the law, in all cases, going upon the false supposition of the supremacy of man, and giving all power into his hands.

After depriving her of all rights as a married woman, if single and the owner of property, he has taxed her to support a government which recognizes her only when her property can be made profitable to it.

He has monopolized nearly all the profitable employments, and from those she is permitted to follow, she receives but a scanty remuneration.

He closes against her all the avenues to wealth and distinction, which he considers most honorable to himself. As a teacher of theology, medicine, or law, she is not known.

He has denied her the facilities for obtaining a thorough education—all colleges being closed against her.

He allows her in Church as well as State, but a subordinate position, claiming Apostolic authority for her exclusion from the ministry, and, with some exceptions, from any public participation in the affairs of the Church.

He has created a false public sentiment, by giving to the world a different code of morals for men and women, by which moral delinquencies which exclude women from society, are not only tolerated but deemed of little account in man.

He has usurped the prerogative of Jehovah himself, claiming it as his right to assign for her a sphere of action, when that belongs to her conscience and her God.

He has endeavored, in every way that he could to destroy her confidence in her own powers, to lessen her self-respect, and to make her willing to lead a dependent and abject life.

Now, in view of this entire disfranchisement of one-half the people of this country, their social and religious degradation,—in view of the unjust laws above mentioned, and because women do feel themselves aggrieved, oppressed, and fraudulently deprived of their most sacred rights, we insist that they have immediate admission to all the rights and privileges which belong to them as citizens of these United States.

In entering upon the great work before us, we anticipate no small amount of misconception, misrepresentation, and ridicule; but we shall use every instrumentality within our power to effect our object. We shall employ agents, circulate tracts, petition the State and national Legislatures, and endeavor to enlist the pulpit and the press in our behalf. We hope this Convention will be followed by a series of Conventions, embracing every part of the country.

Firmly relying upon the final triumph of the Right and the True, we do this day affix our signatures to this declaration.

Resolutions
Whereas, the great precept of nature is conceded to be, "that man shall pursue his own true and substantial happiness," Blackstone, in his Commentaries, remarks, that this law of Nature being coeval with mankind, and dictated by God himself, is of course superior in obligation to any other. It is binding over all the globe, in all countries, and at all times; no human laws are of any validity if contrary to this, and such of them as are valid, derive all their force, and all their validity, and all their authority, mediately and immediately, from this original; Therefore,

Resolved, That such laws as conflict, in any way, with the true and substantial happiness of woman, are contrary to the great precept of nature, and of no validity; for this is "superior in obligation to any other."

Resolved, That all laws which prevent woman from occupying such a station in society as her conscience shall dictate, or which place her in a position inferior to that of man, are contrary to the great precept of nature, and therefore of no force or authority.

Resolved, That woman is man's equal—was intended to be so by the Creator, and the highest good of the race demands that she should be recognized as such.

Resolved, That the women of this country ought to be enlightened in regard to the laws under which they live, that they may no longer publish their degradation, by declaring themselves satisfied with their present position, nor their ignorance, by asserting that they have all the rights they want.

Resolved, That inasmuch as man, while claiming for himself intellectual superiority, does accord to woman moral superiority, it is pre-eminently his duty to encourage her to speak, and teach, as she has an opportunity, in all religious assemblies.

Resolved, That the same amount of virtue, delicacy, and refinement of behavior, that is required of woman in the social state, should also be required of man, and the same transgressions should be visited with equal severity on both man and woman.

Resolved, That the objection of indelicacy and impropriety, which is so often brought against woman when she addresses a public audience, comes with a very ill grace from those who encourage, by their attendance, her appearance on the stage, in the concert, or in the feats of the circus.

Resolved, That woman has too long rested satisfied in the circumscribed limits which corrupt customs and a perverted application of the Scriptures have marked out for her, and that it is time she should move in the enlarged sphere which her great Creator has assigned her.

Resolved, That it is the duty of the women of this country to secure to themselves their sacred right to the elective franchise.

Resolved, That the equality of human rights results necessarily from the fact of the identity of the race in capabilities and responsibilities.

Resolved, therefore, That, being invested by the Creator with the same capabilities, and the same consciousness of responsibility for their exercise, it is demonstrably the right and duty of woman, equally with man, to promote every righteous cause, by every righteous means; and especially in regard to the great subjects of morals and religion, it is self-evidently her right to participate with her brother in teaching them, both in private and in public, by writing and by speaking, by any instrumentalities proper to be used, and in any assemblies proper to be held; and this being a self-evident truth, growing out of the divinely implanted principles of human nature, any custom or authority adverse to it, whether modern or wearing the hoary sanction of antiquity, is to be regarded as self-evident falsehood, and at war with the interests of mankind.

Notes

1 "Report of the Women's Rights Convention," August 1848, p. 3. National Park Service, www.nps.gov.
2 Ibid.
3 See Penny Weiss, "Revolution: The Declaration of Sentiments," in *Canon Fodder: Historical Women Political Thinkers* (University Park: Pennsylvania State University Press, 2009).
4 "Declaration of Sentiments and Resolutions." *Elizabeth Cady Stanton and Susan B. Anthony Papers Project*, 2010, accessed Sept. 25, 2013, ecssba.rutgers.edu.

14

Statutes
Viennese Democratic Women's Association
Vienna, Austria
October 16, 1848

Photo of Karoline von Perin, *Währinger Frauenweg.*

The goal of this organization[1] was to spread democracy in Germany, to establish equal education for women, and to care for the victims of the Revolution. The Revolution was the people's protest against Emperor Ferdinand; the people wanted the right to vote and a written constitution, and many who championed the cause had been injured or killed by Ferdinand's forces. This declaration delineates three areas of work for the group—political, social, and charitable—refusing to cast only the latter as of proper concern to women. The association emphasized a free-thinking, democratic population, women's equality, and assistance for the victims of revolutionary fighting. A great deal of attention is given to organizational matters, from who has a right to speak to who may vote. (While men were allowed to attend group meetings on special occasions, only women were permitted as active, voting members.) Attention is also paid to class, in at least two places in the document: acknowledgment that many members work, and the call for attention "to the state of the poorer girls."

The group formed in August as one of at least ten women's organizations devoted to democracy during the Revolution, and over three hundred women joined the organization that wrote this declaration. The association disbanded in November 1848, when its president, Karoline Perin, pictured in figure 14.1, was arrested and imprisoned. For more about this declaration in an international context, we recommend Bonnie S. Anderson's book *Joyous Greetings: The First International Women's Movement, 1830–1860*.

Statutes of the First Viennese Democratic Women's Association

1. The name of the association is: Viennese Democratic Women's Association
2. The task of the association is threefold: political, social, and charitable:
   a) political, to inform oneself through reading and instructive lectures about the welfare of the Fatherland, to disseminate the democratic principle in all women's circles, to inspire the love of freedom in a child's heart from the very beginning of a child's upbringing, and at the same time to strengthen the German element;
   b) social, to strive for the equality of women by establishing public primary schools [*Volksschulen*] and higher educational institutions, to reform the curriculum for women, and to improve the state of the poorer girls through loving advancement;
   c) charitable, to express the deeply-felt gratitude of the women of Vienna for the blessings of liberty by providing conscientious care for all victims of the Revolution.
3. The association shall consist of active (female) and supporting male and female members.
4. Active members are obliged to exert themselves on behalf of the association as best they can and in every way. Consideration is given to each member's self-chosen primary occupation.
5. Active members pay 30 kr. the first month and 20 kr. C.M. a month thereafter, supporting members pay 20 kr. C.M. monthly. The former contributions flow into the association's treasury, the latter into the support fund.
6. Each member shall receive a card with the association's seal, which is shown at the meetings.
7. Only women of good character and a free-thinking disposition can be members, both active and supporting. Should it happen, against all hope, that a member has joined who does not meet these criteria, she can be excluded by a majority vote.
8. Gentlemen can be included in the meetings as honorary members only by way of exception, but they must refrain from voting.
9. Female supporting members may attend the meetings, but they must refrain from voting.
10. No differences in social rank shall exist among the members. The form of address is simply "Mrs." [*Frau*] and "Miss" [*Fräulein*]. Married women take no precedence over unmarried women.
11. The association is governed by a committee of five members (with three substitute members), of which one is the permanent chair, one the secretary, and one the treasurer.
12. The committee runs all the affairs of the association.

13. The committee must step down after three months, though it may be re-elected in whole or in part. The entire committee, or part of it, can also be compelled to resign earlier through a majority vote.

14. The chairwoman grants the right to speak in the order in which speakers have asked to be recognized and moderates the debate. She can ask the speaker to stay on topic or issue a call to order only if a speaker departs substantially from the topic of the speech, if she engages in personal attacks, or if this is necessary to re-establish an orderly debate. After twice issuing a call to stay on topic or a call to order without success, she may revoke the speaker's right to speak.

15. In urgent cases the committee has the right to make decisions and carry them out, though it has the responsibility and obligation to bring the matter up for consideration at the next meeting.

16. The clerks [*Schriftführerinnen*] keep a record of members and guests and a brief account of the debates and decisions, which are published. They also attend to the association's correspondence and write down the names of those who wish to speak in the order in which they have asked to be recognized, for or against the topic of the debate.

17. Every motion that is supported by three members must be brought to a vote.

18. The member who proposed the motion is the last to speak. Like any other member, she can ask to be recognized three times during the debate.

19. Once a vote has been taken, no further debate about the same motion is allowed to take place at the same meeting.

20. All votes are decided by a majority vote. Voting is by written ballot.

21. Every meeting requires half the members plus one.

22. At least two regular meetings shall take place every week.

23. Selecting the location and the weekdays for the meetings is left up to the association.

24. Plenary sessions—which one-third of the members must attend—must be called for committee elections, changes to the statutes, larger expenses (over 50fl. C.M.), important decisions that affect the welfare and existence of the association, and the intended dissolution of the association.

25. The committee has the right to summon extraordinary sessions, just as every active member is called upon to come to their association's premises on important occasions, if possible without being summoned.

26. The committee will report on the state of the association's treasury at the end of each month.

27. Every three months, at a general meeting of all active and supporting members, a report will be given about the charitable work of the association (with respect to 2c) and the state of the support fund; the supporting members shall appoint five from among themselves as a commission to audit the report.

28. All requests must be submitted in writing, and only delegations representing groups can be admitted.

29. Placards will be signed by the committee on behalf of the association. Addresses and petitions shall be signed at a meeting by all members present.

30. The chairwoman shall propose members for delegation, and the association shall decide by a majority vote.

31. The association shall make it its task to set up similar associations throughout the country, which shall correspond with the association in Vienna as the central association.

32. A commission shall be appointed for every suburb of Vienna, and it shall be composed, if possible, of members who live in the district in question. They shall reinforce themselves with female helpers, and shall establish branch or affiliated associations for the purely charitable purposes of the central association.

33. For the public's greater convenience, every active member may receive donations of every kind in her home, provide receipts for them, and then hand them over to the treasurer.—To that end, every member shall be given a subscription sheet and a certain number of cards embossed with the association's seal.

34. Every member is free to leave the association. Only members of the committee must provide notice eight days ahead of time.

Note

1 "Statutes of the First Viennese Democratic Women's Association (1848)." *GHDI*, accessed Feb. 25, 2016, germanhistorydocs.ghi-dc.org.

15

Appeal of the Married Women and Maidens of Württemberg to the Soldiers of Germany
Württemberg, Germany
May 7, 1849

This Appeal to German[1] soldiers indeed shows women as active participants in the revolutionary period, a role that included their participation in riots and print campaigns to end the counterrevolutionary movement. Here they use the tactic of threatening to deny love and marriage to those who support "a princely tyranny hostile to the people." It is an early version of today's tactic of refusing to date men who aren't feminists.[2]

Apparently, there is some precedent for this Appeal.

The "married women and maidens" of the west German textile town of Elberfeld met in a "public meeting" on 31 March 1848. Explaining that their "hearts beat faster and stronger at the hope of a united Germany, yet bleed at the thought of the desperate condition of our workers," they called on their sisters just to wear the products of the nation's industry, so that their sex might assist in both the movement of national unification and help resolve the social crisis of the working class.

Their determination to have a voice in the issues confronting their nation despite opposition to women having a role in public life may explain why their protest takes place "largely in terms of their private role in the household and family."[3] The tactics suggested are reminiscent of the 1774 Edenton petition, and the stance taken against conflict is but one of a long series of such appeals found throughout this volume.

Appeal of the Married Women and Maidens of Württemberg to Our German Soldiers

German soldiers! A mighty spirit is blowing through all the districts of our common Fatherland! It is the spirit of the awakened, true liberty of the German people! And to you too, young German men, you who are following the brave German army, goes the admonitory call to participate in the spirit of freedom, so that this treasure so long yearned for will finally become the inalienable possession of the entire nation. But you, German soldiers, will not help to win the delightful gift of German liberty with the path you have so far embarked upon!

If civic prosperity and happiness, which can only flourish in the liberty of the people, are priceless, sacred goods to you, you can no longer consecrate your bodies and your strength to a princely tyranny hostile to the people, by continuing to aim your weapons at the heart of the people from whom you have emerged and to whose midst you will one day wish to return! You have sworn to serve the Fatherland against external enemies, but not to stain the heart of your own Fatherland, the peaceful district your own homeland with the blood of its sons, your brothers.

Come, now, German youngsters [*Jünglinge*] and men, listen to the call of German married women and maidens: think of your future, think of the peaceful civilian estate you wish to rejoin one day, think of the peaceful happiness of love and marriage, and of the domestic hearth, which smiles pleasantly at you from afar. Hear the oath of German women, which we swear in sacred patriotism:

"Never shall we give our hand at the altar to him whose hand was stained by the blood of his fellow German citizens!"

"Never shall we share our domestic hearth with him who destroyed this—our shrine—with fire and sword!"

"Never shall we approach in faithful love him whose hostile weapon brought misery and destruction upon the German lands!"

Hear our oath, young German men, and may the wrath of Heaven fall upon us if we do not keep this oath! German soldiers! By the decree of your fathers you are stripped of their inheritance, which you blasphemously seek to destroy with your arms! It will benefit those whom you, in blind madness, have made into widows and orphans! Think of this abyss that is opening up before your blinded eyes and throw in your lot with the people, otherwise the spirit of a happy future for you will conceal its face in mourning.

Notes

1 "Women's Activism in the Revolution of 1848/49: Appeal of the Married Women and Maidens of Württemberg to the Soldiers of Germany (1849)." *GDHI*, accessed Feb. 10, 2017, germanhistorydocs.ghi-dc.org.

2 See, for example, Ana Marie Cox, "Padma Lakshmi Won't Date Men Who Aren't Feminists." *New York Times*, March 17, 2016, www.nytimes.com.

3 Jonathan Sperber, *The European Revolutions, 1848–1851*, 2nd ed. (New York: Cambridge University Press, 2005), pp. 185–86.

16

Resolutions
First Ohio Woman's Rights Convention
Salem, Ohio
April 19, 1850

Historical marker on the outskirts of Salem, Ohio. *The Salem, Ohio 1850 Women's Rights Convention Proceedings*, ed. Robert W. Audretsch (Salem, OH: Salem Public Library, 1976), www.salem.lib.oh.us.

It is probably the first public meeting in the U.S. where the planners, participants, and officers were exclusively women.[1]

In the call for the Salem convention, undersigned by eighty women and placed in antislavery publications, the convenors proposed "to secure to all persons the recognition of Equal Rights, and the extension of the privileges of Government without distinction of sex or color." The call set the task

[t]o inquire into the origin and design of the rights of humanity, whether they are coeval with the human race, of universal heritage, and inalienable, or merely conventional, held by sufferance, dependent for a basis on location, position, color and sex, and like government scrip or deeds on parchment, transferrable, to be granted or withheld, made immutable or changeable, as caprice, popular favor, or the pride of power and place may dictate; changing ever as the weak and the strong, the oppressed and the oppressor, come in conflict or change places.[2]

"Both the women who called the Salem convention and those who attended were from different locations in Ohio, from different religious backgrounds, and from different occupations. One thing they had in common was that their consciousness had been raised either through educational work, temperance work, abolition work, or church work. In many cases they were the backbones of the organizations."[3] The diverse backgrounds show through in the breadth of the document. Hundreds of women from all over Ohio came to Salem to participate in this convention and signed their names to the Resolutions.

This was the first women's rights convention west of the Allegheny Mountains and into what is now the U.S. Midwest. It happened just two weeks before the Ohio Constitutional Convention was to discuss and potentially amend the state's Constitution, and was timed, like the New York petition, to present the woman's rights agenda to the Constitutional Convention. This explains the political character especially of the final set of resolutions, and the claim that women are "equally entitled with men to a voice in creating and administering the governmental and religious institutions under which they and those who are dear to them live." The document also points out that while the United States calls itself a republic, forms of tyranny based on color and sex nonetheless live on in the nation.

It is especially interesting that in a gathering that included abolitionists, and that was advertised in antislavery publications, we find analogies made between the relation of men to women and that of masters to the enslaved. Especially on the basis of married women's lack of right to property and lack of custody over their children, "[W]e recognize only the modified code of the slave plantation, and . . . we are brought more nearly in sympathy with the suffering slave, who is despoiled of all his rights." Hence follows the eerily contemporary language of the document, which declares that "all rights are *human* rights . . . without distinction of sex," perhaps the earliest mention of a now-famous saying.

The document[4] acknowledges that it takes "courage" to step outside the established norms, and to confront the "frowns and scorns" and the "public sentiment" that opposes change. But it nonetheless places heavy demands on women and uses harsher language than we have seen before. Women are not only degraded by patriarchy but might also "perpetuate their own degradation" by leading "an idle, aimless life." The Resolutions thus confront internalized oppression and pay attention to how patriarchy is maintained and might be changed.

The Salem convention repeats parts of but deepens and broadens the contents of the Declaration of Sentiments from the Seneca Falls gathering. It established the tradition of Ohio Woman's Rights Conventions, as Ohio was the only state that regularly held meetings apart from the national conventions. Betsy Mix Cowles was elected president of the convention. She remained single as part of her fight for women's rights, and she was a teacher and active reformer as an abolitionist and a women's rights leader.[5]

Photo of Betsy Mix Cowles.

Resolutions of the Ohio Woman's Rights Convention

WHEREAS, all men are created equal and endowed with certain God-given rights, and all just government is derived from the consent of the governed; and whereas, the doctrine that "man shall pursue his own substantial happiness" is acknowledged by the highest authority to be the great precept of Nature; and whereas, this doctrine is not local, but universal, being dictated by God himself; therefore—

1. Resolved, That all laws contrary to these fundamental principles, or in conflict with this great precept of nature, are of no binding obligation, not being founded in equity or justice.

2. Resolved, That the prohibition of Woman from participating in the enactment of the laws by which she is governed is a direct violation of this precept of Nature, as she is thereby prevented from occupying that position which duty points out, and from pursuing her own substantial happiness by acting up to her conscientious convictions; and that all statutes and constitutional provisions which sanction this prohibition are null and void.

3. Resolved, That all rights are *human* rights, and pertain to human beings, without distinction of sex; therefore justice demands that all laws shall be made, not for man, or for woman, but for mankind, and that the same legal protection be afforded to the one sex as to the other.

4. Resolved, That the servile submission and quiet indifference of the Women of this country in relation to the unequal and oppressive laws by which they are governed, are the fruit either of ignorance or degradation, both resulting legitimately from the action of those laws.

5. Resolved, That the evils arising from the present social, civil and religious condition of women proclaim to them in language not to be misunderstood, that not only their *own* welfare, but the highest good of the race demands of them, as an imperative duty, that they should secure to themselves the elective franchise.

6. Resolved, That in those laws which confer on man the power to control the property and person of woman, and to remove from her at will the children of her affection, we recognize only the modified code of the slave plantation; and that thus we are brought more nearly in sympathy with the suffering slave, who is despoiled of all his rights.

7. Resolved, That we, as human beings, are entitled to claim and exercise all the rights that belong by nature to any members of the human family.

8. Resolved, That all distinctions between men and woman in regard to social, literary, pecuniary, religious or political customs and institution, based on a distinction of sex, are contrary to the laws of Nature, are unjust, and destructive to the purity, elevation and progress in knowledge and goodness of the human family, and ought to be at once and forever abolished.

9. Resolved, That the practice of holding women amenable to a different standard of propriety and morality from that to which men are held amenable, is unjust and unnatural, and highly detrimental to domestic and social virtue and happiness.

10. Resolved, That so long as women oppose the examination of the position and duties of woman in all the various relations of human life, they do not enhance and perpetuate their own degradation, and put far off the day when social laws and customs shall recognize them as equally entitled with men to a voice in creating and administering the governmental and religious institutions under which they and those who are dear to them live.

11. Resolved, That the political history of Woman demonstrates that tyranny, the most degrading, cruel and arbitrary, can be exercised and produced the same in effect under a mild and republican form of government as by an hereditary despotism.

12. Resolved, That while we deprecate thus earnestly the political oppression of Woman, we see in her social condition, the regard in which she is held as a moral and intellectual being, the fundamental cause of that oppression.

13. Resolved, That amongst the principal causes of such social condition we regard the public sentiment which withholds from her all, or almost all, lucrative employments, and enlarged spheres of labor.

14. Resolved, That in the difficulties thus cast in the way of her self-support, and in her consequent *dependence* upon man, we see the greatest influence at work in imparting to her that tone of character which makes her to be regarded as the "weaker vessel."

15. Resolved, That as all things work in a circle, such places as we have spoken of will only be opened to woman as she shows by the cultivation of her own mind, and the force of her own character, that she is capable of filling them, and that herself must prove her courage by calmly putting forth her hand to grasp them, in disregard of the usages which have hitherto withheld them from her.

16. Resolved, That we regard those women who content themselves with an idle, aimless life, as involved in the guilt as well as the suffering of their own oppression; and that we hold those who go forth into the world, in the face of the frowns and the sneers of the public, to fill large spheres of labor, as the truest preachers of the cause of Woman's Rights.

WHEREAS, one class of society dooms woman to a life of drudgery, another to one of dependence and frivolity; and whereas, the education she generally receives is calculated to cultivate vanity and dependence, therefore—

17. Resolved, That the prevalent ideas of female education are in perfect harmony with the position allotted her by the laws and usages of society.

18. Resolved, That the education of woman should be in accordance with her responsibility in life, that she may acquire that self-reliance and true dignity so essential to the proper fulfillment of the important duties devolving on her.

19. Resolved, That, as woman is not permitted to hold office, nor have any voice in the government, she should not be compelled to pay taxes out of her scanty wages to support men who get eight dollars a-day for taking the right to *themselves* to enact laws for *her*.

20. Resolved, That we, the Women of Ohio, will hereafter meet annually in Convention to consult upon and adopt measures for the removal of various disabilities—political, social, religious, legal and pecuniary—to which women as a class are subjected, and from which results so much misery, degradation and crime.

21. Resolved, That we appoint a Committee to attend to all the interests of this Cause, and to fix upon the time and place of holding our next Convention.

22. Resolved, That we will personally interest ourselves in promoting the circulation of those periodicals which endeavor to promote this great cause of Justice and Equal Rights.

Notes

1 "Introduction," in *The Salem, Ohio 1850 Women's Rights Convention Proceedings,* ed. Robert W. Audretsch (Salem, OH: Salem Public Library, 1976), p. 11.

2 *The Salem, Ohio 1850 Women's Rights Convention Proceedings,* p. 17.

3 "Introduction," p. 11.

4 *The Salem, Ohio 1850 Women's Rights Convention Proceedings*, pp. 23–24.

5 Photo of Betsy Mix Cowles from Ashtabula County Historical Society website, www.ashtcohs.com.

17

Resolutions
First National Woman's Rights Convention
Worcester, Massachusetts

October 23–24, 1850

Paulina Kellogg Wright Davis, who organized and presided over the convention.

Paulina Wright Davis, Lucy Stone, Lucretia Mott, and Abby Kelley organized the first national convention devoted entirely to women's rights, or at least the first women's "national" after the three female antislavery conventions in the late 1830s. The decision to hold the meeting came during a discussion at the New England Anti-Slavery Convention earlier the same year, more evidence of the enduring links between the movements. Despite the fact that "many newspapers [were] depicting the female advocates of woman's rights as unfeminine at best, dangerous at worst, and their male supporters as radicals and infidels determined to overthrow the social order,"[1] it is estimated that thousands of people were present for some part of the convention. Official delegates came from twelve states, including one from the just-added state of California. As the size of the crowd grew to well over three times that at Seneca Falls at any given moment, it spilled outside Brinley Hall. "Both the *New-York Daily Tribune* and the *New York Herald* published detailed accounts of each day's sessions, as did several Boston papers."[2] A decision was explicitly made on the grounds of democracy to have the Resolutions serve as the declaration of principles. Some contend that this meeting, rather than Seneca Falls, spearheaded the feminist movement.[3] It certainly was another grand moment.

Eighty-nine people from six states signed the call for the convention, a lengthy invitation and argument that included a paragraph about how the rights and interests of woman are not antagonistic to those of man:

One half of the race are its immediate objects, and the other half are as deeply involved, by that absolute unity of interest and destiny which nature has established between them. . . . The sexes should not, for any reason or by any chance, take hostile attitudes towards each other, either in the apprehension or amendment of the wrongs which exist in their necessary relations; but they should harmonize in opinion and co-operate in effort, for the reason that they must unite in the ultimate achievement of the desired reformation.

The call also delineated the proposed subject matter: "[T]he general question of Woman's Rights and Relations comprehends these: Her Education, Literary, Scientific, and Artistic; Her Avocations, Industrial, Commercial, and Professional; Her Interests, Pecuniary, Civil, and Political; in a word Her Rights as an Individual, and her Functions as a Citizen." Many items included in the convention debates and in the document had appeared before then, including legal equality and education, and evidence was brought to show that similar problems existed in other places in the world. There was more emphasis in Worcester on the need for employment opportunities so that wider use could be made of women's education, on the need for women to be economically independent, and on the need to end discrimination based on race as well as sex.

Importantly, the 1850 convention and document ended in a set of standing committees, which led to sustained, organized work for women's rights. The four committees were on Education, Industrial Avocations, Civil and Political Rights and Regulations, and Social Relations. They were charged with holding meetings, gathering information, raising funds, and guiding public sentiment through the press.

The meeting may be most memorable for the speakers there, which included famous activists and inspiring orators, such as William Lloyd Garrison, Ernestine Rose, Antoinette Brown, Frederick Douglass, Lucretia Mott, and Sojourner Truth. The meeting opened with a speech by the convention president, Paulina Davis. She said, in unforgettable language,

The reformation which we purpose, in its utmost scope, is radical and universal. It is not the mere perfecting of a progress already in motion, a detail of some established plan, but it is an epochal movement—the emancipation of a class, the redemption of half the world, and a conforming re-organization of all social, political, and industrial interests and institutions. Moreover, it is a movement without example among the enterprises of associated reformations, for it has no purpose of arming the oppressed against the oppressor, or of separating the parties, or of setting up independence, or of severing the relations of either.

A speech by Abby Price included the following treatment of sexual differences:

In contending for this co-equality of woman's with man's rights, it is not necessary to argue, either that the sexes are by nature equally and indiscriminately adapted to the same positions and duties, or that they are absolutely equal in physical and intellectual ability; but only that they are absolutely equal in their rights to life, liberty, and the pursuit of happiness—in their rights to do, and to be, individually and socially, all they are capable of, and to attain the highest usefulness and happiness, obediently to the divine moral law. These are every man's rights, of whatever race or nation, ability or situation, in life. These are equally every woman's rights, whatever her comparative capabilities may be—whatever her relations may be. These are human rights, equally inherent in male and female. To repress them in any degree is in the same degree usurpation, tyranny, and oppression.

Lucy Stone, who would become a formidable organizer and orator, spoke on the last evening.

> We want to be something more than the appendages of Society; we want that Woman should be the coequal and help-meet of Man in all the interest and perils and enjoyments of human life. We want that she should attain to the development of her nature and womanhood; we want that when she dies, it may not be written on her gravestone that she was the relict of somebody.

This convention should be remembered for advocating that "[a]ll men and women of any color, including slaves, were proclaimed to have the same rights as any white man at the pinnacle of American society."[4]

Resolutions

RESOLVED, That every human being of full age, and resident for a proper length of time on the soil of the nation, who is required to obey law, is entitled to a voice in its enactment; that every such person, whose property or labor is taxed . . . is entitled to a direct share in such government; therefore,

RESOLVED, That women are clearly entitled to the right of suffrage, and to be considered eligible to office; the omission to demand which on her part, is a palpable recreancy to duty, and the denial of which is a gross usurpation, on the part of man, no longer to be endured; and that every party which claims to represent the humanity, civilization, and progress of the age, is bound to inscribe on its banners, "Equality before the law, without distinction of sex or color."

RESOLVED, That political rights acknowledge no sex, and, therefore, the word "male" should be stricken from every State Constitution.

RESOLVED, That the laws of property, as affecting married parties, demand a thorough revisal, so that all rights may be equal between them; that the wife may have, during life, an equal control over the property gained by their mutual toil and sacrifices, be heir to her husband . . . and entitled at her death to dispose by will of the same share of the joint property as he.

RESOLVED, That since the prospect of honorable and useful employment . . . for the faculties we are laboring to discipline, is the keenest stimulus to fidelity in the use of educational advantages, . . . therefore, it is impossible that woman should make full use of the instruction already accorded to her, or that her career should do justice to her faculties, until the avenues to the various civil and professional employments are thrown open to arouse her ambition and call forth all her nature.

RESOLVED, That every effort to educate woman, until you accord to her rights, and arouse her conscience by the weight of her responsibilities, is futile, and a waste of labor.

RESOLVED, That the cause we have met to advocate—the claim for woman of all her natural and civil rights—bids us remember the two millions of slave women at the South, the most grossly wronged and foully outraged of all women; . . . we will [remember] . . . the trampled womanhood of the plantation, and omit no effort to raise it to a share in the rights we claim for ourselves.

PLAN AND PRINCIPLES [William Channing offered "a plan for organization, and the principles which should govern the movement for establishing women's co-sovereignty with man. . . ."]

RESOLVED, That as women alone can learn by experience and prove by works, what is their rightful sphere of duty, we recommend, as next steps, that they should demand and secure:

1st. Education in primary and high-schools, universities, medical, legal, and theological institutions, as comprehensive and exact as their abilities prompt them to seek and their capabilities fit them to receive.

2d. Partnership in the labors, gains, risks, and remunerations of productive industry, with such limits only as are assigned by taste, intuitive judgment, or their measure of spiritual and physical vigor, as tested by experiment.

3d. A co-equal share in the formation and administration of law, Municipal, State, and National, through legislative assemblies, courts, and executive offices.

4th. Such unions as may become the guardians of pure morals and honorable manners—a high court of appeal in cases of outrage which can not be, and are not touched by civil or ecclesiastical organizations, . . . and a medium for expressing the highest views of justice dictated by human conscience and sanctioned by holy inspiration.

RESOLVED, That a Central Committee be appointed by this Convention, empowered to enlarge its numbers, on (1st) Education; (2d) Industrial Avocations; (3d) Civil and Political Rights and Regulations; (4th) Social Relations; who shall correspond with each other and with the Central Committee, hold meetings in their respective neighborhoods, gather statistics, facts, and incidents . . . , raise funds for the movement; and through the press, tracts, books, and the living agent, guide public opinion upward and onward in the grand social reform of establishing woman's co-sovereignty with man. . . . [The second national woman's rights convention was held at Worcester the next year; the first chair of the Central Committee was Paulina Wright Davis].

Notes

1 "First National Women's Rights Convention Ends in Worcester: October 24, 1850." Mass Moments, accessed Feb. 10, 2017, www.massmoments.org.

2 "Proceedings." *Worcester Women's History Project*, accessed Feb. 10, 2017, www.wwhp.org. All references to comments at the convention are to this version. Also see Lisa Connelly Cook, "Why Was the First National Women's Rights Convention Swept under the Rug?" Unpublished dissertation, Feb. 16, 1998, History Department, Clark University.

3 "Why Commemmorate the 1850s Woman's Rights Convention?" *Worcester Women's History Project*, accessed Feb. 10, 2017, www.wwhp.org.

4 Cook.

18

Resolutions
Women's Rights Convention
Akron, Ohio
May 28–29, 1851

Sojourner Truth, participant in the Akron, Ohio, Women's Rights Convention.

This conference was called "to consider the Rights, Duties, and Relations of Women." Frances Gage served as president. There were highly objectionable words about the conquering of "savage" Native Americans in her opening address, as well as some eloquence, as she touched on matters ranging from the illegitimate source of men's power over women to the expected resistance encountered by every progressive social movement. There is language we recognize today of "voice" in her remarks, asking men "to allow the voice of woman to be heard," to "let woman speak for herself," but it is a universalized voice she appeals to, ruing that if only

all women could be impressed with the importance of their own, and with one united voice speak out in their own behalf, in behalf of humanity, they could create a revolution without armies, without bloodshed, that would do more to ameliorate the condition of mankind, to purify, elevate and ennoble humanity, than all that has been done by reformers in the last century.[1]

The document calls patriarchy a combination of "criminal injustice" and "reprehensible submissiveness." It recognizes that sexism has infiltrated all institutions and practices. Despite the fact that feminist abolitionists believed in immediate, rather than gradual emancipation of the enslaved, almost the opposite stance is taken here with regard to those oppressed by sex. Bold language regarding the oppression of women as workers appears, though perhaps not as uncompromising as that in the earlier Lowell documents. It supports women workers organizing, and seeks to inquire into "the monopoly of capital, or . . . the control of the means of living is not the primary cause of the wrongs woman suffers in regard to compensation for labor." It urges that "the means of honest livelihood" not be denied "those females who have lost their reputation for chastity." It calls on parents, the pulpit, and, newly, the press, to be agents of change, and sets up the tools for future research and gatherings.

The proceedings include reports given at the convention on the legal status of women, on women's education, and on the condition of women laborers, among other subjects. They also include many letters. Most often, they only mention that someone spoke, or that resolutions[2] were discussed. This is the case with regard to the most famous talk, that given by Sojourner Truth. Fortunately, we have records of Truth's talk from outside the proceedings. "The first reports of the speech were published by the *New York Tribune* on June 6, 1851, and by *The Liberator* five days later. . . . The first complete transcription was published on June 21 in the *Anti-Slavery Bugle* by Marius Robinson, an abolitionist and newspaper editor who acted as the convention's recording secretary."[3] We include the version here that has been revised from the nineteenth-century dialect style in which Truth's words are often published:

Well, children, where there is so much racket there must be something out of kilter. I think that 'twixt the Negroes of the South and the women at the North, all talking about rights, the white men will be in a fix pretty soon. But what's all this here talking about?

That man over there say that women needs to be helped into carriages, lifted over ditches, and to have the best place everywhere. Nobody ever helps me into carriages, or over mud-puddles, or gives me any best place! And ain't I a woman? Look at me! Look at my arm! I have ploughed, and planted, and gathered into barns, and no man could head me! And ain't I a woman? I could work as much and eat as much as a man—when I could get it—and bear the lash as well! And ain't I a woman? I have borne thirteen children, and seen most sold off to slavery, and when I cried out with my mother's grief, none but Jesus heard me. And ain't I a woman?

Then they talk about this thing in the head; what's this they call it? [member of audience whispers, "intellect"] That's it, honey. What's that got to do with women's rights or Negroes' rights? If my cup won't hold but a pint, and yours holds a quart, wouldn't you be mean not to let me have my little half-measure full?

Then that little man in black there, he says women can't have as much rights as men, because Christ wasn't a woman! Where did your Christ come from? Where did your Christ come from? From God and a woman! Men had nothing to do with Him.

If the first woman God ever made was strong enough to turn the world upside down all alone, these women together ought to be able to turn it back, and get it right side up again! And now they are asking to do it. The men better let them! Obliged to you for hearing me, and now old Sojourner ain't got nothing more to say.

Much outstanding research has been done on the speech that exceeds the confines of this introduction to the document the convention produced. But it is essential to note that

eyewitness reports of Truth's speech told a . . . story, one where all faces were "beaming with joyous gladness" at the session where Truth spoke; that not "one discordant note" interrupted the harmony of the proceedings. [. . .] Truth was warmly received by the convention-goers, the majority of whom were long-standing abolitionists, friendly to progressive ideas of race and civil rights.[4]

Resolutions

Inasmuch as it is self-evident that Woman has been created with as high intellectual and moral endowments, and subjected to similar necessities as Man, it is also self-evident that she is possessed naturally of a perfect equality with him in her legal, political, pecuniary, ecclesiastical and social rights, therefore:

1. *Resolved,* That the inequalities that manifestly exist in the privileges of the sexes as bestowed or allowed by institutions or customs, demonstrate in their creation and perpetuation the practice of criminal injustice on the part of man, and in her unresisting toleration of them a reprehensible submissiveness on the part of Woman.

2. *Resolved,* That as the unjust distinction between the sexes which vitiate all known civil and ecclesiastical institutions, and so large a proportion of legislative statutes and social usages, have received an apparent consecration in the opinions of a large majority of mankind by their antiquity and the blinding influence of custom, we can rely alone for their correction upon such means as will enlighten public sentiment and improve public morals; and this we can only hope to achieve in a gradual manner, though in a constantly increasing ratio.

3. *Resolved,* That as the religious instructors of the people exercise a most potent influence in moulding public sentiment, we call upon them, as we desire to promote a religion which is pure and undefiled, to afford special instruction in those principles of natural justice and equity on which alone all true religion rests, and to point out the violation of them in those oppressions which are endured by the female sex.

4. *Resolved,* That as the periodical press possesses an equal if not superior influence with the pulpit, in giving shape to that public sentiment which sustains all our political, ecclesiastical and educational relations, and general usages, we ask the conductors thereof not only to tolerate but to promote and urge through their columns the investigation of the subject.

5. *Resolved,* That as the main hope of beneficial change and effectual reform of public evils depends upon the direction given to the mind of the rising generation, we urge upon all teachers, upon all parents, and especially upon mothers, the duty of training the mind of every child to a complete comprehension of those principles of natural justice which should govern the whole subject of Human Rights, and, of course, Woman's rights, and to an accurate perception of those departures from them in human institutions and laws, which necessarily oppress woman primarily, and thereby injure man as well as woman ultimately.

6. *Resolved,* That we demand an immediate modification or repeal of all constitutional provisions and legislative enactments which create a difference in the privileges of individuals in consequence of a difference in sex.

7. *Resolved,* That Labor is a physical and moral necessity, binding upon all of both sexes; but as many females—especially the seamstresses—might improve their condition by the formation of Labor Partnerships, in which each can obtain all that her labor can command in the markets of the world,

we earnestly invite their attention to this subject and solicit on their behalf the sympathy, encouragement and patronage of the public.

8. *Resolved*, That as in the pecuniary oppressions to which woman is subjected are to be found the principal reasons for any deficiency of feminine purity and virtue, we call upon the philanthropic among mankind to unite in the effort to give woman the same opportunities to labor which men possess, and the same reward for its performance.

9. *Resolved*, That all avocations and pursuits which in their nature are honorable and conducive to the happiness and welfare of man, should be open to woman, if her capacity qualify her for the various duties, and her attractions impel her to enter them.

10. *Resolved*, That the Standing Committee appoint some individual to inquire, whether the monopoly of capital, or in other word, the control of the means of living, is not the primary cause of the wrongs woman suffers in regard to compensation for labor.

11. *Resolved*, That seven persons, with power to add to their number, be appointed as a Standing Committee, whose duties shall be to take charge of all matters pertaining to the interest of this cause, during the interval of the Convention, and make arrangements for the next meeting.

12. *Resolved*, That this Convention deem it of imminent importance to collect all facts relating to Woman and her position, and for this purpose authorize the Standing Committee to select suitable persons to report upon the number of attendants upon select Schools and Colleges, their adequacy and amount of funds, common schools and general education, industrial avocations and compensations, civil and political functions, social relations, common law and statutory law, and report at our next Convention.

13. *Resolved*, That we recommend the formation of District Societies throughout the State for discussion and action, in reference to the rights, duties, responsibilities and relation of the sexes.

14. *Resolved*, That we will not withhold the means of honest livelihood from those females who have lost their reputation for chastity.

15. *Resolved*, That the Standing Committee consist of Emily Robinson, of Morlboro', Cordelia L. Smallery, of Randolph, Martha J. Tilden, of Akron, K. G. Thomas, M.D., of Marlboro', Sarah N. M'Millan, of Salem, Lydia Irish, of New Lisbon, Betsey M. Cowles, of Canton.

Notes

1 *The Proceedings of the Women's Rights Convention, Held at Akron, Ohio, May 28 and 29, 1851.* Conference proceedings available online from the Library of Congress: hdl.loc.gov.

2 Ibid.

3 "Ain't I a Woman?" civil-rights-and-conflict-in-the-united-states-selected-speeches-001-aint-i-a-woman.pdf.

4 "Sojourner Truth," modified Sept. 15, 2017. *Wikipedia*, www.wikipedia.org.

19

Resolutions
Second National Convention
Daughters of St. Crispin
Stoneham, Massachusetts
April 12–14, 1870

Image of the Daughters of St. Crispin, 1869.

This organization of women shoemakers, founded on July 28, 1869 (and preceded in 1860 by a large strike of women workers), is thought to be the *first national women's workers group* in the United States. It represents women's increasing participation and struggles as paid laborers in the public sphere during the Industrial Revolution. St. Crispin, the patron saint of cobblers, tanners, and leather workers, had already inspired male shoemakers to establish the Order of the Knights of St. Crispin.

The Daughters' first meeting in 1869 did not seem to result in a lasting document, though there were "30 delegates present, representing the local lodges at Lynn, South Abington, Stoneham, Danvers, North Easton and North Bridgewater, Mass.; Auburn, Maine; Rochester, N.Y.; Philadelphia, Chicago and San Francisco."[1] Locals were as many as four hundred, and the organization lasted in some places until the industrial depression began around 1873.

By the time of this convention, twenty-four lodges of the Daughters existed across the country. Thirty delegates from thirteen locals in six states attended the 1870 meeting. Carrie Wilson served as president, and Abbie Jacques as secretary. Their Resolutions,[2] unanimously adopted, called the idea of employers that women should be paid less for work of equal quality "a usurpation and a fraud." They focused on equal pay and the "power of organization" and argued that improving their conditions at work would improve their social condition generally. The Daughters of St. Crispin influenced women's later participation in labor unions in the Progressive Era and women's and workers' rights generally.

Resolutions

WHEREAS the common idea among employers has been and still is that women's labor should receive a less remuneration, even though equally valuable and efficient, than is paid men even on the same qualities of work; and

WHEREAS in every field of human effort the value and power of organization is fully recognized; therefore be it

RESOLVED, by this National Grand Lodge of the Daughters of St. Crispin, that we demand for our labor the same rate of compensation for equal skill displayed, or the same hours of toil, as is paid other laborers in the same branches of business; and we regard a denial of this right by anyone as a usurpation and a fraud.

RESOLVED, That we condemn and promptly veto one sister's making a percentage on another sister's labor.

RESOLVED, That we assure our fellow-citizens that we only desire to so elevate and improve our condition as to better fit us for the discharge of those high social and moral duties which devolve upon every true woman.

Notes
1 Ruth Delzell, "1869: The Daughters of St. Crispin," in *Life and Labor*, vol. 2 (National Women's Trade Union League, 1912), p. 303.
2 Ibid.

20

Declaration of Rights of the Women of the United States
National Woman Suffrage Association
Philadelphia, Pennsylvania
July 4, 1876

The National Woman Suffrage Association. Undated photo.

We ask of our rulers, at this hour, no special favors, no special privileges, no special legislation. We ask justice, we ask equality, we ask that all the civil and political rights that belong to citizens of the United States, be guaranteed to us and our daughters forever.
—Susan B. Anthony

Written by Susan B. Anthony, Elizabeth Cady Stanton, and Matilda Joslyn Gage on behalf of the National Woman Suffrage Association (NWSA), this Declaration was drafted and presented in Philadelphia at the centennial celebration to demonstrate that, despite the principles of the Declaration of Independence and of republican government, women were still second-class citizens. It evokes "commemorative" speeches such as Frederick Douglass's "What to the Slave Is the Fourth of July?"

The NWSA was founded in 1869 as a result of a split of the American Equal Rights Association into two groups, primarily over the Fifteenth Amendment. The NWSA opposed giving Black men the vote before granting women suffrage. While its agenda was broader than suffrage (including unionizing women workers and obtaining the right to divorce), the group led the drive for the constitutional amendment that eventually passed in 1920. Men could join, but only women held leadership positions. "In 1872, it supported Victoria Woodhull, the first woman candidate for president of the United States."[1]

The original intention of the NWSA at the centennial was simply to have the Declaration included in the record so it would be historically preserved in the proceedings. General Joseph Hawley regretfully refused because he felt that the Declaration would distract from the message of unity and progress the ceremony intended to foster. Such tactics are part of an epistemology of ignorance. A dissenting perspective was apparently deemed more of a problem than recognition of the absence of equal rights.

Anthony and the NWSA were unwilling to sit back and celebrate when half of the country was excluded from progress and effective citizenship. In the middle of the ceremony, they respectfully, and without purposeful disruption, delivered a copy of the Declaration to Senator Thomas Ferry and many people in the crowd. Anthony and the protesters moved from the square to a nearby stage to read the document and discuss its purpose. Such neighboring gatherings perfectly capture the division of the United States without equal rights based on sex; men sat steeped in tradition and ceremony, while blocks away women were standing up and speaking out for revolution. The men saw what had been done. The women saw what must be done.

The document shows in great detail just how gendered law can be and with what consequences. Contrasting America's celebrated achievements with the "degradation of disenfranchisement" experienced by its women, it concludes that "[t]he history of our country the past hundred years, has been a series of assumptions and usurpations of power over woman, in direct opposition to the principles of just government, acknowledged by the United States at its foundation." Laying out exactly which rights and principles have been violated by what specific practices, it presents "articles of impeachment." It argues that "[w]oman's degraded, helpless position is the weak point in our institutions to-day." The Declaration is a stark presentation of the betrayal felt by many female citizens, the power of a patriarchal government, and what is at stake in gender equality.

Declaration of Rights of the Women of the United States

While the Nation is buoyant with patriotism, and all hearts are attuned to praise, it is with sorrow we come to strike the one discordant note, on this hundredth anniversary of our country's birth. When subjects of Kings, Emperors, and Czars, from the Old World, join in our National Jubilee, shall the women of the Republic refuse to lay their hands with benedictions on the nation's head? Surveying America's Exposition, surpassing in magnificence those of London, Paris, and Vienna, shall we not rejoice at the success of the youngest rival among the nations of the earth? May not our hearts, in unison with all, swell with pride at our great achievements as a people; our free speech, free press, free schools, free church, and the rapid progress we have made in material wealth, trade, commerce, and the inventive arts? And we do rejoice, in the success thus far, of our experiment of self-government. Our faith is firm and unwavering in the broad principles of human rights, proclaimed in 1776, not only as abstract truths, but as the corner stones of a republic. Yet, we cannot forget, even in this glad hour, that while all men of every race, and clime, and condition, have been invested with the full rights of citizenship, under our hospitable flag, all women still suffer the degradation of disfranchisement.

The history of our country the past hundred years, has been a series of assumptions and usurpations of power over woman, in direct opposition to the principles of just government, acknowledged by the United States at its foundation, which are:

First. The natural rights of each individual.

Second. The exact equality of these rights.

Third. That these rights, when not delegated by the individual, are retained by the individual.

Fourth. That no person can exercise the rights of others without delegated authority.

Fifth. That the non-use of these rights does not destroy them.

And for the violation of these fundamental principles of our Government, we arraign our rulers on this 4th day of July, 1876,—and these are our

Articles of Impeachment.

Bills of Attainder have been passed by the introduction of the word "male" into all the State constitutions, denying to woman the right of suffrage, and thereby making sex a crime—an exercise of power clearly forbidden in Article 1st, Sections 9th and 10th of the United States Constitution.

The Writ of Habeas Corpus, the only protection against *lettres de cachet*, and all forms of unjust imprisonment, which the Constitution declares "shall not be suspended, except when in cases of rebellion or invasion, the public safety demands it," is held inoperative in every State in the Union, in case of a married woman against her husband,—the marital rights of the husband being in all cases primary, and the rights of the wife secondary.

The Right of Trial by a Jury of One's Peers was so jealously guarded that States refused to ratify the original Constitution, until it was guaranteed by the 6th Amendment. And yet the women of this nation have never been allowed a jury of their peers—being tried in all cases by men, native and foreign, educated and ignorant, virtuous and vicious. Young girls have been arraigned in our courts for the crime of infanticide; tried, convicted, hung—victims, perchance, of judge, jurors, advocates—while no woman's voice could be heard in their defence. And not only are women denied a jury of their peers, but in some cases, jury trial altogether. During the war, a woman was tried and hung by military law, in defiance of the 5th Amendment, which specifically declares: "no person shall be held to answer for a capital or otherwise infamous crime, unless on a presentment or indictment of a grand jury, except in cases . . . of persons in actual service in time of war." During the last Presidential campaign, a woman, arrested for voting, was denied the protection of a jury, tried, convicted and sentenced to a fine and costs of prosecution, by the absolute power of a judge of the Supreme Court of the United States.

Taxation Without Representation, the immediate cause of the rebellion of the Colonies against Great Britain, is one of the grievous wrongs the women of this country have suffered during the century. Deploring war, with all the demoralization that follows in its train, we have been taxed to support standing armies, with their waste of life and wealth. Believing in temperance, we have been taxed to support the vice, crime, and pauperism of the Liquor Traffic. While we suffer its wrongs and abuses infinitely more than man, we have no power to protect our sons against this giant evil. During the Temperance Crusade, mothers were arrested, fined, imprisoned, for even praying and singing in the streets, while men blockade the sidewalks with impunity, even on Sunday, with their military parades and political processions. Believing in honesty, we are taxed to support a dangerous army of civilians, buying and selling the offices of government and sacrificing the best interests of the people. And, moreover, we are taxed to support the very legislators, and judges, who make laws, and render decisions adverse to woman. And for refusing to pay such unjust taxation, the houses, lands, bonds, and stock of women, have been seized and sold within the present year, thus proving Lord Coke's assertion, "that the very act of taxing a man's property without his consent, is, in effect, disfranchising him of every civil right."

Unequal Codes for Men and Women. Held by law a perpetual minor, deemed incapable of self-protection, even in the industries of the world, woman is denied equality of rights. The fact of sex, not the quantity or quality of work, in most cases, decides the pay and position; and because of this injustice thousands of fatherless girls are compelled to choose between a life of shame and starvation.

Laws catering to man's vices have created two codes of morals in which penalties are graded according to the political status of the offender. Under such laws, women are fined and imprisoned if found alone in the streets, or in public places of resort, at certain hours. Under the pretence of regulating public morals, police officers seizing the occupants of disreputable houses, march the women in platoons to prison, while the men, partners in their guilt, go free.

While making a show of virtue in forbidding the importation of Chinese women on the Pacific coast for immoral purposes, our rulers, in many states, and even under the shadow of the National Capitol, are now proposing to legalize the sale of American womanhood for the same vile purposes.

Special Legislation for Woman has placed us in a most anomalous position. Women invested with the rights of citizens in one section—voters, jurors, office-holders—crossing an imaginary line, are subjects in the next. In some states, a married woman may hold property and transact business in her own name; in others, her earnings belong to her husband. In some states, a woman may testify against her husband, sue and be sued in the courts; in others, she has no redress in case of damage to person, property, or character. In case of divorce, on account of adultery in the husband, the innocent wife is held to possess no right to children, or property, unless by special decree of the court. But in no state of the Union has the wife the right to her own person, or to any part of the joint earnings of the co-partnership, during the life of her husband. In some States women may enter the law schools and practice in the courts; in others they are forbidden. In some universities, girls enjoy equal educational advantages with boys, while many of the proudest institutions in the land deny them admittance, though the sons of China, Japan and Africa are welcomed there.

But the privileges already granted in the several states are by no means secure. The right of suffrage once exercised by women in certain States and Territories, has been denied by subsequent legislation. A bill is now pending in Congress to disfranchise the women of Utah, thus interfering to deprive United States citizens of the same rights, which the Supreme Court has declared the National Government powerless to protect anywhere. Laws passed after years of untiring effort, guaranteeing married women certain rights of property, and mothers the custody of their children, have been repealed in States where we supposed all was safe. Thus have our most sacred rights been made the football of legislative caprice, proving that a power which grants, as a privilege, what by nature is a right, may withhold the same as a penalty, when deeming it necessary for its own perpetuation.

Representation for Woman has had no place in the nation's thought. Since the incorporation of the thirteen original states, twenty-four have been admitted to the Union, not one of which has recognized woman's right of self-government. On this birthday of our national liberties, July 4th, 1876, Colorado, like all her elder sisters, comes into the Union, with the invidious word "male" in her Constitution.

Universal Manhood Suffrage, by establishing an aristocracy of sex, imposes upon the women of this nation a more absolute and cruel despotism than monarchy; in that, woman finds a political master in her father, husband, brother, son. The aristocracies of the old world are based upon birth, wealth, refinement, education, nobility, brave deeds of chivalry; in this nation, on sex alone; exalting brute force above moral power, vice above virtue, ignorance above education, and the son above the mother who bore him.

The Judiciary of the Nation has proved itself but the echo of the party in power, by upholding and enforcing laws that are opposed to the spirit and letter of the Constitution. When the slave power was dominant, the Supreme Court decided that a black man was not a citizen, because he had not the right to vote; and when the Constitution was so amended as to make all persons citizens, the same high tribunal decided that a woman, though a citizen, had not the right to vote. Such vacillating interpretations of constitutional law unsettle our faith in judicial authority, and undermine the liberties of the whole people.

These Articles of Impeachment Against Our Rulers we now submit to the impartial judgment of the people.

To all these wrongs and oppressions woman has not submitted in silence and resignation. From the beginning of the century, when Abigail Adams, the wife of one President and the mother of another, said, "we will not hold ourselves bound to obey laws in which we have no voice or representation," until now, woman's discontent has been steadily increasing, culminating nearly thirty years ago in a simultaneous movement among the women of the nation, demanding the right of suffrage. In making our just demands, a higher motive than the pride of sex inspires us; we feel that national safety and stability depend on the complete recognition of the broad principles of our government. Woman's degraded, helpless position is the weak point in our institutions to-day; a disturbing force everywhere, severing family ties, filling our asylums with the deaf, the dumb, the blind, our prisons with criminals, our cities with drunkenness and prostitution, our homes with disease and death.

It was the boast of the founders of the republic, that the rights for which they contended, were the rights of human nature. If these rights are ignored in the case of one half the people, the nation is surely preparing for its own downfall. Governments try themselves. The recognition of a governing and a governed class is incompatible with the first principles of freedom. Woman has not been a heedless spectator of the events of this century, nor a dull listener to the grand arguments for the equal rights of humanity. From the earliest history of our country, woman has shown equal devotion with man to the cause of freedom, and has stood firmly by his side in its defence. Together, they have made this country what it is. Woman's wealth, thought and labor have cemented the stones of every monument man has reared to liberty.

And now, at the close of a hundred years, as the hour hand of the great clock that marks the centuries points to 1876, we declare our faith in the principles of self-government; our full equality with man in natural rights; that woman was made first for her own happiness, with the absolute right to herself—to all the opportunities and advantages life affords, for her complete development; and we deny that dogma of the centuries, incorporated in the codes of all nations—that woman was made for man—her best interests, in all cases, to be sacrificed to his will.

We ask of our rulers, at this hour, no special favors, no special privileges, no special legislation. We ask justice, we ask equality, we ask that all the civil and political rights that belong to citizens of the United States, be guaranteed to us and our daughters forever.

Note

1   "National Woman Suffrage Association," Jan. 21, 2011. Social Welfare History Project, Virginia Commonwealth University Libraries, www.socialwelfarehistory.com.

21

Series of Resolutions
First International Congress of Women's Rights
Paris, France
Summer 1878

Maria Deraismes, *left*, and Léon-Pierre Richer, co-organizers.

Last evening a gentleman who seemed a bit skeptical about the advantages of our congress asked me, "Well Madame, what great truth have you proclaimed to the world?" I replied to him, "Monsieur, we have proclaimed a woman is a human being." He laughed. "But, Madame, that is a platitude." So it is; but when this platitude . . . is recognized by human laws, the face of the world will be transformed. Certainly, then, there would be no need for us to assembly in congress to demand the rights of woman.
—Emily Venturi, representative from France[1]

The First International Congress of Women's Rights was held to coincide with the third Paris World's Fair, and it was organized by Leon Richer and Maria Deraismes, who also ran a periodical together, *Le Droit des Femmes* (Women's Rights). The meeting was attended by "a sizable number of French republican leaders as well as representatives from abroad."[2] While about two hundred attended the closing banquet, some four hundred other "unofficial" participants heard parts of the three days of speeches. At this first international women's rights gathering, the participants were "from eleven countries and sixteen feminist organisations,"[3] including representatives from Switzerland, Holland, the United States, Russia, Italy, and France.

The goal of the congress was to establish equal civil rights for men and women in all countries, though the group deliberately left out the question of suffrage (and other political rights) in their Resolutions as a matter of timing and in order to maintain unity. The congress was also a protest against the French republic's Civil Code of 1804, which limited the rights of women. The overriding principle of the gathering is found in the first resolution, which urges that "the entire body of civil legislation be revised in the direction of the most absolute and complete equality between the two sexes."

The Resolutions[4] proposed by this congress focus mainly on marriage and morality, asserting the importance of legal divorce to prevent abuse against women, the need for equal punishments for men and women for the crime of adultery, stricter punishments for men who seduce underage girls with false promises of marriage, and the ability of illegitimate children to inherit from both parents equally with legitimate children (an issue that gained visibility in Olympe de Gouge's 1791 "Declaration of the Rights of Woman and the Female Citizen"). The bias of French laws and laws from around the world favored men in matters of sexual morality, and this congress established both a vocabulary and a forum for women's rights to be discussed in terms of human rights.

Series of Resolutions

I. Considering that woman is a civil personality;

Whereas, according to natural law, the adult woman is the equal of the adult man, The Congress resolves that, in every country where woman is made inferior, the entire body of civil legislation be revised in the direction of the most absolute and complete equality between the two sexes.

II. Convinced as we are that the legislation presently in force is inadequate; that the system of legal separation is immoral and should be eradicated; that the indissolubility of marriage is contrary both to the principle of individual liberty and to morality and has the most unfortunate and terrible consequences; that divorce is necessary from the perspective of humanity, of morals, and, in a word, of the future of society;

The Section concerned with legislation—illuminated by the debates and drawing inspiration from the hopes common to all nations as expressed by the members that represent them; leaving to the legislators the task of formulating the text of the law and determining a mode of special jurisdiction—puts forth the following propositions, which it believes respond to the wishes of the majority and which it submits to the consideration of the Congress:

The Congress demands:

1. The suppression of the regime of bodily separation [*régime de la séparation de corps*].
2. The establishment or reestablishment of divorce, according to the principle of equality between the spouses.

III. The Congress considers the absolute freedom to divorce as the best remedy against the inequality of the man and the woman with regard to the laws on adultery.

IV. Whereas there is only one morality;

Whereas the degree of guilt for the same crime or misdemeanor cannot vary according to sex.

With regard to the misdemeanor of adultery:

Considering that adultery by the man is as sinful as that of the woman, since the man, like the woman, can introduce into someone else's family bastards of his authorship.

Considering that, even apart from this circumstance, the adultery of man, no less than that of woman, carries in its wake social disorders whose seriousness, whether from the perspective of family bonds or of public morality, is not contested by anyone.

Considering that if the reestablishment of divorce on the foundation of the greatest liberty should result in the decrease of instances of adultery, it will not be able to prevent them at all:

The Congress resolves that the penal laws should not acknowledge any difference between the adultery of the wife and the adultery of the husband, wherever the act is committed.

V. The Congress expresses its ardent desire to see enacted as soon as possible, in those nations currently deprived of it, a law establishing as a misdemeanor the act of seduction of an underage girl, accomplished with the help of lies and a false promise of marriage.

Such a law should empower the appropriate tribunals to sentence, when appropriate, the guilty party to pay damages to the plaintiff.

VI. The Congress,

Considering that both morality and social order require equally that the parentage of every human being should be a matter of record:

Resolves that the search for paternity [*recherché de paternité*] by judicial process be allowed and pursued, without charge, on behalf of any child who has not been legally recognized, and also at the request of an underage girl whose seduction by lies and promises of marriage has been verified.

The Congress adds that it would be useful to have the laws on the right of inheritance of the father's estate be equalized for all his children, with no distinctions being made between them.

VII. Considering the first and most sacred right of the human being is his right to absolute sovereignty over his own person:

Considering that citizens (*citoyens*) and citizenesses (*citoyennes*) are equal in common law;

Considering that the arbitrary powers accorded to the morals police are in flagrant violation of the juridical guarantees assured by the law to each individual, even to the worst criminal;

The Congress demands the suppression of the morals police.

Notes

1 Karen Offen, *European Feminisms: A Political History, 1700–1950* (Stanford, CA: Stanford University Press, 2000), p. 152.

2 "Women and the Civil Law," in *Women, the Family, and Freedom: The Debate in Documents*, ed. Susan Groag Bell and Karen M. Offen (Stanford, CA: Stanford University Press, 1983), p. 409.

3 James McMillan, *France and Women, 1789–1914: Gender, Society, and Politics* (Abingdon, UK: Routledge, 2000), p. 136.

4 "Women and the Civil Law."

22

Official Statement of the First International Council of Women

First International Council of Women
Washington, D.C.
March 25–April 1, 1888

Logo of the International Council of Women (ICW-CIF).

Men have granted us, in the privileges and civil rights of society, which
we have been demanding, everything, almost, but the pivotal right . . .
—Susan B. Anthony[1]

The first meeting of the International Council of Women[2] was held to celebrate the progress made in the forty years since the Seneca Falls convention, which some were trying to establish as a decisive historical moment.[3] Elizabeth Cady Stanton and Susan B. Anthony conceived of and made arrangements for the convention, and forty-nine delegates from nine countries (England, Ireland, France, Norway, Denmark, Finland, India, Canada, and the United States) were appointed to the council. Hundreds, possibly thousands, of people attended the convention to hear the delegates speak on the conditions of various aspects of women's lives across the globe. The council is the oldest existing transnational feminist organization.[4]

According to the *Women's Studies Encyclopedia*,

In its early years ICW stressed equal access to schools and training programs, equal pay for equal work, state-supported maternity leaves and benefits, protection of workers, and the development of machinery and programs to alleviate the drudgery of housework as well as to promote better working conditions for domestic workers. In the 1920s, ICW standing committees worked closely with the League of Nations, especially in matters of health, welfare, peace, racial equality, and the rights of national minorities. . . . Through the 1960s, the membership of the ICW expanded to include many African and Asian countries, and the organization became directly involved in programs of economic development in those areas. The stress ICW placed on the involvement of women in development was picked up by the United Nations in its 1973–1983 Decade of Women.[5]

After 1945, the ICW began to "defend and advocate the notion of Human Rights for women," an argument we have already seen emerging. Today, nongovernmental organizations of women from more than sixty countries belong to the ICW, whose present-day headquarters are in Lausanne, Switzerland.

The leaders of the International Council of Women.

The organization works to stay nonpartisan in order to support women across the world. Some of its specific issues stem from its founders at the 1888 meeting, including work against "violence, discriminations, trafficking and poverty," and its central aim "towards a re-moralised society is nothing less than restoring the dignity for all men and women whatever their origin, race, creed or social condition may be."[6] It has long stood for sexual equality in education, employment, pay, and moral standards.

The group was intended to be an umbrella organization of independent national councils. A constitution was drafted with international assemblies to be held every five years and national meetings occurring every three; however, it took many years for independent national groups to develop globally.

Official Statement of the International Council

The International Council of Women, in session in the city of Washington from March 25 to April 1, inclusive, in closing makes public announcement that fifty-three different organizations of women have been represented on its platform by eighty speakers and forty-nine delegates from England, France, Norway, Denmark, Finland, India, Canada, and the United States. All of these organizations but four are of national scope, and these are of national value. The subjects of Education, Philanthropies, Temperance, Industries, Professions, Organization, Legal Conditions, Social Purity, Political Conditions, and Religion have been discussed. While no restriction has been placed upon the fullest expression of the most widely divergent views upon these vital questions of the age, it is cause for rejoicing that the sessions, both executive and public, have been absolutely without friction.

It is the unanimous voice of the Council; that all institutions of learning and of professional instruction, including schools of theology, law, and medicine, should, in the interests of humanity, be as freely opened to women as to men; that opportunities for industrial training should be as generally and liberally provided for one sex as for the other, and the representatives of organized womanhood in this Council will steadily demand that in all avocations in which both men and women engage equal wages shall be paid for equal work; and, finally, that an enlightened society should demand, as the only adequate expression of the high civilization which it is its office to establish and maintain, an identical standard of personal purity and morality for men and women.

Notes

1 *Report of the International Council of Women: Assembled by the National Woman Suffrage Association, Washington, D.C., U.S. of America, March 25 to April 1, 1888*, vol. 1 (Rufus Darby, 1888). Made from stenographic report by Mary F. Seymour and assistants, 1888.

2 *Report of the International Council of Women*, p. 454.

3 See Lisa Tetrault, *The Myth of Seneca Falls: Memory and the Women's Suffrage Movement, 1848–1898* (Chapel Hill: University of North Carolina Press, 2014).

4 Leila Rupp, "The International Council of Women, 1888 to the Present" (Alexandria, VA: Alexander Street Press, 2016), wasi.alexanderstreet.com. Leila Rupp argues for seeing the organization as historically Euroamerican and Christian in Thomas Dublin and Kathryn Kish Sklar, *Women and Social Movements, International: 1840–Present* (Alexandria, VA: Alexander Street Press, 2017), wasi.alexanderstreet.com.

5 "International Council of Women," in *Women's Studies Encyclopedia*, ed. Helen Tierney (Santa Barbara, CA: Greenwood Press, 2002), gem.greenwood.com.

6 "History," International Council of Women. Accessed Sept. 15, 2017, www.icw-cif.com.

23

Resolutions *and* Objectives
The National Colored Woman's Congress and the National Association of Colored Women's Clubs
Washington, D.C.
January and July 21, 1896

Logo of the National Association of Colored Women's Clubs.

The work which we hope to accomplish can be done better, we believe, by the mothers, wives, daughters, and sisters of our race than by the fathers, husbands, brothers, and sons.
—Mary Church Terrell's presidential address

This organization of colored women means much; through it our women are brought more closely in touch with the world and the great questions of the day; by organization, not only are their own minds and talents strengthened and developed, but they are enabled to give a helping hand to those less favored; through it the inspiration of congeniality is felt, besides this each organization is a strong factor for the general elevation of the race. A certain independence of action in the leagues is admirable, but still, even here the power of organization should be recognized and used, a general interest in each other's work is not enough to gain the greatest power. To do the most good the leagues should be united to a certain degree.[1]

The oldest African American secular organization in existence today was established in 1896, a time of much local and national organizing by Black women, who were playing a crucial role in the development of the African American community and in reform movements. Jim Crow laws and social Darwinism provided the immediate background for such organizing. In addition to general threats to the well-being and political participation of Black people, some attacks were directed specifically at Black women.

> To discredit the successful antilynching activities of American journalist and reformer Ida B. Wells in England, James W. Jacks, president of the Missouri Press Association, published a letter denouncing all blacks. But he dismissed the credibility of black women: "[They] were prostitutes and all were thieves and liars." The Jacks article fueled the debate in the press and among the intelligentsia. Unlike the antebellum era, however, a new significant ingredient entered the playing field. A large body of articulate, college-educated women had emerged during the first generation of freedom. In response to Jacks' letter, Josephine St. Pierre Ruffin of Boston issued a call to women to meet in Boston because, she argued, only in that environment could they educate the public mind "to a just appreciation of us."[2]

Little did Jacks suspect that his "unjust and unholy charges," as St. Pierre Ruffin called them, would lead to greater consolidation of Black women's organizations and an increase in their clout. This Boston meeting culminated in the establishment of the National Association of Colored Women's Clubs (NACWC), based on a merger of the National League of Colored Women of Washington, D.C. (organized in 1893), the National Federation of Afro-American Women (founded in 1895), and the Women's Era Club of Boston (1894), as well as some smaller clubs.

The founders of NACWC included some of the best-known Black women of the time, including Frances Harper, Ida B. Wells-Barnett, Harriet Tubman, Margaret Murray Washington, and Mary Church Terrell, who was elected as the first president. Its motto, "Lifting as We Climb," signaled its positive aims to "an ignorant and suspicious world." There was in this motto a somewhat classist idea that middle-class (and above) Black women must "lift" those beneath them, who might be something of an embarrassment, and an establishment of common ground with some White women's organizations that the goal for women is moral improvement.

At the founding convention, reports by prominent individuals and local clubs addressed prison reform, care of the aged, care of orphans, the separate car system, and the ideal home. Terrell's broad agenda for NACWC included job training, wage equity, and childcare, and from the outset the group raised money for early education, vocational schools, summer camps, and retirement homes. Like the groups from which it was composed, the NACW opposed segregated transportation systems and supported the antilynching campaign. Early in the twentieth century, it started a national scholarship fund for college-bound African American women, and supported the suffrage movement—two years before its white counterpart,

The Woman's Era was the first U.S. publication by and for African American women, started by Ruffin and published from 1894 to 1897. From the first issue there were calls for a "Congress of colored women's leagues and clubs."[3]

the General Federation of Women's Clubs. The two documents featured here[4] overlap considerably, which makes sense given that the group behind the Resolutions[5] became part of the larger coalition. The second, however, gives more substance to the briefly outlined objectives of the first.

National Association of Colored Women's Clubs Objectives

1. To promote the education of women and children
2. To raise the standards of the home
3. To improve conditions for family living
4. To work for the moral, economic, social, and religious welfare of women and children
5. To protect the rights of women and children
6. To secure and enforce civil and political rights for the African-American race
7. To promote interracial understanding so that justice may prevail among all people

Resolutions of the Colored Women's Congress

Recognizing that there is a great need of bringing before the Anglo-Saxons of these United States the capabilities of the Negro, and feeling assured that this may best be done by contact with them, therefore be it

Resolved, That we, the women of this Congress, endorse the Cotton States Exposition in giving the Negro the chance to show what he is doing and the possibilities of his future, *but* be it further

Resolved, That we condemn in strongest terms the sale of liquor and all intoxicants in the lunch room of the Negro Building of the Cotton States Exposition, and consider it a direct reflection upon the intelligence and respectability of our race.

WHEREAS, it has come to our observation and knowledge that for years the convict lease system of the Southern States has been a Subject of national slander, in which the indiscriminate mixing of males and females has been the most abhorrent feature, therefore

Resolved, That the women of this Congress upon the legal authorities of the states where the convict lease system is in force, to at least make proper provision for the separation of the sexes, in common justice and as an honest concession to our common human nature.

Resolved, That we ask the co-operation of the generous white women of the South to assist us in all honorable ways to correct the evil here complained of.

Resolved, That this Congress express its sense of appreciation of the efforts already put forth by Gov. Atkinson of Georgia to correct evils acknowledged to exist in the penal system of this state, and that we would be grateful to the governors of all states concerned if they would emulate his noble example.

Resolved, That as the National W.C.T.U. offers so many opportunities through which the women of our race may be enlightened and encouraged in their work for humanity, therefore be it further resolved that we, as Afro-American women, accept these opportunities by entering this open door, and heartily endorse the work taken up by the W.C.T.U., but insist that their attitude in regard to the lynching evil and color prejudice question generally be less equivocal.

WHEREAS, many women of this Congress, coming from points remote, have had experience with the separate car system prevailing in many states of the south, of its brutal, inhuman and degrading nature, and

WHEREAS, the separate car system is contrary, not only to the law of contract but to the genius of our liberal institutions, tending to accentuate unduly discriminations on account of color and condition, and

WHEREAS, it is the proud boast of Southern white men that the ennobling of womanhood is the basis of all chivalric manhood,

Resolved, That we call upon the Southern legislators, in the name of the common womanhood, to adopt a first and second class fare, so that the womanhood of the race may be protected from every outrage and insult. We trust that the white men of the South now in power will heed this just petition.

WHEREAS, all forms of lawlessness is prejudicial to the best interest, the highest development and fair fame of all the people of America, our common country, and

WHEREAS, there does exist in many parts of our country a most deplorable disregard for law and order, and in many commonly reported cases for humanity itself, and

WHEREAS, all tendency toward mob rule, lynching, burning, midnight marauding, and all unlawful and unjust discriminations, is not only contrary to the fundamental principles of our government, but a menace to every department of justice and the well being of posterity,

Resolved, That we condemn every form of lawlessness and miscarriage of justice, and demand, without favor or compromise, the equal enforcement of the law for all classes of American citizens.

WHEREAS, one Dr. S. A. Steele, a prominent minister in the Methodist Episcopal Church, south, and editor of the *Epworth Era*, the official organ of the southern Epworth League, has in that paper made one of the most scurrilous attacks that has yet appeared against the Negro,

Resolved, That we, the women of this Congress, most severely condemn this article and all such articles which may hereafter appear, as they seriously misrepresent us and are detrimental to the work we are doing and what we hope to accomplish.

WHEREAS, organization among women has proved a most active agent in stimulating and inaugurating needed reforms and wise movements for the advancement of progress, not only of women, but mankind in general, and

WHEREAS, there are efforts now being made for the unification and concentration of existing national associations among women at this time in Atlanta, and

WHEREAS, it is the policy of the National Federation of Afro-American Women, Mrs. B. T. Washington, president, to unite in one common bond of mutual sympathy and kindly interest the women of all sections, with the view of serving the common good by establishing one strong organization which shall truly represent the colored women of the country,

Resolved, That this Congress endorse and co-operate with the National Federation of Afro-American Women in the final establishment of one truly representative national body of colored women.

Miss Lucy Moten, of Washington, objected, on the ground that the resolution as it stood gave the Federation the advantage of the National League. Mrs. Matthews offered an amendment, and the resolution as amended was adopted. The amendment was as follows:

Resolved, That this Congress recommend to the various organizations here represented, local, state and national, the wisdom of uniting for the establishment of one national organization of women.

WHEREAS, we as a race have never been taught to feel and appreciate the value of good homes, and

WHEREAS, to this day there are to be seen in many of our country communities the one room log cabin where many live together in an unwholesome atmosphere which is detrimental both morally and physically to the best growth and development of the masses,

Resolved, That as a body of women we do urge upon the teachers and leaders of our race the necessity and importance of mother's meetings, social purity talks and such other agencies as shall most forcibly impress upon the mothers of our race the evil influences generated by the admission of frivolous or obscene books or pictures into their homes.

WHEREAS, the colored women of this country stand very greatly in need of all the aid and assistance that the more fortunate and intelligent members of the race can offer them, and

WHEREAS, the elevation of the motherhood and womanhood of the race is the most effectual and powerful means for raising the mental and moral standard of the masses of our people, therefore be it

Resolved, That we hereby pledge ourselves individually and collectively to use every effort in our power,

1. To establish homes among our people the influence of which will tend to the development of men and women of strong character and purity of purpose in life.

2. To demand of our leaders and teachers the highest standard of character, refinement and culture.

3. That we require the same standard of morality for men as for women, and that the mothers teach their sons social purity as well as their daughters.

4. We condemn the universal prodigality of the race and urge upon our people, having the best interests of the race at heart, to give permanence to our present progressiveness by practising strict economy in their homes and business relations, and to count no effort insignificant which is made in the interest or with a view toward the purchase of a home.

Resolved, That it is the duty of the colored women of the country to take a more practical interest in the condition and treatment of the unfortunate members of our race and in making proper provision for the establishment of reformatories and institutions for the orphans, the aged, and the infirm, not excepting those institutions that have steadily adhered to the broadest of philanthropic principles, and thrown wide their doors to suffering humanity regardless of color, past condition or creed.

Realizing the gravity of our social and economic condition, and the wide influences of our teachers in assisting in the formation of the character of our children,

Resolved, That we urge upon those in authority to exercise the greatest diligence in selecting trained, competent teachers, who are imbued with the love and true spirit of their work. Further we urge upon parents the necessity of co-operating with the teachers in all matters that pertain to the successful development of those intrusted to their care.

Resolved, That in order to secure healthful bodies in which to contain healthful minds and souls we do heartily encourage all teachers, parents and guardians to make physical culture a prominent feature in their training of our youth.

WHEREAS, since every race must possess intelligence, energy, industry and enterprise in order that it may rank among the great and powerful races of the world, and,

WHEREAS, we feel that the life and prosperity of the home depends largely upon its women who are entrusted with its making, therefore be it

Resolved, That we endorse and encourage every phase of higher industrial education and urge all persons to take such training as will elevate and make the noblest types of woman and man, and thus fit themselves for the actual responsibilities of life.

Resolved, That the tone of the Negro press should be elevated and placed upon such high standard so that none but those having special training for that calling may be encouraged to continue in such work. In the publication of race journals the personality of the editor should either be wholly eliminated or subordinated to questions of public importance. The advocacy of the selfish ends of any person or persons as against the public interests should be condemned, and no article that is not elevating in its character and pure in its purpose should ever appear in the columns of our newspapers.

Resolved, That we endorse the work of the John Brown Memorial Association of the state of Minnesota, of which Mrs. T. H. T. Lyles is president, and suggest instead of the proposed marble statue, that the funds collected by the association be devoted to the purchase and maintenance of a home farm for helpless and dependent children, the same to be dedicated to the memory of John Brown, and located in that section furnishing the most money for the purpose.

Resolved, That the very courteous invitation to the Afro-American women of the country, as here represented, to hold a meeting in the city of Nashville, Tenn., in the fall or winter of 1896 on such days as shall be hereafter determined upon, from the Mayor and City Council of that city, the Board of Public Works and Affairs, the Chamber of Commerce, the Director-General of the Tennessee Centennial and Executive Committee of the Negro Department of the Centennial, be accepted.

Resolved, That we, the colored women of America, insist upon the highest degree of excellence as the standard of attainment for our race and pledge ourselves to do all in our power to help our artisan, business and professional men and women, who have shown themselves fitted for the respective pursuits in which they may be engaged.

Notes

1 This is from the May 1894 edition of the *Woman's Era.* Courtesy of the Emory Women Writers Resource Project, Emory University, womenwriters.digitalscholarship.emory.edu.

2 Lillian Serece Willaims and Randolph Boehm, "Records of the National Association of Colored Women's Clubs, 1895–1992: Part I—Minutes of National Conventions, Publications, and President's Office Correspondence" (University Publications of America and National Association of Colored Women's Clubs, 1994), www.nacwc.org.

3 Francesca Sawaya, *Modern Women, Modern Work: Domesticity, Professionalism, and American Writing, 1890–1950* (Philadelphia: University of Pennsylvania Press, 2011), p. 41.

4 "Who Are We." National Association of Colored Women's Clubs. Accessed Sept. 2017, www .nacwc.org.

5 This is from the April 1895 edition of the *Woman's Era.* Courtesy of the Emory Women Writers Resource Project, Emory University, womenwriters.digitalscholarship.emory.edu.

Part III

1900–1949

24

Declaration of Principles
International Woman Suffrage Alliance
Berlin, Germany
June 2–4, 1904

The first meeting of the International Alliance of Women was organized by Susan B. Anthony, Millicent Fawcett, Anita Augspurg, and Carrie Chapman Catt for the purpose of gaining the right to vote and making equal legal rights for women in all of the countries who sent delegates to the conference. Members of women's organizations from Australia, Germany, Great Britain, the Netherlands, Sweden, the United States, Denmark, and Norway attended the meeting. Its motto became "Equal Rights—Equal Responsibilities." By 1928, women in all of these countries had gained the electoral franchise.[1]

The group is still operational today (womenalliance.org), and it is composed of forty-one women's organizations that are "involved in the promotion of women's human rights, of equality and of the empowerment of women."[2] It changed its name to the International Alliance of Women in 1946, after suffrage had been gained in most European and many African and South American countries.

The Declaration of Principles[3] is mainly concerned with the natural equality between men and women; it emphasizes the right of each to equal exercise of their liberty and individuality and, consequently, the importance of cooperation between the sexes instead of the dependence of women on men, and the right of all to equal exercise of their liberty and individuality. The Principles see sexual inequality as an injustice itself, founded on falsehoods in laws, creeds, and customs, and as the cause of other "social, legal and economic injustice." Precisely who is excluded in the restriction of equal rights to "every normal adult" is unclear; probably, the intent was simply to "normalize" equality. The Declaration asserts that representation in government, education, and personal development, and the right to vote, are the best and most reasonable ways to resolve the governmental, economic, and societal ills caused by inequality between men and women. Today, the IAW still builds on these foundational principles with its

The International Woman Suffrage Alliance Banner. Photo from the International Alliance of Women, www.womenalliance.org.

active commissions on Democracy, Human Rights, Violence Against Women, and Gender and the Economic Crisis.

Declaration of Principles

That men and women are born equally free and independent members of the human race, equally endowed with intelligence and ability, and equally entitled to the free exercise of their individual rights and liberty.

That the natural relation of the sexes is that of inter-dependence and cooperation, and that the repression of the rights and liberty of one sex inevitably works injury to the other, and hence to the whole race.

That in all lands, those laws, creeds and customs which have tended to restrict women to a position of dependence, to discourage their education, to impede the development of their natural gifts and to subordinate their individuality, have been based upon false theories and have produced an artificial and unjust relation of the sexes in modern society.

That self-government in the home and the State is the inalienable right of every normal adult, and the refusal of this right to women has resulted in social, legal and economic injustice to them, and has also intensified the existing economic disturbances throughout the world.

That governments which impose taxes and laws upon their women citizens without giving them the right of consent or dissent, which is granted to men citizens, exercise a tyranny inconsistent with just government.

That the ballot is the only legal and permanent means of defending the rights to the "life, liberty and the pursuit of happiness" pronounced inalienable by the American Declaration of Independence, and accepted as inalienable by all civilised nations. In any representative form of government, therefore, women should be vested with all political rights and privileges of electors.

Notes

1 With the exception of Indigenous Australian women and men, who were not granted suffrage until 1962.
2 "What Is IAW," 2013. *International Alliance of Women*, accessed Nov. 11, 2014, womenalliance.org.
3 "Declaration of Principles," 2013. *International Alliance of Women*, accessed Oct. 7, 2013.

25

Resolutions and Motions *and* Excerpt
First International Conference of Socialist Women and
Second International Conference of Socialist Women
Stuttgart, Germany, and Copenhagen, Denmark
August 18–24, 1907, and 1910

This first conference was held in conjunction with the International Socialist Congress. Clara Zetkin (perhaps most famous for proposing March 8 as International Women's Day), a leader of the German women's rights movement, convened the conference in her own home. Fifty-eight delegates from fifteen countries participated, including representatives from Germany, Austria, the United States, and Russia; representatives from each of the Scandinavian countries; female members of Parliament from Finland; British delegates from the Women's Labour League, the Independent Labour Party, and the Social Democratic Party; and a single delegate from the Portuguese Tailoresses Union. Rosa Luxembourg (pictured in figure 25.2) was another attendee, who earlier in 1907 had attended the Congress of the Russian Social Democrats in London, England. International connections were growing in every direction.

The Stuttgart conference is most notable for its position on women's suffrage. Up until this conference, many socialist women suspected that female suffrage would extend the right to vote to women on the same conditions as men, meaning only "bourgeois" or propertied women would be granted the right. This conference was among the first to express a "clear commitment to suffrage for all men and women, as opposed to a strategy of male universal suffrage first."[1] This conference is thus a key moment in the movement towards universal suffrage, which it defines as "open to all adults and bound by no conditions of property, payment of taxes, or degrees of education or any other qualifications." The International Socialist Conference later adopted this demand.

The Resolutions are interesting for other reasons, as well. While supporting universal suffrage, socialist feminists see the legal equality of women in class society as of limited consequence, since those with more property, including women, necessarily have more social power. Where other groups and gatherings largely

Clara Zetkin, *left*, and Rosa Luxemburg, 1910.

tried to build bridges among women across race, class, religion, and national boundaries, socialists spoke directly about "class antagonisms between women" that result in the fact that "the bourgeois woman's movement does not march united, with closed ranks and the highest development of force." Their argument was that proletarian women would have to look elsewhere for justice and full political and economic rights.

This document[2] foreshadows many others in emphasizing antimilitarization. It is the first to advocate for paid maternity leave and for giving "mothers with children dependent upon them . . . continued adequate support to enable them to attend to their children without having to work for wages." At the Second International Conference of Socialist Women, held in 1910 in Copenhagen, these sorts of provisions were greatly expanded upon. Because such detailed attention remains unusual, we include that part of the 1910 Resolutions[3] along with the 1907 Resolutions.

Resolutions and Motions from the First International Conference of Socialist Women

I. Resolutions on Woman Suffrage

The demand for Woman Suffrage arises from the economic and social transformation caused by the capitalist system of production, especially, however, from the revolutionising of woman's labour, of her position and her mind. It is by its nature a consequence of the bourgeois democratic principle, which calls for the setting aside of all social distinctions that do not rest on property, and proclaims in the sphere of public as well as of private life the complete legal equality of all adults as a right of personality. For this reason Woman Suffrage has always been demanded by individual thinkers in connection with every struggle which the bourgeoisie ever took up for the democratization of political rights as a necessary condition of their political emancipation and class rule. Efficient force as a demand from the masses has, however, first accrued to it from the increasing number of women who have to earn their living, and especially owing to the numbers of the female proletariat who have been drawn into the modern industry. Woman Suffrage is necessarily bound up with the economic emancipation of woman from the household and her economic independence of the family on the strength of her activity as an earner.

From the standpoint of principle the active and passive suffrage means for the female sex, as a whole, the recognition of their social maturity; from the practical point of view it is the means to obtain political power, so as to remove the legal and social hindrances which stand in the way of the development of woman's life and activity. But owing to the class antagonisms, which are just as influential in the world of women as in that of men, the value and main object of the suffrage is different for women of the different classes. The value of the suffrage as a weapon in the social struggle is in inverse proportion to the size of the property possessed by the individual and the social power conferred by that property. Its principal object differs, according to the class position: it is either the complete legal equality of the female sex, or it is the social emancipation of the proletariat through the conquest of political power for the purpose of abolishing class-rule and bringing about the Socialist society which alone affords a guarantee for the complete emancipation of woman as a human being.

In consequence of the class antagonisms between women, the bourgeois woman's movement does not march united, with closed ranks and the highest development of force, in support of Universal Woman Suffrage. The proletarian women, consequently, must rely on their own strength and on that of their class for the conquest of their full political rights. The practical needs of their struggle for emancipation, together with their historic insight and sense of justice, make the proletariat the most consistent champion of the complete political emancipation of the female sex. . . . Social-Democracy, as the political fighting organisation of the class-conscious proletariat, supports, therefore, Woman Suffrage both in principle and in practice. The question of Woman Suffrage gains increased importance as the class-war increases in severity. In the ruling reactionary parties the tendency grows to strengthen the political power of property by the introduction of a limited Woman Suffrage. The limited Woman's Suffrage is not so much to be looked on as the first step to political emancipation of the female sex, as far more the last step in the social emancipation of property. It emancipates Woman not as a personality but as the bearer of a certain income and property, and thus becomes in effect a plural suffrage for the propertied classes, leaves large numbers of the proletariat Women without political rights and in consequence does not mean the political equality of the entire female sex. For the proletariat the necessity grows of revolutionising the minds and of placing their adult members, without distinction of sex, well armed in the front of the battle. The fight for Universal Woman Suffrage is the best means of making the situation serve the interest of the proletariat's struggle for emancipation.

In accordance with these considerations the first International Conference of Socialist Women declares:

The Socialist Woman's movement of all countries repudiates the limited Woman's Suffrage as a falsification of and insult to the principle of the political equality of the female sex. It fights for the only living concrete expression of this principle: the universal woman's suffrage which is open to all adults and bound by no conditions of property, payment of taxes, or degrees of education or any other qualifications, which exclude members of the working class from the enjoyment of the right. They carried on their struggle not in alliance with the bourgeois Women's Righters, but in alliance with the Socialist Parties, and these fight for Woman's Suffrage as one of the demands which from the point of view of principle and practice is most important for a complete democratization of the suffrage.

The Socialist Parties in all countries are bound to fight with energy for the introduction of Woman Suffrage. Consequently their fight for the democratization of the Suffrage in the legislative and administrative bodies in the State and Commune must especially be fought also as a struggle in favour of Woman Suffrage and this demand they must raise in their propaganda as well as in Parliament and insist on it with all their power. In countries where manhood Suffrage is already far advanced or completely achieved the Socialist Parties must take up the fight for the universal Woman's Suffrage, and with that naturally put forward all the demands which remain in order to obtain complete citizenship for the male proletariat.

I. It is the duty of the Socialist Woman's movement in all countries to take part in all struggles which the Socialist Parties fight for the democratization of the Suffrage, and that with all possible energy, but also to see that in this fight the question of the universal Woman Suffrage is insisted on with due regard to its importance of principle and practice.

The Socialist Women of Germany.

II. That as all Socialists recognise that the freedom of women must include both economic as well as political freedom before it can be complete, every effort should be made by Socialists to assist the Women's Suffrage, the Women's Trade Union, and the Women's Co-operative movements in their respective countries and to arouse the workers in all these movements to the necessity for uniting together for the realisation of Socialism.

Women's Labour League, England.

III. That the women of the Socialist and Labour movement, standing especially for the protection of home and family and believing that the interests of the different countries are identical, and not antagonistic, urge that strong efforts should be made to spread anti-military feeling and to promote international fraternity.

IV. That this Conference urges the adoption of a system whereby necessitons [indigent] mothers shall receive monetary assistance at the time of the birth of children, and whereby mothers with children dependent upon them shall receive continued adequate support to enable them to attend to their children without having to work for wages.

The Women's Labour League.

Excerpt, 1910 Second International Conference of Socialist Women

To Point 4 of the Agenda—Social Protection and Provision for Motherhood and Infants.

1. That this Congress, demanding as it does the National and International ownership of the means of production and distribution, affirms, that it is the duty of the community to maintain the child-bearing women, infants, and children attending school.–*British International Socialist Women's Bureau, London.*

2. The Second International Conference of Socialist Women at Copenhagen demands the following measures of social protection for mother and child:
I. Of the Labor Legislation
   a. The legal eight hours' day for all women workers above 18 years of age, the six hours' day for girls above 16 and under 18 years of age; the four hours' day for children above 14 and under 16 years; the prohibition of all wage-earning labor for children under the age of 14.
   b. The prohibition to employ women in such operations which by their whole nature must be particularly injurious for mother and child.
   c. The prohibition of such methods of work which endanger particularly the female organism and thereby injure not only that one, but also the child.
   d. For pregnant women the right to stop work without previous notice eight weeks before the confinement.
   e. For women in childbed the prohibition of working for eight weeks, if the child lives, for six weeks after abortions or if the child dies within this time.

f. For nursing women the establishment of nursing-rooms in the factories.

II. Of the State, Sickness or Motherhood Insurance.

    a. In case of unemployment caused by pregnancy an obligatory subsidy for eight weeks.

    b. For women in childbed an obligatory subsidy for eight weeks, if the child lives, for thirteen weeks, if the mother is able and willing to nurse the child herself; for six weeks, if the child dies within this time or in case of abortions.

    c. Levelling the subsidies paid to pregnant women, women in childbed and nursing ones with the average daily wages.

    d. Granting of obstetric services, medical treatment of pregnancy and childbed ailments and care for women in childbed at their home by skilled nurses.

    e. Extension of these measures on all laboring women—including agricultural laborers, home workers and maid servants—as well as on all women whose families do not earn more than 250 £.

III. Of the Communality.

    Establishment of lying-in hospitals, asylums for pregnant women, women in childbed and infants; organization of attendance to women in childbed at their home by special nurses; granting of benefits for nursing women as long as the mothers do not get subsidies during the nursing period by the state insurance; providing good, sterile babies' milk.

IV. Of the State.

    a. Contributions paid to the Sickness and Motherhood Insurance and communalities in order to enable them to satisfy our demands.

    b. Enlightenment of women how to perform suitably their maternal duties by introducing into the obligatory continuation classes training for girls in the care and management of infants. Distribution of leaflets containing instructions about nursing women in childbed, managing and feeding infants.

    The Conference requests the following social provisions for the child, besides granting a uniform, gratuitous and lay instruction based on the integral education in schools whose leading principle is to develop the child's capacities by labor and for labor:

    a. Establishment of lay nursery schools and "kindergarten" (play schools).

    b. Obligatory, gratuitous feeding of all school children, in school times, of unprovided ones even in holidays and vacancies.

    c. Establishment of school homes where unprovided children are looked after in physical and moral respect in leisure times, including holidays.

    d. Establishment of sport, trips and camps for holidays.

    e. Establishment of baths, halls for swimming and gymnastic exercises and school gardens.

    f. Appointment of school physicians and school dentists.

    g. Foundation of sanatoriums and wood schools for sickly and weakly children.—*The Social Democratic Women of Germany.*

3. That the tendency to make use of boy and girl labor in monotonous and uneducational work is destructive in its results upon the health, character and subsequent industrial efficiency of the boys and girls themselves and upon the rates of wages and chance of continued employment of men and women, this confer-

ence therefore urges the desirability of so raising the standard of education as to secure to every boy and girl up to the age of 18 efficient physical and technical training, and of making where necessary some provision for their maintenance during that period.—*Women's Labor League, Great Britain.*

4. That in view of the prevalence of preventable diseases and the inability of large masses of the population in every civilized country to pay for skilled attendance and care, this congress demands that national provision should be made for the medical and nursing services, including the setting up of school clinics, hospitals, sanatoria, and convalescent homes, at the public expense.—*Women's Labor League, Great Britain.*

5. That in view of the number of distressing cases where after the death of the father of the family the widow is unable to provide the necessities of life for herself and her children and of the resultant injury to the community, this congress urges the universal establishment of State Insurance for widows in the interests especially of those with young children and those incapacitated by age or illness.—*Women's Labor League, Great Britain.*

6. The conference declares it an absolute duty of the state to protect defenseless and poor citizens. To provide for mother and child, the conference has to recommend in first line such reforms as public obligatory motherhood insurance, viz., the right of unmarried mothers and their children to a real subsidy paid by the father during the pregnancy and for education of the child. The conference urges our comrades in the parliaments to strive for a rational reform according to really modern and just points of view.—*General Women's Club, Stockholm.*

7. Considering the success obtained in Sweden by arranging "lectures of fairy tales and legends" and the importance of a clear understanding of women of the great danger of the English Book Control Movement as being full of clerical and militarist spirit, the conference is earnestly invited to commission the delegation. —*Women's Club, Stockholm-South.*

Notes

1 Ruth Rubio-Marin and Blanca Rodriguez-Ruiz, *The Struggle for Female Suffrage in Europe: Voting to Become Citizens* (Leiden: Brill, 2012), p. 14.
2 Sources on the Development of the Socialist International (1907–1919), Friedrich Ebert Stiftung Library. Accessed September 28, 2017, library.fes.de.
3 Second International Conference of Socialist Women. Pamphlet. Friedrich Ebert Stiftung Library. Accessed September 28, 2017, library.fes.de.

26

Constitution *and* Proclamation
Women's Freedom League
Britain
September 1909 and 1908

The Women's Freedom League on a promotional tour.

The London-based Women's Freedom League (WFL) was founded in 1907 by former members of the Women's Social and Political Union (WSPU) who disagreed with the direction, influence, and methods of leaders Christabel and Emmeline Pankhurst. Teresa Billington-Greig, Charlotte Despard, Elizabeth How-Martyn, Margaret Nevinson, and seventy other women fought to gain the right to vote and attain sexual equality through the use of militant nonviolent actions.

Compared to the WSPU, the WFL was less concerned with suffrage per se, and more focused on the negative social conditions that arose from exclusions from elections and gendered inequality. At its peak, the league boasted more than four thousand members and sixty active branches throughout Great Britain. The WFL was critical of property damage, ranging from vandalism to arson, carried out by the WSPU as part of an official campaign. The WFL objected to the violence and destruction of these tactics rather than their illegality, since they supported "vigorous agitation" and "militant action." The WFL was committed to responsible and accessible leadership. The WSPU, overwhelmed with the mountainous task of attaining the vote, began to run in an authoritarian manner. Power was consolidated to the Pankhursts and a handful of wealthy and influential members.

Early acts of the WFL—which included public demonstrations, refusing to pay taxes, and refusing to fill out 1911 census data—resulted in more than one hundred arrests. Most of the WFL were pacifists who strongly opposed the military recruitment campaigns launched in World War I. While this drew their focus for some time, the Constitution, published in 1909,[1] reflects the young militants' commitment to nonviolent actions, the promotion of peace, and equal participation within the organization.

Also included below is the Proclamation[2] printed on a banner that was unfurled from the Ladies' Gallery in the chamber of the House of Commons by suffragettes during a protest on October 28, 1908. Banners were highly visible, important features in suffrage marches. In both documents women are treated as full citizens, and the government is urged to respond to their demands. Strategies dominate the Constitution, however. The WFL did the opposite of siding with a party, simply opposing any government that did not grant suffrage.

Constitution of the Women's Freedom League

Objects—To secure for Women the Parliamentary Vote as it is or may be granted to men; to use the power thus obtained to establish equality of rights and opportunities between the sexes, and thereby to promote the social and industrial well-being of the community.

Methods—The objects of the League shall be promoted by:
1. Action entirely independent of all political parties.
2. Opposition to whatever Government is in power until such time as the franchise is granted.
3. Participation in Parliamentary Elections; at Bye-elections in opposition to the Government candidate and independently of all other candidates.
4. Vigorous agitation upon lines justified by the position of outlawry to which women are at present condemned.
5. The organising of women all over the country to enable them to give adequate expression to their desire for political freedom.
6. Education of public opinion by all the usual methods, such as public meetings, demonstrations, debates, distribution of literature, newspaper correspondence, and deputations to public representatives and other bodies and their members.

Membership—Women of all shades of political opinion who approve the objects and methods of the League, and who are prepared to act independently of party, are eligible for membership. All members must approve, though they need not actually participate in militant action.

Proclamation

Whereas	the nation depends for its progress and existence upon the work and services of women as well as of men;
Whereas	the State is organised for the mutual protection and co-operation of all its citizens, women as well as men;
Whereas	the Government conducts the national business by means of taxes levied upon women as well as men;
Whereas	the women of the Nation have made clear their need for political rights, and their desire to posses the Parliamentary Vote;
[Wh]ereas	working women, and women in the home, are in especial need of the protection of the Vote since legislation is interfering more and more with their interest;
	The
	[WOME]N'S FREEDOM LEAGUE
	calls upon the Government to remove the sex disability which deprives qualified women of their just right of voting in the Parliamentary elections, and

DEMANDS

DEMANDS

the immediate extension of the Franchise to Women on the same terms as it is, or may be enjoyed by men.

The Nation can never be free until the law recognises and establishes

VOTES FOR WOMEN

THE DEMAND IS JUST.   THE REFORM INEVITABLE.

DELAY IS UNWISE AND UNJUST.

Therefore   in the Name of Liberty and Humanity the Women's Freedom League claims the Vote

THIS SESSION.

Notes

1   "Votes for Women," 1909. Learning Collection, British Library, accessed Feb. 12, 2014, http://www.bl.uk.

2   Women's Freedom League Banner, 1908. UK National Archives, www.nationalarchives.gov.uk.

27

Platform *and* Resolutions
Second Biennial Convention of the
National Women's Trade Union League of America

Chicago, Illinois
September 25–October 1, 1909

National Women's Trade Union League seal.

An orchestra of union women musicians played as delegates settled in the Fine Arts Building, decorated with banners from national and local leagues. President Robins welcomed delegates from across the country, as well as representatives from the British Women's Trade Union League and the German Verband Kaufmannischer Angestellten. Vice-President O'Sullivan then set the agenda:

The Women's Trade Union League extends its hand to every man and woman who stands for the living wage and it opens to us the door of opportunity to limit the working day to eight hours and to eliminate the children from the factories and mills of the world and give them a growing chance—just a growing chance and a chance for education.[1]

Since women were not allowed to join unions as active members, the National Women's Trade Union League of America was established at the Twenty-third Convention of the American Federation of Labor in 1903. Women were determined to protect the rights of women as workers. The league was most active from 1907 to 1922, when Margaret Dreier Robins was president. During this time, the NWTUL met its goals of creating "an eight-hour workday, a minimum wage, and the abolition of child labor."[2] Eleanor Roosevelt became a member of the NWTUL in 1922. When the organization folded in 1950, its goals had largely been accomplished.

The NWTUL was a cross-class organization aiming to reform working conditions for women and the entire factory system; middle- and upper-class women donated money, helped provide legal representation, and even participated in strikes. The overall purpose of the group, however, was to "assist in the organization of *women wage workers* into trade unions and thereby to help them secure conditions necessary for healthful and efficient work and to obtain a just reward for such work."[3] Two very important strikes, the Rising of 20,000 and Bread and Roses, were supported by the NWTUL. Although the demands of the strikers were not met immediately, the league gained publicity and credibility for this work.

The proceedings of this convention show the league to have been dynamic, well-organized, and enthusiastic at the time of its second major national meeting. Local union representatives from San Francisco, Saint Louis, New York, and Boston were heard, as were some international voices. The record shows that the national and local organizations collaborated well, as in the national publication of a "diary" tracking labor legislation throughout the states that was compiled by a local group. Further, in their individual reports, it is also evident that the local groups truly wanted to learn from one another. As Helen Marot from New York said, "I am going to tell you a few of our failures as well as some of our accomplishments." The attendees tell of working with male unions and with the suffrage movement; of establishing libraries and schools; and of the frustrations of misrepresentations of their work, as well as the joys of legislative victories.

The Resolutions testify to a rich understanding of intersecting systems of domination, especially capitalism, militarism, and patriarchy. The lengthiest one explains how "[t]he interests of working women as women, as workers and as mothers are peculiarly bound up in the maintenance of peace and in the avoidance of armaments." Thus, in addition to urging changes in labor laws, the Resolutions argue for a Court of Arbital Justice.

The first independent convention of the NWTUL was held in Norfolk, Virginia, in 1907, but the official Constitution of the league was not unanimously adopted until the second meeting, in 1909. Below are the Platform[4] and Resolutions[5] adopted after the Constitution was approved. A final proposed resolution, "that we earnestly support the strenuous efforts of the people of the West to obtain exclusion laws against all Asiatics, similar to those now in force against the Chinese," was rejected after much discussion. While seemingly simply racist, the failed resolution blamed "our present industrial and economic conditions" for allowing employers to exploit "this reservoir of cheaper labor," and said that once workers "obtained for themselves such safeguards for our American standard of life . . . [it] would render alien competition harmless."

Platform of the National Women's Trade Union League

1. Organization of all workers into trade unions.
2. Equal pay for equal work.
3. Eight-hour day.
4. A minimum wage scale.
5. Full citizenship for women.
6. All principles involved in the economic program of the American Federation of Labor.

Resolutions from the Second Biennial Convention of the National Women's Trade Union League

Whereas, The out-of-town delegates to the Convention of the National Women's Trade Union League have received invitations from Marshall Field & Company to visit their department store, the Convention on behalf of the out-of-town delegates unanimously and respectfully declines to accept that invitation because of the known opposition of this firm to the organization of women workers and to efforts to raise the industrial status of women. (Applause.)

Whereas, To establish a uniform eight-hour work day among all our women workers in the various industries, be it
Resolved, That each Local League present an eight-hour bill at the next General Assembly in their state, if possible, and that we urge all State Federations of Labor to assist us in securing such legislation.

Whereas, All wars in our day are wars for the extension of markets; and
Whereas, The interests of women workers in every industrial country are one and their industrial and social conditions are in time of peace disastrously influenced by the enormous expenditure of civilized nations upon battleships and other preparations for war, and in time of war by the depredations, cruelties, and horrors of war; and
Whereas, The interests of working women as women, as workers and as mothers are peculiarly bound up in the maintenance of peace and in the avoidance of armaments; be it
Resolved, That the delegates to the National Women's Trade Union League in convention assembled, urge the establishment of the Court of Arbital Justice, provided for by the second Hague conference and awaiting only the appointment of its judges under some form of international agreement, and that they also protest against further increase of the United States Navy as unnecessary for our protection and as tending to aggravate the rivalry of the nations in building costly armaments.

Notes
1 National Women's Trade Union League of America, *Proceedings of the Second Biennial Convention of the National Women's Trade Union League of America*, ed. Alice Henry and

S. M. Franklin (Chicago: National Women's Trade Union League, 1909–1936). Second (1909), p. 4. Baker Library, Harvard Business School, Harvard University, accessed Feb. 10, 2017, nrs.harvard.edu.

2 "Women's Trade Union League." Eleanor Roosevelt Glossary, George Washington University. Accessed Aug. 2017, www.gwu.edu.

3 "National Women's Trade Union League of America," *Women Working, 1800–1930*. Harvard University Library Open Collections Program, ocp.hul.harvard.edu. Emphasis added.

4 *Proceedings of the Second Biennial Convention of the National Women's Trade Union League of America*, ed. Alice Henry and S. M. Franklin (Chicago: National Women's Trade Union League, 1909–1936), p. 1. Baker Library, Harvard Business School, Harvard University, accessed Feb. 10, 2017, nrs.harvard.edu.

5 Ibid., pp. 48–50.

28

Conclusions
First International Feminist Congress of Argentina
Buenos Aires, Argentina
May 18-23, 1910

The International Women's Congress advocates for all the women of the world to unite in order to work for universal peace, as well as so that the principle of arbitration might be applied both to international issues and to all challenging issues. We desire that this principle be the main orientation for the education of children.

The leaders of the Cofederacion Femenina Argentina.

This congress was organized by people such as Julie Madeleine Lanteri and Petrona Eyle, who also cofounded the first university student association for women in 1904, the Asociación de Universitarias Argentinas. Other local feminist efforts around this time include the establishment of the Argentine Council of Women in 1901, the Center for Feminism in 1906, and the National League for Freethinking Women in 1909, as well as the publication of the journal *Union and Labor* from 1910 to 1914. Such "first wave" efforts were led by women working together and clearly identifying as feminists. They were also active in other movements and conferences, including a series of Latin American scientific congresses held from 1898 to 1909.[1]

Some four hundred women attended the congress, including representatives from Italy, Chile, Uruguay, Peru, and the United States. "Prominent foreign feminists were made honorary sponsors,"[2] including Marie Curie, Ellen Key, and Maria Montessori, who, while not present, sent papers to be read and influenced the group's efforts to set up a Children's House (which included an orphanage, school, and home for unwed mothers). Sponsoring groups reflect the diversity of feminist activism and of the city of Buenos Aires, and include the National Argentine Association against the White Slave Trade, the Socialist Women's Center, the Women's Union and Labor group, the National League of Women Freethinkers, and the Association of Normal School Teachers.

> The Congress brought together representatives of women's groups that had formed in very different ways, ways in which their class interests were directly reflected: telephone operators and factory workers whose interests lay with the trade union movement; teachers and professors and lawyers who sought the right of entry into professional fields; and volunteer workers whose charitable activities were directed at alleviating the conditions of poverty. The women were not insensitive to these divisions of class but believed that the overwhelming discrimination against all women gave them common ground.[3]

Feminism at the congress was broadly defined as "the evolution of women toward superior ideals and woman's participation in the progress of humanity."[4] Debated issues at the congress included divorce, protective labor legislation for women and children, and strategies for political change (for example, should expanded qualified suffrage come before universal suffrage?). The National League of Women Freethinkers and the Socialists disagreed about whether protective labor legislation would support or hurt women workers, and the congress ended up advocating stronger protection for all workers. Debates included talk not only about what rights were desirable but about how they would

Cecilia Grierson.

play out in conservative political regimes. Less controversial were efforts such as the Children's House, support for equal pay, and advocacy of laws that would stop women losing civil rights and property upon marriage. Women's suffrage, though supported, was not won until 1947. The gathering supported secular state education (including for immigrants, delinquents, the "weak," and the orphaned) for both sexes, "scientific" if sometimes gendered, but always geared toward expanding the borders of women's lives. Like gatherings elsewhere, this one opposed child abuse and child labor. It argued for social change over charity. It mentioned human trafficking and prison conditions. Clearly, this gathering suggested and creatively confronted a broad agenda.[5]

Cecilia Grierson, the first woman to receive a medical degree in Argentina, was an active feminist who presided over the First International Feminist Congress. These two areas of medicine and feminist activism frequently overlapped in medical innovations, as she introduced a course in massage therapy, provided free services for children with special needs, and founded the first school of nursing. She was vice-president of the 1889 meeting of the International Council of Women, and founder of the Argentine Women's Council.[6]

Conclusions

Education—Letters—Arts and Industry

The International Women's Congress [I.W.C.], considering that primary education is the most important element for progress, affirms a vote such that:

- Governments will use all means necessary to serve elementary education, without allowing any social or religious consideration to siphon the resources that the State has set aside for said education.

The I.W.C. affirms a vote such that: education should be secular as well as mixed, and equal for both sexes.

The I.W.C. formulates the following vote: That the National Educational Council of the Federal Capital of the Argentine Republic pass a law regulating fees for those parents who do not send their children to school, or, who having enrolled their children, cause their children to repeatedly be absent from class without cause.

The I.W.C. affirms a vote such that the children in our schools be taught patriotism, while simultaneously avoiding disrespect for others' patriotism or an exclusivist feeling.

The I.W.C. affirms a vote such that the elementary school's work may not be just to instruct the child, but also to give attention to the formation of the child's character, and to prepare the child for the struggles of life.

The I.W.C., considering that the State must broadly carry out its charge regarding the great number of weak children as well as its duty to provide for their betterment and instruction, affirms a vote such that:

- Modern pedagogy is taken into account regarding this issue. Educational methods should adapt to the student and not the student to the method.

- School camps and vacation camps should be created and expanded, in mountainous and wilderness settings, and in seaside beaches, where a child can stay until he regains strength, as well as during the vacation months, according to the case and the nature of the institution.
- The quantity of homework should be reduced to a minimum—right now it is excessive—so that the student can recharge outside of class hours. Currently, homework deprives the student of necessary rest, with a deleterious effect on his health.
- It should be officially instituted that a cup of milk, or another snack, be served at some interval during class hours.

The I.W.C., considering that school hours are an issue of vital importance for the health of the students, affirms a vote such that the hours for the Education Schools of the Federal Capital of the Argentine Republic be reformed so that teachers-in-training attend class in the mornings only.
- In consequence, programs should be modified: they should condensed, combining related materials and subjects that are now taught separately. The specialization required for a teaching position can be simplified, making this change possible.

The I.W.C. affirms a vote such that, given the physiological condition of women, female students and teachers should be given the right to be excused from classes for two consecutive days each month.

The I.W.C. affirms a vote such that, as History is taught, special preference be given to those things that reveal the various progressive aspects of communities and societies, more than to the narration of wars and battles.

The I.W.C. formulates a vote such that scholastic authorities in countries with immigrants establish schools designated for immigrant children. The purpose of these schools should be to teach these children the language of the country of residence, because without the language immigrant children will not be able to attend primary schools.

The I.W.C., considering that is it important to educate a child's imagination with appropriate stories which, while maintaining links to reality, contribute to the development of children's ideas, affirms a vote such that the woman should cultivate this type of literature.

The I.W.C. affirms a vote such that the primary education in boys' schools should be complemented by two years of vocational school.

The I.W.C., considering that educational direction for orphans does not generally correspond to current ethical-social necessities, and considering too the necessity that each orphan will need to possess—at the end of her education—an art or office by which she can achieve her own economic independence, formulates the following votes:

I. That girls' orphanages be established, with a strictly scientific organization following the norms of modern pedagogy, and that the residence of the orphan girls in these institutions be until they reach the age of majority.

II. That the orphanages be centered in Capital cities, under the vigilance of the State, without having to exclude particular initiatives, which might be divided into elementary or general-studies orphanages, vocational school orphanages, and agricultural orphanages.

III. That commissions of protection and support be named, from among female personages with particular competence in ethical-social activity, with the goal of aiding the girls' integration, from the time that they leave the orphanage until they reach the age of twenty-five years, or before, in the case of matrimony.

The I.W.C. affirms a vote such that orphans should not be objects of exploitation.

- That orphanages in which the maintenance and education of orphans is free be exonerated from paying taxes.
- That assets of a person who has died without an heir be given for the aid of abandoned children.

The I.W.C. formulates a vote for the creation of female reformatories for girls who are minors:

As it is necessary to improve the moral culture of the category of girl for whom these reformatories are created, and since it is also necessary for each of these girls to possess an art or an office with which she can achieve her own economic independence, the I.W.C. considers:

I. That the educational orientation of these institutions should be strictly scientific, following the norms of the modern correctional pedagogy, under the triple focus: psycho-physical-pathological.

II. That the reformatories should be divided according to age: elementary or general-studies reformatories, and vocational, industrial, and agricultural reformatories. Each reformatory should be classified according to the type of delinquent girls there: unruly girls and seduced minors, common delinquents, sexual delinquents.

III. That in order to integrate and ease the work of direction, a commission of female inspectors should be named from among female personages who have a particular competence in ethical-social activities. This commission will also provide a motherly watchfulness of the girls from the moment they leave the reformatory until they reach the age of twenty-five years, or before, in the case of matrimony.

That these establishments should fall under the vigilance of the State.

The I.W.C., considering that it is necessary to engage fully in the instruction of the domestic sciences, affirms a vote such that:

- These sciences should be included in primary and secondary schools, as well as in teaching colleges.
- The creation of special schools will be managed in cooperation with the authorities for the purpose of preparing teachers for this kind of teaching.
- May these domestic sciences replace the empirical teaching of home economics.

The I.W.C., considering that commercial and professional careers are each day becoming more accessible to women, and that, in order to obtain the most just

salaries or wages for their work it is crucial that they possess the necessary technical instruction, declares that:
- It applauds every initiative of the State, of associations, or of individual citizens who provide to women a full understanding of their future careers along with a practical base of knowledge that relates to current needs.

The I.W.C., considering that the growth of industry and of commerce is necessary for the world's progress, advocates that:
- In any population of more than five thousand inhabitants, vocational and trade schools be created for women.

The I.W.C. would be pleased to see that, whether through public or private initiative, gardening and horticulture schools be founded for women, as a means of making women skillful in a productive occupation that also is of general benefit.

The I.W.C. formulates a vote such that vocational schools, especially in the provinces, teach and perfect the national industries of women. For the Republic of Argentina, these would be: weaving blankets and ponchos, crocheting lace, braiding straw and leather, fruit preservation, and confectionery.

The I.W.C. affirms a vote such that feminine physical education should be encouraged in schools, and that gymnasia and recreational plazas be officially created. Feminine clubs that contribute to the development of physical education should be founded.

The I.W.C. affirms a vote such that popular libraries be promoted. There, women can come across books that broaden their culture.

The I.W.C., considering that woman is called to be the soul of the school, of the home, and of the workshop, declares that she should receive an adequate understanding of aesthetic culture, and it affirms a vote such that women be given aesthetic education in primary school.
- This education should tend toward a practical end, so that it may later be useful in industrial work, in the workshop, in the home, and in the school.

The I.W.C. affirms a vote such that women should be educated to understand the social dangers of extravagance.

The I.W.C. affirms a vote such that feminine education be given a scientific orientation which will allow women to perform their roles, within the development of social progress.

Sociology
The International Women's Congress advocates for all the women of the world to unite in order to work for universal peace, as well as so that the principle of arbitration might be applied both to international issues and to all challenging issues. We desire that this principle be the main orientation for the education of children.

The I.W.C. affirms a vote such that beneficent societies provide complete religious liberty of conscience to those they aid.

The I.W.C. formulates a vote such that laws to protect childhood be passed, and that societies for the protection of children be encouraged.

The I.W.C. affirms a vote such that laws be passed regarding children's labor. Also, that those that already exist be enforced.

The I.W.C. declares that homes for abandoned babies are an attack on the rights of childhood, and, in order to see their suppression, the congress demands for every woman—mother, whether or not she is a spouse, the right to social status and aid.

The I.W.C. formulates a vote to support the project of the "Juana Manuela Gorriti" center in this Capital city, in support of the creation of a Home for Unwed Mothers for abandoned women.

The I.W.C. affirms a vote such that homes for unwed mothers be founded wherever there is a population of more than five thousand inhabitants.

The I.W.C. agrees with the foundation of the society that will call itself the "Women's Pan-American Federation," whose purpose is to safeguard the rights of women and children, as well as their protection.

The I.W.C. affirms a vote such that the human personality be fully integrated in women. For this to occur, it is imperative to give them higher education, economic independence, and a more profound understanding of their place in society and in the home: as an instrument of universal progress.

The I.W.C. affirms a vote such that the current condition of women be given dignity, both in the moral aspect as in the economic, so that the battle of the sexes may disappear in our future collective life.

The I.W.C. declares that it does not seek a fight between the sexes, but it does seek that women be respected, in their ideals and in their rights.

The I.W.C. intercedes so that a new tendency will begin, substituting the reign of homes for orphans with parental institutions in which up to 25 children are under the direction of one matrimony, living family life, as would be done in a well-organized home.

The I.W.C. advocates for freedom of scientific, artistic, and industrial work in order to raise the dignity of women.

The I.W.C., considering that the most poorly paid and strenuous work that women do is that which occurs in their homes, affirms a vote such that feminine societies give serious consideration to this reality in order to better the situation of these workers as rapidly as possible.

The I.W.C. affirms a vote such that industrial cooperatives, as well as associations and homes of solidarity for women, be encouraged.

The I.W.C., with respect to beneficent societies, declares itself to be against any institution that functions simply as a charity. The congress advocates, instead, that reformers and institutions ensure for women the full enjoyment of social integration, inasmuch as having been born implies the right to live.

The I.W.C. affirms a vote such that, as long as Newspaper Boys work in the Argentine Republic, homes should be founded to take them in and educate them.

The I.W.C. appeals to the reason of society, that it might advocate for severe sanctions against immoral conduct of men. Such behavior should be judged with the same stringency for both sexes.

The I.W.C. advocates for laws to be passed illegalizing the existence of brothels.

The I.W.C., considering that female prostitution is the most severe suffering and shame for the modern woman, formulates a vote of protest against governments' tolerance regarding the maintenance and exploitation of female prostitution.

The I.W.C. asks that women's and mixed associations be created in order to abolish human trafficking.

The I.W.C. would be pleased to see educated women dedicate themselves to journalism, as a means of disseminating positive ideas to a wider public.

The I.W.C. declares that all women are the natural mothers of all children.

The I.W.C. affirms a vote such that the conditions in the prisons be improved. Thus, prisons might truly become moral sanatoria, with workshops, schools, etc.
- And such that inspections be made by females in women's prisons.

Sciences

The International Women's Congress would be pleased to see, with the goal of avoiding the evils that alcoholism can bring:
- That, to reach the lower classes, small printed pamphlets in plain language, without technical vocabulary, be distributed in homes, making clear the path that an alcoholic takes, starting with the first drink and ending with delirium tremens.
- That the appropriate authorities be solicited for the formation of ad-hoc sanatoria, where those who still have time can go to be cured.
- That a large financial prize be offered by governments for those who discover an efficacious remedy for alcoholism.
- That the PERMANENT PEACE CONGRESS be solicited to present the title HUMANITARIAN PRIZE RECIPIENT for he who discovers said efficacious remedy for alcoholism.
- That anti-alcoholic maxims be added to daily newspapers.

The I.W.C. votes such that women unite in order to fight the advance of alcoholism, whose social and individual consequences so often include female victims.

The I.W.C. affirms a vote such that: propaganda be spread in schools as well as homes in order to make known the deleterious effects of the kiss and of mating.
  The kiss should be eliminated from greetings.

The I.W.C. affirms a vote such that:
- Ad-hoc schools be formed for pedagogically retarded students, accompanied by a medical annex in the institution.
- School refectories should be installed in public schools.
- Heating should be installed in classrooms, where necessary.

The I.W.C. would be pleased to see propaganda against the use of tobacco in schools and homes.

The I.W.C., considering that women, and above all mothers, should be aware of the basic symptoms and prophylaxis for infectious and contagious diseases, votes to organize courses that make this knowledge available to non-professionals.

The I.W.C. advocates that academic women study and present statistics of female mortality, including type of illness and the woman's occupation.

The I.W.C. declares that women should cooperate in the fight against tuberculosis.

The I.W.C., considering that the bias that inspires the vulgarization of the knowledge needed to treat syphilis is greatly harmful for both public and individual health, affirms a vote such that this bias be abolished.

The I.W.C. affirms a vote such that women's education be given a scientific orientation, permitting women to carry out her part in society's progress.

The I.W.C. affirms a vote such that the number of houses for unwed mothers be increased. In addition, that they be organized according to the progress of scientific discovery and the best humanitarian feelings.

The I.W.C. affirms a vote such that childcare classes be organized for girls between the ages of 15 and 20.

The I.W.C. affirms a vote such that the knowledge of first aid be disseminated by every method possible.

The I.W.C. votes that women should become aware of the social importance of the popularization of science, and contribute to it.

Law
The International Women's Congress declares that divorce is a law of moral sanitation for marriage.

The I.W.C. advocates for absolute divorce, so long as in the process of its regulation, necessary limits are established so that said divorce does not degenerate into abuse.

The I.W.C., considering that women are capable of exercising their political and civil rights, affirms a vote such that her right to suffrage be recognized.

The I.W.C. affirms a vote such that, in all the countries of the world, laws be passed providing for the same civil and juridical rights to be applied to both women and men.

The I.W.C. affirms a vote such that working hours for adults and children be regulated in the following way: eight hours of work for adults, and six hours for children until they reach sixteen years of age. Children should be given thirty-six continuous hours to rest.

The I.W.C. advocates that female clerks in shops, as well as female employees in workshops and factories, be given seats.

The I.W.C. advocates that the employed woman and female laborer be given forty days of rest before and after delivering a child, along with the enjoyment of her complete wages. These are a means of protecting maternity.

The I.W.C. advocates that obligatory instruction, in the form of daily classes, be given to children who work in factories and workshops, along with the enjoyment of their complete daily wages.

The I.W.C. affirms a vote such that tribunals for delinquent youth be created within all countries. Women should form part of these tribunals.

The I.W.C. affirms a vote such that governments adopt retirement laws for workers.

The I.W.C. affirms a vote such that the following modifications be made to the Civil Code of Argentina and to those of other countries in similar conditions:

1.—A woman, when she contracts marriage, will not lose the rights that the law provides to adults in possession of sane mental faculties.

2.—A mother will be able to exercise the same authority and responsibilities as a father (administration of assets, etc.).

3.—An investigation into paternity will be permitted always, in every case.

4.—A natural father or mother who exercises legal custody will be in charge of the administration of their children's assets and have usufructuary rights regarding his or her children, barring an exceptional legal case.

5.—A married woman will be able to exercise any legal profession, and she will possess the free administration of the assets that she may have brought to the matrimony, as well as of those assets that she may have gained through her own industry or profession.

6.—A married woman will be able to sell, mortgage, acquire, or donate assets that belong to her, under the same conditions as a man.

7.—When it comes to common assets or joint property, one spouse cannot dispossess the other of said assets or property without the express consent of the other.

8.—When, by express agreement, one of the two spouses takes on the full administration of assets, said spouse will be obliged to inform the other regarding their financial, business, and investment status.

9.—A woman, without requiring authorization from her husband, will be able to fully manage her assets, have a checkbook, and be a member of cooperative societies and of mutual aid societies.

10.—A divorced woman, in every case of divorce, will have access to all of her assets, including those joint assets that correspond to her. If there are children, an amount will be determined, equal for both the man and the woman, with which they should cooperate to pay the costs of care, clothing, education, etc.

11.—While the divorce is being processed, and once it has been decreed, if there is no objectionable cause or legal exception regarding the mother, the children should stay under her care.

12.—A woman, being of age, whether single, widowed, or married, can be a legal guardian.

13.—A woman can be a witness of public instrument as well as of wills, under the same conditions as a man.

Notes

1 Francesca Miller, *Latin American Women and the Search for Social Justice* (Lebanon, NH: University Press of New England, 1991), p. 72.
2 Marifran Carlson, *¡Feminismo! The Woman's Movement in Argentina* (Chicago: Chicago Review Press, 2005), p. 141.
3 Miller, p. 74.
4 Cited in Carlson, p. 142.
5 Centenario del Primer Congreso Femenino Internacional de la República Argentina. Ciudad Autónoma de Buenos Aires: Comité Organizador del II Congreso Feminista Internacional de la República Argentina, 2010. Library Edition. Translation by Madeleine Brink and Violeta Morones Martinez of Ardilla Translators.
6 "Cecilia Grierson," last edited August 1, 2017. *Wikipedia*, www.wikipedia.org.

29

Resolutions
International Congress of Women
The Hague, Netherlands
April 28–May 1, 1915

The American delegates to the International Congress of Women traveling the "Peace Ship" to the Netherlands.

There could be nothing negative in the idea of peace. War is the negative. Peace is the highest effort of the human brain applied to the organization of the life and being of the peoples of the world on a basis of cooperation.
—Emmeline Pethick Lawrence[1]

Women had been meeting internationally over the issue of suffrage before this congress. The 1915 meeting planned by the International Woman Suffrage Alliance could not be held in Berlin, however, because of World War I.

> A committee of Dutch women, headed by Dr. Aletta Jacobs, who met in Amsterdam last February with a group of women from Germany, Belgium and Holland, issued a Call for an International Congress of Women. They all believed in the solidarity of the Woman's Movement and were confident that even in war times a meeting might be organised to discuss the principles of constructive peace.[2]

The alliance did not officially support or oppose the congress, and the war surely divided some suffragists. Nonetheless, this remarkable congress was attended by some twelve hundred women in the neutral country of the Netherlands, many of them enduring ideological resistance and physical hardship to get there. The opening speech was delivered by Jacobs, who was the first female medical doctor in the Netherlands:

> With mourning hearts we stand united here. We grieve for many brave young men who have lost their lives on the battlefield before attaining their full manhood; we mourn with the poor mothers bereft of their sons; with the thousands of young widows and fatherless children, and we feel that we can no longer endure in this twentieth century of civilisation that governments should tolerate brute force as the only solution to international disputes. (4)

As the organizers set things up, delegates were not to argue about who had responsibility for the present war, or about how to regulate future wars. Procedurally, speakers were limited to five minutes, unless presenting resolutions. There were three days of debates and discussion, all translated into English, French, and German, some in public, some in committee.

President Jane Addams's closing speech explained the distinct role women might play in peace:

> It is possible that the appeals for the organisation of the world upon peaceful lines have been made too exclusively to man's reason and sense of justice (quite as the eighteenth century enthusiasm for humanity was founded on intellectual sentiment). Reason is only a part of the human endowment; emotion and deep-set racial impulses must be utilised as well—those primitive human urgings to foster life and to protect the helpless, of which women were the earliest custodians, and even the social and gregarious instincts that we share with the animals themselves. These universal desires must be given opportunities to expand, and the most highly trained intellects must serve them rather than the technique of war and diplomacy. (6)

The official attendees from twelve countries (United States, Sweden, Norway, Netherlands, Italy, Hungary, Germany, Great Britain, Denmark, Canada, Belgium, and Austria) met to forward two ideas: "that international disputes should be settled by pacific means, and that the Parliamentary franchise should be extended to women."[3] Over the course of the meeting, the congress decided to send the president and vice-president of the organization, Jane Addams and Aletta Jacobs, to both belligerent and neutral countries' capitals, to attempt to persuade them to end the war and resolve differences through negotiation. Astonishingly, the women met with the leaders of fourteen countries following the congress. Still, "how many textbooks dealing with World War I include an account of the women who visited fourteen heads of state with a peace plan for a neutral nations' conference of mediation?"[4] Jane Addams did win the Nobel Peace Prize in 1931.

Though the efforts of the delegation, as expected, did not bring a sudden end to the war, they did enable warring parties to understand each other's positions and for the public to understand that many heads of state agreed that the war was one of blame and media inflation rather than deep-seated conflict. Further, with this congress and the actions that followed, women's visible participation in international politics had begun. It began, in the words of the document, with a simple, universal "protest against the madness and the horror of war, involving as it does a reckless sacrifice of human life and the destruction of so much that hu-

Women's International League for Peace and Freedom logo.

manity has laboured through centuries to build up," and a fundamental, equally universal appeal to a common humanity that surpasses national boundaries.

The document shows a gender-conscious and holistic understanding of the causes of and solutions to war. It links democratic international politics with women's rights, grants men *and* women of each territory the right to consent to the state of their choosing, emphasizes the education of children "toward the idea of constructive peace," and insists that peace settlements include the claims of women. The Resolutions[5] note the "horrible violation of women which attends all war," and thus ridicules the idea of "protecting" women in any state that goes to war. The congress founded the Women's International League for Peace and Freedom, which still exists under that name today.

Resolutions of the International Congress of Women at The Hague

I. WOMEN AND WAR
I. Protest
We women, in International Congress assembled, protest against the madness and the horror of war, involving as it does a reckless sacrifice of human life and the destruction of so much that humanity has laboured through centuries to build up.

2. Women's Sufferings in War
This International Congress of Women opposes the assumption that women can be protected under the conditions of modern warfare. It protests vehemently against the odious wrongs of which women are the victims in time of war, and especially against the horrible violation of women which attends all war.

II. ACTION TOWARDS PEACE
3. The Peace Settlement
This International Congress of Women of different nations, classes, creeds and parties is united in expressing sympathy with the suffering of all, whatever their nationality, who are fighting for their country or labouring under the burden of war.

Since the mass of the people in each of the countries now at war believe themselves to be fighting, not as aggressors but in self-defence and for their national existence, there can be no irreconcilable differences between them, and their common ideals afford a basis upon which a magnanimous and honourable peace might be established.

The Congress therefore urges the Governments of the world to put an end to this bloodshed, and to begin peace negotiations. It demands that the peace which follows shall be permanent and therefore based on principles of justice, including those laid down in the resolutions adopted by this Congress, namely:

That no territory should be transferred without the consent of the men and women in it, and that the right of conquest should not be recognized.

That autonomy and a democratic parliament should not be refused to any people.

That the Governments of all nations should come to an agreement to refer future international disputes to arbitration or conciliation and to bring social, moral and economic pressure to bear upon any country which resorts to arms.

That foreign politics should be subject to democratic control.

That women should be granted equal political rights with men.

4. Continuous Mediation

This International Congress of Women resolves to ask the neutral countries to take immediate steps to create a conference of neutral nations which shall without delay offer continuous mediation. The Conference shall invite suggestions for settlement from each of the belligerent nations and in any case shall submit to all of them simultaneously, reasonable proposals as a basis of peace.

III. PRINCIPLES OF A PERMANENT PEACE

5. Respect for Nationality

This International Congress of Women, recognizing the right of the people to self-government, affirms that there should be no transference of territory without the consent of the men and women residing therein, and urges that autonomy and a democratic parliament should not be refused to any people.

6. Arbitration and Conciliation

This International Congress of Women, believing that war is the negation of progress and civilisation, urges the governments of all nations to come to an agreement to refer future international disputes to arbitration and conciliation.

7. International Pressure

This International Congress of Women urges the governments of all nations to come to an agreement to unite in bringing social, moral and economic pressure to bear upon any country, which resorts to arms instead of referring its case to arbitration or conciliation.

8. Democratic Control of Foreign Policy

Since war is commonly brought about not by the mass of the people, who do not desire it, but by groups representing particular interests, this International Congress of Women urges that Foreign Politics shall be subject to Democratic Control; and declares that it can only recognise as democratic a system which includes the equal representation of men and women.

(The Congress declared by vote that it interpreted no transference of territory without the consent of the men and women in it to imply that the right of conquest was not to be recognized.)

9. The Enfranchisement of Women

Since the combined influence of the women of all countries is one of the strongest forces for the prevention of war, and since women can only have full responsibility and effective influence when they have equal political rights with men, this International Congress of Women demands their political enfranchisement.

IV. INTERNATIONAL COOPERATION

10. Third Hague Conference

This International Congress of Women urges that a third Hague Conference be convened immediately after the war.

11. International Organization

This International Congress of Women urges that the organization of the Society of Nations should be further developed on the basis of a constructive peace, and that it should include:

a. As a development of the Hague Court of Arbitration, a permanent International Court of Justice to settle questions or differences of a justiciable character, such as arise on the interpretation of treaty rights or of the law of nations.

b. As a development of the constructive work of the Hague Conference, a permanent International Conference holding regular meetings in which women should take part, to deal not with the rules of warfare but with practical proposals for further International Cooperation among the States. This Conference should be so constituted that it could formulate and enforce those principles of justice, equity and good will in accordance with which the struggles of subject communities could be more fully recognized and the interests and rights not only of the great Powers and small nations but also those of weaker countries and primitive peoples gradually adjusted under an enlightened international public opinion.

This International Conference shall appoint:

A permanent Council of Conciliation and Investigation for the settlement of international differences arising from economic competition, expanding commerce, increasing population and changes in social and political standards.

12. General Disarmament

The International Congress of Women, advocating universal disarmament and realizing that it can only be secured by international agreement, urges, as a step to this end, that all countries should, by such an international agreement, take over the manufacture of arms and munitions of war and should control all international traffic in the same. It sees in the private profits accruing from the great armament factories a powerful hindrance to the abolition of war.

13. Commerce and Investments

a. The International Congress of Women urges that in all countries there shall be liberty of commerce, that the seas shall be free and the trade routes open on equal terms to the shipping of all nations.

b. Inasmuch as the investment by capitalists of one country in the resources of another and the claims arising therefrom are a fertile source of international complications, this International Congress of Women urges the widest possible acceptance of the principle that such investments shall be made at the risk of the investor, without claim to the official protection of his government.

14. National Foreign Policy

a. This International Congress of Women demands that all secret treaties shall be void and that for the ratification of future treaties, the participation of at least the legislature of every government shall be necessary.

b. This International Congress of Women recommends that National Commissions be created, and International Conferences convened for the scientific study and elaboration of the principles and conditions of permanent peace, which might contribute to the development of an International Federation.

These Commissions and Conferences should be recognized by the Governments and should include women in their deliberations.

15. Women in National and International Politics

This International Congress of Women declares it to be essential, both nationally and internationally to put into practice the principle that women should share all civil and political rights and responsibilities on the same terms as men.

V. THE EDUCATION OF CHILDREN

16. This International Congress of Women urges the necessity of so directing the education of children that their thoughts and desires may be directed towards the ideal of constructive peace.

VI. WOMEN AND THE PEACE SETTLEMENT CONFERENCE

17. This International Congress of Women urges, that in the interests of lasting peace and civilisation the Conference which shall frame the Peace settlement after the war should pass a resolution affirming the need in all countries of extending the parliamentary franchise to women.

18. This International Congress of Women urges that representatives of the people should take part in the conference that shall frame the peace settlement after the war, and claims that amongst them women should be included.

VII. ACTION TO BE TAKEN

19. Women's Voice in the Peace Settlement

This International Congress of Women resolves that an international meeting of women shall be held in the same place and at the same time as the Conference of the Powers which shall frame the terms of the peace settlement after the war for the purpose of presenting practical proposals to that Conference.

20. Envoys to the Governments

In order to urge the Governments of the world to put an end to this bloodshed and to establish a just and lasting peace, this International Congress of Women delegates envoys to carry the message expressed in the Congress Resolutions to the rulers of the belligerent and neutral nations of Europe and to the President of the United States.

These Envoys shall be women of both neutral and belligerent nations, appointed by the International Committee of this Congress. They shall report the result of their missions to the International Committee of Women for permanent Peace as a basis for further action.

Notes

1 Jane Addams, Emily Balch, and Alice Hamilton, eds., *Women at The Hague: The International Congress of Women and Its Results* (New York: Macmillan, 1915). Subsequent page references are to these proceedings.

2 *Report of the International Congress of Women: The Hague—The Netherlands, April 28th to May 1st, 1915* (Woman's Peace Party, 1915), p. 3.

3 Ibid.

4 Catherine Foster, *Women for All Seasons: The Story of the Women's International League for Peace and Freedom* (Athens: University of Georgia Press, 1989), pp. 1–2.

5 "Resolutions Adopted at the Hague Congress," in *Women at The Hague*, pp. 150–59. From Thomas Dublin and Kathryn Kish Sklar, eds., *Women and Social Movements in the United States, 1600–2000*. Accessed Sept. 28, 2017, www.womhist.alexanderstreet.com.

Resolutions
First Feminist Congress
Méridia, Yucatán, Mexico
January 13, 1916

Announcement of the First Feminist Congress in Diario Oficial del Gobierno Constitucionalista del Estado de Yucatan (Republica Mexicana) Year XIX, Number 5580. J4 .Y8 January–March 1916. Law Library, Library of Congress.

Advertising announcing this gathering acknowledged that in order "[t]o create free and strong generations, women must attain a legal status that elevates them."[1] The socialist governor of Yucatán, Salvador Alvarado, apparently influenced by his own knowledge of European socialist feminist gatherings and by local women, called for the convention in October of 1915.[2] At least 620 delegates, many of them teachers, attended this feminist conference, the first in Mexico and the second in Latin America. The proceedings were published at the time, and then again in 1975, to celebrate International Women's Year, though this may be their first appearance in English. There were not a great number of events leading up to this congress, although there was a newspaper, *La Mujer Mexicana*, and a Women's Loyalty Club (1913), whose "gatherings became massive and a symbol of resistance to the usurper's government";[3] too, women had played many roles in the violent 1910 Revolution.

This congress differed from that in 1910 in Argentina in many important ways. First, the instigating force here was the governor, rather than a range of feminist groups and individuals. Second, Alvarado set up the questions that would be debated, while the 1910 feminists determined their own issues. Third, suffrage was more central. Finally, the earlier gathering strove to be international, while this one was framed in national and even nationalist terms.

The topics discussed at the congress were raised in a series of questions that appeared in Article VII of the "Regulations Governing the First Feminist Convention of Yucatan," and appear in the document translated below. The Resolutions[4] below are perhaps best considered as very early deliberations on feminist questions.

Resolutions

1. The gates of all fields of activity in which man wages his daily struggle for bread should be open to women.

2. The woman of the future can fulfill any civic charges which do not demand a vigorous physical constitution; since there is no difference in intellectual status between woman and man, the former is equally capable of being a guiding element in society.

Report from the Congress

Report submitted by the Board of Directors of the First Feminist Congress in Yucatan to the Executive Power of the State. Written before the closure of the Congress, in response to the reasons for which it was convened.

I am privileged to communicate to the honorable Government the conclusions, based on Article 17 from the Interior Policies of the First Feminist Congress, that the women of the Congress approved by a majority vote during the sessions that took place on the 13th, 14th, 15th and 16th of this month. Said sessions were proposed by the commissions that were given the charge of resolving those issues that you opportunely suggested for discussion.

The first issue inquires: What social methods should be utilized to liberate women from the burden of tradition? The following was agreed:

I. In all cultural centers, including both those that require citizen participation and those of voluntary nature, women will be made aware of their potential. They will also be made aware of the variety of practical applications for their capabilities. Their practical applications shall include occupations performed, until the present, by men.

II. To work with the Government on the modification of current Civil Law, granting women more freedom and rights, so they are able to climb toward new aspirations.

III. This has already been accomplished. The successful implementation of secular education.

IV. To avoid in churches religious teaching to minors under the age of 18, since children accept everything without rational thought and personal judgment.

V. To instill in women high moral, as well as humane and fraternal, principles.

VI. To help women understand the responsibility of their actions. "Do good for the sake of goodness itself."

VII. To encourage performances with socialist tendencies that inspire women with the ideal of free thought.

VIII. To introduce periodical conferences at schools. The purpose of these conferences will be to banish children's dark fears of a vengeful and irate God who inflicts eternal punishments resembling those of Talion: "An eye for an eye, a tooth for a tooth."

IX. That women should have a profession, an occupation that allows them to earn a living if necessary.

X. That women should receive an intellectual education so that both women and men can support each other through any difficulty, and so that a man may always find in a woman a being equal to him.

XI. That young women, upon getting married, should be made aware of what they are facing, and what their duties and obligations are. They should never have any spiritual guide other than their conscience.

The second issue: What role does Elementary school play in the recognition and affirmation of women in society, given that this institution's objective is to educate for life? The following was agreed to:

I. To introduce public conferences meant to be attended principally by teachers and parents, that they might become acquainted with the noble objectives of Rational Education, founded on total freedom. This freedom, far from leading to licentiousness, guides new generations to a society in which harmony and an awareness of rights and duties prevail.

II. To eliminate current schools with their textbooks, summaries, and oral lectures, and to replace them with Institutes of Rational Education, where free actions, beneficial to society, can flourish.

The third issue: What arts and occupations should be encouraged and sustained by the State, so as to prepare women for a life paced by progress? The question was answered as follows:

I. To immediately build an Art and Design Academy in order to encourage fondness for painting. Also, to begin Music lessons in the main cities of the State.

II. To add speech classes to the Schools of Music and Education.

III. Photography, silver-smithing, agave fiber-craft, printing, bookbinding, lithography, photoengraving, steel and copper engraving, flower arrangement, and pottery in adult education centers. Remuneration should be equal for every instructor. Scholarships should be granted to young ladies who come to the Capital City with the intention of studying these classes. All courses should also take place in the evening.

IV. To build as many co-educational School-Farms as possible.

V. To encourage, through conferences and news articles, an affinity for medicine and pharmaceutical studies in the fairer sex.

VI. To encourage an affinity for literature, as well as for writing books on hygiene, arts, and any other topic that counts in favor of women's progress.

Fourth issue: What are the public functions women can and should perform in order that they not only be followers, but also leaders in society? It was resolved as follows:

I. Doors must be opened to women so that they, too, might access all of the areas in which men now work for their livelihoods.

II. Women from future generations can perform any public charge that does not demand a vigorous physical build, since there is no difference between their intellectual capability and that of a man. Women are as capable as men of being leaders in society.

Notes

1 "100th Anniversary of the First Feminist Congress of Mexico," *Secretaría de Relaciones Exteriores, Mexico* (blog), Jan. 15, 2016, https://www.gob.mx/sre/. articulos/100th-anniversary-of-the-first-feminist-congress-of-mexico.

2 Alaide Foppa, "First Feminist Congress in Mexico, 1916." *Signs* 5.1 (Autumn 1979): 193. Translated by Helene de Aguilar.

3 Heather Dasher Monk, "Mexican Women—Then and Now," *Against the Current*, Sept./Oct. 2010. *Solidarity*, www.solidarity-us.org.

4 Translation by Violeta Martinez Morones and Madeleine Brink.

31

Manifesto
Australia's Women's Peace Army
Melbourne, Australia
October 2, 1916

We war against war.

Vida Goldstein, 1912.

The Australian Women's Peace Army was led by Vida Goldstein (pictured in figure 31.1 with the *Australian Herald*) and Cecilia Annie John, who organized women from Melbourne, Sydney, and Brisbane in an attempt to join all women who believed war was wrong, no matter what their political affiliation. These women did not want young Australian men conscripted to fight for the British Empire in World War I, as Britain was asking the Australian government to do. The Women's Peace Army held peace demonstrations, encouraged voters to elect candidates who supported peace for Australia, sent petitions to government officials, and offered practical help to those disadvantaged by the war.[1]

The Manifesto[2] argues that military and commercial supremacy do not give a country the right to order its young men to break the commandment, "Thou shalt not kill." It also protests against the misuse of workers who are "crushed" by the war machine and the arms race. Perhaps the strongest language the Manifesto uses is in its appeal to women voters, especially mothers, who they believe have an especially strong duty to vote against conscription: "As the Mothers of the Race, it is your privilege to conserve life, and love, and beauty, all of which are destroyed by war. Without them, the world is a desert. You, who give life, cannot, if you think deeply and without bias, vote to send any mother's son to kill, against his will, some other mother's son." The language of the entire manifesto is a passionate defense of "Right" against the power of "Might."

The Australian Women's Peace Army was not successful in stopping conscription during World War I, and it disbanded in 1919 when the war was over. The Women's Peace Army, however, continued a tradition of women protesting against military and economic violence and aggression that started with the workplace and antislavery protests of the 1830s, continued through the world wars, and still occurs today. It revealed the costs of unrestrained militarism and

This poster was used as propaganda against conscription in Australia during World War I. The poem features a mother who realizes she has sentenced a man to death by voting for conscription, and she imagines the pain of his widow and orphaned children because of her careless decision.

capitalism, working together, on wage earners, unions, conscripted soldiers, "every conception of right and freedom," and world peace. It contained an argument for bringing "the gifts" of womanhood to the state—"the gifts of order, of beauty, of forbearance, of harmony, of love." There is an argument against "separate spheres" for the sexes encountered for the first time here in precisely this way.

Manifesto of the Australian Women's Peace Army

Conscription: VOTE NO.

Women of Australia! On October 28 we shall have had laid upon us the greatest responsibility and the greatest privilege that could be placed upon the women of any country.

For the first time in history, the people of a whole nation are being asked whether they shall declare their allegiance to the force of Might or the force of Right.

The A.B.C. of the Case

Down the ages, the rulers of the world have held that Might is a nation's only defence, and in the twentieth century this doctrine has been carried to such a point that no nation can claim to be a "Great Power" unless it is so great in naval or military strength as to excite the fear and suspicion of other "Great Powers."

The "Great Powers" of Europe, which have hostile neighbours on one or more frontiers, have, in deadly fear of one another, accepted the principle of conscript armies as being necessary for defensive purposes; but England, with her sea-girt shores, considered a voluntary navy and army sufficient to defend her from possible enemies. Her people, deploring the supposed necessity for conscription in Europe, gloried in the fact that no Britisher need be a fighting man against his will.

It has been universally recognised that conscription and freedom are mutually destructive, and in conscript countries the aim of the masses, in contradistinction to the classes, has always been to throw off the crushing yoke of conscription and militarism.

* * *

While European countries were engaged in protecting themselves, or fighting against each other, our island England was free to develop her manufactures and find markets and possessions overseas, to protect which, an ever-increasing navy was needed.

We have become, accordingly, such a far-flung mighty Empire, that we have excited the fear and jealousy of other "Great Powers," some of which, with the aid of electricity and chemistry, have been endeavouring to catch up with us in production, and, in turn, seek outlets for their surplus products, and profitable investments. International commercial rivalry has developed to such an extent that the peace of the world has trembled in the balance many times during the past decade.

Desire for commercial supremacy, or fear of losing it, has kept all the nations armed to the teeth. This weight of armaments, upon which our capitalistic system depends, and on whose maintenance the bulk of the national income must be expended, has kept the working classes (without whose labour no wealth could be created) in such an oppressive condition of wage slavery, that in every country they were building up their industrial and political organisations with the object of bringing about a complete change of the commercial system—so that production should be for use and not for profit. Sometimes, when conditions became more than usually oppressive, the double-edged weapon of the strike had to be resorted to.

* * *

Their teaching so aroused the fear of the Great Powers of Industry, whose enormous profits depend on a docile wage-earning working class, that in every country certain of these financial magnates, backed up by their newspaper and naval and military tools, have openly declared that the only way to bring the working men to their senses was to have a great war, which would destroy the growing power of Trade Unionism, which was directly opposed to the established power of Capitalism.

We do not say that this war was promoted with the deliberate object of crushing the workers, but we do say that the belief in Might, the fear of enemies without and within national boundaries, the use of the press, or armament firms, of secret diplomacy, of naval and military strength, to bolster up a social system under which the great mass of the people live in avoidable anxiety, wretchedness and ugliness, has made such a Clash of Interests that a Clash of Arms between Nations prepared for War, some more, some less, became inevitable when Circumstance and Opportunity sounded the tocsin of alarm.

* * *

Now that war has come, Britishers who believe that Might is the guardian angel of Right, are driven to jettison all their cherished ideas of freedom and conscience in the frantic effort to get enough men to do enough killing to wipe out the enemy.

* * *

When British men believed that they were going out to protect a "Little Nation," and to do their part in the "War to end War and Prussian Militarism," they came forth in their thousands as Free Men. But as time went on, they found that "Little Belgium" was forgotten, that the rights of "Little Ireland," "Little Finland" and "Little Greece" seemed to be set aside by other "Big Nations."

They found that, while they were destroying a European menace, they were setting up what they believed was another and nearer menace. They found that, instead of Prussian militarism being destroyed, it was being hailed as the saviour of the British Empire. They found that instead of England being the

> "Land where girt by friends or foes,
> A man may speak the thing he will."

She had become the land of military and industrial slaves, of shackled speech and shackled conscience.

They found that, instead of this being the "war to end all war," all nations, neutral as well as belligerent, are preparing for future wars, and arming more and more feverishly.

* * *

Under these circumstances, do you wonder that free Australian men have come to see that the war is not being fought for the great ideals of freedom that were held before them at the beginning, and that, therefore, the few men who might still volunteer in the cause of freedom refuse to volunteer in a cause that aims at rivetting the chains of European militarism on Australia?

They begin to see that the belief in Might throws the nations into a bottomless pit of hate, and oppression, and debt. They begin to see that conscription entrenches militarism still more deeply and breeds endless war, to which every conception of Right and Freedom must be ruthlessly sacrificed.

They say.
Therefore, they say, "To 'vote NO' means the beginning of the end of militarism in Australia, and of every other nation; the beginning of the reign of Right as the only Might there is or can be."

And You?
And you, women of Australia, are asked to say the same thing, and more; for as women you are faced with a greater responsibility in this matter than men.

As the Mothers of the Race, it is your privilege to conserve life, and love, and beauty, all of which are destroyed by war. Without them, the world is a desert.

You, who give life, cannot, if you think deeply and without bias, vote to send any mother's son to kill, against his will, some other mother's son.

You may, if you choose, send your own son, but you are guilty in the first degree if you take upon yourself the responsibility of forcing someone else's son to break the Sixth Commandment, and, defying God, say to him,

Thou Shalt Kill.

We ask you to tell us what MORAL RIGHT you have to do this thing?

* * *

A sorrowing mother, who had lost a brave son at Gallipoli, said to us:–

"It was not the thought of his being killed that was a nightmare to me. That was terrible, but more terrible still was the thought of his killing another dear boy like himself, a boy whose mother loved him as passionately as I loved mine."

Which is the noble spirit? That woman's or that of the woman who would say on October 28 to all men in Australia:–

"You SHALL Go, and KILL, KILL, KILL, till you have helped bring about 'THE DAY' when Germany is utterly crushed and every German mother has lost every son of military age?"

Which Australian woman, do you think, will stand the more fearlessly before her Maker?

* * *

Man-made laws that defy eternal laws of God, of Right, of Reason, of Love, can never produce good. We cannot gather grapes of thorns, not figs of thistles.

And so we ask you to be true to your womanhood, and, with your vote, bring to the State the same gifts that you bring to your homes, the gifts of order, of beauty, of forbearance, of harmony, of love. The nations are dying for lack of these gifts from women. Give them freely, give them gladly, but GIVE THEM YOU CANNOT IF YOU VOTE FOR CONSCRIPTION.

Therefore Vote NO.

Notes

1   "Women's Peace Army (1915–1919)." *Trove: National Library of Australia*, accessed Nov. 11, 2014, trove.nla.gov.au.
2   "Manifesto," *Woman Voter*, Oct. 6, 1914. *Reason in Revolt: Source Documents of Australian Radicalism*, http://www.reasoninrevolt.net.au.

32

Program
National Association of Spanish Women
Madrid, Spain
October 1918

María Espinoza.

While Spain's feminist movement at this time was not as strong as that in some other countries, there were several active groups, including the Lyceum Club, the Union of Spanish Women (which held a street demonstration for suffrage in 1921), and the National Association of Spanish Women (Asociación Nacional de Mujeres Española), which was active from 1918 until 1936. Its members included Clara Campoamor, Victoria Kent, Celsia Regis, and María Espinosa de los Monteros, and it published a journal, *Mundo Femenino*. Another journal, *El Pensamiento Femenino*, began publication in 1913.[1] The association gave rise to several smaller women's organizations and even founded a political party, the Acción Política Feminista Independiente. The association and the party were dissolved due to the Spanish Civil War.

Pictured in figure 32.1 is a young María Espinosa de los Monteros y Díaz de Santiago (1875–1946). She was the first president of Asociación Nacional de Mujeres Española, and president of the Supreme Feminist Council of Spain (Consejo Supremo Feminista de España), an umbrella organization that brought five feminist groups together.

The politics of this group are complex. Spain at the time had a liberal government that was being challenged by a nationalist Right and a conservative Catholic Church. A political Left was active, as well, that included anarchists and Marxists. Negotiating among these movements, wholly aligned with none, the largely middle-class members of the association developed a program that shared certain elements with both the Left and the Right.

The liberal feminist aspects of the Program include an understanding of women's precarious legal status, and the call for a long list of rights, from the rights to vote,[2] own property, and serve on juries to equal pay, equal educational opportunity, and equal employment options. Nationalist elements come through in the very first two items, defending the territorial integrity of the nation, and calling on mothers to raise patriotic children. Conservative elements appear in the various calls for moral behavior and the unwillingness to challenge outright gender-specific jobs, in the home or for wages. In terms of class, while much attention is on greater access to the professions for "women of merit," several items address the working class, though clearly not from their perspective, such as their rights to unions, to higher wages, and to minimal literacy.

The Program of the National Association,[3] overall, resounds with the cautiousness of first steps, as seen in the need to assert the most basic rights for at least many women. It contains a qualified but definite critique of the status quo that recognizes many of women's daily sufferings, whether at the hands of a drunken spouse, an all-male jury, or an exploitative employer. It imagines women with increasing moral and economic independence, with more arenas in which to move, and with greater decision-making power and positions.

Program of the National Association of Spanish Women

Politico-Social Part

1. To oppose, by any means the Association may have, any proposal, act, or manifestation that harms the integrity of the national territory.
2. To try to see that every Spanish mother, in perfect parallel with the schoolteacher, inculcates in the child, from the earliest childhood, love for our one and indivisible mother the fatherland [*la madre patria*].
3. Scrupulous examination and revision of the existing laws for the protection and defense of women. . . .
4. To consider women eligible for public popular positions.
5. To give women access to the exercise of all those public positions involving the governing and administration of the moral and material interests of their sex.
6. Extensive study of the rights that belong to women under the existing Civil Code to demonstrate her precarious condition and to solicit from the Codes Committee the reform of those articles of the Civil Code that very specifically refer to marriage, to the powers of the father, and to the administration of conjugal property.
7. To obtain for women the right to take part in juries, especially in crimes committed by their sex, or in which women are victims.
8. Joint matrimonial administration, that is to say, the signature of both should be needed for any public document related to this matter. . . .
9. The same rights over the children as the father has in a legal marriage.
10. The legal right of the wife to the salary or wages of the husband, like that of the husband to those of the wife.
11. Complete legal personality for women, with the husband being able to represent her only by her delegating that power.
12. The right to keep the natural daughters recognized by the father.
13. Equality in legislation on adultery.
14. Punishment for the spouse for abandoning the home without the other's consent. . . .
15. Punishment of habitual drunkenness and making it grounds for marital separation.
16. Punishment for abuse of the wife, even if it does not threaten her life.
17. Greater punishment for crimes against decency. . . .

18. Suspension of the regulation of prostitution.
19. Enforcement of the White Slave Act.
20. To seek the creation of public schools in sufficient number that one can demand the observance of the legal principle that makes schooling obligatory, and to establish this same legal principle for the creation of schools for the mentally abnormal.
21. That pedagogical licenses be required of professors in private educational establishments.
22. Support and assistance for the study of medicine by women.
23. Support for the studies of physicians and dentists.
24. The right to rise in the professions that are already exercised, in the same conditions as men, and with the same pay.
25. The right to other new ones in these conditions.
26. To grant representation to women in the chambers of commerce, industry, and property.
27. To see to it that women participate in the syndicates and trade unions for the classification of the industries specific to their sex. . . .
28. To establish educational centers for domestic service and schools for women working in cooking, ironing, etc.
29. To found hospitals for domestic service.
30. To declare the elementary education of maids obligatory, asking the ladies who employ them that on the days of the week of their choice . . . they allow their female servants who do not know how to read or write to spend one hour attending classes that will be established, pursuing the goal that . . . there should be no maid who does not know how to read or write, thus carrying out one of the finest works of Christianity, that of "teaching those who do not know." The same can be extended to those [male] workers who find themselves in the same situation. . . .

Economic Part

1. To do away with the capitalist intermediary in the manual labor of women, seeking by all possible means for the female worker to receive the maximum pay for her work. . . .
   a. In this broad field there is so much labor that the true emancipation of the working classes can be achieved as much by this means as by establishing feminine industries, workshops, factories, and other such things; so, with the Association acting as representative, contractor, or boss, one can manage to avoid the great exploitation of which they are the object by persons or entities which, not knowing anything about the work that is done, reserve for themselves or for great beneficiaries enormous and disproportionate profits.
   b. Any capital invested has the right to remunerative, but limited, interest, so that it allows the female worker to receive the due benefits. The regulation of women's work to obtain an equal economic result will be in the hands of the National Association of Spanish Women, once producers and consumers have given their allegiance to its constitution and program.
   c. We must do away with the traditional commercial custom of excessively exploiting the work of the producing woman, paying a pittance for rich embroidery, valuable lace, and elegant products, for those who charge

and receive from the consuming women extremely high prices and exorbitant profits.

2. The creation of establishments for the children of female workers, offering . . . excellent food and childcare from the youngest infancy to those who are old enough to have to go to work in workshops or public schools. . . .

3. A duly authorized body of feminine vigilance will be created, chosen by the Association among its associates, to put an end to the abuses and pernicious habits of many [female] schoolteachers, mistresses, and nannies who abandon or mistreat the children in the streets, boulevards, and parks. . . .

In some ways, the childhood of the upper classes of society is just as deprived of protection and external oversight as that of the poorest; everything primarily comes down to mothers being more assured of believing their children to be free from all danger while in the care of a well-paid person. . . .

4. The intellectual classes will also benefit greatly from this Association, which proposes to publish on its own those literary works of true merit whose female authors do not have the economic wherewithal to do so, thus making it possible to avoid losing their property, through usury, of so many works that now enrich certain industrialists. . . .

5. In this way, . . . one will seek to sustain and elevate the social situation of women who because of their exceptional qualifications for the arts, sciences, education, etc., deserve it, thus putting an end to the exploitation and neglect of women of merit who can be useful to the fatherland.

Notes

1 "Spain's Women's Movements," in *Women's Studies Encyclopedia*, ed. Helen Tierney (Santa Barbara, CA: Greenwood Press, 2002), gem.greenwood.com; Rosa Ballester, "The Historical Framework: Women in Spain in the 20th Century." *Unlearned Lessons*, accessed Sept. 28, 2017, www.unless-women.eu.

2 Although suffrage is not in the program, the association supported it.

3 Jon Cowans, *Modern Spain: A Documentary History* (Philadelphia: University of Pennsylvania Press, 2003), 115–18. Ellipses in translation.

33

Resolutions
First International Congress of Working Women
Washington, D.C.
October 28–November 6, 1919

Women labor leaders around the world decided to call this meeting, named the International Congress of Working Women (ICWW). Margaret Dreier Robins, who was also president of the Women's Trade Union League (see Chicago 1909), served as president of the gathering. Their primary goal was to establish labor guidelines with women workers in mind, in hopes of influencing the newly formed International Labor Organization (ILO), which was meeting concurrently. The ICWW presented the document below to the first ILO conference, which addressed international labor standards, and also formed the International

Federation of Working Women. The meeting involved representatives of nineteen countries.

The Resolutions[1] demanded changes in the workplace, including a universal eight-hour workday, a minimum of 1.5 days off work per week, a break during the workday, and paid maternity leave. The women at this congress also addressed concerns with child labor, working at night and at hazardous occupations, immigration, and unemployment. They raised the issues of workplace inspections and research on matters including maternity and infant care, and the causes of unemployment. While they express support for protective labor laws for women and children, they say that except under special circumstances, men, too, should not labor at night, and that research should take place on eliminating hazardous working environments for all. They also protested the Russian blockade, showing their concern for working women across the globe. The multifaceted approach the congress took shows some ability to dialogue across national and social boundaries, yet it did not address the role of race in labor unions since, as Laura Vapnek shows, they did not cover domestic or agricultural labor, where most women of color worked at the time. The same exemption exists in much union and state policy.

The International Federation of Working Women met two more times (Geneva, 1921, and Vienna, 1923). Nearly two hundred women attended, though only ten from each country were allowed to vote. After the 1923 congress, the group became the Women's Department of the International Federation of Trade Unions because the funding and ability for women in trade unions to meet was not available to sustain the independent organization.

Resolutions of the First International Congress of Working Women

Countries with voting power: Argentina, Belgium, Canada, Czecho-Slovakia [sic], Denmark, France, Great Britain, Italy, Japan, Norway, Poland, Sweden, United States.

Additional countries represented: Cuba, India, Netherlands, Serbia, Spain, Switzerland.

The First International Congress of Working Women requests the First International Conference of Labor of the League of Nations that an international convention establish:

I. Eight Hour Day and Forty-Four Hour Week
    1. For all workers a maximum eight hour day and a forty-four hour week.
    2. That the weekly rest period shall have an uninterrupted duration of at least one day and a half.
    3. That in continuous industries a minimum rest period of one-half hour shall be accorded in each eight hour shift.

II. Child Labor
    1. Employment of Children
        a. Minimum Age: No child shall be employed or permitted to work in any gainful occupation unless he is 16 years of age, has completed the

elementary school and has been found by a school physician or other medical officer especially appointed for that purpose to be of normal development for a child of his age and physically fit for the work at which he is to be employed.

No young person under 18 years of age shall be employed in or about a mine or quarry.

The legal work day for young persons between 16 and 18 years of age shall be shorter than the legal work day for adults.

b. During the Night: No minor shall be employed between the hours of 6 p.m. and 7 a.m.

c. In Unhealthy Processes: Prohibition of the employment of minors in dangerous or hazardous occupations or at any work which will retard their proper physical development.

Administration

1. Work Permits: A yearly medical inspection by medical officer appointed for that purpose by the authorities, records of which inspections shall be kept.

2. Lists of employed minors with their hours of work shall be posted in all workrooms in which they are employed.

3. The number of inspectors, and especially women inspectors, employed by the factory or labor commission shall be sufficient to insure regular inspection of all establishments in which children are employed and such special inspections and investigations as are necessary to insure the protection of the children.

4. We further recommend compulsory continuation schools for minors until the age of 18.

III. Maternity Insurance

1. The method of administration of maternity benefits shall be left to the individual nations to determine.

2. No woman shall be employed for six weeks before or six weeks after child birth.

3. Every woman shall be entitled during maternity to free medical, surgical and nursing care, either in a hospital or at home, and also to a monetary allowance.[2]

4. The monetary allowance given to mothers shall be adequate for the full and healthy maintenance of mother and child during the aforesaid period.[3]

5. In each country government commissions shall be created to study the best methods of maternity and infant care, and to devise and put into operation effective methods of securing such care.

6. A bureau shall be established in the labor office of the League of Nations to collect information on the best methods of maternity and infant care, said information to be furnished [by] countries represented in the Labor Conference.

IV. Night Work

This Congress adheres to the Berne Convention of 1906 prohibiting night work for all women in industrial employment;

It further urges that night work shall be prohibited by law for men except in so far as it may be absolutely necessary through the special nature of, or the continuity of the occupation, or in the case of essential public service.

Night work shall be defined as the hours between 9 p.m. and 6 a.m.

V. Unemployment

Whereas, The problem of unemployment is such that it cannot be viewed in isolation from wage standards as a whole nor separated from the social and industrial organizations at present prevailing in all countries, and

Whereas, The causes of unemployment have been obscured and remedies obstructed by lack of adequate governmental and international research and control, and

Whereas, Unemployment today results in unwarranted poverty, disease, child labor, incompetency, expense to the State, and unrest; and

Whereas, the problems of unemployment are closely allied with the fluctuations of commerce between nations, therefore be it

Resolved: That the first International Congress of Working Women adopt the following recommendations:

1. That a special Bureau of Employment be established in the International Labor Office to act as the International Bureau of Information between nations on all matters relating to employment and unemployment.
2. That the International Labor Conference recommend to each nation in the League of Nations the establishment of a free employment service in all cities and industrial towns in the nation; and that a system of unemployment insurance be made effective in each country in cooperation with the Labor Unions.
3. That the International Labor Office shall coordinate the research work to be undertaken by the National Labor Departments into the possible causes of unemployment, including maldistribution of raw material, migration, labor turnover and bad management. The results of such research to form the basis of International law for the prevention of unemployment.
4. That with a view to the prevention of unemployment each Nation be required to provide for the allocation of public contracts in such way as to minimize protracted periods of unemployment for both men and women.
5. That no propaganda of misrepresentation for the exportation of foreign labor be carried on by transportation companies of private corporations.
6. That in the International Labor Office and in the national and local labor offices there must be a woman as director of the departments specifically relating to women.

VI. Hazardous Occupations

1. Prohibition of home work in occupations involving the use of poisonous material.
2. No exception of small factories from the regulations governing the industry.
3. Prohibition of the employment of women only in trades which cannot be made healthy for women as potential mothers.
4. An international inquiry to be instituted in order to ascertain the scope of measures which have been adopted in different countries to control dangerous occupations and to publish the results, with the object of

making clearly known which countries fall short of the standards already established in the more advanced countries.

5. The appointment of a committee including women under the League of Nations, international in personnel, to coordinate the work of national research in the dangerous trades, with a view to eliminating poisonous substances through the substitution of non-poisonous, and where this is impossible to devise new and efficient methods of protection.

VII. Immigration

Whereas emigration is a direct consequence of unemployment and

Whereas it is in the highest interests of the workers of all countries that emigration be regulated and protected:

Therefore Be It Resolved, that every nation interested in this question should base its legislations on the subject in conformity with the following principles:

1. Emigration, regulated by Labor Treaties, through agreements between the governments concerned and the trade unions.

2. Equal rights for the foreign worker and his family as far as social labor legislation is concerned.

3. Equal wages for foreign and native born workers.

4. Right of nations whose citizens emigrate to appoint officials to the country to which they emigrate for their assistance and protection.

5. Agreement between the Trade Unions of the several countries for the organization of the immigrant workers and for securing exchange of information of their respective labor movements.

VIII. Distribution of Raw Materials

1. To ask the League of Nations to appoint a Committee to consider and plan for the equal distribution of the raw materials existing in the world, as well as the international control of maritime transports which determine the increase of price of the raw materials.

IX. Russian Blockade

Whereas, neither the United States nor any of the Allied and Associated Powers is officially at war with Russia; and

Whereas, the blockade of the greater part of Russia, in Europe, is in effect directed against millions of women and children, and has brought in its train starvation, disease, and death, to countless victims; therefore be it

Resolved, that we, the delegates to the First International Congress of Working Women in congress assembled, at Washington, hereby protest against this blockade, and we demand the removal of all restrictions upon the shipment of food and other necessities to the people of Russia.

X. A Permanent Bureau

For the purpose of calling another Congress, be it resolved, that there be a Provisional Committee elected by this Congress consisting of a president, five vice-presidents and a secretary-treasurer, and that the present members of the executive committee, or alternates nominated by the trade union groups of the various nations, be corresponding members of this Provisional Committee.

1. The basis of representation for the next Congress shall be the same as the basis for this Congress.

2. That the officers be empowered to transact any necessary business.
3. That the International Office be in the United States.

Notes

1   International Congress of Working Women, *Resolutions Adopted by First International Congress of Working Women, Washington, U.S.A., October 28 to November 6, 1919* (Chicago: National Women's Trade Union League of America, [1919?]), p. 3 (seq. 3.), Collection Development Department, Widener Library, HCL, Harvard University.

2   Belgium, Czechoslovakia, Poland, Italy, and Canada voted to change this clause to read, "Every wage-earning woman or the wife of a wage earner shall be entitled during maternity to free medical, surgical and nursing care, either in a hospital or at home, and also to a maternity allowance."

3   Belgium, Czechoslovakia, Poland, and Italy voted to change this clause to read, "The indemnity given to mother shall be based on the living wage in the district."

34

Declaration of Principles
United States National Woman's Party
Washington, D.C.
November 11, 1922

The National Women's Party pickets at the White House, January 26, 1917. National Women's Party Records, Library of Congress.

In 1916 the Congressional Union for Woman Suffrage merged with the Woman's Party to form the National Woman's Party (NWP). During their short (though effective) suffrage campaign, the NWP adopted a range of tactics. They lobbied members of Congress and President Wilson (rather than running state-by-state campaigns), held rallies and parades, campaigned against politicians (mainly Democrats) who voted against suffrage, picketed the White House, and held hunger strikes. In figure 34.1, NWP sentinels famously make the argument that it is hypocritical for the United States to fight for democracy in Europe while denying its benefits to half of the U.S. population. When members were held in D.C. jails, some underwent the ordeal of being force-fed. After women's suffrage was ratified by the Nineteenth Amendment in 1920, some officers wanted to disband the NWP while others wanted to reorganize to advocate for women's full legal, social, and economic equality: the organization moved from suffrage to equality in the fullest sense.

To this end, Alice Paul drafted the Equal Rights Amendment. For the next few decades the NWP promoted the Equal Rights Amendment and participated in international women's rights campaigns. Senator Charles Curtis and Representative Daniel Anthony (nephew of Susan B. Anthony) introduced the ERA to Congress as early as December 1923; it passed the House and Senate in 1971, but was never ratified by the required number of states. The NWP managed to get the ERA introduced to Congress almost every year of this fifty-year campaign. During the 1920s, the NWP Legal Research Department also drafted over six hundred pieces of legislation concerning child custody rights, access to juries, property rights, divorce rights, reinstatement of maiden names after marriage, estate administration, and general contract powers. More than three hundred of these bills were passed by state legislatures during this decade alone.[1]

The Declaration of Principles[2] was passed at the 1922 conference of state and national officers of the National Woman's Party. They begin by stating what aspects of women's subjection the long and ultimately successful campaign for suffrage did not in itself change, in "the law, in government, in educational opportunities, in professions, in the church, in industry, and in the home." In the language of the document, "that women no longer shall" emphasizes the problems with the status quo, while "but shall" puts emphasis on how things should be. In every instance, the solution is for "the same" treatment, for equal laws. The document thus takes a principled stance against gendered protective labor legislation, and for women's full and equal participation in every aspect of civil and government service.

The document addresses legal changes but does not stop there. Looking to culture, it sees a still-existing sense of female inferiority, and looks forward to the day when women regard themselves and are regarded as equals. It urges that employers and professions open their doors to women. The full meaning of women having the "same right to control of their persons as have men" is not clear, but given that it comes in a sentence addressing double moral standards, the allusion is probably to sexuality.

Some of the most interesting and novel aspects of the document concern the family—the one place where identical treatment does not dominate. Regardless of how they contribute to the well-being of their family, "the wife shall no longer be considered as supported by the husband, but their mutual contribution to the family maintenance shall be recognized." The NWP recommends democracy in

The *Suffragist* was the paper of the Congressional Union. The cover pictured here was drawn by Nina Allender. The text, turning President Wilson's words against him, reads, "We shall fight for the things we have always carried nearest our hearts, for democracy, for the right of those who submit to authority to have a voice in their own governments. W.W."

the family—there being no "head of household," or any different consequences of marriage for men and women in terms, for example, of name or citizenship or legal independence.

Declaration of Principles

WHEREAS, Women today, although enfranchised, are still in every way subordinate to men before the law, in government, in educational opportunities, in professions, in the church, in industry, and in the home:

BE IT RESOLVED, That as a part of our campaign to remove all forms of the subjection of women, we shall work for the following immediate objects:

That women shall no longer be regarded and shall no longer regard themselves as inferior to men, but the equality of the sexes shall be recognized.

That women shall no longer be the governed half of society, but shall participate equally with men in the direction of life.

That women shall no longer be denied equal educational opportunities with men, but the same opportunities shall be given to both sexes in all schools, colleges and universities which are supported in any way by public funds.

That women shall no longer be barred from any occupation, but every occupation open to men shall be open to women and restrictions upon the hours, conditions, and remuneration of labor shall apply alike to both sexes.

That women shall no longer be discriminated against in the legal, the medical, the teaching, or any other profession, but the same opportunities shall be given to women as to men in training for professions and in the practice of these professions.

That women shall no longer be discriminated against in civil and government service, but shall have the same right as men to authority, appointment, advancement and pay in the executive, the legislative, and the judicial branches of the government service.

That women shall no longer be discriminated against in the foreign trade, consular and diplomatic service, but women as well as men shall represent our country in foreign lands.

That women shall no longer receive less pay than men for the same work, but shall receive equal compensation for equal work in public and private employment.

That women shall no longer be barred from the priesthood or ministry, or any position of authority in the church, but equally with men shall participate in ecclesiastical offices and dignities.

That a double moral standard shall no longer exist, but one code shall obtain for both men and women.

That exploitation of the sex of women shall no longer exist, but women shall have the same right to the control of their persons as have men.

That women shall no longer be discriminated against in treatment of sex diseases and in punishment of sex offenses, but men and women shall be treated in the same ways for sex diseases and sex offenses.

That women shall no longer be deprived of the right of trial by a jury of their peers, but jury service shall be open to women as to men.

That women shall no longer be discriminated against in inheritance laws, but men and women shall have the same right to inherit property.

That the identity of the wife shall no longer be merged in that of her husband, but the wife shall retain her separate identity after marriage and be able to contract with her husband concerning the marriage relationship.

That a woman shall no longer be required by law or custom to assume the name of her husband upon marriage, but shall have the same right as a man to retain her own name after marriage.

That the wife shall no longer be considered as supported by the husband, but their mutual contribution to the family maintenance shall be recognized.

That the headship of the family shall no longer be in the husband alone, but shall be equally in the husband and the wife.

That the husband shall no longer own his wife's services, but these shall belong to her alone as in the case of any free person.

That the husband shall no longer own his wife's earnings, but these shall belong to her alone.

That the husband shall no longer own or control his wife's property, but it shall belong to her and be controlled by her alone.

That the husband shall no longer control the joint property of his wife and himself, but the husband and wife shall have equal control of their joint property.

That the husband shall no longer obtain divorce more easily than the wife, but the wife shall have the right to obtain divorce on the same grounds as the husband.

That the husband shall no longer have a greater right to make contracts than the wife, but a wife shall have equal right with her husband to make contracts.

That married women shall no longer be denied the right to choose their own citizenship, but shall have the same independent choice of citizenship as is possessed by their husbands.

That women shall no longer be discriminated against in the economic world because of marriage, but shall have the same treatment in the economic world after marriage as have men.

That the father shall no longer have the paramount right to the care, custody, and control of the child, to determine its education and religion, to the guardianship of its estate, and to the control of its services and earnings, but these rights shall be shared equally by the father and mother in the case of all children, whether born within or without the marriage ceremony.

That no form of the Common Law or Civil Law disabilities of women shall [any] longer exist, but women shall be equal with men before the law.

IN SHORT—THAT WOMAN SHALL NO LONGER BE IN ANY FORM OF SUBJECTION TO MAN IN LAW OR IN CUSTOM, BUT SHALL IN EVERY WAY BE ON AN EQUAL PLANE IN RIGHTS, AS SHE HAS ALWAYS BEEN AND WILL CONTINUE TO BE, IN RESPONSIBILITIES AND OBLIGATIONS.

Notes

1 The National Women's Party Pamphlet Collection, ca. 1923–1946, Archives and Special Collections Library, Vassar College Libraries, specialcollections.vassar.edu.

2 Library of Congress website https://www.loc.gov/resource. Accessed September 2017.

35

Manifesto *and* Declaration
Women's Suffrage League
Tokyo, Japan
1924 and 1925

文字通りの 公明選挙で当選
得選生みの親 市川房枝女史
（地方区・東京） 無所属⑯

Pictured here is Fusae Ichikawa, who cofounded the New Women's Association and the League for the Realization of Women's Suffrage, later called the Women's Suffrage League. While purged and excluded from political office after World War II, she later served four terms in the Diet.

Advocacy for women's political rights soared in Japan in the 1920s. Article 5 of the Police Security Act banned women from joining political parties, attending political meetings, and even expressing political views; in 1922, however, the Diet ended the last two bans (but not that on joining political parties), thus giving women the right to organize and participate in political assemblies. The first national women's group, the New Women's Association, was established in 1919, and a socialist organization, Red Wave, was founded in 1921. There was also a Japanese Christian Women's Organization that worked on prohibition, and a Federation of Women's Associations, an umbrella group of forty-three women's interest groups that first formed to help with disaster relief following the 1923 Tokyo earthquake, but that ultimately became a large, multi-issue activist group. It developed five subgroups to tackle gender issues in education, government, society, labor, and employment. "The Tokyo Federation's government section focused on issues of political rights, discussing means of gaining full membership in the state. In November 1924, government section director Kubushiro Ochimi called a meeting of women interested in working for women's political rights. This meeting (on December 13, 1924) spawned the League for the Realization of Women's Suffrage."[1]

Despite work by the league and many other organizations, women did not win the right to vote until 1946, while universal male suffrage was granted in 1925. After suffrage for men only was passed, a Declaration[2] was issued, part of which is copied here. The Declaration resists the demand to "prove" that women are intelligent, etc., and urges a singular focus on political rights.

The Manifesto[3] of the suffrage group was written at its founding. It contains grievances and proposals for ending abuses suffered by Japanese women. It asserts that women, despite differences between them, are a class that can work together and that deserves protection and inclusion. It holds that all women need political rights, whether mothers, workers, or both, and that political rights require suffrage. Women already receive an education (basic literacy), it notes, but that is not enough for

Members of the Japanese Women's Suffrage League delivering twenty thousand petitions to the Imperial Diet urging them to consider a bill for women's suffrage.

them or for the creation of "a new Japan" that, unlike the Japan of the past twenty-six hundred years, will not have destructive customs that deny the natural rights of women and men. This frank challenge to custom in a place that honors many traditions probably reflects both the authors' boldness and their frustration.

Manifesto

1. It is our responsibility to destroy customs which have existed in this country for the past twenty six hundred years and to construct a new Japan that promotes the natural rights of men and women;
2. As women have been attending public school with men for half a century since the beginning of the Meiji period and our opportunities in higher education have continued to expand, it is unjust to exclude women from international suffrage;
3. Political rights are necessary for the protection of nearly four million working women in this country;
4. Women who work in the household must be recognized before the law to realize their full human potential;
5. Without political rights we cannot achieve public recognition at either the national or local level of government;
6. It is both necessary and possible to bring together women of different religions and occupations in a movement for women's suffrage.

Declaration

The foundation for the construction of a new Japan has been laid and, as expected, the [male] suffrage bill was passed by the fiftieth Diet session. However, women, who comprise half of the country's population, have been left without political rights, along with males under the age of 25 years of age or who "receive public or private assistance." We women feel ourselves no longer compelled to explain the reasons why it is at once natural and necessary for us, who are both human beings and citizens, to participate in the administration of our country. . . . Therefore, women should put aside their emotional, religious, and ideological differences and cooperate as women. . . . We women must concentrate our efforts solely on one thing, namely, the acquisition of political rights. We should work closely with the political parties but maintain a position of absolute neutrality [in partisan matters].

Notes

1 Barbara Molony, "Women's Rights, Feminism, and Suffragism in Japan, 1870–1925." *Pacific Historical Review* 69.4 (Nov. 2000): 656.
2 *Transforming Japan: How Feminism and Diversity Are Making a Difference,* ed. Kumiko Fujimura-Fanselow (New York: Feminist Press at CUNY, 2011. The editor's source is Sen Katayama, "The Political Position of Women." *Japanese Women* 2.6 (Nov. 1939): 2. I combined this with a version found in Molony, p. 660.
3 "Feminism in Japan," last edited Aug. 25, 2017. *Wikipedia*, www.wikipedia.com.

36

Resolutions
All India Women's Conference on Education
Women's Indian Association
Poona, India
January 5–8, 1927

All India Women's Conference logo.

"Never" was a word that should be banned in a Conference on reform. . . .
Hope was one of the humanity's greatest heritages. . . . Let our hope
and our effort be as boundless as the sky, as immense as the ocean,
regardless of time and opposing forces. We may achieve our purpose
to-day . . . or fifty years hence. We may not be able to achieve it for this
generation but still let us go on with an undying spirit to make this
world more beautiful for the unborn humanity so that when it opens
its eyes it will be on a world more lovely than the one we looked upon.
—Ms. Chattopadhyaya, a conference participant (37)[1]

The All India Women's Conference is the oldest national women's organization in
the country. It was the fruition of a call to reform women's education, first given
by Mr. E. F. Oaten at Bethune College in Calcutta. Several Irish women, including
Mrs. A. L. Huidekoper and Mrs. Margaret Cousins, responded to this call by sending
it out to many educational institutions across India, and women from across
the country enthusiastically supported education reform for women and girls.
Impressively, at least twenty-two preliminary conferences were held to elect representatives to attend the All India Women's Conference, from September through

December of 1926, where some two thousand people met.[2] The conference focused almost exclusively on education but also voted to raise the legal marriage age to allow girls more opportunity for education before they were married.

"The present system . . . was thought out primarily [. . .] in the interest of boys, and was formulated by men. The time has now come for women to review and reform this system" (26). This statement was part of Cousins's remarks just before the discussion and votes on the Resolutions; it seems fitting, then, to read the Resolutions as the work of women, "representing all communities and races in India" (26), advocating reform of male-designed practices in the name of female inclusion. In fact, the discussion of each resolution contains a critique of the status quo. Resolution I, for example, which speaks to education of the whole person, criticizes current practice for having "catered only to the mind and starved the emotions" (27), not developing the imagination and creativity of children, and suppressing intuition. The regime of testing that a later resolution rejected is also part of this critique. The Resolutions thus begin to provide a distinctly feminist perspective on education, one that envisions female students as responsible, altruistic "members of a great nation" (27). Resolution II, on moral training, which included the study of comparative religions, was justified as contributing to developing a "broad outlook" (28) and "understanding among races and individuals" (28), deemed important to women. Resolution III was defended with an image of girls "fit in health and physique" (31). The resolution on medical examinations was seen as a way for the schools to work with families, the first being the place where disease might be diagnosed, the second, where treatment would be determined. Resolution V, however, supports keeping the family and home as the top priority for girls. It was supported, interestingly, on the basis of the effect of beauty in the home on the development of beauty within, while motherhood was equated with "a loving and protective spirit" (33), and emphasis on fatherhood was suggested but voted down. How interesting to note both that Resolution V also advocates "social service" and that it was followed by a resolution urging an end to child marriage, with its "ruinous" and "disastrous effect" (34). Again support for girls having "a chance to develop all their potentialities" (35) comes through. In a lengthy discussion, some wanted an even stronger version that put more pressure on the government or would include eighteen as the age of consent, while others thought change would only come from the people. Unanimous opposition to purdah was also clear, but accommodating it with special purdah schools was seen as a way to end it. The conference rejected the idea that compulsory education for girls should "wait" until universal education for boys was accomplished. It also came out in support of women's economic independence, discussed because of the resolution on vocational training, beginning with increased wages for primary school teachers. The language in which older students would be taught, and the other languages that would be compulsory and optional, was the most divisive issue, involving as it does concerns of indigenous versus foreign influences, and how important it is that all Indians speak a common tongue and that East-West dialogue (in English, presumably) be promoted.

There was open discussion and dissent in the gathering. Those who opposed religious training, for example, were concerned about how to accommodate different religions and maintain state neutrality on religion. Resolutions were introduced by a variety of individuals and voted on separately at the end of discussion on each. In case after case they considered the impact of recommendations on various populations, those in and out of purdah, those with more and less money, those desiring work outside versus inside the home, those married with husbands supporting them versus those without husbands or unsupported by them, etc. Similarly, they considered what the obstacles to education were for various groups as well as how it could be promoted.

The All India Women's Conference still exists today, and it continues to work for emancipation, education, and empowerment of women. In its nearly one hundred years of advocacy, the AIWC has helped passed the Sarda Act, which raised the age of marriage for girls; the Hindu Code Bills, which standardized legal parent-child relationships; Universal Adult Franchise, allowing all adults to vote; the Factory and Mines Act, which regulated working conditions; and the Maternity Benefits Act, which created maternity leave for working women. It also has consultative status with the UN and has established focus organizations to support needs specific to women and children, including schools and hospitals.[3]

Resolutions

Women representing all communities and races in India, having gathered together in 22 Constituent Conferences in order to express their opinions on education in general in India to-day, and on the education of girls and women in particular and from those Conferences having elected representatives to exchange views in a final All-India Conference of Women on Education Reforms, hereinafter record the result of their serious study of the problems, and express as Resolutions their convictions, based on their practical [. . .] experiences and intuition, regarding the broad general line on which they believe it to be imperative for the good of their children and the future welfare of the Nation that reforms in education should be carried out.

Women are grateful for the immense services rendered to the Indian people by the various educational authorities, official and non-official, in India. The present system, however, was thought out primarily, they believe, in the interest of boys, and was formulated by men. The time has now come for women to review and reform this system. This Conference aims at offering a constructive Programme, through its Memorandum of Resolutions, to those who have already shown a sincere desire to promote the advancement of education.

A. GENERAL
Resolution I: This Conference defines Education as training which will enable the child and the individual to develop his or her latent capacities to their fullest extent, for the service of humanity. It must therefore, include elements for physical, mental, emotional, civic and spiritual development. The courses of study arranged for this purpose must be so flexible as to allow of adaptation to the needs of the individual, the locality and the community. (Passed unanimously)

Resolution II: Moral training, based on spiritual ideals, should be made compulsory for all schools and colleges. (Passed 35–4)

Resolution III: That a complete course of physical training should be compulsory in all boys' and girls' schools, and that it should include as much cheerful recreation out of doors as possible. (Passed unanimously)

Resolution IV: That this Conference is of [the] opinion that systematic medical inspection should be made compulsory in all schools and colleges, and in the case of girls the inspections should [be] carried out by lady doctors. Where possible school clinics should be started. (Passed unanimously)

Resolution V: That in all education of girls in India teaching in the ideals of motherhood and in the making of the home beautiful and attractive, as well as training in social service, should be kept uppermost. (36–3)

Resolution VI: That this Conference deplores the effect of early marriage on education, and demands the raising of the Age of Consent to 16. It urges parents and guardians to see that no marriage takes place before that age.

> Amended version: This Conference deeply deplores the effect of early marriage on education and urges the Government of India to pass legislation making marriage under sixteen a penal offence. It demands that the Age of Consent be raised to 16. It whole-heartedly support[s] as a step to this end SIR HARI SINGH GOUR's Bill which will come before the Assembly this session. It sends a Deputation from its Delegates to the Legislate Assembly to convey to its Members the Demand of women on this vital subject. (Carried unanimously)

Resolution VII: That for girls who observe purdah proper facilities should be provided in purdah education[al] institution. (Passed unanimously)

Resolution VIII: This Conference is of the opinion that the undue importance attached to examinations has greatly hindered the educational progress of pupils and it recommends that investigation be made into the problem of testing knowledge. (Passed unanimously)

B. PRIMARY EDUCATION

Resolution I: That Primary education should be made compulsory for all boys and girls. The present series of vernacular Text-books should be revised, and should be supplemented by illustrated books suitable for children. That facilities and financial provision should be made at the same time in all schemes of compulsion for both boys and girls. That women should be on all Attendance Committees. (Passed unanimously)

Resolution II: That preparatory vocational and manual training should be included in the curriculum suited to the child's needs and daily experience. (Unanimous approval)

Resolution III: That the first essential for improving primary education is that the Scale of salary for primary teachers be raised. That the standard required for the entrance examination for training institutions be also raised and that a better training be provided. That well educated men and women be invited, and afforded opportunities, to act as honorary teachers while the supply of trained teachers is inadequate. (Each sentence passed without opposition, but with some delegates abstaining)

Resolution IV: That special schools for Defectives (Physical, mental and moral) should be established and that private enterprise in this direction should be encouraged and aided by Government. (Passed unanimously)

C. SECONDARY EDUCATION

Resolution I: That the Vernacular should be the medium of instruction, English being a compulsory second subject. (Passed 21–15)

> Amended version: "That Hindi or English might be the compulsory second language." (Lost 24–7)

> Final version: That the Vernacular should be the medium of instruction, English being a compulsory second subject. Hindi or Urdu should be included in the curriculum, and should be an alternative to the classical languages one of which should be compulsory.

Resolution II: That alternative Courses should be established to suit the needs of girls who do not intend to take up college education, these to include Domestic Science, the Fine Arts, Handicrafts and Industries. (Passed unanimously)

Resolution III: That it is desirable that Sex Hygiene be taught in all Secondary Schools and Colleges by competent teachers. (Unanimously passed)

Resolution IV: That separate Middle and High Schools should be established in places where there are no such schools and where a demand for them exists. (Unanimously passed)

D. COLLEGE EDUCATION

Resolution I: That the following subjects should be added as optionals to the present curricula—The Fine Arts, Advanced Domestic Science, Journalism, Social Science and Architecture. (Unanimously supported)

Resolution II: That special encouragement in the way of Scholarships should be offered to women students to attract them to take their Degrees in Law, Medicine, Social Science and the Fine Arts. (Passed unanimously)

> (a): That classes and lectures in literary, industrial and general subjects should be organized for adult women by all women's Associations. (Unanimously passed)

> (b): That the University Extension Scheme should include special courses for women. (Passed unanimously)

Resolution III: That Residential Colleges for women should be established in connection with the Universities. That Hostels for women teachers and students should be aided by Government. (Unanimously agreed to)

Resolution IV: That a Lady Professor be appointed (to act also as Advisor) in all colleges where there are women students. (Unanimously passed)

E. ADULT EDUCATION

Resolution I: That the Mussalman community request the Government to provide teachers to instruct women in their homes.

> Amended version: That this Conference calls on the Government to provide Teachers to instruct purdah women in their homes. (Carried unanimously)

F. GENERAL RECOMMENDATIONS

Resolution I: That the All-India Conference appoints a Standing Committee for the current year to continue the work inaugurated at its first session at Poona, namely, (1) to collect and deal with suggestions on educational matters sent from the Constituent Provinces and States represented at the Conference (and others who later may wish to reap the benefits of this Committee), (2) to make known to each the work done in other parts, (3) to bring public opinion to bear on matters of general educational principle or policy where necessary, and (4) to arrange for the next session of the All-India Women's Conference at Delhi, in February, 1928. (Carried, and Officers and Members of Standing Committees elected)

Resolution II: That all Women's Associations should appoint Educational Committees to continue the work of the All-India Women's First Conference on Educational Reform and to co-operate with all educational institutions in their locality, and report to the Standing Committee of the Conference.

Resolution III: The Women's Conference recommends that Government recognition should be given to successful educational [institutions] which have been working on experimental lines advocated by this Conference (such as the Indian Women's University and others) and which desire such recognition. (Passed unanimously and with acclamation)

Resolution IV: That Indian women Graduates should have a larger number of seats allocated to them on the Senates of all Indian Universities. (Passed unanimously)

Notes

1 All page numbers in this introduction, and the Resolutions below, are from the published conference proceedings, *Call to Action: Extracts from the Speeches & Resolutions at the First Session of the All India Women's Conference—1927*. Copies can be located through WorldCat, www.worldcat.org.
2 Usha Nair, "AIWC at a Glance: The First Twenty-Five Years, 1927–1952." Report for All India Women's Conference, aiwc.org.in. Accessed 2015.
3 All India Women's Conference website, www.aiwc.org.in. Accessed 2015.

37

Resolutions
The Oriental (Eastern) Women's Congress
General Union of Syrian Women
Damascus, Syria
July 1930

The development of a social and political movement referred to as "first wave feminism" in Europe and other regions culturally belonging to the "West" is sufficiently well known, but it was not limited to the "West." In the second half of the nineteenth century and the beginning of the twentieth century women in China, Japan, Persia, Egypt and also the Ottoman Empire developed many activities to improve their position in society.[1]

The first Women's Congress in Damascus, July 1930.

This entry is the only one in the book for which we are dependent on an account of the resolutions of a feminist conference,[2] rather than having the resolutions themselves as part of conference proceedings, etc. It appears that the surviving original source is two accounts in the *International Women's News*, one by Congress president Nour Hamada, the other by Avra Theodoropoulos, an official observer at the Congress for the International Alliance of Women whose imperial stance could hardly be more obvious. There is no conflict in the content of the Resolutions in the two accounts.

The first call for a gathering of "Eastern" women was probably made by Saiza Nabarawi following the 1929 congress of the International Alliance of Women in Berlin, though the main actor organizing the 1930 Congress was Nour Hamada. Approximately one hundred women attended, and they discussed cultural and nationalist topics including "equality in divorce laws, child marriage, labour, education, alcohol, social hygiene, Arabic literature, handicrafts, and national industry."[3]

According to Charlotte Weber, this congress, and that in Teheran in 1932, "in organizing across national boundaries, in seeking recognition from the international women's movement, and above all in articulating a uniquely 'Eastern' framework in which to ground women's rights, . . . tried to create an autonomous women's movement that was allied with but independent from both Middle Eastern male nationalists and Western feminists."[4] The conference marks the first attempt to create an "Eastern" feminist alliance, with Pan-Arab feminist women choosing to work with each other, opposed to Western imperialism and for women's activism. Delegates came from Turkey, Iraq, Syria, Egypt, India, Persia, Afghanistan, Hedjaz (now Saudi Arabia), and Lebanon.

The absence of resolutions on veiling or suffrage is notable. The focus on family matters is clear. This is the earliest document to oppose polygamy, and the second to raise the issue of child marriage (see India 1927). Attention to family does not, however, entail acceptance of whatever is "traditional" in a given time and place. The right to divorce on the same grounds as men and the right of all children to some education inherently change the patriarchal institution to some extent, as does the call for equal employment opportunities.

Resolutions

After long discussions on each subject, the following resolutions were adopted:
- Polygamy. That in all countries where polygamy is legally recognised, it be abolished entirely in all its forms.
- Divorce. That a woman should have the same rights as a man to divorce and under the same conditions.
- Age of Marriage. That the minimum age of marriage be fixed at 16 for girls and 18 for boys, and that child marriage should be abolished by legislation.
- Women's Work. That women should get equal pay with men for equal work, and that all avenues of employment and advancement be equally open to women as to men.
- Education. That compulsory elementary education be established and equally applied to women as to men, and that the law should prohibit the employment of children in industry below the age of 14.

At the end of the Congress the following Commissions were appointed to work between Congresses:—
1. Commission on marriage laws.
2. Commission for social work (cleanliness in towns, prisons, etc.).
3. Commission for the development of national industries and handicrafts.
4. Commission for the encouragement of the study of the Arab language and the propagation of popular books in Arabic.

Notes
1 Nicole Van Os, "Ottoman Muslim and Turkish Women in an International Context." *European Review* 13.3 (2005): 459.
2 Nour Hamada, "The Oriental Women's Congress in Damascus: The President's Report." *International Women's News,* Sept. 1930, pp. 189–90.
3 Hamada, p. 189.
4 "Between Nationalism and Feminism: The Eastern Women's Congresses of 1930 and 1932." *Journal of Middle East Women's Studies* 4.1 (Winter 2008): 83.

38

Statement of Purpose *and* How to Organize
Free Women (Mujeres Libres)
Madrid and Barcelona, Spain
May 1936

Mujeres Libres poster, c. 1936.

Mujeres Libres was formed in revolutionary Spain to end the "triple enslavement of women, to ignorance, to capital, and to men." Founded by Lucía Sánchez Saornil, Mercedes Comaposada, and Amparo Poch y Gascón, the group wanted to empower working-class women who were participating in the Libertarian, anarchist cause. These women believed a separate women's group was necessary to support the anarchist movement because men did not listen to or take seriously women's voices in the main anarchist groups, CNT and FAI. The group in Madrid joined with a similar group, Grupo Cultural Feminino, founded by Soledad Estroach in Barcelona, in May 1936, and Mujeres Libres was born.

The aim of the main anarchist groups in the Spanish Civil War was to give the power to the people, especially in large industries and agriculture, to cut out middlemen and administrators so the workers would benefit more directly. In some areas, these practices worked for almost ten months. Although the women of Mujeres Libres supported these successes, they were also very interested in educating working women, not only in literacy but also in equality. They did not necessarily identify as feminist but saw women's equality as an essential part of solving the social problems rampant in revolutionary Spain. Their two main goals were to raise awareness about women's equality and to directly act to make women equal with men in the anarchist movement. In order to accomplish these goals, Mujeres Libres reported on sexist behavior, established day-care centers, produced a journal called *Mujeres Libres*, and set up classes for literacy, technical skills, and social studies. In Barcelona, the group also created a lying-in hospital that provided pre- and postnatal care, classes on "child and maternal health, birth control, and sexuality."[1]

Different sources report between twenty and thirty thousand active members in Mujeres Libres during the Spanish Civil War.[2] These women took classes, taught each other, and worked together to establish equality in their homes and in public. Although the Republicans lost the Civil War, the role of women was culturally changed in Spain, and complete public segregation of the sexes was no longer expected or enforced.[3]

Given the three forms of subordination women experience, as uneducated, female workers, Mujeres Libres focused on education as a path to ending the other forms of servitude. Their purposes,[4] as stated here, center on creating educational opportunities to help develop awareness and intelligence in the women who would benefit from an anarchist revolution. Their goals include making women more conscientious, responsible, connected, powerful, and effective. The document here also reveals some daily realities of women's lives at the time, and how to use anarchist organizing strategies to move beyond those limits. It is an early document briefly addressing fascism and refugees, as well.

Statement of Purpose

I. To emancipate women from the triple slavery to which they have often been, and are still, subjected: the slavery of ignorance, the slavery of being female, and economic slavery.

II. To make our Organization a conscious and responsible feminine force in society, acting creatively in the vanguard of the revolutionary movement.

III. To combat ignorance by providing our *compañeras* with social and cultural education through basic classes, conferences, talks, interactive lectures, film projections, etc.

IV. To establish relationships with Unions, municipal Arts & Sciences Associations, and Libertarian Youth chapters in order to design more synchronized mechanisms among us, thereby invigorating the revolutionary movement. For example, a Union sends a compañera to a group of our Organization, where she can receive basic instruction as well as expand her social consciousness through her contact with more experienced, older compañeras. Once she is ready, this younger compañera enters a municipal Arts & Sciences Association or a chapter of the Libertarian Youth.

V. To achieve a real camaraderie among our sisters and brothers: to live together and work together, without excluding anyone. To unite our energies in our common endeavors.

VI. To make possible a powerful female contribution to our creative revolutionary work, offering our services as nurses, teachers, doctors, artists, chemists, childcare experts, and intelligent workers. This is much more effective than ignorant good will alone.

How to Organize a Free Women Group
Have You Heard of Our Groups?
Perhaps you don't know who we are, *compañera*. Let us introduce ourselves to you. Among the questions, What is the group like? How does it work? and, What are your goals? This last question is likely the most important to you. So we'll start there.

The Free Women Organization proposes the following:

1st. To emancipate women from the triple slavery to which they have often been, and are still, subjected: the slavery of ignorance, the slavery of being female, and economic slavery.

2nd. To make our Organization a conscious and responsible feminine force in society, acting creatively in the vanguard of the revolutionary movement.

3rd. To achieve a real camaraderie among our sisters and brothers: to live together and work together, without excluding anyone. To unite our energies in our common endeavors.

In order to achieve these aims, our organization creates schools, academies, and libraries; it organizes conferences, talks, lectures, etc. In other words, the Organization is involved in awakening women's interest about social issues, encouraging in women a spirit for remaking customs and improving women's circumstances.

We think that you, our reader, likely feel some concern about these things. The fact that you have decided to look at these pages tells us that. We would like to work with your intrigued spirit to address causes that will benefit us all.

Do you live in a town where women have been relegated to hidden, insignificant lives, thought of as little more than helpful objects, dedicated exclusively to housework and to the care of the family? No doubt you have thought uneasily about these things. Likely, when you think of the freedom that your brothers, the men of the house, have enjoyed you have felt some sadness about having been born a woman. We would guess that at some time you've suffered when, attempting to speak your opinion about a matter that you understood clearly while those around you were having trouble understanding, you've been told sourly, "What are you doing? You belong in the kitchen!" Are we wrong? No, we are certain that this has happened to you. Maybe you even wished, even if timidly for fear of what people might say, to leave it all behind and create a new life for yourself, on your own. Is this accurate?

The Free Women work against all of this, against what you've been told to suffer. We want you to have the same freedom as your brothers. No one has the right to look at you with contempt; you have a right to have your voice heard with the same respect as your father's. We want you to be able to attain, without worrying about others' opinions, that independent life that at some point you desired.

Keep in mind that everything requires effort; things don't happen automatically. To achieve these goals you will need the help of your *compañeras*. You need others who want similar things in life. You need to find support in them, and they need to find support in you. In a word, you need community. You need a group of women. If you would like, we can help you and guide you with our experience. Our organization is called Free Women.

How You Can Organize a Free Women Group in Your Town
Are you seriously interested in this idea? Then let's get started.

With our experience, we have a notion of the things you might be thinking. You might ask yourself, How could I even go about this? Read patiently, we'll explain.

Surely you know some young women of more or less your age. Naturally, you get along with some better than others. These preferences aren't random; rather they're the result of having things in common: things you enjoy, tastes, ways of thinking. What if you were to talk with these friends, to read or communicate this document to them? Surely you all would be in agreement and want to start a Group.

So now you have a small Group. They ask you, What do we do now?

Are there three of you, four? Let's say it's small, just three. But all of you are ready to get to work.

You can start by thinking about what could be the most interesting project for the largest number of young women in your town. Let's see. Certainly, more than one of your compañeras has a brother, a cousin, or a boyfriend fighting on the front lines, and if you spoke with these young women about improving the situation for those young men, they would soon join you. Try it! Some afternoon, a Sunday maybe when you don't have to work, speak with these girls. You can say something like this:

"In this town we have six or seven (however many there are) boys on the front lines. In other places (this is true) the girls take care of them, helping make their lives more bearable. Maybe the boys don't have tobacco, or they lack paper and pencils to write to their families. They really suffer because, while they are there fighting for our lives, it feels to them that nobody thinks of them, that no one feels gratitude. We could get together weekly. 10 cents, 20 cents, even 1 *real* per week will not break our wallets. By creating a common fund from these fees, we could periodically buy something for our comrades on the front: some tobacco, a piece of candy, a trinket. We could write cards to them, signed by all of us or with all our names. They will see that we care about their health, their needs. It would do them so much good."

If it's necessary, make your meetings not only for young *compañeras*. You can also invite older *compañeras*, to give the meeting more gravity.

Speak kindly to the girls and bring the warmth of generosity to your work. Remind them of the sacrifices that the soldiers make while we live in peace in the rearguard, living our day-to-day, having our neighborhood arguments. Surely you will win them over.

But, of course, the Group cannot do just this and no more. Or, maybe this is not the best way to start a Group because your town has no one on the front lines, or sadly, because people just don't care or pay attention. In that case, you should look for another common interest that can attract the attention of your *compañeras*.

It's clear that you know how to read because you are doing it now. Do you have at least one friend who also can read? Then let's get started. In your town there are some girls, more than just one or two, who haven't received much education. Start there. Offer to teach them what you know, even if you just know a little bit. Teach them and be patient. This will be an exercise for you all to learn more and better. No doubt you will find many girls who are willing to learn. This is, of course, only a beginning. Later, if you keep working earnestly, you will receive teachers and anything else you need from us.

Don't forget for a moment to stay in contact with us, the National Committee of the Federation of Free Women. We will send you our materials and literature, direct you, help resolve your dilemmas, and if necessary send a *compañera* to aid you.

As you, new *compañera*, can see, it's not so difficult to gather a good number of girls together when you know how to manage yourself with a little bit of skill. We will be here to guide you.

Organize a Committee

Do you already have ten *compañeras* together? Then you can organize a Committee. A Committee is a group of *compañeras* in charge of the following: arranging—*not commanding*—the activities of the Group, establishing relationships with other bodies, studying the means of spreading our aims, and addressing other issues that may arise.

Let's go over how a Committee is formed.

First, you will need a Secretary. Make sure that the person named to this position has the most knowledge of reading and writing, since she will have to read and write many letters.

The Secretary will be in charge of communicating directly, in the Group's name, with other organizations. In meetings, she will guide discussions so that they don't turn messy. She will have the final word, but she should never forget one thing: being Secretary does not give her any rights over the others. On the contrary, she must listen attentively and openly always, paying attention to the suggestions, ideas, and even the complaints of all.

After the Secretary, name the Vice-secretary. Her mission is to help the Secretary, to stand in when the Secretary is absent, and to provide the minutes from the Committee's meetings. To take minutes is to write down the agreements made during the meeting in an organized way.

The Bookkeeper, whom you should also appoint, is in charge of receiving dues or fees, and of recording all income. She will carefully write the origin of the income—dues, donations, etc. The income will be given to the Treasurer.

The Treasurer will always provide to the Bookkeeper a receipt that corresponds to the amounts in question. The Treasurer will use a book similar to the Bookkeeper's to balance the accounts. If both compañeras do their jobs correctly, both books will have the same balances. The Treasurer is always accountable for the group's funds, and will never pay out any funds unless she has the "Stamp of Approval" of the Bookkeeper, as well as a receipt.

Now that we have the Administrative Area of the Committee set up, the next step is to study what activities the Group can do in its local context, and how many *compañeras* are needed for these activities. The heads of each Area will be the representatives of the Committee and each will have a specific mission.

Since we have said that you are no more than ten, and we have already appointed four, we only have six *compañeras* left. Let's see what we can do.

In your town as in all towns, one feels the war in a thousand different ways. Yours *could be* the only place where there are no speculators (unscrupulous businessmen), but we highly doubt it. Those people try to take advantage of the difficult circumstances to fatten their wallets.

Another thing that you have surely seen is that you have refugees in your town. One of your *compañeras*, then, can be in charge of Community Assistance. She will find out why certain provisions are in short supply in town, and if someone is hiding these provisions, she should report him or her to the authorities. At the same time, she will make sure the refugees are well taken care of, that they lack nothing. The refugees have already suffered enough by having to abandon their homes. Many of them have also left their families without knowing if they will ever see their loved ones again.

Caring for these people is a very delicate task, so the *compañera* in charge of Community Assistance should try hard to free herself from the smallness of local pride that makes one feel bothered by the refugees, thinking that they are disturbing, changing the rhythm of town life. A member of Free Women should feel equally bound to all anti-fascists. She should endeavor to understand justice well, not allowing herself to be swayed by outdated ideas or by friendships that lead her away from reason. We will keep in mind the fundamental reasons our *compañeras* created our Organization: they felt the need to break with the stifling and narrow life that was inherited and imposed upon them throughout the generations.

Another of the tasks of the Community Assistant is to make sure the doctor fulfills his or her obligations, that no infirm individual is left without care, that no child or refugee is treated poorly by anyone or obliged to work in gross excess.

All of these, and other functions that arise in her day-to-day work, will be included in the scope of the Community Assistant. The *compañera* nominated for this post need not be intimidated by the scale of her work. She doesn't have to solve all of the problems personally. Rather, she will bring issues and ideas to the Committee, based on what she observes in her work. Together, the Committee will study the issues and ideas in order to find solutions. Then, the Community Assistant will carry out the Committee's decisions.

That is probably enough for now about the Community Assistant. Let's keep going.

It wouldn't be a bad idea to have a post, an Aid for Combatants. Remember what we said at the beginning about common points of interest. One could organize a festival in the town to raise funds, and with that money buy things for the boys at the front. You could announce times to collect things for them in the neighborhoods. Give gifts to the comrades who come home on leave. There are a thousand things that could be done to create ties between the front and the rearguard, fostering a good relationship and mutual understanding between the two. The first task, though, is to obtain a list of the names and locations of the comrades who are in the front lines, and to keep the list up-to-date as they are transferred and move to new locations.

If this job is done well, it can be of utmost importance for your group's happy coexistence with townspeople, who can feel that they are involved in, and affected by, the work you are doing.

We would bet that the town where you live, dear *compañera*, is of some size and has some shops, a factory, or other places of employment. Therefore, it would make sense to create an Area of Work. The *compañera* who is nominated to head this position will be in charge of visiting the Union. Her goal there will be to influence the Union to make sure there is space for a group of women—that you already have gathered or will gather—to learn to work in the Union's corresponding industry. In other words, you will work so that the factories or other places of employment will admit a certain number of female trainees that you will have ready. This is important since, soon, there will be very few men available to work because they are needed at the front. Without women workers, the national economy may not survive. These *compañeras*, whose names and personal information the woman in charge of the Area of Work will record as is necessary, will go to the factory daily. The head of Work will determine the necessary amount of time required for training at the factory. The *compañeras* training in the factories will understand that training will be unpaid, that they are performing a social service that is imperative if the war is to be won. You must make sure they know that what they are doing now, on their own accord, is something that they will have to do tomorrow anyway, but under the unforgiving command of the Government. It can only benefit them to be ahead of the game. If we follow this plan, in a relatively short amount of time, these women can be ready to contribute effectively in all of the areas of production and distribution in the New Society.

And now let's talk about the most important part of the Committee in every town, large or small: Culture.

This Area is fundamental, so it is vital that the *compañera* in charge of it be in continual contact with the National Cultural Council of Free Women, which in turn will send initiatives and guidance at all times. Our immediate goals regarding culture are that all of our *compañeras* in the Local Groups are able to read and write very soon. Without excluding anyplace or anyone, short classes teaching specialties should be created according to the needs of each town: for example poultry farming, rabbit breeding, horticulture, etc. in the rural areas.

Finally, our last crucial Area is Propaganda.

For this task we need a *compañera* who is poised and proactive, someone who can hand out manifestos, put up posters on the street, sell newspapers and pamphlets, organize parties and speeches. Her job encompasses everything that could help people become familiar with our Groups, while simultaneously raising interest in them.

In the larger towns, another interesting Area could be created: Sports. We don't mean to say that smaller locales may not be interested in sports, but that it would be more difficult to organize sports there. We will leave our instructions for forming this Area for another publication. Those who are interested can contact the National Committee.

We find ourselves now with a Committee composed of the following areas: Administration, four *compañeras*; Community Assistance, one; Assistant to the War Effort and Combatants, one; Work, one; Culture, one; and Propaganda, one. In the occasion that your town requires the area of Work, this adds up to nine *compañeras*. Since we said that there were ten to start with, we should make sure all ten can contribute. So we will add another person to the area of Propaganda, which is likely to give us lots of work.

All of the Committee's programs have been allotted. In your Group, all decisions are made in common, then each *compañera* will carry out her work and duties according to her post. But don't forget, this is very important, *don't worry* about your doubts and problems. You can send a letter to the Committee nearest yours, and surely you will find solutions from their experience.

Now it's time to work zealously. If you do, you will have soon gained the affection of the town, and the Group will keep growing. If the soldiers know they are being aided, if the townspeople feel defended by your rigorous position of justice against any attack, if the girls learn, if everyone sees that you are working with faith and sacrificing yourselves for the war effort and the common good, have no doubt that your town will be on your side and help you grow.

Within very little time you may have to expand your Committee. It won't be enough to have just one *compañera* per Area, you'll need two or three, or more.

Dear friend, you don't yet know how good it feels to work toward the common good. Every sacrifice, every obstacle that you overcome is an incomparable pleasure, a unique joy like none other. Try to make it happen. Write to the Committee that is closest to your town today, to the Provincial, Regional, or National Committee of Free Women. We will help you.

Work for the Revolution: toward progress for your town and toward your own emancipation. We look forward to receiving your letter. All the best.

THE NATIONAL COMMITTEE

Notes

1 "Mujeres Libres." *Works Solidarity* no. 54, June 1998. flag.blackened.net/revolt.

2 "Mujeres Libres," last modified June 24, 2017. *Wikipedia*, www.wikipedia.org.

3 Martha Ackelsberg, "'Separate and Equal'? Mujeres Libres and Anarchist Strategy for Women's Emancipation." *Feminist Studies* 11.1 (1985): 63–83.

4 Translated by Madeleine Brink. We have chosen to maintain the Spanish word "*compañera/as*" throughout this document, since it maintains the fraternal connotation of equality of all humans (comrades), while also designating the female comrades in particular with the "*a/as*" ending, compañera/as. Also, note that one *real* equals twenty-five cents, or one quarter of a *peseta*.

39

Australian Woman's Charter
Australian Women's Conference for Victory in War and Victory in Peace
Sydney, New South Wales, Australia
November 19–22, 1943

Jessie Street, prominent Australian suffragist.

Despite wartime restrictions on travel, representatives of ninety-one women's organizations met to discuss postwar reconstruction, especially issues that would affect women and children. Concerned about having a say in postwar planning, the authors of this document[1] argue that winning the peace requires "the Government to make fuller use of the vision, enthusiasm, practical wisdom and capabilities of women in the planning of reconstruction." The groups present ranged from housewives' associations to the Communist Party, and from the Women's Christian Temperance Union to the Jewish Red Cross Society. They hailed from New South Wales, Queensland, Victoria, Tasmania, South Australia, and West Australia. The Charter was produced at the conference, which was organized by Jessie Street, pictured in figure 39.1, and other members of the United Associations of Women.

The document critiques the status quo on three grounds:

[T]he indispensable contribution that women make to all phases of human life is at present inadequately recognised; . . . they are not accorded the same status, opportunities, responsibilities and rewards as are accorded to men in the community; and . . . they are submitted to many discriminations and limitations imposed on account of their sex.

At this particular historic moment, the authors believe, "[W]omen have earned the right and proven themselves capable to take an active and comprehensive part in every aspect of the making of peace and the subsequent planning and control which will be necessary to win lasting peace." The call for women to have an equal role in peacemaking and reconstruction, we have seen, goes back at least to 1915.

The Charter envisions a postwar Australia that includes women in greater numbers in both elective and appointed offices, the latter a new concern and essential to what is sometimes called "state feminism" in Australia. Sex discrimination would be illegal, as would unequal pay or unequal opportunity "in the professions, in the Public Service, in industry." Domestic work, done in one's own home or for others, gets attention, as does the desire and need of women to hold onto jobs that wartime exigencies allowed them to take on. Trade unions are applauded for admitting women and working for them. Research is urged in many areas, including on "educational problems" and to gather statistics regarding "women wage-earners, breadwinners, grade of occupation, rate of wages, age, conjugal conditions, number of persons wholly or partly supported and relationship to breadwinners." Other issues addressed include the needs of Aboriginal and rural women, and childcare.

The most radical element in the document may be the argument for paying mothers:

> We believe the indispensable service rendered to the community by mothers, accompanied as it is by inevitable and specific handicaps, and responsibilities, demands special consideration and provision; We further believe that economic independence strengthens character and develops a greater sense of responsibility, whereas dependent economic status denies liberty and opportunity and justice to the individual. In order to alleviate these disabilities, we recommend that the mother and/or homemaker be remunerated for her work in the home.

This is the first explicit mention of "wages for housework," though, as noted, the 1907 Conference of Socialist Women addresses maternal compensation. Other relatively novel and progressive elements include attention to services for cognitively impaired children and adults, support for sex education, and attention to adult education as well as to that of children, which should include teaching about "the causes of war and the foundations of peace." The most conservative element in the document, on the other hand, is the unfortunate support for "the removal of obstacles to early marriage," an issue that relates to concerns about increasing the population.

After the conference, twenty thousand copies of the Charter booklet were distributed in Australia and overseas. The Australian Women's Charter Movement provided concrete follow-up activity based on the resolutions. Too, state conferences were organized, charter deputations lobbied members of the federal parliament on specific points, and a follow-up conference was organized in 1946.[2]

Australian Woman's Charter

(1) WOMAN IN WAR AND PEACE.

This Australian Women's Conference, representing every State and 90 organisations in the Commonwealth, called after four years of war, affirms its unshakeable belief that the hopes of all women for a world in which justice and liberty and equality will exist depends entirely upon winning the war and eradicating Fascism in any form in every country.

Therefore this Conference calls upon every woman to take her full share in the war effort by either enlisting in the defence forces, undertaking work on the land or in industry, or enrolling as a voluntary worker, and by subscribing to war loans.

This Conference further affirms its belief that if we are to win the peace it is necessary to plan for peace while carrying on the war, and while noting with satisfaction the action of the Government in creating a Ministry of Reconstruction, exhorts the Government to make fuller use of the vision, enthusiasm, practical wisdom and capabilities of women in the planning of reconstruction.

(2) WOMAN IN PUBLIC LIFE.

The Australian Women's Conference affirms its belief that women have a special contribution to make in public life, as citizens of a democratic community, and in order that their capabilities may be developed and utilised for the national good.

We recommend that
  a. every encouragement should be given to women to stand as candidates for all elected legislative bodies;
  b. women be appointed in adequate numbers to national and international conferences, diplomatic posts, to administrative positions of authority and responsibility, and on boards, commission, etc.

(3) WOMEN AT THE PEACE CONFERENCE.

Whereas in every country women have taken a full share in their country's struggle to win the war, and in all the war centres shared the dangers and privations of war and have shown courage, resource and endurance;

This Australian Women's Conference affirms its belief that women have earned the right and proven themselves capable to take an active and comprehensive part in every aspect of the making of peace and the subsequent planning and control which will be necessary to win lasting peace.

We declare that qualified Australian women with full status as delegates should be included in sufficient numbers to participate effectively in the delegation attending the peace settlement as representatives of the Australian people.

(4) EQUAL STATUS, OPPORTUNITY, RESPONSIBILITY AND REWARD.

Whereas the indispensable contribution that women make to all phases of human life is at present inadequately recognised; and

Whereas they are not accorded the same status, opportunities, responsibilities and rewards as are accorded to men in the community; and

Whereas they are submitted to many discriminations and limitations imposed on account of their sex; and

Whereas it has been found to be essential to develop the capabilities of women and to utilise the resources of woman power in order to achieve victory in war; and

Whereas it will be equally necessary to continue the development and utilise the potential capacity of women in the post-war period in order to achieve victory in peace;

Therefore, this Australian Women's Conference affirms the need for the immediate application of the principle of equality as between men and women in all laws and regulations.

(5) EQUAL RIGHTS LEGISLATION.

Whereas past history and contemporary conditions demonstrate that many laws, regulations and statements purporting to confer rights, status and opportunity on all people are, in fact, only applied to male persons;

We request the Commonwealth Government to introduce a Blanket Bill, designed to abolish sex discrimination and to establish and maintain equality for all citizens without distinctions based on sex, and to provide that any sex discriminations embodied in any laws or regulations be invalid;

We further request the Commonwealth Government that when the Referendum is held for the amendment to the Constitution an amendment shall be submitted to provide that women shall be entitled to equal rights, status and opportunity with men, and to provide that any sex discrimination embodied in any laws or regulations be invalid.

(6) EMPLOYMENT AND SOCIAL SECURITY.

We believe that a progressive and democratic society should guarantee economic security by providing employment, education, health services, and adequate maintenance during illness and old age for all its members.

We therefore request the Commonwealth Government to survey the needs, resources and labour power of the community, to develop and implement a plan to provide employment, educational and health services for all, and to care for all persons in old age, ill-health and unemployment.

We further believe that it is vital to the interests of the community as a whole that we should achieve demobilisation without unemployment.

We therefore request the Commonwealth Government

a. to plan training and employment with the object of absorbing the men and women in the Services and in the war industries into useful occupations;

b. to pay a wage to persons, irrespective of sex, awaiting employment, on a scale which will enable them and their dependents to maintain a reasonable standard of living;

c. to pay particular attention to the 200,000 women newly employed in industry in response to the war emergency situation who may need or wish to continue in paid employment.

(7) EMPLOYMENT OF WOMEN, WAGE EARNERS AND PROFESSIONAL WOMEN.

We believe that the standard of living of the whole community is threatened, and animosity between men and women wage-earners is engendered by cheap female labour within the community.

We believe that experience has shown that whenever women have been given the opportunity to do work previously performed by men in the professions, in the Public Service, in industry, etc., they have proved themselves capable of measuring up to the established standards.

We recommend that

a. there should be no sex discrimination limiting the opportunities for women, and that they should be given equal pay, equal status, equal opportunity and equal responsibility with men in all appointments and spheres of employment;

b. all restrictions be abolished on the right of women to work (a) at night, (b) in any specific occupation, (c) at any particular period, and (d) when they marry;

c. in all laws and awards, adult female labour should be classified with adult labour instead of being classified with the labour of young persons;

d. all sex discrimination in the Public Service be eliminated and the principle established throughout the Public Service of equal pay and equal opportunity for men and women;

e. the Government eliminate in its plans for training for post-war employment the sex discrimination introduced by fixing lower rates of sustenance allowance for women than men, and give to men and women the same rates of sustenance allowance;

f. canteen services be provided in all industrial establishments where the number of employees is in excess of 250;

g. provision be made for domestic workers in private homes to obtain an award governing their wages and conditions.

(8) WOMEN'S EMPLOYMENT BOARD AND AMENDMENT TO COMMONWEALTH CONCILIATION AND ARBITRATION ACT.

We record our appreciation of the action of the Commonwealth Government in appointing the Women's Employment Board to assess the value and standard of women's work as compared with the work of men, thus for the first time affording women the opportunity to justify their claim for equal pay.

We urge the Commonwealth Government to pass the necessary legislation or regulation to direct the Women's Employment Board to proceed immediately with the complete elimination of sex differentiation in all wage raises for women coming within its jurisdiction.

We believe that the evidence given before the Board has shown that women have earned the right to equal pay and equal opportunity; and

We request the Commonwealth Government to implement the policy of equal pay by amending the Commonwealth Conciliation and Arbitration Act, 1904–32, to provide that the basic wage for females shall be the same as the basic wage for males.

(9) TRAINED NURSES.

In view of the long and arduous period of training which must be undertaken by nurses, and in view of their indispensable services to the community,

We recommend,

a. that the status of nurses be raised by granting them higher rates of pay, a shorter working day with consecutive hours on duty, and better living conditions;

b. that the status of qualified trained nurses be protected by enacting legislation to prohibit the use of the title of "nurse" by other than registered nurses;

c. that the nurse's veil be registered as the official uniform of a registered nurse and that none other than registered nurses be permitted to wear the nurse's veil;

d. that the nursing staff in public hospitals be represented on the Board of their hospital by a representative or representatives nominated and elected by the nurses;

e. that nurses when off duty be permitted the same independence and freedom of movement as are accorded to other workers.

(10) TRADE UNIONS AND WOMEN'S EMPLOYMENT.

We record our recognition of the vital part played by the Trade Unions in moulding and controlling the conditions of employment in the community.

We congratulate those Trade Unions which have granted women members equal rights with men members in the organisation and administration of the Union.

We record our appreciation of the pressure brought to bear by the Trade Unions for the maintenance of the Women's Employment Board and of the consistent advocacy by the Unions of higher wages and better working conditions for women.

We request the Trade Unions to press for the immediate implementation of the policy of equal pay for men and women in all occupations.

We recommend that all women's organisations working for the improvement of the status of women workers co-operate with the Trade Unions in all campaigns for the betterment of the conditions and wages of women workers.

(11) SERVICEWOMEN.

As special provision is made for the wives, children and other dependents of Servicemen,

We recommend that

a. Servicewomen, including the Nursing Service, be granted the same status, pay, dependents' allowances and other benefits and opportunities afforded to Servicemen of equivalent rank;

b. Servicewomen under 21 years of age be granted the same pay and status as servicemen under 21 years of age.

(12) VOLUNTARY WORKERS.

As the spirit of fellowship and co-operation which is so essential to progress is fostered by the common interest and common effort of persons working together,

We recommend that

a. provision be made to give ample scope to the initiative and energies of voluntary workers to take a full part in the great work of reconstruction that must follow the war;

b. opportunities be made available for women who wish to continue giving voluntary services to assist in welfare work in association with other voluntary workers, but not in competition with paid employment, in order that they should not undermine the conditions of paid workers.

(13) WOMAN AS MOTHER AND/OR HOME-MAKER.

We believe the indispensable service rendered to the community by mothers, accompanied as it is by inevitable and specific handicaps, and responsibilities, demands special consideration and provision;

We further believe that economic independence strengthens character and develops a greater sense of responsibility, whereas dependent economic status denies liberty and opportunity and justice to the individual.

In order to alleviate these disabilities, we recommend that

    a. the mother and/or home-maker be remunerated for her work in the home by a personal endowment of a minimum of 30/- [shillings] a week, operated on the same principle as Child Endowment.

    b. the existing system of Child Endowment apply to all dependent children in a family and be increased to an adequate sum.

(14) HEALTH.

As it is to the advantage of the community as a whole that the health of every man, woman and child should be developed and maintained at the maximum standard, and as many factors are responsible for undermining the health of the community,

We recommend to the Commonwealth Government that

    a. a comprehensive health programme be adopted that will take into consideration the part that economic security, satisfactory occupation, proper housing, nutrition and education standards play in the maintenance of the health of the community;

    b. a nationally-planned comprehensive system of free health services, including medical, dental and hospital treatment and provision of free medical examinations, be developed;

    c. an adequate system of free pre-natal and baby clinics and maternity hospitals and nursing services be developed;

    d. such preventive health measures as child welfare, general hygiene, industrial hygiene and immunisation services be extended;

    e. regular medical and psychological supervision and advice be provided for all children during their pre-school and school life, so that variations can be observed and dealt with as early as possible;

    f. hospital construction and equipment be extended, especially for maternity cases, for sufferers from tuberculosis and mental diseases, and for the chronically ill and infirm;

    g. an adequate number of institutions and special schools, including handicraft centres and farm colonies, be provided for mentally retarded and mentally defective adults and children;

    h. special sanatoria be provided for the treatment of incipient nervous cases of women;

    i. at least one-third of the members of the Board of any hospital or health institution or committee be women;

    j. an intensive government campaign be developed and maintained for the education of the public in all matters pertaining to health;

    k. the public be educated in the early signs of disease, especially tuberculosis, cancer and venereal disease, and that additional diagnostic clinics, X-ray units and pathological laboratories be established wherever required;

    l. the exchange of medical certificates by persons about to marry be made compulsory, provided that there shall be no interference with the existing rights of any persons to marry;

    m. medical students and nurses be given the most up-to-date gynaecological training.

(15) EDUCATION.

As it is of paramount importance for the future development of Australia that the potential capacities of every man, woman and child should be developed to the maximum,

We recommend that

a. nation-wide plans on an adequate scale be developed by the Federal Government to provide free schools, technical and cultural colleges and Universities, sports and recreational facilities for all children, youths and adults;

b. academic and technical training be designed to fit the students to meet the expanding needs of modern community life;

c. schools of all grades include in their curricula the teaching of the principles of the Atlantic Charter, the causes of war and the foundations of peace;

d. nature study, elementary biology, anatomy, hygiene, nutrition and physical development be introduced into the curricula of all schools;

e. a widespread public campaign of health, recreation and culture be organised by the educational authorities by means of films, radio, press, posters, leaflets and lectures;

f. Governments provide on a much more generous scale than at present teachers, buildings and equipment in schools;

g. the Commonwealth Government set up and endow generously a committee on the lines of the British Council for the Encouragement of National Art to carry out a nation-wide cultural education campaign and to provide libraries, national theatres, film libraries and facilities for artistic and cultural appreciation and achievement;

h. the Commonwealth Government set up a body for research into educational problems and for publicising new ideas and developments in educational principles and practices;

i. more holiday homes and holiday camps be established by the Government for the purpose of providing country vacations for city children;

j. full provision be made for regional sharing of control and responsibility in the above matters in order to develop the maximum local interest and pride in cultural achievement.

(16) HOUSING.

We believe that the moral and physical well-being of the community is adversely affected by bad housing conditions.

We recommend that

a. adequate national housing and slum-clearance plans, as part of national town-planning schemes, be formulated by the Commonwealth authorities, and that the building of homes be commenced immediately;

b. Federal and State authorities co-operate with local regional boards in the execution of the national plan;

c. the Government fix a reasonable minimum standard of home for town and country in regard to size, area and equipment and that no building below this standard be permitted;

d. the services of women be fully employed in official capacities in planning, developing and administering housing schemes;

e. the Commonwealth Government makes funds available from the Commonwealth Band for (a) building homes at low rental for those who do not desire to purchase them; (b) providing loans at a service rate of interest for the purchase of homes; (c) assisting genuine co-operative building societies;

f. fares be zoned in order to encourage home-building in the outer suburbs of cities;

g. industry be decentralised and linked up with local housing and town-planning schemes;

h. homes for aged married people be built so that they may live together instead of being sent to separate institutions.

(17) COMMUNITY CENTRES.

As education is a continuous, living process essential to the adult as well as the child; and

As art, culture, leisure and recreation will train the citizen in constructive self-expression and social responsibility;

We recommend that the Federal and State Governments establish as part of their post-war reconstruction programme, Community Centres, wherever needed, equipped with public libraries, auditoria, playgrounds, nursery schools, community kitchens, meetings rooms and other facilities, and provide that the Education Departments, the local Councils and elected citizen bodies in each State co-operate on a regional basis in the administration of such Centres in order to develop local interest to the maximum.

(18) CHILD CARE.

As experience has shown that the mental and physical well-being of children is developed, and delinquency prevented by the existence of day nursery and nursery schools and supervised playground facilities,

We recommend the Commonwealth Government to

a. establish a National Children's Bureau with Headquarters at Canberra, under the aegis of either the Department of Reconstruction, of Health, or of Social Services to

  (i)   formulate a National Programme for promoting the welfare of children;
  (ii) assemble information from scientific sources;
  (iii) interpret this information for the public;
  (iv) disseminate this information throughout the Commonwealth;
  (v)   educate systematically public opinion in the best standards of child care;

b. subsidise a national scheme for the establishment of a network of child centres wherever needed and provide that Education Department, local Councils and elected citizens bodies in each State co-operate in the development and administration of these Centres in order to develop local interest and effort to the maximum.

(19) BIRTHRATE.

This Conference is of the opinion that an increase in the birthrate is of vital importance to Australia, and that the low birthrate is largely attributable to lack of economic security, of adequate housing, and of facilities for the care of babies and children to relieve the mother of the continuous care and strain of a young family;

We recommend

a. the removal of obstacles to early marriage;

b. the guaranteeing of economic security (as outlined in Resolutions on "Employment and Economic Security" and "Woman as Mother and/or Home-maker");

c. the provision of suitable family homes;

d. adequate child endowment;

e. provision of day nurseries, nursery schools and supervised playgrounds in all residential areas;

f. safeguarding maternal health;

g. the development of a baby nurses' scheme through baby clinics which would make casual nursing service available to parents of families.

(20) ALCOHOL.

We believe that the abuse of alcohol is an important contributing cause of poverty, disease, immorality and crime;

We recommend that

a. every community shall have the democratic right restored to them to vote whether alcoholic liquour shall, or shall not, be sold in their district;

b. direct or indirect advertising of alcoholic beverages be prohibited;

c. an educational publicity campaign be directed against the evils of indulgence in alcohol, through the schools, Press, radio and other agencies.

(21) MORAL STANDARDS.

Whereas the experiences of many countries over the last 100 years has demonstrated that the regulation of prostitution encourages vices, stimulates the white slave traffic, creates a false sense of security from venereal infection, and imposes cruel injustice and humiliation upon the women concerned while allowing men to go free; and

Whereas the economic inequality of women tends to lower their dignity and status;

Therefore we declare our unswerving opposition to the licensing of vice by the registration of prostitution, registration of brothels, or any other form of regulation, including the compulsory examination and detention of women on suspicions, and

We recommend

a. an equal moral standard for men and women;

b. a widespread publicity campaign on (i) the need for early treatment of sufferers from venereal disease; (ii) the causes of venereal disease such as promiscuous sex relation, ignorance about sex matters, bad housing, economic insecurity, the existence of undesirable places of amusement, abuse of the use and sale of alcohol, etc.;

c. that sufferers from venereal disease be under the supervision of officers of the Health Department assisted by social workers and almoners, instead of the Police Department;

d. the provision of adequate facilities for the free and secret treatment of venereal disease;

e. the adoption of scientific methods for the rehabilitation of girls and women who have contracted promiscuous habits;

f. the education of children in the laws of reproduction through the scientific approach of botany and biology, leading up to education of adolescents in the emotional and ethical aspects of sex relations and the significance and responsibilities of family life;

g. that men partners in immorality and patrons of prostitutes be regarded as equally guilty of an offence under the law;

h. that ample facilities for healthy recreation be provided;

i. that the sale of liquour be strictly controlled;

j. the prohibition of the publication or distribution of literature calculated to stimulate crime, sexual laxity and other anti-social behaviour.

(22) REHABILITATION.

In view of the number of young men and women and boys and girls whose mental and moral life has been affected by war conditions,

We recommend that the Federal Government be asked to establish institutions and colonies where men and women, and boys and girls who have developed immoral habits and anti-social behaviour and are classed as delinquents, may be re-educated by modern methods, including occupational therapy, to re-establish them economically and socially in society.

(23) COUNTRY WOMEN.

As much of the development of Australia has depended, and much of the future development of Australia will inevitably depend upon the men and women in rural areas, it is vitally important that the amenities of life should be made available in country districts.

We recommend that

a. special rail transport facilities be made available for families;

b. telephone services at special rates be provided;

c. water conservation, and schemes for the generation of electricity be developed so that, as far as possible, water and electricity may be supplied to all homes in the country at a reasonable cost;

d. classes for mothers, giving instruction on baby and child care and nutrition, be organised on the same lines as the correspondence school classes;

e. bush nursing systems be extended to cover all districts, traveling medical clinics to provide adequate maternal, infant and general health services to isolated country areas be organised, and the country schools be made available for these services.

(24) ABORIGINES.

The Conference deplores the continued neglect of the native race and demands immediate measures by the Federal Governments to arrest the process of extinction and to provide the Aborigines with all the means for a secure and prosperous life. These immediate measures to include the following:—

a. Federal control over all questions concerning the welfare of the Aborigines;

b. Tribal Aborigines to be given reserves; such native reserves to be inviolable, the land and natural resources to be the property of the Aborigines;

c. adequate medical services to be provided for the Aborigines throughout Australia;

d. no contact with the natives in the reserves to be permitted except by members of the Medical Services and other specially qualified persons responsible to the Government;

e. the potential equality of the Aboriginal Race be recognised; education be directed to preparation for full citizenship rights and responsibilities, including technical and other training and the opportunity to use this training;

f. the term Australian Aboriginal be interpreted in the law to mean full blood Australian Aboriginal;

g. suitable advisers be appointed to assist in the gradual economic development of the Aborigines. Native enterprises to be developed on a co-operative basis;

h. the abolition of the system of employment by licence; the aboriginal worker to be entitled to receive the full amount of his or her wages as a legal right;

i. that women be urged to use their influence to eliminate colour prejudice from the social life of the nation.

(25) LEGAL REFORMS.

We believe that nationality, domicile, legitimation, parental right and guardianship of children and property of children should be the concern of the Commonwealth, and that legislation thereon should contain no discrimination between men and women;

We recommend that

a. the Commonwealth Government submit an amendment vesting in the Commonwealth such of these powers as it does not already possess when the Referendum is taken;

b. the Commonwealth pass legislation to ensure to a married woman the same rights in regard to nationality as a man or a single women;

c. the Commonwealth pass legislation to ensure to a married woman the same rights in regard to domicile as a man or a single woman.

We further recommend that the competent authority pass legislation

a. to provide that a child shall be automatically legitimated by the marriage of its parents;

b. to provide that the mother and father should have the same right in regard to the guardianship of children and the property of children;

c. to provide that all investments or savings made by or placed in the name of a married woman should be regarded as her undisputed property;

d. to declare joint ownership of property used by married persons as their home or business jointly conducted or property acquired after marriage by either party, other than by inheritance.

(26) DIVORCE.

Whereas at the present time marriage and divorce laws are controlled by the State Parliament, and

Whereas the various provisions of these laws differ in their grounds for divorce,

We recommend

a. that the marriage and divorce laws of the individual State be amended to provide that the grounds for divorce in the laws of each State shall be common to all States, and that when this has been achieved the Commonwealth Parliament shall take over the control of marriage and divorce;

b. that Courts of Conciliation to arbitrate in matrimonial disputes be set up throughout the Commonwealth and that petitions for divorce or separation be heard only after the parties have submitted their case to this Court;

c. that women should be included on the Bench of the Conciliation Courts.

(27) WIDOWS' PENSIONS.

Whereas at the present time the male basic wage is computed to maintain a family at the minimum standard, and

Whereas a widow's pension is reduced if she earns more than 12/6 [shillings and pence] per week,

We recommend that widows with dependents shall be eligible to supplement their pensions to a sum equivalent to the male basic wage.

(28) CENSUS.

We request that when the census is taken fuller particulars of the status, responsibilities, etc., of women be required, so that data will be available in respect of women wage-earners, breadwinners, grade of occupation, rate of wages, age, conjugal conditions, number of persons wholly or partly supported and relationship to breadwinners.

FINIS.

Special Resolution passed at Australian Woman's Conference:—

RACIAL PERSECUTION.

Realising that the Jewish people were the first victims of Hitler's barbarism; that already over 4,000,000 Jewish men, women and children have been massacred; and that the Jewish people alone have been selected by the Nazis for complete annihilation,

We Australian women, in conference assembled, urge that in accordance with uprooted European Jewry's desperate need, relief and rehabilitation be provided, and equal status restored to them by the United Nations at the earliest moment possible;

Further, we urge, in the name of justice and mercy, that those who can escape shall be provided with opportunity for migration and settlement in Palestine and elsewhere, and that the Australian Government be asked to approach the authorities concerned to further these purposes.

Notes

1 Australian Women's Conference, "Australian Woman's Charter, 1943: Which Comprises the Resolutions Adopted by the Australian Women's Conference for Victory in War and Victory in Peace, November 19–22, 1943, Sydney, New South Wales, Australia." National Library of Australia, nla.gov.au.

2 Nikki Henningham, "The Australian Women's Conference for Vicory in War and Victory in Peace (1943)." *Australian Women's Register*, June 12, 2009, www.womenaustralia.info.

Part IV
1950–1980

40

Purposes *and* Resolutions
International Association of Radio Women Conference
Amsterdam, Holland, and Stockholm, Sweden
October 1951 and 1972

IAWRT logo.

We urge broadcasting organizations to recognize that women have special expertise, knowledge and understanding of human affairs.

As early as 1954, the International Federation of Journalists urged that media programming avoid discrimination based on gender, sexual orientation, race, ethnicity, national origin, language, religion, or political or other opinions.[1] Nonetheless, a recent six-country research project by the International Association of Women in Radio and Television shows that still, today, majority-race men literally have greater "voice" in the public media than do women. For example, 63 percent of speaking characters are male, 37 percent female (25). Diversity is not much of a priority, either. For instance, 75 percent of radio and 95 percent of television programs are broadcast in the official language of a country (24). Further, "there is little to no diversity among categories of characters examined, and in particular among journalists and experts, in regards to sexual orientation, age, ethnicity, and ability," a lack that is correlated "with a lack of focus on the lives and concerns of those of more diverse backgrounds globally" (8) and that "reinforce[s] the relative invisibility of those who already have less power in the public sphere. Additionally, since those who get to speak in the media also get to influence public opinion, it can be argued that influencers primarily remain male, of middle age, and of the majority population of a country" (8).

The founding of the International Association of Radio Women involves an interesting story. During the wartime occupation, Lilian van der Groot, a doctor of economics and head of women's programming in radio at AVRO (Algemeene Vereeniging Radio Omreop),

> heard some BBC programmes that showed her the power of radio—one about a German prisoner-of-war who found a common bond in an English household through the shared craft of shoemaking; another by some miners' wives who met miners' wives in neighbouring France and found a link in the unique way of life dictated by their husbands' work. Those examples convinced her of how this powerful instrument used by women might perhaps serve the cause of mutual understanding in a world recovering from war. . . . Already in 1949 she had a vision of women radio journalists coming together to discuss their profession, the audience, the programming, the need for programmes for women and the hope that women have a special talent for peace.[2]

Van der Groot started making contacts, and a few women met informally in Holland in the fall of 1949, and then more officially in London in 1950. In October 1951 the International Association of Radio Women (IARW) began with a gathering in Amsterdam of delegates from eight countries: Denmark, Austria, Germany, Belgium, Holland, Canada, the United States, and Switzerland. At that meeting the women discussed the group's purposes. Those goals are reproduced below.

Because the historical record of the IAWRT is still incomplete, because their resolutions are brief, and because we do not often get to see a group's evolution over time in this volume, below also are some later versions of the group's goals and resolutions.[3] The contents show that the group has long addressed the issues of who controls the media and what messages it conveys, has tried to make the working environment more just, and has becoming increasingly inclusive. They also provide an example of how women use their skills and positions in their workplaces for feminist ends, changing themselves, their work environments, and the political culture.

Purposes

Purposes (1951):
1) to promote exchange between radio women of various countries,
2) to exchange techniques of radio and television in the women's field,
3) to improve methods of contacting and serving the listeners,
4) to extend the range of programme content in order to improve the practice and ideals of the profession.

Goals (2005):
IAWRT aims to work worldwide to promote the entry, development and advancement of women working in the media in order to broaden their perspectives and raise the quality of radio and television programmes by:
- supporting the professional development of members through exchange of ideas, experience and technical knowledge;
- raising awareness of the privilege of free speech and of the responsibility it entails in the profession;
- utilizing media skills to ensure that the points of view of women are respected and their needs are recognized;
- utilizing member access to media in support of women in developing countries;
- supporting the full integration of women within all areas of society.

Research goals (2014–2015):[4]
Goals of the research
The 2014–2015 IAWRT media monitoring research project has attempted to make a contribution toward gaining a comprehensive understanding of where media currently stand in regards to equality by:
- Moving beyond the already well scrutinized news programs and monitoring prime time entertainment, public interest, and educational programs;
- Looking specifically at public radio and television;
- Analyzing gender in conjunction with other social justice aspects such as sexual orientation, age, ethnicity, and ability.

Resolutions

Stockholm, 1972:

1) [W]e call upon the United Nations and all Broadcasting stations within their influence to redouble their efforts to expose the danger of pollution throughout the world. This can be done in the following ways:

. . . by extending the practice of broadcasting the atmospheric pollution count in conjunction with the daily weather forecasts

. . . by exchange of programmes on the subject

. . . by emphasizing the urgent need that children should understand the dangers of pollution

2) that we seek to further a better understanding of the need to integrate the traditional male and female role in order to achieve a common society

3) that we seek to establish better contacts with women colleagues in Africa, Asia and Latin America . . .

4) that we believe that problems facing the world as a result of overpopulation are of paramount importance, we ask the United Nations to urge all member states to regard contribution to the United Nations Fund for Population Activities as a first priority

Helsinki, September 1974:

1. That the IAWRT should continue to make every effort to strengthen our ties with colleagues in Eastern Europe, Africa, Asia and South America. To this end, the Board will try to ensure that as many delegates as possible attend the next Conference and redouble their efforts to obtain financial assistance for those who may require it.

2.a) That all radio and TV stations do everything they can to further the aims and reflect the activities of the U.N. International Women's Year 1975—both by producing new programmes and through exchange of programmes.

2.b) That the planning and production of such programmes should not be restricted to the departments traditionally dealing with women's programmes. In this way, it will be made clear that there is no section of society where women do not have a part to play—since whatever decisions are made affect women as much as men.

3. That we urge every broadcasting corporation/company to instigate an inquiry into the relative position of women in its organisation. That such an inquiry includes in the terms of reference:

i) Equal pay.

ii) Equal opportunity for promotion, especially to decision-making positions.

iii) Similar terms and conditions on retirement.

Munich, September 1976:

1. In view of the fact that women comprise fifty percent of the population, we urge broadcasting organisations: a) to recognize that women have special expertise, knowledge and understanding of human affairs. b) to emphasise the importance of women's place in society by representing women and their views more widely both in radio and television programmes by involving more women at policy making levels.

Notes

1   Greta Gober and Diana Iulia Natasia, "Gender Equality and Social Justice in Public Media: Media Monitoring Research in Eight Countries across Four Continents," 2015, p. 8. Report

for International Association of Women in Radio and Television, www.iawrt.org.
Subsequent page references are to this source.

2 Christina Ruhnbro, ed., "Voices/Pictures: The Story of the International Association of Women in Radio and Television," 2008, p. 10. Report for International Association of Women in Radio and Television, www.iawrt.org.

3 Ibid.

4 Gober and Natasia.

41

Women's Charter and Aims
Federation of South African Women
Johannesburg, South Africa
April 17, 1954

Poster advertising FEDSAW.

It is our duty and privilege to enlist all women in our struggle for emancipation and to bring to them all realisation of the intimate relationship that exists between their status of inferiority as women and the inferior status to which their people are subjected by discriminatory laws and colour prejudices.

This organization and declaration were created as a reaction against increased discrimination imposed when the National Party, which made apartheid even more extreme, came into power in 1948. The Federation of South African Women (FEDSAW) elected Dora Tamana as its first president, and Ray Simons, Helen Joseph, Lillian Ngoyi, and Amina Cachalia as executive committee members. At the inaugural meeting, 146 delegates from all parts of South Africa attended with the goal of bringing "the women of South Africa together to secure full equality of opportunity for all women, regardless of race, colour or creed; to remove social and legal and economic disabilities; to work for the protection of the women and children."[1]

FEDSAW was a multiracial federation of women's organizations based primarily on opposition to apartheid, a shared experience of motherhood, and a common desire for change. Organizations centrally involved included the African National Council Women's League, and the Food and Canning Workers' Union.

The Charter shows that women in South Africa in 1954 lacked basic rights, including the rights to vote and be elected, and to own property. During apartheid, both women and men lived in the presence of color prejudice, and in a society where free compulsory education did not exist for all. Linking themselves with trade unions and national liberatory movements, the people in this organization strove "for permanent peace throughout the world."

The authors of this document, "wives and mothers, working women and housewives, African, Indians, European and Coloured," argue against laws and traditions "keeping our sex in a position of inferiority and subordination" even as they simultaneously acknowledge that they "share with our menfolk the cares and anxieties imposed by poverty and its evils." Further, they see the connection "between their status of inferiority as women and the inferior status to which their people are subjected by discriminatory laws and colour prejudices." They call on men to recognize the need for cooperation, not segregation, of the sexes in order to reach true empowerment. The Charter aims to create legal equality for women as well as a more democratic society, including universal, free public education. This document may be the earliest modern one to represent the tensions and coalitions involved in being oppressed female members of a group also discriminated against on another basis—in this case, race. The tone is personal ("We know," they repeat) and the analysis directed at broad social and economic conditions. They argue recurrently for progress, and see inequality as an obstacle to it.

During its lifetime, FEDSAW "supported the Bantu Education boycotts and campaigned against rent increases, housing problems and passes for women,"[2] as well as fought against the evils of poverty. It was disbanded in 1994 after the first democratic national elections were held in South Africa.

On August 9, 1956, FEDSAW, together with the African National Congress Women's League and the Black Sash movement, organized a march of some twenty thousand women of different racial groups from all across the country. They "marched to the Union Buildings in Pretoria where they stood in silence as petitions against the pass laws were handed over to the Prime Minister's office. The women chanted the phrase 'wathinth, abafazi, wathinth, imbokodo,' which is translated to 'you strike a woman, you strike a rock'—it became a symbol of the strength and courage of women in the movement. August 9 is now celebrated as Women's Day in South Africa."[3]

The leaders of the 1955 Women's March holding petitions against "pass laws" in South Africa, which limited movement around the country for Black South Africans during apartheid.

The Women's Charter

Preamble: We, the women of South Africa, wives and mothers, working women and housewives, African, Indians, European and Coloured, hereby declare our aim of striving for the removal of all laws, regulations, conventions and customs that discriminate against us as women, and that deprive us in any way of our inherent right to the advantages, responsibilities and opportunities that society offers to any one section of the population.

A Single Society: We women do not form a society separate from the men. There is only one society, and it is made up of both women and men. As women we share the problems and anxieties of our men, and join hands with them to remove social evils and obstacles to progress.

Test of Civilisation: The level of civilisation which any society has reached can be measured by the degree of freedom that its members enjoy. The status of women is a test of civilisation. Measured by that standard, South Africa must be considered low in the scale of civilised nations.

Women's Lot: We women share with our menfolk the cares and anxieties imposed by poverty and its evils. As wives and mothers, it falls upon us to make small wages stretch a long way. It is we who feel the cries of our children when they are hungry and sick. It is our lot to keep and care for the homes that are too small, broken and dirty to be kept clean. We know the burden of looking after children and land when our husbands are away in the mines, on the farms, and in the towns earning our daily bread.

We know what it is to keep family life going in pondokkies and shanties, or in overcrowded one-room apartments. We know the bitterness of children taken to lawless ways, of daughters becoming unmarried mothers whilst still at school, of boys and girls growing up without education, training or jobs at a living wage.

Poor and Rich: These are evils that need not exist. They exist because the society in which we live is divided into poor and rich, into non-European and European. They exist because there are privileges for the few, discrimination and harsh treatment for the many. We women have stood and will stand shoulder to shoulder with our menfolk in a common struggle against poverty, race and class discrimination, and the evils of the colour bar.

National Liberation: As members of the National Liberatory movements and Trade Unions, in and through our various organisations, we march forward with our men in the struggle for liberation and the defence of the working people. We pledge ourselves to keep high the banner of equality, fraternity and liberty. As women there rests upon us also the burden of removing from our society all the social differences developed in past times between men and women, which have the effect of keeping our sex in a position of inferiority and subordination.

Equality for Women: We resolve to struggle for the removal of laws and customs that deny African women the right to own, inherit or alienate property. We resolve to work for a change in the laws of marriage such as are found amongst our African, Malay and Indian people, which have the effect of placing wives in the position of legal subjection to husbands, and giving husbands the power to dispose of wives' property and earnings, and dictate to them in all matters affecting them and their children.

We recognise that the women are treated as minors by these marriage and property laws because of ancient and revered traditions and customs which had their origin in the antiquity of the people and no doubt served purposes of great value in bygone times.

There was a time in the African society when every woman reaching marriageable stage was assured of a husband, home, land and security.

Then husbands and wives with their children belonged to families and clans that supplied most of their own material needs and were largely self-sufficient. Men and women were partners in a compact and closely integrated family unit.

Women who Labour: Those conditions have gone. The tribal and kinship society to which they belonged has been destroyed as a result of the loss of tribal land, migration of men away from the tribal home, the growth of towns and industries, and the rise of a great body of wage-earners on the farms and in the urban areas, who depend wholly or mainly on wages for a livelihood.

Thousands of African women, like Indians, Coloured and European women, are employed today in factories, homes, offices, shops, on farms, in professions as nurses, teachers and the like. As unmarried women, widows or divorcees they have to fend for themselves, often without the assistance of a male relative. Many of them are responsible not only for their own livelihood but also that of their children.

Large numbers of women today are in fact the sole breadwinners and heads of their families.

Forever Minors: Nevertheless, the laws and practices derived from an earlier and different state of society are still applied to them. They are responsible for their own person and their children. Yet the law seeks to enforce upon them the status of a minor.

Not only are African, Coloured and Indian women denied political rights, but they are also in many parts of the Union denied the same status as men in such matters as the right to enter into contracts, to own and dispose of property, and to exercise guardianship over their children.

Obstacle to Progress: The law has lagged behind the development of society; it no longer corresponds to the actual social and economic position of women. The law has become an obstacle to progress of the women, and therefore a brake on the whole of society.

This intolerable condition would not be allowed to continue were it not for the refusal of a large section of our menfolk to concede to us women the rights and privileges which they demand for themselves.

We shall teach the men that they cannot hope to liberate themselves from the evils of discrimination and prejudice as long as they fail to extend to women complete and unqualified equality in law and in practice.

Need for Education: We also recognise that large numbers of our womenfolk continue to be bound by traditional practices and conventions, and fail to realise that these have become obsolete and a brake on progress. It is our duty and privilege to enlist all women in our struggle for emancipation and to bring to them all realisation of the intimate relationship that exists between their status of inferiority as women and the inferior status to which their people are subjected by discriminatory laws and colour prejudices.

It is our intention to carry out a nation-wide programme of education that will bring home to the men and women of all national groups the realisation that freedom cannot be won for any one section or for the people as a whole as long as we women are kept in bondage.

An Appeal: We women appeal to all progressive organisations, to members of the great National Liberatory movements, to the trade unions and working class organisations, to the churches, educational and welfare organisations, to all progressive men and women who have the interests of the people at heart, to join with us in this great and noble endeavour.

Our Aims
We declare the following aims:

This organisation is formed for the purpose of uniting women in common action for the removal of all political, legal, economic and social disabilities. We shall strive for women to obtain:

1. The right to vote and to be elected to all State bodies, without restriction or discrimination.
2. The right to full opportunities for employment with equal pay and possibilities of promotion in all spheres of work.
3. Equal rights with men in relation to property, marriage and children, and for the removal of all laws and customs that deny women such equal rights.
4. For the development of every child through free compulsory education for all; for the protection of mother and child through maternity homes, welfare clinics, creches and nursery schools, in countryside and towns; through proper homes for all, and through the provision of water, light, transport, sanitation, and other amenities of modern civilisation.
5. For the removal of all laws that restrict free movement, that prevent or hinder the right of free association and activity in democratic organisations, and the right to participate in the work of these organisations.
6. To build and strengthen women's sections in the National Liberatory movements, the organisation of women in trade unions, and through the peoples' varied organisation.
7. To cooperate with all other organisations that have similar aims in South Africa as well as throughout the world.
8. To strive for permanent peace throughout the world.

Notes
1 "Federation of South African Women (FEDSAW)," updated Aug. 8, 2017. *South African History Online*, www.sahahistory.org.za.
2 "Women Unite for People's Power." *South African History Online*. Accessed Feb. 13, 2017, www.saha.org.za.
3 "African Women in Liberation Struggles." *Is This Africa? Creating Conversation about Africa* blog, isthisafrica.tumblr.com/post/18963678511, accessed Feb. 13, 2017.

42

Mission Statement
Daughters of Bilitis
San Francisco, California
1955

Phyllis Lyon and Del Martin.

Phyllis Lyon and Del Martin, pictured in figure 42.1, founded, along with three other lesbian couples, the Daughters of Bilitis (DOB), the first lesbian education and civil rights society, in 1955. The name of the organization was meant to prevent authorities from recognizing the group as lesbian, since homosexuality was not only a diagnosable medical disease but also a criminal offense in 1950s America. The name held other significance, as well: "*Bilitis* is the name given to a fictional lesbian contemporary of Sappho, by the French poet Pierre Louÿs in his 1894 work *The Songs of Bilitis*, in which Bilitis lived on the Isle of Lesbos alongside Sappho."[1] The organization was eventually infiltrated by the FBI, and the members of the group and recipients of its magazine, the *Ladder*, were blacklisted during the McCarthy era.

The *Ladder* was one of the group's most successful endeavors, achieving its goal of educating and providing reading material for isolated lesbians across the country. (It was perhaps the second lesbian periodical in the United States, as *Vice Versa* was published in 1947–1948.) The group formed as an alternative to lesbian bar culture, and the police harassment that often accompanied it. The Daughters of Bilitis were mostly middle-class white women, though they provided support for a broader network of women.

DOB held a national convention in 1960. The group fought sexism in the gay rights movements and homophobia in the women's movement and stayed involved in both. Martin and Lyon also started the Council on Religion and the Homosexual and the Alice B. Toklas Democratic Club.[2] Leslie Feinberg provides some context:

> The systematic and sensationalized witch hunt carried out against lesbian, gay, bisexual and trans people in the 1950s Cold War era aided the economic efforts underway to reinforce the heterosexual nuclear family as the primary economic unit under capitalism. . . . How could even such a politically moderate demand by lesbians—the right to fit in and just live their lives—be articulated at the mid-fifties height of the Cold War, a time of the most focused persecution of gays and lesbians in U.S. history? . . . In effect, lesbian organizing rode the crest of turbulent swells of militant political organizing and resistance.[3]

The October 1957 issue of *The Ladder*.

The Daughters of Bilitis gradually lost steam after Lyon and Martin stepped down as leaders, though another couple took over the publication of the *Ladder* in the mid-1960s. Although the group disintegrated, it lasted for fourteen years and took the first step toward normalizing homosexuality in America and educating the whole population about lesbians' rightful place in society. Their mission statement,[4] printed below, makes four claims that may appear modest now but really hit the heart of the group's purpose: they wished to help lesbians understand themselves, create public acceptance for lesbians, invite medical professionals to study lesbians more fully and accurately, and revise laws to make them fair across gender orientations. Other lesbian and feminist groups would expand these principles in later declarations. Readers should note that the word "variant" was less negative than "lesbian" at the time.

Mission Statement of the Daughters of Bilitis

1. Education of the variant, with particular emphasis on the psychological, physiological and sociological aspects, to enable her to understand herself and make her adjustment to society in all its social, civic and economic implications—this to be accomplished by establishing and maintaining as complete a library as possible of both fiction and non-fiction literature on the sex deviant theme; by sponsoring public discussions on pertinent subjects to be conducted by leading members of the legal, psychiatric, religious and other professions; by advocating a mode of behavior and dress acceptable to society.

2. Education of the public at large through acceptance first of the individual, leading to an eventual breakdown of erroneous taboos and prejudices; through public discussion meetings aforementioned; through dissemination of educational literature on the homosexual theme.

3. Participation in research projects by duly authorized and responsible psychologists, sociologists, and other such experts directed towards further knowledge of the homosexual.

4. Investigation of the penal code as it pertains to the homosexual, proposal of changes to provide an equitable handling of cases involving this minority group, and promotion of these changes through due process of law in the state legislatures.

Notes

1 "Daughters of Bilitis," last modified Aug. 3, 2017. *Wikipedia*, www.wikipedia.org.
2 LHA Daughters of Bilitis Video Project: Del Martin & Phyllis Lyon. *Lesbian Herstory Archives*, accessed Sept. 29, 2017, herstories.prattinfoschool.nyc.
3 Leslie Feinberg, "1955: First Lesbian Organization Rises on Waves of Militant Struggles." *Workers World*, Jan. 26, 2006, www.workers.org, accessed Feb. 13, 2017.
4 Chrislove, "Top Comments: Remembering Lesbian History: The Daughters of Bilitis Edition," *Daily Kos*, April 18, 2012, www.dailykos.com.

43

Objectives and Purposes
Women's Rights Movement of the Philippines
Global City, Philippines
May 5, 1958

Women's Rights Movement of the Philippines logo.

[W]e shall [. . .] remove discrimination, restrictions and limitations
on women's rights and forestall further imposition of the same.

Fifteen professional women with different but complementary civic concerns met in 1958 to found the Women's Rights Movement of the Philippines (WRMP). This is the third document from a third continent showing groups working for sexual equality still several years before what would be called the second wave of feminism—more documentation of the never-ending stream of feminist activism globally—and twenty-one years after women activists won the vote in the Philippines. WRMP's foremost goal was to encourage women to assert their equality with men, in the home as well as in the workplace and in politics. Stressing awareness and education, they used outreach tools such as seminars, lectures, and workshops, and made strides in girls' and women's education.

As so often seen, this group, too, gathered to "protect" existing rights and "promote" additional ones for Filipinas "irrespective of individual political convictions, affiliations or religious belief." Despite the middle-class nature of the group, their objectives and purposes share ground with those of diverse other groups, from eliminating discrimination to urging "women to exercise their rights and assert proper influence in public life." Their goal of stimulating discussion of gender issues shows a group and a nation in the early stages of grappling with sexual inequality, but also aware of the power of consciousness raising and the importance of women's voices.

Objectives and Purposes

We pledge ourselves to protect and promote women's rights, irrespective of individual political convictions, affiliations or religious belief.

TO PROTECT women's rights we shall:
- Provide information on the status, rights and obligations of women in our country and in other nations.
- Urge women to exercise their rights and assert proper influence in public life.
- Uphold and safeguard the rights of women.
- Remove discrimination, restrictions and limitations on women's rights and forestall further imposition of the same.

TO PROMOTE women's rights we shall:
- Stimulate an intelligent and vigorous public opinion through community education.
- Initiate support for women to be elected or appointed to responsible positions.
- Pursue projects to help improve the quality of family living.
- Obtain legislative and other measures to advance the Movement's Objectives.

44

Statement of Purpose
The National Organization for Women
Washington, D.C.
October 29, 1966

National Organization for Women logo.

We do not accept the token appointment of a few women to high-level positions in government and industry as a substitute for serious continuing effort to recruit and advance women according to their individual abilities.

NOW is often cited as a prominent example of liberal feminism and second-wave feminism, though its influence as a social and political actor has carried into the "third-wave feminism" of the twenty-first century. NOW declares itself "the largest organization of feminist activists in the United States, with hundreds of thousands of contributing members and more than 500 local and campus affiliates in all fifty states and the District of Columbia." Its organizational structure is often referred to as a "federalist framework," meaning that its operations and priorities are multilevel, from the national to the local or "grassroots." This framework has also been described as "formalized and hierarchical." The national-level office identifies priorities and sets organizational policies; regional and state branches manage memberships and coordinate actions; local offices contribute to national and local initiatives.

The multiplicity of levels and affiliates leads to a multiplicity of activist approaches. Tactics include electoral work, lobbying, and legislative activism; mass marches, rallies, and street theater; and pickets and nonviolent civil disobedience. NOW is a multi-issue organization, whose scope has grown to include violence against women, reproductive freedom and other health issues, and discrimination based on race and sexual orientation.

The reason NOW's Statement of Purpose gets labeled as "liberal" is its emphasis on bringing women "into full participation in the mainstream of American society," rather than challenging what constitutes the mainstream, and its treatment of discrimination as isolable and removable rather than fully integrated into social structures. Further, its goals are truly rooted in liberal political thought: equality of opportunity and freedom of choice. It does, however, look to social solutions to social problems that confront women, as in the case of daycare for children, and sees itself "as part of the world-wide revolution of human rights."

Those "conditions that now prevent women from enjoying the equality of opportunity and freedom of choice which is their right, as individual Americans, and as human beings" include "prejudice and discrimination against women in government, industry, the professions, the churches, the political parties, the judiciary, the labor unions, in education, science, medicine, law, religion and every other field of importance in American society"—a list virtually unchanged from

Group portrait of NOW founders at NOW's organizing conference in Washington, D.C., October 1966. Photo by Vince Graas. Records of the National Organization for Women, Schlesinger Library, Radcliffe Institute for Advanced Study, Harvard University.

Seneca Falls. The job market is sex segregated and women are underpaid; further, "proper recognition" is not "given to the economic and social value of homemaking and child-care"—the first economic recognition of such work in a "liberal" document. Some of what makes change possible now, the document claims, has nothing to do with activism for social transformation; instead, the causes are an expanded lifespan and technological developments that mean that women are not consigned primarily to lives as child-bearers and child-rearers and that sheer physical strength is a rare requirement for labor. Those developments may be necessary, but they are not sufficient, so the document recommends a civil rights movement for women, enforcement of new antidiscrimination laws, and coalition building with other human rights groups. The document attacks socialization in general and institutional practices that "undermine [women's] confidence in their own abilities and foster contempt for women."

Statement of Purpose

We, men and women who hereby constitute ourselves as the National Organization for Women, believe that the time has come for a new movement toward true equality for all women in America, and toward a fully equal partnership of the sexes, as part of the world-wide revolution of human rights now taking place within and beyond our national borders.

The purpose of NOW is to take action to bring women into full participation in the mainstream of American society now, exercising all the privileges and responsibilities thereof in truly equal partnership with men.

We believe the time has come to move beyond the abstract argument, discussion and symposia over the status and special nature of women which has raged in America in recent years; the time has come to confront, with concrete action, the conditions that now prevent women from enjoying the equality of opportunity and freedom of choice which is their right, as individual Americans, and as human beings.

NOW is dedicated to the proposition that women, first and foremost, are human beings, who, like all other people in our society, must have the chance to develop their fullest human potential. We believe that women can achieve such equality only by accepting to the full the challenges and responsibilities they share with all other people in our society, as part of the decision-making mainstream of American political, economic and social life.

We organize to initiate or support action, nationally, or in any part of this nation, by individuals or organizations, to break through the silken curtain of prejudice and discrimination against women in government, industry, the professions, the churches, the political parties, the judiciary, the labor unions, in education, science, medicine, law, religion and every other field of importance in American society.

Enormous changes taking place in our society make it both possible and urgently necessary to advance the unfinished revolution of women toward true equality, now. With a life span lengthened to nearly 75 years it is no longer either necessary or possible for women to devote the greater part of their lives to childrearing; yet childbearing and rearing which continues to be a most important part of most women's lives—still is used to justify barring women from equal professional and economic participation and advance.

Today's technology has reduced most of the productive chores which women once performed in the home and in mass-production industries based upon routine un-skilled labor. This same technology has virtually eliminated the quality of muscular strength as a criterion for filling most jobs, while intensifying American industry's need for creative intelligence. In view of this new industrial revolution created by automation in the mid-twentieth century, women can and must participate in old and new fields of society in full equality—or become permanent outsiders.

Despite all the talk about the status of American women in recent years, the actual position of women in the United States has declined, and is declining, to an alarming degree throughout the 1950's and 60's. Although 46.4% of all American women between the ages of 18 and 65 now work outside the home, the overwhelming majority—75%—are in routine clerical, sales, or factory jobs, or they are household workers, cleaning women, hospital attendants. About two-thirds of Negro women workers are in the lowest paid service occupations. Working women are becoming increasingly—not less—concentrated on the bottom of the job ladder. As a consequence full-time women workers today earn on the average only 60% of what men earn, and that wage gap has been increasing over the past twenty-five years in every major industry group. In 1964, of all women with a yearly income, 89% earned under $5,000 a year; half of all full-time year round women workers earned less than $3,690; only 1.4% of full-time year round women workers had an annual income of $10,000 or more.

Further, with higher education increasingly essential in today's society, too few women are entering and finishing college or going on to graduate or professional school. Today, women earn only one in three of the B.A.'s and M.A.'s granted, and one in ten of the Ph.D.'s.

In all the professions considered of importance to society, and in the executive ranks of industry and government, women are losing ground. Where they are present it is only a token handful. Women comprise less than 1% of federal judges; less than 4% of all lawyers; 7% of doctors. Yet women represent 51% of the U.S. population. And, increasingly, men are replacing women in the top positions in secondary and elementary schools, in social work, and in libraries—once thought to be women's fields.

Official pronouncements of the advance in the status of women hide not only the reality of this dangerous decline, but the fact that nothing is being done to stop it. The excellent reports of the President's Commission on the Status of Women and of the State Commissions have not been fully implemented. Such Commissions have power only to advise. They have no power to enforce their recommendation; nor have they the freedom to organize American women and men to press for action on them. The reports of these commissions have, however, created a basis upon which it is now possible to build. Discrimination in employment on the basis of sex is now prohibited by federal law, in Title VII of the Civil Rights Act of 1964. But although nearly one-third of the cases brought before the Equal Employment Opportunity Commission during the first year dealt with sex discrimination and the proportion is increasing dramatically, the Commission has not made clear its intention to enforce the law with the same seriousness on behalf of women as of other victims of discrimination. Many of these cases were Negro women, who are the victims of double discrimination of race and sex. Until now, too few women's organizations and official spokesmen have been willing to speak out against these dangers facing women. Too many women have been restrained by the fear of being called "feminist." There is no civil rights movement to speak for women, as there has been for Negroes and other victims of discrimination. The National Organization for Women must therefore begin to speak.

WE BELIEVE that the power of American law, and the protection guaranteed by the U.S. Constitution to the civil rights of all individuals, must be effectively applied and enforced to isolate and remove patterns of sex discrimination, to ensure equality of opportunity in employment and education, and equality of civil and political rights and responsibilities on behalf of women, as well as for Negroes and other deprived groups.

WE REALIZE that women's problems are linked to many broader questions of social justice; their solution will require concerted action by many groups. Therefore, convinced that human rights for all are indivisible, we expect to give active support to the common cause of equal rights for all those who suffer discrimination and deprivation, and we call upon other organizations committed to such goals to support our efforts toward equality for women.

WE DO NOT ACCEPT the token appointment of a few women to high-level positions in government and industry as a substitute for serious continuing effort to recruit and advance women according to their individual abilities. To this end, we urge American government and industry to mobilize the same resources of ingenuity and command with which they have solved problems of far greater difficulty than those now impeding the progress of women.

WE BELIEVE that this nation has a capacity at least as great as other nations, to innovate new social institutions which will enable women to enjoy the true equality of opportunity and responsibility in society, without conflict with their responsibilities as mothers and homemakers. In such innovations, America does not lead the Western world, but lags by decades behind many European countries. We do not accept the traditional assumption that a woman has to choose between marriage and motherhood, on the one hand, and serious participation in industry or the professions on the other. We question the present expectation that all normal women will retire from job or profession for 10 or 15 years, to devote their full time to raising children, only to reenter the job market at a relatively minor level. This, in itself, is a deterrent to the aspirations of women, to their acceptance into management or professional training courses, and to the very possibility of equality of opportunity or real choice, for all but a few women. Above all, we reject the assumption that these problems are the unique responsibility of each individual woman, rather than a basic social dilemma which society must solve. True equality of opportunity and freedom of choice for women requires such practical, and possible innovations as a nationwide network of child-care centers, which will make it unnecessary for women to retire completely from society until their children are grown, and national programs to provide retraining for women who have chosen to care for their children full-time.

WE BELIEVE that it is as essential for every girl to be educated to her full potential of human ability as it is for every boy—with the knowledge that such education is the key to effective participation in today's economy and that, for a girl as for a boy, education can only be serious where there is expectation that it will be used in society. We believe that American educators are capable of devising means of imparting such expectations to girl students. Moreover, we consider the decline in the proportion of women receiving higher and professional education to be evidence of discrimination. This discrimination may take the form of quotas against the admission of women to colleges, and professional schools; lack of encouragement by parents, counselors and educators; denial of loans or fellowships; or the traditional or arbitrary procedures in graduate and professional training geared in terms of men, which inadvertently discriminate against women. We believe that the same serious attention must be given to high school dropouts who are girls as to boys.

WE REJECT the current assumptions that a man must carry the sole burden of supporting himself, his wife, and family, and that a woman is automatically entitled to lifelong support by a man upon her marriage, or that marriage, home and family are primarily woman's world and responsibility—hers, to dominate—his to support. We believe that a true partnership between the sexes demands a different concept of marriage, an equitable sharing of the responsibilities of home and children and of the economic burdens of their support. We believe that proper recognition should be given to the economic and social value of homemaking and child-care. To these ends, we will seek to open a reexamination of laws and mores governing marriage and divorce, for we believe that the current state of "half-equity" between the sexes discriminates against both men and women, and is the cause of much unnecessary hostility between the sexes.

WE BELIEVE that women must now exercise their political rights and responsibilities as American citizens. They must refuse to be segregated on the basis of sex into separate-and-not-equal ladies' auxiliaries in the political parties, and they must demand representation according to their numbers in the regularly constituted party committees—at local, state, and national levels—and in the informal power structure, participating fully in the selection of candidates and political decision-making, and running for office themselves.

IN THE INTERESTS OF THE HUMAN DIGNITY OF WOMEN, we will protest, and endeavor to change, the false image of women now prevalent in the mass media, and in the texts, ceremonies, laws, and practices of our major social institutions. Such images perpetuate contempt for women by society and by women for themselves. We are similarly opposed to all policies and practices—in church, state, college, factory, or office—which, in the guise of protectiveness, not only deny opportunities but also foster in women self-denigration, dependence, and evasion of responsibility, undermine their confidence in their own abilities and foster contempt for women.

NOW WILL HOLD ITSELF INDEPENDENT OF ANY POLITICAL PARTY in order to mobilize the political power of all women and men intent on our goals. We will strive to ensure that no party, candidate, president, senator, governor, congressman, or any public official who betrays or ignores the principle of full equality between the sexes is elected or appointed to office. If it is necessary to mobilize the votes of men and women who believe in our cause, in order to win for women the final right to be fully free and equal human beings, we so commit ourselves.

WE BELIEVE THAT women will do most to create a new image of women by acting now, and by speaking out in behalf of their own equality, freedom, and human dignity—not in pleas for special privilege, nor in enmity toward men, who are also victims of the current, half-equality between the sexes—but in an active, self-respecting partnership with men. By so doing, women will develop confidence in their own ability to determine actively, in partnership with men, the conditions of their life, their choices, their future and their society.

45

Redstockings Manifesto
Redstockings
New York, New York
July 7, 1969

Redstockings logo.

The founders of the Redstockings, Shulamith Firestone and Ellen Willis, formed the radical collective after the dissolution of the New York Radical Women, where they were both former members. The name is a play on the word "bluestockings," which was a historically negative term used to describe a woman who was interested in academic pursuits. They reclaimed the name and substituted red to exemplify their more radical revolution. Valuing both intellectual inquiry and activism, the Redstockings began to publish and recruit members to their "radical feminist activist group."

Initially, the Redstockings called for widespread consciousness raising. The Redstockings were highly critical of both the political Left and "reformist" feminist groups, condemning each for working within the existing oppressive system.

Much of the early work of the Redstockings consisted of speak-outs, which mirrored the topics of but contrasted sharply with existing legislative hearings. Providing a public space for sharing the personal became a sort of trademark for the radical group. The collective sparked a national movement of women speaking from their experiences as experts, on issues including rape, sexual harassment, and domestic violence.

The Redstockings Manifesto[1] was inspired by Kathie Sarachild's paper "Principles," which was submitted anonymously to represent the thematic core of the

The Redstockings hold a childcare sit-in. New York City, 1971.

Redstockings at the New Left Women's Conference in New York City on June 27, 1969. The declaration was condensed and published within the following month. The Manifesto makes clear that where there is oppression there are oppressed and oppressors, and that it is men who benefit from women's inferior status. It sees male supremacy infiltrating every aspect of society and enforced through violence, not only socialization. It emphasizes that the personal is political, and thus commits itself to learning from and acting on the basis of women's stories of their own lives.

Redstockings Manifesto

I. After centuries of individual and preliminary political struggle, women are uniting to achieve their final liberation from male supremacy. Redstockings is dedicated to building this unity and winning our freedom.

II. Women are an oppressed class. Our oppression is total, affecting every facet of our lives. We are exploited as sex objects, breeders, domestic servants, and cheap labor. We are considered inferior beings, whose only purpose is to enhance men's lives. Our humanity is denied. Our prescribed behavior is enforced by the threat of physical violence.

Because we have lived so intimately with our oppressors, in isolation from each other, we have been kept from seeing our personal suffering as a political condition. This creates the illusion that a woman's relationship with her man is a matter of interplay between two unique personalities, and can be worked out individually. In reality, every such relationship is a class relationship, and the conflicts between individual men and women are political conflicts that can only be solved collectively.

III. We identify the agents of our oppression as men. Male supremacy is the oldest, most basic form of domination. All other forms of exploitation and oppression (racism, capitalism, imperialism, etc.) are extensions of male supremacy: men dominate women, a few men dominate the rest. All power structures throughout history have been male-dominated and male-oriented. Men have controlled all political, economic and cultural institutions and backed up this control with physical force. They have used their power to keep women in an inferior position. All men receive economic, sexual, and psychological benefits from male supremacy. All men have oppressed women.

IV. Attempts have been made to shift the burden of responsibility from men to institutions or to women themselves. We condemn these arguments as evasions. Institutions alone do not oppress; they are merely tools of the oppressor. To blame institutions implies that men and women are equally victimized, obscures the fact that men benefit from the subordination of women, and gives men the excuse that they are forced to be oppressors. On the contrary, any man is free to renounce his superior position, provided that he is willing to be treated like a woman by other men.

We also reject the idea that women consent to or are to blame for their own oppression. Women's submission is not the result of brain-washing, stupidity or mental illness but of continual, daily pressure from men. We do not need to change ourselves, but to change men.

The most slanderous evasion of all is that women can oppress men. The basis for this illusion is the isolation of individual relationships from their political context and the tendency of men to see any legitimate challenge to their privileges as persecution.

V. We regard our personal experience, and our feelings about that experience, as the basis for an analysis of our common situation. We cannot rely on existing ideologies as they are all products of male supremacist culture. We question every generalization and accept none that are not confirmed by our experience.

Our chief task at present is to develop female class consciousness through sharing experience and publicly exposing the sexist foundation of all our institutions. Consciousness-raising is not "therapy," which implies the existence of individual solutions and falsely assumes that the male-female relationship is purely personal, but the only method by which we can ensure that our program for liberation is based on the concrete realities of our lives.

The first requirement for raising class consciousness is honesty, in private and in public, with ourselves and other women.

VI. We identify with all women. We define our best interest as that of the poorest, most brutally exploited woman.

We repudiate all economic, racial, educational or status privileges that divide us from other women. We are determined to recognize and eliminate any prejudices we may hold against other women.

We are committed to achieving internal democracy. We will do whatever is necessary to ensure that every woman in our movement has an equal chance to participate, assume responsibility, and develop her political potential.

VII. We call on all our sisters to unite with us in struggle.

We call on all men to give up their male privilege and support women's liberation in the interest of our humanity and their own.

In fighting for our liberation we will always take the side of women against their oppressors. We will not ask what is "revolutionary" or "reformist," only what is good for women.

The time for individual skirmishes has passed. This time we are going all the way.

Note

1 "1968–72 Consciousness Raising Papers." *Redstockings.org*, accessed 2014.

46

The Woman-Identified Woman
Radicalesbians
New York, New York
May 1, 1970

Members carry a Radicalesbians flag.

As long as the label "dyke" can be used to frighten women into a less militant stand, keep her separate from her sisters, keep her from giving primacy to anything other than men and family—then to that extent she is controlled by the male culture.

This manifesto was written as a way to protest homophobia within the feminist movement in 1970, and it was delivered first to the Second Congress to Unite Women. The congress was a feminist gathering, but no open lesbians had been invited to speak or present. The group calling itself the "Lavender Menace,"[1] including Artemis March, Lois Hart, Rita Mae Brown, Ellen Shumsky, Cynthia Funk, and Barbara XX, decided to take over the stage on the opening night. They staged a "zap" action where they turned off all the lights and the microphone so the organizers of the congress would get off the stage. They then surrounded the audience and took the microphone, voicing their indignation that lesbians were not included and explaining to the crowd the importance of lesbianism to feminism. The audience responded very positively to the "zap," and the organizers of the congress invited the Radicalesbians to give workshops later during the meeting.

This positive response gave momentum to lesbian feminists, who eventually organized as the Radicalesbians, a subsection of the National Organization of Women. The feminist movement became increasingly inclusive, and many remember this moment as the spark that lit the fire for incorporating lesbian voices.[2]

The manifesto[3] gives several definitions of lesbian that are fairly different from twenty-first-century understandings. Lesbianism, for this group of women at this time, is as much of a rebellion against a repressive patriarchal society as it is a sexual identity. For example, the manifesto defines a lesbian as "the rage of all women condensed to the point of explosion. She is the woman who . . . acts in accordance with her inner compulsion to be a more complete and freer human being than her society . . . cares to allow her." This definition focuses on the freedoms denied women by society, strengthened by a later claim: "Lesbian is a label invented by the Man to throw at any woman who dares to be his equal, who dares to challenge his prerogatives (including that of all women as part of the exchange medium among men), who dares to assert the primacy of her own needs." Lesbianism, then, is seen as a way for women to operate without men, or without concern for meeting men on equal terms, in order to meet women's needs. One powerful idea in the declaration is what it could mean to be "woman-identified"—when "the label 'dyke' can[not] be used to frighten women into a less militant stand."

Another aspect of this manifesto that may be surprising to some twenty-first-century readers is the idea that lesbianism is a temporary category, required only because of repressive social structures: "In a society in which men do not oppress women, and sexual expression is allowed to follow feelings, the categories of homosexuality and heterosexuality would disappear." This language is reminiscent of Karl Marx's reference to the state withering away as its political functions become obsolete. Once the norm of patriarchal marriage passes, "lesbian" would be an obsolete category, for there would be no "condition which keeps women within the confines of the feminine role." Finally, in likening "femininity" to "slavery," the document evokes memories of our earliest antislavery and labor documents; it is this relationship to men captured by "femininity" that must be cast off in the name of freedom.

The impact of this document has been lasting for lesbian women, and it has enabled the feminist movement across the world to become more inclusive not only of sex and gender minorities but of other minority and identity groups as well. As the writers of the manifesto declared, inclusion of all women "is no side issue. It is absolutely essential to the success and fulfillment of the women's liberation movement that this issue be dealt with."

The Woman-Identified Woman

What is a lesbian? A lesbian is the rage of all women condensed to the point of explosion. She is the woman who, often beginning at an extremely early age, acts in accordance with her inner compulsion to be a more complete and freer human being than her society—perhaps [not] then, but certainly later—cares to allow her. These needs and actions, over a period of years, bring her into painful conflict with people, situations, the accepted ways of thinking, feeling and behaving, until she is in a state of continual war with everything around her, and usually with herself. She may not be fully conscious of the political implications of what for her began as personal necessity, but on some level she has not been able to accept the limitations and oppression laid on her by the most basic role of her society—the female role. The turmoil she experiences tends to induce guilt proportional to the degree to which she feels she is not meeting social expectations, and/or eventually drives her to question and analyze what the rest of her society more or less accepts. She is forced to evolve her own life pattern, often living much of her life alone, learning usually much earlier than her "straight" (heterosexual) sisters about the essential aloneness of life (which the myth of marriage obscures) and about the reality of illusions. To the extent that she cannot expel the heavy socialization that goes with being female, she can never truly find peace with herself. For she is caught somewhere between accepting society's view of her—in which case she cannot accept herself—and coming to understand what this sexist society has done to her and why it is functional and necessary for it to do so. Those of us who work that through find ourselves on the other side of a tortuous journey through a night that may have been decades long. The perspective gained from that journey, the liberation of self, the inner peace, the real love of self and of all women, is something to be shared with all women—because we are all women.

It should first be understood that lesbianism, like male homosexuality, is a category of behavior possible only in a sexist society characterized by rigid sex roles and dominated by male supremacy. Those sex roles dehumanize women by defining us as a supportive/serving caste in relation to the master caste of men, and emotionally cripple men by demanding that they be alienated from their own bodies and emotions in order to perform their economic/political/military functions effectively. Homosexuality is a by-product of a particular way of setting up roles (or approved patterns of behavior) on the basis of sex; as such it is an inauthentic (not consonant with "reality") category. In a society in which men do not oppress women, and sexual expression is allowed to follow feelings, the categories of homosexuality and heterosexuality would disappear.

But lesbianism is also different from male homosexuality, and serves a different function in the society. "Dyke" is a different kind of put-down from "faggot," although both imply you are not playing your socially assigned sex role . . . are not therefore a "real woman" or a "real man." "The grudging admiration felt for the tomboy, and the queasiness felt around a sissy boy point to the same thing: the contempt in which women—or those who play a female role—are held. And the investment in keeping women in that contemptuous role is very great. Lesbian is a word, the label, the condition that holds women in line. When a woman hears this word tossed her way, she knows she is stepping out of line. She knows that she has crossed the terrible boundary of her sex role. She recoils, she protests, she reshapes her actions to gain approval. Lesbian is a label invented by the Man to throw at any woman who dares to be his equal, who dares to challenge his prerogatives (including that of all women as part of the exchange medium among men), who dares to assert the primacy of her own needs. To have the label applied to people active in women's liberation is just the most recent instance of a long history; older women will recall that not so long ago, any woman who was successful, independent, not orienting her whole life about a man, would hear this word. For in this sexist society, for a woman to be independent means she can't be a woman—she must be a dyke. That in itself should tell us where women are at. It says as clearly as can be said: women and person are contradictory terms. For a lesbian is not considered a "real woman." And yet, in popular thinking, there is really only one essential difference between a lesbian and other women: that of sexual orientation—which is to say, when you strip off all the packaging, you must finally realize that the essence of being a "woman" is to get fucked by men.

"Lesbian" is one of the sexual categories by which men have divided up humanity. While all women are dehumanized as sex objects, as the objects of men they are given certain compensations: identification with his power, his ego, his status, his protection (from other males), feeling like a "real woman," finding social acceptance by adhering to her role, etc. Should a woman confront herself by confronting another woman, there are fewer rationalizations, fewer buffers by which to avoid the stark horror of her dehumanized condition. Herein we find the overriding fear of many women toward being used as a sexual object by a woman, which not only will bring her no male-connected compensations, but also will reveal the void which is woman's real situation. This dehumanization is expressed when a straight woman learns that a sister is a lesbian; she begins to relate to her lesbian sister as her potential sex object, laying a surrogate male role on the lesbian. This reveals her heterosexual conditioning to make herself into an object when sex is potentially involved in a relationship, and it denies the lesbian her full humanity. For women, especially those in the movement, to perceive their lesbian sisters through this male grid of role definitions is to accept this male cultural conditioning and to oppress their sisters much as they themselves have been oppressed by men. Are we going to continue the male classification system of defining all females in sexual relation to some other category of people? Affixing the label lesbian not only to a woman who aspires to be a person, but also to any situation of real love, real solidarity, real primacy among women, is a primary form of divisiveness among women: it is the condition which keeps women within the confines of the feminine role, and it is the debunking/scare term that keeps women from forming any primary attachments, groups, or associations among ourselves.

Women in the movement have in most cases gone to great lengths to avoid discussion and confrontation with the issue of lesbianism. It puts people up-tight. They are hostile, evasive, or try to incorporate it into some "broader issue." They would rather not talk about it. If they have to, they try to dismiss it as a "lavender herring." But it is no side issue. It is absolutely essential to the success and fulfillment of the women's liberation movement that this issue be dealt with. As long as the label "dyke" can be used to frighten women into a less militant stand, keep her separate from her sisters, keep her from giving primacy to anything other than men and family—then to that extent she is controlled by the male culture. Until women see in each other the possibility of a primal commitment which includes sexual love, they will be denying themselves the love and value they readily accord to men, thus affirming their second-class status. As long as male acceptability is primary—both to individual women and to the movement as a whole—the term lesbian will be used effectively against women. Insofar as women want only more privileges within the system, they do not want to antagonize male power. They instead seek acceptability for women's liberation, and the most crucial aspect of the acceptability is to deny lesbianism—i.e., to deny any fundamental challenge to the basis of the female. It should also be said that some younger, more radical women have honestly begun to discuss lesbianism, but so far it has been primarily as a sexual "alternative" to men. This, however, is still giving primacy to men, both because the idea of relating more completely to women occurs as a negative reaction to men, and because the lesbian relationship is being characterized simply by sex, which is divisive and sexist. On one level, which is both personal and political, women may withdraw emotional and sexual energies from men, and work out various alternatives for those energies in their own lives. On a different political/psychological level, it must be understood that what is crucial is that women begin disengaging from male-defined response patterns. In the privacy of our own psyches, we must cut those cords to the core. For irrespective of where our love and sexual energies flow, if we are male-identified in our heads, we cannot realize our autonomy as human beings.

But why is it that women have related to and through men? By virtue of having been brought up in a male society, we have internalized the male culture's definition of ourselves. That definition consigns us to sexual and family functions, and excludes us from defining and shaping the terms of our lives. In exchange for our psychic servicing and for performing society's non-profit-making functions, the man confers on us just one thing: the slave status which makes us legitimate in the eyes of the society in which we live. This is called "femininity" or "being a real woman" in our cultural lingo. We are authentic, legitimate, real to the extent that we are the property of some man whose name we bear. To be a woman who belongs to no man is to be invisible, pathetic, inauthentic, unreal. He confirms his image of us—of what we have to be in order to be acceptable by him—but not our real selves; he confirms our womanhood—as he defines it, in relation to him—but cannot confirm our personhood, our own selves as absolutes. As long as we are dependent on the male culture for this definition, for this approval, we cannot be free.

The consequence of internalizing this role is an enormous reservoir of self-hate. This is not to say the self-hate is recognized or accepted as such; indeed most women would deny it. It may be experienced as discomfort with her role, as feeling empty, as numbness, as restlessness, as a paralyzing anxiety at the center. Alternatively, it may be expressed in shrill defensiveness of the glory and destiny of her role. But it does exist, often beneath the edge of her consciousness, poisoning her existence, keeping her alienated from herself, her own needs, and rendering her a stranger to other women. They try to escape by identifying with the oppressor, living through him, gaining status and identity from his ego, his power, his accomplishments. And by not identifying with other "empty vessels" like themselves. Women resist relating on all levels to other women who will reflect their own oppression, their own secondary status, their own self-hate. For to confront another woman is finally to confront one's self—the self we have gone to such lengths to avoid. And in that mirror we know we cannot really respect and love that which we have been made to be.

As the source of self-hate and the lack of real self are rooted in our male-given identity, we must create a new sense of self. As long as we cling to the idea of "being a woman, " we will sense some conflict with that incipient self, that sense of I, that sense of a whole person. It is very difficult to realize and accept that being "feminine" and being a whole person are irreconcilable. Only women can give to each other a new sense of self. That identity we have to develop with reference to ourselves, and not in relation to men. This consciousness is the revolutionary force from which all else will follow, for ours is an organic revolution. For this we must be available and supportive to one another, give our commitment and our love, give the emotional support necessary to sustain this movement. Our energies must flow toward our sisters, not backward toward our oppressors. As long as woman's liberation tries to free women without facing the basic heterosexual structure that binds us in one-to-one relationship with our oppressors, tremendous energies will continue to flow into trying to straighten up each particular relationship with a man, into finding how to get better sex, how to turn his head around—into trying to make the "new man" out of him, in the delusion that this will allow us to be the "new woman." This obviously splits our energies and commitments, leaving us unable to be committed to the construction of the new patterns which will liberate us.

It is the primacy of women relating to women, of women creating a new consciousness of and with each other, which is at the heart of women's liberation, and the basis for the cultural revolution. Together we must find, reinforce, and validate our authentic selves. As we do this, we confirm in each other that struggling, incipient sense of pride and strength, the divisive barriers begin to melt, we feel this growing solidarity with our sisters. We see ourselves as prime, find our centers inside of ourselves. We find receding the sense of alienation, of being cut off, of being behind a locked window, of being unable to get out what we know is inside. We feel a real-ness, feel at last we are coinciding with ourselves.

With that real self, with that consciousness, we begin a revolution to end the imposition of all coercive identifications, and to achieve maximum autonomy in human expression.

Notes

1 Purportedly, this was a term used against lesbians to prevent them from becoming a major part of the women's rights movement sponsored by NOW. The Radicalesbians took the term as their own and made it an empowering part of their drive to be included in feminist organizations of the time.

2 Karla Jay, *Tales of the Lavender Menace: A Memoir of Liberation* (New York: Basic Books, 1999).

3 Radicalesbians, "The Woman-Identified Woman" (Pittsburgh, PA: Know, Inc., 1970).

47

Manifesto
Female Revolt (Rivolta Femminile)
Rome, Italy
July 1970

Rivolta Femminile manifesto pamphlet.

The transmission of life, respect for life, awareness of life are intense experiences for woman and values that she claims as her own.

Italy has a history of feminism dating back to the fifteenth-century works of Christine de Pizan (including her 1405 *Book of the City of Ladies*) and the nineteenth-century journal *La Donna* (Woman), which covered international feminist news. Rivolta Femminile was established in Rome and Milan in 1970, while Feminist Struggle (Lotta Femminista) began in 1971.

Student and worker activism marked this period in Italy, which influenced the forms feminism took there. Yasmin Ergas remarks, "[T]he basic tenets of the New Left's ideology (especially its egalitarian antiauthoritarianism and anti-institutionalism) played an important role in undermining the legitimacy of the rules of the game by which women had apparently been placed in a subordinate position within these organizations. . . . The formation of collectives and the adoption of consciousness-raising techniques generated closely-knit female networks."[1] The Left, rather than the Church, helped shaped Italian feminism of the era. "As in

France, in Italy women started denouncing the pervasive sexism of the new Left and began thinking that one outlet from oppression was the development of a personal consciousness of female oppression."[2] That development is seen in Rivolta Femminile's Manifesto,[3] which the group posted in the streets of Milan and Rome.

The feminism in this document emphasizes difference more than sameness, views domestic labor as reproducing the capitalist workforce, blasts the myth of equality, and "emphasize[s] the separation between gender as a social construction and sex as a biological foundation as a means to unveil the cultural and political discourses that legitimate discrimination." Put (relatively) succinctly, "[F]eminists theorized that the oppression of women does not result from socioeconomic determinants only, nor can it be affected by means of juridical struggles alone. More radically, subordination is about structures of meaning and power played out at the level of the symbolic."[4] That argument explains the focus in the Manifesto on not defining women in relation to men, an idea also raised by the Radicalesbians. Feminists must reject the multiple myths, images, institutions, and ideologies that have contributed to women's subordination. It is a mammoth task, but necessary given that "[c]ivilization had despised us as inferior, the church has called us sex, psychoanalysis has betrayed us, Marxism has sold us to hypothetical revolution."

Shortly after its founding, Rivolta Femminile opened its own publishing house, Scritti di Rivolta Femminile. In fact, the group has exercised influence primarily through their publications, especially those of founder Carla Lonzi, rather than through direct action. The group published a second Manifesto in 1977.

Manifesto

Will women always be divided one from another? Will they never be
a single body?
Olympe de Gouges, 1791

Woman must not be defined in relation to man. This awareness is the foundation of both our struggle and our liberty.

Man is not the model to hold up for the process of woman's self-discovery.

Woman is the other in relation to man. Man is the other in relation to woman. Equality is an ideological attempt to subject woman even further.

The identification of woman with man means annulling the ultimate means of liberation.

Liberation for woman does not mean accepting the life man leads, because it is unlivable; on the contrary, it means expressing her own sense of existence.

Woman as subject does not reject man as subject but she rejects him as an absolute role. In society she rejects him as an authoritarian role.

Up until now the myth that the one complements the other has been used by man to justify his own power.

Women are persuaded from infancy not to take decisions and depend on a "capable" and "responsible" person: father, husband, brother.

The image with which man has interpreted woman has been his own invention.

Virginity, chastity, fidelity are not virtues; but bonds on which to build and to maintain the institution of the family. Honour is its consequent repressive codification.

In marriage, the woman, deprived of her name, loses her identity, signifying the transfer of property which has taken place between her father and the husband.

She who gives birth is unable to give her name to her children: the woman's right has been coveted by others whose privilege it had become.

We are forced to reclaim as our own the issue of a natural fact.

We identify marriage as the institution that has subordinated woman to male destiny. We are against marriage.

Divorce is a welding of marriages which actually reinforces the institution.

The transmission of life, respect for life, awareness of life are intense experiences for woman and values that she claims as her own.

Woman's first reason for resentment against society lies in being forced to face maternity as a dilemma.

We denounce the unnatural nature of a maternity paid for at the cost of exclusion.

The refusal of the freedom of abortion is part of the global denial of woman's autonomy.

We do not wish to think about motherhood all our lives or to continue to be unwitting instruments of patriarchal power.

Woman is fed up with bringing up a son who will turn into a bad lover.

In freedom she is able and willing to face the son and the son is humanity.

In all forms of cohabitation, feeding, cleaning, caring and every aspect of daily routing must be reciprocal gestures.

By education and by mimesis men and women step into their roles in very early infancy.

We understand the mystifying character of all ideologies, because through the reasoned forms of power (theological, moral, philosophical, political) they have constrained humanity into an inauthentic condition, suppressed and consenting.

Behind every ideology we can see the hierarchy of the sexes.

From now on we do not wish to have any screen between ourselves and the world.

Feminism has been the first political moment of historical criticism of the family and society.

Let's unite the situations and episodes of historical feminist experience: through it woman has manifested herself, interrupting for the first time the monologue of patriarchal civilization.

We identify in unpaid domestic work the help that allows both private and state capitalism to survive.

Shall we allow that which happens again and again at the end of every popular revolution, when woman, who has fought with the others, finds herself and her problems pushed to one side?

We detest the mechanisms of competitiveness and the blackmail exercised in the world by the hegemony of efficiency. We want to put our working capacity at the disposal of a society that is immune to this.

War has always been the specific activity of the male and his model for virile behaviour.

Equality of remuneration is one of our rights but our suppression is another matter. Shall we be content with equal pay when we already carry the burden of hours of domestic work?

We must re-examine the creative contributions made by woman to society and defeat the myth of her secondary industry.

Attributing high value to "unproductive" moments is an extension of life proposed by woman.

Whoever is in power states "loving an inferior being is part of eroticism." Maintaining the status quo is therefore an act of love.

We welcome free sexuality in all its forms because we have stopped considering frigidity an honourable alternative.

Continuing to regulate life between the sexes is a necessity for power, the only satisfactory choice is a free relationship.

Curiosity and sexual games are a right of children and adolescents.

We have looked for 4,000 years; now we have seen!

Behind us is the apotheosis of the age-old masculine supremacy. Institutionalized religions have been its firmest pedestal. And the concept of "genius" has constituted its unattainable step. Woman has undergone the experience of seeing what she was doing destroyed every day.

We consider incomplete any history which is based on non-perishable traces.

Nothing, or else misconception, has been handed down about the presence of woman. It is up to us to rediscover her in order to know the truth.

Civilization had despised us as inferior, the church has called us sex, psychoanalysis has betrayed us, Marxism has sold us to hypothetical revolution.

We ask for testimonials for centuries of philosophical thought that has theorized about the inferiority of woman.

We hold systematic thinkers responsible for the great humiliation imposed on us by the patriarchal world. They have maintained the principle of woman as an adjunct for the reproduction of humanity, as bonded with divinity, or as the threshold of the animal world, a sphere of privacy and pietas. They have justified by metaphysics what was unjust and atrocious in the life of woman.

We spit on Hegel.

The servant-master dialectic is a settling of accounts between groups of men: it does not foresee the liberation of woman, the great oppressed by the patriarchal civilization.

Class struggle, as a revolutionary theory that developed from the servant-master dialectic, also excludes woman. We question socialism and the dictatorship of the proletariat.

By not recognizing herself in male culture woman deprives it of the illusion of universality.

Man has always spoken the name of humanity but half the world population now accuses him of having sublimated a mutilation.

Man's strength lies in identifying with culture, ours in refuting it.

After this act of conscience man will be distinct from woman and will have to listen to her telling what concerns her.

The world will not explode just because man will no longer hold the psychological balance based on our submission.

From the bitter reality of a universe that has never revealed its secrets we take much of the credit given to the obstinacies of culture. We wish to rise to be equal to an answerless universe.

We look for the authenticity of the gesture of revolt and will sacrifice it neither to organization nor to proselytism.

We communicate only with women.

Notes

1 "1968–79—Feminism and the Italian Party System: Women's Politics in a Decade of Turmoil." *Comparative Politics* (April 1982): 261–62.

2 Elena Dalla Torre, "French and Italian Feminist Exchanges: Queer Embraces in Queer Time," PhD diss., University of Michigan, 2010, p. 7.

3 *Italian Feminist Thought: A Reader,* ed. Paola Bono and Sandra Kemp (Oxford, UK: Blackwood, 1991), pp. 37–40.

4 Miguel Malagreca, "Lottiamo Ancora: Reviewing One Hundred and Fifty Years of Italian Feminism." *Journal of International Women's Studies* 7.4 (May 2006): 83.

48

Young Lords Party Position Paper on Women
Young Lords Women's Caucus
New York, New York
September 25, 1970

"Machismo Es Fascismo—Women from the Young Lords." Silkscreen. Juan Carlos, 1970. New York, New York.

Third World Women have an integral role to play in the liberation of all oppressed people as well as in the struggle for the liberation of women.

Darrel Enck-Wanzer writes,

> One of the fundamental paradoxes of "new social movements" arising in the late 1960s and early 1970s was the disjuncture between their theoretical and practical stances on equality. . . . While sometimes (though not always) featuring demands for the equality of all people, groups like the Black Panthers, Nation of Islam, ME-ChA (Movimiento Estudiantil Chicanode Aztlan), and the early Young Lords frequently paid only lip service to the equality of a large portion of their membership: women. . . . But in the New York Young Lords, women banded together and demanded more than the theoretical equality announced by the organization.[1]

As in many other "progressive" groups, women in the Young Lords were relegated to a subordinate position before they rose to challenge such sexism. They formed a women's caucus in the summer of 1970, and published a newspaper that covered women's oppression, *La Luchadora.* "The Young Lords' 'Position Paper on Women' is the only comprehensive position on the subject of equality and women of color of any ethnic nationalist organization of the period."[2] The challenge to the practice of *machismo* is central in the document below, and it transformed the group's daily practices.

Influenced by the Black Panthers, the New York Young Lords (there were other chapters) began in the summer of 1969. While primarily thought of as radical Puerto Rican activists, in fact the group was broader than that. The Position Paper on Women opens with a claim about the growing consciousness of "Puerto Rican, Black, and other Third World (colonized) women," and ends with a section on "Revolutionary Women" that includes five Puerto Rican women, four Black women, and two Vietnamese women. The analysis is intersectional throughout, especially clear in the treatment of prostitution and of reproduction; too, connections between Third World men and women are as important as the tensions between them.

Denise Oliver Velez remembers the Young Lords this way:

Too often when you see pictures of the Panthers, or the Lords, or AIM or other radical groups from the 60's and 70's communities of color the images are those of men. Hard for me to believe it was 40 years ago that a group of young Puerto Ricans, African-Americans and other Latinos, most under the age of 20, would found an organization that would radically change the future of Puerto Ricans in the US, and affect issues around health care, education, culture, and justice for years to come. The Young Lords challenged racism, redefined what it meant to be Puerto Rican; no longer "Spanish," but Afro-Taino, in culture. To be proud to be "Boricua" or Nuyorican. To fight for basic human rights of food, clothing, shelter, health care, and justice. But most important to me as a woman, and former Young Lord, was the hard won stance taken by the YLP, as a whole, to address issues of "machismo," sexism and male chauvinism in our community as part of our political platform. For this I salute my sisters, and those brothers who struggled with us to throw off centuries of patriarchal enculturation to embrace our own brand of feminism.[3]

Young Lords Party Position Paper on Women

Puerto Rican, Black, and other Third World (colonized) women are becoming more aware of their oppression in the past and today. They are suffering three different types of oppression under capitalism. First, they are oppressed as Puerto Ricans or Blacks. Second, they are oppressed as women. Third, they are oppressed by their own men. The Third World woman becomes the most oppressed person in the world today.

Economically, Third World women have always been used as a cheap source of labor and as sexual objects. Puerto Rican and Black women are used to fill working class positions in factories, mass assembly lines, hospitals and all other institutions. Puerto Rican and black women are paid lower wages than whites and kept in the lowest positions within society. At the same time, giving Puerto Rican and Black women jobs means the Puerto Rican and Black man is kept from gaining economic independence, and the family unit is broken down. Capitalism defines manhood according to money and status; the Puerto Rican and Black man's manhood is taken away by making the Puerto Rican and Black woman the breadwinner. This situation keeps the Third World man divided from his woman. The Puerto Rican and Black man either leaves the household or he stays and becomes economically dependent on the woman, undergoing psychological damage. He takes out all of his frustrations on his woman, beating her, repressing and limiting her freedom. Because this society produces these conditions, our major enemy is capitalism rather than our own oppressed men.

Third World Women have an integral role to play in the liberation of all oppressed people as well as in the struggle for the liberation of women. Puerto Rican and Black women make up over half of the revolutionary army, and in the struggle for national liberation they must press for the equality of women; the woman's struggle is the revolution within the revolution. Puerto Rican women will be neither behind nor in front of their brothers but always alongside them in mutual respect and love.

Historical

In the past women were oppressed by several institutions, one of which was marriage. When a woman married a man she became his property and lost her last name. A man could have several wives in order to show other men what wealth he had and enhance his position in society. In Eastern societies, men always had several wives and a number of women who were almost prostitutes, called concubines, purely sexual objects. Women had no right to own anything, not even their children; they were owned by her husband. This was true in places all over the world.

In many societies, women had no right to be divorced, and in India it was the custom of most of the people that when the husband died, all his wives became the property of his brother.

In Latin America and Puerto Rico, the man had a wife and another woman called la corteja. This condition still exists today. The wife was there to be a homemaker, to have children and to maintain the family name and honor. She had to be sure to be a virgin and remain pure for the rest of her life, meaning she could never experience sexual pleasure. The wife had to have children in order to enhance the man's concept of virility and his position within the Puerto Rican society. La corteja became his sexual instrument. The man could have set her up in another household, paid her rent, bought her food, and paid her bills. He could have children with this woman, but they are looked upon as by-products of a sexual relationship. Both women had to be loyal to the man. Both sets of children grew up very confused and insecure and developed negative attitudes about the role.

Women have always been expected to be wives and mothers only. They are respected by the rest of the community for being good cooks, good housewives, good mothers, but never for being intelligent, strong, educated, or militant. In the past, women were not educated, only the sons got an education, and mothers were respected for the number of sons they had, not daughters. Daughters were worthless and the only thing they could do was marry early to get away from home. At home the role of the daughter was to be a nursemaid for the other children and kitchen help for her mother.

The daughter was guarded like a hawk by her father, brothers, and uncles to keep her a virgin. In Latin America, the people used "duenas" or old lady watchdogs to guard the purity of the daughters. The husband must be sure that his new wife has never been touched by another man because that would ruin the "merchandise." When he marries her, her purpose is to have sons and keep his home but not to be a sexual partner.

Sex was a subject that was never discussed, and women were brainwashed into believing that the sex act was dirty and immoral, and its only function was for the making of children. In Africa, many tribes performed an operation on young girls to remove the clitoris so they would not get any pleasure out of sex and would become better workers.

The Double Standard, Machismo, and Sexual Fascism

Capitalism sets up standards that are applied differently to Puerto Rican and Black men from the way they are applied to Puerto Rican and Black women. These standards are also applied differently to Third World peoples than they are applied to whites. These standards must be understood since they are created to divide oppressed people in order to maintain an economic system that is racist and oppressive.

Puerto Rican and Black men are looked upon as rough, athletic and sexual, but not as intellectuals. Puerto Rican women are not expected to know anything except about the home, kitchen and bedroom. All that they are expected to do is look pretty and add a little humor. The Puerto Rican man sees himself as superior to his woman, and his superiority, he feels, gives him license to do many things—curse, drink, use drugs, beat women, and run around with many women. As a matter of fact these things are considered natural for a man to do, and he must do them to be considered a man. A woman who curses, drinks, and runs around with a lot of men is considered dirty scum, crazy, and a whore.

Today Puerto Rican men are involved in a political movement. Yet the majority of their women are home taking care of the children. The Puerto Rican sister that involves herself is considered aggressive, castrating, hard and unwomanly. She is viewed by the brothers as sexually accessible because what else is she doing outside the home. The Puerto Rican man tries to limit the woman's role because they feel the double standard is threatened; they feel insecure without it as a crutch.

Machismo has always been a very basic part of Latin American and Puerto Rican culture. Machismo is male chauvinism and more. Machismo means "mucho macho" or a man who puts himself selfishly at the head of everything without considering the woman. He can do whatever he wants because his woman is an object with certain already defined roles—wife, mother, and good woman.

Machismo means physical abuse, punishment and torture. A Puerto Rican man will beat his woman to keep her in place and show her who's boss. Most Puerto Rican men do not beat women publicly because in the eyes of other men that is a weak thing to do. So they usually wait until they're home. All the anger and violence of centuries of oppression which should be directed against the oppressor is directed at the Puerto Rican woman. The aggression is also directed at daughters. The daughters hear their fathers saying "the only way a woman is going to do anything or listen is by hitting her." The father applies this to the daughter, beating her so that she can learn "respeto." The daughters grow up with messed up attitudes about their role as women and about manhood. They grow to expect that men will always beat them.

Sexual fascists are very sick people. Their illness is caused in part by this system which mouths puritanical attitudes and laws and yet exploits the human body for profit.

Sexual Fascism is tied closely to the double standard and machismo. It means that a man or woman thinks of the opposite sex solely as sexual objects to be used for sexual gratification and then discarded. A sexual fascist does not consider people's feelings; all they see everywhere is a pussy or a dick. They will use any rap, especially political, to get sex.

Prostitution

Under capitalism, Third World women are forced to compromise themselves because of their economic situation. The facts that her man cannot get a job and that the family is dependent on her support mean she hustles money by any means necessary. Black and Puerto Rican sisters are put into a situation where jobs are scarce or nonexistent and are forced to compromise body, mind, and soul; they are then called whores or prostitutes.

Puerto Rican and Black sisters are made to prostitute themselves in many other ways. The majority of these sisters on the street are also hard-core drug addicts, taking drugs as an escape from oppression. These sisters are subjected to sexual abuse from dirty old men who are mainly white racists who view them as the ultimate sexual objects. Also he has the attitude that he cannot really prove his manhood until he has slept with a Black or Puerto Rican woman. The sisters also suffer abuse from the pimps, really small time capitalists, who see the women as private property that must produce the largest possible profit.

Because this society controls and determines the economic situation of Puerto Rican and Black women, sisters are forced to take jobs at the lowest wages; at the same time take insults and other indignities in order to keep the job. In factories, our men are worked like animals and cannot complain because they will lose their jobs—their labor is considered abundant and cheap. In hospitals, our women comprise the majority of the nurse's aides, kitchen workers, and clerks. These jobs are unskilled, the pay is low, and there is no chance for advancement. In offices, our positions are usually as clerks, typists and no-promotion jobs. In all of these jobs, our sisters are subjected to racial slurs, jokes, and others indignities such as being leered at, manhandled, propositioned, and assaulted. Our sisters are expected to prostitute themselves and take abuse of any kind or lose these subsistence jobs.

Everywhere our sisters are turned into prostitutes. The most obvious example is the sisters hustling their bodies on the streets, but the other forms of prostitution are also types of further exploitation of the Third World women. The only way to eliminate prostitution is to eliminate this society which creates the need. Then we can establish a socialist society that meets the economic needs of all the people.

Birth Control, Abortion, Sterilization = Genocide

We have no control over our bodies, because capitalism finds it necessary to control the woman's body to control population size. The choice of motherhood is being taken out of the mother's hands. She is sterilized to prevent her from having children, or she has a child because she cannot get an abortion.

Third World sisters are caught up in a complex situation. On one hand, we feel that genocide is being committed against our people. We know that Puerto Ricans will not be around on the face of the earth very long if Puerto Rican women are sterilized at the rate they are being sterilized now. The practice of sterilization in Puerto Rico goes back to the 1930's when doctors pushed it as the only means of contraception. In 1947–48, 7% of the women were sterilized; between 1953–54, 4 out of every 25; and by 1965, the number had increased to about 1 out of every 3 women. In many cases our sisters are told that their tubes are going to be "tied," but are never told that the "tying" is really "cutting" and that the tubes can never be "untied."

Part of this genocide is also the use of birth control pills which were tested for 15 years on Puerto Rican sisters (guinea pigs) before being sold on the market in the u.s. Even now many doctors feel that these pills cause cancer and death from blood clotting.

Abortions in hospitals that are butcher shops are little better than the illegal abortions our women used to get. The first abortion death in NYC under the new abortion law was Carman Rodriguez, a Puerto Rican sister who died in Lincoln Hospital. Her abortion was legal, but the conditions in the hospital were deadly.

On the other hand, we believe that abortions should be legal if they are community controlled, if they are safe, if our people are educated about the risks and if doctors do not sterilize our sisters while performing abortions. We realize that under capitalism our sisters and brothers cannot support large families and the more children we have the harder it is to support them. We say, change the system so that women can freely be allowed to have as many children as they want without suffering any consequences.

Day Care Centers

One of the main reasons why many sisters are tied to the home and cannot work or become revolutionaries is the shortage of day care centers for children. The centers that already exist are over-crowded, expensive, and are only super-babysitting centers. Day care centers should be free, should be open 24 hours a day, and should be centers where children are taught their revolutionary history and culture.

Many sisters leave their children with a neighbor, or the oldest child is left to take care of the younger ones. Sometimes they are left alone, and all of us have read the tragic results in the newspapers of what happens to children left alone—they are burned to death in fires, or they swallow poison, or fall out of windows to their death.

Revolutionary Women

Throughout history, women have participated and been involved in liberation struggles. But the writers of history have never given full acknowledgement to the role of revolutionary women. At the point of armed struggle for national liberation, women have proved themselves as revolutionaries.

MARIANA BRACETTI was a Puerto Rican woman who together with her husband fought in the struggle for independence in Lares. She was called "el brazo de oro" [golden arm] because of her unlimited energy. For her role in the struggle, she was imprisoned. She sewed the first flag of El Grito de Lares.

Another nationalist woman was LOLA RODRIGUEZ DE TIO, a poet who expressed the spirit of liberty and freedom in "La Borinquena." Besides being a nationalist, she was a fighter for women's rights. She refused to conform to the traditional customs concerning Puerto Rican women and at one point cut her hair very short.

Only recently, a 19 year old coed, ANTONIA MARTINEZ, was killed in Puerto Rico in a demonstration against the presence of amerikkkan military recruiting centers. She was murdered when she yelled "Viva Puerto Rico Libre!"

SOJOURNER TRUTH was born a slave in New York around 1800. She traveled in the north speaking out against slavery, and for women's right. She was one of the most famous black orators in history.

KATHLEEN CLEAVER is a member of the Central Committee of the Black Panther Party. The Black Panthers are the vanguard of the Black liberation struggle in the united states. Another Panther sister, ERICA HUGGINS, is imprisoned in Connecticut for supposedly being a member of a conspiracy. She was forced to have her child in prison, and was given no medical attention while she was pregnant. Her child was later taken away from her because of her political beliefs.

ANGELA DAVIS is a Black revolutionary sister who is being hunted by the f.b.i. and is on their 10 most wanted list because she always defended her people's right to armed self-defense and because of her Marxist-Leninist philosophy.

In other parts of the world, women are fighting against imperialism and foreign invasion. Our sisters in Vietnam have struggled alongside their brothers for 25 years, first against the French colonizer, then against the japanese invaders, and now against the amerikkkan aggressors. Their military capability and efficiency has been demonstrated in so many instances that a women's brigade was formed in the National Liberation Front of the North Vietnamese Army.

BLANCA CANALES was one of the leaders of the revolution in Jayuya in 1950.

LOLITA LEBRON, together with three other patriots, opened fire on the House of Representative in an armed attack in 1954, bringing the attention of the world on the colonial status of Puerto Rico. She emptied a 45 automatic from the balcony of the Congress on to the colonial legislators. She then draped herself in the Puerto Rican flag and cried "Viva Puerto Rico Libre." The result was 5 legislators shot, and one critically wounded. She was imprisoned in a federal penitentiary and sentenced to 50 years. She is still in prison for this heroic act of nationalism.

LA THI THAM was born in a province which was constantly bombarded by u.s. planes. After her fiance was killed in action, she sought and got a job with a time bomb detecting team. She scanned the sky with field glasses and when the enemy dropped bombs along the countryside, she would locate those which had not exploded and her teammates would go and open them and clear the road for traffic.

KAN LICH, another Vietnamese sister, fought under very harsh and dangerous conditions. She became a brilliant commander, decorated many times for her military ability. Her practice to "hit at close quarters, hit hard, withdraw quickly" proved to be valid.

The Central Committee of the Young Lords Party has issued this position paper to explain and to educate our brothers and sisters about the role of sisters in the past and how we see sisters in the struggle now and in the future. We criticize those brothers who are "machos" and who continue to treat our sisters as less than equals. We criticize sisters who remain passive, who do not join in the struggle against our oppression.

We are fighting every day within our PARTY against male chauvinism because we want to make a revolution of brothers and sisters—together—in love and respect for each other.

FORWARD SISTERS IN THE STRUGGLE!
ALL POWER TO THE PEOPLE!

Notes

1 "Gender Politics, Democratic Demand, and Anti-Essentialism in the New York Young Lords," in *Latina/o Discourse in Vernacular Spaces: Somos De Una Voz?* ed. Michelle A. Holling and Bernadette Calafell (Lanham, MD: Lexington Books, 2011), p. 59.
2 "1040 Lounge: Women of the Young Lords." Bronx Museum (press release), accessed Feb. 13, 2017, www.bronxmuseum.org.
3 Denise Oliver Valdez, "We Were Young Lords, not Young Ladies." *Daily Kos,* Aug. 22, 2009, accessed Feb. 13, 2017, www.dailykos.com.

49

Manifesto
Women's Liberation
Adelaide, South Australia
1971

March by Women's Liberation and Women's Electoral Lobby.

Men must have demonstrated to them the destruction of human relations that they perpetuate in clinging to their dominance as males.

There was a very visible "first wave" feminist movement in Australia and, as seen in earlier documents, it continued through the world wars. Among the most active groups of the earlier era were the Women's Suffrage League, the Women's Christian Temperance Union, and the Working Women's Trade Union. Most Australian women won the vote in 1902, yet Indigenous women had to work another sixty years for suffrage. The second wave tackled a broad gamut of issues, from childcare and equal employment opportunities to domestic violence and unpaid care work.

Australia had an active feminist movement around the time of this Manifesto. The Adelaide Women's Liberation group started at the University of Adelaide in 1968 and spread to several other locations.[1] They had their first national conference in Melbourne in 1970. They engaged in protest and actions against the campus Miss Fresher competition, for women's studies, for access to abortion, and for working women's rights. They are credited with many long-term gains, including establishment of a Women's Health Center, a Rape Crisis Center, a Women's Community Center, and a Women's Studies Resource Centre. Until 1989, they were housed in Bloor House, which gave them a space to meet, hold consciousness-raising groups, and publish a newsletter.

Many Australian women entered the women's movement from other political campaigns—in this case, from Young Labor and anti–Vietnam War—where they experienced sexism. As was popular at the time, Women's Liberation tried to operate by more democratic (less male-identified) principles and believed in linkages between personal and political change. As Susan Magarey has described it, "Women's Liberation was developing an analysis of power that reached from the most traditional and public to the most intimate and private—challenging conventional distinctions between public and private as well as showing a household to be quite as much a political arena as a house of parliament."[2]

Like Italy's "Female Revolt," this Manifesto[3] rejects women being identified in relation to men, or aspiring to be what men have been; it does, however, emphasize more than most that men, too, need to be freed from prescribed sex roles. The critique focuses on systems of domination, and how they influence the behavior of individuals. When compulsion ends, individual choice reigns. The document makes a familiar distinction between structural changes and reforms. The list of reforms, however, is pretty dramatic, as it includes such changes as free childcare in all workplaces, pay for domestic work, free abortion on demand, and democratization of families.

Manifesto

We appeal to women to combine in solidarity to make these demands
and simultaneously to secure the understanding and cooperation of
men in making them.
Women's Liberation Movement. Adelaide.
[*Camp Ink* July 1971]

Women's Liberation is *not* a feminist movement, i.e., it is not narrowly confined to the struggle of women for equality with men in the present society. The aims of Women's Liberation are TOTAL in the sense that the liberation of women must concur with the liberation of *all individuals* from a situation in which the only socially accepted mode of self-expression or development is in terms of predefined sexual roles.

A woman is never taken for *herself*: she is always "Bill's bird," "the little woman" or just "mum." Her greatest humiliation lies in the situation where her decorated body, being the subject of male phallic fantasies and the consequent source of much commercial profit, determines her VALUE both in her own ideas and those of the male.

But that the male regards the female in this way indicates that he, too, is imprisoned within a sexual role: potency and/or virility become for him fetishized and, in worshipping them, symbols of his *power* over woman. (The woman, knowing herself to be desired, exploits this male obsession; in this sense, and in others, the power relationship is reciprocal.) This situation, because no male can ever measure up to such absolute potency, leads to male fears, real though false, as to his "virility," his "masculinity." Just as the woman is required to fulfil expectations of her role as sexual object, wife, mother, so is the male required to fulfil expectations of him as actor in the outside world. To *succeed* as bread-winner he must develop qualities required for success in our society: aggressiveness, competitiveness, emotional detachment and, since he is always involved in authoritarian work, structure, authoritarianism. Moreover, in a national society that relates to other societies in terms of power (economic and military), he has to be trained, psychologically and physically, for the military role, as instrument of his nation's power-obsession. If he rejects this role on political/moral grounds, society calls him "coward," "sissy"; and since much of self definition and security is based in the dominant role of "masculinity," his whole being in relation to the existing world may be called into doubt.

"Masculinity," like "femininity," is a role socially imposed; it is a role reflecting the historical process in which man's ("man" used as to signify the male human species in abstract) greater physical strength determined him as, progressively, hunter, armed protector, commander of armies, ruler of society. This role derives from the first division of labour, which was sexual, required for man's management of basic scarcity.

In modern society, where basic scarcity no longer exists and there is productive potential to satisfy all needs, where technological mastery has removed the need for human physical strength, the masculine role and its counterpart, the feminine role, need no longer exist. This is true not only of the primary social roles (the sexual ones) but of all social roles. That is to say, we are now in an historical situation that has the *potential* for individuals to free themselves of being defined by role structures, of a situation in which, the role having defined the behaviour appropriate to it, the individual has become a *reactive* being, not an *active subject*. The historical possibility now exists for individuals to realise *themselves* in terms of human creative potential and sociability.

Our society talks of "love" between male and female; but this "love" is a mystification, the rationale for the modern marriage/family institution—for how can spontaneous feeling or communication of self take place when individuals relate not to each other as individuals, but to each other as the occupiers of pre-defined roles? How can the generous free reciprocity that is human occur when the nature of these sexual roles is to make the male dominant over the female? For reciprocity can only occur in a situation between *equals*.

Accordingly, the freeing of woman from her subservient role, the assertion of her freedom as an individual, must *simultaneously* involve an attack on the male *role*. Men must have demonstrated to them the destruction of human relations that they perpetuate in clinging to their dominance as males. For males are frustrated in their possible wish for communication of their dreams and despairs to the individual closest to them by the obstacles arising from the pre-definition of the other (the female)—a pre-definition usually mutually established and maintained—as illogical, irrational, ignorant of the affairs of the world, gossipy, frivolous, etc, particularly when that other expects him to know how to handle the world and despises him if he admits any failure here.

If we believe that men and women are individuals, each with an experience of the world unique to them, who can relate to this world as active critical subjects rather than passively behaving as the occupants of pre-defined roles, then why does this individuality not express itself, throw off these chains? The answer lies in the nature of the social system in which they exist. As Herbert Marcuse says: "*Domination* is in effect whenever the individual's goals and purposes and the means of striving for and attaining them are prescribed to him and performed by him as something prescribed."

In a society where hierarchical top-down organisation predominates, a minority (of men) will dominate the rest. This domination is based not just in their actual power (control of the economy, of the political and military systems) but in their more or less conscious perpetuation of domination as *natural*. This cultural control successfully whittles down the imagination of most to conceive that society might be organised so as to minimize domination and allow each individual effective participation in the decisions governing his/*her* life. Domination, in requiring effective control of the many by the few determined to hold on to their power, requires that people be *taught* to *behave* in organised, predictable patterns that service the structure of domination. This is why sexuality and human relations have to be *institutionalized* in the marriage-family. Spontaneity is the arch-enemy of this system, and spontaneity arises when individuals exercise their right to *act*, to choose, to determine their lives, because it is then that the particular chain of behaviour is broken. This is the meaning of the "Anarchy" that so patently terrifies not only our own rulers but ourselves. We are terrified because in adjusting to this structure of domination, we have had to repress our natural spontaneity and life-instincts, and instead of living life in itself, we have subordinated our lives to gaining the means (work-wage, salary) merely to exist, the standard of subsistence becoming more developed, more comfortable as the productive capacity of society increases. Life as an end in itself. The distortion and oppression of life in this way is experienced by the psyche as so natural, so ordinary—for it has become automatic—that *freedom* becomes *almost* inconceivable and, into the bargain, a terrifying spectre in the threat it presents to the already established personality in the world. And it is much "easier" to live, as far as possible, life as a patterned routine than to choose freedom.

We can change this situation, which is historical, not natural.

It is significant that Women's Liberation, in being the first expression of political radicalism to be consciously and directly concerned with the individual, in effect, with the intimate relation between two human beings, with human relations generally, has erupted in the modern, western societies in this time of affluence and of the struggle for acceptance of the common humanity of other (women constituting the largest group with minority status) minority groups, the negroes and the Vietnamese.

Women's Liberation has to evoke what woman already, if only partially, know—that they are denied individual creative potential, denied recognition as individuals in their own right. Every women [sic] who has looked ahead, passively and/or despairingly, to a *closed* future of marriage, children and housework knows this; every women [sic] who has wanted education sufficient to get a job in which she can express herself to some degree, who has sought after good jobs or who has suffered routine jobs knows the brutal, discriminatory practice all along that line. We should be more inclined to believe the myth of the "happy housewife" if it could be demonstrated that woman ever had any choice to be otherwise. Such "happiness" may be the symptom of more or less mature, more or less tenuous adaptation to a virtually inescapable situation, rather than *real* happiness. That the situation is inescapable for most middle-class women as for working class women suggests the obstacles to be not only, or even primarily, material. On the whole, middle-class women only escape the pressure of *Women's Day* ideology and social expectations, made most effectively by the family, if they, by educational attainment or some "break," have partial refuge in a community (university, bohemian/deviant social groups) which goes part or all of the way in accepting her as an individual first, a woman second. As the last phrase indicates even here she is likely to be fragmented into roles with their respective functions.

Women's Liberation can spearhead the change, but to do this it must show itself as *human* (individual) *liberation. It must,* in this latter sense, *always remember there is little point in claiming equality if the nature of the latter is to make us equal to unfree men.*

Yet while men are unfree, women are materially, socially and psychologically more unfree—hence *Women's* Liberation. *Women's = Human* Liberation since, in freeing ourselves, we must free men (and vice versa).

Programme
The following aims and demands may be classified as two types:

a) *Structural*—those that would challenge and eventually destroy the existing system of domination

b) *Reforms*—ie, although significant change would be required for their achievement, they do not challenge the basis of the system of domination.

A. STRUCTURAL
(The general critique made above is already assumed; only specific points are made here)

We are working towards:

1. An end to the socialisation of children and adults—by the family, the education system, the mass media and socio-cultural agencies in general—into their respective sexual roles.

2. The abolition of institutionalisation of relationships between men and women. This means abolition of the family as an institution, an end to the laws bonding together the members of a family.

There is no reason why people may not freely choose to live in a familial situation; but they should remain in that situation only by their free will.

Equally, people should be free to choose other relational situations—eg, small communal groupings.

3. The democratisation of inter-sexual and inter-generational relationships. In the relations between man and woman, between parents and children, there should exist reciprocal recognition of each as an individual in his/her own right, with capacity and right to participate in the decisions governing that relational situation and with freedom to pursue his/her own life as he/she deems fit. (While small children may not be able to exercise such rights, nonetheless, they should still be respected as individuals; the age at which they can exercise such rights is problematic and should be left flexible to accommodate the differences in growth of individuals.)

4. The end of commercial exploitation of women as sex-objects, of human sexuality in general. This would require the ends of the economic system to be human, rather than profit and production as overriding ends in themselves.

5. The end of a situation in which most individuals, for the bulk of their working lives, are involved in alienated labour. The development of a situation in which, so far as we have to meet material necessity, we do so communally and democratically, in which, therefore, the labour process and product are our own and not another's. A situation in which each and all, having met material necessity, possess the means whereby to develop and express themselves.

B) REFORMS
We Demand:

1. Democratisation of the existing family institution, at least so far as the limits of institutionalisation allow it.

2. The equal sharing of housework and child-care between husband and wife, with the work situation adjusted accordingly. (eg, guarantee of women's right to work; the granting by employers of free shopping time during working time to both men and women.)

3. The rationalisation of housework in the provision of communal facilities, such as local and cheap dining facilities, child-minding centre, and laundries for those who want to use them.

4. If women are forced by temporary necessity (the care of infants) or *choose* to undertake the bulk of the domestic work, that they be paid a wage by the state for what is essential productive labour.

5. That women have the right to control their own bodies:
   - that the government initiate and finance a widespread education campaign on birth control and establish local community birth control centres for the dissemination of birth control information and devices
   - that such information and centres be extended to cover the various physiological disorders the female body is susceptible to.
   - the abolition of sales tax—at present 27 ½%—on contraceptives
   - that free abortion on demand be instituted.

6. The removal of all barriers for women in work.
   - the full integration of all areas of work , ie an end to the labelling of some areas as being fit only for men or only for women. (Only if this occurs can "equal pay for equal work" really mean economic equality.)
   - Equal pay
   - the payment of maternity allowances to women workers at least three months before births and one to two years after births.
   - guarantee of the same or similar job to a woman returned after absence through pregnancy.
   - the establishment of free, small, professionally staffed child centres in every work place (factories, offices, stores, universities, schools); these centres could be directed by a committee of elected parents and staff.
   - that further training, promotion, etc, be equally open to women as to men.
7. The abolition of all sexual differentiation in education:
   - the establishment of all schools as co-educational in every sense
   - the abolition of any sexual differentiation in subjects and vocational choices
   - if there exists training in schools in health, cooking, etc, that boys and girls be required to undertake it. (This demand is important in the present situation so as to legitimize male interest in cooking, etc, to destroy the inbuilt male resistance to such tastes and thereby free girls from their future burden of having been the only ones inducted into these "arts." Once this has occurred, compulsion should give way to individual choice.)
   - the encouragement of and provision of opportunities for all girls to develop their education as far as possible, to develop interest in the traditional male preserves of politics and technology and to secure equal training in these fields.
8. The provision of educational training or retraining schemes and employment for women of an age no longer burdened by the care of children, so that they may regain their self-respect as individuals in developing their capacities and contributing to the community.
9. The repeal of the law that makes it an offence for male homosexuals to express their homosexuality as they choose; the end of all discrimination in employment and in social life generally, against homosexuals.
10. That women be written back into history; that analysis of their historical role, of the source and development of the division of labour between the sexes be made.

Notes

1 "Women's Liberation Movement (Adelaide, S.A.), (1969–1989)," 2008. *Trove*, accessed Feb. 14, 2017, trove.nla.gov.au.
2 Susan Magarey, *Dangerous Ideas* (Adelaide, SA: University of Adelaide Press, 2014), pp. 27, 30.
3 Women's Liberation Movement, "Manifesto." *Camp Ink*, July 1971. Writings from the Australian Gay Left Library (online), accessed Feb. 13, 2017, www.anu.edu.au.

50

Women of *La Raza* Unite!
First National Conference of *Raza* Women
Houston, Texas
May 28–30, 1971

As *hermanas* [sisters], we have a responsibility to help each other in problems that are common to all of us. . . . Therefore, in order to reduce rivalry, we must disseminate our knowledge and develop strong communications.

The Raza Unida Party (RUP), made up of Mexican Americans mostly in southern Texas, was "established on January 17, 1970, at a meeting of 300 Mexican Americans at Campestre Hall in Crystal City, Texas."[1] The party aimed to elect members of La Raza (the Hispanic people) to governmental positions across Texas in order "to bring greater economic, social, and political self-determination to Mexican Americans in Texas, especially in South Texas."[2] Although the RUP supported a candidate for governor and several other members ran for other governmental positions, the group was not successful in electing members to influential positions in Texas.

The RUP did, however, provide a platform for Chicana women—"workers, unemployed women, welfare recipients, housewives, students"—to organize as a social, economic, and political group. Led by Elma Barrera, more than six hundred Chicanas from twenty-three states met at the first interstate gathering of Mexican American feminists: Conferencia de Mujeres por la Raza, or the National Conference of Raza Women.[3] The main resolutions that came from this conference were made at the workshops on "Sex and the Chicana" and "Marriage—Chicana Style." The women were concerned about reproductive rights, advocating for safe, free, and legal abortions, for birth control, and against involuntary sterilization. They also wanted to create a Chicana-run childcare system to enable La Raza women to go to school and work but also have a safe, culturally similar place for their children to stay while they were outside the home. According to Mirta Vidal, the conference discussed these resolutions in the context of "a rising consciousness of the Chicana about her special oppression in this society."[4]

The declaration below focuses on including women's perspectives in all social issues the RUP confronted from a Chicano perspective. The women address working conditions and wages; reproductive and sexual rights, including prostitution and women's health care; the legalization of marijuana possession and racially equal sentencing for drug abuse; cultural education and research; and an end to the war in Vietnam. Each of these sections includes advocating for legislation to change the policies and social systems that discriminate against or damage members of the Chicano/a race in very specific and culturally insensitive ways. Also included below are the resolutions made at the two major workshops of the session[5] to illustrate the most important concerns of the Women of La Raza at this conference. These resolutions specifically target the Catholic Church as one of the main repressive social organs in Chicana communities, and they advocate leaving the church or creating major changes in it to allow women greater sexual freedom and respect from men. The declaration is one of the few documents since the very earliest ones to address prostitution. While it endorses marriage, it

Chicana pride poster.

insists that traditional marital roles must change and that children must be educated, by "men, women, young and old," about new attitudes toward gender.

This declaration,[6] like the earlier South African Women's Charter (1954) and Radicalesbian document (1970), addresses the needs of a specific group of women that shares some conditions with other women and some with similarly situated men. While centered in a specific Texas community, the declaration from the Women of La Raza participates in the demand for equal human rights that was a major part of women's movements across the globe during the late twentieth century.

Women of *La Raza* Unite!

We, as *Chicanas*, are a vital part of the *Chicano* community. (We are workers, unemployed women, welfare recipients, housewives, students.) Therefore, we demand that we be heard and that the following resolutions be accepted.

Be it resolved that we, as *Chicanas*, will promote *la hermanidad* [sisterhood] concept in organizing *Chicanas*. As *hermanas*, we have a responsibility to help each other in problems that are common to all of us. We recognize that the oldest example of divide-and-conquer has been to promote competition and envy among our men and especially women. Therefore, in order to reduce rivalry, we must disseminate our knowledge and develop strong communications.

Be it also resolved, that we as *Raza* must not condone, accept or transfer the oppression of *La Chicana*.

That all *La Raza* Literature should include *Chicana* written articles, poems, and other writings to relate the *Chicana* perspective in the *Chicano* movement.

That *Chicanas* be represented in all levels of *La Raza Unida* party and be run as candidates in all general, primary, and local elections.

JOBS
Whereas the *Chicana* on the job is subject to unbearable inhumane conditions, be it resolved that:

Chicanas receive equal pay for equal work; working conditions, particularly in the garment-factory sweatshops, be improved; *Chicanas* join unions and hold leadership positions within these unions; *Chicanas* be given the opportunity for promotions and be given free training to improve skills; there be maternity leaves with pay.

PROSTITUTION

Whereas prostitution is used by a corrupt few to reap profits for themselves with no human consideration for the needs of *mujeres* [women], and *whereas* prostitutes are victims of an exploitative economic system and are not criminals, and *whereas* legalized prostitution is used as a means of employing poor women who are on welfare, be it resolved that:

1. those who reap profits from prostitution be given heavy prison sentences and be made to pay large fines;
2. that *mujeres* who are forced to prostitution not be condemned to serve prison sentences;
3. that prostitution not be legalized.

ABORTIONS

Whereas we, as *Chicanas*, have been subjected to illegal, dehumanizing, and unsafe abortions, let it be resolved that we endorse legalized medical abortions in order to protect the human right of self-determination. Be it also resolved that *Chicanas* are to control the process to its completion. In addition, we feel that the sterilization process must never be administered without full knowledge and consent of the individual involved.

COMMUNITY-CONTROLLED CLINICS

We resolve that more *Chicano* clinics (self-supporting) be implemented to service the *Chicano* community:

1. for education about medical services available (birth control, abortion, etc.);
2. as a tool for further education of *Chicana* personnel into medical areas, returning to the *barrios* [neighborhoods];
3. as political education for our people in view of the contracting bandaid programs now in existence.

CHILD-CARE CENTERS

In order that women may leave their children in the hands of someone they trust and know will understand the cultural ways of their children, be it resolved that *Raza* child-care programs be established in *nuestros barrios* [our neighborhoods]. This will allow time for women to become involved in the solving of our *Chicano* problems and time to solve some of their own personal problems. In order that she will not be deceived by these programs, be it further resolved that these programs should be run and controlled by *nuestra raza* [our race].

DRUGS

Whereas drug administration and drug abuse is a big problem among our people, and *whereas Chicanos* and *Chicanas* are not presently adequately represented in drug-education programs, be it resolved that: this conference go on record as advising all local public health and public schools and *La Raza* that the possession of marijuana must be decriminalized; and that a study on *Chicanas* in prison on drug-abuse charges be made as soon as possible; and that *Chicanos* and *Chicanas* who are bilingual and related to *La Raza* must be employed on a parity basis in all drug-abuse programs.

EDUCATION

Whereas we resolve that legislation concerning sex discrimination in education be supported and carried out by the *Chicano* community, we further resolve that a legislative clearinghouse be established to disseminate information pertaining to *Chicanas*.

That *Chicana* classes educating the *Chicana, Chicano,* and community in education growth together be implemented on all campuses. That these classes be established, controlled, and taught by *Chicanas*. The classes should deal with existing problems faced by the *Chicana* as a wife, mother, worker, and as a member of *La Raza*, and historical research should also be done by the classes into the discrimination against *Chicana* women.

RESEARCH

Whereas we resolve that research information be gathered and disseminated on the *Chicana* in the following areas: (1) health, education, and welfare, (2) labor, (3) women's rights, (4) funding sources.

INTERPRETERS

Whereas many *La Raza* women do not speak English, and *whereas* this poses a problem in their support of their minor children, be it resolved that juvenile justice courts be petitioned to provide interpreters for Spanish-speaking mothers, and be it further resolved that *Chicanos* form a committee to offer time and moral support to mothers and children who have juvenile justice court actions.

VIETNAM

Whereas the Vietnam war has victimized and perpetuated the genocide of *La Raza*, and has been used as a vehicle of division within our community and *familia* [family], be it resolved that we as Chicanas demand an immediate halt to the bombing and withdrawal from Vietnam.

Workshop Resolutions

SEX AND THE CHICANA

We feel that in order to provide an effective measure to correct the many sexual hang-ups facing the Chicano community the following resolutions should be implemented:

I. Sex is good and healthy for both Chicanos and Chicanas and we must develop this attitude.

II. We should destroy the myth that religion and culture control our sexual lives.

III. We recognize that we have been oppressed by religion and that the religious writing was done by *men* and interpreted by *men*. Therefore, for those who desire religion, they should interpret their Bible, or Catholic rulings according to their own feelings, what they think is right, without any guilt complexes.

IV. Mothers should teach their sons to respect women as human beings who are equal in every respect. *No double standard.*

V. Women should go back to the communities and form discussion and action groups concerning sex education.

VI. Free, legal abortions and birth control for the Chicano community, controlled by *Chicanas*. As Chicanas we have the right to control our own bodies.

VII. Make use of church centers, neighborhood centers and any other place available.

"Liberate your mind and the body will follow. . . ."

"A quitarnos todos nuestros complejos sexuales para tener una vida mejor y feliz"
(Let's cast off all our sexual complexes to have a better and happier life).

MARRIAGE—CHICANA STYLE

Reaffirmation that Chicano marriages are the beginnings of Chicano families which perpetuate our culture and are the foundation of the movement.

Points brought up in the workshop:

1. Chicano Marriages are individual and intimate and solutions to problems must be primarily handled on an individual basis.
2. A woman must educate and acquaint herself with outside issues and personal problems (sexual hangups, etc.).
3. It is the responsibility of Chicanas with families to educate their sons and thus change the attitudes of future generations.
4. Chicanas should understand that Chicanos face oppression and discrimination, but this does not mean that the Chicana should be a scapegoat for the man's frustrations.
5. With involvement in the movement, marriages must change. Traditional roles for Chicanas are not acceptable or applicable.

RESOLUTIONS:

I. We, as *mujeres de La Raza* [women of the Race], recognize the Catholic Church as an oppressive institution and do hereby resolve to break away and not go to it to bless our unions.

II. Whereas: Unwanted pregnancies are the basis of many social problems, and

III. Whereas: The role of Mexican-American women has traditionally been limited to the home, and

IV. Whereas: The need for self-determination and the right to govern their own bodies is a necessity for the freedom of all people, therefore,

BE IT RESOLVED: That the National Chicana Conference go on record as supporting free family planning and free and legal abortions for all women who want or need them.

[I.] Whereas: Due to socio-economic and cultural conditions, Chicanas are often heads of households, i.e., widows, divorcees, unwed mothers, or deserted mothers, or must work to supplement family income, and

[II.] Whereas: Chicana motherhood should not preclude educational, political, social, and economic advancement, and

[III.] Whereas: There is a critical need for a 24-hour child-care center in Chicano communities, therefore,

BE IT RESOLVED: That the National Chicana Conference go on record as recommending that every Chicano community promote and set up 24-hour day-care facilities, and that it be further resolved that these facilities will reflect the concept of La Raza as the united family, and on the basis of brotherhood (La Raza), so that men, women, young and old assume the responsibility for the love, care, education, and orientation of all the children of Aztlan.

[I.] Whereas: Dr. Goldzieher of SWRF has conducted an experiment on Chicana women of westside San Antonio, Texas, using a new birth control drug, and

[II.] Whereas: No human being should be used for experimental purposes, therefore,

BE IT RESOLVED: That this Conference send telegrams to the American Medical Association condemning this act. Let it also be resolved that each Chicana women's group and each Chicana present at the conference begin a letter writing campaign. . . .

RELIGION

I. Recognize the *Plan de Aztlan*

II. Take over already existing Church resources for community use, i.e., health, Chicano awareness—public information of its resources, etc.

III. Oppose any institutionalized religion.

IV. Revolutionary change of Catholic Church or for it to get out of the way.

V. Establish communication with the barrio and implement programs of awareness to the Chicano movement.

Notes

1 Teresa Palomo Acosta, "A Historical Snapshot: El Partido de La Raza Unida," *La Voz de Austin*, July 18, 2012. Reprinted in *Latina Lista* online, www.latinalista.com.

2 Ibid.

3 Mirta Vidal, "Women: New Voice of La Raza," 1977. *Documents from the Women's Liberation Movement*, Duke University, library.duke.edu.

4 Ibid.

5 "Workshop Resolutions: First National Chicano Conference," in *Chicanas Speak Out: Women; New Voice of La Raza*, ed. Mirta Vidal (New York: Pathfinder Press, 1971).

6 "Women of La Raza Unite!" in *Dear Sisters: Dispatches from the Women's Liberation Movement*, ed. Rosalyn Baxandall and Linda Gordon (New York: Basic Books, 2000).

51

Statement of Purpose
Chicago Women's Liberation Union
Chicago, Illinois
1972

Della Leavitt, CWLU member, and the CWLU emblem in the 1970s

The Chicago Women's Liberation Union is a way for us to work together and experience, perhaps for the first time, the excitement and sense of purpose that comes when you are working with other women for a better life for everyone.[1]

The Chicago Women's Liberation Union (CWLU), founded in 1969, worked to unite women in an attempt to change society to better women's lives. The CWLU strongly believed in democracy; it was radical, anticapitalist, and feminist, which made its cause revolutionary. The union was made of different work groups that created proposals and programs. Some of the most successful programs included the Liberation School for Women, which taught about political analysis and women's liberation; *Womankind*, a newspaper published by the CWLU; Jane, the underground illegal abortion provider; Blazing Star, which fought against homophobia; DARE, which worked to end discrimination in employment; and even the Chicago Women's Liberation Rock Band and the Women's Graphics Collective, which "spread information about women's liberation and the CWLU."[2] During its existence, the CWLU included some of the most prominent feminist activists in Chicago, including Heather Booth, Vivian Rothstein, Naomi Weisstein, Estelle Carol, and Diane Horowitz.

The organization defined itself as radical, aimed at a redistribution of power and restructuring of society. Their primary target was sexism—"the systematic oppression of women for the benefit of the people in power"; they reckoned, however, with other forms of oppression, and thought that those in power made the weaker people (which the CWLU defines as "women, blacks, Latins, and the poor and working people of this country") fight against each other to make it easier to maintain power. They saw sexism as pervasive, and as requiring both internal and social transformation. They wanted to change this structure to suit human needs, not those of the capitalist profit-making machine. Their programs addressed this desire and worked to educate and change women's attitudes toward their position in American society. Experience in the antiwar movement had again made clear the need for a women's movement.

As a socialist feminist organization, the CWLU defined itself in contrast to liberal and radical groups. Its eight years of existence were filled with hope and action for democracy.[3]

Statement of Purpose

The Chicago Women's Liberation Union is a radical women's liberation organization that is over three years old. We have over 300 members, and many different programs aimed at changing the lives of all women and building a new society in which all people will have the opportunity to develop their full potential.

WHAT WE BELIEVE

Changing women's position in society is going to require changes in expectations, jobs, childcare, and education. It also means changing the distribution of power from the few having power over the rest of us to all people sharing power and sharing in the decisions that affect our lives. These are major, radical changes. We consider our struggle revolutionary because it will require a total restructuring of society, not merely making room for more women within this structure.

Our primary purpose is to attack sexism—that's the systematic oppression of women for the benefit of the people in power. Sexism exists everywhere in this society—for example, on the job, in family roles, and in the laws. We are fighting for changes in ourselves and other individuals, and in the institutions and policies that set up our lives in sexist patterns.

We do not think that women are the only people in this society who are oppressed[.] We think that it is easier for the people in power to keep women, blacks, Latins, and the poor and working people of this country down when we're fighting against each other instead of learning to work together against the unequal distribution of wealth and opportunity that comes with this arrangement of society—an arrangement where decisions are based on making profits, not on human needs.

We believe in democracy. By that we do not mean just voting in elections, but responsible participation of the people affected by a decision. We are trying to act on our ideas to test and improve them. Ours is not an organization that one just joins—it is a working organization, trying to involve more people in change, and trying to create a society where our principles are at work.

Notes

1 Chicago Women's Liberation Union, "About the Herstory Project." *CWLU Herstory Project*, accessed Aug. 8, 2017, https://www.cwluherstory.org.

2 Chicago Historical Society, Chicago Women's Liberation Union Records, 1954, 1967–78. Chicago History Museum, www.chsmedia.org.

3 *Womankind*, Dec. 1972. *Womankind* was the CWLU newspaper from 1971 to 1973.

52

Jewish Women Call for Change
Ezrat Nashim
New York
March 14, 1972

This document[1] is reminiscent of the 1846 "Petition for Women's Rights." Both were written by a small group of women urging the larger group of which they are a part, and to which they feel committed, to reconsider past discriminatory practices based on a commitment to women's rights. The earlier petition was sent to the New York Constitutional Convention; this one was taken to the 1972 convention of the Conservative Rabbinical Assembly. Both became parts of long-term feminist struggles.

The signatories were ten young members of a *havurah*, or religious fellowship. They called themselves "Ezrat Nashim," which refers to the women's section in Orthodox synagogues, and also literally means "women's help." Their document was included in the rabbis' convention packet, was presented during a meeting with the rabbis' wives, and was written about in the *New York Post*.

There are four denominations of Judaism in the United States: Reform, Reconstructionist, Conservative, and Orthodox. Ezrat Nashim was a study group of Conservative women. Calling the "second-class status of women in Jewish life" "disgraceful" and "entirely unacceptable," and asserting the sexes' equality "in intellectual capacity, leadership ability and spiritual depth," the document below challenges women's confinement to private roles and worship.

In separate meetings with rabbis and their wives, the women of Ezrat Nashim issued a "Call for Change" that put forward the early agenda of Jewish feminism. That agenda stressed the "equal access" of women and men to public roles of status and honor within the Jewish community. It focused on eliminating the subordination of women in Judaism by equalizing their rights in marriage and divorce laws, counting them in the *minyan* (the quorum necessary for communal prayer), and enabling them to assume positions of leadership in the synagogue as rabbis and cantors. In recognition of the fact that the secondary status of women in Jewish law rested on their exemption from certain *mitzvot* (commandments), the statement called for women to be obligated to perform all *mitzvot*, as were men.[2]

Reformed Judaism ordained its first female rabbi in 1972, Reconstructionist in 1974, and Conservative in 1985. Orthodox Jews still ordain only men, but groups such as Jewish Orthodox Feminist Alliance continue to work for change from within. The first national conference of Jewish women, held in 1973, drew over five hundred people.

> Conservatism is Judaism's largest American branch. When Ezrat Nashim assailed its Rabbinical Assembly, a truly agonizing examination of Conservative Judaism's law on women in the *minyan* [prayer quorum] took place. And the law was reversed: women became equals. This legal change inspired more and more Conservative synagogues to reassess the role of women in their congregations; long-standing prohibitions pertaining to public ritual and institutional governance were overturned. The "women's issue" has touched virtually every Conservative synagogue in the United States, and, not surprisingly, vain efforts to alter a particular congregation's policy one year, have with continued pressure, achieved some success in subsequent attempts.[3]

Jewish Women Call for Change

The Jewish tradition regarding women, once far ahead of other cultures, has now fallen disgracefully behind in failing to come to terms with developments of the past century.

Accepting the age-old concept of role differentiation on the basis of sex, Judaism saw woman's role as that of wife, mother, and home-maker. Her ritual obligations were domestic and familial: nerot, challah, and taharat ha-mishpachah. Although the woman was extolled for her domestic achievements, and respected as the foundation of the Jewish family, she was never permitted an active role in the synagogue, court, or house of study. These limitations on the life-patterns open to women, appropriate or even progressive for the rabbinic and medieval periods, are entirely unacceptable to us today.

The social position and self-image of women have changed radically in recent years. It is now universally accepted that women are equal to men in intellectual capacity, leadership ability and spiritual depth. The Conservative movement has tacitly acknowledged this fact by demanding that their female children be educated alongside the males—up to the level of rabbinical school. To educate women and deny them the opportunity to act from this knowledge is an affront to their intelligence, talents and integrity.

As products of Conservative congregations, religious schools, Ramah camps, LTF, USY, and the Seminary, we feel this tension acutely. We are deeply committed to Judaism, but cannot find adequate expression for our total needs and concerns in existing women's social and charitable organizations, such as Sisterhood, Hadassah, etc. Furthermore, the single woman—a new reality in Jewish life—is almost totally excluded from the organized Jewish community, which views women solely as daughters, wives, and mothers. The educational institutions of the Conservative movement have helped women recognize their intellectual, social and spiritual potential. If the movement then denies women opportunities to demonstrate these capacities as adults, it will force them to turn from the synagogue, and to find fulfillment elsewhere.

It is not enough to say that Judaism views women as separate but equal, nor to point to Judaism's past superiority over other cultures in its treatment of women. We've had enough of apologetics: enough of Bruria, Dvorah, and Esther; enough of Eshet Chayil [the woman of valor]!

It is time that:

- Women be granted membership in synagogues
- Women be counted in the minyan
- Women be allowed full participation in religious observances—(aliyot, ba'a lot kriyah, shlichot tzibur) [being called to the Torah, reading torah, leading services]
- Women be recognized as witnesses before Jewish law
- Women be allowed to initiate divorce
- Women be permitted and encouraged to attend Rabbinical and Cantorial schools, and to perform Rabbinical and Cantorial functions in synagogues
- Women be encouraged to join decision-making bodies, and to assume professional leadership roles, in synagogues and in the general Jewish community
- Women be considered as bound to fulfill all mitzvot equally with men.

For three thousand years, one-half of the Jewish people have been excluded from full participation in Jewish communal life. We call for an end to the second-class status of women in Jewish life.

Notes

1 Ezrat Mashim, "Jewish Women Call for Change," 1972. Jewish Women's Archive, www.jwa. org.

2 Paula Hyman, "Jewish Feminism in the United States." Jewish Women's Archive Encyclopedia, accessed Feb. 14, 2017, www.jwa.org/encyclopedia/article.

3 Steven Cohen, "American Jewish Feminism: A Study in Conflicts and Compromises." *American Behavioral Scientist* 23.4 (March–April 1981): 556.

53

Manifesto #2
Radicalqueens
Philadelphia, Pennsylvania
1973

Issue #2 of *Radicalqueen* magazine.

Trans issues have become increasingly visible in feminist discourse and activism. This Manifesto is an early piece that deeply and positively connects trans and feminist issues. A trans collective located in Philadelphia, Pennsylvania,

> Radicalqueens was in the forefront of questioning not only why boys and girls are assigned different and unequal tasks in our society, but also the very existence of such cherished institutions as marriage and the nuclear family. In our often controversial magazine, *Radicalqueen*, we as a collective espoused the not-so-new idea (Marx and Engels beat us to it) that marriage and family were the means society used to control behavior, sexual and otherwise.[1]

In their Manifesto, the Radicalqueens challenge socialization into male and female roles, and see being trans as thus inherently subversive. They portray some of the forms of violence those who are "nonmen" are subjected to, violence pervasive still today. Their critique of roles centers on male socialization into disdain for the feminine and unmanly, a feminine they join feminism in reconceiving. Their analysis sees gender roles as individually and socially destructive, and they distance themselves from multiple forms of oppression.

Trans activism has a history, this is to say, linked with both gay and women's liberation but also containing some critiques of each. The first trans journal may have been the short-lived 1952 *Transvestia: The Journal of the American Society for Equality in Dress*.[2] Trans street prostitutes first rioted against police harassment in 1966. The role of queens in the Stonewall riots has also been recovered as central. "The signs of a more militant queer spirit were always there among the most vulnerable queers, the street queens who couldn't pass as anything other than what they were."[3]

Radicalqueens Manifesto #2

Having been born men, having been socialized to be independent, aggressive, competitive, assertive, task-oriented, outward-oriented, innovative, self-disciplined, stoic, active, objective, analytic-minded, courageous, unsentimental, rational, confident, emotionally controlled, having been made to consider makeup, dresses, crying, touching other men, kissing other men and related traits "sissyish" or "faggoty," having been made to play war games as a child and to believe that life is a battle to be fought in Vietnam, and against the communists and against those men who are not "manly," having been made to believe that women are the weaker sex, and frail, passive, unexciting, intuitive, emotional, things which real men are not supposed to be, thing which only "faggots" are, having been told as men that real men are not hairdressers, that real men are not artists, actors or female impersonators, having been slapped when we tried on our mother's dresses or jewelry, or when we played with our sister's dolls, having been part of movements that, though liberal, still held onto the definition of man as aggressive, competitive, etc., and still reduced women in the movement to secretaries and typists, having been part of gangs in school, gangs that taunted effeminate boys, kicking and spitting on them, calling them names, pushing them, stealing their books, sometimes beating them up or forcing them to suck us off, having as men defined ourselves as the creators, the conquerors, the scientists, having as men resisted seeing how ugly these images of men are, how destructive they are!

Radicalqueens are not men, we are non-men. We are not women. We do not accept the attributes of femininity, that is, passivity, non-aggressiveness, fragility, etc., things which our sisters in the Women's Movement see as oppressive and undesirable traits socialized into women. We do not accept the traditional role of women as any alternative to the oppressor role of the male. Both roles are inventions of the oppressor, both are oppressive to those who accept them.

We of radicalqueens feel it is only by becoming non-men, that is, by throwing off the needs of the machismo man, the need to conquer, to suppress, the need to be like john wayne or any other symbol of strength and "manliness." We feel being sensitive, being compassionate, being able to cry, to touch, to feel, yet without being totally passive, totally non-aggressive, is revolutionary, is Gay. Being homosexual is not the answer to being oppressors. Men have been raised to be the oppressor. All men.

We of radicalqueens will not be the oppressors, we have been working against our own oppressive tendencies. We recommend that all Gay men begin questioning their own feelings. It is only by questioning everything that we can find anything, can find a bit of the truth, by slicing through all of the lies!

Notes

1 Tommi Avicolli Mecca, "The Lavender Picket Fence," in *Do I Don't*, ed. Greg Wharton and Ian Philips (San Francisco: Suspect Thoughts Press, 2004), www.avicollimecca.com, accessed Feb. 14, 2017.

2 Some of this history is from GLBTQ Spark Network, *GLBT History: Transgender Activism* board, www.sparkpeople.com/myspark/team_messageboard_thread. asp?board=0x940x45855093.

3 Tommi Mecca, *Smash the Church, Smash the State: The Early Years of Gay Liberation* (San Francisco: City Lights Press, 2009), p. 10.

54

Statement of Purpose
The National Black Feminist Organization
New York, New York

May 1973

Florynce "Flo" Kennedy, cofounder of the NBFO, at a protest rally in support of Joann Little, a young African American accused of murdering her jailor-rapist in 1974.

I can't be Black three days and woman four days when I'm a Black woman
seven days a week.
—Margaret Sloan

During the course of their work as feminist activists, Florynce Kennedy (a lawyer, pictured in figure 54.1) and Margaret Sloan (a founding editor of *Ms.* magazine) heard from Black women who felt alone in their fight for equality. Sloan suggested that these feelings of isolation were a consequence of two major trends: (1) common media narratives that implied there was a "lack of Black women's interest in feminism" and (2) a sense that "Black women shouldn't declare priorities outside of the existing civil rights movement."[1] In response, Kennedy and Sloan organized the first NBFO meeting for May 1973. Thirty founding members (including Michele Wallace, Faith Ringgold, and Doris Wright) attended this meeting, where they discussed Black women's relationship to feminism and drafted this Statement of Purpose. Sloan soon after released an announcement, on August 15, 1973, inviting all Black women to join the organization. Sloan and Kennedy were right to question the assumption that Black women were uninterested in feminist politics, for around four hundred women responded with inquiries, and by February 1974 the NBFO had over two thousand members from ten chapters all across the country.[2] The NBFO is often cited as the first national Black women's organization that explicitly identified itself as feminist, though earlier ones, as we have seen, speak from the experiences and for the betterment of Black women's lives.

Many NBFO members were associated with other women's organizations, like the National Organization for Women (NOW), leading up to and following the group's founding. In fact, NBFO founding members borrowed the office of the New York City chapter of NOW. However, NBFO members felt there was a "need to establish ourselves as an independent black feminist organization." Evidence of this need can be found from their agendas, which were distinct in the types of issues prioritized. For example, the first regional conference from November 30 to December 2, 1973, included twenty workshops focusing on Black women's access to childcare, welfare, media, homosexuality, prisons, addiction, and education.[3]

Ollie Johnson and Karin Stanford's study of Black women's organizations following World War II suggests that the NBFO's interest in welfare as a fundamental women's issue set it apart from many other contemporary organizations. They argue that "mainstream feminist organizations such as the National Organization for Women (NOW) were preoccupied with the Equal Rights Amendment and thus did not make explicit political alliances with the . . . ranks of the Welfare Rights Movement."[4]

In this document,[5] blame is placed on "the distorted male-dominated media image of the Women's Liberation Movement" for turning people away from what is a "serious political and economic revolutionary force." It also mourns that "we have virtually no positive self-images to validate our existence." It criticizes racism's effects on Black women and men as well as sexism's effects on White and Black women. It forcefully portrays the no-win situation of the Black woman in America at the time, which it traces back to the era of enslavement.

Statement of Purpose

The distorted male-dominated media image of the Women's Liberation Movement has clouded the vital and revolutionary importance of this movement to Third World women, especially black women. The Movement has been characterized as the exclusive property of so-called white middle-class women and any black women seen involved in this movement have been seen as "selling out," "dividing the race," and an assortment of nonsensical epithets. Black feminists resent these charges and have therefore established The National Black Feminist Organization, in order to address ourselves to the particular and specific needs of the larger, but almost cast-aside half of the black race in Amerikkka, the black woman.

Black women have suffered cruelly in this society from living the phenomenon of being black and female, in a country that is *both* racist and sexist. There has been very little real examination of the damage it has caused on the lives and on the minds of black women. Because we live in a patriarchy, we have allowed a premium to be put on black male suffering. No one of us would minimize the pain or hardship or the cruel and inhumane treatment experienced by the black man. But history, past or present, rarely deals with the malicious abuse put upon the black woman. We were seen as breeders by the master; despised and historically polarized from/by the master's wife; and looked upon as castrators by our lovers and husbands. The black woman has had to be strong, yet we are persecuted for having survived. We have been called "matriarchs" by white racists and black nationalists; we have virtually no positive self-images to validate our existence. Black women want to be proud, dignified, and free from all those false definitions of beauty and womanhood that are unrealistic and unnatural. *We*, not white men or black men, must define our own self-image as black women and not fall into the mistake of being placed upon the pedestal which is even being rejected by white women. It has been hard for black women to emerge from the myriad of distorted images that have portrayed us as grinning Beulahs, castrating Sapphires, and pancake-box Jemimas. As black feminists we realized the need to establish ourselves as an independent black feminist organization. Our above ground presence will lend enormous credibility to the current Women's Liberation Movement, which unfortunately is not seen as the serious political and economic revolutionary force that it is. We will strengthen the current efforts of the Black Liberation struggle in this country by encouraging *all* of the talents and creativities of black women to emerge, strong and beautiful, not to feel guilty or divisive, and assume positions of leadership and honor in the black community. We will encourage the black community to stop falling into the trap of the white male Left, utilizing women only in terms of domestic or servile needs. We will continue to remind the Black Liberation Movement that there can't be liberation for half the race. We must, together, as a people, work to eliminate racism, from without the black community, which is trying to destroy us as an entire people; but we must remember that sexism is destroying and crippling us from within.

Notes

1 Beverly Davis, "To Seize the Moment: A Retrospective on the National Black Feminist Organization." *Sage* 5.2 (Fall 1988): 43–44.

2 Kayomi Wada, "National Black Feminist Organization (1973–1976)." BlackPast.Org, accessed Feb. 14, 2017, www.blackpast.org.

3 Davis, p. 44.

4 *Black Political Organizations in the Post–Civil Rights Era* (New Brunswick, NJ: Rutgers University Press, 2002), p. 185.

5 "The National Black Feminist Organization's Statement of Purpose, 1973." University of Michigan–Dearborn, accessed Oct. 9, 2013, http://www-personal.umd.umich.edu.

55

Working Women's Charter
London Trades Council
London, England
March 1974

Working Women's Charter Campaign badges, 1974–1975. TUC Library Collections, London Metropolitan University.

In 1968, women sewing machinists at Ford's Dagenham car plant in East London won a victory for increased (though not equal) wages. A National Joint Action Campaign Committee for Women's Equal Rights was formed, and an Equal Pay Act was passed.[1] Following these events, in 1974 the Working Women's Charter was drafted by women in trade unions and trades councils. It clearly links together what happens in schools, workplaces, and homes.

The status quo to which the Working Women's Charter is reacting is not unfamiliar: unequal educational opportunities, unequal opportunities for apprenticeships, pregnancy marking the end of or a setback to one's job or career, inadequate family planning, inadequate childcare options, unequal pay, and the double shift for women. The Charter is a challenge to the labor movement, which often supported equal pay but never considered these broader social issues part of their mandate. This document is another attempt to merge labor and feminist issues.

While the Working Women's Charter[2] was launched by the London Trades Council, the push for its acceptance came from local charter campaign groups established around the country. The Brent Working Women's Charter Group, for example, worked hard in support of this bill, translating the document into Gujarati to reach Asian workers, supporting a group of workers fighting for equal pay, speaking to local groups, and holding a conference on November 10, 1974. "At its height it had 27 groups across the UK and was supported by 12 national unions, 55 trade union branches, 37 trade councils and 85 other organizations."[3]

The union ended up not approving the Charter at its 1975 Trades Union Congress conference. The union then proposed its own.[4] While the two have several features in common, the later one does not mention a minimum wage, family allowances, *free* childcare, *paid* maternity leave, or contraception and abortion at all, free or otherwise. It does, however, support retraining courses for women returning to the paid labor force after years home with children, advocate part-time work to enable women "to meet their commitments as mothers," and oppose allowing women to work with materials that might endanger them or future offspring.

Working Women's Charter

We pledge ourselves to agitate and organize to achieve the following aims:

1. The rate for the job regardless of sex, at rates negotiated by the trade unions, with a national minimum wage below which no wages should fall.
2. Equal opportunity of entry into occupations and in promotion, regardless of sex and marital state.
3. Equal education and training for all occupations and compulsory day-release for all 16–19 year olds in employment.
4. Working conditions to be, without deterioration of previous conditions, the same for women as for men.
5. The removal of all legal and bureaucratic impediments to equality—e.g. with regard to tenancies, mortgages, pension schemes, taxation, passports, control over children, social security payments, hire purchase agreements.
6. Improved provisions of local authority day nurseries, free of charge, with extended hours to suit working mothers. Provision of nursery classes in day nurseries. More nursery schools.
7. 18 weeks maternity leave with full net pay spread before and after the birth of a live child; 7 weeks after birth if the child is stillborn. No dismissal during pregnancy or maternity leave. No loss of security, pension or promotion prospects.
8. Family planning clinics supplying free contraception to be extended to cover every locality. Free abortion to be readily available.
9. Family allowances to be increased to L2.50 per child, including the first child.
10. To campaign amongst women to take part in the trade unions and in political life so that they may exercise influence commensurate with their numbers and to campaign amongst men trade unionists that they may work to achieve this aim.

Notes

1 Cathy Nugent, "Restarting Our Women's Work," April 14, 2007. Alliance for Workers' Liberty, accessed Feb. 14, 2017, www.workersliberty.org.
2 "Charter for Women," March 1974. London Trades Council, www.unionhistory.info.
3 *Working Women.* Film, 1975. North East Film Archive/BFI, www.bfi.org.uk.
4 Trade Union Congress, "Charter" (London: Victoria House Printing Company/Trade Union Congress, 1975).

56

Wages for Housework
New York Wages for Housework Committee
New York
1975

Wages for Housework logo.

The women of the world are serving notice. We clean your homes and factories. We raise the next generation of workers for you. Whatever else we may do, we are the housewives of the world. . . . We are serving notice to you that we intend to be paid for the work we do.

Wages for Housework (WFH) was an international campaign with its roots in the Italian International Feminist Collective, whose founding members included Selma James, Brigitte Galtier, Mariarosa Dalla Costa, and Silvia Federici. Federici, who wrote *Wages for Housework* (1975) and *Revolution at Point Zero: Housework, Reproduction, and Feminist Struggle* (2012), came from Italy to the United States and helped start groups there. The New York Wages for Housework Committee opened an office in Brooklyn in 1975. Many other groups organized across the country, including Black Women for Wages for Housework and Wages Due Lesbians.

The idea of compensation for domestic work goes back further in history; for example, "Crystal Eastman called for 'a generous endowment of motherhood provided by legislation' in her opening address to the First Feminist Congress in 1919," and "the idea that the work of raising children should be recognized and remunerated as well as any other job surfaced again among American welfare-rights activists in the 1960s, who demanded that welfare be dignified with the title of a 'wage.'"[1]

Wages for Housework Campaign poster. Image courtesy of Labor and Love: An Ongoing Conversation about Mothers, Children, Housework, and Wages exhibit by Norene Leddy, Newark Museum and Gallery Aferro.

WFH incorporated Marxist themes into their feminist analysis. While the idea of compensating women for domestic labor was at the forefront, behind all of the group's work were broader arguments about the importance of reproductive and affective labor, the unequal access of men and women to leisure time, and the economic exploitation of women in paid and unpaid work under capitalism. WFH agreed with the Italian intellectual movement *operaismo* that wages are essential to worker control. It challenges the idea that women working in the home are somehow outside social production and the capitalist market.

Its proponents insisted that the binary between work and home, "productive" and "reproductive" work, was not only a fiction, but a necessary fiction at the basis of capitalism. Capital accumulation depended on unwaged household work: giving birth to the future workforce, yes, but also feeding husbands, children, and parents, cleaning up after them, placating them when the world frustrated their ambitions, and so on. Seeing this more clearly than its predecessors, Wages for Housework understood how much damage a refusal to do unwaged labor could inflict on a capitalist system.[2]

As one might guess, "the Left" did not always respond positively.[3]
The document below[4] shows that Wages for Housework reached out to more women than those working primarily in the home, seeing in the affective labor that women do a "common problem" that could be the basis of a "common struggle." It emphasizes just how much is at stake for women in having some degree of economic independence, linking it with social power and freedom. They demand that women have social, sexual, and economic autonomy regardless of their position within or outside of the formal workforce. They write elsewhere, "Wages for Housework, then, is not a demand, one among others, but a political perspective which opens a new ground of struggle, beginning with women, for the entire working class."[5]

Wages for Housework

The New York WAGES FOR HOUSEWORK COMMITTEE is part of a nationwide organization that is campaigning for WAGES FOR HOUSEWORK from the government for ALL WOMEN

married or not   with or without children   with or without a second job
native or immigrant   lesbian or straight

HOUSEWORK IS OUR COMMON PROBLEM
LET'S MAKE IT OUR COMMON STRUGGLE

We demand WAGES FOR HOUSEWORK because we cannot afford to work endless hours in the home and then depend on a man or on welfare or have to take a second job BECAUSE WE HAVE NO MONEY we can call our own. Nobody works as much as we do. WE ALL NEED

MORE MONEY NOT MORE WORK.
WE DEMAND WAGES FOR HOUSEWORK

To cut down on housework—to eat out, get machines to do some of the work, and refuse to be slaves to the house
    To be able to decide working conditions and wages on the second job, and if we want it in the first place
    To stand up to men when we work WITH them and when we work FOR them—if we had our own money we could
    To decide what our sex lives should be like
    To decide if, when and under what conditions to have children
    To give our children what we want them to have
    To demand and WIN paid holidays away from ALL work
    To demand and WIN decent housing

JOIN OUR CAMPAIGN
All over the US and in several other countries of the world women are organizing speak outs, rallies, marches for WAGES FOR HOUSEWORK. We speak in different languages but we are all saying the same thing.

NOTICE TO ALL GOVERNMENTS
The women of the world are serving notice. We clean your homes and factories. We raise the next generation of workers for you. Whatever else we may do, we are the housewives of the world. In return for our work, you have only asked us to work harder.

We are serving notice to you that we intend to be paid for the work we do. We want wages for every dirty toilet, every painful childbirth, every indecent assault, every cup of coffee and every smile. And if we don't get what we want, then we will simply refuse to work any longer.

We have brought [up] our children to be good citizens and to respect your laws and you have put them in factories, in prisons, in ghettos and in typing pools. Our children deserve more than you can offer and now we will bring them up to EXPECT more.

We have borne babies for you when you needed more workers, and we have submitted to sterilization when you didn't. Our wombs are not government property any longer.

We have scrubbed and polished and oiled and waxed and scoured until our arms and backs ached, and you have only created more dirt. Now you will rot in your own garbage.

We have worked in the isolation of our homes when you needed us to and we have taken on a second job too when you needed that. Now we want to decide WHEN we work, HOW we work, and WHO we work for. We want to be able to decide NOT TO WORK AT ALL—like you.

We are teachers and nurses and secretaries and prostitutes and actresses and childcare workers and hostesses and cooks and cleaning ladies—and workers of every variety. We have sweated while you have grown rich. Now we want back wealth we have produced.

WE WANT IT IN CASH, RETROACTIVE AND IMMEDIATELY. AND WE WANT ALL OF IT.

The crime against us internationally, from which all other crimes against us flow, is our life sentence of housework at home and outside, servicing men, children, and other women, in order to produce and reproduce the working class. For this work we are never paid a wage.

This crime of work and wagelessness brands us for life as the weaker sex and delivers us powerless to employers, government planners and legislators, doctors, the police, prisons and mental institutions as well as the individual men for a lifetime of servitude and imprisonment.

Our campaign for wages for housework is our demand for power to refuse the social and sexual onslaught on our minds, our bodies and our relations—in a word, our demand for power to refuse this destiny of work which we carry in every country, wherever we find ourselves.

We have been divided by the status and income of the men we marry, by whether or not we work fulltime in the home, by whether or not we are with men, by whether or not we have children, by whether or not we are natives or immigrants, and by language, race, and nation and the technology of our exploitation.

But our destiny and the roots of our exploitation—our wageless work in the home—are the same in every country of the world, and so is our struggle against it.

LET'S UNITE TO WAGES FOR HOUSEWORK
FROM ALL GOVERNMENTS
FOR ALL WOMEN

Notes

1 Dayna Tortorici, "More Smiles? More Money." *N+1 Magazine*, 2013, www.nplusonemag.com.

2 Ibid.

3 The New York group responded comprehensively to these criticisms in their November 1974 newsletter. See Nicole Cox and Silvia Federici, "Counter-Planning from the Kitchen," in *Wages for Housework: A Perspective on Capital and the Left* (New York: New York Wages for

Housework Committee and Falling Wall Press, 1975). Barnard Center for Research on Women Archive, accessed Feb. 14, 2017, bcrw.barnard.edu.

4 Wages for Housework Committee, "The Campaign for Wages for Housework," 1975. Barnard Center for Research on Women Archive, accessed Feb. 14, 2017, bcrw.barnard.edu.

5 Cox and Federici, p. 3.

57

Founding Manifesto
Women's Liberation Front (Frente de Liberación de la Mujer)
Madrid, Spain
January 25, 1976

In Madrid, on January 25, 1976, a group of feminist women launched the independent Women's Liberation Front (WLF). Spain was practically awash in feminist groups and actions at the time.[1] Due to Franco's death, International Women's Year, and the Tribunal of Crimes Against Women held in Brussels in March of 1976, some five hundred delegates secretly gathered for the First National Conference for Women's Liberation and wrote a common set of demands. Too, all this activity led to the formation of additional organizations (including the Catalonian Association of Women, the Barcelona Women's Coordinating Committee, and the People's Union of Women), a new magazine (*Vindicacion Feminista*), and self-help groups (one called the Feminist Pelvis Collection).

The WLF defined "itself as for the 'feminism-class struggle,' fighting for a socialist society, and openly espousing 'double militancy [for party and feminist ideals].' Women like Felioidad Orquin and Fini Rubio were members."[2] "Dual activists" may have been the majority at the First National Conference.[3]

This debate was known as the opposition between monism and dualism, or unique militancy (*"militancia única"*) and double militancy (*"doble militancia"*). Feminist women from the first groups stated that feminist goals were part of a bigger fight in favor of democracy and political rights. Thus, they accepted participation in political parties because they thought that fighting against a dictatorship and supporting citizen rights would also help in meeting feminist goals. Women's Democratic Movement (Movimiento Democrático de Mujeres) and Women's Democratic Association (Asociación Democrática de Mujeres) agreed with these ideas and were connected to workers' parties.

On the other hand, feminist women of the second group (*dualismones*) argued that the feminists' fight should be independent from other political claims, and they rejected any alliance with political parties or state machinery. Thus, they stated that the fight in favor of democracy didn't necessarily mean that feminist claims would be satisfied. In this group, we can mention Seminars and Feminist Associations (Seminarios y Colectivos Feministas). Finally, there was an attempt to find a "third way," exemplified by the Women's Liberation Front (Frente de Liberación de la Mujer). These women accepted double militancy, but they were not connected to a concrete political party.[4]

It is true both that "Spanish feminism was . . . marked by the political context in which it was born, the democratic movement against Franco's dictatorship in the mid-1970s,"[5] and "that four decades of Franco's dictatorship had not been able to kill progressive ideas."[6] Pretty impressive.

Stickers from the WLF.

The WLF "focused its activity on impacting the media, using its network of women journalists, thus winning popularity for women's demands and discourses. It focused on abortion rights, divorce (both unlawful in Spain at that point), and free expression of women's sexuality, including lesbianism. It was mainly influenced by cultural feminism, and by the French/Italian ideas of *feminisme de la difference*, but it also participated in the pro-democracy political struggles, alongside communist and socialist women's organizations."[7] The Founding Manifesto[8] supports coalition building. Just a year after its founding, WLF signed a manifesto written by the Homosexual Revolutionary Action Front against the Law of Social Dangers.[9] Nonetheless, the choice for autonomy meant a split from the Socialist Party, where women had (once again) experienced sexism and exploitation; though the claim below is that this split does not amount to division on the Left, in fact many divisive battles took place.

Founding Manifesto

The FLM is an autonomous group, consisting of only women and independent of political parties, the Spanish State and sectarian organizations. We are autonomous because women, as an oppressed group, must take control of our struggle—it has never been the case in history that any oppressed group has been emancipated without carrying out their own struggle. Our autonomy does not imply a division among the forces of the left. Division comes, however, as a result of forgetfulness in action. Defending our real goals and the exclusive acceptance of all female protest programs tend to improve our situation, and keep us together as a group apart. Therefore, we do not want women to start their own battle, we want, on the contrary, to recognize and be recognized as full citizens and unite our own to all the struggles of the exploited.

While there ha[s] been oppression of women in all societies, capitalism generates specific forms of exploitation that [necessitate] the existence of marginalized social sectors of production which can not absorb but at the same time [require] a sector of society, women, which guarantees the maintenance and reproduction of the labor force. Therefore, we affirm that the feminist struggle is directed against capitalism and the division of society into classes, and it aims to secure a socialist society. We also believe that this society will only be genuinely socialist if it fulfills the following objectives:

- Dismantling of all the structures of domination: economic, legal and ideological.
- Abolition of the traditional family and the economic and ideological relations that it supports.
- Elimination of the sexist division of labor.
- Dissolution of the institution of marriage; in its place we propose free choice in equal relationships between the sexes.

- Conscious and voluntary motherhood.
- Incorporation of all women into productive, political, and creative social tasks.
- Socialization of domestic work and the education of children, and monitoring of its implementation by the whole society.

We characterize the current political moment as a continuation of the Franco dictatorship. In this situation, feminist struggle is linked to the combined action of all oppressed sectors to achieve democratic freedoms:

- Freedom of assembly, expression, association, strikes and demonstrations.
- General amnesty and return of exiles.
- Repeal of all legislation that discriminates against and penalizes women.
- Repeal of anti-terrorist decree law, special jurisdiction, the death penalty and, in general, all repressive legislation.
- Self-determination for the nations of the Spanish state.

Our struggle, whose ultimate objective is the destruction of capitalist and patri-archal society, is captured in the present moment in the following demands:

- Equal pay for equal work.
- No female unemployment.
- Women's access to all jobs with equal decision-making power.
- Equal education and vocational training in a co-educational system at all levels.
- The right of women to control their bodies.
- Free and legal contraceptives and widely disseminated information about them.
- Sex education.
- Free and legal abortion paid for by Social Security.
- Free day-care centers, open 24 hours a day, with specialized and responsible personnel.
- Public cafeterias in workplaces and neighborhoods.
- Equality of responsibility between men and women for domestic work.
- Elimination of moral double standards.
- Disappearance from the media of sexist roles and of the image of woman as consumer and demander of consumption.
- An end to discriminatory treatment of women based on their marital status.

The FLM invites all women who are conscious of these issues to join it.

The FLM also wishes all groups of feminist women who are struggling for their liberation to unite for concrete action.

Women, unite for your liberation!!

Notes

1   This information is from Maria-Jose Rague-Arias, "Spain: Feminism in Our Time," in *The Women's Liberation Movement: Europe and North America*, ed. Jan Bradshaw (Amsterdam: Pergamon Press, 2013), p. 473.

2   Ibid.

3   Anny Brooksbank Jones, *Women in Contemporary Spain* (Manchester, UK: Manchester University Press, 1997), pp. 7–8.

4   Silvia López, Elin Peterson, and Raquel Platero, *Quing: Quality in Gender+ Equality Policies* (Vienna: Institute for Human Sciences, 2007), pp. 17–18.

5   Manuel Castells, *The Power of Identity*, 2nd ed. (Hoboken, NJ: Wiley-Blackwell, 2010), p. 248.

6 Gisela Kaplan, *Contemporary Western European Feminism* (New York: Routledge, 2012), p. 207.

7 Castells, p. 248.

8 Translation consulted: Jon Cowans, *Modern Spain: A Documentary History* (Philadelphia: University of Pennsylvania Press, 2003), pp. 259–61.

9 Paul Garlinger, *Confessions of the Letter Closet: Epistolary Fiction and Queer Desire in Modern Spain* (Minneapolis: University of Minnesota Press, 2005), p. 129.

58

Working Women's Charter
Working Women's Council
New Zealand
1977

The New Zealand Working Women's Council sponsored a convention of about four hundred women from all around the country where the Working Women's Charter was debated and approved. After being endorsed by two annual general meetings of the Working Women's Council, and two years of discussion, the Federation of Labour endorsed the Charter at its annual conference in 1980. It "became the focus of activism in the late 1970s and early 1980s. Provisions 8 and 15 dealing with working hours and sex education were particularly controversial."[1]

A pamphlet provided in support of the Charter discusses the status quo in New Zealand. It claims that women on average earn 75 percent of what men earn, due to lack of opportunity for women and consignment to low-wage jobs. It boldly states, "If a woman is to control her working life, she must be able to control her fertility."[2]

The New Zealand Working Women's Charter[3] shows the connection between the feminist and union movements in that country, and this document is more radical than its 1974 British counterpart. In addition to what the other mentions, it includes a right to work; speaks against discrimination based on race, sexuality, ethnicity, and age, as well as sex; advocates a shorter working week and improved working conditions for all; supports twenty-four-hour childcare; and asks for paid maternity *and* paternity leave.

Sandi Beattie, WWC national convenor, and other women from Auckland, New Zealand, prepare signs for a march supporting the Working Women's Charter, 1981. This photo appeared in the *New Zealand Herald*.

"Once the Federation of Labour and the Labour Party had adopted the Working Women's Charter's provisions as policy in 1980 opposition was very active. The anti-abortion lobby and traditional churches led a campaign that included the claim that the charter was a communist document."

New Zealand Working Women's Charter

1. The right to work for everyone who wishes to do so.
2. The elimination of all discrimination on the basis of sex, race, marital or parental status, sexuality or age.
3. Equal pay for work of equal value—meaning the same total wage plus other benefits.
4. Equal opportunity of entry into occupations and of promotion regardless of sex, sexuality, marital or parental status, race or age.
5. Equal education opportunity for all.
6. (a) Union meetings be held in working hours. (b) Special trade union education courses for women unionists to be held with paid time off for participants.
7. Equal access to vocational guidance and training, including on-the-job training, study and conference leave.
8. Introduction of a shorter working week with no loss of pay, flexible working hours, part-time opportunities for all workers.
9. Improved working conditions for women and men. The retention of beneficial provisions which apply to women. Other benefits to apply equally to men and women.
10. Removal of legal, bureaucratic and other impediments to equality of superannuation, social security benefits, credit, finance, taxation, tenancies, and other related matters.
11. Special attention to the needs and requirements of women from ethnic communities as they see them.
12. Wide availability of quality child care with Government and/or community support for all those who need it, on a 24-hour basis, including after-school and school holiday care.
13. Introduction of adequate paid parental leave without loss of job security, superannuation or promotion prospects.
14. Availability of paid family leave to enable time off to be taken in family emergencies, e.g. when children or elderly relatives are ill.
15. Sex education and birth control advice freely available to all people. Legal, financial, social and medical impediments to safe abortion, contraception and sterilisation to be removed.
16. Comprehensive Government-funded research into health questions specific to women.

Notes

1 Megan Cook, "Women's Labour Organisations: Unions, 1970s to 2000s," May 5, 2011. *Te Ara: The Encyclopedia of New Zealand*, accessed Aug. 29, 2017, http://www.TeAra.govt.nz.
2 "Working Women's Charter," in *The Vote, the Pill, and the Demon Drink: A History of Feminist Writing in New Zealand, 1869–1993*, ed. Charlotte Macdonald (Wellington, New Zealand: Bridget Williams Books, 1993), p. 217.
3 Christine Dann, *Up from Under: Women and Liberation in New Zealand, 1970–1985* (Wellington, New Zealand: Allen and Unwin/Port Nicholson Press, 1985), p. 80.

59

A Black Feminist Statement
Combahee River Collective
Boston, Massachusetts
April 1977

The Combahee River Collective.

Being on the bottom, we would have to do what no one else has done:
we would have to fight the world.
—Michelle Wallace

The Combahee River Collective (named after an 1863 military action along the Combahee River in South Carolina led by Harriet Tubman) started as a group of African American women meeting in Boston to talk about intersections of systems that promote racial, gendered, heteronormative, and class-based oppression. Barbara Smith attended the first National Black Feminist Organization (NBFO) regional meeting in 1973. She and other delegates intended to start an NBFO chapter in Boston, but they formed a new organization, instead, to follow a different political framework. Like the members of the NBFO, members of the Combahee River Collective rejected the notion that their political loyalties were necessarily divided between feminist and civil rights movements. They chose to shape this complicated intersection of political identities in distinctive ways.

Estelle Freedman's *Essential Feminist Reader* describes the collective's politics as "radical" with traces of socialist feminism, lesbian feminism, and Black nationalism. She contrasts this political approach to that of the NBFO, which she describes as "liberal."[1] Joy James's *Seeking the Beloved Community* similarly states that the collective emerged "to contest the liberalism" of the the NBFO.[2] James makes a compelling case for why we should make the effort to see the differences between NBFO and Combahee politics, arguing that the tendency to erase distinctions essentializes both Black women and Black feminism.

At a basic level, liberal and radical Black feminisms will identify similar instances of marginalization, though they may disagree when identifying the source of this marginalization and thus the proper response. James suggests that "Black feminisms that accept the political legitimacy of corporate state institutional and police power, but posit the need for humanistic reform, are considered liberal. Black feminisms that view (female and black) oppression as stemming from capitalism, neocolonialism and the corporate state that enforces both, are generally understood to be radical" (53). Radical Black feminisms thus address racial, gendered, heteronormative, and class-based oppression by confronting corporate powers, complicit state powers, and systems of policing that enforce corporate and state powers. The numerous documents in this collection may make the picture even richer, and more complicated.

Despite differences, the Combahee Statement explicitly identifies the NBFO as an important forerunner to its own brand of politics. Specifically, it lists 1973 as an important turning point when "Black feminists, primarily located in New York, felt the necessity of forming a separate Black feminist group." The NBFO helped to identify many of the problems that became a priority for the collective, as illustrated by the following similarities:

- Both documents identify racism as a problem in traditional, Western women's movements and sexism as a problem in traditional manifestations of the civil rights movement.
- Both documents reject popular media representations of Black women ("mammy, matriarch, Sapphire").
- Both recognize the roles and the needs of lesbians in the Black feminist movement.

However, the Combahee Statement confronts corporate powers as important material forces of oppression: "We realize that the liberation of all oppressed peoples necessitates the destruction of the political-economic systems of capitalism and imperialism as well as patriarchy."

The Combahee River Collective Statement[3] is often credited with dispersing the concept of identity politics. Identity politics can be a means of understanding identities that are influenced by multiple forces of power. It can also refer to a preferred type of political action, as when the Statement declares, "We believe that the most profound and potentially the most radical politics comes directly out of our own identity, as opposed to working to end somebody else's oppression." Thus, the collective showed a preference for group retreats where they discussed the material experience of being a Black woman along with participating in general consciousness-raising sessions. The additional impact of the CRCS is difficult to overstate given that the organization did not have ready access to models of political action from around the globe that account for multiple systems of oppression simultaneously. Barbara Smith recalls Demita Frazier explaining, "'This is not a mix cake. We have got to make it up from scratch.'" Thus, they "built strong friendships networks, community, and a rich Black women's culture where none had existed before."[4] This has provided a compelling example even after their dissolution in 1981.

A Black Feminist Statement

We are a collective of Black feminists who have been meeting together since 1974. During that time we have been involved in the process of defining and clarifying our politics, while at the same time doing political work within our own group and in coalition with other progressive organizations and movements. The most general statement of our politics at the present time would be that we are actively committed to struggling against racial, sexual, heterosexual, and class oppression, and see as our particular task the development of integrated analysis and practice based upon the fact that the major systems of oppression are interlocking. The synthesis of these oppressions creates the conditions of our lives. As Black women we see Black feminism as the logical political movement to combat the manifold and simultaneous oppressions that all women of color face.

We will discuss four major topics in the paper that follows: (1) the genesis of contemporary Black feminism; (2) what we believe, i.e., the specific province of our politics; (3) the problems in organizing Black feminists, including a brief herstory of our collective; and (4) Black feminist issues and practice.

1. The Genesis of Contemporary Black Feminism

Before looking at the recent development of Black feminism we would like to affirm that we find our origins in the historical reality of Afro-American women's continuous life-and-death struggle for survival and liberation. Black women's extremely negative relationship to the American political system (a system of white male rule) has always been determined by our membership in two oppressed racial and sexual castes. As Angela Davis points out in "Reflections on the Black Woman's Role in the Community of Slaves," Black women have always embodied, if only in their physical manifestation, an adversary stance to white male rule and have actively resisted its inroads upon them and their communities in both dramatic and subtle ways. There have always been Black women activists—some known, like Sojourner Truth, Harriet Tubman, Frances E. W. Harper, Ida B. Wells Barnett, and Mary Church Terrell, and thousands upon thousands unknown—who have had a shared awareness of how their sexual identity combined with their racial identity to make their whole life situation and the focus of their political struggles unique. Contemporary Black feminism is the outgrowth of countless generations of personal sacrifice, militancy, and work by our mothers and sisters.

A Black feminist presence has evolved most obviously in connection with the second wave of the American women's movement beginning in the late 1960s. Black, other Third World, and working women have been involved in the feminist movement from its start, but both outside reactionary forces and racism and elitism within the movement itself have served to obscure our participation. In 1973, Black feminists, primarily located in New York, felt the necessity of forming a separate Black feminist group. This became the National Black Feminist Organization (NBFO).

Black feminist politics also have an obvious connection to movements for Black liberation, particularly those of the 1960s and 1970s. Many of us were active in those movements (Civil Rights, Black nationalism, the Black Panthers), and all of our lives were greatly affected and changed by their ideologies, their goals, and the tactics used to achieve their goals. It was our experience and disillusionment within these liberation movements, as well as experience on the periphery of the white male left, that led to the need to develop a politics that was anti-racist, unlike those of white women, and anti-sexist, unlike those of Black and white men.

There is also undeniably a personal genesis for Black Feminism, that is, the political realization that comes from the seemingly personal experiences of individual Black women's lives. Black feminists and many more Black women who do not define themselves as feminists have all experienced sexual oppression as a constant factor in our day-to-day existence. As children we realized that we were different from boys and that we were treated differently. For example, we were told in the same breath to be quiet both for the sake of being "ladylike" and to make us less objectionable in the eyes of white people. As we grew older we became aware of the threat of physical and sexual abuse by men. However, we had no way of conceptualizing what was so apparent to us, what we knew was really happening.

Black feminists often talk about their feelings of craziness before becoming conscious of the concepts of sexual politics, patriarchal rule, and most importantly, feminism, the political analysis and practice that we women use to struggle against our oppression. The fact that racial politics and indeed racism are pervasive factors in our lives did not allow us, and still does not allow most Black women, to look more deeply into our own experiences and, from that sharing and growing consciousness, to build a politics that will change our lives and inevitably end our oppression. Our development must also be tied to the contemporary economic and political position of Black people. The post World War II generation of Black youth was the first to be able to minimally partake of certain educational and employment options, previously closed completely to Black people. Although our economic position is still at the very bottom of the American capitalistic economy, a handful of us have been able to gain certain tools as a result of tokenism in education and employment which potentially enable us to more effectively fight our oppression.

A combined anti-racist and anti-sexist position drew us together initially, and as we developed politically we addressed ourselves to heterosexism and economic oppression under capitalism.

2. What We Believe

Above all else, our politics initially sprang from the shared belief that Black women are inherently valuable, that our liberation is a necessity not as an adjunct to somebody else's but because of our need as human persons for autonomy. This may seem so obvious as to sound simplistic, but it is apparent that no other ostensibly progressive movement has ever considered our specific oppression as a priority or worked seriously for the ending of that oppression. Merely naming the pejorative stereotypes attributed to Black women (e.g. mammy, matriarch, Sapphire, whore, bulldagger), let alone cataloguing the cruel, often murderous, treatment we receive, indicates how little value has been placed upon our lives during four centuries of bondage in the Western hemisphere. We realize that the only people who care enough about us to work consistently for our liberation are us. Our politics evolve from a healthy love for ourselves, our sisters and our community which allows us to continue our struggle and work.

This focusing upon our own oppression is embodied in the concept of identity politics. We believe that the most profound and potentially most radical politics come directly out of our own identity, as opposed to working to end somebody else's oppression. In the case of Black women this is a particularly repugnant, dangerous, threatening, and therefore revolutionary concept because it is obvious from looking at all the political movements that have preceded us that anyone is more worthy of liberation than ourselves. We reject pedestals, queenhood, and walking ten paces behind. To be recognized as human, levelly human, is enough.

We believe that sexual politics under patriarchy is as pervasive in Black women's lives as are the politics of class and race. We also often find it difficult to separate race from class from sex oppression because in our lives they are most often experienced simultaneously. We know that there is such a thing as racial-sexual oppression which is neither solely racial nor solely sexual, e.g., the history of rape of Black women by white men as a weapon of political repression.

Although we are feminists and Lesbians, we feel solidarity with progressive Black men and do not advocate the fractionalization that white women who are separatists demand. Our situation as Black people necessitates that we have solidarity around the fact of race, which white women of course do not need to have with white men, unless it is their negative solidarity as racial oppressors. We struggle together with Black men against racism, while we also struggle with Black men about sexism.

We realize that the liberation of all oppressed peoples necessitates the destruction of the political-economic systems of capitalism and imperialism as well as patriarchy. We are socialists because we believe that work must be organized for the collective benefit of those who do the work and create the products, and not for the profit of the bosses. Material resources must be equally distributed among those who create these resources. We are not convinced, however, that a socialist revolution that is not also a feminist and anti-racist revolution will guarantee our liberation. We have arrived at the necessity for developing an understanding of class relationships that takes into account the specific class position of Black women who are generally marginal in the labor force, while at this particular time some of us are temporarily viewed as doubly desirable tokens at white-collar and professional levels. We need to articulate the real class situation of persons who are not merely raceless, sexless workers, but for whom racial and sexual oppression are significant determinants in their working/economic lives. Although we are in essential agreement with Marx's theory as it applied to the very specific economic relationships he analyzed, we know that his analysis must be extended further in order for us to understand our specific economic situation as Black women.

A political contribution which we feel we have already made is the expansion of the feminist principle that the personal is political. In our consciousness-raising sessions, for example, we have in many ways gone beyond white women's revelations because we are dealing with the implications of race and class as well as sex. Even our Black women's style of talking/testifying in Black language about what we have experienced has a resonance that is both cultural and political. We have spent a great deal of energy delving into the cultural and experiential nature of our oppression out of necessity because none of these matters has ever been looked at before. No one before has ever examined the multilayered texture of Black women's lives. An example of this kind of revelation/conceptualization occurred at a meeting as we discussed the ways in which our early intellectual interests had been attacked by our peers, particularly Black males. We discovered that all of us, because we were "smart" had also been considered "ugly," i.e., "smart-ugly." "Smart-ugly" crystallized the way in which most of us had been forced to develop our intellects at great cost to our "social" lives. The sanctions in the Black and white communities against Black women thinkers is comparatively much higher than for white women, particularly ones from the educated middle and upper classes.

As we have already stated, we reject the stance of Lesbian separatism because it is not a viable political analysis or strategy for us. It leaves out far too much and far too many people, particularly Black men, women, and children. We have a great deal of criticism and loathing for what men have been socialized to be in this society: what they support, how they act, and how they oppress. But we do not have the misguided notion that it is their maleness, per se—i.e., their biological maleness—that makes them what they are. As Black women we find any type of biological determinism a particularly dangerous and reactionary basis upon which to build a politic. We must also question whether Lesbian separatism is an adequate and progressive political analysis and strategy, even for those who practice it, since it so completely denies any but the sexual sources of women's oppression, negating the facts of class and race.

3. Problems in Organizing Black Feminists

During our years together as a Black feminist collective we have experienced success and defeat, joy and pain, victory and failure. We have found that it is very difficult to organize around Black feminist issues, difficult even to announce in certain contexts that we are Black feminists. We have tried to think about the reasons for our difficulties, particularly since the white women's movement continues to be strong and to grow in many directions. In this section we will discuss some of the general reasons for the organizing problems we face and also talk specifically about the stages in organizing our own collective.

The major source of difficulty in our political work is that we are not just trying to fight oppression on one front or even two, but instead to address a whole range of oppressions. We do not have racial, sexual, heterosexual, or class privilege to rely upon, nor do we have even the minimal access to resources and power that groups who possess any one of these types of privilege have.

The psychological toll of being a Black woman and the difficulties this presents in reaching political consciousness and doing political work can never be underestimated. There is a very low value placed upon Black women's psyches in this society, which is both racist and sexist. As an early group member once said, "We are all damaged people merely by virtue of being Black women." We are dispossessed psychologically and on every other level, and yet we feel the necessity to struggle to change the condition of all Black women. In "A Black Feminist's Search for Sisterhood," Michele Wallace arrives at this conclusion:

> We exist as women who are Black who are feminists, each stranded for the moment, working independently because there is not yet an environment in this society remotely congenial to our struggle—because, being on the bottom, we would have to do what no one else has done: we would have to fight the world.

Wallace is pessimistic but realistic in her assessment of Black feminists' position, particularly in her allusion to the nearly classic isolation most of us face. We might use our position at the bottom, however, to make a clear leap into revolutionary action. If Black women were free, it would mean that everyone else would have to be free since our freedom would necessitate the destruction of all the systems of oppression.

Feminism is, nevertheless, very threatening to the majority of Black people because it calls into question some of the most basic assumptions about our existence, i.e., that sex should be a determinant of power relationships. Here is the way male and female roles were defined in a Black nationalist pamphlet from the early 1970s:

> We understand that it is and has been traditional that the man is the head of the house. He is the leader of the house/nation because his knowledge of the world is broader, his awareness is greater, his understanding is fuller and his application of this information is wiser ... After all, it is only reasonable that the man be the head of the house because he is able to defend and protect the development of his home ... Women cannot do the same things as men—they are made by nature to function differently. Equality of men and women is something that cannot happen even in the abstract world. Men are not equal to other men, i.e. ability, experience or even understanding. The value of men and women can be seen as in the value of gold and silver—they are not equal but both have great value. We must realize that men and women are a complement to each other because there is no house/family without a man and his wife. Both are essential to the development of any life.

The material conditions of most Black women would hardly lead them to upset both economic and sexual arrangements that seem to represent some stability in their lives. Many Black women have a good understanding of both sexism and racism, but because of the everyday constrictions of their lives, cannot risk struggling against them both.

The reaction of Black men to feminism has been notoriously negative. They are, of course, even more threatened than Black women by the possibility that Black feminists might organize around our own needs. They realize that they might not only lose valuable and hardworking allies in their struggles but that they might also be forced to change their habitually sexist ways of interacting with and oppressing Black women. Accusations that Black feminism divides the Black struggle are powerful deterrents to the growth of an autonomous Black women's movement.

Still, hundreds of women have been active at different times during the three-year existence of our group. And every Black woman who came, came out of a strongly-felt need for some level of possibility that did not previously exist in her life.

When we first started meeting early in 1974 after the NBFO first eastern regional conference, we did not have a strategy for organizing, or even a focus. We just wanted to see what we had. After a period of months of not meeting, we began to meet again late in the year and started doing an intense variety of consciousness-raising. The overwhelming feeling that we had is that after years and years we had finally found each other. Although we were not doing political work as a group, individuals continued their involvement in Lesbian politics, sterilization abuse and abortion rights work, Third World Women's International Women's Day activities, and support activity for the trials of Dr. Kenneth Edelin, Joan Little, and Inéz García. During our first summer when membership had dropped off considerably, those of us remaining devoted serious discussion to the possibility of opening a refuge for battered women in a Black community. (There was no refuge in Boston at that time.) We also decided around that time to become an independent collective since we had serious disagreements with NBFO's bourgeois-feminist stance and their lack of a clear political focus.

We also were contacted at that time by socialist feminists, with whom we had worked on abortion rights activities, who wanted to encourage us to attend the National Socialist Feminist Conference in Yellow Springs. One of our members did attend and despite the narrowness of the ideology that was promoted at that particular conference, we became more aware of the need for us to understand our own economic situation and to make our own economic analysis.

In the fall, when some members returned, we experienced several months of comparative inactivity and internal disagreements which were first conceptualized as a Lesbian-straight split but which were also the result of class and political differences. During the summer those of us who were still meeting had determined the need to do political work and to move beyond consciousness-raising and serving exclusively as an emotional support group. At the beginning of 1976, when some of the women who had not wanted to do political work and who also had voiced disagreements stopped attending of their own accord, we again looked for a focus. We decided at that time, with the addition of new members, to become a study group. We had always shared our reading with each other, and some of us had written papers on Black feminism for group discussion a few months before this decision was made. We began functioning as a study group and also began discussing the possibility of starting a Black feminist publication. We had a retreat in the late spring which provided a time for both political discussion and working out interpersonal issues. Currently we are planning to gather together a collection of Black feminist writing. We feel that it is absolutely essential to demonstrate the reality of our politics to other Black women and believe that we can do this through writing and distributing our work. The fact that individual Black feminists are living in isolation all over the country, that our own numbers are small, and that we have some skills in writing, printing, and publishing makes us want to carry out these kinds of projects as a means of organizing Black feminists as we continue to do political work in coalition with other groups.

4. Black Feminist Issues and Projects

During our time together we have identified and worked on many issues of particular relevance to Black women. The inclusiveness of our politics makes us concerned with any situation that impinges upon the lives of women, Third World and working people. We are of course particularly committed to working on those struggles in which race, sex, and class are simultaneous factors in oppression. We might, for example, become involved in workplace organizing at a factory that employs Third World women or picket a hospital that is cutting back on already inadequate heath care to a Third World community, or set up a rape crisis center in a Black neighborhood. Organizing around welfare and daycare concerns might also be a focus. The work to be done and the countless issues that this work represents merely reflect the pervasiveness of our oppression.

Issues and projects that collective members have actually worked on are sterilization abuse, abortion rights, battered women, rape and health care. We have also done many workshops and educationals on Black feminism on college campuses, at women's conferences, and most recently for high school women.

One issue that is of major concern to us and that we have begun to publicly address is racism in the white women's movement. As Black feminists we are made constantly and painfully aware of how little effort white women have made to understand and combat their racism, which requires among other things that they have a more than superficial comprehension of race, color, and Black history and culture. Eliminating racism in the white women's movement is by definition work for white women to do, but we will continue to speak to and demand accountability on this issue.

In the practice of our politics we do not believe that the end always justifies the means. Many reactionary and destructive acts have been done in the name of achieving "correct" political goals. As feminists we do not want to mess over people in the name of politics. We believe in collective process and a nonhierarchical distribution of power within our own group and in our vision of a revolutionary society. We are committed to a continual examination of our politics as they develop through criticism and self-criticism as an essential aspect of our practice. In her introduction to *Sisterhood is Powerful* Robin Morgan writes:

> I haven't the faintest notion what possible revolutionary role white heterosexual men could fulfill, since they are the very embodiment of reactionary-vested-interest-power.

As Black feminists and Lesbians we know that we have a very definite revolutionary task to perform and we are ready for the lifetime of work and struggle before us.

Notes

1 Freedman, *The Essential Feminist Reader* (New York: Modern Library, 2007), p. 325.

2 James, *Seeking the Beloved Community: A Feminist Race Reader* (New York: SUNY Press, 2014), p. 50. Subsequent page references are to this text.

3 Zillah Eisenstein, "The Combahee River Collective Statement," 2010. *Circuitous.org*, accessed Oct. 14, 2013.

4 Barbara Smith, "Doing It from Scratch: The Challenge of Black Lesbian Organizing," in *The Truth That Never Hurts: Writings on Race, Gender, and Freedom* (New Brunswick, NJ: Rutgers University Press), p. 172.

60

Every Woman's Bill of Rights *and* Workshop Resolutions
Black Women's Conference
National Alliance of Black Feminists
Chicago, Illinois
October 21–23, 1977

A 1976 National Alliance of Black Feminists march in Chicago. Photo from the Harsh Research Collection, Brenda Eichelberger/ National Alliance of Black Feminists Papers.

Dedicated to advancing Black feminism, the 1976 National Alliance of Black Feminists (NABF) started as the Chicago Chapter of the National Black Feminist Organization (NBFO). When NBFO dissolved in 1975, Chicago chapter president Brenda Eichelberger organized the NABF and served as its first executive director. The group held a three-day conference, "A Meeting of the Minds: A National Conference for, by, and about Black Women" in Chicago in 1977, at which the Resolutions reproduced here were passed.

The Resolutions[1] touch on a broad range of topics, covering everything from recent legal decisions to interpersonal relationships. The means they suggest are, for the most part, mainstream: lobbying, educating, forming coalitions, boycotting, etc. Yet their approaches are comprehensive—regarding education, for example, they support affirmative action, busing, nonsexist teaching, drug education, prison-diversion programs, accessible childcare, community forums, and sex education, all as complementary means to achieve equal educational opportunity and empowerment enacted together by schools, families, churches, and communities. The same can be said about their approach to work, which covers job training, exploitation, parental leave, childcare, etc. They address other problems especially plaguing Black women, including drug abuse and economic exploitation, and broad clusters of issues such as sexual and reproductive justice. Noteworthy is how often they mention the need for additional information or wider distribution of it. The organization itself answered this call, serving as a networking center for Black women through the Black Women's Center, a Black Women's Speaker's Bureau, consciousness-raising groups, and issue-specific task forces.

Another noteworthy activity of NABF included the compilation of a bill of rights for Black women,[2] which is reprinted below, still relevant, and reinforces the Resolutions. Their documents have not been widely available before this printing.

Every Woman's Bill of Rights

1. The right to be treated with respect.
2. The right to have and express your own feelings and opinions.
3. The right to be listened to and taken seriously.
4. The right to set your own priorities.
5. The right to say no without feeling guilty.
6. The right to ask for what you want.
7. The right to get what you pay for.
8. The right to ask for information from professionals.
9. The right to make mistakes.
10. The right to choose not to assert yourself.

Resolutions

EDUCATION WORKSHOP

1. BE IT RESOLVED, that the National Alliance of Black Feminists support a national scope and sequence[d] approach to sex/family life education to enhance a quality of life that is desirable, and to promote an awareness of a freedom to choose alternative lifestyles, emphasis should be placed on training teachers/parents to teach the above mentioned topics.

BE IT RESOLVED, that NABF support a national focus on non-sexist teaching in our educational systems, and the employment of Title IX enforcers to assist the national changes.

WHEREAS, the case of Alan Bakke, which attacks the special admission programs at the University of California at Davis Medical School is an attack on the gains won by Blacks and our supporters during the Civil Rights Movement and;

WHEREAS, a ruling by the Supreme Court, which is now reviewing the Bakke case, that supports the California decision will be a threat to special admissions and affirmative action programs across the country;

BE IT RESOLVED, that the participants at the Black Women's Conference sponsored by the National Alliance of Black Feminists go on record in opposition to the California Bakke decision. NABF should join with other groups like the NAACP and National Coalition to Overturn the Bakke Decision to organize and protest actions to pressure the Supreme Court to reverse the California court decision that ruled in favor of Bakke.

2. WHEREAS, Black children in Chicago, Boston, Louisville and other cities who are being bused to get a chance to have an equal education are being physically attacked by racist mobs and;

WHEREAS, the racist cuts in government funds for education ha[ve] provided an atmosphere favorable to these physical attacks;

BE IT RESOLVED, that participants at the Black Women's Conference sponsored by the National Alliance of Black Feminists join with community organizations to demand protection of Black children being bused, that the racists carrying out [...] physical attacks on Black children, Black women and Black men, be arrested, prosecuted and jailed, and that our rights as Blacks to equal access to educational facilities guaranteed by the 14th Amendment be implemented.

3. BE IT RESOLVED, that the National Alliance of Black Feminists develop a series of booklets concerning the relationship of the Black female to her children e.g.: 1) how to communicate your work-a-day world to your children; 2) rearing the independent child—both female and male; 3) the responsibility of the child to her/his parents and; 4) role stereotypes;

BE IT RESOLVED, that NABF develop an ad-hoc committee as a possible resource bank for female offenders and ex-offenders, of existing programs as they relate to funding, the writing of resumes and job applications; and prevention and diversion programs.

WOMEN'S HEALTH CARE

4. WHEREAS, the feminist movement must take the lead in the fight for women's rights and;

WHEREAS, all [feminist] groups will maintain a united front to challenge the attacks on women's rights;

BE IT RESOLVED, that NABF work with other women, independent[ly] and in organizations, to fight for abortion rights for all women, against [sterilization] abuse, and support the right for lesbian women in the fight against discrimination in health care.

5. WHEREAS, 50% of all active alcoholics and many drug abusers are women and;

WHEREAS, alcoholism and drug abuse [affect] these women emotionally, physically and mentally;

BE IT RESOLVED, that NABF support national educational campaigns on the subject of alcoholism and drug abuse as it affects women.

ECONOMICS

6. WHEREAS, Black and minority women are victims of economic and social exploitation from an unyielding and unrewarding society, more information is needed on what the federal department of HEW is doing about the plight of women in programs that HEW supports. How do the many millions of dollars funnelled through these programs affect Black women;

BE IT RESOLVED, that NABF and their affiliated organizations examine the plight of Black and working class women in federally funded programs.

7. WHEREAS, Black women in attendance at the Black Women's Conference sponsored by the NABF, see the need in the total economic climate of this country to once again reply to the outgrowth of our oppressive status and;

WHEREAS, we the women supporters and delegates at the National Black Women's Conference recognize the rights of women to pursue and continue a position in the labor force and;

WHEREAS, women constitute an important and substantial element of the labor force;

8. BE IT RESOLVED, that NABF support the current legislation before Congress to define maternity leave as a right deserving of the [same] status and recognition as other health disabilities.

BE IT RESOLVED, that NABF give every woman at the conference feedback concerning the resolutions that are voted on in these workshops. (although this resolution was voted out of this workshop, the voting body present on Sunday agreed that this [resolution] would pertain to the entire Conference)

WOMEN RELATING TO WOMEN

9. BE IT RESOLVED, that it is important to reinforce our female bond by positive acknowledgment upon meeting another sister, whether through physical contact and/or some other form of verbal or non-verbal communication.

BE IT RESOLVED, that we shall accept the individual responsibility for being supportive of and give affirmation to, other Black women.

BE IT RESOLVED, that we shall help other Black women in their endeavors by sharing knowledge and expertise.

ACCURATE MEDIA PORTRAYAL

10. BE IT RESOLVED, that the Black women in attendance at this Conference take a stand against all media portrayal of negative images of Black people, especially Black women. That we make our disapproval known throughout the nation. Further to support specialized boycotts against advertisers in sexist and racist publications and those advertisers that refuse to advertise their products in Black publications.

BE IT FURTHER RESOLVED, that we seek to create regular career day conferences designed to educate women about career opportunities and possibilities in the media.

BE IT RESOLVED, that NABF should develop a resource bank that is designed to educate Black women about all aspects of funding possibilities available to persons interested in pursuing a career in the media.

BLACK WOMEN RELATING TO MEN

11. WHEREAS, Black Women have not been traditionally viewed by men as having the right to define her role in relationships;

BE IT RESOLVED, that NABF continue to sponsor workshops and seminars that will enable Black women and men to develop skills in defining roles in such relationships and that NABF work with educational institutions to promote courses in human sexuality for adolescents.

BLACK FEMINISM

12. BE IT RESOLVED, that NABF organize on the local level to address itself to the needs of the Black community in relation to [economic], spiritual, social, medical and political areas.

13. BE IT RESOLVED, that NABF embrace all struggles for liberation and freedom; the struggles of Blacks, women, oppressed nationalities, gays and workers.

14. BE IT RESOLVED, that NABF provide a means of reaching more Black women and furthering the commitment of Black feminism to expand the scope and membership of the organization.

15. BE IT RESOLVED, that NABF develop a mechanism of communication for the purpose of uniting and solidifying the bond of feminism among other individuals and women's groups including a forum on black prostitutes; to provide greater access to feminist activities and to facilitate the flow of information among Black women and the women's movement by organizing discussions, panels, forums, news letters, rallies on women['s] rights; issues like legal abortion, affirmative action programs, equal rights amendment, pregnancy disability benefits and other issues.

WOMEN IN RELIGION

16. WHEREAS, the Black church has been a foundation for the Black family and was historically the only institution in the Black community;

WHEREAS, women have been relegated to supportive roles and have never been truly recognized, appreciated or encouraged in leadership roles of the church;

WHEREAS, church services are traditionally segregated;

BE IT RESOLVED, that the women attending the NABF, Black Women's Conference go on record as:

a) Denouncing the racist and sexist ideals fostered by religious institutions;
b) Encouraging the fuller participation of the Black church in the social, political and economic problems of the total black church community;
c) Recognizing the positive potential of women as leaders in the church.

POLITICAL AWARENESS

17. WHEREAS, the Hyde Amendment will deny Black and poor women the right to abortions through the use of Medicaid and public funds;

WHEREAS, the Bakke case, if upheld by the Supreme Court, will set a precedent for halting affirmative action programs for Blacks and women;

WHEREAS, the ERA will be an important step for Black women in gaining equality in the country if passed;

WHEREAS, January 20, 1978 is the anniversary of the Supreme Court abortion ruling;

BE IT RESOLVED, that NABF hereby calls for a day, January 20, 1978 of nationally coordinated actions, teach-ins, forums, demonstrations and press conferences to reaffirm our stand on these issues and to reach, involve and educate other Black sisters.

18. WHEREAS, there is a need for more Black women to be involved in government as elected and appointed officials;

WHEREAS, it is essential that Black women be effectively organized to participate in the political process;

BE IT RESOLVED, that the NABF endorse the concept of a Black Women's
Political Caucus which would sponsor political education forums and workshops
and form a nationwide task force of politically astute and experienced Black
women in order to develop a format for promoting and assisting the election of
Black women to political offices.

19. BE IT RESOLVED, that NABF Black Women's Conference supports the ERA
and that conferees join other women's organizations in working for the passage
of the amendment.

INTERNATIONAL WOMEN'S YEAR

20. BE IT RESOLVED, that NABF support a national resolution created by the
Minority Caucus of IWY to assure that minority women are represented in all
levels of policy and decision making positions created by the IWY and any outgrowth thereof for its duration.

21. BE IT RESOLVED, that there shall be compiled and kept current a national
directory of women's organizations for direct communication purposes.

22. BE IT RESOLVED, that resolutions passed by the NABF Women's Conference be used as a guide in the consideration of proposed resolutions at the National IWY Conference in Houston.

LIFESTYLES

23. BE IT RESOLVED, that NABF supports the right of women to choose her
lifestyle.

24. BE IT RESOLVED, that NABF support and develop programs to facilitate
the discussion of the lifestyles of Black women.

CHILD CARE/ADOLESCENTS

25. BE IT RESOLVED, that NABF develop female sexuality awareness programs
for adolescents. We are encouraging the development of sex education programs
and referrals to other programs.

BE IT RESOLVED, that NABF organize a task force together to develop a proposal for the female sexuality program.

BE IT RESOLVED, that NABF find ways to inform young Black females of existing information on child care programs via the use of the media and other means.

BE IT RESOLVED, that NABF give support to Black women and their children who are having problems in the area of child abuse or any problems relating
to being a parent.

COMMUNITY AWARENESS

26. BE IT RESOLVED, that NABF in concert with other groups seek representation on Boards and Commissions that will advocate for Black women's issues at
every Government level.

BE IT RESOLVED, that NABF develop a data base resource listing eligible
and available Black women for these appointments.

BE IT RESOLVED, that NABF prepare and distribute a directory of Conference attendees to be received by all Conference attendees.

SEXUALITY

27. BE IT RESOLVED, that a NABF task force on sexuality initiate workshops throughout the Black community that will be available at no cost to Black women.

BE IT RESOLVED, that NABF be supportive of each Black woman's right to exercise her sexuality in a manner which is fulfilling to her.

BLACK WOMEN RELATING TO MEN

28. WHEREAS, Black women in management and similar positions previously held only by white males face embarrassing situations due to the insensitivity and ignorance of co-workers;

BE IT RESOLVED, that NABF produce consciousness-raising material dealing specifically with the problems of white males with black female bosses and the problem of black women being solicited for prostitution on business trips and make such material available to companies with affirmative action programs.

WOMEN IN THE ARTS

29. WHEREAS, the images of Black women in the arts have been distorted and negative images have prevailed;

WHEREAS, it is important to maintain a flow of information regarding opportunities and developments in this field;

WHEREAS, control over money and resources is used to manipulate artistic talent and stifle creativity;

BE IT RESOLVED, that NABF work towards establishing a Black women's task force on the arts which would act as a communication network, compile a listing of past and present black women artists, and encourage research, participation and assumption of leadership roles and otherwise aid and support Black women in this field and form political coalitions with other organizations to combat the derogatory images of Black women in the arts.

Notes

1. The 1977 Resolutions are located in the Brenda Eichelberger/National Alliance of Black Feminists Papers [Box 1, Folder 22], Vivian G. Harsh Research Collection of Afro-American History and Literature, Chicago Public Library. Handwritten corrections are incorporated into this version.

2. Everywoman's Bill of Rights is located in the Brenda Eichelberger/National Alliance of Black Feminists Papers [Box 9, Folder 7], Vivian G. Harsh Research Collection of Afro-American History and Literature, Chicago Public Library. An eleven-page document accompanies this list and develops each item on it.

Part V

1981–1999

61

We Cannot Wait
Association of Salvadoran Women (AMES)
San Jose, Costa Rica
November 1981

Our struggle as Latin American women is different from that of women
in developed countries.... Nobody can be free in a system that destroys
everything human in both men and women.

Patricia Hipsher's essay "Right- and Left-Wing Women in Post-Revolutionary El
Salvador" makes the claim that "[m]ost of the women involved in today's feminist
movement served as guerillas and political activists for the revolutionary forces
that sought the overthrow of right-wing military rule."[1] This claim has important
implications for the ways in which we interpret the work of the Association of
Women in El Salvador (AMES). For, as Hipsher notes, AMES and other contemporary feminist organizations from El Salvador were shaped by the simultaneous
movement against political dictatorship. For this reason, Salvadoran women's
organizations have not commonly been seen as autonomous feminist movements
working for gender-specific interests but rather as extensions of revolutionary
groups dedicated to "broader" class-based reforms. This is true even among
feminist scholars like Hipsher, who argues that "[i]t was not until the end of the
revolution and the signing of the peace accords in 1992 that women's movement
organizations demanded autonomy from the popular movement and developed a
distinctly feminist agenda that emphasized women's political, economic, and sexual rights" (135). She argues that feminists' ties to left-wing politics delayed their
eventual autonomy, restricted the focus of their agendas, and, more importantly,
prevented them from forging connections with politically right-wing women.

Whether or not one accepts this claim, it is clear that one must interpret the
AMES declaration in the context of the civil war in El Salvador (1980–1992).
Since Spanish colonialism in the sixteenth century, El Salvador has been organized around plantations that grow commodity crops for foreign markets: cacao,
indigo, coffee, etc. After independence, El Salvador was managed by a "small
minority of landholders called the 'Fourteen Families' [of primarily European
ancestry] through a long series of military dictatorships."[2] A group of officers led
a coup that ousted the dictator, Carlos Humberto Romero, on October 15, 1979.
They formed the Revolutionary Government Junta (JRG). No women were included in this ruling junta.[3]

Robin Morgan's *Sisterhood Is Global: The International Women's Movement Anthology* states that the Association of Women in El Salvador (AMES) was founded
in 1979 to incorporate women from all sectors of society into the movement for
liberation. Hipsher similarly describes AMES as one of over half a dozen "party-
linked" women's organization that emerged around this time. Ilja A. Luciak's
*After the Revolution: Gender and Democracy in El Salvador, Nicaragua, and Gua-
temala* describes AMES as a "precursor" to the Farabundo Martí National Liberation Front (FMLN) women's groups that followed shortly after.[4]

In September 1980, five major revolutionary organizations combined as the
Farabundo Martí National Liberation Front to oppose government and right-
wing forces. Morgan notes that "[w]omen made up 29.1 percent of FMLN

combatants and 35.52 percent of political personnel during the war. Women commanded troops, worked as radio operators, became demolition experts, and served as mass organizers and public relations officers" (138). The conflict continued for twelve years, and over seventy-five thousand civilian casualties were attributed to government forces until the Chapultepec Peace Accords were brokered on January 16, 1992.

Distinguishing between exploitation and oppression, "We Cannot Wait"[5] names capitalism and patriarchy as the major sources of inequality. It delineates how both men and capitalism gain from the oppression of women. It emphasizes that life, and therefore what is needed for liberation, varies according to one's sex, class, and the degree of development of one's country. The association explains the dynamics of internalized oppression more thoroughly than most. It argues that women have long been political actors and now must also participate in their own liberation.

We Cannot Wait

Traditionally the mode of development of the Latin American economies has been structured around the production of raw materials and oriented toward satisfying the demands of the foreign market and the interests of the bourgeoisie. Concomitant with this was high concentration of income, large foreign debt, inflation, and military dictatorship. Permanent economic, political, and social crisis is therefore characteristic of the great majority of the countries of the continent; and in its wake, poverty, super-exploitation, and repression.

Latin American women, who face double oppression, have not been exempt from this dramatic reality. Although the principal source of our subjection is capitalism, even before its advent feudal society had already assigned a subordinate role to women. The oppression of women is a suffocating cultural heritage, and, as Simone de Beauvoir has pointed out, "one is not born, but rather learns to be, a woman." We Latin American women have undoubtedly been learning: learning *not* to be accomplices of the myth of Cinderella, who waited for Prince Charming to free her from misery and convert her into the happy mother of numerous little princes; learning to take to the streets to fight for the elimination of poverty; learning to be active protagonists in the forging of our social destiny.

To be a member of the working class is not the same as being a member of the upper class; to be a North American or a European is not the same as being a Chilean or a Salvadoran. We are all, to some degree, exploited and we all carry the burden of our patriarchal heritage, but unquestionably our class interests transcend those of gender. What has a Domitila, a working-class woman of the Bolivian mines, to do with the wife of Abdul Gutiérrez the bloody colonel of the Christian Democratic military junta of El Salvador? For women of low-income sectors, joining the labor force is linked with a survival strategy similar to that of men of the same class and obeying the same necessities. However, for the women of the middle and higher strata, incorporation into production is determined by the number and age of their children, by their level of education, by the gap between the family wage and their consumer expectations.

There are also differences arising from the degree of development of a region, or from the pattern of urban and rural zones. Our struggle as Latin American women is different from that of women in developed countries. Like us, the latter play a fundamental role as reproducers of labor power and ideology, but *our* problematic arises fundamentally from the economic, political, and cultural exploitation of our people. Our struggle is, thus, not only for immediate demands; nor is it an individual one or against men. We seek the liberation of our countries from imperialism, dictatorship, and the local bourgeoisie—although we work simultaneously around the question of the specific condition of women and our oppression within the capitalist and patriarchal system.

While in the developed countries there is a struggle for contraception and abortion, in Latin America we must also fight against forced sterilization and certain birth-control projects agreed to under pressure from the United States. For us women, it is not a question of demanding collective services such as day-care centers or laundries, but rather of demanding general community services such as water, light, housing, and health care.

For Latin American women the "double day" has another dimension which converts "wages for housework" into a remote goal; our short-term goals are related to employment and job opportunities, to the exploitation of the principal wage earner, and the impossibility of survival with starvation wages. It makes no sense to struggle against the consumerism of one part of society if we are faced with poverty and the impossibility of consuming by the other part, which constitutes the majority of the people.

In sum, we are fighting for a thoroughgoing change which will include women in the production process, which will free both women and men from exploitation and poverty. At the same time the search for solutions to the specific problems of women must not be neglected.

Invisible Work

Man's work in capitalist society is carried out at the cost of women's work within the home, which saves him the extra hours required for the reproduction of his labor power: hence the higher level of masculine skill and the male monopoly of political power. Both factors are characteristic of class society, and are due to an enormous amount of invisible labor done by women and appropriated by men through the mechanism of the family as an economic unit.

The family has been the foundation stone of all class societies and has given stability to the system based on private property. The family nucleus is the economic and legal formation through which the dominant classes put at their service and confiscate the labor of the female population. The toil of the male laborer is not sufficient to reproduce his labor power; another phase of production is required, namely domestic labor. Carried out by women, it produces goods and services: laundered, ironed, and mended clothing; meals; a tidy house; and children educated in accordance with the requirements laid down for the new generation of workers.

If formerly the capitalists obtained a given amount of surplus value from the male worker, the principal family wage-earner, with the growing incorporation of women into the paid labor force they obtain a further benefit. In addition to the male workers, who are responsible for family subsistence, the women also work (and are paid lower wages), thus making up the deficit of income necessary to survival of the family unit. It is vitally important for the reproduction of class society that we women not exhaust our strength in social production, but rather that we conserve our energy for the private economic nucleus. Thus women, because of this contradiction between the two kinds of labor we perform, are obliged to accept unskilled jobs which leave us with a reservoir of energy for domestic tasks.

In other words, the fundamental aspect of women's problem, exploitation, is the direct result of capitalist relations of production. However, there exists another dimension, *oppression*, which is useful to the system and whose cultural and social roots go back to the dawn of civilization: female subordination to the male and the division of labor (along gender lines), which predate capitalist society. They are found in most societies known to the history of humanity. So we can conclude that the problem of women is a fundamental social and cultural reality.

In the nineteenth century, socialist thinkers assumed that the cause of women was identical with the cause of the working class. Although these thinkers acknowledged that women's subordination predated capitalism, they thought that the abolition of that social system would simultaneously abolish both workers' exploitation and commercialized human relations, freeing women from economic dependence on men and consequently from subordination. However, we think that to achieve our total emancipation such a change is a necessary but not sufficient condition.

It is indispensable that we also transform the ideological superstructures that perpetuate a male-female relationship based on the equation domination-subjection and reproduced fundamentally in the family. The family nucleus is the locus where models and values useful to the system are transmitted through the sexual division of labor; on the legal level through inheritance through the male line; on the economic level, as a unit of production and consumption and as a mediator between needs and resources; and on the social plane, by relegating women to the "private" domestic sphere and hampering our social and political participation.

Inasmuch as our specific situation of oppression and subordination is a centuries-old state of affairs which by now we have internalized, it can be said that we women share a specific condition. And it is in function of this specificity that we have been marginalized from history and the values inherent in our subordinate role have been exalted. We must acknowledge that we have internalized these values which now form part of our personalities.

We are conscious of the fact that the alleged separation between the "private" and the "public" is merely a sophism. The private is directly political because patriarchal ideology permeates the individual lives of men and women. It is important to recognize the link between the two areas and understand that although women will not be liberated without a change in society, it is equally true that there can be no genuine social transformation without women's emancipation

To the extent to which we women are kept isolated and confined to the domestic sphere we will continue to accept our role, to accept the postulate that, due to biological differences, we are weak beings—docile, inferior to men, but also beautiful and noble—to whom have been assigned the important roles of wife and mother.

Changes That Don't Change Anything

There is a daily growing contingent of women who question our passive role, the defense of the status quo, and our being distanced from political activity on our continent; there is a daily growing number of women who question why we work as much as 80 hours a week on the "double shift" which prevents us from participating in the social process and in decision-making.

In the light of this situation, many ruling regimes promulgate paternalistic legislation which establishes "equality before the law," even "no sex discrimination," including certain measures in favor of mothers and children. These are formal measures which do not affect the daily reality of the great majority of people. Such is the case with education, for example, access to which is limited for the majority of both men and women of the lower classes, but especially women. Six out of ten Salvadorans are illiterate; well over half are women. In the cities twice as many women as men are illiterate.

In order to avert the threat of a genuine change in the specific role of women and our active participation in the liberation processes which would follow upon a massive increase of female consciousness, many governments have promoted modernist or developmental solutions. They point to the betterment of general living conditions in capitalist countries and to the introduction of new technology; they claim that this economic prosperity offers women the possibility of participating in the labor market and, consequently, of having "access to and participation in social life."

These seductive conceptions of women's liberation are almost always associated with conservative or reformist values, which do not conduce to effective changes in social relations. They provide a basis for exalting the role of women within the family as an institution which creates consensus and continuity of a culture, and which is an outgrowth of the capitalist system—macho, repressive, and based on the commercialization of human relations.

We think that the integration of women into capitalist society does not constitute liberation. Nobody can be free in a system that destroys everything human in both men and women. Nor can our problem be solved by the "insertion" (the very word implies passivity) of women into such a system, without our full participation as subject, not object, and without full awareness of the process of change. To postulate our insertion into development, without determining what kind of development, resolves nothing.

First Steps toward Liberation

The struggle of Latin American women to transcend the domestic takes place on several levels. It begins with middle- and high-income women who in part delegate their domestic tasks to other women; some of the privileged women fulfill their social vocation through works of charity, some are political militants who focus on the structural roots of the system.

The condition of the *mujer del pueblo* [literally, woman of the people] on our continent during the last decade has been affected in two different ways. In terms of repression, thousands of women have been harassed and tortured, and have disappeared or been assassinated by the dictatorships. We have also been affected in our specific roles as mother, wife, or daughter of an unemployed, persecuted, or assassinated man. We have had to face the sudden destruction of our families and the need to find a way to manage without our *compañeros*, who frequently had been the only wage-earners in the household.

Then, as a result of the unpopular economic policies of the dictatorships, we women began to organize in *frentes*—of shantytown dwellers and housewives affected by economic, social, and political repression; of factory workers, peasants, and professionals who organized to defend the gains won through long years of struggle. The *frentista* format has become one of the principal responses utilized by Latin American women for dealing with specific demands. Women's mobilizations in defense of, and in solidarity with, the struggles of men have grown from day to day, as a frequent expression of mass participation helping to lay bare certain prevailing contradictions and exposing the true nature of military regimes. Conceived within a liberal context and subject to penetration by bourgeois ideology, the defense of women's traditional role is the precondition of women's mobilization: it is not easy for the state to repress those who, as mothers, wives, daughters, confront it in the very roles which constitute the pillar and foundation of domination.

When the private, domestic realm is altered from the outside, Latin American women come out of their homes and take to the streets. In strikes of miners, industrial workers, and building workers, women have pounded at the doors of ministries and parliaments. They have pressured the authorities and employers to demand wage increases or jobs for their male family members, or to demand their release from prison. That is to say, their demands are not their own, but are rather familial. Responding to moments of crisis and deterioration of living conditions, women participate massively; as the foundation stone of the home, they defend their families; as the ones who gave life to their children, they demand that their lives be respected.

Historically, however, both the strength and the weakness of such movements have resided in their spontaneity. Arising as support groups for male struggles, many of these groups dissolve when the conflicts that gave rise to them are ended; when husbands, fathers, sons return to center stage, we women retreat to our homes, leaving to the men, once again, the sphere of public activity. Perhaps that is why in Latin American history threats to traditional roles have frequently been converted into factors of women's mobilization. However, many of us, as a result of this experience, have recognized the implications of this dynamic, which opens up a terrain bordering on the political and gives us the objective possibilities of losing the "fear of power," of transcending our traditional condition, of beginning to open up our political space.

The Difficult Task of Being Members of an Organized Movement

If men have, for centuries, devoted themselves to political work and fulfilled themselves in it, it is because they have always had the support of one or several women who have provided them with children, with affection, with domestic services; to these women are diverted all psychological tensions, thereby freeing men from the problems of domestic life.

We women, on the other hand, do not have such support systems available to us, and in order to utilize our intellectual potential must organize ourselves in such a way that the private sphere does not interfere with our specific political work. It is indeed dramatic to organize ourselves physically and psychologically to exercise this role without experiencing guilt vis à vis the "neglected" roles of mother and wife which relegate us to the domestic sphere.

For a woman to be active in sociopolitical organizations implies the assumption of a definitive commitment, a commitment which, she feels, will have repercussions on her activities as woman, wife, mother, and, in some cases, as paid worker. This situation is aggravated by the fact that until now it has not appeared that men have the intention of truly assuming some of the responsibility which for centuries has been delegated to women. It is not easy for men, even with good intentions, to raise their consciousness concerning the privileges conveyed by masculinity and to relinquish their role as the star members of the cast, becoming instead comrades who share daily life and struggle.

Consequently, for those of us who have decided to make a leap onto the stage of history and to become organized political women, protagonists of social and political transformation, the task as we see it is not an easy one.

The parties and movements of the democratic Left have, in general, not dealt with the problems of women with the same consistency with which they confront other social problems. Their pronouncements in this regard are limited to the realm of class struggle and thus appear to be detached from political discourse. They do not make reference to the specific condition of women or to our integration in the struggle as a key factor in the liberation of our societies.

This omission implicitly assumes that feminism and socialism are opposed to each other. Women's liberation is not presented in terms of the liberation of the oppressed. The resolution of our struggle is, for the moment, conceived of as technical and private, becoming collective and social only after the exploited sectors have won their liberation, that is to say, in some distant and unpredictable future.

In other words, the failure to integrate the female problematic into the broad political project has, until now, left a large vacuum: a change in the relations of production is advocated, but not in the relations of reproduction; society is to be overturned economically and ideologically, but nothing is said of changes in the family, which is the sphere not only of consumption but also of reproduction of labor power, as well as the strategic locale for the transmission of ideology.

Will the people's organizations be capable of focusing on the specifics of daily life, or will they leave this to the mercy of the dominant ideology? Will they be capable of breaking the female tradition of conservatism and fear, transforming women on a mass scale into organized political activists? Indicative of the political and ideological maturity of an organization is its analysis and proposals vis-à-vis the present role of women as reproducers of an ideology of domination, and therefore the perpetuation of a social system.

Participation of Women in the Process of National Liberation

We Salvadoran women have become aware of our situation: we understand that our revolution for [national] liberation will provide the fundamental solution for our problems. We Salvadoran women have participated, in this century, in all the political movements against domination by the oligarchy, but in the last two decades our participation has grown by leaps and bounds. In the 1970s we adopted a clear revolutionary strategy.

In 1922 there was a demonstration of women in mourning, demanding the release of their imprisoned family members. It was repressed by the regime in power, with several *compañeras* assassinated. Women also played a part in the heroic insurrection of 1932, which left 30,000 workers and peasants murdered. We also played an active role in the general sit down strike in 1944, which succeeded in removing General Martínez from power.

A women's organization remembered with respect in El Salvador is the *Fraternidad de Mujeres*, which, in 1960, organized spirited struggles and, together with other organizations belonging to the National Front of Civic Orientation, removed Colonel Lemus from power. (At that time the level of consciousness was not what it is today, and a new tyrant took over.)

A national strike movement known as the "strike of Steele, Inc.," involving 35,000 workers, took place in 1967. Women workers took part in it massively and militantly. There were also two big national strikes of teachers, the majority of whom were women. These strikers took to the streets in a broad struggle around union and political issues and against the military dictatorship, which had violently repressed these movements. The firm revolutionary spirit of women began to be forged in those struggles.

The revolutionary student movement also provided the setting for the combativity and revolutionary consciousness of many of our heroic *compañeras* who are still struggling today and for many others who have fallen in combat against the military dictatorship.

The political-military organizations currently offering a new alternative for people's struggle, and which led our people toward our present level of development, arose early in the 1970's. At the beginning, women's participation was minimal, and was limited primarily to students and teachers. But with the advent of revolutionary peasant-workers' organizations, peasant women have also joined the struggle in large numbers. Children are also participating, together with their parents, since they also experience exploitation and repression.

In the mid-1970's, the mass struggle reached new, qualitatively higher, levels of struggle; there were qualitative leaps in respect to combativity, and there was an acceleration in the process of self-defense in mass political actions. Salvadoran women are participating in diverse and exemplary ways—in tasks of agitation, propaganda, and organization, as well as in the military struggle of our people.

In 1977, organizations arose, composed primarily of women, which demanded the freedom of the many captured and disappeared prisoners taken by the government. The Committee for the Freedom of Prisoners and the Disappeared and the Committee of Disappeared Prisoners carried on spirited struggles—hunger strikes, demonstrations, appeals to international organizations for the freeing of their family members. At the same time the class struggle, which had been characterized by legalistic thinking since 1967, underwent a transformation. With the advent of the revolutionary trade-union movement, women workers also joined the struggle.

In 1978 the first steps were taken toward forming the organization that was to become AMES (the Association of Salvadoran Women) as a way of incorporating in to political life those sectors of women (housewives, professionals, teachers, secretaries, shantytown dwellers, students, etc.) who, because of their special circumstances, had not yet joined the people's struggle. The year 1978 saw also the organizing of market and street vendors. AUTRAMES (the Association of Market Vendors and Workers) and the Luz Dillian Arévalo Coordinating Committee of Market Vendors led spirited struggles, occupying markets and demonstrating to better their working and living conditions.

Salvadoran women also have been joining mass organizations which today form part of the Democratic Revolutionary Front (FDR). Concurrently women have been joining the political-military organization and armed units of the people. Thousands of women fight with weapons in the militia, the guerrilla forces, and the popular army of liberation, participating at the rank-and-file level and in the leadership.

Our revolutionary struggle is a political and military war of the entire people against a minority supported by US imperialism. Salvadoran women constitute half the population and we are participating in this effort on a massive scale. There is no area of struggle today where we are not present. This is an indication of the profundity of the revolutionary struggle in our country, and the way in which women participate demonstrates the high revolutionary level of our liberation process.

For centuries the women of our country have been suffering double oppression and exploitation. Today we are fighting as part of a people who have taken up arms to end oligarchic and imperialist domination. Our presence is felt, from the members of AMES to the highest leadership levels of the FDR. In our country, as in Nicaragua, new procedures are being developed not only in revolutionary organization and leadership, but also in the transformation of human relations. Strategies, speeches, guidelines—these are no longer the prerogatives of men. And they too are aware of the need for, and accept being participant in, an educational process in that respect, a process that will result in human relations that are morally binding on everyone.

We think that in a revolutionary organization there can be no contradictions between professed ideas and behavior. There must be consistency between the choices made, the values affirmed, and daily life—with no exceptions, no ambiguity.

No real change in society is ever brought about painlessly, nor will the problem of women's organized participation be resolved by the insertion of stipulated quotas of women in the leadership. It is necessary to face seriously and self-critically the male-female relationship with all its implications and to understand the gravity of our exclusion from, or relegation to a minor role in, the process of change. We constitute half of humanity and we constitute an objectively exploited and oppressed social group with enormous revolutionary potential.

Keeping clearly in mind that the struggle for women's liberation must be immersed in the struggle for the liberation of our peoples, it is also necessary to point out that we women are a group defined by our own conditions and specific demands and that we cannot wait for socialism or a change of structures to solve tomorrow the very problems that are today the source of our limitations, of our backwardness as integral human beings, as agents of change.

A woman's conscious decision to join in organized struggle implies a transition much longer and more arduous than that of men, inasmuch as we must overcome an endless number of hurdles. If we evaluate these hurdles, we see that, qualitatively speaking, a dual leap has been taken. Obviously this does not mean that we have solved our specific problems of "being a woman," nor is organized participation a panacea that will permit us to achieve our full identity. However, we think that the hallmark of revolutionary feminism is that it locates itself within a context of total transformation of society. We also know that the liberation of women requires a level of generalized collective consciousness which is the result of a development of a new ideology. And that new ideology must be the result of a project for a new structuring of society—a society without private property and without exploitation of one human being by another.

We Salvadoran women ask the peoples of the world to increase your solidarity with the people of El Salvador so as to isolate the junta and bring to a halt the nefarious efforts toward direct and massive military intervention in our country by U.S. imperialism.

Notes

1 Hipsher, "Right- and Left-Wing Women in Post-Revolutionary El Salvador: Feminist Autonomy and Cross-Political Alliance Building for Gender Equality," in *Radical Women in*

Latin America: Left and Right, ed. Victoria Gonzalez and Karen Kampwirth (University Park: Pennsylvania State University Press, 2001), p. 133. Subsequent page references are to this text.

2 "El Salvador: 125 Years of Civil War." Center for Justice & Accountability, accessed Feb. 14, 2017, www.cja.org.

3 Ibid.

4 Luciak, *After the Revolution: Gender and Democracy in El Salvador, Nicaragua, and Guatemala* (Baltimore, MD: John Hopkins University Press, 2001), p. 14.

5 The Association of Salvadoran Women, "Participation of Latin American Women in Social and Political Organizations: Reflections of Salvadoran Women." *Monthly Review*, June 1982, pp. 10–23. Freedom Archives, accessed Feb. 14, 2017, www.freedomarchives.org.

62

Anarchafeminist Manifesto
Third Congress of the Anarchist Federation of Norway
Oslo, Norway
June 1–7, 1982

The Anarchafeminist symbol.

A serious anarchism must also be feminist otherwise it is a question of patriarchal half-anarchism and not real anarchism. It is the task of the anarcha-feminists to secure the feminist feature in anarchism. There will be no anarchism without feminism.

Like so many other groups, anarchist feminists work to bridge two movements— anarchism and feminism, in this case. They see women's oppression in economic exploitation, violence, and ideology, as do most feminists, but also as rooted in the state, and manifested in lack of other organizations and individual responsibility. They want women and men, and the voluntary social organizations they join, to have the power to decide upon the important questions in their lives. Anti-authoritarian, the Manifesto is critical of both Marxist and liberal feminisms, and offers a simultaneous critique of patriarchy, capitalism, and statism. In rejecting values and practices of domination and competition, it sides with cooperation and mutual aid, virtues and practices long associated with women.

The Anarchist Federation of Norway dates back to 1872, but the Anarchafeminist sector was established in 1982. There is very little written about the gathering in June 1982 that established this Manifesto, and we have not been able to discover who wrote or contributed to it. The group's writings focus almost exclusively on what anarchy and anarchism mean in both theoretical and practical terms, and they aim to create equality for all people. Perhaps purposely, they have left off names and descriptions of specific people in order to create a shared experience for all who read the Manifesto.

The declaration itself[1] is clear, straightforward, and forceful. The group wants equality in all spheres, achieved by "organization without power" or hierarchical systems. The writers declare there will be no feminism without anarchism and no anarchism without feminism: the two are necessarily part of one another. Most of all, the writers advocate autonomy. Women and all people must be able to make their own decisions about everything, but especially about issues that affect them most deeply. They urge cooperation, but never at the cost of losing personal autonomy: "[W]e must make decisions all by ourselves in personal matters, together with other women in pure female matters, and together with the male fellows in common matters."

Anarchafeminist Manifesto

All over the world most women have no rights whatsoever to decide upon important matters which concern their lives. Women suffer from oppressions of two kinds: 1) the general social oppression of the people, and 2) secondly sexism—oppression and discrimination because of their sex.

There are five main forms of oppression:
1. Ideological oppression, *brainwash* by certain cultural traditions, religion, advertising and propaganda. Manipulation with concepts and play upon women's feelings and susceptibilities. Widespread patriarchal and authoritarian attitudes and capitalistic mentality in all areas.
2. State oppression, hierarchical forms of organization with command lines downwards from the top in most interpersonal relations, also in the so-called *private life*.
3. Economic exploitation and repression, as a consumer and a worker in the home and in low-salary *women's jobs*.
4. Violence, under the auspices of the society as well as in the private sphere—indirectly when there is coercion because of lack of alternatives and direct physical violence.
5. Lack of organization, *tyranny of the structurelessness* which pulverizes responsibility and creates weakness and inactivity.

These factors work together and contribute simultaneously to sustain each other in a vicious circle. There is no panacea to break the circle, but it isn't unbreakable.

Anarcha-feminism is a matter of consciousness. The consciousness which puts guardians off work. The principles of a liberating society thus stand perfectly clear to us.

Anarcha-feminism means women's independence and freedom on an equal footing with men. A social organization and a social life where no-one is superior or inferior to anyone and everybody is coordinate, women as well as men. This goes for all levels of social life, also the private sphere.

Anarcha-feminism implies that women themselves decide and take care of their own matters, individually in personal matters, and together with other women in matters which concern several women. In matters which concern both sexes essentially and concretely women and men shall decide on an equal footing.

Women must have self-decision over their own bodies, and all matters concerning contraception and childbirth are to be decided upon by women themselves.

It must be fought both individually and collectively against male domination, attitudes of ownership and control over women, against repressive laws and for women's economic and social autonomy and independence.

Crisis centers, day care centers, study and discussion groups, women's culture activities etc. must be established, and be run under women's own direction.

The traditional patriarchal nuclear family should be replaced by free associations between men and women based on equal right to decide for both parts and with respect for the individual person's autonomy and integrity.

Sex-stereotyping in education, media and at the place of work must be abolished. Radical sharing of the work by the sexes in ordinary jobs, domestic life and education is a suitable mean.

The structure of working life must be radically changed, with more part-time work and *flat* organized cooperation at home as well as in society. The difference between men's work and women's work must be abolished. Nursing and taking care of the children must concern men just as much as women.

Female power and female prime ministers will neither lead the majority of women to their ends nor abolish oppression. Marxist and bourgeoisie feminists are misleading the fight for women's liberation. For most women it is not going to be any feminism without anarchism. In other words, anarcha-feminism does not stand for female power or female prime ministers, it stands for organization without power and without prime ministers.

The double oppression of women demands a double fight and double organizing: on the one hand in feminist federations, on the other hand in the organizations of anarchists. The anarcha-feminists form a junction in this double organizing.

A serious anarchism must also be feminist otherwise it is a question of patriarchal half-anarchism and not real anarchism. It is the task of the anarcha-feminists to secure the feminist feature in anarchism. There will be no anarchism without feminism.

An essential point in anarcha-feminism is that the changes must begin today, not tomorrow or *after the revolution.* The revolution shall be permanent. We must start today by seeing through the oppression in the daily life and do something to break the pattern here and now.

We must act autonomously, without delegating to any leaders the right to decide what we wish and what we shall do: we must make decisions all by ourselves in personal matters, together with other women in pure female matters, and together with the male fellows in common matters.

Note

1 Anonymous, "The Anarchafeminist Manifesto." *Bulletin C.R.I.F.A.* no. 44 (March–April 1983): 13. Anarchist Library Online, accessed Feb. 14, 2017, www.anarchistlibrary.org.

63

Women in Prison Manifesto
Women in Prison
England
1985

Women in Prison is a national organization established in 1983 in England to help women avoid, survive in, and transition out of the criminal justice system. The organization envisions a world without women's prisons and campaigns for *social justice* instead of *criminal justice*. Imprisoned women, usually disproportionately women from already marginalized groups, are surely a relatively invisible and silenced population. The group was started by Pat Carlen, a criminologist, and Chris Tchaikovsky, a former inmate, who felt "the specific needs of women in prison and the damaging effect prison sentences were having on women scarcely figured in public or political discourse."[1]

The following serves as a preamble to the 1985 Manifesto:[2]

During the last decade the number of British women prisoners has increased by 65 per cent. The average daily population of women in British prisons in 1981 were 1,407 in England and Wales and 135 in Scotland. In 1980 the average daily population of women in prison in Northern Ireland was 69. As prisoners, women suffer the same deprivations, indignities and violations of civil rights as male prisoners. Additionally as women in prison they suffer from sexist and racist discriminatory practices which result, for instance, in them receiving fewer leisure, work and educational opportunities, closer surveillance and much greater control by drugs than male prisoners. Yet women prisoners have been largely ignored by prison campaigners, prison writers and officials in the penal and judicial systems. Women In Prison therefore seeks to unite women of all classes, ethnic background and sexual orientation in a campaign which whilst highlighting, and attempting to redress, the injustices presently suffered by Britain's hitherto neglected women prisoners, will also contribute to the wider campaigns for democratic control of the criminal justice and penal systems.

A later document, "Women in Prison: A Manifesto for Change," was issued by the group in 2015 to garner support for the group's agenda in the upcoming elections. It notes that as of 2015, twelve thousand women are sentenced to prison annually in the UK, most still serving short sentences for nonviolent crimes, as they were in 1985. It emphasizes that most females in prison were first victims of crimes, primarily domestic abuse and sexual violence, and experienced poverty and mental health challenges, as well.[3] It advocates addressing these root causes of women being in prison, as well as housing for women leaving prison and, as with the 1985 document, noncustodial solutions. Other issues include discrimination against certain groups of women—those enduring multiple forms of oppression and those suffering from inadequate reproductive and mental health care. Just as in other documents, feminists argue for the democratization of numerous institutions and social structures, so this one demands it of the prison system.

In many countries, the number of women in prison is increasing at a rate higher than that for men, though everywhere there are fewer women than men behind bars. Consequently there are often fewer facilities housing women, who are then more likely to be incarcerated farther from their homes. "Because of women's unique stabilizing and caretaking roles, incarcerating women exacts a devastating toll not only on the women themselves, but also on their children, families and communities. Nearly three-quarters of women in prison are mothers, and many were the primary caregivers for their children prior to incarceration."[4] Women in Prison makes visible the harm to women and their children from imprisonment, and demands that the incarcerated have greater access to their children.

Women in Prison Manifesto

Women In Prison—campaigning for WOMEN PRISONERS—demands:

1. Improved safety conditions, particularly in Holloway Prison where women have been burned to death in their cells.

2. The introduction of a range of facilities (e.g more visits, including family and conjugal visits in relaxed surroundings, more association with other prisoners, fewer petty rules) aimed both at reducing tension and, subsequently, the number of drugs prescribed for behaviour and mood control rather than the benefit of prisoners.

3. Improved, non-discriminatory and non-paternalistic education, job-related training, leisure and work facilities.

4. Improved training and supervision of prison officers, aimed at reducing their present discriminatory practices against women from ethnic minorities and lesbian, disabled or mentally or emotionally disturbed women.

5. A mandatory and non-discriminatory income entitlement to meet the basic needs of women prisoners.

6. Improvement of the existing child care facilities in prisons together with the introduction of a whole new range of child-care facilities for mothers receiving a custodial sentence (e.g. new centres specially for mothers and children; contacts with local nurseries and parents' groups).

7. Improved medical facilities in general and specialized facilities for women during pregnancy, childbirth and menstruation.

8. Dismantling of the punitive disciplinary structure coupled with the development of official recognition of prisoner participation in the organization of the prison.

9. Non-discriminatory sentencing of women.

10. Unrestricted access to the Boards of Visitors for representatives from women's organizations, community, ethnic minority and other minority (e.g. Lesbian) organizations.

Women In Prison—campaigning for ALL PRISONERS—demands:

1. Democratic control of the criminal justice and penal systems with: suspension of Official Secrets Act restrictions on the availability of information about

prisons; public accountability of the Home Office Prison Department for its administration of the prisons; public inquiries replacing Home Office internal inquiries into the deaths of prisoners, injuries and complaints in general together with Legal Aid to enable prisoners' families to be represented at any such inquiry.

2. Reduction in the length of prison sentences.

3. Replacement of the parole system with the introduction of half-remission on all sentences. Access to a sentence-review panel after serving seven years of a life sentence.

4. Increased funding for non-custodial alternatives to prisons (e.g. community service facilities, sheltered housing, alcohol recovery units) together with greater use of the existing sentences alternatives (e.g. deferred sentence, community service order, probation with a condition of psychiatric treatment etc.), with the aim of removing from prisons all who are there primarily because of drunkenness, drug dependency, mental, emotional or sexual problems, homelessness or inability to pay a fine.

5. Abolition of the censorship of prisoners' mail.

6. Abolition of the Prison Medical Service and its replacement by normal National Health Service provision coupled with abolition of the present system whereby prison officers vet, and have the power to refuse, prisoners' requests to see a doctor.

7. Provision of a law library in prisons so that prisoners may have access to information about their legal rights in relation to DHSS entitlement, employment, housing, marriage and divorce, child-custody, court proceedings, debt, prison rules etc.

8. Improved living and sanitary conditions together with a mandatory income entitlement to meet basic needs.

9. Non-discretionary rights to call witnesses and to full legal representation of prisoners at Visiting (internal) Court proceedings together with the abolition of the charge of "making false and malicious allegations against an officer."

10. A review of the existing methods of the recruitment and training of prison discipline staff.

Notes

1 Women in Prison, "Our History." Women in Prison, accessed Feb. 14, 2017, www.womeninprison.org.uk.

2 Women in Prison, "The Women in Prison Manifesto." Women in Prison, accessed Feb. 14, 2017, www.womeninprison.org.uk.

3 Women in Prison, "Women in Prison's Manifesto: General Election 2015." Women in Prison, accessed Feb. 14, 2017, www.womeninprison.org.uk.

4 "Women and the Criminal Justice System." Correctional Association of New York, accessed Feb. 14, 2017, www.correctionalassociation.org.

64

World Charter for Prostitutes' Rights
First World Whores' Congress
International Committee for Prostitutes' Rights
Amsterdam, Netherlands
February 1985

ICPR logo.

One of the position papers from the First Congress, stated that the word "whore" is used to stigmatize women, the word "prostitute" is used to criminalise women. Rather than disassociate from the social or legal labels used against us, we identify with both.
—Gail Pheterson

The relationships among feminism, prostitution, and sexual freedom remain complicated and contentious, as is clear from documents in this book. While feminist attention has long been paid to prostitution (recall resistance to the Contagious Diseases Acts of the 1860s in England, for example), and while individuals have long protested the abuse of prostitutes, the *movement* of sex workers and their allies advocating for the respect and rights due them as workers and as human beings dates only to the 1970s. Several groups emerged around the world in the 1970s, such as COYOTE (Cast Off Your Old Tired Ethics) in San Francisco (1973) and the French Collective of Prostitutes (1975). Today, numerous local, regional, and international organizations address a wide range of concerns, from child welfare and police harassment to AIDS and the right of all to sexual integrity and choice. Such groups range from Brooklyn's "small and feisty" activist "Red Umbrella" (redupnyc.tumblr.com) to the expansive "Durbar Mahila Samanwaya Committee," described as a collective of "65000 sex workers" (www.durbar.org).

The First World Whores' Congress was itself the result of years of local organizing and coalition building in many sites around the world. About 150 people attended, including some from the United Kingdom, the United States, France, Switzerland, the Netherlands, Sweden, and Germany; this dominance of the West would be remedied in later years. Only those who self-identified as sex workers or former sex workers had voting and speaking rights, while the rest had various roles as organizers and resources. Coming out of the first-ever convention on the rights of prostitutes, the Charter helped shape the then-fledgling movement.

The World Charter for Prostitutes' Rights[1] uses a human rights framework. It distinguishes between forced and voluntary prostitution (later documents will reject this distinction). Liberal at its core, it affirms individuals' decisions to engage in prostitution and their right to create the working conditions they prefer. They should have freedom from criminal prosecution, it asserts, and their work should have no impact on their possession of human rights and civil liberties. They condemn forced prostitution and support services that help those wishing to leave the life.

Margo St. James and Gail Pheterson, who organized the First World Whores' Congress, continued their collaboration in *A Vindication of the Rights of Whores* (Seal Press, 1989). The anthology both evokes history, in that the title references Mary Wollstonecraft's 1792 *Vindication of the Rights of Woman*, and contributes to historical records, by, for example, including unedited workshop transcripts from both World Whores' Conferences (the second was in Brussels in October 1986) and interviews with some of the participants. As Penelope Saunders commented fifteen years after the First World Whores' Congress, "Clearly sex worker activists and their organizations have a long road ahead before their rights are accepted, institutionalized as part of human rights doctrine, and made widely accessible to those who need them."[2]

World Charter for Prostitutes' Rights

Laws
- Decriminalize all aspects of adult prostitution resulting from individual decision.
- Decriminalize prostitution and regulate third parties according to standard business codes. It must be noted that existing standard business codes allow abuse of prostitutes. Therefore special clauses must be included to prevent the abuse and stigmatization of prostitutes (self-employed and others).
- Enforce criminal laws against fraud, coercion, violence, child sexual abuse, child labor, rape, racism everywhere and across national boundaries, whether or not in the context of prostitution.
- Eradicate laws that can be interpreted to deny freedom of association, or freedom to travel, to prostitutes within and between countries. Prostitutes have rights to a private life.

Human Rights
- Guarantee prostitutes all human rights and civil liberties, including the freedom of speech, travel, immigration, work, marriage, and motherhood and the right to unemployment insurance, health insurance and housing.
- Grant asylum to anyone denied human rights on the basis of a "crime of status," be it prostitution or homosexuality.

Working Conditions
- There should be no law which implies systematic zoning of prostitution. Prostitutes should have the freedom to choose their place of work and residence. It is essential that prostitutes can provide their services under the conditions that are absolutely determined by themselves and no one else.

- There should be a committee to insure the protection of the rights of the prostitutes and to whom prostitutes can address their complaints. This committee must be comprised of prostitutes and other professionals like lawyers and supporters.
- There should be no law discriminating against prostitutes associating and working collectively in order to acquire a high degree of personal security.

Health
- All women and men should be educated to [engage in] periodical health screening for sexually transmitted diseases. Since health checks have historically been used to control and stigmatize prostitutes, and since adult prostitutes are generally even more aware of sexual health than others, mandatory checks for prostitutes are unacceptable unless they are mandatory for all sexually active people.

Services
- Employment, counseling, legal, and housing services for runaway children should be funded in order to prevent child prostitution and to promote child well-being and opportunity.
- Prostitutes must have the same social benefits as all other citizens according to the different regulations in different countries.
- Shelters and services for working prostitutes and re-training programs for prostitutes wishing to leave the life should be funded.

Taxes
- No special taxes should be levied on prostitutes or prostitute businesses.
- Prostitutes should pay regular taxes on the same basis as other independent contractors and employees, and should receive the same benefits.

Public Opinion
- Support educational programs to change social attitudes which stigmatize and discriminate against prostitutes and ex-prostitutes of any race, gender or nationality.
- Develop educational programs which help the public to understand that the customer plays a crucial role in the prostitution phenomenon, this role being generally ignored. The customer, like the prostitute, should not, however, be criminalized or condemned on a moral basis.
- We are in solidarity with workers in the sex industry.

Organization
- Organizations of prostitutes and ex-prostitutes should be supported to further implementation of the above charter.

Notes

1 International Committee for Prostitutes' Rights, "World Charter for Prostitutes' Rights" (Amsterdam: ICPR, 1985). Commercial Sex Information Service, June 11, 1997, accessed Feb. 14, 2017, www.walnet.org/csis.

2 Penelope Saunders, "Fifteen Years after the World Charter for Prostitutes' Rights," 2000. Carnegie Council for International Affairs, accessed Feb. 14, 2017, www.carnegiecouncil.org.

65

Resolution *and* The Comilla Declaration
*Feminist International Network of Resistance against the New Reproductive
Technologies and Genetic Engineering*
Sweden and Bangladesh
July 1985 and March 19–25, 1989

We call for a halt to the research and application of reproductive and
genetic engineering in all its forms. . . . Initial experiences with reproductive and genetic engineering all over the world show that these
technologies are aggravating the deteriorating position of women
in society and intensifying the existing differences among people in
terms of race, class, caste, sex, and religion.

The Feminist International Network of Resistance against the New Reproductive Technologies and Genetic Engineering (FINRRAGE) provides a radical,
"unambiguous oppositional voice" in debates about reproductive technology
and genetic engineering.[1] The basis for its opposition has at least two related
prongs: (1) the various harmful effects of reproductive and genetic technologies
on women, and (2) the drive for control that directs and is reinforced by these
technologies: "attempting to control population quantity and quality through
controlling women's reproductive capacities."[2] Even while criticized for a variety
of feminist wrongs, from essentialism to biological reductionism, FINRRAGE
has held onto and evolved its critique, and is given credit for "publiciz[ing]
the dangers of eugenicism."[3] While many documents in this collection express
concern with the way reproduction is regulated, FINRRAGE's agenda is unique.

Feminists discussed reproductive and genetic engineering at the Second International Interdisciplinary Congress of Women in the Netherlands, in April
1984, and created a network called FINNRET (Feminist International Network
on New Reproductive Technologies). A year later (July 1985), this network held
the Women's Emergency Conference on the New Reproductive Technologies
in Sweden, attended by seventy-four women from perhaps twenty countries.
Changing their name to FINRRAGE (adding "resistance" and "genetic"), they
came to see that reproductive technologies harmed women around the world in
diverse ways, and became part of a feminist resistance to them. The Resolution
is from that conference in Sweden, and is the group's first statement of purpose.[4]

FINRRAGE addresses a large range of reproductive medicines and practices,
including contraceptives, fertility drugs, in-vitro fertilization, embryo transfer,
surrogacy, sex selection and determination, research and reproductive cloning,
genetic screening, and genetic manipulation.[5] They focus on "the implications of
these and related technologies for the socio-economic position and wellbeing of
women in different situations, cultures, and countries, as well as the impacts on
the environment and other life forms." Strategically, they work to raise awareness,
to build knowledge and tactics with women internationally, and to understand
"the relationship between science, technology, and social relations in patriarchal
societies which underlie these technologies . . . and the development of alternatives which respect women and nature."

The Resolution[6] criticizes the "genetic reconstruction of nature" as a violation
of "the autonomy and integrity of all life on earth," and argues that it is "oriented

around profit motives and military aims—motives which are glossed over with promises of alleviating pain and suffering," benefiting infertile women, and being for women's good. It calls reproductive scientific advances eugenics, practices that dangerously divide women and fetuses into the worthy and unworthy.

At the Comilla, Bangladesh, conference,[7] which was cosponsored by UBINIG (Policy Research for Development Alternatives, a social research organization in Bangladesh), FINRRAGE's geographical representation expanded, as the 145 attendees came from thirty-five countries, this time including Asia, Africa, and Latin America. The attendees "were natural and social scientists, doctors, lawyers, health workers, journalists, demographers, development workers, community organisers, teachers, social workers and academics."[8] In the face of "the rapid development and increasing application of [reproductive and genetic] technologies," they addressed selling contraceptives to people in the developing world that have been banned elsewhere; testing contraceptives on poor women; forced sterilization; risky and expensive fertility treatments with low success rates; a growing business in sex determination to allow abortion of female fetuses; and seed genetics that benefit multinational corporations rather than farmers and reduce diversity.

Resolution

The women present at the First European Conference of the Feminist International Network of Resistance against the New Reproductive Technologies and Genetic Engineering (FINRRAGE) from Austria, Australia, Bangladesh, Canada, Denmark, England, France, Holland, Ireland, Norway, Spain, Sweden, Switzerland, the United States and West-Germany declare the following:

We believe that the New Reproductive Technologies and Genetic Engineering violate the autonomy and integrity of all life on earth now and will do so even more so in the future. Both the technologies and the ideology behind them are based on the idea that human life—and in the case of the New Reproductive Technologies, specifically women's bodies—can be and should be dissected, manipulated and controlled as raw material for the production of human beings and other life forms to exact specification.

The Genetic Engineering of plants, animals and microorganisms is being propagated by scientists, industry and the state as a new way of constructing man-made life-forms which are more efficient than what has evolved in nature. This genetic reconstruction of nature is oriented around profit motives and military aims—motives which are merely being glossed over with promises of alleviating pain and suffering when these technologies are applied to human beings.

We reject the elimination and destruction of life forms through the use of genetic engineering not only in humans, but also in plants, animals and microorganisms. With specific reference to women we reject the attempts of scientists and doctors to interfere with women's reproductive capacities. We oppose the New Reproductive Technologies—in particular in vitro fertilisation (IVF) in all its forms and plans for "gene therapy" and disagree with the claim of their makers that they are beneficial for infertile women and contribute to alleviate human pain. We are opposed to any attempt to use the new genetic techniques including forms of pre- and postnatal screening, in particular in connection with IVF and other reproductive technologies for the purpose of determining and for modifying individuals' genetic identity and developing new forms of eugenics. For us there are no technological solutions to the ecological and social destruction already caused by industrialisation.

Our point is that women do not need to transform our bodies for patriarchal use, for industrial profit-making, population control, medical experimentation and woman-hating science. We believe that enforced sterilisation and the distribution of harmful contraceptives around the globe under the guise of population policies is a violation of women's human dignity as is the prohibition of abortion and the practice of not informing women of dangers and the low success rate of IVF procedures under the guise of doing it all for women's "own good."

We also reject the classification of women into "worthy" and "unworthy" bearers of children on the basis of our race, class, language, sexuality, disability and marital status. This holds true for women from so-called first world and third world countries, as well as poor women from within all our countries.

We also reject state control with respect to women's pro-creativity. We do not want laws that focus on the fetus rather than putting women's needs and interests first. We believe that at their core these technologies and their makers act against women's human dignity and we have serious doubts and negative historical precedents about whether women's interests will be met through state regulations.

We call for a halt to the research and application of reproductive and genetic engineering in all its forms: in human beings, specifically women, in all animal and plant life and in its use in the construction of devastating biological weapons.

With regard to women we demand the setting of priorities for women's health programmes according to the expressed concerns of women. This includes programmes for the prevention of infertility and alternatives for infertile women.

With regard to the international development of medicine and science we propose to use decision-making models which enable genuine participation of people on the basis of concern for the survival of life on earth and a better future. In sum, we call for a different science which specifically takes into account women's realities and uses the method of empassioned-curiosity to fulfill people's desire to know about the complexity of life on earth.

Comilla Declaration

1. We, the women from Australia, Austria, Bangladesh, Brazil, Canada, Denmark, Egypt, Fiji, France, Federal Republic of Germany, Hong Kong, Holland, India, Indonesia, Japan, Malaysia, Mauritius, Norway, Pakistan, Peru, Philippines, Sri Lanka, South Korea, Spain, Sweden, Switzerland, United Kingdom, Uganda, United States of America, and Zambia, have met in Comilla, Bangladesh, to share our concern about reproductive and genetic engineering and women's reproductive health.

We feel an urgent need to halt the political decisions which are leading to the rapid development and increasing application of these technologies.

2. Initial experiences with reproductive and genetic engineering all over the world show that these technologies are aggravating the deteriorating position of women in society and intensifying the existing differences among people in terms of race, class, caste, sex, and religion. These technologies also contribute to the further destabilizing of the already critical ecological situation.

3. Genetic and reproductive engineering are part of an ideology of eugenics which we oppose! In this ideology, human beings are viewed as inherently inferior or superior. This leads to degradation, discrimination and elimination of oppressed groups; be they women, disabled, people of certain colors, races, religions, class, or caste. Similarly, traits of animals and plants are arbitrarily valued as being desirable or undesirable and become subject to genetic manipulation.

4. Eugenics justifies the political strategy used by those in power to divide and rule.

5. Women from the participating countries described how eugenic ideology and racism are the basis of population control policies. We resist population control policies and methods. They hide the true roots of poverty as exploitation by the rich. They reduce women to their reproductive organs. We object to women being used as experimental subjects by science, industry and government.

6. Genetic and reproductive engineering, as well as population control, are introduced and promoted on the grounds that they solve problems such as hunger, disease, and pollution. In reality, however, they divert attention from the real causes and are incapable of solving these problems. Nor do they reflect women's demands and needs.

7. Genetic and reproductive engineering claim to offer unlimited control over all life forms, but tinkering with genetic codes opens up a truly uncontrollable situation of "runaway designer genes" and unintended consequences. These changes will be particularly hazardous because a chain reaction will be set in motion which cannot be traced back to its origins. The effects produced cannot be countered. They will be irreversible.

8. In our increasingly materialistic and consumer-oriented world, genetic engineering is promising unlimited diversity. But to live in a man-made patriarchal world, where everything has been tampered with, will be to live with the ultimate limitation. Our present finite world of resources offers a richer diversity than that promised by genetic engineering with its selective, eugenic, and patriarchal philosophy.

9. Genetic and reproductive engineering are a product of the development of science which started off by viewing the whole world as a machine. Just as a machine can be broken down into its components, analyzed and put back, living beings are seen as consisting of components which can be viewed in isolation. Aspects of

nature which cannot be measured or quantified are seen as subjective and of no value and are, therefore, neglected. In their ignorance or disregard of the complex interrelationships in life, scientists collaborate with industry and big capital and believe they have finally acquired the power to create and reconstruct plants, animals, and other forms of life and, possibly soon, even human beings. We oppose this patriarchal, industrial, commercial and racist domination over life.

10. In our work of bearing and raising children, caring for the sick or disabled, growing, preserving, and preparing food, materials for clothes and other basic human needs, we women have developed and passed on for generations a wealth of knowledge and skills about dealing with all of nature in a compassionate, humane, and ecologically sustainable way. We realize that this knowledge and these skills, as well as the contributions of women to the arts, crafts, culture and social relations are generally not recognized as having value in mainstream science, philosophy, or technology. But these have been and still are vital for the survival of human beings and all of nature. They are valuable human achievements and resources. We want to renew, reaffirm and build upon this female tradition.

11. We strongly believe that reproductive and genetic engineering cannot meet the needs of women or enhance their status in today's societies. We, therefore, demand the participation and recognition of women in all spheres of life. We want women to have access to resources, income, employment, social security, and a safe environment at work and at home. Quite fundamentally, we demand living and working conditions that assure a life of human dignity for all women worldwide.

12. We demand access for girls to practical knowledge, resources, and skills that are in women's best interest and further women's well being. These include an education about taking care of primary health needs, including nutrition. This will empower women and increase women's general health, reduce morbidity and mortality of women and children. Such primary health care will reduce the number of children born with mental and physical disabilities and also reduce infertility.

13. We demand knowledge and access to safe contraception which does not harm women's bodies. We reject any coercion, be it through force, incentives or disincentives in the name of population control policies, such as enforced sterilization, particularly in camps and in target oriented policies. We demand a stop to the use of dangerous IUDs, unsafe injectables, hormonal implants, such as Norplant, and other hormonal contraceptives, as well as antifertility vaccines.

14. We support the recovery by women of knowledge, skill and power that gives childbirth, fertility and all women's health care back into the hands of women. We demand recognition, support and facilitation of the work of midwives and reestablishment of midwifery services under the control of women.

15. We demand literature be distributed and education be given about adverse effects of all contraceptive methods.

16. We demand contraceptives for men be developed and also that men be made responsible for contraception.

17. We demand the United Nations and the governments of the respective countries stop population control policies as preconditions for developmental aid.

18. We support the exclusive rights of all women to decide whether or not to bear children without coercion from any man, medical practitioner, government or religion. We demand that women shall not be criminalized for choosing and performing abortion.

19. We oppose the medicalization and commercialization of the desire of women for motherhood.

20. Internationally, we demand that conditions be created under which social parenthood in a variety of forms meets the needs of children and people who wish to care for children. In particular, maternity and child care should be a social concern rather than the responsibility of individual women.

21. We condemn men and their institutions that inflict infertility on women by violence, forced sterilization, medical maltreatment and industrial pollution, and repeat the damage through violent "repair" technologies.

22. Given the continuing deterioration of women's lives through the application of patriarchal science and technology, we call for an international public trial on medical crimes against women to be organized by women.

Notes

1 Hilary Rose, "Moving On from Both State and Consumer Eugenics?" in *Remaking Reality: Nature at the Millenium*, ed. Bruce Braun and Noel Castree (London: Routledge, 1998), p. 91.

2 FINRRAGE: Feminist International Network of Resistance to Reproductive and Genetic Engineering, accessed Feb. 14, 2017, www.finrrage.org.

3 See, for example, Hilary Rose, *Love, Power, and Knowledge: Towards a Feminist Transformation of the Sciences* (Cambridge, UK: Polity, 1994).

4 Extensive notes from that meeting include country reports. See "FINRRAGE Conference: Lund, Sweden, 1985, Conference Report." Feminist International Network of Resistance to Reproductive and Genetic Engineering, accessed Feb. 14, 2017, www.finrrage.org.

5 "Aims of the Network." Feminist International Network of Resistance to Reproductive and Genetic Engineering, accessed Feb. 14, 2017, www.finrrage.org.

6 "Resolution of the First European Conference of FINRRAGE." Feminist International Network of Resistance to Reproductive and Genetic Engineering, accessed Feb. 14, 2017, www.finrrage.org.

7 "History of FINRRAGE." Feminist International Network of Resistance to Reproductive and Genetic Engineering, accessed Feb. 14, 2017, www.finrrage.org.

8 "Conference Report: FINNRAGE-UBINIG International Conference, Reproductive and Genetic Engineering and Women's Reproductive Health." Feminist International Network of Resistance to Reproductive and Genetic Engineering, accessed Feb. 14, 2017, www.finrrage.org.

66

South Asian Feminist Declaration
Bangalore, India
January 1989

The state in our countries is chauvinist, authoritarian, militaristic
and patriarchal.

This document[1] could only emerge from a transnational regional meeting, this
time in South Asia. Twenty-three women from Bangladesh, Pakistan, Sri Lanka,
and India "explicitly focused on collective reflection on and conceptualiza-
tions of feminism, the relationship of the women's movement with other social
movements, and developing a Southasian Perspective."[2] The result is a powerful account of the historical and contemporary situation in the region, and the
numerous, complex ways in which issues involved in peace, development, militarization, democracy, and gender are intertwined.

South Asian feminists confront many of the same gendered and racialized
stereotypes, confront the same forms of gender-based violence, and share not
only a similar colonial history but also histories rife with women activists in independence and democracy movements. Their feminism is challenged on similar
grounds, both fundamentalist and nationalist. Still, the countries have different
major religions and different feminist histories, and so conversation is crucial.

Another South Asian Feminist Declaration was issued in 2007, building on the
1989 document.[3] The belief that a regional network of feminists is essential to
creating space for transformative gender work is behind contemporary work by
groups such as Sangat, the South Asian Feminist Alliance for Economic, Social
Cultural Rights, and the South Asian Women's Network.

South Asian Feminist Declaration

We come from different countries in South Asia—Bangladesh, India, Pakistan,
and Sri Lanka. Divided by geopolitical boundaries, we are all bound together by
a common South Asian identity. This identity expresses itself both in the linkages
we have with each other and in the struggles each of us is involved in within the
women's movement in our respective countries.

These links have strengthened us individually and have led to a growing sense
of regional solidarity. Today, in the context of the contemporary socio-political
environment, we feel it is imperative to develop and further strengthen a South
Asian perspective for women's liberation in the region. This declaration is an
expression of our personal/political commitment to a broad based South Asian
feminist platform and a call for support to strengthen such a platform.

Our countries, although far from being homogenous, having different social, and
economic conditions, share great similarities. The South Asian region has been a
mosaic, a pentimento through which layers of history have been created through
alignments and realignments as people moved from one part of the region to
another, mixing, mingling and internalising different cultures. These alignments

and movements were ones of conflict as well as of collaboration; whatever their specific history, these migrations created corresponding structures of kinship, caste and community within each region. Each country today is internally constructed by these structures. Each mirrors the other in richness and diversity of religions, cultures and social institutions.

The way we eat, dress, build our homes, the songs we sing, the pictures we paint are all of a common mode, shaped more by local environments (cultural and ecological) than by political boundaries.

Who we are today is as much a product of a common heritage of the legacy of colonialism and the struggle of earlier generations to create a just and equal society in the region. In the post independence period however, we have continued to be subject to common structure[s] of oppression and exploitation imposed by dominant class/caste and patriarchal rule, reinforced by almost identical government responses to the legitimate aspirations of people.

As women our lives are subject to control through predominantly patriarchal structures and family laws and institutions, often justified on the basis of religion. The onslaught of capitalism and imperialism in the post independence period, has led to increasing restrictions on our space and access to resources, and a destruction of our traditional skills and knowledge systems.

Along with other marginalised communities we have been subject to increasing levels of state, community and family violence. Our voices are not heard as we are excluded from the political process which projects class privileged dynastic rule, whether by men or women leaders. The disintegration of civil society; the increasing centralization of authority in the hands of the state, often backed with fundamentalist sanction leaves us vulnerable to constant attack inside and outside our homes. Growing statistics on rape, dowry deaths, incidents of acid throwing, the stripping of women as acts of revenge, the concerted attack by religious fundamentalists to keep us propertyless and resourceless, the continued denial of our contribution to subsistence, production and reproduction, are shared experiences of an orchestrated campaign to keep us forever silent, invisible and subhuman.

These similarities of experience (and internal diversities) are however denied by the centralizing and homogenizing actions of the state in each country. Some countries in the region project a monolithic Islamic or Hindu nation, often defined in opposition to their neighbours. Pakistan and Bangladesh are now Islamic states, Sri Lanka is virtually a Sinhala Buddhist state and India is being increasingly identified as a Hindu state. Relations between the countries are determined by national security interests. India and Pakistan have had 3 wars and numerous border clashes in the last 43 years. Periodically there are hostile exchanges, and on each side the flames of false patriotism, xenophobia and chauvinism are aroused. Such an imagery feeds into traumatic memories of partition and resurrects the fears of either Hindu or Muslim domination, further widening the gulf between the two countries.

Indian ships police the waters of the Indian Ocean and the presence of Tamils across the sea in Tamilnadu, has led to fears about "Indian imperialism," being whipped up among the Sinhala people. As a result the Tamils in the North and Eastern provinces of Sri Lanka and the Tamil plantation workers imported by colonialism are viewed as the Indian fifth column. Although Indian intervention in Sri Lanka was requested by militant groups and supported by democratic forces in Sri Lanka, the record of the atrocities by the IPKF has raised serious questions about India's geopolitical interests in the region.

The neighbouring country is the main enemy or the cause for internal tensions we are told. Although there is some opening up, it is still difficult to cross borders to meet friends or colleagues, to visit familial villages or read each others['] books and papers. Today barbed wire fences are being erected between India, Pakistan and Bangladesh, while Sri Lankans are said to disappear in green boats in the seas controlled by the Indian navy.

When we reach out in support of other women fighting against patriarchal and state violence in the region we are labelled anti-national. Activists and intellectuals who take a democratic stand in Sri Lanka are branded as traitors to the Sinhala nation. Support for women in Pakistan and Bangladesh, in their fight against religious fundamentalism by the women's movement in India is seen as a Hindu reaction and these organisations are seen as Indian agents. Conversely, when organisations in India have highlighted the protofascist tendencies of Hindu fundamentalists and raised the issue of attacks against minority communities, they are suspected of being Pakistani agents and betrayers of "national interests."

The notion of "national interests" becomes a ready rationale for governments in our countries to increase their level of militarisation. National and religious chauvinism built on mutual hostility becomes the binding force to maintain the nation state. It becomes possible, even commendable to kill, humiliate, maim and threaten the citizens of another country, religious or ethnic group or nationality in the name of preserving the unity of one's own country. Justified on the grounds of external defence, the armies are used more often for internal suppression rather than against each other. Rightful citizens are suddenly treated as enemy agents.

A declining proportion of yearly budgets are being allocated to health and education while there are massive increases in defence spending. Since the 1980's defence expenditure has escalated phenomenally in all the countries of the region. In addition, military assistance in the form of weapons and training have been provided for instance by the U.S. and Israel to the Sri Lankan government. The diversion of resources for military spending results in unproductive consumption of energy and non-energy materials and the diversion of labor and industrial production from socially useful production. The existence of a manufacturing base for armament production in India creates a demand for more and more wars and lays the material basis for Indian dominance in the region. In the 1980's India's defence expenditure shot up from Rs. 4,329 crore in 1981–82 to Rs. 14,500 crore in 1989–90.

The militarisation of our societies has made brutalisation a way of life. War toys, daily violence in films and on the television have created a militarized culture. For women this means a sanctioning of and an increase in violence within the home and by the "uniformed guardians of the state." The disruption of "normal life" in military situations adds additional burdens and dangers to women's continuing responsibility for subsistence and household provisioning.

Each shaky regime is seeking legitimacy through projecting military power as a symbol of independent strength, prowess and national virility. The acquisition of arms from the superpowers has led to the creation of an interest lobby of influential political, military and bureaucratic groups who would push for higher and higher defence expenditures.

The most significant threat is that of nuclearisation. The use of nuclear energy only for peaceful purposes is denied by the fact that each country uses the threat of the "other side[']s bomb" as a justification to have its own bomb for national security. The global nuclear arms race and its horrific capacity to eliminate life on earth has shown that nuclear weapons are instruments of mass annihilation and cannot ever lead to security. The subcontinent particularly lies under the threat of a mushroom cloud. Statements issued by the Indian and Pakistani governments to not attack each other[']s nuclear intallations do not rule out the nuclear option.

The increasing crisis of legitimacy facing our governments today is rooted in the conditions of the birth of these separate nations, and the inherently divisive nature of the nation state itself. The colonial policy of divide and rule led to the political bifurcation of the subcontinent into two mutually hostile states of India and Pakistan. In Pakistan, Punjabi domination rested on the suppression of other nationalities and the process of Islamisation attempted to impose a homogeneity that suppressed other Islamic minority sects and created two classes of citizens— muslims on one side and non-muslims and women on the other side. Further intensification of ethnic and sectarian conflict has now led to the situation where Muhajirs are also demanding recognition as a separate nationality. In Sri Lanka, the control of state power by a Sinhala majority together with the projection of a Sinhala Buddhist identity led to the demand for a separate homeland by the Tamils. Today the violence and bloodshed continues and further divisions are being created on a religious basis.

In Bangladesh by the late seventies, the tensions between the Bengalis and the tribal population intensified as a reaction to the state's attempt to colonise tribal areas along with the use of constitutional/extra constitutional measures to contain tribal demands. The projection of Islam as a state religion, backed by foreign powers, has become a strategy to contain the economic and political crisis in the country.

In India, regional tensions have extended to communal conflicts between Hindus and Muslims, Hindus and Sikhs, with caste conflicts also being transformed into communal tensions. Caste conflicts and attacks on dalits have been heightened by the onslaught of capitalist development, the manipulation of political parties and the intervention of hindu fundamentalists. Indian secularism has contained the seeds of communalism which are now being aggressively articulated by the Hindu majority in their equation of nationalism with a Hindu state.

The state in our countries is chauvinist, authoritarian, militaristic and patriarchal. Historical evidence from the earliest times indicates that the very institution of the state was not only class defined but also based on patriarchal authority right from the onset and the contradictions of patriarchy and class have been further developed by capitalism and imperialism. Anti-colonial nationalism incorporated particular notions of womanhood and manhood which ideologically circumscribed the proper roles of women within the limits of social work and domesticity. The maintenance of separate personal laws by post-colonial South Asian states reflects their patriarchal bias, since all these reinforce the patrilineal, patrilocal family. Equal rights legislation remains unimplemented whether it concerns equal right to property or wages.

The homogenising and centralizing thrust of the state in our region is an expression of the spread, albeit unevenly, of capitalism. Although there are differences in the specific constellation of dominant classes, and the degree of dependence or independence from foreign capital between our countries, development programmes for agricultural and industrial growth have resulted in the appropriation of resources by a dominant class/caste group and increasing impoverishment of large sections of working people. Due to an energy and resource intensive strategy of development, our region, like others in Africa and Latin America, is in the throes of a severe ecological crisis. Water and land have been poisoned and polluted. Forests have been destroyed and river systems have been disrupted with dams. Waterlogging and salinity have turned vast tracts of fertile land into deserts.

Women, adivasis, dalits and small peasants have been the most debilitated in this process. Women now work longer hours than before, seeking fodder and fuel to maintain increasingly impoverished families. The acceleration of the twin processes of privatization and commercialisation, exacerbated in our regions due to varied combinations of capitalism with feudalism, has had very specific effects on women, particularly poor rural women. The provisioning of families has shifted even more onto the bodies of women as the number of female headed households increase in the countryside. More women are being drawn into wage work in the invisible, irregular and low paid sectors of the economy. New avenues of employment in the world market factories has [sic] instituted another form of exploitation as women are barricaded into restricted industrial production zones subject to patriachal control within and outside the factory. IMF conditionality and structural adjustment programmes intensify these processes, particularly with the withdrawal of already scanty social and welfare services.

Although the processes of capitalist development have led to certain changes in the traditional structures of patriarchy, especially within the family, women are still subject to violent forms of control by the family, community, village and the state, as they begin to enter male space. Not only is women's labor and mobility regulated but the state in our countries is adopting more and more sophisticated and dangerous techniques to control women's fertility.

Over the past decades strong social movements have emerged in our countries, resisting and struggling against these manifestations of class and patriarchal rule. One of the most important movements of challenge and resistance to the various systems of exploitation and oppression that exist in South Asia, has been the women's movement. At both material and ideological levels feminists of the region have been active in challenging the authoritarianism and violence of the state, its repressive laws, fundamentalist tendencies, militarism and chauvinism: they have challenged the economic exploitation of workers and peasants, social oppression through the use of religion, culture and the cast system as well as discrimination based on ethnicity, language, caste or religious allegiance. They have also highlighted the use of violence against women within the family and in the workplace. In recent years they have raised the issue of human rights violations. Apart from such challenges feminists have also been involved in resistance to all forms of patriarchy, a resistance that has historic roots but also been sharpened in recent decades.

However, feminists have been called western, bourgeois, anti men, at various times. We have watched with amazement and often a feeling of regret at the strange alliance of the bourgeois controlled press, right wing fundamentalists and sections of the progressive forces in our countries as they mocked, ridiculed and attacked the assertions of women's autonomy from capitalist/patriachal controls. We see this labelling as a deliberate blindness and refusal to acknowledge the issues which have been taken up by the feminist movement in our countries. These issues have ranged from confronting the government on the withdrawal of equal rights for women, confronting dominant class/caste and patriarchal forces when they have suppressed, attacked and raped us for demanding our rights to land, wages or simply a job, to raising questions about the link between development models based on ecological destruction and violence against women within and outside the home.

More importantly, such labelling is a denial of our history within the region—a history which is rich with the stories of many women and men who struggled for democratic rights for women in the 19th and early 20th century. It is a denial of the contributions of the masses of women in national movements and in peasant and working class struggles who raised both class and gender issues, who struggled and fought within wider political movements and within their families for recognition as equal human beings.

In the 1980's we see feminism as an awareness of patriarchal control, exploitation and oppression at the material and ideological level, over women's labour, fertility and sexuality, within the family, at the workplace and in society in general; committed to conscious action to transform society.

The feminist struggle is guided by a vision of a society where people can live free of class, caste and state domination.

Although there are different tendencies within feminism, we locate ourselves within a broad tradition committed to democracy and socialism. In our actions and our ideas we combine a vision of socialism and feminism, seeing both as essential to a struggle against patriarchy, capitalism and imperialism.

We believe that feminism is the expression of women in struggle and is therefore a political movement and consciousness which will develop in practice as more and more women begin to join together against the structures which oppress and exploit them.

Feminism as a movement in South Asia has asserted the principle of autonomous organisation for women, while linking with broader movements at the same time. It rejects separatism and a narrow focus on individualism. It has opened the way to look at alternative ways of living, of building relationships, of an alternative decentralized economy and polity. It has struggled for dignity and for the humanization and democratisation of the family.

Linking together in concrete actions, formulating and campaigning for a joint charter of women's rights, sharing visions and developing alternatives to existing development models at the South Asian level from a feminist perspective would be an important contribution towards the overcoming of the tensions, distrust, and political, economic, social and cultural crisis affecting our countries today. We see this as one step in a broader process which would draw on and link together broader social movements, political organisations and progressive individuals who share this vision of transformation of both political and economic structures and relationships between people.

Notes

1 "South Asian Feminist Declaration, 1989." South Asia Citizens Web, accessed Feb. 14, 2017, www.sacw.net.
2 Rawwida Baksh and Wendy Harcourt, eds., *The Oxford Handbook of Transnational Feminist Movements* (New York: Oxford University Press, 2015), p. 560.
3 "South Asian February Declaration, 2006." Sangat, accessed Feb. 14, 2017, www.sangatnetwork.org.

67

Who We Are *and* Reproductive Justice Agenda
Native American Women's Health Education Resource Center
Yankton, South Dakota
1990

The Native American Women's Health Education Resource Center staff, as of 2001.

The Native American Women's Health Education Resource Center was founded by the Native American Community Board, a group of men and women living on or near the Yankton Sioux Reservation in Yankton, South Dakota. The center was founded primarily to create healthcare resources for women and to raise awareness about fetal alcohol syndrome, and it was the first such center on a Native American reservation in the United States.

In 1990 the group held a three-day conference, "Empowerment through Dialogue," that resulted in the Reproductive Justice Agenda that follows. Over thirty Native women from at least eleven Northern Plains nations came together for the event in Pierre, South Dakota, May 16–18. The document embodies a sense of reproductive justice specific enough to address coerced sterilization and Two Spirited women, and broad enough to encompass nonsexist, nonracist childrearing and age-appropriate education on sexuality and reproduction.

Knowing that "[t]hree-fourths of Native women have experienced some type of sexual assault and or domestic violence in their lives,"[1] in 1991 the center opened a Women's Lodge to provide protection for women and children who are victims of domestic or sexual violence. This shelter is still an important part of the center's work, and coexists with a men's reeducation group, Batterers Intervention Program.

Since its founding, the center has expanded its focus from women's health education to many other projects important to Native American women, including preservation of the Dakota language, environmental justice and preservation, and reproductive justice. Today, the center supports programs including the Domestic Violence Program, AIDS Prevention Program, Youth Services—which include the Child Development Program and the Youth Wellness Program—Adult Learning Program, Environmental Awareness and Action Project, Cancer Prevention, Fetal Alcohol Syndrome Awareness Program, Clearinghouse of Educational Materials, Food Pantry, Wicozanni Wowapi Newsletter, Diabetic Nutrition Program, Scholarships for Native American Women, Reproductive Health and Rights, "Green Thumb" Project, and Community Health Fairs.[2]

Who We Are

The Native American Community Board (NACB) was incorporated as a nonprofit (501)(c)(3) organization in 1985 by a concerned and well-informed group of Native Americans living on or near the Yankton Sioux Indian Reservation in South Dakota.

The Native American Women's Health Education Resource Center (NAWHERC)—which provides direct services to Native women and families in South Dakota and advocates for Native women at the community, national, and international levels to protect our reproductive health and rights—is a project of the NACB (the NACB is the governing board). NAWHERC's activities range from community education to preserve our culture, campaigns to end violence against Indigenous women, coalition building to fight for our reproductive justice, and environmental justice.

Since its founding in 1988, NAWHERC has become the *leading pathfinder in the country in addressing Indigenous women's reproductive health and justice issues* while working to preserve and protect our culture. NACB and NAWHERC serve reservation-based Indigenous women at the local, national, and international levels.

Reproductive Justice Agenda

1. The right to knowledge and education for all family members concerning sexuality and reproduction that is age-, culture-, and gender-appropriate.
2. The right to all reproductive alternatives and the right to choose the size of our families.
3. The right to affordable health care, including safe deliveries within our communities.
4. The right to access safe, free, and/or affordable abortions, regardless of age, with confidentiality and free pre- and post-counseling.
5. The right to active involvement in the development and implementation of policies concerning reproductive issues, which include but are not limited to pharmaceuticals and technology.
6. The right to include domestic violence, sexual assault, and AIDS as reproductive justice issues.
7. The right to programs which meet the nutritional needs of women and families.
8. The right to programs to reduce the rate of infant mortality and high-risk pregnancies.
9. The right to culturally specific comprehensive chemical dependency prenatal programs including, but not limited to, prevention of Fetal Alcohol Syndrome and Effects.
10. The right to stop coerced sterilization.
11. The right to a forum for cultural/spiritual development, culturally-oriented health care, and the right to live as Native Women.
12. The right to be fully informed about, and to consent to any forms of medical treatment.
13. The right to determine who are members of our Nations.
14. The right to continuous, consistent, and quality health care for Native People.
15. The right to reproductive justice and support for women with disabilities.
16. The right to parent our children in a non-sexist, non-racist environment.
17. The right of Two Spirited women, their partners, and their families to live free from persecution or discrimination based on their sexuality and/or gender, and the right to enjoy the same human, political, social, legal, economic, religious, tribal and governmental rights and benefits afforded all other Indigenous women.
18. The right to give birth and be attended to in the setting most appropriate, be it home, community, clinic or hospital and to be able to choose the support system for our births, including but not limited to, Traditional Midwives, Families and community members.
19. The right to education and support for breastfeeding that include but not limited to, individuals and communities that allow for regrowth of traditional nurturing and parenting of our children.

In order to accomplish the foregoing stated rights, Native Women for Reproductive Justice will create conditions and alliances to network with other groups.

Notes

1 "Programs and Services." Native American Women's Health Education Resource Center, accessed Feb. 14, 2017, www.nativeshop.org.
2 "History." Native American Women's Health Education Resource Center, accessed Feb. 14, 2017, www.nativeshop.org.

68

Declaration from the Founder Members' Meeting
Independent Women's Democratic Initiative (NEZHDI)

Voronez, Soviet Union

July 24, 1990

NEZHDI emblem.

In Russian, the acronym "NEZHDI" means "Don't wait."[1] The organization behind this acronym, the Independent Women's Declaration Initiative, has its roots in the first ever Centre for Gender Studies in the USSR. This center was established in 1989. Anastasia Posadskaya played a central role in the Centre for Gender Studies and in NEZHDI, which soon followed. She recalls that the center's members hosted a seminar in the spring of 1990, titled "Women, Politics, and Policy," primarily to elicit feedback on the center's position paper from people "outside the academic milieu." An association of women's groups formed organically from these meetings; by July there was a "core of women representing informal women's groups," which was codified as the NEZHDI.[2]

During its early years, NEZHDI placed itself in contrast to the Soviet Women's Committee: a "formal" women's organization convened by the state. The organization's name, the language found in the Declaration itself, and members' personal statements show that they emphasized "independence" as a crucial value missing from other women's movements in the USSR. When they use the term "independent women's movements," NEZHDI members generally mean independence from "party control" or any other "state-organized control."

Of course, the value of "independence" has resonance for individual women's lives, as well. This Declaration[3] addresses the need for Soviet women's economic independence from both individual men and the state. At the time, the state was an especially potent force in maintaining women's economic dependence; however, the looming dissolution of the Soviet Union caused members to fear that the fall of the state would simply direct women to become more economically dependent on the men in their households. The women who drafted this resolution acknowledge that the Soviet Union failed to deliver promises of equality to its female citizens, but they simultaneously express a fear that the transition towards a new social and economic system will be used to justify regressive policies towards women's rights. Specifically, the Declaration's first main claim affirms that approaching unemployment is not to be solved through the redomestication of women. The founding members of NEZHDI saw this as a likely scenario, although at times there is a sense of optimism. Posadskaya reflects in an interview (frequently included alongside this Declaration) that the USSR had been "a society flattened out under a heavy weight, it was just smashed flat like a plate. This weight is now lifting, and the shape of society is changing, it is becoming rounded, more transparent. Now there will be something of everything in this society."

The Declaration also addresses the need for previously lacking social and political independence. In the Soviet Union, quotas ensured that women played a role in the political process. However, the Declaration expresses concern that women's participation has up to this point often been purely symbolic. This Declaration notes that women in positions of public power who nonetheless lack the ability to act and speak and choose independently can often cause more harm than good. Posadskaya recalls that "[t]hese women were seen as people who raised their hands from time to time, so as a result . . . the idea of women in positions of power, is now discredited."

Over seventy women from five cities in the Soviet Union attended the July meeting, in the context of a dissolving Soviet Union. Thus, overall the Declaration can be read as a fascinating opportunity to reconsider the language of social equality and women's rights often appropriated or misused by previously dominant social and political forces. Once again, Posadskaya's interview provides helpful insight into the purpose of the Declaration. "The danger now, however, is that we cannot use the old language because it was discredited by hypocritical usage," she notes. "Wonderful concepts like equality, emancipation, solidarity, can no longer be used. They were used to describe a reality which was quite their opposite. . . . We have a real linguistic crisis, and this affects our ability to communicate." The Declaration is thus a new attempt to communicate using a language of women's own choosing in the hope for women's independence.

Declaration from the Founder Members' Meeting of the Association

We, the participants in the seminar "Women in Politics and Politics for Women," recognizing that the process of social renewal cannot be truly democratic without an active, independent women's movement, have taken the decision to establish the association Independent Women's Democratic Initiative—NEZHDI.

NEZHDI is an association of independent, democratically run women's groups, societies and individual women, coming together with the aim of providing moral support, advice and other help to members of the association, and also joint action in solving problems of general interest.

Tasks of the association
1. Economic independence via mutual aid
NEZHDI believes that a woman's economic independence is the foundation of her dignity in society and family. By conjuring up the horrors of approaching unemployment, attempts are being made to get us to return to the home, "protected" by allowances and part-time work. But this is only part of the truth. Along with these "rights" we also acquire obligations, the greatest of which is unpaid housework instead of paid work, the obligation to submit to economic dependence on husband and state.

NEZHDI is for the raising of family values in society, for women as well as men having more opportunities for high-quality leisure, for contact with family and friends, for bringing up children. But we believe in a strong and economically independent family, whose fate depends on the productive labour of its members, and not on the charity of the state. We are against society hypocritically using its failure to establish family values as a reason for forcing women out of the sphere of paid and visible labour into unpaid and invisible labour.

NEZHDI considers that the past seventy years of socialism have propagated one of the most dangerous myths—the myth that women have been over-emancipated. How can one speak of the liberation of one sex if in our society the individual, the family, the town and the republic have not been emancipated? Or has the state been only half totalitarian, only for men? NEZHDI is convinced that in reality there has been no emancipation, that there is a patriarchy which is expressed at the level of social production: women's professions and occupations are the least prestigious, the worst paid, women's work is to carry out orders, routine, heavy and uncreative; even in "female" occupations the directors are men. In the new sectors of the economy—joint ventures, firms, corporations—at best we are graciously invited to be secretaries, translators, etc. The widely advertised reduction of the administrative apparatus in ministries and institutions has been in more than 80 percent of the cases carried out at the expense of women! We can only ask a rhetorical question: how many of those people were the ones who took the decision, the ones who really controlled things? And the remaining high-ranking men discovered a fine consolation for the reduction in the number of their subordinates: they divided those people's salaries among themselves.

NEZHDI considers that our government statistics more readily conceal the true situation of women than reveal it. This is particularly intolerable now in a period of transition to the market.

We are in favour of the market, we recognize that our present difficulties are the reward for years of incompetent and criminal administration. But we want to know what price women will pay for the curing of society's problems. We want to know, so that we can act. NEZHDI supports the full and systematic publication of all social statistics affecting the situation of women.

Among the association's tasks are:
- the provision of legal, advisory and financial support to women's organizations whose aim is women's independence;
- the organization of business and management schools for women and assertiveness-training courses [courses in psychological and social steadfastness];
- the organization of campaigns against the preferential sacking of women in the reorganization of industry and the reduction of staff;
- solidarity and also financial and legal support for members of the association who find themselves in a crisis;
- the establishment of an insurance fund to support women living in poverty;
- the exertion of pressure on the new economic structures to stop or prevent discrimination against women;
- the mandatory inclusion of women on a proportional basis in both state and local schemes for professional training and retraining of specialists;
- the revision of pay scales and wage rates in "women's" occupations, according to the quality of the work.

2. Social and political tasks

"Puppet-women" in representative organs of power and "iron ladies" in the director's chair, women elected by no one but appointed by one or other state institution, obedient to the will of the bosses and always ready to carry out any directive issued from on high—thus has a negative image been created of the woman director, the woman political leader. They have built an invisible and unappealing barrier for women as candidates in the reformed soviets, which every female candidate felt and which allowed only a handful of individuals to win.

For decades the political system shamelessly used female qualities such as discipline, conscientiousness, women's emotional nature, their readiness to suffer together and offer assistance, expecting nothing in return. We formed the majority of those engaged in so-called public work, many of us were rank-and-file members of the Party and of various public organizations. Even during the period of perestroika, the stillborn organism of the women's councils [zhensouety] was formed from our ranks, under the nominal leadership of the State Committee of Soviet Women, which no one had elected. However, we were permitted to share the thing men value most—power. The central feature of that power, which has brought the country to the brink of economic and social catastrophe, is its domination by a militaristic consciousness, the urge to use force to resolve all social conflicts, the infringement of the interests of the individual in the service, allegedly, of the public interest. In such an environment, the men who created it destroy themselves under the constant pressure of incompetence and mutual conflict.

Yes, we lost the elections. Yes, today we are outsiders in high politics and local politics. At present the vast majority of those who formulate and discuss political issues and take the decisions over our heads and on our behalf are men.

But this is not perestroika's last word. NEZHDI considers politics to be a matter for women as well. There are thousands of our female compatriots who are well qualified and ought in future to enter the institutions of power—women who exercise the highest degree of responsibility towards the people who elected them, and possessing a political culture rooted in competence, openness, goodwill and commitment to the interests of the individual.

NEZHDI will support those female political leaders who uphold the values of humanity.

NEZHDI will support women's democratic political clubs and organizations.

NEZHDI will facilitate the organization of schools for women in political leadership.

NEZHDI will advocate the involvement of independent women's organizations in issues of military politics: for social security for servicemen and their families—soldiers and their mothers and fathers should not have to pay for the incompetence of their generals. For the transfer to a professional army—a professional army is cheaper than a nonprofessional, as professionals make fewer mistakes for which we have to pay. Better 600 competent generals than 6,000 Mukashovs [incompetent leaders]! Let us have a woman as minister of defence in the RSFSR! There must be a conversion not only in words, but in deed—and that includes a conversion of ideology.

The association advocates a democratically elected committee to observe the Declaration forbidding all forms of discrimination against women and to implement the UN Nairobi guidelines. Women in the USSR ought to know what sort of report the government makes about their situation to international organizations and who produces these reports.

NEZHDI is opposed to a one-sided protectionism that demeans women, and it will support a policy of equal opportunities.

NEZHDI is convinced that no one will help women if we cannot help ourselves. We have been organized "from above" for so long, have we really lost the ability to do it ourselves and for ourselves?

3. Information
One of the foundations of patriarchy, men's power, is the monopoly on information. Therefore NEZHDI intends to set up a Women's Information Bureau (ZHIB) which would collect and disseminate information about:
- women's movements, groups and organizations;
- the situation of women in various countries, regions, social and political structures;
- academic research and publications on women's issues;
- conferences, seminars, symposia and also information which will help women acquire the essential knowledge to integrate themselves into the process of social renewal and the stabilization of the country during the transition to a market economy. Information will be collected and stored in a computerized data bank. ZHIB will publish a bulletin for the association's members, arrange for the sale of information to nonmembers of the association and publish a newspaper, *Woman and Democracy*.

4. Research support for the association's work
NEZHDI considers that one of the reasons for the lamentable situation of women has been the long-standing belief that the "woman question" had been solved, which made it impossible for systematic and unprejudiced research to be conducted into existing problems.

An independent women's movement must be able to depend on independent research. The association supports the setting up of centres of research, education and information on women's (gender) issues; it will develop links with equivalent centres abroad and facilitate the exchange of students and scholarship holders.

The Centre for Gender Studies, which has joined the association, will undertake research to monitor the situation of women around the country, summarize the experience of other countries, make its data base available and prepare a report for the association's annual conference.

In this way we confirm our intention to be subjects and not objects in the transformation of society, to participate on equal terms in the construction of the country's democratic future. We, the participants in the founding meeting of the NEZHDI association, call on the entire independent women's movement, groups, organizations and individual women to join the association and prepare for its first conference early in 1991.

Notes

1 Independent Women's Democratic Initiative (NEZHDI), accessed Feb. 14, 2017, www.owl.ru.
2 Quotations are from Maxine Molyneux and Anastasya Posadskaya, "Interview with Anastasya Posadskaya (25 September 1990)." *Feminist Review* 39 (Autumn 1991): 133–40. Subsequent quotations are from this interview.
3 Independent Women's Democratic Initiative (NEZHDI) and Linda Edmondson. "Feminist Manifesto: 'Democracy without Women Is No Democracy!'" *Feminist Review* 39 (1991): 127–32, www.jstor.org/stable/1395448. Brackets in document are in the original.

69

Charter of Intentions
The Serbian Women's Party (ZEST)
Belgrade, Yugoslavia
Fall 1990

The genocide in Bosnia and Herzegovnia in the early 1990s spurred many women in the region to organize groups protesting both war and the violence done to women in times of political unrest. One of these groups was the Women's Party (Zenska Stranka, or ZEST), which was formed in the fall of 1990. The founding members of the political party included Marina Blagojevic, Vesna Gojkovic, Maja Korac, Andjelka Milic, Zarana Papic and Lina Vuskovic, and their platform was women (Z), ethics (E), solidarity (S), and tolerance (T), with the greater goal of peace in the Yugoslavian region. Within two months, the group had over five hundred members and was receiving a lot of media attention.

In an interview, the six founding members stated that their intent was to create "a decentralized and non-authoritarian democratic structure, an independent judiciary, a mixed economy, free- and high-quality health care, educational reforms, environmental protection, and democratic and accessible media."[1] This reformation of the Yugoslavian government would enable women to participate more fully and encourage women to vote—something women in the Yugoslavian region rarely did. The party's objectives also included "energizing a women's movement at the grass roots" (156) and, "in five years' time, 'a women's organization active in every location in Serbia' and growing activity too in all other localities of Yugoslavia, not as party branches but as a women's movement" (157). ZEST desired to create societal change, not just through governmental positions but through local, grassroots changes in the ways women see themselves and their role in their community.

During its brief existence, ZEST put forward candidates for many governmental offices, but its most radical proposition was that of a "job share" reform of the presidential role: they wanted a man and a woman to share the presidential position, and they received a surprising amount of support. This proposal also inspired other political parties to put forward women candidates to gain support of the populace. ZEST was strongly committed to being a political party, not just an organization for women, because the group felt that "women simply 'needed a legal space in the power system'" (157).

Because of tensions surrounding the position ZEST should take on nationalism, ZEST only existed for one year. Its Charter, however, makes strong claims to empower women and other marginalized groups. The Charter explains that the current androcentric government is power-hungry and self-centered, focusing on its own desires rather than the democratic good of the whole society. ZEST wants to give women confidence and resources to implement social change that benefits them and all of society, not just a powerful elite. Its programmatic goals illustrate a dedication to peace and an increase in quality of life for all citizens, especially those who are marginalized. To achieve this, the Charter proposes reform in executive, legislative, and judicial branches of government, health care, the environment, education, family life, culture, and media. This multifaceted program, it was hoped, would enable Yugoslavia to recover from its economic and social depression and create a society that supported and cared for all of its citizens.

The Women's Party Charter of Intentions

By this Charter women of the Steering Committee of the Women's Party make known to all women and the general public their resoluteness to take an active part in the resolution of the ongoing social crisis. Women make up half of the population, almost half of an active and employed labour force, one third of the educated and skilled population and half of the electorate. This is an enormous and unrealized potential.

The Women's Party appeals to all who feel socially marginalized. All feeling excluded from the public scene and willing to change that, could find themselves in the ideas of the Women's Party. Female situation is the first symptom of a sick situation and its suppression of individuality, neglect of particular human desires, powers and potentials in the name of abstract and imposed higher goals. As a half of humankind, women have to engage themselves in the change of this state of affairs, and the way to accomplish this is but one—affirmation of all still-hidden and disregarded human qualities and potentials.

Why a Women's Party?

The prolonged economic and social crisis of Yugoslav society has only worsened the already imperiled existence of women. Although legally equal and free, women have for decades been living the life of second-rate citizens and unrealized and subjected individuals in the family and society alike. Instead of real progress, the prevailing part of society, and within it women in the first place, has been deprived of its right to independent political thinking and organization; unemployment and the accompanying economic emigration, an inadequate educational system, poor living standards, despicable family conditions, bureaucratized institutions uncaring for citizens, their self-centredness—have been affecting women as the most neglected part of the population. And besides, women have never ceased to be subject to the repressive influences of a backward patriarchal social consciousness, which recognizes and appreciates woman only as the sexual and reproductive object, with the outcome of her ever more tragic susceptibility to physical and psychic maltreatment and exploitation in the family and society.

In the existing situation the Women's Party will act in conformity with the following urgent goals, claiming no right to voice the interests of all women:
- It will promote women's self-confidence and their faith in their own abilities, strength and maturity to fight independently for legal rights and genuine interests of their own;
- It will support the emergence and further development of the women's movement as the firm guarantee of continuity in accomplishing the equality of the sexes and social reform processes leading to that end;
- It will act so as to facilitate the unveiling and recognition of the forms and holders of authoritarian consciousness and behaviour who hardly care for the genuine democratization of society, overwhelmed with lust for power and dictatorship over human needs.

Association Principles of the Women's Party
The Women's Party is a voluntary, independent political organization. It enrolls women and men approving its programme, regardless of occupation, education, religious or national affiliation.

The Party will initiate various forms of association and gatherings of women on all levels—from territorial all the way to interest and professional organizations of women in economic, cultural, educational, scientific and technical and health-care spheres, in arts and creativity of all kinds.

The Party will advocate dialogue and co-operation with all existing and new forms of female organizations and associations determined to further the spread and strength of female self-consciousness and their influence in all the domains of social work and decision-making.

As the political party of the by far most numerous social minority, the Women's Party will initiate and propose changes on behalf of marginalized social groups. To this end the Party will co-operate with associations of citizens and institutions engaged in solving the problems of all deprived groups and individuals in the society.

Principles of Activity of the Women's Party
By this Charter, the Women's Party obliges itself to stick to the following principles of organization of social life and relations in its public declarations, political activities, electoral campaigns and parliamentary engagement:
1. For democracy and against all forms and aspects of discrimination and authoritarian power and authority in society.
2. For peace, tolerance and co-operation among nations and peoples.
3. For quality of life as a crucial aim of development.

At this moment the Women's Party has the following PROGRAMMATIC GOALS:

- The creation of a system of mixed economy with different forms of ownership; stimulation of development of small and medium enterprises; rational use of human and natural resources; orientation towards regional development; stimulation of self-employment; development of clean technologies; stimulation of private initiative in all spheres; a unified tax system; direct and progressive taxation of enterprises and citizens; control of budget spendings;
- An independent judiciary as a guarantee of functioning of the legal state and responsibility of those holding public posts for the passing and implementation of laws and decisions; laws that won't endanger individual freedoms and will ensure and protect the integrity and dignity of personality;
- Good essential health care, compulsory and free, based on minimal deductions from personal income;
- Struggle for a healthy environment as the imperative of the future; stimulation of research and introduction of clean technologies and use of alternative sources of energy; preservation of natural goods and development of ecological consciousness;
- Radical reform of the educational system not only regarding curricula, but also organization of life and work in educational institutions which will provide for the development of individuality, creativity and solidarity of pupils and teachers; change of stereotype notions of sex roles; development of alternative forms of upbringing and education on all levels;
- Realization and improvement of quality of family life; establishment of equality in relations among its members; equal participation in housework and the upbringing of children and social recognition of household labour, as a condition of further development of emancipated and creative personality; individual freedom to choose, according to his/her needs a form of community of life and equal legal treatment of different forms of community of life;
- Autonomous culture and adequate cultural policy as the only genuine protection of critical consciousness in creation and communication of cultural values;
- Equal opportunities for communication, implying access to media and participation of all citizens; right to answer; right to information quota for women and children; change of stereotyped mass-media notions of women and men.

Note

1 Cynthia Cockburn, "A Women's Political Party for Yugoslavia: Introduction to the Serbian Feminist Manifesto." *Feminist Review* 39 (1991): 155–60. Subsequent page references are to this text.

70

Riot Grrrl Manifesto

Bikini Kill
Washington, D.C.
1991

Riot Grrrl logo.

We're Bikini Kill and we want Revolution Girl-Style Now![1]

Kathleen Hanna yells this rallying cry at the beginning of Bikini Kill's Riot Grrrl anthem "Double Dare Ya." Riot Grrrl was an underground feminist hardcore punk movement that was part of the new feminism of the 1990s in the West. The movement protested silencing, rape, domestic violence, patriarchy, and capitalism, among other things, in order to empower women and allow all voices to be heard. Riot Grrrl groups specifically acted through the music scene with bands such as Bikini Kill, Bratmobile, Calamity Jane, and Heavens to Betsy. They created music and magazines that expressed their punk ideology and activism.

The Riot Grrrl movement originated on both coasts, specifically in Washington, D.C., and New York on the East Coast and Olympia, Washington, on the West. These groups had a do-it-yourself ethic that enabled women to express not only their music but also their opinions and experiences through magazine and handbill publishing. Their unique style, which emphasizes the rough cut-and-paste look, can be seen in the group's logo and the pages of the Riot Grrrl zines.

Riot Grrrls proclaimed their power and angst in the most unladylike of musical genres—punk rock. Girls had been alienated from the "beergutboyrock" of punk music for years. Riot Grrrls carved a space for themselves in male-dominated punk music, bringing "girls to the front" of the audience so they could safely watch their performances without men pushing them out of the way, as had been the case at many punk shows.[2] They employed the strategies used by punk musicians to combat social injustice, such as zines and loud music. Punk's aggression served as a perfect vehicle for girls to express their anger with gender inequality and defy gender norms.

The emphasis on girlhood, indicated in the name of the movement and Hanna's cry for "Revolution Girl-Style," distinguishes Riot Grrrls. Joanne Gottlieb and Gayle Wald write, "Instead of tirelessly insisting on the right to be called 'women,'

Riot Grrrl art. Midge Blitz, via etsy.com.

as mainstream feminism has long been advocating, riot grrrls foreground girl identity, in its simultaneous audacity and awkwardness—and not just girl, but a defiant 'grrrl' identity that roars back at the dominant culture."[3] Riot Grrrls challenged feminism's failure to take girls seriously by advocating the power of girls to start their own movement. Riot Grrrls reclaimed girlhood in their performance style as well: Hanna and other musicians often wore girly outfits, such as cheerleader skirts and Girl Scout uniforms, while yelling about discrimination and sexual abuse, subverting traditional notions of girls as weak.[4]

The movement fizzled out in the late 1990s after frequent misrepresentation by mainstream media. According to Corin Tucker of the bands Heavens to Betsy and Sleater-Kinney, "I think it was deliberate that we were made to look like we were just ridiculous girls parading around in our underwear. They refused to do serious interviews with us, they misprinted what we had to say, they would take our articles, and our fanzines, and our essays and take them out of context."[5] Despite its end, Riot Grrrl continues to influence music and young feminists, especially with Bikini Kill's reissue of their albums and Sleater-Kinney's new album, which were released in 2015.

The focus on art in this document is usually more subdued in others, though it appears, for example, in some form in the 2015 Charter of Female Comics Creators and the 1977 Resolutions of the National Alliance of Black Feminists. The arts have been both a location of sexism and a source of feminist resistance, and both of those aspects come through in this Manifesto.[6]

Riot Grrrl Manifesto

BECAUSE us girls crave records and books and fanzines that speak to US that WE feel included in and can understand in our own ways.

BECAUSE we wanna make it easier for girls to see/hear each other's work so that we can share strategies and criticize-applaud each other.

BECAUSE we must take over the means of production in order to create our own moanings.

BECAUSE viewing our work as being connected to our girlfriends-politics-real lives is essential if we are gonna figure out how what we are doing impacts, reflects, perpetuates, or DISRUPTS the status quo.

BECAUSE we recognize fantasies of Instant Macho Gun Revolution as impractical lies meant to keep us simply dreaming instead of becoming our dreams AND THUS seek to create revolution in our own lives every single day by envisioning and creating alternatives to the bullshit christian capitalist way of doing things.

BECAUSE we want and need to encourage and be encouraged in the face of all our own insecurities, in the face of beergutboyrock that tells us we can't play our instruments, in the face of "authorities" who say our bands/zines/etc are the worst in the US and

BECAUSE we don't wanna assimilate to someone else's (boy) standards of what is or isn't.

BECAUSE we are unwilling to falter under claims that we are reactionary "reverse sexists" AND NOT THE TRUEPUNKROCKSOULCRUSADERS THAT WE KNOW we really are.

BECAUSE we know that life is much more than physical survival and are patently aware that the punk rock "you can do anything" idea is crucial to the coming angry grrrl rock revolution which seeks to save the psychic and cultural lives of girls and women everywhere, according to their own terms, not ours.

BECAUSE we are interested in creating non-hierarchical ways of being AND making music, friends, and scenes based on communication + understanding, instead of competition + good/bad categorizations.

BECAUSE doing/reading/seeing/hearing cool things that validate and challenge us can help us gain the strength and sense of community that we need in order to figure out how bullshit like racism, able-bodieism, ageism, speciesism, classism, thinism, sexism, anti-semitism and heterosexism figures in our own lives.

BECAUSE we see fostering and supporting girl scenes and girl artists of all kinds as integral to this process.

BECAUSE we hate capitalism in all its forms and see our main goal as sharing information and staying alive, instead of making profits of [sic] being cool according to traditional standards.

BECAUSE we are angry at a society that tells us Girl = Dumb, Girl = Bad, Girl = Weak.

BECAUSE we are unwilling to let our real and valid anger be diffused and/or turned against us via the internalization of sexism as witnessed in girl/girl jealousism and self defeating girltype behaviors.

BECAUSE I believe with my wholeheartmindbody that girls constitute a revolutionary soul force that can, and will change the world for real.

Notes

1 Bikini Kill, "Double Dare Ya," qtd. in Kevin Dunn and May Summer Farnsworth, "'We Are the Revolution': Riot Grrrl Press, Girl Empowerment, and DIY Self-Publishing." *Women's Studies* 41 (2012): 136–57, 140.

2 Kathleen Hanna and Eugenia Williamson, "Interview: Kathleen Hanna on Sexism at Shows, Being like George W. Bush, and Her Riot Grrrl Lecture at the Wilbur." *Vanyaland*, March 30, 2015, accessed March 20, 2016, www.vanyaland.com.

3 Joanne Gottlieb and Gayle Wald, "Smells like Teen Spirit: Riot Grrrls, Revolution, and Women in Independent Rock," in *Microphone Fiends: Youth Music and Youth Culture*, ed. Andrew Ross and Tricia Rose (New York: Routledge, 1994), p. 266.

4 Alexandria Symonds, "Kathleen Hanna Revisits Her Riot Grrrl Past." *New York Times*, Sept. 1, 2015, accessed March 20, 2016, www.nytimes.com.

5 Interview for "What Got Lost," qtd. in Dunn and Farnsworth, pp. 141–42.

6 Bikini Kill, "Riot Grrrl Manifesto." *History Is a Weapon*, 2012, accessed Oct. 16, 2013, http://onewarart.org.

71

Declaration of Intent
Feminist Network of Hungary (Feminsta Hálózat)
Budapest, Hungary
June 1991

Feminsta Hálózat emblem.

The Feminist Network aims to achieve the recognition of specific female interests and points of view, the participation of women in public life and decision-making, the realization of women's and men's real emancipation, and the abolition of all kinds of discrimination.

After years of suppression by the Communist Party after World War II, women in Hungary finally were able to form a feminist group in June of 1990. This group was part of a larger movement in Hungary for women to be heard and for women to have a greater voice in society and government. By 1999, there were women's studies programs in three different Hungarian universities, five governmental research departments focused on women, gender studies collections in libraries, and several official women's movement groups and NGOs active in Hungary.[1] The Feminist Network was part of the beginning of this new movement in Hungary, and it focused on connecting women and promoting their participation in public and governmental life.

Led by Judit Acsady, a sociology student, about fifty women from various backgrounds came together in 1990 with the following aims:

1. to promote the equality of men and women in Hungarian society and to fight against all kinds of discrimination
2. to increase awareness of women's issues and women's situation in Hungarian society
3. to promote the participation of women in public life
4. to lobby for legal, administrative and policy reforms in areas which affect women. (Toth)

Their work to achieve these aims included translating and publishing feminist literature, holding talks and seminars, and supporting and teaching women's and gender studies in universities. They also published *Nöszemély*, a magazine with articles "written from women's points of view on reproductive rights, violence against women, women's movements around the world, and other women's issues" (Toth).

In 1991–1992, the Feminist Network of Hungary fought with other women's groups against the restriction of abortion, succeeding when the government "passed relatively liberal legislation" (Toth). The organization lasted until about 1995; besides its pro-choice work, the Feminist Network created a hotline for battered women and joined the pacifist Women in Black movement. Although the network dissolved, more women since the 1990s have been elected to political office, mostly on the local level.[2]

The Declaration of Intent[3] from the Feminist Network emphasizes the second-class status of women in Hungary and calls for change, especially to prevent women from accepting "the scapegoat role they are often given." It specifically focuses on equal employment opportunities and wages, deflating male egos, and equal sexual moral standards. The Declaration also advocates better support for unmarried and battered women in an attempt to make equality of the sexes a reality in all aspects of life.

Declaration of Intent

During the past forty years, just as before the Second World War, women have not been able to play an active role in social and political life. In the countries behind the Iron Curtain women could not join in the positive and progressive actions taken by women's movements around the world. Despite the recent political changes that have taken place in Hungary, women still must face their virtual nonrecognition as full citizens.

The founding of the Feminist Network demonstrates the persistence of needs long declared nonexistent. The Feminist Network aims to achieve the recognition of specific female interests and points of view, the participation of women in public life and decision-making, the realization of women's and men's real emancipation, and the abolition of all kinds of discrimination. We intend to change the political, economical and employment practices that have been perpetuating women's current disadvantageous situation both in society and in the family. Through dialogue and public debates we wish to reshape the structure of interests so as to make possible a real, rather than a forced and false harmonization of interests.

We will fight for the improvement of our life conditions, our right to work, our autonomy, our health and for our basic and broadly defined existential security.

We hope to join in a united Europe, and we are convinced that these specific women's interests are also the values of a civilized society, serving women, men and children.

The 1949 Constitution recognized women's emancipation. In practice, this was reduced to the right to work, and under the given economic conditions this right became a necessity. This emancipation granted by the state without any previous public discussion or grass-roots organization in a basically conservative society with a double standard of morality has only succeeded in producing deeply uncertain and self-doubting women prone to accept the scapegoat role they are often given.

In order for this situation to change:
- The impact of the last forty years on women's roles, status, and self-conceptions of male-female relations, and on family, must be analyzed and these analyses must be widely disseminated.
- The current efforts of the renewed and strengthened conservative religious groups, aided by the mass media, to secure the dominance of their moral views in society must be opposed.
- The parliament, with its overwhelming majority of men as members, must be prevented from making decisions in haste and without social debate, especially such decisions that can have particularly far-reaching consequences for women.

If these tasks are not accomplished, the great majority of women—surrendering the few positive developments of the past forty years—will have to choose resignation and submission in order to survive. The former omnipotence of state power, disabling or deforming all members of society, destroyed support communities and exploited the natural forces of human life, including human relationships. Women, men and children have been forced to bear their burdens alone. Women have become a bad but cheap workforce. State social policies have made them responsible for the size of the population. With the degradation of human relationships they have become sexual objects. The lack of decent educational institutions and service infrastructure has ensured both that they remain unpaid household servants, and that they do not have an equal chance with men in the world of paid work.

Those few women who have been in sufficiently favourable situations to become independent modern women, have seldom found similarly modern men to be their companions. Authoritarianism and paternalism, in addition to their everyday burdens, have also made men vulnerable (rising mortality rates) and distorted their personalities. The consequences of their inability to renounce their privileges and dominance shapes private and public life in Hungary even today.

The Feminist Network commits itself to the goal of extending to children, women, and men equally opportunities for self-realization with regard to gender, religion, nationality, racial origin or social class. From this it follows that our understanding of emancipation is universal and is directed toward the whole of society. To this end, the Feminist Network demands that effective steps be taken against unemployment; that the employment structure which is so disadvantageous to women be changed; that the formation and operation of strong trade unions with proportionate numbers of women in leadership positions be facilitated within all ownership sectors of the economy; and that the introduction of new technologies not be permitted to force women into jobs with low prestige and obsolete technology. Legal opportunities should be created for flexible working hours and part-time work for both men and women.

The concept of work must be redefined so that the work required to care for family and children and the tasks needed to sustain everyday life should be included within the sphere of important activities deserving social and material recognition. Men and women must be assured equal rights and obligations to participate in these activities. A high-quality system of childcare institutes and family services must be created out of public funds. A free and high-quality health system, including a more enlightened women's health network, is essential for the entire population. The availability of abortion must be legally guaranteed and contraception must become a responsibility of men as well as women.

Social and moral constraints which penalize forms of cohabitation outside of the traditional marriage and family must be struggled against and must not characterize state policy. The possibility for participation in social insurance must be created for and extended to every man and woman regardless of family status. Strong efforts must be made to increase society's tolerance of all otherness— whether cultural, sexual, racial or religious—and its acceptance of mentally and physically disabled people, and of pensioners. The books and activities of nurseries and schools must be examined critically in order to prevent the continued propagation of obsolete and destructive prejudices regarding gender roles.

We protest against violence within families against women and children, which is widely known about but not discussed. Now is the time for it to be given the public attention it deserves, for only with public education can this tragic situation be ameliorated. We urge stricter and stronger judicial handling of such cases, as well as the creation of refuges, telephone and taxi crisis services for those suffering from such violence.

The feminist movement is an organic part of Western democracy. The political activity of feminists is aimed at overcoming those aspects of male-female relations which are based on a relation of unequal power. We too are working for the real—not simply formal or legal—equality between the sexes in every area of social life. We hope finally to free the word "feminist" from the misunderstanding and uninformed prejudices under which it currently labours.

Notes

1 Andrea Toth, "The Feminist Network," 1999. Feminist Theory Website: Feminism in Hungary, Center for Digital Discourse and Culture, Virginia Tech University, accessed Feb. 14, 2017, www.cddc.vt.edu. Subsequent parenthetical references are to this text.

2 John Feffer, "The Flowering of Feminism in Hungary." *World Post* (*Huffington Post*), April 28, 2014, accessed Feb. 14, 2017, www.huffingtonpost.com.

3 Feminist Network of Hungary, "Declaration of Intent." *Feminist Review* 39 (1991): 171–73.

72

Joint Resolution
First Asian Solidarity Conference on Military Sexual Slavery by Japan
Korean Council for the Women Drafted for the Military Sexual Slavery by Japan
Seoul, South Korea
October 10–11, 1992

Military sexual slavery by Japan, which occurred during 1932–1945, was not simply the incidental raping of women by occupying soldiers, as has often accompanied war in the world. It was a deliberate, long-term, and systematic institution which was planned, designed, and enforced by the Supreme Commander of the Japanese army. Women between the ages of 11 to 32, 80% of whom were Korean women, were taken to the Japanese occupied areas by force, deceit, or kidnapping in order to be used as military sex slaves for the Japanese soldiers. They were forced to serve about 30 soldiers daily on weekdays and 50 soldiers a day on weekends. These women were euphemistically called "comfort women." They were often called "Sen Pees" ("Sen" is a derogatory term for Koreans in Japanese, and "Pees" means "vulva" in Chinese).[1]

Many documents in this book confront the impact of war on women. This document[2] addresses one specific, massive case of women's human rights being violated, the result of a concurrence of colonialism, militarism, and patriarchy. Women have worked within and across national borders to bring the situation to light and win reparations. Charges of a military system of sexual slavery are today being made against ISIS.

No known documents precisely reveal the number of women forced into military sexual slavery, but it is likely that between fifty thousand and two hundred thousand Korean girls and women under Japan's colonial control constituted the majority. Perhaps three-fourths of them died during their enslavement, and many survivors suffered from sexual trauma, infertility, disease, and the physical effects of torture. Today those still living are often called "Halmoni," meaning "grandmother," a term of respect and affection.

Korean Church Women United was, in 1988, the first group to gather survey-based information about Japanese "comfort stations" (which they link to the current sex tourism industry). Various individuals and groups came together in 1990 to form the Korean Council for the Women Drafted for the Military Sexual Slavery by Japan. In 1991 they organized a news conference at which Kim Hak-sun became the first "comfort woman" to speak publicly about what happened to her during the war, leading many others to come forward. The council has held protests every Wednesday since 1992 in front of the Japanese Embassy in Seoul.

This photo was taken for this book by the Korean Council for the Women Drafted for Military Sexual Slavery by Japan.

That was also the year of the First Asian Solidarity Conference, which resulted in the document below.

Delegates to the conference came from six countries: Taiwan, the Philippines, Korea, Thailand, Hong Kong, and Japan. This international solidarity is both a strategy for obtaining justice for those trafficked and an end in itself, in that it represents peaceful, constructive relationships. But issues remain, and as the Twelfth Solidarity Conference noted in 2014, "Resolution of this issue is the first step towards normalization of relations with neighboring countries, and a necessary foundation in order to contribute to world peace."[3]

Japan denied that military sexual slavery existed until making the Kono Statement in 1993. In 1995, the Japanese government endorsed the Asian Women's Fund, a private effort that collected money to compensate the women. Many of them refused the money, on the grounds that it did not come from the government and was not accompanied by any formal apology.[4] Hundreds of archived government documents began to be unearthed starting in 2007, revealing more information about what happened, where, and how. A statue outside the Japanese embassy in Seoul represents the victims of Japanese military sexual slavery. A controversial 2015 agreement included a demand by the Japanese government that it be removed.

In terms of the "apology" desired, the 2014 Asian Solidarity Conference summed up well what constitutes an acceptable apology:

An apology is one of the important elements of the resolution sought by the survivors. The key issue here is for the perpetrating country to accurately recognize who conducted which kind of violating acts, to acknowledge responsibility, to clearly and unambiguously express this apology both domestically and internationally, and take continuing measures to make it credible and sincere. Only then will the survivors be able to accept it as a genuine apology.[5]

Starting with the First Conference, the goals have been for the Japanese government and military to acknowledge their war crimes, to make reparations, and to take actions to prevent a recurrence.

Joint Resolution

With the reconsideration of atrocities and women slavery during the military colonial period, the following resolution was adopted with the realization of seriousness of military sexual slavery by Japanese colonial invasion with the attendance of six nations; Korea, the Philippines, Taiwan, Thailand, Hong Kong, and Japan during the Seoul Asian Coalition Conference for Comfort Women During the Japanese Colonial Period from Oct. 10–11, 1992.

"Military Sexual Slavery" is a cold-blooded act which was fulfilled systematically by Japanese military power and autocracy. This is a model example of how patriarchy and militarism-oriented war could dishonor women sexually. Therefore, we strongly believe that taking good care of the military sexual slavery incident during the Japanese colonial rule is the very solution to prevent any possible war and build up peace around the neighboring area.

However, the Japanese government's apology against the military sexual slavery issue[d] on July 6 was hardly satisfactory. Japan's never admitted its brutal wrongdoing and just tried to avoid any responsibility. Furthermore, the Junichiro Koizumi administration has passed PKO bill and opened a gate for Self-defense Forces. That's why we cannot ignore the resurrection of Japanese autocracy. Japan must admit its wrongdoing and take the responsibility of its brutal and cruel actions during World War II, in order to become a real friend with neighboring nations.

We have realized that we need to build up a strong coalition among Asian countries such as South Korea, North Korea, China, Taiwan, Thailand, the Philippines, Indonesia, and Malaysia as well as Japan to solve the past military sexual slavery problem. For this, the six nations (Korea, Taiwan, the Philippines, Hong Kong, Thailand, and Japan) have adopted the Asian Coalition Conference for Comfort Women during the Japanese Colonial Rule. Empowered by this coalition, the military sexual slavery issue will be dealt with as follows:

1. We will continue doing the research on Japan's sexual slavery atrocity during World War II.
2. We urge that the post-war actions (ex: examining the real truth, compensation, correcting history textbook, etc.) could be properly made with regard to sexual slavery issue.
3. To solve the sexual slavery issue, we will work together with the UN's human rights organization and others.
4. We will make decent efforts to make the other absent nations participate in the Asian coalition above.
5. We will also do our best for world peace and women's rights.
The attendants of the Asian Coalition Conference for Comfort Women during the Japanese Colonial Period have agreed that it's our duty to make the Japanese government admit the following issues:

1. The Japanese government admits its sexual slavery atrocity in several Asian countries during the World War II.
2. The Japanese government forms a special organization and closely investigates the Military Sexual Slavery issue. Then, it announces the results worldwide to prevent the tragedy from reoccurring.

3. The Japanese government must admit that it trampled on human rights and publicly apologize for its atrocity especially to the victims from many Asian nations.

4. The Japanese government has to compensate the victims and their family based on related international law.

5. The Japanese government must have its school textbooks include its brutal and cruel atrocities such as forcing prostitution and violation of human rights by the name of "Military Sexual Slavery."

Notes

1 Hee Soon Kwon, "The Military Sexual Slavery Issue and Asian Peace." Paper presented at the First East Asian Women's Forum, Oct. 20–22, 1994, Japan.

2 "Solidarity Conference 1992." Asian Solidarity Conference for the Issue of Military Sexual Slavery by Japan, Deutsche Ostasienmission, accessed Feb. 15, 2017, www.doam.org.

3 "Solidarity Conference 2014." Asian Solidarity Conference for the Issue of Military Sexual Slavery by Japan, Deutsche Ostasienmission, accessed Feb. 15, 2017, www.doam.org.

4 Christine Ahn, "Seeking Truth for 'Comfort Women.'" *Asian Times*, June 26, 2014, accessed Feb. 15, 2017, www.atimes.com.

5 "Recommendations to the Government of Japan for Resolution of the Japanese Military 'Comfort Women' Issue." Twelfth Asian Solidarity Conference on the Issue of Military Sexual Slavery by Japan, June 2, 2014. Deutsche Ostasienmission, accessed Feb. 15, 2017, www.doam.org.

73

Dyke Manifesto
Lesbian Avengers
New York
1994

Lesbian Avengers button.

"On June 28, 1992 six activist dykes threw down the gauntlet: 'LESBIANS! DYKES! GAY WOMEN! . . . We're wasting our lives being careful. Imagine what your life could be. Aren't you ready to make it happen?' By 1994, a multitude had responded. Twenty thousand dykes marched on Washington. More than sixty chapters sprang up worldwide. The Lesbian Avengers also took 'out' gay activism where it had never been before."[1] Started by Ana Simo, Sarah Schulman, Maxine Wolfe, Anne-christine d'Adesky, Marie Honan, and Anne Maguire, the Avengers focused on direct action that would bring visibility to lesbian lives and issues, which were marginalized within both the feminist and the gay rights movements.

Their activism was striking and creative. In response to opposition to what was called the "Rainbow Curriculum" in New York, the Avengers showed up at a grade school with a marching band and handed out balloons stamped "Ask about Lesbian Lives." Thousands of copies of the Dyke Manifesto were handed out at the March on Washington. The group defaced antichoice billboards. It held a kiss-in at an ABC affiliate in the face of opposition to airing "the lesbian kiss" on the TV show *Roseanne*.[2] The Avengers were disruptive, loud, lovely, inventive, and energetic. They challenged homophobic stereotypes and policies. They published a *Lesbian Avenger Organizing Handbook*, still available, that "explained step by step how to shape effective actions, write press releases, design flyers, even how to run meetings. . . . Tools like this enabled independent groups to get up and running without an experienced activist present, and without the professional journalists and designers."[3]

The Dyke Manifesto was a two-sided handout, filled with attention-getting capital letters and bold print on shocking pink paper. It moves from the present invisibility and danger lesbians confront to direct action through a repeated cry to "wake up!" It celebrates lesbian sex, forgoes conventional forms of activism, and expresses confidence in the potential political power of dykes working together.

Dyke Manifesto

lesbian avengers DYKE MANIFESTO lesbian avengers
CALLING ALL LESBIANS
WAKE UP! WAKE UP! WAKE UP!
IT'S TIME TO GET OUT OF THE BEDS, OUT OF THE BARS AND INTO THE STREETS
TIME TO SEIZE THE POWER OF DYKE LOVE, DYKE VISION, DYKE ANGER
DYKE INTELLIGENCE, DYKE STRATEGY.
TIME TO ORGANIZE AND IGNITE. TIME TO GET TOGETHER AND FIGHT.
WE'RE INVISIBLE AND IT'S NOT SAFE—NOT AT HOME, ON THE JOB, IN THE
STREETS OR IN THE COURTS
WHERE ARE OUR LESBIAN LEADERS?
WE NEED YOU
WE'RE NOT WAITING FOR THE RAPTURE. WE ARE THE APOCA-LYPSE.
WE'LL BE YOUR DREAM AND THEIR NIGHTMARE.
LESBIAN POWER
BELIEVE IN CREATIVE ACTIVISM: LOUD, BOLD, SEXY, SILLY, FIERCE, TASTY
AND DRAMATIC. ARREST OPTIONAL.
THINK DEMONSTRATIONS ARE A GOOD TIME AND A GREAT PLACE TO CRUISE.
WOMEN DON'T HAVE PATIENCE FOR POLITE POLITICS. ARE BORED WITH THE

BOYS. BELIEVE CONFRONTATION FOSTERS GROWTH AND STRONG BONES.

BELIEVE IN RECRUITMENT. NOT BY THE ARMY; NOT OF STRAIGHT WOMEN.

ARE NOT CONTENT WITH GHETTOS: WE WANT YOUR HOUSE, YOUR JOB, YOUR

FREQUENT FLYER MILES. WE'LL SELL YOUR JEWELRY TO SUBSIDIZE OUR

MOVEMENT. WE DEMAND UNIVERSAL HEALTH INSURANCE AND HOUSING. WE

DEMAND FOOD AND SHELTER FOR ALL HOMELESS LESBIANS. WE ARE THE

13TH STEP. THINK GIRL GANGS ARE THE WAVE OF THE FUTURE.
LESBIAN SEX

THINK SEX IS A DAILY LIBATION. GOOD ENERGY FOR ACTIONS. CRAVE,

ENJOY, EXPLORE, SUFFER FROM NEW IDEAS ABOUT RELATIONSHIPS:

SLUMBER PARTIES, POLYGAMY, PERSONAL ADS, AFFINITY GROUPS.

USE LIVE ACTION WORDS: lick, waltz, eat, fuck, kiss, bite, give it up, hit the dirt
LESBIAN ACTIVISM

THINK ACTIONS MUST BE LOCAL, REGIONAL, NATIONAL, GLOBAL, COSMIC.

THINK CLOSETED LESBIANS, QUEER BOYS AND SYMPATHETIC STRAIGHTS

SHOULD SEND US MONEY.

PLAN TO TARGET HOMOPHOBES OF EVERY STRIPE AND INFILTRATE THE

CHRISTIAN RIGHT.

SCHEME AND SCREAM AND FIGHT REAL MEAN
the lesbian
AVENGERS
THE LESBIAN AVENGERS: WE RECRUIT
WELCOME AVENGER!

WHO ARE THE LESBIAN AVENGERS?

The Lesbian Avengers is a *direct action* group focused on issues vital to *lesbian survival and visibility*. There are many ideas in the lesbian community about what kind of strategies to employ—electoral and legal reform, therapy groups, social services, theoretical development. These are all valid strategies, but they are not the strategies of the Avengers. Direct action is what the Lesbian Avengers do. It is the reason for our existence.

WHAT IS DIRECT ACTION?

The real question is "Do we have to spray paint billboards to be a Lesbian Avenger?" Direct Action is a *public intervention* ranging in creative form from marches to street theatre to speakouts to cathartic spray painting of anti-hate slogans. Direct action is about getting attention, and that means media coverage. The purpose of direct action is *visibility*, so we can't be shy. As a direct action group, the Lesbian

Avengers is for women who want to be activists, want to take responsibility for making things happen, want to do the shit work, have their minds blown, change their opinions, share organizing skills, and work in community. You don't have to spray paint billboards (although it's really fun)! You have to be willing to act-out publicly. We want to *empower* lesbians as leaders!

WHY NO ABSTRACT THEORETICAL DISCUSSION?

How many of us have sat in meetings arguing political theory to the point of mental and physical exhaustion, to the point where we run screaming to the nearest dance floor for release from the frustrations?! To keep our work pro-active and fulfilling and successful, we focus our political discussions on the creations and purpose of an *action*. We agree to disagree on political ideology—it is too easy to create false polarities. We also encourage women to *take responsibility* for their own suggestions—be willing to make them happen. Instead of saying "someone should . . ." try saying "I will . . ." or "Who will do this with me?" In our meetings, if you disagree with a proposal on the floor, instead of tearing it apart, propose another way of realizing the goal. The Avengers is a place where ideas are realized, where lesbians can have an impact. A crucial part of that is learning how to *propose alternatives* instead of just offering critiques. Be willing to put your body where your brain is—matter over mind!

Notes

1 The Lesbian Avengers, accessed Feb. 15, 2017, www.lesbianavengers.com.
2 These examples come from "Shaping Lesbian Avenger Actions." Lesbian Avengers, accessed Feb. 15, 2017, www.lesbianavengers.com.
3 Ibid.

74

The Zapatista Women's Revolutionary Law
Zapatista Army of National Liberation (Ejercito Zapatista de Liberación Nacional)
Chiapas, Mexico
January 1, 1994

EZLN Women's Revolutionary Laws poster (2007). Art by Melanie Cervantes and Jesus Barraza.

A mostly indigenous, rural group in southern Mexico, the revolutionary Zapatistas combine Mayan beliefs with elements from South American leftist movements. They mobilized at first against NAFTA, and broadened these concerns about indigenous rights, globalization, and neoliberalism to advocate for greater democracy, equality, and control over their land. At the time, "most families in the Chiapas region lived in dire poverty. And for women, an already difficult situation was often made worse because of gender discriminatory cultural practices, beliefs, and behaviors. The culture in Chiapas dictated a subordinate and oppressive position in the family for women—who were often the victims of unpunished spousal abuse and rape—and a macho role for men."[1] After early military forays, the Zapatistas committed themselves to nonviolence.

Changes in the lives of indigenous Mayan women are advocated in the Women's Revolutionary Law, which was passed by consensus within the Zapatista Army for National Liberation (EZLN) in 1993. Anonymous suggestions collected from Zapatista, Tojobal, Chol, Tzotzil, and Tzeltal women by Comandante Ramona, Major Ana María, and EZLN activist Susana formed the foundation of the ten sections listed in the document. Reactions to it were varied, and it had to be defended as part of the struggle. "Both Comandanta Ramona and Comandanta Susana spent over four months travelling throughout those then-Zapatista communities. They visited each and every community dialoguing with the Zapatistas collectively through community assemblies, as is the custom of the people of the region. Once accepted in each Zapatista community and village, it was proposed that the Law be included in the EZLN publication, *El Despertador Mexicano, Organo Informativo del EZLN*."[2] The centrality of women's rights to the Zapatista agenda was remarkable at the time, and is a commitment the group continues to honor and wrestle with in its daily practices, where obstacles to equality remain.

Given the commitments of the Zapatistas to human rights and democracy, and the important role that women have played in the Zapatista movement, it has been fertile territory for the struggle for gender equality. The list of laws[3] contain basic and revolutionary rights, some that apply to all and some drawn to address the specific wrongs women have experienced. The freedom and autonomy women have in the law is combined with their right to participate in their cherished community. Women hold positions of authority in their communities' commissions and among EZLN insurgents. The Women's Revolutionary Law has become a symbol of women's equality. It has been said that the EZLN spurred indigenous women to organize, but that Zapatista women have gone on to become important advocates for indigenous women's rights.[4]

Zapatista Women's Revolutionary Law

In their just fight for the liberation of our people, the EZLN incorporates women in the revolutionary struggle regardless of their race, creed, color or political affiliation, requiring only that they meet the demands of the exploited people and that they commit to the laws and regulations of the revolution. As well as taking account of the situation of the woman worker in Mexico, the revolution incorporates their just demands of equality and justice in the following Women's Revolutionary Law.

First—Women, regardless of their race, creed, color or political affiliation, have the right to participate in the revolutionary struggle in any way that their desire and capacity determine.

Second—Women have the right to work and receive a just salary.

Third—Women have the right to decide the number of children they have and care for.

Fourth—Women have the right to participate in the matters of the community and have charge if they are free and democratically elected.

Fifth—Women and their children have the right to Primary Attention in their health and nutrition.

Sixth—Women have the right to education.

Seventh—Women have the right to choose their partner and are not obliged to enter into marriage.

Eighth—Women have the right to be free of violence from both relatives and strangers. Rape and attempted rape will be severely punished.

Ninth—Women will be able to occupy positions of leadership in the organization and hold military ranks in the revolutionary armed forces.

Tenth—Women will have all the rights and obligations which the revolutionary laws and regulations give.

Notes

1   Devon Hansen and Laura Ryan, "Teaching Women in the Zapatista Movement: Gender, Health, and Resistance," in *World History Connected* (Urbana: University of Illinois Press, 2007), worldhistoryconnected.press.illinois.edu.
2   Sylvia Marcos, "The Zapatista Women's Revolutionary Law as It Is Lived Today," July 22, 2014. openDemocracy, www.opendemocracy.net.
3   EZLN, "Zapatista Women's Revolutionary Laws." *El Despertador Mexicano*, Jan. 1, 1994. Schools for Chiapas, www.schoolsforchiapas.org.
4   R. Hernandez Castillo, "Zapatismo and the Emergence of Indigenous Feminism." *NACLA Report on the Americas* 35.6 (May/June 2002).

75

The Women's Charter for Effective Equality
Women's National Coalition of the African National Congress
Johannesburg, South Africa
February 25–27, 1994

ANC banner.

The African National Congress, or ANC, was established in 1912 to fight against colonizers and apartheid factions in South Africa. The ANC aims to create unity and peace in South Africa by implementing a nonracist, nonsexist government in which the laws are made and enforced by the people. In particular, this has meant liberating African and Black people from the oppression of apartheid and of colonizers. Today, the ANC is affiliated with the South African Communist Party and the Congress of South African Trade Unions. Its struggle has persisted for over one hundred years, and in the past twenty-five years it has had some significant victories. In 1994, ANC candidates were elected to office, and the new Constitution created by the party was adopted by South Africa.[1]

The Women's League branch of the ANC was established in April 1992. The Women's League attracted women from many different walks of life and geographical regions, who united across political, racial, religious, economic, and cultural lines. This diverse group of women worked together toward the goal of helping to write the new South African Constitution, which they did through the vehicle of the Women's Charter for Effective Equality, printed below. The Charter maps the women's demands for their societal and governmental rights, focusing on equality in nearly every sphere of life, from healthcare to education to legal rights.[2] Today, this branch is called the Women's National Coalition, and it now focuses "on lobbying (of government), training (for parliamentary and local government candidates and community leaders) and play[ing] a key role in Adult Basic Education and Gender training."[3]

This document was directly used in the writing of the country's new democratic Constitution. It describes what women from across South Africa believed was fair and deserved for themselves and their mothers, sisters, and daughters. They protest the basic structure of South African society, demanding equality in no uncertain terms—and not just equality, but effective equality that would give women authority, voice, and influence over not only their homes but also their workplaces and communities. Each area addressed in the Charter[4] is undergirded with the basic assertion of equality between sexes, races, and all other distinguishing demographics, and the areas of concern address all aspects of women's lives in South Africa: law and the administration of justice, economy, education and training, development, infrastructure and the environment, social services, political and civic life, family life and partnerships, custom, culture and religion, violence against women, health, and media.

The Women's Charter for Effective Equality

Note: This is the second draft of the Charter drawn up through the National Women's Coalition structures, and approved at the National Conference on 27 February 1994.

PREAMBLE:

As women, citizens of South Africa, we are here to claim our rights. We want recognition and respect for the work we do in the home, in the workplace and in the community. We claim full and equal participation in the creation of a non-sexist, non-racist democratic society.

We cannot march on one leg or clap with one hand. South Africa is poorer politically, economically, and socially for having prevented more than half of its people from fully contributing to its development.

Recognising our shared oppression, women are committed to seizing this historic moment to ensure effective equality in a new South Africa.

For decades, patriarchy, colonialism, racism and apartheid have subordinated and oppressed women within political, economic and social life.

At the heart of women's marginalisation is the patriarchal order that confines women to the domestic arena and reserves for men the arena where political power and authority reside. Conventionally, democracy and human rights have been defined and interpreted in terms of men's experiences. Society has been organised and its institutions structured for the primary benefit of men.

Women want to control their lives. We bear important responsibilities but lack the authority to make decisions in the home and in society.

We want shared responsibility and decision-making in the home and effective equality in politics, the law, and in the economy. For too long women have been marginalised, ignored, exploited and are the poorest and most disadvantaged of South Africans.

If democracy and human rights are to be meaningful for women, they must address our historic subordination and oppression. Women must participate in, and shape the nature and form of our democracy.

As women we have come together in a coalition of organisations and engaged in a campaign that has enabled women to draw on their experience and define what changes are needed within the new political, legal, economic and social system.

The development of the potential of all our people, women and men, will enrich and benefit the whole of society.

We set out here a programme for equality in all spheres of our lives, including the law, the economy, education, development and infrastructure, political and civic life, family life and partnerships, custom, culture and religion, health and the media.

ARTICLE 1: EQUALITY

Equality underlies all our claims in this Charter. We recognise that the achievement of social, economic, political and legal equality is indivisible. Our struggle for equality involves the recognition of the disadvantage that women suffer in all spheres of our lives. As a result similar treatment of women and men may not result in true equality. Therefore the promotion of true equality will sometimes require distinctions to be made. No distinction, however, should be made that will disadvantage women. Within this context programmes of affirmative action may be a means of achieving equality.

We demand that equality applies to every aspect of our lives, including the family, the workplace and the state. The right to equality shall not be limited to our relationship with the state.

- The principle of equality shall be embodied at all levels in legislation and government policy. Specific legislation shall be introduced to ensure the practical realisation of equality.
- The state shall establish appropriate institutions to ensure the effective protection and promotion of equality for women. These institutions shall be accessible to all women in South Africa.

ARTICLE 2: LAW AND THE ADMINISTRATION OF JUSTICE

Women demand equality in the development, application, adjudication, interpretation and enforcement of the law. This can only be achieved if the social, economic and political position of women is taken into account in deciding policy, determining legislative priorities, and in formulating, applying, interpreting, adjudicating and enforcing all laws.

- At all times the law, and its application, interpretation, adjudication and enforcement, shall promote and ensure the practical realisation of equality for women.
- There shall be equality in the treatment of women in all legal and quasi-legal proceedings.
- Women shall have equal legal status and capacity in civil law, including, amongst others, full contractual rights, the right to acquire and hold rights in property, the right to equal inheritance and the right to secure credit.
- All public and private institutions shall enable women to exercise their legal capacity.
- Positive and practical measures shall be taken to ensure equality for women complainants in the criminal justice system.
- There shall be equality for women offenders.
- There shall be equality for women in the legal profession.
- Women shall be equally represented on, and participate in the selection of, the constitutional court, the judiciary, the magistracy, all tribunals and commissions, including the Human Rights Commission, and in the Department of Justice.
- There shall be educational programmes to address gender bias and stereotypes and to promote equality for women in the legal system.
- Women shall have equal representation on, and participation in all traditional courts, alternative dispute resolution mechanisms and local community courts.
- There shall be accessible and affordable legal services for women. In particular the position of paralegals in assisting women to claim their rights shall be recognised.

ARTICLE 3: ECONOMY

Conventional definitions of the economy do not include a major proportion of the work performed by women. The key sectors of the South African economy are occupied and dominated by men. Women face social, economic and ideological barriers to full and equal participation in the economy. Women are perceived in terms of their domestic and reproductive role. Women participate in large numbers in sectors of the economy which are characterised by low wages and poor working conditions. Low remuneration is worsened by discrimination against women in the receipt of social benefits. As a result, many women are forced to make a living outside the formal economy.

- Gender stereotyping and the categorisation of jobs on the basis of sex and gender, must be eliminated.
- Equal benefits must be provided including housing, pensions and medical aid, amongst others.
- There should be no discriminatory taxation. All dependents supported by women breadwinners should be recognised for tax deductions for women.
- Legal mechanisms are needed to protect women against unfair, monopolistic and other exploitative business practices that affect women's participation in the informal economy.
- Safe and healthy facilities must be provided for women in the informal sector.
- Women must be protected from sexual harassment and violence in all the places where women are working.
- Group benefits are needed for women outside formal employment, such as accident and disability insurance, group housing schemes, sick leave and maternity benefits.
- Women need access to credit which is not based on the need for collateral or linked to their marital status.
- Health and safety for commercial sex workers and their clients are needed. Prostitution should be decriminalised.
- Economic policy must secure a central place for women in the economy.
- The full participation of women in economic decision-making should be facilitated.
- The definition of what constitutes economic activity must include all women's work.
- Unpaid labour should be recognised as contributing to the creation of national wealth and should be included in the national accounts.
- Gender stereotyping of work in the home needs to be combatted.

ARTICLE 4: EDUCATION AND TRAINING

Education and training in South Africa has historically focused on schooling, higher education and vocational training in the workplace. It has been male oriented, inaccessible, inappropriate and racially discriminatory. It has ignored women's needs and experience. Education and training is a continuous lifelong process. Education includes educare, adult basic and continuing education, primary, secondary and tertiary education and vocational training for the formal and informal economy. Education and training must meet the economic, social, cultural and political needs of women in South Africa.

- Every woman shall have the right to education and training at any stage of her life in order to realise her full potential.

- Every person has the right to equality within education irrespective of sex, gender, pregnancy, race, sexual orientation, age, disability, urban or rural location, domestic and child care responsibilities and financial status.
- Accessible and appropriate institutions shall be established to provide education to enable active participation by women, particularly rural women, single mothers, and disabled women.
- There shall be no negative gender stereotyping in both curriculum development and educational practice.
- Women shall be represented at all levels of the policy-making, management and administration of education and training.
- Women shall have special access to funds for education and training.
- Childcare facilities shall be provided at all education and training institutions.
- Human rights education to develop awareness of women's status, to build women's self confidence, and enable them to claim their constitutional and legal rights should be implemented.
- Girls and women in educational institutions must be protected against sexual harassment and abuse.
- Sex education shall be provided for boys and girls at all levels of schooling.

ARTICLE 5: DEVELOPMENT, INFRASTRUCTURE AND THE ENVIRONMENT

Women are primarily responsible for maintaining the household and the community. The majority of South Africans have been denied access to the full range of basic development resources and services necessary to sustain a healthy and productive life. Rural women and informal settlement residents in particular have been denied vital resources. The gradual destruction of the natural environment [through] soil erosion, deforestation and air pollution increases women's household, agricultural and community work responsibilities.

Women should participate in designing and implementing development programmes to meet their needs.
- Employment generated from development and infrastructure programmes should benefit women.
- Adequate, accessible and safe water supplies and sanitation should be made available to all communities, including those in rural areas and informal settlements.
- Services such as communications and electricity or other appropriate sources of energy must be extended to all communities as a matter of priority.
- Women need safe transport networks.
- Women need affordable and secure housing with non-discriminatory subsidies and loans.
- Women must have equal access to land and security of tenure, including women living under customary law.
- Accessible health care, recreational, educational and social welfare facilities should be provided to women.
- There shall be protection of natural resources to benefit women.

ARTICLE 6: SOCIAL SERVICES

- Social services should be a right and not a privilege. Inadequate social services place the burden for providing these on women, since women are primarily responsible for maintaining the household and the community.

- Social welfare services should be provided by both the state and the private sector in accordance with the principles of social justice, equality, appropriateness and accessibility.
- Social services should apply to all areas of women's lives, in particular in the home, the workplace, health and education.
- The system of social services should pay special attention to the needs of rural and disabled women.
- State pensions should be provided to all women on an equal basis.
- Accessible and affordable social services should be provided to women.

ARTICLE 7: POLITICAL AND CIVIC LIFE

Women have traditionally been excluded from participation and decision-making in political, civic and community life. Democracy requires that the political playing field between men and women be levelled by acknowledging women's right to participate equally in all political activities.

- Women shall have equal opportunity and access to leadership and decision-making positions at all levels of government.
- Rural women have the right to be part of decision-making structures in traditional communities.
- Women shall have equal access to, and representation on, public bodies.
- Traditional institutions shall be restructured in accordance with the principles of equality and democracy.
- There shall be adequate and appropriate support services to facilitate the full political participation of women.
- Women shall have the right to acquire, change or retain their nationality and to pass it on to their children.
- Women shall be free from political intimidation and threat to her person.

ARTICLE 8: FAMILY LIFE AND PARTNERSHIPS

There are many different types of families which have not enjoyed the same rights, duties and benefits. Women bear an unequal burden in maintaining the family and yet have little power to make decisions.

- All family types shall be recognised and treated equally.
- Women shall have equality within the family and within marriages and intimate relationships.
- Women shall have the right to choose the partner of their choice.
- Women shall have equal rights during, and at the dissolution of, a marriage.
- Women married under customary law shall have the right to inherit from their husbands.
- Women must have the right to decide on the nature and frequency of sexual contact within marriage and intimate relationships.
- Partners and all members of the household should endeavour to share domestic responsibilities.
- Women should have equal access to the financial resources of the household.
- Women should have equal decision-making powers and access to information with regard to the economic management of the household.
- The integrity of the partnership has to be maintained without external and familial interference, except where physical, sexual and emotional abuse occurs.

- Women shall have guardianship over their children.
- Women shall have adequate, effective and enforceable maintenance and/or social welfare benefits for themselves and their children.

ARTICLE 9: CUSTOM, CULTURE AND RELIGION

Customary, cultural and religious practice frequently subordinates women. Roles that are defined for women are both stereotypical and restrictive Women are often excluded from full participation, leadership and decision-making in religious and cultural practice.

- Custom, culture and religion shall be subject to the equality clause in the Bill of Rights.
- All women shall have the freedom to practise their own religion, culture or beliefs without fear.

ARTICLE 10: VIOLENCE AGAINST WOMEN

Violence in all its forms is endemic to South African society. Both sexual and domestic violence are pervasive and all women live under the threat of or experience violence. Women experience secondary victimization at all stages of the criminal justice system.

- Women shall be entitled to security and integrity of the person which shall include the right to be free from all forms of violence in the home, in communities, in the workplace and in public spaces.
- The state should be responsible for public education about the dignity and integrity of the person.
- There shall be legal protection for all women against sexual and racial harassment, abuse and assault.
- Facilities staffed by trained personnel where women can report cases of rape, battery and sexual assault, undergo medical examination and receive appropriate treatment and counselling shall be provided.
- Appropriate education and training for police, prosecutors, magistrates, judges, district surgeons and other persons involved in dealing with cases of rape, battery, sexual assault and incest must be provided.
- There shall be accessible and affordable shelters and counselling services for survivors of rape, battery and sexual assault.

ARTICLE 11: HEALTH

Health services in South Africa have traditionally been unequal, inaccessible and inappropriate. Women in particular are unaware of their rights in relation to health services. Health services have not been appropriately oriented to meet women's health needs and priorities. The lack of basic life sustaining services, such as water and sanitation, has denied the majority of South Africans access to the resources necessary to ensure good health.

- Equal, affordable and accessible health care services which meet women's specific health needs shall be provided.
- Women have the right to control over their bodies which includes the right to reproductive decisions.
- Access to Information and knowledge to enable women to make informed choices about their bodies and about health care should be provided.

- Education about family planning and family planning services should be provided free of charge to both men and women.
- Every person shall have access to adequate nutrition.
- Appropriate and accessible mental health care services must be provided to women.

ARTICLE 12: MEDIA

In South Africa women do not enjoy equal access to, or coverage in the film, print and electronic media. Very few women own or control media institutions or occupy executive or editorial decision-making positions. Women are marginalised and trivialised in the media. The principles of freedom of speech and the press should not justify the portrayal of women in a manner that is degrading and humiliating or promotes violence against them.
- Women must have equal access to all media and media institutions.
- The contribution of women in all areas of public and private life must be reflected in the media.
- The promotion of equality, including affirmative action, in employment must redress current imbalances in the status of women in the media.
- There is a need to monitor the representation of women in the media.
- Negative or injurious stereotypes of women must be eliminated.

This Charter gives expression to the common experiences, visions and aspirations of South African women. We are breaking our silence. We call for respect and recognition of our human dignity and for a genuine change in our status and material conditions in a future South Africa.

Notes

1 "About." African National Congress. Accessed March 8, 2016. www.anc.org.za.
2 "Women's Protection and Representation in South Africa after 20 Years of Democracy." History of Women's Struggle in South Africa, *South African History Online*, accessed Aug. 8, 2016, www.sahistory.org.za.
3 "Women's National Coalition," Women's Struggle Timeline 1905–2006. *South African History Online*, accessed July 20, 2015, www.sahistory.org.za.
4 African National Congress, accessed March 8, 2016, www.anc.org.za.

76

Brighton Declaration on Women and Sport
First World Congress on Women and Sport
International Working Group on Women and Sport
Brighton, England
May 1994

The Brighton conference had a specific focus: "how to accelerate a process of change to rectify the imbalances faced by women in their involvement in sport and their under-representation in sports leadership, particularly at the higher levels."[1] Underrepresentation and unequal involvement are, of course, gender issues people confront in a wide range of fields, from politics and STEM disciplines to sports. What, then, did the Brighton Declaration[2] recommend? Its aim, it says,

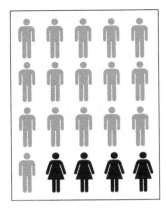

The IWG launched the Sydney Scoreboard, a global index that reports on women's representation on sports boards of national sport organizations and international federations. This graphic shows that "at a national level, based on 38 countries and 1,599 National Sport Organisations, the average percentage of women directors barely increased from 19.7 in 2010 to 20.7 in 2014." Figure from the Sydney Scoreboard: A Global Index for Women in Sport Leadership website, www.sydneyscoreboard.com.

"is to develop a sporting culture that enables and values the full involvement of women in every aspect of sport."

The first noteworthy strategy is to involve "all those governments, public authorities, organisations, businesses, educational and research establishments, women's organisations and individuals who are responsible for, or who directly or indirectly influence, the conduct, development or promotion of sport or who are in any way involved in the employment, education, management, training, development or care of women in sport." Second, the Declaration maintains this breadth when it addresses "policies, structures and mechanisms," and when it simultaneously emphasizes increased participation of women in sport and a greater voice for women in the development of sports. Third, it reckons with diversity, advocating for the right of all women to participate, "regardless of race, colour, language, religion, creed, sexual orientation, age, marital status, disability, political belief or affiliation, national or social origin." Finally, it links its agenda to "equality, development and peace."

Brighton Declaration on Women and Sport

Scope and Aims of the Declaration

This Declaration is addressed to all those governments, public authorities, organisations, businesses, educational and research establishments, women's organisations and individuals who are responsible for, or who directly or indirectly influence, the conduct, development or promotion of sport or who are in any way involved in the employment, education, management, training, development or care of women in sport. This Declaration is meant to complement all sporting, local, national and international charters, laws, codes, rules and regulations relating to women or sport.

The overriding aim is to develop a sporting culture that enables and values the full involvement of women in every aspect of sport.

It is in the interests of equality, development and peace that a commitment is made by governmental, non-governmental organisations and all those institutions involved in sport to apply the Principles set out in this Declaration by developing appropriate policies, structures and mechanisms which:

- ensure that all women and girls have the opportunity to participate in sport in a safe and supportive environment which preserves the rights, dignity and respect of the individual;
- increase the involvement of women in sport at all levels and in all functions and roles;
- ensure that the knowledge, experiences and values of women contribute to the development of sport;
- promote the recognition by women of the instrinsic value of sport and its contribution to personal development and healthy lifestyle.

The Principles

1. Equity and Equality in Society and Sport

Every effort should be made by state and government machineries to ensure that institutions and organisations responsible for sport comply with the equality provisions of the Charter of the United Nations, the Universal Declaration of Human Rights and the UN Convention on the Elimination of all Forms of Discrimination Against Women.

Equal opportunity to participate and be involved in sport whether for the purpose of leisure and recreation, health promotion or high performance, is the right of every woman, regardless of race, colour, language, religion, creed, sexual orientation, age, marital status, disability, political belief or affiliation, national or social origin.

Resources, power and responsibility should be allocated fairly and without discrimination on the basis of sex, but such allocation should redress any inequitable balance in the benefits available to women and men.

2. Facilities

Women's participation in sport is influenced by the extent, variety and accessibility of facilities. The planning, design and management of these should appropriately and equitably meet the particular needs of women in the community, with special attention given to the need for childcare provision and safety.

3. School and Junior Sport

Research demonstrates that girls and boys approach sport from markedly different perspectives. Those responsible for sport, education, recreation and physical education of young people should ensure that an equitable range of opportunities and learning experience, which accommodate the values, attitudes and aspirations of girls, is incorporated in programmes to develop physical fitness and basic sport skills of young people.

4. Developing Participation

Women's participation in sport is influenced by the range of activities available. Those responsible for delivering sporting opportunities and programmes should provide and promote activities which meet women's needs and aspirations.

5. High Performance Sport

Governments and sports organisations should provide equal opportunities to women to reach their sports performance potential by ensuring that all activities and programmes relating to performance improvements take account of the specific needs of female athletes.

Those supporting elite and/or professional athletes should ensure that competition opportunities, rewards, incentives, recognition, sponsorship, promotion and other forms of support are provided fairly and equitably to both women and men.

6. Leadership in Sport

Women are under-represented in the leadership and decision making in all sport and sport-related organisations. Those responsible for these areas should develop policies and programmes and design structures which increase the number of women coaches, advisers, decision makers, officials, administrators and sports personnel at all levels with special attention given to recruitment, development and retention.

7. Education, Training and Development

Those responsible for the education, training and development of coaches and other sports personnel should ensure that education processes and experiences address issues relating to gender equity and the needs of female athletes, equitably reflect women's role in sport and take account of women's leadership experiences, values and attitudes.

8. Sports Information and Research

Those responsible for research and providing information on sport should develop policies and programmes to increase knowledge and understanding about women and sport and ensure that research norms and standards are based on research on women and men.

9. Resources

Those responsible for the allocation of resources should ensure that support is available for sportswomen, women's programmes and special measures to advance this Declaration of Principles.

10. Domestic and International Cooperation

Government and non-government organisations should incorporate the promotion of issues of gender equity and the sharing of examples of good practice in women and sport policies and programmes in their associations with other organisations, within both domestic and international arenas.

International Women and Sport Strategy

Governments and organisations committing to be a part of an International Women and Sport Strategy will:

- endorse and commit to the application of the Declaration of Principles, to be known as the "Brighton Declaration of Women and Sport";
- develop and execute an implementation plan which reflects full and practical fulfilment of the principles contained in the Brighton Declaration;
- nominate a representative for the purposes of communications with the International Working Group on Women and Sport;

- support international cooperation by striving to send qualified representatives to future international conferences conducted to discuss issues, share exemplary practices and model programmes, network and monitor progress in aplication of the principles;
- provide feedback to the working group on the effectiveness of their actions taken to advance the principles.

Notes

1 Karen Hennessy, "Brighton Declaration: Its Impact on Irish Sport, 10 years On." Unpublished paper, 2004, accessed Sept. 30, 2017, https://www.easm.net.
2 International Working Group on Women and Sport, "Brighton Declaration on Women and Sport," 1994. WomenSport International, www.sportsbiz.bz/womensportinternational.

77

Women's Declaration on Population Policies
International Women's Health Coalition Delegation
New York, New York
September 1994

IWHC logo.

As women involved directly in the organisation of services, research and advocacy, we focus this declaration on women's reproductive health and rights. We call for a fundamental revision in the design, structure and implementation of population policies, to foster the empowerment and well-being of all women.

The International Women's Health Coalition was formed in 1984, when Joan Dunlop took over an abortion-training program and broadened its goals to women's holistic healthcare. Based in New York City, the coalition first established connections with grassroots organizations in Bangladesh, Colombia, Indonesia, the Philippines, and Venezuela. In 1985, Adrienne Germain, a woman with vast experience working with women's grassroots organizations across the globe, joined Dunlop as the vice-president of the coalition, strengthening the organization's connections and ability to work internationally.[1]

Today, the IWHC's mission is to advance "the sexual and reproductive health and rights of women and young people, particularly adolescent girls, in Africa, Asia, Latin America, and the Middle East. IWHC furthers this agenda by supporting and strengthening leaders and organizations working at the community, national, regional, and global levels, and by advocating for international and U.S. policies, programs, and funding." Since their founding in 1984, the IWHC has "helped build and strengthen nearly 80 organizations in Africa, Asia, Latin America, and the Middle East. [They] have provided mentorship and more than

$31 million in grants to women and youth advocates across these regions." This enormous impact and widespread reach has made the IWHC one of the most successful women's health organizations in the world.[2]

In 1992, the IWHC served as secretariat for a meeting of women's health advocates "representing women's networks in Asia, Africa, Latin America, the Caribbean, the USA, and Western Europe." The purpose of this meeting was "to discuss how women's voices might best be heard during preparations for the 1994 Cairo Conference on Population and Development, and in the conference itself."[3] The Declaration that arose from this meeting was approved by over one hundred women's organizations across the globe before being presented at the 1994 Cairo Conference. Many of the objectives, goals, and attitudes presented in this Declaration were adopted at the Cairo Conference, especially in the "Principles" and "Reproductive Rights and Reproductive Health" sections.[4]

The point of view that this Declaration challenges holds that population growth causes poverty and environmental challenges, and it is up to women to control population growth. In contrast, this document starts with the gendered inequality of material and social resources, and holds that this inequality affects reproduction, so that population programs must focus on quality of life and ending discrimination. The Declaration[5] asserts a number of basic ethical principles that privilege women's rights to make decisions about their bodies. It outlines actions that create governmental equality between men and women and governmental support for and access to women's healthcare, including birth control. Finally, the Declaration concludes by creating a set of conditions necessary to make this kind of social change effective, including putting women in decision-making positions and making sure that women are financially supported.

Women's Declaration on Population Policies: Women's Voices '94

Preamble
Just, humane and effective development policies based on principles of social justice promote the well-being of all people. Population policies, designed and implemented under this objective, need to address a wide range of conditions that affect the reproductive health and rights of women and men. These include unequal distribution of material and social resources among individuals and groups, based on gender, age, race, religion, social class, rural-urban residence, nationality and other social criteria; changing patterns of sexual and family relationships; political and economic policies that restrict girls' and women's access to health services and methods of fertility regulation; and ideologies, laws and practices that deny women's basic human rights.

While there is considerable regional and national diversity, each of these conditions reflects not only biological differences between males and females, but also discrimination against girls and women, and power imbalances between women and men. Each of these conditions affects, and is affected by, the ability and willingness of governments to ensure health and education, to generate employment, and to protect basic human rights for all. Governments' ability and willingness are currently jeopardised by the global economic crisis, structural adjustment programmes, and trends toward privatisation, among other factors.

To assure the well-being of all people, and especially of women, population policies and programmes must be framed within and implemented as a part of broader development strategies that will redress the unequal distribution of resources and power between and within countries, between racial and ethnic groups, and between women and men.

Population policies and programmes of most countries and international agencies have been driven more by demographic goals than by quality of life goals. Population size and growth have often been blamed inappropriately as the exclusive or primary causes of problems such as global environmental degradation and poverty. Fertility control programmes have prevailed as solutions, when poverty and inequity are root causes that need to be addressed. Population policies and programmes have typically targeted low-income countries and groups, often reflecting racial and class biases.

Women's fertility has been the primary object of both pro-natalist and anti-natalist population policies. Women's behaviour rather than men's has been the focus of attention. Women have been expected to carry most of the responsibility and risks of birth control, but have been largely excluded from decision-making in personal relationships as well as in public policy. Sexuality and gender-based power inequities have been largely ignored, and sometimes even strengthened, by population and family planning programmes.

As women involved directly in the organisation of services, research and advocacy, we focus this declaration on women's reproductive health and rights. We call for a fundamental revision in the design, structure and implementation of population policies, to foster the empowerment and well-being of all women. Women's empowerment is legitimate and critically important in its own right, not merely as a means to address population issues. Population policies that are responsive to women's needs and rights must be grounded in the following internationally accepted, but too often ignored, ethical principles.

Fundamental ethical principles
1. Women can and do make responsible decisions for themselves, their families, their communities, and, increasingly, for the state of the world. Women must be subjects, not objects, of any development policy, and especially of population policies.
2. Women have the right to determine when, whether, why, with whom, and how to express their sexuality. Population policies must be based on the principle of respect for the sexual and bodily integrity of girls and women.
3. Women have the individual right and the social responsibility to decide whether, how, and when to have children and how many to have; no woman can be compelled to bear a child or be prevented from doing so against her will. All women, regardless of age, marital status, or other social conditions have a right to information and services necessary to exercise their reproductive rights and responsibilities.
4. Men also have a personal and social responsibility for their own sexual behaviour and fertility and for the effects of that behaviour on their partners and their children's health and well-being.

5. Sexual and social relationships between women and men must be governed by principles of equity, non-coercion, and mutual respect and responsibility. Violence against girls and women, their subjugation or exploitation, and other harmful practices such as genital mutilation or unnecessary medical procedures, violate basic human rights. Such practices also impede effective, health- and rights-oriented population programmes.
6. The fundamental sexual and reproductive rights of women cannot be subordinated, against a woman's will, to the interests of partners, family members, ethnic groups, religious institutions, health providers, researchers, policy makers, the state or any other actors.
7. Women committed to promoting women's reproductive health and rights, and linked to the women to be served, must be included as policy makers and programme implementors in all aspects of decision-making including definition of ethical standards, technology development and distribution, services, and information dissemination.

To assure the centrality of women's well-being, population policies and programmes need to honour these principles at national and international levels.

Minimum programme requirements
In the design and implementation of population policies and programmes, policy makers in international and national agencies should:
1. Seek to reduce and eliminate pervasive inequalities in all aspects of sexual, social and economic life by:
   - providing universal access to information, education and discussion on sexuality, gender roles, reproduction and birth control, in school and outside;
   - changing sex-role and gender stereotypes in mass media and other public communications to support more egalitarian and respectful relationships;
   - enacting and enforcing laws that protect women from sexual and gender-based violence, abuse or coercion;
   - implementing policies that encourage and support parenting and household maintenance by men;
   - prioritising women's education, job training, paid employment, access to credit, and the right to own land and other property in social and economic policies, and through equal rights legislation;
   - prioritising investment in basic health services, sanitation, and clean water.
2. Support women's organisations that are committed to women's reproductive health and rights and linked to the women to be served, especially women disadvantaged by class, race, ethnicity or other factors, to:
   - participate in designing, implementing and monitoring policies and programmes for comprehensive reproductive health and rights;
   - work with communities on service delivery, education and advocacy.
3. Assure personally and locally appropriate, affordable, good-quality, comprehensive reproductive and sexual health services for women of all ages, provided on a voluntary basis without incentives or disincentives, including but not limited to:
   - legislation to allow safe access to all appropriate means of birth control;

- balanced attention to all aspects of sexual and reproductive health, including pregnancy, delivery and post-partum care; safe and legal abortion services; safe choices among contraceptive methods including barrier methods; information, prevention and treatment of sexually-transmitted diseases, AIDS, infertility, and other gynaecological problems; child-care services; and policies to support men's parenting and household responsibilities;
- non-directive counselling to enable women to make free, fully informed choices among birth-control methods as well as other health services;
- discussion and information on sexuality, gender roles and power relationships, reproductive health and rights;
- management information systems that follow the woman or man, not simply the contraceptive method or service;
- training to enable all staff to be gender-sensitive, respectful service providers, along with procedures to evaluate and reward performance on the basis of the quality of care provided, not simply the quantity of services;
- programme evaluation and funding criteria that utilise the standards defined here to eliminate unsafe or coercive practices, as well as sexist, classist or racist bias;
- inclusion of reproductive health as a central component of all public health programmes, including population programmes, recognising that women require information and services not just in the reproductive ages but before and after;
- research into what services women want, how to maintain women's integrity, and how to promote their overall health and well-being.

4. Develop and provide the widest possible range of appropriate contraceptives to meet women's multiple needs throughout their lives:
   - give priority to the development of women-controlled methods that protect against sexually transmitted infections, as well as pregnancy, in order to redress the current imbalances in contraceptive technology research, development and delivery;
   - ensure availability and promote universal use of good-quality condoms;
   - ensure that technology research is respectful of women's right to full information and free choice, and is not concentrated among low-income or otherwise disadvantaged women, or particular racial groups.

5. Ensure sufficient financial resources to meet the goals outlined above. Expand public funding for health, clean water and sanitation, and maternity care, as well as birth control. Establish better collaboration and co-ordination among UN, donors, governments and other agencies in order to use resources most effectively for women's health.

6. Design and promote policies for wider social, political and economic transformation that will allow women to negotiate and manage their own sexuality and health, make their own life choices, and participate fully in all levels of government and society.

Necessary conditions

In order for women to control their sexuality and reproductive health, and to exercise their reproductive rights, the following actions are priorities:

1. Women decision makers

   Using participatory processes, fill at least 50 per cent of decision-making positions in all relevant agencies with women who agree with the principles described here, who have a demonstrated commitment to advancing women's rights, and who are linked to the women to be served, taking into account income, ethnicity and race.

2. Financial resources

   As present expenditure levels are totally inadequate, multiply at least four-fold the money available to implement the programme requirements listed in this Declaration.

3. Women's health movement

   Allocate a minimum of 20 per cent of available resources for women's health and reproductive rights organisations to strengthen their activities and work towards the goals specified in this declaration.

4. Accountability mechanisms

   Support women's rights and health advocacy groups, and other non-governmental mechanisms, mandated by and accountable to women, at national and international levels, to:
   - investigate and seek redress for abuses or infringements of women's and men's reproductive rights;
   - analyse the allocation of resources to reproductive health and rights, and pursue revisions where necessary;
   - identify inadequacies or gaps in policies, programmes, information and services and recommend improvements;
   - document and publicise progress.

Meeting these priority conditions will ensure women's reproductive health and their fundamental right to decide whether, when, and how many children to have. Such commitment will also ensure just, humane and effective development and population policies that will attract a broad base of political support.

Notes

1 "History." International Women's Health Coalition, accessed Feb. 15, 2017, www.iwhc.org.
2 Quotations in the preceding paragraph are from "About Us." International Women's Health Coalition, accessed Feb. 15, 2017, www.iwhc.org.
3 "Women's Declaration on Population Policies: International Women's Health Coalition." *Development in Practice* 3.2 (1993): 116–21.
4 "Programme of Action—Adopted at the International Conference on Population and Development, Cairo 5–13 September 1994. 20th Anniversary Edition," 2014. United Nations Population Fund, www.unfpa.org.
5 Ibid.

78

Platform Papers
National Asian Pacific American Women's Forum
Los Angeles, California
September 1996

National Asian Pacific American Women's Forum logo.

The very diverse population of Asian and Pacific Islanders (APIs) is a fast-growing group in the United States. Given this, it is perhaps surprising that the National Asian Pacific American Women's Forum (NAPAWF) is the only multi-issue women's organization dealing with the specific issues that API women confront.

NAPAWF was founded in 1996. Interestingly, some Asian and Pacific Islander American women found themselves at the 1995 UN Conference on Women with no organized voice with which to participate, and no coalition at home linking their work. They got together in Beijing, and discussed building a multi-issue, national, progressive movement of API women. A year later, 157 women (the "founding sisters") gathered in Los Angeles and developed the Platform Papers included here.

This collection of Platform Papers describes the six issue areas that form the basis for NAPAWF's work: civil rights, economic justice, educational access, ending violence against women, health, and immigrant and refugee rights. "The Platform Papers are not meant to provide a complete list of issues and concerns in these areas. Nor does the format of this collection assume that the issues discussed can be neatly separated into six areas. Rather, the Platform Papers are intended to be works-in-progress that serve as companions to the organization's grassroots work."[1] Each section begins with a strong statement delineating the problems, and proceeds to develop goals and strategies for their accomplishment.

The Platform Papers[2] subscribe to a civil rights and human rights approach. The status quo they address is described thus:

> API women and girls are systematically marginalized from the decision-making processes and structures that impact their daily lives. As a result, API women and girls are left vulnerable to misinformed, misguided or misanthropic legislation and policies that not only violate their civil and human rights, but also perpetuate their inability to fully participate in effecting meaningful social, economic and political change.

Issues of immigrant status, guest workers, and English-language skills complicate their situation, and thus take a more prominent role in this document than in most. Culturally sensitive childcare appears here, as it does in some Latina documents, as well as the intersection of sex and race discrimination.

Platform Papers

I. CIVIL RIGHTS
PHILOSOPHICAL STATEMENT
Through the use of a variety of creative strategies, our civil rights struggle includes advancing the expression of our identities, access to basic human resources and necessities, and justice for Asian Pacific Islander American women and girls. Beyond the U.S. context, NAPAWF asserts the importance of linking our issues with international human rights movements, recognizing that domestic and global struggles shape and inform each other.

ISSUE AREAS
- Political empowerment
- Enforcing and expanding civil rights
- Bias and discrimination based on gender, racial and/or sexual identity
- Same-sex marriage
- Bilingual education
- Affirmative action
- Hate speech and hate crimes
- Other issues that do not fit neatly into other Platform Areas

PROBLEM STATEMENTS
API women and girls are systematically marginalized from the decision-making processes and structures that impact their daily lives. As a result, API women and girls are left vulnerable to misinformed, misguided or misanthropic legislation and policies that not only violate their civil and human rights, but also perpetuate their inability to fully participate in effecting meaningful social, economic and political change. This is illustrated by the blatant targeting of immigrant communities in recent "reform" policies (e.g., immigration reform, welfare reform, English-only) which disproportionately disaffect [sic] women and by the failure of current employment discrimination laws to include sexual orientation or to address the intersection of race and gender in the categories of protected classes.

Gender, race, class, age, and sexual biases within as well as beyond the API community play a prominent role in undermining the rights and limiting the opportunities of API women and girls. This is complicated by biases in the dominant American culture about immigration status and English-speaking ability. Stereotypes about API women and girls (e.g., "exotic and erotic dragon women" and "dutiful daughters and wives") lead to accepted and institutionalized forms of oppression, exploitation, and/or victimization. A lack of understanding and dialogue about the intersecting gender, racial and sexual identities of API women and girls exacerbates and reinforces discrimination against them in their families, communities, and society at large. This is exemplified by the ongoing invisibility of API issues in mainstream feminist organizations and of lesbian/bisexual/trans gendered issues in API organizations.

PLATFORM GOALS
- To promote the leadership and visibility of API women and girls in the political process and legal system.
- To enforce and expand civil rights laws and protections for API women and girls.

- To provide a safe and supportive forum space for open discourse and political support for all API women and girls.
- To be the leading organization representing the issues of importance to API women and girls.

ISSUE AREA OBJECTIVES

- Expand civil rights protections for all API women and girls to include unprotected classes of people (e.g., sexual minorities) and additional categories of prohibited activities (e.g., hate crimes).
- Address bias and discrimination that limit the rights and opportunities of API women and girls.
- Serve as the primary resource on issues pertaining to API women and girls.
- Involve API women in redefining "civil rights" and in reframing a progressive civil rights agenda.

ISSUE AREA STRATEGIES

- Develop a Political Empowerment program to promote voter education and participation; to groom progressive API women candidates and community leaders; and to educate, lobby and hold policymakers accountable to the issues affecting API women and girls.
- Develop a national resource and information network to promote a progressive civil rights agenda that benefits API women and girls [protect affirmative action, restore welfare benefits to immigrants, expand protected classes (sexual minorities) and prohibited activities (hate crimes), protect immigrant labor rights, legalize same-sex marriage].
- Provide political leadership on specific legislation or policies that protect, enforce and expand civil rights for API women and girls by testifying before legislative and policy-making bodies, engaging in letter-writing campaigns, and developing position papers.
- Work with Identity Forum Committee to develop and implement programs that address the intersecting gender, race, and sexual identities of API women and girls to continually inform and refresh NAPAWF's Platform.

II. ECONOMIC JUSTICE
ISSUE AREAS

- Discrimination in employment opportunities and conditions
- Deterrents to economic independence
- Support and "safety nets" for the economically poor
- Economic exploitation of immigrant API women and girls in sweatshop industries
- Sexual exploitation of API women and girls

PROBLEM STATEMENTS

API women and girls encounter a diversity of experiences in the American labor force and workplace. These experiences are largely conditioned by pervasive racism and oppressive patriarchal cultural norms in both API and mainstream communities. Although U.S.-born and English-proficient API women and girls generally hold "white- or pink-collar" jobs, they face ongoing racial and gender discrimination in the workplace: pay inequities, employment typecasting, and limited career mobility. Immigrant and non-English-speaking API women and girls are often concentrated in industries characterized by excessively long working hours, labor intensive work, and subsistence wages: garment "sweatshops," restaurants, and domestic service. Economic class, citizenship status and limited English language skills make these workers especially vulnerable to exploitation as exemplified by the global trafficking of primarily API women and girls.

This complex interplay of racism, sexism, and economic exploitation impedes economic independence for API women and girls, which involves the power to control and define the conditions of their work and their lives. In the long run, the wage inequities experienced by API women at their peak working ages directly contribute to subsequent inequities in their pension benefits, thereby condemning many API women to poverty in their old age. Inadequate protections and lax enforcement of U.S. labor laws as well as legislative policies that weaken the social and economic "safety net" for politically and economically marginalized members of society reinforce the continued subjugation of API women.

PLATFORM GOALS
- To eliminate discrimination against and exploitation of API women and girls in the workplace.
- To achieve economic independence and create economic opportunities for API women.
- To secure stable "safety net" support resources for economically poor API women and girls.
- To combat the international trafficking and exploitation of API women.
- To eliminate sweatshop conditions in industries where immigrant API women are employed.

ISSUE AREA OBJECTIVES
- Secure all API working women's rights to fair livable wages and benefits, to safe and decent working conditions, and to collectively organize and represent their labor.
- Increase educational and job training opportunities that are sensitive to the social, cultural, and economic realities of API women.
- Advocate for culturally sensitive, affordable child care to enable API women to manage work and family responsibilities.
- Increase API women's economic and social power to control and define the conditions of their work and their lives by combating patriarchal cultural norms in both the API and mainstream communities.
- Increase accessibility to and capacity of safety nets to support economically poor API women and their families in culturally appropriate ways by developing alternative resources and improving community accountability. Safeguard the safety net for older API women in retirement.
- Raise national and international public awareness about the global trafficking of API women and girls by creating linkages and building coalitions with other activists. Develop and implement a strategy that leverages our unique position as API women in the United States to effect national policies addressing this issue.

ISSUE AREA STRATEGIES
- Compile data about API women's labor to inform the development of policies and advocacy strategies that address API women's labor and economic issues

and to establish accountability benchmarks for employers, labor organizations, and governments.

- Provide and support a variety of educational, advocacy, organizing, and outreach activities, programs and materials (e.g., position papers, public workshops and events, speakers bureaus, mentoring programs, labor organizing and media campaigns, etc.) that increase knowledge and understanding about the myriad issues affecting API women and girls and that uphold API women's rights to control and define their labor and their lives. Issues to include: employment discrimination; sexual harassment; self-advocacy and empowerment; trafficking of women and girls; access to education and job-training, including non-traditional occupations; etc.

- Collaborate with other community-based organizations and activists to improve awareness of, access to and advocacy for particular "safety net" support services needed by economically poor API women and their families (culturally competent outreach, language accessibility, etc.). Create community accountability for augmenting publicly supported "safety net" programs with resources available within the API community (e.g. collaborating with API bar associations to provide pro bono services to economically poor API women and their families).

- Develop effective internal organizational structures that enable NAPAWF to implement a variety of strategies (e.g. national media strategy, national legislative strategy, etc.) and to proactively respond to issues affecting API women and girls.

- Engage in and create an information/resource bank about national and international organizing efforts to combat the exploitation of API women and girls and their labor (e.g. global trafficking, sweatshops, etc.).

NATIONAL CAMPAIGN PROPOSAL

Young Chinese women are working as indentured servants of a garment manufacturing business operating in the Mariana Islands, a U.S. territory exempt from U.S. labor and immigration laws. The business, which is owned by a local government of mainland China, contracts these "guest workers" for a period of two years but can unilaterally extend the contract which prohibits the workers from striking, asking for higher wages, dating or marrying, engaging in local politics or in religious activities, or returning to their homes. These women work 18-hour days (8 a.m. to 2 a.m.) six days a week and live 8 to a room. In addition, some women work for 6 months before receiving their pay and, at the end of two years, may take home only $300.00.

This exploitation of Asian women has domestic and international dimensions since the business is sited on U.S. territory, involves foreign nationals working for a business owned by their home government, and potentially affects API immigrants in the United States who may lose job opportunities if businesses operating in the U.S. relocate their manufacturing facilities offshore.

NAPAWF could co-sponsor a national educational and advocacy campaign with Sweatshop Watch, a sister organization currently investigating the situation, as well as Asian Pacific American Labor Alliance (APALA). While the details of such a campaign can be developed at a later date, NAPAWF should target API women and consumers as a particular audience for future mobilization and action (e.g., boycotts).

III. EDUCATIONAL ACCESS
ISSUE AREAS
- Data and information on the status and needs of API women and girls
- Access to education
- Relevant curricula, programs, and services for students
- Employment opportunities
- Parental involvement in schools

PROBLEM STATEMENTS
The educational issues and needs of API women and girls are often invisible due to gaps in collecting and analyzing relevant information. Educational status and progress are typically tracked along lines of race or gender, but statistics involving the intersection of race and gender are lacking. Consequently, the basic information needed to assess the particular situations of API women and girls is hidden. In addition, lost within the general category of "Asian and Pacific Islander" are women of specific ethnic classifications, sexual identities, economic classes, and other differing characteristics. Thus, the needs and status of some API women and girls remain hidden even more deeply than others.

Access to appropriate and relevant educational opportunities, including employment in the field of education, must support and reflect the full diversity of API women and girls. Educational institutions, from K–12 to colleges and universities, must adopt curricula, policies and programs that encourage rather than hinder the full participation and success of API women and girls as students and as employees. To these ends, the gathering and analysis of information about the status and needs of API women and girls is imperative.

PLATFORM GOALS
- To increase access to appropriate and relevant educational opportunities, including employment in the field of education, for API women and girls.
- To improve the availability of information necessary to analyze the diverse needs and status of API women and girls.

ISSUE AREA OBJECTIVES
- Increase the number of API women employed and promoted in every field of education and at all levels of education from K-12 through colleges and universities.
- Reform educational programs, services and curricula to address the diverse needs of API students (e.g., bilingual education or support services for lesbian, gay, bisexual students) and to reflect the diversity of their communities and identities (e.g., multicultural and gender sensitive curricula).
- Promote the involvement and leadership of API mothers in school-based and educational activities.
- Promote awareness within and beyond the API community about the issues that affect API girls and women and that hinder their full participation and development in school and in their jobs.

ISSUE AREA STRATEGIES
- Develop a network and strategies to support and advocate for the mentoring, recruitment, hiring, development and promotion of API women at all levels of education.

- Advocate for multicultural curricula and materials that reflect and address the diversity of API women and girls and their issues, including issues of gender, sexuality, culture, difference and power. Link curriculum to the development of effective pedagogical strategies for all students.
- Advocate for effective bilingual education programs that address the needs of diverse API students and their families and that are gender- and culturally-inclusive. Support pedagogical strategies that attend to issues of gender and culture.
- Advocate for culturally sensitive support services for lesbian, gay, and bisexual API students. Support the development and distribution of appropriate educational materials that address issues of sexual diversity in API communities. Eliminate hostile environments that permit harassment and violence against racially and sexually diverse students. Develop strategies for protecting students from such harassment and violence.
- Monitor the effectiveness of educational programs and policies designed to target "underrepresented" groups to ensure responsiveness to the complexities and intersections of ethnicity, gender, sexuality, and class. Work with civil rights organizations to identify and confront segregationist educational districting as well as biased achievement "tracking" systems.
- Promote the involvement and leadership of API mothers in a variety of school-based and educational activities. Work with parents, teachers, and other community members to develop strategies for keeping API female students engaged and motivated in their own education. Support informal information networks for the transformation of knowledge "from the ground up."
- Develop strategies for enabling parents to integrate their children's education with family life.
- Develop workshops and materials to educate non-API teachers, educational administrators, and school board members about:
    1. The impact of stereotypes in hiring, promotions, workplace environments, and the development of leadership in educational settings.
    2. The problems of "tracking" students based on stereotypical assumptions.
    3. Cultural, pedagogical, and curricular issues that affect the success of API girls and women.
- Develop educational workshops and strategies to inform and transform API community attitudes toward the participation of women and girls in a broad range of educational and extracurricular activities and opportunities.
- Develop strategies for educating parents, students and other community members about the benefits of specific educational programs so that they can make informed choices about opportunities. Develop workshops and materials to inform API parents and students about the availability of scholarships, fellowships, grants, and other educational opportunities.

NATIONAL CAMPAIGN PROPOSAL

Educational institutions are increasingly linked by Internet technologies; NAPAWF should draw from the growing networking opportunities that are opening up. New networks not only allow for increased communications (local and national) but also for organizing opportunities between educational institutions and various local communities. NAPAWF should seize upon funding and programmatic opportunities that are becoming available as the result of growing interest in this area. The various levels of networks could be used for sharing information, organizing, and strategizing on local and national levels.

The networking opportunities and strategies developed by this initiative would not be limited to the area of Educational Access. NAPAWF in general will need to confront the difficult communications issues related to the attempt to organize nationally. Work done in the area of Educational Access could provide the starting point for developing such communications, information-sharing, and organizing possibilities to be gained from the Internet. Because many members working in educational institutions are probably already linked, beginning stages of such a network could begin immediately.

Objective:
- To develop a network that facilitates both national and local strategizing around issues of educational access for API girls and women.

Strategies: Research grant opportunities for funding technological initiatives. For example, the National Endowment for the Humanities has a special grants program for funding the use of new technologies. The NEH seems to be particularly interested in funding initiatives that link institutions of higher education to public schools and local communities. NAPAWF's work in obtaining grants would benefit a network of educators in higher education and public schools, as well as communities that may not have sufficient funds to hook up to the Internet on a large scale. NAPAWF would thus be working to fight the troubling gap between those who can benefit from the new information and communications possibilities and those who cannot.

Investigate local models where such networks are in place. NAPAWF ought to learn from initiatives that work well in linking educational institutions to communities.

Investigate and develop national communications networks using the new technologies. Again, because institutions of higher education are increasingly linked, NAPAWF should build from the resources that are already in place. NAPAWF members interested in Educational Access could develop a listserv (specialized email list), a Website that both provides information and facilitates communications, and a method for connecting to existing organizations working on educational access and affirmative action.

Notes

1 Platform Papers, 1999. National Asian Pacific American Women's Forum, www.napawf.org.
2 Ibid.

79

Final Statement: Women and Children, Militarism, and Human Rights

International Women's Working Conference
International Women's Network Against Militarism
Naha City, Okinawa, Japan
May 1–4, 1997

Document from the International Women's Working Conference. Image courtesy of Gywn Kirk.

We see militarism as a system of structural violence which turns its members into war machines and creates victims among women and children in our local communities.

For four days, activists, policymakers, advocates, and researchers from mainland Japan, Korea, Okinawa, the Philippines, and the United States discussed the impact of U.S. military bases on each country, especially focusing on the consequences for women, children, and the environment. The conference was sponsored by the International Women's Network Against Militarism, which "envision[s] a world of genuine security free of militarism, based on justice, people's participation, and compassion for others; a world where people's fundamental human dignity and respect for cultural identities are honored; a world of peace, wellbeing and abundance for the common good; a world where people live in harmony with the environment that sustains us all."[1] They question what the real meaning of security is, and for whom.

Both "the importance and the challenge of building anti-militarist alliances of women across boundaries of culture, class, race, age, and nation" cannot be overstated.[2] "During the meeting, both in formal sessions and in informal conversations, [attendees] talked about the importance of acknowledging the complex inequalities among participants, and the relationships of dominance and oppression that exists [sic] among our countries."[3] Such is grassroots, transnational feminism.

"Participants at the Okinawa meeting worked in small groups on four related themes: women and children, the environment, legal agreements between the U.S. and host countries, and base conversion, with economic development that will benefit local people, especially women."[4] They emphasized the discrimination experienced by Amerasian children, the hypermasculine character of the military and subsequent objectification of women in "GI towns," the military as a major polluter, and the problematic nature of military agreements. They challenged the rationales given for U.S. military spending and for the presence of U.S. military bases abroad—of which there are about two thousand, "located strategically."[5] Finally, they claimed that "military violence against women also occurs in situations of military occupation, colonial domination, military political control, and even U.N. military forces' peacekeeping activities, and that all military activity must be analyzed and challenged from a gendered perspective."[6]

Both the conference and the document below[7] engage in considerable reframing of the familiar. Military bases do not offer protection but threaten security and local culture. Military "rest and recreation," better known as "R and R," becomes sexual exploitation. Women, usually marginalized in military discussions, are to be included "in all levels of base-conversion decision-making." This is dramatic, powerful revisioning.

Two of the participants at the conference wrote about the alternatives they envisioned:

> Our vision . . . includes the creation of true local democracies, the empowerment of local people, and the inclusion of women and children in decision-making. It will involve base conversion as well as nonmilitary approaches to resolving conflicts. . . . We agreed that we need a deeper understanding of demilitarization that goes beyond bases, land, and weapons, to include cultures, consciousness, and national identities. Given that masculinity in many countries, including the United States, is defined in military terms, it will also involve a redefinition of masculinity, strength, power, and adventure. It will involve more harmonious ways of living among people, and between people and the nonhuman world that sustains us.[8]

Final Statement

We are a group of women activists, policy-makers, and scholars from Okinawa, mainland Japan, Korea, the Philippines, and the U.S. who share a deep concern for the impact of the U.S. military presence on women and children in all our communities.

For four days we have exchanged information and strategized together about the situation of victims of violence committed by U.S. military personnel against civilians, especially women and children. We have shared information about the plight of Amerasian children who are abandoned by their G.I. fathers, and the effects of U.S. military bases on the social environment, in particular on women who are absorbed into the dehumanizing and exploitative system of prostitution around U.S. bases. We have considered the current status of the various official agreements governing U.S. bases and military personnel; also the effects of high rates of military spending on women and children in the U.S. We see militarism as a system of structural violence which turns its members into war machines and creates victims among women and children in our local communities. Underlying our discussion this week is the clear conviction that the U.S. military presence is a threat to our security, not a protection. We recognize that the governments of Japan, South Korea, and the Philippines are also complicit in this.

This is the first time that women have sat down together to discuss these issues, which are usually marginalized in discussion concerning U.S. military operations. As a result of our work this week, we see the many striking similarities in our various situations more clearly than ever before. As women activists, policy-makers, advocates, and scholars, we have strengthened our commitment to work together toward a world with true security based on justice, respect for each other across national boundaries, and economic planning based on local people's needs, especially the needs of women and children. We will continue to support women and children affected by U.S. militarism in all our countries, and to create alternative economic systems based on local people's needs. We will establish new guidelines to prevent military violence against women that are quite separate from existing official agreements.

In addition we demand the following:
- that the Status of Forces Agreements between the United States and the governments of Japan and South Korea be significantly revised to protect the human rights of women and children, and to include firm environmental guidelines for the clean-up of toxic contamination to restore our land and water and to protect the health of our communities;
- that the U.S. government cease circumventing constitutional provisions and national laws in imposing their continued military access or presence;
- that our governments pursue sincere efforts to support the democratization and reunification of Korea;
- that our governments take full responsibility for violence against women perpetrated by U.S. military personnel;
- that all military "R and R," which has meant widespread sexual abuse and exploitation of local women and children, be banned;
- that all military personnel receive training aimed at preventing the sexual exploitation, harassment, and abuse of women and children who live and work around bases;
- that our governments provide substantial funding for the health care, education, training, and self-reliance of women who service GIs, and their children, including Amerasian children;
- that the U.S. government and the governments of Japan, South Korea, and the Philippines take full financial responsibility for Amerasian children, and that the U.S. government introduce immigration law that provides for all Amerasians in these three countries;
- that all U.S. bases, weapons, and military personnel be removed from Japan and South Korea;
- that our governments take full financial responsibility for environmental clean-up of U.S. military bases in a way that meets local people's needs;
- that our governments and public agencies recognize the central importance of women's issues in all base conversion projects and include women in all levels of base-conversion decision-making;
- that the money currently spent on the U.S. military by taxpayers in the U.S., Japan, and Korea be devoted to socially useful programs that benefit women and children;
- that the lands currently in U.S. military use be developed to benefit local people rather than investors and transnational corporations as has happened at the former Subic Bay Naval Base and Clark Air Base in the Philippines;

- that local, national, and international media investigate and report the issues and concerns referred to here, and educate people on the effects of the U.S. military presence in our countries.

We have committed ourselves to establishing an international network to hold our governments accountable on these issues, and to build a broad base of support to create a secure and sustainable world for future generations.

Notes

1 "Vision and Mission." International Women's Network Against Militarism, accessed May 8, 2015, www.iwnam.org.

2 Gwyn Kirk and Margo Okazawa-Rey, "Making Connections: Building an East Asia–U.S. Women's Network against U.S. Militarism," in *The Women and War Reader*, ed. Lois Ann Lorentzen and Jennifer Turpin (New York: NYU Press, 1998), pp. 308–22.

3 Ibid.

4 Ibid.

5 Gwyn Kirk and Carolyn Bowen Francis, "Redefining Security: Women Challenge U.S. Military Policy and Practice in East Asia." *Berkeley Women's Law Journal* 15 (2000): 230.

6 Ibid., p. 262.

7 Rachel Cornwell, "International Women's Planning Meeting Seeks Alternative to Militarism and a New Definition of Security." *OKINAWA: Peace. Human Rights. Women. Environment*, no. 6. Reprinted in *Voices from Japan* 3 (Oct. 1997): 82–83. Asia-Japan Women's Resource Center, www.ajwrc.org.

8 Kirk and Okazawa-Rey.

80

Priorities for Action *and* Conclusions
Changing Borders Conference
Disabled Women on the Web
Oakland, California
June 3, 1998

Disabled Women on the Web logo. Image from the Disability Social History Project.

It's not very often that we are able to be in a room with people who are so similar to ourselves. I love being around people where I don't have to prove anything. I can just be at home, and it's so wonderful. And of course, if I said anything stupid like, "what's the use, I'm going to kill myself," or whatever, I think I'd have the whole room here descending on me and saying, "no, no, don't you do that."
—Cheryl Green, Keynote Speaker[1]

Disabled Women on the Web is a branch of the Disabled Women's Alliance, and it is mainly a resource guide for disabled women and others who support the disabled rights movement. The website supports a wide variety of resources, including categories like Advocacy & Activism, Art & Culture, Disability Studies, Disabled Women of Color, Economics & Employment, Education, Feminism, Health, Lesbians & Queers with Disabilities, Mothers with Disabilities, Sexuality, Violence, and Young Women with Disabilities. The website provides the ability for women to establish networks and makes available outlines for high school curricula and conference information.[2]

The organization held conferences in 1998, 1999, and 2002, helping bring disabled women together to form networks and gain access to resources and community. Laura Hershey, Corbett O'Toole, and Tanis Doe organized the first conference, in 1998. Over 120 women with a wide variety of disabilities attended the conference, and many had never been to an event for disabled women before. The organizers reported that their objectives were met at the conference: "The experienced women and 'new' women were able to meet each other, discuss both successes and struggles, and come up with concrete steps for action to address their personal and professional goals. Changing Borders helped women to collectively and personally set their objectives beyond the artificial lines."

This great success was repeated with modifications the next year and in 2002, and all three conferences were completely planned and organized online—one of the first times the Internet had been used to this extent by a grassroots group of women. This planning especially included making the conference accessible for all women; the organizers recruited women of many different racial and ethnic backgrounds as well as women with a wide range of physical and developmental disabilities. They attempted to organize the day in ways that would enable women to take breaks, transition easily, and have enough stamina to engage in all the activities of the conferences.

The Priorities for Action[3] illustrate continuity with many other women's groups included in this collection. The foremost of these was the need for increased self-esteem; as noted in the quotation above, many women with disabilities struggle with self-worth, something women have discussed since the earliest declarations. This issue is different because compounded for women with disabilities, and Changing Borders attempts specifically to address disabled women's need for more resources to prevent self-loathing and suicide. Changing Borders was also concerned with disabled women's need to be trained for work and to have a network of mentors available to them, something women have identified and demanded since the earliest labor declarations, which often mention though do not center the differently abled.

The Conclusions[4] reached by the Changing Borders conference create a specific plan to reach the organization's goals. The group plans here to continue expanding its network and make its resources more widely available to all women, including those who have trouble reading. The Conclusions also focus on making the network function on a regional and community level as well as the national level. These goals seem to have been met, at least in part, by the next two conferences held by the organization.

Priorities for Action

Women participating in the event had a diversity of experiences. Despite the range of needs and interests, several common themes emerged as urgent areas to be addressed. These themes can best be understood as areas which need attention for all women with disabilities but for which the form of intervention may be very different depending on the type of disability or experience levels. Information about all of these issues, or services designed to address them, desperately needs to be available and accessible to women with disabilities.

Self-Esteem and Personal Development

From the keynote presentations to the individual comments on evaluations, there was a consensus that women with disabilities need support to develop positive self-esteem. That girls and adult women with disabilities need to be told that they are valued, need to see images of themselves in the media and in schools, and that they need to be able to improve their skills. Feeling better about who we are as women with disabilities is central to empowerment and independent living as well as accessing services.

Violence and Suicide Prevention

Abuse of many types is a serious threat to the well-being of women with disabilities. Sexual abuse, physical abuse, psychological and financial abuse, by caregivers, family members and professionals is a major problem leading to mental health problems and for some women, suicide. Suicide issues for girls and women with disabilities need to be addressed nationwide—particularly where phone lines and crisis intervention are not currently accessible or do not accommodate people with disabilities. Shelters for battered women, respite programs and violence prevention programs should also all be accessible.

Training Opportunities

Women with disabilities also identified the need for improved and increased training for a range of skills. Women wanted the skills to participate in the workforce, in their communities and in the arts. Many of the women wanted computer and internet training that suited their needs and their disabilities. Other women were interested in self-employment but needed training on how to manage a small business, how to apply for loans and how to make the transition to the workplace. Many of the women had exciting and creative ideas for marketing their products or services but limited knowledge about how to proceed. Other women wanted training around self-defense, interpersonal communication, parenting or family relationships. When providing training to women with disabilities it is important that instructional methods take into account various types of disabilities, including learning disabilities. Accessible, appropriate training is needed and information should be disseminated about programs which are currently available.

Peer Support and Mentoring

Women with disabilities need to have contact with other women with disabilities who share experiences and issues. To put women together in a society which isolates us can be difficult. Women who are "voiceless," underserved and marginalized are a particular priority. A focused effort is needed to ensure that women and girls are able to be part of peer support and mentoring programs suited to their needs. These may be at independent living centers, women's centers, through college campuses or connected to specific issues, ethnic identities or disability types. Reducing isolation can reduce problems with self-esteem, mental health difficulties, employment problems and improve overall well-being. Mentoring can also help disseminate information and skills among the community which increases access to the available resources.

Conclusions

1. The conference met the goal of connecting women to each other and having women meet others who shared interests. The objective of providing training was not completely met and should be taken up as a priority for the next event. Resource materials were widely appreciated, but need to be made more accessible and available for women who do not read well. This is a challenge for any dissemination effort.

2. Low self-esteem is a particularly difficult barrier for women with disabilities. For women to be able to look for work, sell their own products, maintain healthy relationships, be mothers, or be active in their communities they need to feel safe, strong and educated. Priority should be placed on eliminating violence, supporting women's personal development and providing access to further vocational training, employment, peer support and independent living services.

3. Women have a range of skills and needs, not all of which can be met in one conference. It would be wise to hold a "first timers" event with ample direction and support as well as a "veterans" event for those more experienced. There should, of course, be a chance for the new and more experienced women to interact. However, their needs are different and could be best met by targeting training accordingly.

4. Longer sessions, and perhaps a two day event, will provide more time for discussion, training and networking. This must also include the breaks between the events and time for transition, resting and networking as many women have disabilities which affect their stamina.

5. Outreach is needed to ensure that women who are "voiceless" are included as well as outreach to women who are not part of the internet and current organizations for women, or for people with disabilities.

6. Local and regional trainings are needed, not just national events. Some women need to have regular access to information at their home community level rather than general information at the national level. In addition women need time to meet with women who share the same disability or same personal situation in addition to having cross-disability and cross-issue workshops.

7. Databases and information sources for women need to be accessible so that skills development, independent living and economic self-sufficiency goals can be pursued. A national or coordinated effort is needed to ensure that women have easy access to essential information.

Notes

1 Changing Borders Conference Proceedings, June 3, 1998. Disabled Women on the Web website, Disability Social History Project, www.disabilityhistory.org.

2 Disabled Women on the Web, Disability Social History Project, accessed April 15, 2017, www.disabilityhistory.org.

3 "Priorities for Action" from Changing Borders: First Conference of Disabled Women on the Web, Oakland, California, June 3, 1998.

4 "Conclusions" from Changing Borders: First Conference of Disabled Women on the Web, Oakland, California, June 3, 1998.

Part VI

The Twenty-First Century

81

Declaration of the Essential Rights of Afghan Women
Dushanbe Conference on Afghan Women
Roqia Center for Women's Rights, Studies and Education in Afghanistan
Dushanbe, Tajikistan
June 28, 2000

Preceding this conference, the Taliban militias, "by force and edict," officially revoked the rights of Afghan women to work, to freedom of movement, to health, and to education. By contrast, in the Declaration below, "[A]ll the twelve million women of Afghanistan are equally included regardless of their social and political affiliations; they not only have these rights but also own them for themselves," and are legitimate Afghans "without regards to language, race, ethnicity, locality, religion, sect or historical background."[1]

Embedded in a human rights framework, this document both brings attention to the "profound distress" experienced by individual women and links the status of women to the well-being of the nation, claiming that the "torture and inhumane and degrading treatment imposed by the Taliban on women . . . have put Afghan society in danger." The signatories believe that the dangers and violence endured by women and their children are the consequence of "discrimination on the basis of gender, race, religion, ethnicity and language." The Declaration[2] offers a list of rights seen as essential to a life of dignity that is, again, linked to the most basic conditions argued for in this collection's earliest documents, including the rights "to freedom of thought, speech, assembly and political participation."

The status quo to which this document objects includes the following:

- The barbaric acts and massive attacks on fundamental rights committed against the women of Afghanistan by the Taliban regime.
- The suppression of freedom to move about, to work and to access healthcare.
- The attacks on woman's dignity and invasion of private and family life, attacks that cause irreparable physical and mental damage and are international crimes against humanity.
- The cynical pretense of the Taliban regime that claims to subscribe to the international laws protecting the rights of women and men.
- The international drug traffic by the Taliban representing 80% of the world production of heroin.
- The fact that the zones controlled by the Taliban have become an epicenter generating international terrorism which has become a threat to democracies.
- Pakistan's active alliance in providing logistics and arms support to the Taliban.
- The "neutrality" of the international communities and organizations, and world states, which in effect constitutes complicity with the criminal acts of the Taliban.[3]

A mere year after this Declaration, the Roqia Center claimed to "have witnessed a drastic deterioration of the plight of Afghan women inside Afghanistan (and in the refugee camps)" that

is tearing asunder the very life structure of Afghanistan. There is no doubt that the Taliban militias and their terror friends' policy of making Afghan women outlawed non-citizens is one of the major causes of the unraveling of Afghanistan that is being reported (and witnessed) today. Within five short years, the effect of this total cancellation of rights, a first in the history of the world, has snowballed into a multidimensional disaster unlike anything the world has experienced. The social fabric of Afghan life, so dependent on its women before, is falling apart. The children who five years ago were six years old are now teenagers with no education who do not know what a book is. The traditional economy, so dependent on the women workforce, has practically died out. The ability of the community to fend for itself, where before women held alive the networks of relationships, is at its lowest ebb.[4]

In response to this oppression, on June 28, 2000, three hundred Afghan women from all segments of the Afghan nation (including many Afghan women's organizations) assembled in Dushanbe, Tajikistan, to draft and promulgate the Declaration of the Essential Rights of Afghan Women. No political groups (which in the current situation are tantamount to political parties) had a role in it. The Dushanbe conference was organized at the initiative of NEGAR—Support of Women of Afghanistan, an international organization established in 1996 by Afghan women to defend their rights. The members are Afghan women and non–Afghan women supporters.

The Roqia Center for Women's Rights, Studies and Education in Afghanistan, and its sister organization in the United States, Kabultec, has held conferences, offered workshops for female political candidates, conducted seminars for the female candidates to the Parliament and Provincial Councils of fourteen provinces, published "Women in the Koran," and offers a literacy program to boys and girls as well as to couples.

On June 7, 8, and 9, 2002, NEGAR organized in Kabul its Second Conference of Afghan Women. Approximately one thousand Afghan women and forty non-Afghan women from four continents attended.

Declaration of the Essential Rights of Afghan Women

SECTION I
Considering that the Universal Declaration of Human Rights, as well as the international statements addressing the rights of women listed in Section II of this document, are systematically trampled in Afghanistan today.

Considering that all the rules imposed by the Taliban concerning women are in total opposition to the international conventions cited in Section II of this document.

Considering that torture and inhumane and degrading treatment imposed by the Taliban on women, as active members of society, have put Afghan society in danger.

Considering that the daily violence directed against the women of Afghanistan causes, for each one of them, a state of profound distress.

Considering that, under conditions devoid of their rights, women find themselves and their children in a situation of permanent danger.

Considering that discrimination on the basis of gender, race, religion, ethnicity and language is the source of insults, beatings, stoning and other forms of violence.

Considering that poverty and the lack of freedom of movement pushes women into prostitution, involuntary exile, forced marriages, and the selling and trafficking of their daughters.

Considering the severe and tragic conditions of more than twenty years of war in Afghanistan.

SECTION II
The Declaration which follows is derived from the following documents:
- United Nations Charter.
- Universal Declaration of Human Rights.
- International Covenant on Economic, Social and Cultural Rights.
- International Covenant on Civil and Political Rights.
- Convention on the Rights of the Child.
- Convention on the Elimination of All Forms of Discrimination Against Women.
- Declaration on the Elimination of Violence Against Women.
- The Human Rights of Women.
- The Beijing Declaration.
- The Afghan Constitution of 1964.
- The Afghan Constitution of 1977.

SECTION III
The fundamental right of Afghan women, as for all human beings, is life with dignity, which includes the following rights:

1. The right to equality between men and women and the right to the elimination of all forms of discrimination and segregation, based on gender, race or religion.
2. The right to personal safety and to freedom from torture or inhumane or degrading treatment.
3. The right to physical and mental health for women and their children.
4. The right to equal protection under the law.
5. The right to institutional education in all the intellectual and physical disciplines.
6. The right to just and favorable conditions of work.
7. The right to move about freely and independently.
8. The right to freedom of thought, speech, assembly and political participation.
9. The right to wear or not to wear the chadari (burqa) or the scarf.
10. The right to participate in cultural activities including theatre, music and sports.

SECTION IV
This Declaration developed by Afghan women is a statement, affirmation and emphasis of those essential rights that we Afghan women own for ourselves and for all other Afghan women. It is a document that the State of Afghanistan must respect and implement.

Notes
1 Nasrine Gross, "The Declaration of the Essential Rights of Afghan Women and the Legitimacy of Afghanistan," Nov. 27, 2000. *Kabultec* blog, www.kabultec.org.

2 "Declaration of the Essential Rights of Afghan Women," Dushanbe, Tajikistan, June 28, 2000. Roqia Center, Kabultec, www.kabultec.org.

3 "Call to Action," June 28, 2000. *Kabultec* blog, www.kabultec.org.

4 Nasrine Gross, "On the Occasion of the First Anniversary of the Declaration of the Essential Rights of Afghan Women," June 28, 2001. *Kabultec* blog, www.kabultec.org.

82

Gender Violence and the Prison Industrial Complex
INCITE! Women, Gender Non-Conforming, and Trans People of Color*
Against Violence
Burbank, California
2001

INCITE! logo.

It is critical that we develop responses to gender violence that do not depend on a sexist, racist, classist, and homophobic criminal justice system.

"INCITE! is a nation-wide network of radical feminists of color working to end violence against women, gender non-conforming, and trans people of color, and our communities. We support each other through direct action, critical dialogue, and grassroots organizing."[1] The group began in 2000 with what was supposed to be a small conference devoted to understanding and addressing violence against women of color, but which two thousand ended up attending (and an equal number had to be turned away). From the start the group understood its charge broadly, "including attacks on immigrants' rights and Indigenous treaty rights, the proliferation of prisons, militarism, attacks on the reproductive rights of women of color, medical experimentation on communities of color, homophobia/heterosexism, hate crimes against queer women of color, economic neo-colonialism, institutional racism, and more."[2] Analysis of colonization and white supremacy is central to their feminism, and they have made greater commitment to those who are gender nonconforming. They address multiple forms of violence and, because they see the state as an organizer of violence, discourage state funding of their work. In their "Principles of Unity,"[3] they seek to link liberation struggles and build coalitions as they develop creative models of organizing and action.

In the document below, INCITE! strives to connect state, international, and interpersonal violence in a number of ways, and to address them outside the criminal justice system they condemn for a variety of reasons. They assert that the movement confronting domestic violence, and the antiprison/anti–police brutality movements both marginalize women of color, and respond by centering precisely those women left out, as well as other ignored groups. They advocate community-based solutions to violence. What follows is a call to more inclusive, more effective action by those already working against interpersonal violence, against mass incarceration, and against police abuse—those working *for* violence-free lives.

Gender Violence and the Prison Industrial Complex

We call social justice movements to develop strategies and analysis that address both state AND interpersonal violence, particularly violence against women. Currently, activists/movements that address state violence (such as anti-prison, anti–police brutality groups) often work in isolation from activists/movements that address domestic and sexual violence. The result is that women of color, who suffer disproportionately from both state and interpersonal violence, have become marginalized within these movements. It is critical that we develop responses to gender violence that do not depend on a sexist, racist, classist, and homophobic criminal justice system. It is also important that we develop strategies that challenge the criminal justice system and that also provide safety for survivors of sexual and domestic violence. To live violence-free lives, we must develop holistic strategies for addressing violence that speak to the intersection of all forms of oppression.

The anti-violence movement has been critically important in breaking the silence around violence against women and providing much-needed services to survivors. However, the mainstream anti-violence movement has increasingly relied on the criminal justice system as the front-line approach toward ending violence against women of color. It is important to assess the impact of this strategy.

1. Law enforcement approaches to violence against women MAY deter some acts of violence in the short term. However, as an overall strategy for ending violence, criminalization has not worked. In fact, [. . .] mandatory arrest laws for domestic violence have led to decreases in the number of battered women who kill their partners in self-defense, but they have not led to a decrease in the number of batterers who kill their partners. Thus, the law protects batterers more than it protects survivors.

2. The criminalization approach has also brought many women into conflict with the law, particularly women of color, poor women, lesbians, sex workers, immigrant women, women with disabilities, and other marginalized women. For instance, under mandatory arrest laws, there have been numerous incidents where police officers called to domestic incidents have arrested the woman who is being battered. Many undocumented women have reported cases of sexual and domestic violence, only to find themselves deported. A tough law and order agenda also leads to long punitive sentences for women convicted of killing their batterers. Finally, when public funding is channeled into policing and prisons, budget cuts for social programs, including women's shelters, welfare and public housing are the inevitable side effect. These cutbacks leave women less able to escape violent relationships.

3. Prisons don't work. Despite an exponential increase in the number of men in prisons, women are not any safer, and the rates of sexual assault and domestic violence have not decreased. In calling for greater police responses to and harsher sentences for perpetrators of gender violence, the anti-violence

movement has fueled the proliferation of prisons which now lock up more people per capita in the U.S. than any other country. During the past fifteen years, the numbers of women, especially women of color in prison has skyrocketed. Prisons also inflict violence on the growing numbers of women behind bars. Slashing, suicide, the proliferation of HIV, strip searches, medical neglect and rape of prisoners has largely been ignored by anti-violence activists. The criminal justice system, an institution of violence, domination, and control, has increased the level of violence in society.

4. The reliance on state funding to support anti-violence programs has increased the professionalization of the anti-violence movement and alienated it from its community-organizing, social justice roots. Such reliance has isolated the anti-violence movement from other social justice movements that seek to eradicate state violence, such that it acts in conflict rather than in collaboration with these movements.

5. The reliance on the criminal justice system has taken power away from women's ability to organize collectively to stop violence and has invested this power within the state. The result is that women who seek redress in the criminal justice system feel disempowered and alienated. It has also promoted an individualistic approach toward ending violence such that the only way people think they can intervene in stopping violence is to call the police. This reliance has shifted our focus from developing ways communities can collectively respond to violence.

In recent years, the mainstream anti-prison movement has called important attention to the negative impact of criminalization and the build-up of the prison industrial complex. Because activists who seek to reverse the tide of mass incarceration and criminalization of poor communities and communities of color have not always centered gender and sexuality in their analysis or organizing, we have not always responded adequately to the needs of survivors of domestic and sexual violence.

1. Prison and police accountability activists have generally organized around and conceptualized men of color as the primary victims of state violence. Women prisoners and victims of police brutality have been made invisible by a focus on the war on our brothers and sons. It has failed to consider how women are affected as severely by state violence as men. The plight of women who are raped by INS officers or prison guards, for instance, has not received sufficient attention. In addition, women carry the burden of caring for extended family when family and community members are criminalized and warehoused. Several organizations have been established to advocate for women prisoners; however, these groups have been frequently marginalized within the mainstream anti-prison movement.

2. The anti-prison movement has not addressed strategies for addressing the rampant forms of violence women face in their everyday lives, including street harassment, sexual harassment at work, rape, and intimate partner abuse. Until these strategies are developed, many women will feel shortchanged by the movement. In addition, by not seeking alliances with the anti-violence movement, the anti-prison movement has sent the message that it is possible to liberate communities without seeking the well-being and safety of women.

3. The anti-prison movement has failed to sufficiently organize around the forms of state violence faced by LGBTI communities. LGBTI street youth

and trans people in general are particularly vulnerable to police brutality and criminalization. LGBTI prisoners are denied basic human rights such as family visits from same sex partners, and same sex consensual relationships in prison are policed and punished.

4. While prison abolitionists have correctly pointed out that rapists and serial murderers comprise a small number of the prison population, we have not answered the question of how these cases should be addressed. The inability to answer the question is interpreted by many anti-violence activists as a lack of concern for the safety of women.

5. The various alternatives to incarceration that have been developed by anti-prison activists have generally failed to provide sufficient mechanism[s] for safety and accountability for survivors of sexual and domestic violence. These alternatives often rely on a romanticized notion of communities, which have yet to demonstrate their commitment and ability to keep women and children safe or seriously address the sexism and homophobia that [are] deeply embedded within them.

We call on social justice movements concerned with ending violence in all its forms to:

1. Develop community-based responses to violence that do not rely on the criminal justice system AND which have mechanisms that ensure safety and accountability for survivors of sexual and domestic violence. Transformative practices emerging from local communities should be documented and disseminated to promote collective responses to violence.

2. Critically assess the impact of state funding on social justice organizations and develop alternative fundraising strategies to support these organizations. Develop collective fundraising and organizing strategies for anti-prison and anti-violence organizations. Develop strategies and analysis that specifically target state forms of sexual violence.

3. Make connections between interpersonal violence, the violence inflicted by domestic state institutions (such as prisons, detention centers, mental hospitals, and child protective services), and international violence (such as war, military base prostitution, and nuclear testing).

4. Develop an analysis and strategies to end violence that do not isolate individual acts of violence (either committed by the state or individuals) from their larger contexts. These strategies must address how entire communities of all genders are affected in multiple ways by both state violence and interpersonal gender violence. Battered women prisoners represent an intersection of state and interpersonal violence and as such provide an opportunity for both movements to build coalitions and joint struggles.

5. Put poor/working class women of color in the center of their analysis, organizing practices, and leadership development. Recognize the role of economic oppression, welfare "reform," and attacks on women workers' rights in increasing women's vulnerability to all forms of violence and locate anti-violence and anti-prison activism alongside efforts to transform the capitalist economic system.

6. Center stories of state violence committed against women of color in our organizing efforts.

7. Oppose legislative change that promotes prison expansion, criminalization of poor communities and communities of color and thus state violence

against women of color, even if these changes also incorporate measures to support victims of interpersonal gender violence.

8. Promote holistic political education at the everyday level within our communities, specifically how sexual violence helps reproduce the colonial, racist, capitalist, heterosexist, and patriarchal society we live in as well as how state violence produces interpersonal violence within communities.

9. Develop strategies for mobilizing against sexism and homophobia WITHIN our communities in order to keep women safe.

10. Challenge men of color and all men in social justice movements to take particular responsibility to address and organize around gender violence in their communities as a primary strategy for addressing violence and colonialism. We challenge men to address how their own histories of victimization have hindered their ability to establish gender justice in their communities.

11. Link struggles for personal transformation and healing with struggles for social justice.

We seek to build movements that not only end violence, but that create a society based on radical freedom, mutual accountability, and passionate reciprocity. In this society, safety and security will not be premised on violence or the threat of violence; it will be based on a collective commitment to guaranteeing the survival and care of all peoples.

Notes

1 "Who Is INCITE!" 2014. INCITE-National.Org, www.incite-national.org.
2 "History," 2014. INCITE-National.Org, www.incite-national.org.
3 "Principles of Unity," 2014. INCITE-National.Org, www.incite-national.org.

83

Resolutions to Member Organisations
First International Conference: Now Is the Time
Women's Ordination Worldwide
Dublin, Ireland
June 29–July 1, 2001

The oppression and poverty of women and girls around the world is reinforced when women and men are not seen as equally imaging God, and this inequality in leadership, governance and ministry is reflected in our Church.[1]

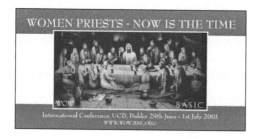

Graphic advertising the first international conference of the Women's Ordination Worldwide, showing women at the last supper.

Women's Ordination Worldwide (WOW) is a network of groups whose top priority is opening Roman Catholic ordained ministries to women. It was founded in 1996, at the First European Women's Synod in Gmunden, Austria. Participants at the 2001 conference numbered 350 and came from twenty-six countries.

The ban on women was introduced in medieval times in canon law and so is not, WOW argues, part of early church history or based on the teachings of Jesus. The exclusion was made more durable with a 1994 papal ban on the very discussion of women's ordination. Even more recently, "[I]n 2010, the Vatican added 'the attempted ordination of a woman' right alongside priest paedophelia to its list of most serious crimes against Church law ('*delicta graviora*')."[2] Today WOW calls the barring of women from the Catholic ministry a sin of sexism that has divided the Church and is inconsistent with the Church's general denunciation of discrimination and regard for individual conscience. Challenging the idea that this matter is "only" about women priests or a familiar division between traditionalists and progressives, Jamie Manson writes, "At its heart, it is a movement to convince one of the largest and most influential religious organizations in the world to lift up women globally as truly equal to men."[3]

According to its website,[4] WOW aims to

- Coordinate the women's ordination movement worldwide
- Bring together organisations working for women's ordination in all Christian churches
- Host regular international conferences to raise awareness about women's ordination in the Roman Catholic Church
- Support women's equality in religions
- Free the Church from the sin of sexism and heal divisions that exist because of it
- Foster awareness and development of women's vocations to renewed ordained ministry

To accomplish its goals, WOW uses such tools as media campaigns, vigils, and women's liturgies. Despite the group's commitment to dialogue, it is difficult to communicate on the subject of women's ordination with an all-male, celibate, and clerical hierarchy still committed to the official silencing of such conversation. Consequently, some women have chosen illegal ordination in the Roman Catholic WomenPriests movement, for which they face excommunication, or have been ordained in independent Catholic churches. Men in the Church have also been punished for speaking out in support of women's ordination.

WOW includes organizations in Australia, Bangladesh, Canada, France, Germany, Great Britain, Ireland, Japan, Malta, Poland, Western Europe, and the United States. Representatives from all member groups form WOW's Steering Committee. Since this first international conference,[5] which was sponsored by the Irish group Brothers and Sisters in Christ, two others have been held, in Ottawa and Philadelphia. Archives of the conferences are available on WOW's website.

Resolutions

Preamble

All of us, people of God, have gathered from twenty-six countries and six continents for the inaugural WOW ecumenical conference in Dublin, June 29–July 1,

2001. As followers of Christ we answer the call to radical discipleship and seek justice so that all may participate in the sacrament of Orders. Conference members wholeheartedly celebrate the freedom of speech and the primacy of conscience proclaimed by the teachings of Vatican II. We consider any obstruction of these to constitute a violation of human rights and an obstacle to the Holy Spirit in guiding the churches into the fullness of truth.

Conference participants hold that vocations are not restricted by gender, race, marital status, sexuality, educational background or life opportunities.

Resolutions

1. That this conference calls on the Pope to revoke the ban on the discussion of women's ordination.

2. That this conference calls on each member organisation of WOW to pursue dialogue with local bishops, religious, priests and laity on the subject of women's ordination in the context of retrieving the discipleship of integrity.

3. That this conference calls on the leaders of the Roman Catholic Church to restore the diaconate to women as was the practice in the early church.

4. That this conference encourages women who feel called, to study for the diaconate and the priesthood and resolves to support the establishment of suitable training courses where they are not available to women at present.

5. That this conference resolves to promote the cause of women's ordination by drawing constant public attention to the issue, through regular demonstrations by each member organisation, by an annual world day of prayer for women's ordination on the 25th [of] March and by a world conference within three to five years.

6. That this conference calls on ministers in all the churches to adapt the language used in liturgy to reflect the equal dignity of all God's people. Images of God need to reflect both the female and the male.

7. That this conference salutes Ludmila Javorova, our sister priest, and the women deacons ordained by courageous bishops in the underground Roman Catholic Church in Czechoslovakia and asks that the Vatican join us in recognising the validity of their orders.

8. That this conference proposes that WOW through its member groups create avenues for the financial support of those who lose their position as a result of their stand on the ordination of women.

9. That this conference calls on WOW through its member groups to encourage those women and men who have been punished for their support of women's ordination to tell their story publicly and expose the Vatican's actions.

10. That this conference proposes the setting up of a rapid response email system by WOW in order to support the networking of women's ordination groups.

11. That this conference proposes that the purple stole/ribbon be adopted as the international symbol for women's ordination.

Notes

1. "Pope Francis Confirms He Has a Blind Spot Regarding Women Priests," press release, November 3, 2016. Women's Ordination Worldwide website, www.womensordinationworldwide.org.

2. "Herstory." Women's Ordination Worldwide website, accessed 2016, www.womensordinationworldwide.org.

3. Jamie Manson, "The Women's Ordination Movement Is about Much More Than Priests." *National Catholic Reporter*, May 22, 2014, www.ncronline.org.

4 "Aims and Mission." Women's Ordination Worldwide website, accessed 2016, www.womens
   ordinationworldwide.org.

5 "Resolutions, WOW Dublin International Conference, 2001," July 1, 2001. Women's
   Ordination Worldwide website, www.womensordinationworldwide.org.

84

Women's Manifesto
Housewives' Trade Union (SAC)
Santa Fe, Argentina
January 17, 2002

SACRA/Housewives' Trade Union emblem.

We women are already building a better present and a better future! We want a different life for ourselves and our families where the priorities are: the welfare of the people rather than the pockets of the usual capitalists, the dignity of the people and social justice rather than charity given for political advantage, accountability rather than corruption. We know that this is possible.

According to the UN, women do 2/3 of the world's work: from breastfeeding and raising children to caring for those who are sick, older or disabled, to growing, preparing and cooking the food that feeds families, communities and continents, . . . to volunteer work and to work in the informal economy as cleaners, seamstresses, street sellers, sex workers, as well as work in the formal economy. Here again women's work is often caring for people, in hospitals and schools, as domestic workers, childminders, personal assistants . . . or in sweatshops—jobs where men who do comparable work also get low pay. But women get the lowest, and often face sexual and racial harassment. Although in every country all this work is basic to the welfare and even survival of humanity, it is devalued and ignored by the Market, and women get only 5% of the world's assets in return.[1]

The Sindicato de Amas de Casa de Santa Fe (Housewives' Trade Union, or SAC) is Argentina's largest working-class women's organization, bridging feminist and labor issues. It insisted on calling itself a union rather than an association: "For SACRA, trade union status was crucial, not only to enable it to carry out functions normally associated with Argentine trade unions, such as the administration of an *obra* social, but also to obtain social recognition of the value of housework, which would enable women to take their place as workers alongside men in the union movement."[2] The Housewives' Trade Union tackles the poverty pervasive among Argentine families and communities, and works for the recognition of women's contributions to the welfare of families and neighborhoods. SAC was formed in 1983, when hopes were high for a transition from military dictatorship to democratic government. It is autonomous, grassroots, and independent, not aligned with any political party. It has fought for the rights of housewives to healthcare, wages, and pensions.

As the introductory note to the Manifesto reveals, this document was written during a time of economic collapse. Four presidents were brought down in rapid succession. There were demonstrations against political parties in general, as well as against politically aligned trade unions and NGOs, and disdain for the concern shown to capital (especially foreign) versus citizens' needs. SAC held regular women's neighborhood assemblies to circulate and discuss their Manifesto, and used "*cacerolazos*," a pots-and-pans noise-making protest symbolizing domestic life and the need to be heard. As a tool of resistance, *cacerolazos* allow for spontaneous protest outside one's front door.

The Manifesto[3] uses the refrain "we are the women" throughout the first half, leading one commentator, Krista Lynes, to read the manifesto itself as a *cacerolazo*.

> In this powerful refrain (which takes up the first half of the manifesto), the repetitions of "we are the women" clamour for social and economic justice, clamour across differential social positions, weaving through the contexts of labour rights, education, health care, domestic violence, racism, sexism, homophobia, exploitation, migration, and scarcity. The feminist language is itself a *cacerolazo*, a persistent beat tied to the very heart of the personal as political, by way of the very publicity of the private sphere. The *cacerolazo* is thus a special drumbeat—a beat that announces through the mundane materiality of kitchen tools the publicity of the private in the face of the privatization of the public sphere.[4]

"We are the women" appeals to commonalities across difference. This document's tone is reminiscent of the 1954 South African Charter. The authors mourn the fates of their children, of the elderly, the involuntarily migratory, the farmers losing their land, and those enduring gender- and race-based violence. "We are each and every woman in Santa Fe, Argentina, Latin America . . ." The document challenges the misuse of social and economic resources, and urges a reassessment of care work. Like other manifestos, it recalls and builds on an often-unacknowledged history of activism by women, "from the Indigenous and slave

In December 2001, just before the SAC drafted this document, Argentina saw widespread protests in response to an economic recession. One of these protests is pictured here.

rebellions at the time of the Conquest, to the movement of the mothers during the dictatorship, to today's '*cacerolazo*.'"

The government since 2004 has made self-employed workers, including homemakers, eligible for a minimum pension at retirement age, regardless of previous contributions to the system. When monies were made available for the unemployed in exchange for community work, SAC argued that women heads of household should receive them in recognition of the care work they already do in their homes and communities. In the midst of rampant distrust of government, SAC also wanted to be an auditor of the funds.

The Sindicato de Amas de Casa de Santa Fe coordinates the Global Women's Strike in Argentina and is part of the WinWages* international network.

Women's Manifesto

The people of Argentina have undergone severe economic and political shocks in the past few months. The government has frozen all bank accounts and people cannot withdraw their money. This is particularly severe in Argentina because people don't tend to use credit cards.

There have been popular protests in response. Two governments resigned because of the protests and Argentina had three presidents within one week. However, bank accounts are still frozen. In addition, the government has said that the money in the accounts, when people can withdraw it, will be available only in pesos, which are worth less than dollars, even though many people had saved the money in dollars.

In the face of the increasingly serious situation of our people, we feel we have the responsibility and also the renewed hope for our voices to be heard. Here is our proposal.

–Sindicato de Amas de Casa

Santa Fe, Argentina

January 17, 2002

We are the women who work outside of the home and get the lowest wages, and those who work only in the home and get no wages.

We are the women who have to send our daughters and sons to the soup kitchens because we have nothing to give them to eat, and those who still have something but don't know for how long.

We are the mothers whose children have had to leave school, and those whose children stayed in school but now are leaving the country because the education they got doesn't help them to get a job.

We are the women in the hospital queues early in the morning waiting to be seen, and the older people and the pensioners who may have social security but this has been bankrupted by successive governments.

We are the women who emigrated from the interior or from other Latin American countries because we had nothing to eat, and who ended up, more discriminated [against], in slums.

We are the teenagers who don't want to be mothers so young but are deprived of that choice.

We are the adult women who want a better present for ourselves and a better future for our daughters. And we are the older women discarded because of age who today have to support our grandchildren because their parents can't.

We are the women farmers who since childhood have worked the land that today is up for auction.

We are the women who have never had anything, and those who had life savings in the bank which today they want to steal from us.

We are the women who suffer violence inside and outside our homes.

We are the women discriminated against because of the color of our skin, because we are domestic workers, because we are sex workers, or because of our sexual preference. We are each and every woman in Santa Fe, Argentina, Latin America . . .

We women are already building a better present and a better future! We want a different life for ourselves and our families where the priorities are: the welfare of the people rather than the pockets of the usual capitalists, the dignity of the people and social justice rather than charity given for political advantage, accountability rather than corruption. We know that this is possible.

Therefore we demand that:
- *The money collected from oil export rights must not be used to save the banks, nor is the country to be further indebted to international creditors for that purpose.*
- *The banks, major supermarkets and privatised companies, must be made to pay employers' contributions, to be used to reactivate the country's economy.*
- *Taxes must be imposed not on essentials but on non-essential luxury goods.*

With these resources, and with what can be counted on from the suspension of the external debt:
- *An employment benefit must be introduced for unemployed heads of households, women and men.*
- *Women must be prioritized for benefits distributed through employment plans without doing community work as a condition for receiving them, so that mothers in the greatest poverty with five, six or more children, are not prevented from taking care of them.*
- *A wage must be paid for caring work since the care of people by women and girls is a priority activity which must be recognised and paid for.*
- *The social and productive value of housewives must be recognised through a pension.*
- *A benefit must be paid for each child, and to ensure it is spent on the children, it must be paid to the mother.*

We also demand that:
- *Small savers' deposits be refunded: these savings are often compensation for redundancy. Their loss has made the situation of those who have nothing to live on even more desperate.*

- *The auction of small farmers' land be suspended: they have become indebted through high-interest bank loans and the loss of value of their produce.*

To ensure accountability, it is essential that:
- *The Supreme Court of Justice, which has shielded the corrupt and violated the most elementary constitutional rights of the citizen, be put on trial.*
- *The families of the 35 people who were murdered in the events of 19th and 20th of December get justice.*
- *The employment plans be submitted to social audits by women in each neighborhood to prevent them from being used politically by those who negotiate with the needs of the poorest.*

We put forward these ideas for the consideration of all women and invite each of you to express your views, to discuss, dissent, propose, and not to allow others to decide for or against us any more. Let us meet in the neighborhoods, in the organizations to which we belong or with which we are active, to discuss alternatives and proposals, and circulate them, using all the means at our disposal: by post, media, telephones, word of mouth.

Although women have always been involved in the popular struggle, from the Indigenous and slave rebellions at the time of the Conquest, to the movement of the mothers during the dictatorship, to today's "cacerolazo," we have not been listened to and our demands have been postponed in the name of "more urgent" needs. Other women in Latin America and in the world are banging their pots not only in support of the Argentinian people but on their own behalf, because beyond national realities, we women have needs and demands which bring us together as sisters.

We will all together find the ways to build a country and a world which starts with people's needs rather than corporate greed. Let us defend with all the energy, intelligence and passion of which we women are capable, the dignity and the future that we deserve. Join this call and invite other women to join. Tell us what you are doing, proposing, how you are organizing.

Notes

1 "Calling All Women!!" *Poor Magazine*, July 18, 2004, www.poormagazine.org.
2 *Hidden Histories of Gender and the State in Latin America*, ed. Elizabeth Dore and Maxine Molyneux (Durham, NC: Duke University Press, 2000), p. 327.
3 Housewives' Trade Union, "Women's Manifesto," *Off Our Backs,* March/April 2002. Caring Labor: An Archive, caringlabor.wordpress.com.
4 Krista Geneviève Lynes, "Clamouring Out: Against the Privative Sphere." *Wi: Journal of Mobile Media Studies* 6.2 (2012), wi.mobilities.ca.

85

Workshop Commitments and Recommendations
Sierra Leone/West African Workshop on Women in Parliament
Freetown, Sierra Leone
February 5–7, 2002

The period after a conflict provides a unique opportunity to reform political institutions and processes in a way that will increase the opportunities for women to participate in decisionmaking. Much of the international peacebuilding effort to build sustainable and peaceful societies has focused on seizing this opportunity. Elections, for example, offer women the chance to translate the new roles they assumed out of necessity during conflict into formal political representation. However, elections also expose women to lingering discriminatory mindsets and cultural practices that are considerable barriers to their greater political participation.[1]

This document reveals just how much it takes to accomplish that seemingly single and straightforward goal of having women participate equally in politics, as voters, appointees, and candidates. From accessible registration centers to freedom from harassment, from political agendas that address gender equality to gender-enlightened media campaign coverage, the workshop recommendations reveal that one change implies others, so that no transformation can be successful if isolated. It may not be immediately apparent to some that obstacles to women's participation include domestic violence and unequal education, but such is the reality portrayed here. That complex approach to a single issue makes this document especially valuable.

"In 1989, UNICEF reported that on average a woman in Sierra Leone worked up to 16 hours a day and that the majority were surviving on just one meal per day. There was a [very high] maternal mortality rate . . . primarily from infections and malnutrition."[2] During the civil war (1991–2002), a time of rampant human rights abuses, women established the Sierra Leone Women's Movement for Peace. "At present, despite legislative changes that have increased women's legal protection, women continue to experience discriminatory practices. Their rights and position are largely contingent on customary law and the ethnic group to which they belong. In addition, secret (*bondo* or *sande*) societies to which most girls and women belong, serve to uphold and reinforce harmful practices such as female genital mutilation (FGM) and early marriage."[3]

The participants in the workshop were the Ministry of Social Welfare, Gender, and Children's Affairs; the Ministry of Development and Economic Planning Sierra Leone; the Commonwealth Secretariat; the Commonwealth Parliamentary Association; the National Democratic Institute; and the British Council, Sierra Leone. The document[4] includes commitments expressed by various parties regarding gender equity in politics that are excluded below.

Workshop Commitments and Recommendations

A VISION OF SIERRA LEONE WOMEN:

We, the women of Sierra Leone, look forward to the day when:

- 50% of holders of all public offices including parliament and candidates, are women.
- Every eligible woman is on the electoral roll.
- Every registered woman votes on polling day, making her own independent choice.
- Every woman can walk into a registration centre which is accessible and convenient for her, be it a market, clinic or school.
- Every woman who is pregnant, taking care of a baby or young child, is elderly or disabled, gets priority treatment when she registers or votes.
- Every woman candidate, campaigner or voter, is safe from sexual harassment or any form of violence, pressure or threats.
- Every woman MP knows that a political agenda without gender equality ignores half of the electorate.
- Every woman knows that if she decide[s] to stand as a candidate, she will not face opposition or stigma from family, friends and the community.
- Every woman candidate is sure that the media will report not on her view in the mirror, but on her views on the needs of the community.
- Every woman will have equal access to a good education, good health and employment opportunities and productive resources, and will be thus better equipped to take a leading role in politics.
- Every woman should be free from domestic violence and sexual abuse so that she can function with pride and confidence as a leader.
- Every woman will become so economically empowered and benefit from poverty reduction strategies that she will be in a stronger position to function as an independent political actor.

His Excellency, the President of Sierra Leone, Alhaji Dr. Ahmad Tejan Kabbah, in his opening address said: "We are committed to supporting and promoting all initiatives aimed at mainstreaming gender into national policies and programmes in line ministries, as defined by the National Policy on gender mainstreaming developed by the Ministry of Gender Affairs."

We have women Paramount Chiefs, Ministers, Deputy Ministers, a woman Deputy Speaker of Parliament, but only 10% women in parliament. The Commonwealth target for women in Parliament is at least 30%. The target of women in Sierra Leone is 50%. Greater participation of women in politics is imperative. The extent to which we succeed in achieving a smooth transition to a stable democracy will depend on whether we have gender equality in politics.

I urge every Sierra Leonean woman to register so she can be on the electoral roll and exercise her constitutional right to vote on polling day. We have also made it clear that women have an equal right to become candidates."

WORKSHOP RECOMMENDATIONS:

In order to meet international standards, the Sierra Leone Government must make provision for the following to ensure free and fair elections:

- The right of an individual to vote on a non-discriminatory basis in the forthcoming elections and beyond.

- The right of an individual to an effective, impartial and non-discriminatory procedure for registration of voters.
- The right of every eligible citizen to be registered as a voter, subject only to disqualification and in accordance with criteria established by law that are objectively verifiable and not subject to arbitrary decision.
- The right of an individual to have equal and easy access to a polling station in order to exercise her right to vote.
- The unrestricted right of the individual to vote in secret, and the right to respect the integrity of her choice.
- The right of the candidate to present herself as a candidate for election.
- The right to express political opinions without interference otherwise than permitted by law.
- The right to move freely within the country in order to campaign for election.
- The right to have access to the media in order to put forward political views.
- The right for women to campaign on an equal basis with men and political parties.

Notes

1 Tim Kellow, "Women, Elections, and Violence in West Africa: Assessing Women's Political Participation in Liberia and Sierra Leone," 2010, p. 5. *International Alert*, http://www.international-alert.org.
2 "Women in Sierra Leone." *Wikipedia*, accessed 2017, www.wikipedia.org
3 "Sierra Leone." Social Institutions & Gender Index, accessed 2017, www.genderindex.org.
4 Sierra Leone/West African Workshop on Women in Parliament, British Council Offices, Freetown, Sierra Leone, Feb. 5–7, 2002. National Democratic Institute, www.ndi.org.

86

International Women's Day Statement
Nicaraguan Autonomous Women's Movement
Anuncio, Nicaragua
March 8, 2002

[W]hat is good for democracy is good for women.

Fighting against patriarchal authoritarianism captures the Autonomous Women's Movement's (MAM) work in the home and in the state, as elsewhere. It is an autonomous organization, believing that it must determine its own issues and strategies independently from the influence of political parties. Many leaders of MAM were Sandinista militants in the 1980s (women made up approximately 30 percent of the revolutionary army),[1] and continue to fight both for women and for the nation. Because "the Nicaraguan Revolution focused on resolving women's practical interests, but left little room to advance women's strategic interests . . . the women's movement was the first social movement in Nicaragua to declare independence from the Frente Sandinista's control," which it did in 1992.[2] Other feminist groups in Nicaragua include the Asociación de Mujeres Nicaragüenses Luisa Amanda Espinoza and Red de Mujeres contra la Violencia (Women's Network Against Violence).

Movimiento Autónomo de Mujeres de Nicaragua

Nicaraguan Autonomous Women's Movement logo.

The Statement[3] begins by recalling the history of feminist activism in Nicaragua, which has encompassed fighting for suffrage and fighting against dictatorship. MAM describes itself in the document as "a plural and inclusive movement with proposals reflecting both the interests of the nation as a whole and the historic demands of . . . women." Its authors determinedly confront the "profound inequalities" in their society. The state is charged with two wrongs: failing to protect and promote women's rights, and "constructing a model of society that impoverishes and divides the Nicaraguan population and particularly discriminates against women." As detailed in several other documents, MAM lists the ways an oppressive state distinctly injures women. The list of wrongs is lengthy and wide-ranging. MAM sees equality as much more than the absence of legal discrimination, touching the very ways we organize communal living, especially for the most disenfranchised. MAM demands a secular state, equality of rights for all, transparency, inclusive political dialogue (including with the autonomous women's movement), a Women's Ministry, money for women's civil society organizations, and fiscal accountability. Like so many other groups, this one sees democracy as critical to equality, and vice versa. As Azahalea Solís, a member of MAM, recently said, "Women are always disproportionately affected by extreme political situations—repression, harassment, imprisonment—and to make it worse, they are also the forgotten ones (never the heroines). Women are demanding justice and we can't have it in a State that belongs to a single individual, where impunity prevails and the enjoyment of your rights depends on who you are."[4]

MAM has issued quite a few statements and manifestos, available on their website.

International Women's Day Statement

Over five decades have passed since the Nicaraguan autonomous women's movement started building to fight for political and social democracy without any form of exclusion.

It fell to us to fight for women's suffrage and our rights to education and paid work. We were part of the fight against the Somoza dictatorship and participated in the revolutionary transformations of Nicaraguan society. We then became critical of the Sandinista Front due to its lack of commitment and political will regarding respect for women's rights, and maintained a pro-active attitude and openness to dialogue during the only government in our country's history to have been headed by a woman. We have made progress in consolidating an autonomous social movement with its own identity and the capacity for self-convocation and self-representation. Ours is a plural and inclusive movement with proposals reflecting both the interests of the nation as a whole and the historic demands of the 51% of the population made up of women.

In drawing up an historical balance sheet of the Nicaraguan women's movement, we can state that we, as different women's organizations with a presence throughout the country, have contributed not only to shaping a new legal and institutional framework that transcends legalized discrimination against women, but also to developing multiple initiatives that nourish solidarity in the face of the progressive weakening of the state and of public policies on behalf of the most dispossessed sectors of the population. The model of society imposed by the state and other hegemonic groups from our society has generated profound inequalities. In the extreme case of women these are expressed, among other ways, by the increasing exploitation of paid and non-paid work; the increase in maternal mortality rates; the increased cruelty of the violence exercised by men against women; the growing impoverishment of women, who in a great number of cases are the only ones responsible for sustaining themselves and their families; and the exclusion of women from decision-making processes at all levels.

Among the concrete facts this situation generates are that the female-headed households in a situation of extreme poverty are the majority; that women with access to land have a smaller area, less credit and fewer possibilities of receiving training; that we occupy inferior posts in the teaching hierarchy; that one in every five women suffers violence; that there is evident deterioration in women's health throughout their life cycle; and that there is limited female representation among the highest governmental leadership posts.

Despite the efforts of the autonomous women's movement both nationally and internationally, we have not succeeded in getting the Nicaraguan state to embrace a comprehensive and long-term vision aimed at overcoming the structural causes of the subordination and discrimination suffered by women, albeit on different levels.

The Nicaraguan state has neither the public policies nor expeditious mechanisms to promote and protect women's rights, both the universal rights we share with all of the citizenry and those aimed at transcending the subordination and discrimination we suffer as a result of our sex. On the contrary, it has been marked by its failure to honor them and, more recently, for allying with backward-looking forces to roll back the potential successes represented by international agreements.

The Nicaraguan state has consistently lacked the political will to use its legitimate forms of representation to be accountable to women for the role it has played in constructing a model of society that impoverishes and divides the Nicaraguan population and particularly discriminates against women.

On International Women's Day, aware that what is good for democracy is good for women, the autonomous women's movement reiterates its historic political proposals to the state and to Nicaraguan society through the following demands:

First: The observation of strict respect for the constitutional precept of the state's lay nature and thus abstention from any religious bias in public policy formulation. Said policies should not be influenced by the religious conceptions of public officials.

Second: The establishment of political and institutional foundations that favor the construction of a state aimed at guaranteeing the full exercise and enjoyment of the rights of all citizens, excluding no one.

Third: The urgency of honestly and transparently reexamining the changes needed to substantially transform the current system of state organization, which is based on a privileged and corrupt sharing that gives important quotas of power to the top party leaders and allows impunity.

Fourth: The creation, regulation and provision of feedback to arenas of political dialogue with the different sectors of civil society, including the legitimate participation of the autonomous women's movement.

Fifth: The attainment of coherence between the different international agreements signed by the Nicaraguan state and national legislation. In this sense, we reiterate our demand that the Action Program of the International Conference on Population and Development and the Action Platform of the Fourth World Women's Conference, respectively signed by the Nicaraguan government in 1994 and 1995, be taken up.

Sixth: The signing of the Facultative Protocol of the Convention on the Elimination of All Forms of Discrimination against Women and of the International Criminal Court, providing the means to protect women's rights in the exercise of human rights and in the context of armed conflicts.

Seventh: The modernization, expansion and strengthening of the current institutional mechanisms to promote and protect women's rights. We reiterate our demand for the creation of a Women's Ministry or the assigning of the Nicaraguan Women's Institute to the Presidency of the Republic. We also demand the strengthening of the Special Office of Ombudsperson for Women.

Eighth: The establishment by the National Assembly commissions of clear mechanisms of dialogue with the autonomous women's movement.

Ninth: The reformulation of the Republic's general budget, assigning specific financial resources for attention to women's demands deriving from their condition of subordination and as victims of discrimination.

Tenth: The regulation of and control over national and foreign capital in accord with the state's role as the main guarantor of the universal rights of men and women, with the aim of preserving the human and environmental resources that belong to the whole of society.

Notes

1 Carlos Arenas, "Endangering Democracy in Nicaragua," Jan. 13, 2015. WCCN, www.wccn.org.

2 Ibid.

3 "The Autonomous Women's Movement Makes 10 Demands on the Government." *Envío*, April 2002, www.envio.org.ni.

4 Gabby De Cicco, "Constitutional Reform and Women's Rights in Nicaragua," *AWID*, April 10, 2014, www.awid.org.

87

Statement of Conscience: A Feminist Vision for Peace
Feminist Peace Network
Online Community
September 1, 2002

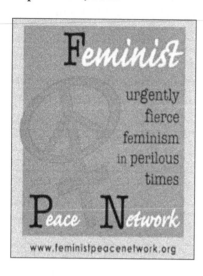

Feminist Peace Network logo.[1]

The Statement of Conscience was written by members of the Feminist Peace Network (FPN) shortly after it was founded in 2002. It began as a listserv, added a website, and then introduced a blog. The origin of the Statement of Conscience was a familiar experience of exclusion.

> The Statement was written partially in response to the original Not in Our Name (NION) statement, from which, conspicuously, all mention of war's impact on women was missing. In the cover letter to the Statement, we wrote, "FPN believes that, in order to effectively address the problems with the current U.S. military policy and the globalization of the so-called war against terror, the global pandemic of violence against women and children must be stopped. It is FPN's contention that, if we are to truly create peace, we must first recognize the horrific violence endured by the women of this planet every day. And, most importantly, we must vow that ending violence—by definition—includes ending violence that specifically endangers women and children. Until we do that, there will not truly be peace."[2]

Women still struggle to have their voices heard, their experiences matter.

WPN believes that every person on the planet should have his or her basic needs for food, safety, shelter, and education met, and that the conditions (economic, environmental, etc.) that would ensure this must be created. It draws on "matriarchal thinking" and asks that only women join the network online. WPN distributes a weekly e-letter, ominously titled "Atrocities," that documents "the global pandemic of violence against women." It continues to fight for women's participation in conflict resolution, as do many other groups in this collection, dating back at least to 1915.

The document below[3] rejects the rhetoric of "good versus evil" as misleading when all sides in war are complicit in killing and rape, and war's many other horrible consequences. They expand the idea of a war zone into the spaces where most women and children live most of the time. Imagine if the so-called war on terror addressed "the terrorism of hunger, thirst, sexual servitude, racism, patriarchy, nationalism, joblessness, homelessness, ableism, homophobia, ignorance, child molestation and elder neglect," as FPN suggests. Imagine if we valued human life, redistributed the resources spent on war machines, and praised peacemakers. FPN tunes in to the overt and subtle forces, from the psychological to the economic, that support war.

Statement of Conscience: A Feminist Vision for Peace

As citizens of Planet Earth we affirm our freedom.

We declare our right to live free from aggression and violence, and we encourage every person who reads this statement to add their own experience of terrorism in all its forms and proclaim the freedom of peace again and again.

We declare the rhetoric of "good" versus "evil" invalid. Every battle pretends to be for "good." But victory is too often celebrated by further loss of life, the rape of mothers and children, and the forced sexual servitude of daughters. Those who create and nurture life are both the first and last casualties of violent conflict. Those who wield violence are declared heroes.

When efforts to quiet violent conflict are made, women, whose stake in the resolution of conflict is at least as high as men's, must be involved as full members of peace negotiation teams. Any "peace" that does not address the worldwide pandemic of violence against women and girls is not Peace.

As women and men of conscience, we call for an end to the terrorism that forces upon women and children the obscene choice between prostitution and starvation, a choice that degrades us all. Warfare and its chaotic aftermath intensify the environment and opportunities for abduction and trafficking. The period following violent conflict exacerbates domestic violence. Usurping the healthy social role of men in neighborhoods under attack must also be addressed. Violent destruction, especially when followed by an apathetic and delayed restoration, effectively demoralizes families and destroys the well-being of communities. War strips men of their livelihood and dignity, and fosters hateful attitudes toward women, even their own wives, mothers, and daughters. The systematic use of rape as a weapon of war increases the alienation between men and their assaulted families. The detention, rape and torture of women and children as a strategy of warfare against their male relatives is evil in its most vile form.

As women and men of conscience, we demand that the use of rape as a weapon of war be stopped. As the linkages between gender, conflict, and a more rapid spread of the deadly HIV/AIDS plague are better understood, so too must be the devastating consequences for the women violated and the babies born of this hellish form of warfare. Special programs must be fielded on an emergency basis in former war zones to prevent, and to address, the widespread suffering faced by victims of rape and forced sexual servitude.

We defy those who would limit our experience of life to the maintenance of a caste system that supports the pursuit of profit and personal aggrandizement at the expense of meeting basic human needs. We challenge world leaders to put an end to the terrorism of hunger, thirst, sexual servitude, racism, patriarchy, nationalism, joblessness, homelessness, ableism, homophobia, ignorance, child molestation and elder neglect that many of the Earth's citizens face daily. When every child of this world is adequately nourished, clothed, educated and healthy; when every adult who wishes to work has life-sustaining employment; when women and children are free from abuse then human life on earth will have become so highly valued that terroristic activity will lose its attraction.

In the meantime, we will defend the lives of our children with our own lives, as necessary, but we refuse to endorse pre-emptive strikes that result in the massacre of thousands of innocents as a response to crimes against humanity.

We oppose terrorism in all its forms, whether sponsored by non-governmental groups or the state. We grieve deeply at the loss of life at the World Trade Center and the Pentagon on September 11, 2001. We also grieve the untold thousands of non-combatants slaughtered in the rain of bombs in Afghanistan in the aftermath of the September 11 attacks. Our hearts ache with sorrow as the slaughter of Iraqi citizens is justified to the world with the marketing of lies and fear. We are thankful that we have not yet become immune to grief.

We oppose terrorism in all its forms, but we steadfastly support the right to a fair trial, in an international court, and based on clear evidence, of all those accused of terrorism. We steadfastly oppose any prejudgment of the guilt of any individual accused of terrorism based on the color of their skin or the mother-blessing of their name. We demand a lifting of the cloak of secrecy, that prevents disclosure of evidence, in the investigations of the mass murder of thousands of our brothers and sisters in New York and Washington on September 11, 2001. We demand accountability for the lack of indictments and statements of progress.

We repudiate payment for a war machine that compromises our capability to feed and educate our children and care for our parents in their old age. We demand a full accounting of expenditures for war during the past year.

We resent and resist the gratuitous encouragement of fear. We become more cynical toward the source and motives of each new rumor of imminent terrorist attack. But our children do not have our insight, and their childhoods are being destroyed by nightmares about powerlessness and destruction.

We lift our heads proudly and boldly, and join our sisters and brothers throughout the world in a call for peace and justice, in full knowledge that our plea will be labeled treasonous by those world leaders who would defend peace by generating war.

We repudiate warlords and praise peacemakers. We are brave enough to step back from the brink of global warfare, and we demand leaders who are strong enough to endure peace.

Notes

1 Graphic from Feminist Peace Network, "Statement of Conscience: A Feminist Vision of Peace," Sept. 1, 2002. Feminist Peace Network online, www.feministpeacenetwork.org.

2 Lucinda Marshall, "Missing in Action: The Peace Movement's Silence on the Impact of War on Women." *Z Commentaries*, March 28, 2007, www.zcomm.org. Not in Our Name was an organization in the United States founded to protest President Bush's bellicose response to the 9/11 attacks.

3 Feminist Peace Network, "Meet Us on the Street to Stop Street Harassment April 7–13," March 31, 2013. Feminist Peace Network online, www.feministpeacenetwork.org.

88

The Manukan Declaration
Indigenous Women's Biodiversity Network
Manukan, Sabah, Malaysia,
February 4–5, 2004

The Indigenous Women's Biodiversity Network meeting on Manukan Island, Malaysia, in 2004.

Indigenous women continue to affirm our cultures, histories, views of creation and ancestry, our views of life and the world, and ways of being. These life-ways are essential to the continued perpetuation, promotion, and development of the world's biodiversity.

Any decisions regarding the use and protection of our traditional knowledge and biological resources must respect the rights of Indigenous peoples.

The Manukan Declaration is unique in its focus on biodiversity. It was signed by seventeen participating organizations from Africa, South America, North America, and Asia. The groups they represent exist in order to do such things as "assist indigenous peoples in the protection of their genetic resources" (Indigenous Peoples Council on Biocolonialism),[1] and "give indigenous peoples a voice and representation where the interests of indigenous and minority peoples are at stake. . . . especially on issues of environment and development such as food, climate change, habitat, health and education" (African Indigenous Women's Network).[2] This particular gathering was held just days before the Seventh Conference of the Parties (COP 7) to the UN Convention on Biological Diversity, to "address concerns about the Convention on Biological Diversity as an institution," which they argue should "support indigenous political and cultural self-determination."[3] Its argument against genetically engineered life forms overlaps with that of the Feminist International Network of Resistance against the New Reproductive Technologies and Genetic Engineering (1985), while its stance on women's role in the community is reflective of other Indigenous environmental declarations.

The Manukan Declaration rues the still ongoing decline in the world's biodiversity, which is happening at the same time as increased corporate control of collective biological resources and biotech-friendly policies. As a result of "mining, logging, hydroelectric projects, nuclear power and waste, toxic dumping, agri-business expansion, commercial fisheries, tourism development and war," it claims, we "devastate our lands, destroy our economies, and threaten our survival within our territories." Indigenous peoples in particular "have been and continue to be expelled from their lands and to be victimized by the despoilment of their lands and sacred sites." The future of indigenous communities, including their knowledge and way of living, is consequently at risk. "Our lifeways, our artistic expressions, are dependent on the bounty of the land. Any erosion of biodiversity can irreversibly impact our cultural heritage."

What are the relationships among biodiversity, women, and feminism, according to the Declaration?[4]

- Women, as "midwives, spiritual leaders, healers, herbalists, botanists and pharmacists," know and protect medicinal plants. In general, Indigenous women's knowledge can help us protect biological resources and use them well.
- Women build bridges between past and future, biologically and culturally, and so are conservationists.
- Indigenous women's relationship to the earth is valued and reciprocal, meaning they recognize "duties to" and not just "rights over."
- Women's ability to produce healthy offspring requires healthy ecosystems.

This document can be read as a claim for the integrity and utility of Indigenous women's knowledge. It urges Indigenous women to continue to play their historical role in environmental conservation—to protect and teach different skills, rituals, values, and relationship to the earth than found in a commercial outlook. It endorses a fascinating sense of women's self-determination, linking what is usually connected to autonomy instead to community self-determination and to fulfilling community responsibilities.

The Manukan Declaration

Preamble

We, the Indigenous women, having met in Manukan, Sabah from the 4th to 5th February 2004 in order to prepare ourselves for the deliberations of the Conference of the Parties to the Convention on Biological Diversity (COP 7) wish to present the following statement:

We are alarmed that despite the existence of the Convention on Biological Diversity the erosion of the world's biodiversity continues.

As Indigenous women, we have a fundamental role in environmental conservation and preservation throughout the history of our Peoples. We are the guardians of Indigenous knowledge and it is our main responsibility to protect and perpetuate this knowledge. Our weavings, music, songs, costumes, and our knowledge of agriculture, hunting or fishing are all examples of some of our contributions to the world. We are daughters of Mother Earth and to her we are obliged. Our ceremonies recognize her and we return to her the placentas of our children. She also safeguards the remains of our ancestors.

We, Indigenous women, continue to affirm our cultures, histories, perspectives on creation and ancestry, our views of life and the world, and ways of being. These ways of life are essential for the perpetuation, promotion and development of the world's biodiversity.

We, Indigenous women, secure the health of our Peoples and our environment. We maintain a reciprocal relationship with Mother Earth because she sustains our lives. Indigenous Peoples have developed our own health systems, and Indigenous women are the fundamental conservers of the diversity of medicinal plants, used since the time of our conception.

We, Indigenous women, strongly affirm our right to self-determination. Our right to self-determination is fundamental to the freedom to carry out our responsibilities in accordance with our cultural values and our customary laws.

We also note the importance of the work still to be done by the States to honor the treaty obligations made with Indigenous Peoples. Many treaties contain specific obligations of the States which guarantee Indigenous rights to protect the flora, fauna, lands, coasts, fishing areas, oceans and lakes.

As Indigenous women, it is our priority to protect our rights over our traditional knowledge and biological resources which have to be preserved and protected for future generations. Any decision on the use and protection of our traditional knowledge and biological resources must respect the rights of Indigenous Peoples.

Our areas of concern:

Indigenous Women as Guardians of Knowledge
Indigenous women are the guardians of knowledge, wisdom and experience in relation to environment. We have an integral role in the transmission of this knowledge, wisdom and experience to the younger generations.

Our systems of traditional knowledge have existed prior to the western systems of education or property rights regimes. In order to maintain our own integrity, we have the right to exist free from external interference.

Non-Indigenous systems of education have had a negative impact on Indigenous knowledge and ways of life. Indigenous Peoples have the right to protect, develop and perpetuate their own systems of education which are consistent with their cultural and spiritual values. This is an integral aspect of self-determination.

There are more than 6000 languages in the world, the majority of which are spoken by Indigenous Peoples. As Indigenous women, we recognize that these languages are disappearing rapidly and this threatens the maintenance and continuance of our knowledge.

As Indigenous women, we are opposed to the development of data banks and registries of Indigenous knowledge without our free, prior informed consent, including our right to say no to the development of data banks and registries.

Biodiversity and Indigenous Women

Indigenous knowledge systems and the diversity of life in our territories are collective resources under our direct control and administration.

Indigenous women have a vital role to play in the protection and conservation of the biodiversity in distinct ecosystems including forests, arid and semi-arid lands, inland waters, oceans and coasts and mountains. Our ways of life, our artistic expressions, are dependant on the land and its abundance. Any erosion of biodiversity has an irreversible impact on our cultural heritage.

The medicinal knowledge of Indigenous women is vast. Our specialized experience has made us midwives, spiritual leaders, healers, herbalists, botanists and pharmacists within our communities. Our knowledge, use and control of medicinal plants, must be protected from outside research and commercialization efforts.

We are opposed to technologies and policies such as regimes on intellectual property rights which violate the rights of Indigenous Peoples to maintain our traditional knowledge, practices, seeds and other food related genetic resources.

We are opposed to the introduction of genetically modified organisms and genetic use restriction technologies which might have very serious impacts on food security, health, the environment and the livelihoods of Indigenous Peoples.

Indigenous Women and Health

Indigenous women recognize that the womb is the first environment of every person. The state of health in this sacred environment is intrinsically linked to, and depends on, the health of the water, the air, the land, the plants and animals.

Our poor health situation as Indigenous women is intimately linked to our access to traditional medicines and to the health of ecosystems. For example, in the Arctic region, mother's milk has the highest levels of polychlorinated biphenols (PCBs) and mercury in the world due to the trans-boundary travel of persistent organic pollutants, their bioaccumulation and their subsequent magnification in the food chain.

As Indigenous women, we are the main producers of food for our communities. Environmental contamination threatens food security, our cultures and ways of life.

We recognize that Indigenous knowledge has contributed greatly to food security and to many of the medicines used throughout the world. We are opposed to any attempts from outside to commercialize and profit from our knowledge and resources.

Indigenous Women and Industrialization

Industrial projects, including but not limited to, mining, clear-cutting, hydroelectric projects, nuclear energy and waste, toxic dumping, agri-business expansion, commercial fisheries, tourism development, and war devastate our lands, destroy our economies, and threaten our survival within our territories.

Power in the government in many countries is largely concentrated in the hands of the industry lobby so they have an opportunity and advantage to make decisions about environmental problems. We need instruments to ensure the participation of Indigenous Peoples in the decision-making processes related to industrial developments and environmental policy.

Indigenous Women and Protected Areas

Indigenous communities have been and continue to be expelled from our territories. We are victims of the destruction of our territories under the pretext of the establishment of protected areas and national parks. We demand that our rights be restored and that these acts which violate our human rights and our rights as women cease immediately.

Indigenous Women, Trade and Globalization

We, Indigenous women, strongly oppose the appropriation and commercialization of our knowledge, ceremonies, songs, dances, rituals, designs, medicines and intellectual property. Any acquisition, use or commercial application of intellectual, cultural and spiritual property of Indigenous women must be done with our free, prior informed consent and respect our customary laws.

Intellectual property regimes must be prevented from asserting patents, copyright, or trademark monopolies for products, data, or processes derived or originating from the biodiversity or knowledge of Indigenous Peoples.

We affirm that natural life processes and prior art and knowledge are clearly outside the parameters of intellectual property rights protection. Therefore intellectual property rights protections over any genes, isolated genes, or other natural properties or processes, for any life forms, or knowledge derived from Indigenous knowledge may not be utilized without the free, prior informed consent of the Indigenous communities involved.

The advancement of policies of free trade through international and regional free trade agreements, state laws, and policies is allowing an increase in the exploitation of Indigenous Peoples['] knowledge and resources.

We oppose trade policies which impose western legal frameworks upon us and do not recognize our rights to maintain and implement our systems of management based on our customary laws.

Indigenous Women, Conflict and Militarization

Indigenous women have been seriously affected by colonialism, armed conflict, resettlement and forced displacement from our communities by discriminatory laws or lack of enforcement of laws.

In regions where conflicts exist, we as Indigenous women are the first victims of the destruction of biodiversity. Dependent and linked to the lands, but displaced as a result of war, they are unable to provide for the needs of our families.

Recalling previous declarations, conventions and decisions which affirm the rights of Indigenous Peoples to full and effective participation in international fora which influence our lives:

Recalling that the Charter of the United Nations, the International Covenant on Economic, Social and Cultural Rights and the International Covenant on Civil and Political Rights affirm the fundamental importance of the right to self-determination of all Peoples, according to which, they can freely determine their political situation and freely pursue their economic, social and cultural development;

Recalling Decision VI/10 on Article 8(j) and related provisions "emphasizing the need for dialogue with representatives of Indigenous and local communities, particularly women for the conservation and sustainable use of biological diversity within the framework of the Convention";

Considering "the vital role of Indigenous Peoples in sustainable development" already affirmed by the political declaration of the World Summit on Sustainable Development, Johannesburg, 2002, para.25; and

Affirming other instruments and mechanisms which guarantee our participation and contribution in the discussions, such as:

The Rio Declaration on Environment and Development (in particular Principle 22), Agenda 21 (in particular chapters 11 and 26); and the Convention on Biological Diversity (in particular Article 8(j) and related provisions); the Convention on the Elimination of all Forms of Racial Discrimination; the Declaration on the Forest Principles and the IPF/IFF/UNFF; ILO Convention 169 on Indigenous and Tribal Peoples, among others;

Further Recognizing, that at the end of the United Nations Decade on the World's Indigenous Peoples there have been achievements and progresses but there still remains a lot of work to be done.

We therefore call upon Conference of the Parties to include the following recommendations in the final decisions of COP7:

We encourage the development of instruments which avoid the expropriation and commercialization of our knowledge and biological resources.

We affirm that natural processes and prior art and knowledge are clearly outside of the parameters of the protection of intellectual property. Therefore, intellectual property rights over genes, isolated genes or other processes or natural properties over any form of life derived from Indigenous knowledge must be eliminated.

The Parties must declare an immediate moratorium on the development, cultivation and use of seeds, plants, fish and other genetically modified organisms.

We request the Parties reaffirm Paragraph 23 of their Decision V/5, in light of the continuing lack of information on negative impacts on Indigenous Peoples and in accordance with the precautionary principle.

We request that the Parties guarantee that Indigenous women are free to implement our own practices and institutions to ensure food sovereignty.

Scientific research and any activity of bioprospecting, conducted without the full consultation and free, prior informed consent of the Indigenous Peoples affected must be stopped and any research must be undertaken in a comprehensive and protective manner.

The Parties must undertake immediate action to urgently stop the introduction of alien species which threaten the health of our traditional territories and food sources.

Knowing that contaminated ecosystems threaten the very survival of our Peoples, Indigenous women urge the Parties to ratify and implement the Stockholm Convention on Persistent Organic Pollutants.

We request that the Parties guarantee decisions to protect and promote the development of sui generis systems based on our customary laws.

That the Parties guarantee that intellectual property regimes are not imposed on Indigenous knowledge, biodiversity and customary systems of management.

Ensure that any benefit sharing regime protects the rights of Indigenous Peoples to prior informed consent as principle parties when our knowledge or resources are impacted, and further protect our right to deny access and/or refuse to participate.

The Parties must ensure that national legislation reflects and is coherent with the norms established by the CBD.

The decisions must recognize and reflect the intrinsic link existing between Indigenous knowledge and biodiversity.

The Conference of the Parties, in its activities of public information and capacity-building, must pay specific attention to the full and effective participation of Indigenous women.

All decisions must recognize and protect the fundamental principle that Indigenous Peoples are rights holders with inherent and inalienable rights over our traditional knowledge and biological resources.

Notes

1 Indigenous People's Council on Biocolonialism website, accessed Aug. 2017, http://www.ipcb
.org.

2 The African Indigenous Women's Organisation, "Advocacy." AIWO-OAFA website, accessed
Aug. 2017, www.indigenouswomen-africa.org.

3 Kylie White, "Indigenous Environmental Movements and Governance," in *The Oxford
Handbook of Environmental Political Theory*, ed. Teena Gabriel et al. (New York: Oxford
University Press, 2016), p. 568.

4 "The Manukan Declaration of the Indigenous Women's Biodiversity Network," Manukan,
Sabah, Malaysia, February 4–5, 2004.website, asianindigenouswomen.org.

89

Chiang Mai Declaration on Religion and Women: An Agenda for Change

International Committee of the Peace Council
Chiang Mai, Thailand
February 29–March 3, 2004

The world's religions play a leadership role in seeking social justice, in the environment, against racism, and for the poor. But religions have been largely silent in response to critical issues of women's human rights, in the family and in the work place.

Fifty-two participants met to discuss how "to reduce barriers to cooperation between women's organizations and faith communities (often perceived as indifferent or even hostile to women's issues)."[1] The attendees were from geographically diverse lands (Africa, the Middle East, Latin America, Europe, the United States, and Asia) and represented numerous religious traditions (among them Protestant, Anglican, Muslim, Buddhist, Hindu, Catholic, and Jewish). They included pastors and professors, religious leaders and leaders of international women's organizations, and, in addition to internal discussions, the attendees held meetings with local NGOs and individuals. The gathering was part of a multiyear effort to "decrease some of the interdependent obstacles to peace and development by focusing on counteracting religious intolerance, patriarchy and social injustice. . . . and [exploring] how religions can help to improve women's status."[2] Discussion was grounded in preconference reading of two papers, one each by Christine Gudorf and Vandana Shiva.

The starting points for deliberations were two: the distinctive effects of globalization on women, and discrimination against women in many world religions. The document produced[3] urges religions to take more active roles in securing women's rights and opportunities. It delineates ways religions have contributed to women's suffering, and points to how they can do better. In particular, it urges that religious institutions oppose violence against women, support the right of women to choose any role, foster positive attitudes toward sexuality, and accept (at least) the decriminalization of abortion.

Interestingly, in failing women, and thus the world, religions themselves are at stake, the document holds. It calls on women and men to end gender injustice in this particular historical moment of "widespread insecurity" under globalized capitalism. The claim that religious institutions have collaborated in patriarchy dates back at least to Seneca Falls, just as the claim that they can do better is reminiscent of the antislavery conventions of the 1830s.

The Chiang Mai Declaration

PREAMBLE:

We, the participants in this conference on women and religion, recognize that contemporary realities have tragic consequences for women's lives. Without a commitment to women's human rights and to the resolution of these tragedies, religions are failing the world. Their own relevance is at stake as they become more and more isolated from the values and needs of their members.

It is urgent that religions address these realities. Religions must be consonant with the cultural evolution in which we are all immersed. Religions must no longer tolerate violence against women. Women are alienated from religions that do. We are committed to working towards change, and we call on others, women and men, to join in this task.

I. WOMEN AND GLOBALIZATION: PROBLEM AND PROMISE

We live in a time of rapid change which provides both challenges and opportunities. This change has profound effects on all our lives.

Our globalized world is ravaged by armed conflict, increasing economic disparity, the feminization of poverty, massive displacement of peoples, violence against women, the pandemic of HIV and AIDS, enduring racism, and extremisms—all of which generate a climate of deep fear and widespread insecurity.

Globalized capitalism has reduced everything to a commodity and everyone to a consumer and commodity. Nowhere is this more evident than in the lives of women:

- Women's and children's bodies are commodified, especially in sexual trafficking.
- Increasingly HIV and AIDS have a woman's face.
- Women and children disproportionately populate the camps of refugees and displaced persons.
- Women make up the greater proportion of exploited laborers.
- Pressures of the globalized economy have led to even greater violence against women and children.

Globalization, however, also bears the promise and possibilities of advancing women's human rights and well-being:

- More women in more places can be gainfully and justly employed.
- Information technology can enable women throughout the world to share strategies, successes, and hope.

II. WOMEN AND RELIGIONS: PROBLEM AND PROMISE

Religions at their best celebrate the dignity of each human being and of all life as valuable parts of a sacred whole. They inspire and empower us to compassion and justice.

Religions, however, have not always been at their best. They have collaborated with dehumanizing values of cultural, economic and political powers. Thus they have contributed to the suffering of women:

- They have made women invisible by denying them religious education and excluding them from decision-making.
- They have been silent when patriarchal systems have legitimated the violence, abuse, and exploitation of women by men.
- This silence has been deafening in the face of such atrocities as rape, incest, female genital mutilation, sex selective abortion, and discrimination against sexual minorities.
- They have not recognized the conscience and moral agency of women, especially in relation to their sexuality and reproductive decisions.

But religions can and must do better. They must reclaim their core values of justice, dignity, and compassion and apply these values to women. We reached consensus that:

A. Within the religions, women's religious literacy should be recognized and fostered. Women are:

- Students: Just as education of women is today understood to be critical in transforming the world, so providing women with religious education is critical in transforming religion. Women seek religious education at both basic and advanced levels. They should be welcomed.
- Scholars: In spite of obstacles, women have developed as religious scholars. That scholarship is an essential resource for the overall development of our understanding of religion. It should be promoted.
- Teachers: Male religious leaders and students have much to gain from exposure to women teachers of religion. Unless we work to change men, the ability of religions to progress in sensitivity to women is impossible.
- Leaders: Women should be full participants in the life and institutional leadership of their religious communities. Women are prepared to be decision-makers, and their gifts should be recognized and used to the fullest extent.

B. Within the world:

- Religions should apply their message of peace in order to oppose the daily reality of violence in family and society. There is a contradiction between the message of peace inherent in all religions and the absence of advocacy for peace in the home and society.
- Women are subjects, not objects, in their own lives. The right to choose any role, including motherhood, should be supported socially, economically, and politically.
- Religions should apply the message of social justice to women. The world's religions play a leadership role in seeking social justice, in the environment, against racism, and for the poor. But religions have been largely silent in response to critical issues of women's human rights, in the family and in the work place.
- This is nowhere more evident than in the area of women's sexuality and reproductive health. Given the moral concern about abortion and the range of stances toward it, the view of any particular religious tradition should not be imposed on the consciences of others. Decriminalization of abortion is a minimal

response to this reality and a reasonable means of protecting the life and health of women at risk.

CONCLUSION:
Our experience of coming together as women leaders and religious leaders has convinced us that the religious traditions and the aspirations of women are not in opposition. We are not enemies. On the contrary, we share the same commitment to human dignity, social justice, and human rights for all.

We therefore commit ourselves and call on other women and other religious leaders to reach out to each other to enhance mutual understanding, support, and cooperation. This can be done on the regional level to expand the consensus achieved here and at the national level to define concrete, joint activities toward advancing women's human rights and well-being.

We came together as women and men to explore how the positive powers of religion could be engaged to advance the well-being of women. Indeed, we believe that when women and religious traditions collaborate, a powerful force for advancing women's human rights and leadership will be created.

This statement was unanimously endorsed by all the participants on March 3, 2004.

Notes

1 Lyda Alpizar qtd. in AWID, "Women and Religions in a Globalized World: Conversations to Advance Gender Equity." *Our Voices* blog, Women's Empowerment & Leadership Development for Democratization, accessed 2016, www.weldd.org.

2 "Women, Globalization, and Religion." Peace Council archives online, accessed 2015, peace-council.org.

3 "The Chiang Mai Declaration," 2012. *International Committee for the Peace Council*, accessed Oct. 30, 2013, www.peacecouncil.org.

90

Letter to Women Legislators of the Coalition of the Willing: Neither Blood nor Rape for Oil
Black Women's Rape Action Project and Women Against Rape
London, England
May 12, 2004

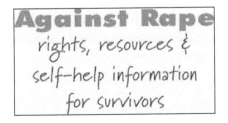

Women Against Rape/Black Women's Rape Action Project logo.

Why are these attacks on women largely invisible? Have you or others asked questions about this? How many men will ask if women do not? If you did ask, what answers have you received? Why are they not yet known to the public?

Unlike all other petitions in this collection, this Letter[1] is addressed to women legislators in the United States and the United Kingdom, countries that formed part of what President George Bush called "the coalition of the willing" for their support of the invasion of Iraq. The signatories ask the legislators to be accountable for their two governments' complicity in war crimes, including rape, given that they owe a debt to the women's movement for their very presence in government. The Letter notes the various ways rape is used in war, despite its "invisibility." It mourns the plight of rape survivors and points out "how convenient [it is] for the troops that the women and girls they rape should be too vulnerable to tell the truth." Given that "those in power seem unwilling to acknowledge what is going on," the groups behind this document attach photographs, which had been treated as pornography rather than evidence of torture and grounds for political asylum. They claim that rape is inevitable in war and tolerated by the political and military hierarchy.

Women Against Rape (WAR) was founded in 1976, Black Women's Rape Action Project (BWRAP) in 1991. The multiracial groups sponsor a joint website. "Both organisations are based on self-help and provide support, legal information and advocacy. [Both] campaign for justice and protection for all women and girls, including asylum seekers, who have suffered sexual, domestic and/or racist violence."

The groups also have an online petition, "End the Rape of Justice."[2] The understanding of rape in that petition mirrors that in the letter to legislators.

Since in cases of rape and sexual assault
- The conviction rate for recorded rape is only 5.7%
- Despite the introduction of legal changes, specialist units and further training, many of those paid to enforce the law on rape are not doing this job
- The police often do not collect all the evidence or lose or misinterpret it
- The Crown Prosecution Service routinely turn down strong cases and often prosecute rape incompetently and negligently
- Judges exercise their own sexism, racism and other prejudice, allowing victims to be put on trial in court (including through the illegal use of their sexual history), misdirecting juries and reinforcing prejudices they may bring
- Incompetent professionals, who would be disciplined or even sacked in other professions, are not dismissed and rarely disciplined in any way.
- Women and girls are endangered by the refusal of the criminal justice system to effectively prosecute violent criminals, i.e. rapists
- Men who are allowed to get away with rape go on to rape again and sometimes to kill

We the undersigned believe that police officers, prosecutors and judges who have shown themselves to be sexist, racist or otherwise prejudiced against victims of sexual violence, or to be negligent and incompetent in the prosecution of rape cases, should be publicly disciplined, moved off rape cases or sacked, depending on the nature of their offence. We the undersigned believe that's the only way those responsible for the criminal justice system will be held to account, so women, children and men are finally protected from the violent crime of rape.

To Women Legislators of the Coalition of the Willing

We are writing to you, women legislators in both the UK and the US. That there are now many more women in Congress and in Parliament is due to a massive women's movement over decades in every area of this planet. In the name of all the women whose movement helped get you there, we ask for your accountability in the present crisis of war, occupation, war crimes and torture, including rape, in which both your governments are complicit.

1. The rape and other torture of women and girls has been largely hidden

Information has exploded onto our screens and in all the media about the sexual humiliation, torture and murder of prisoners in Iraq and the murder of civilians, including children, in the streets and in their own homes. Questions are also being raised about Afghanistan. Yet while the rape of men (and increasingly boys) is beginning to be acknowledged, the rape of women and girls was initially dismissed as "a soldier had sex with a woman prisoner." Greater truth is now emerging.

Iraqi women have told us that women are in prison to be interrogated and tortured to get information on male relatives. For women, torture almost always begins with the torture of rape, often gang rape. A US reporter said that "Last month women prisoners at Abu Ghraib smuggled out leaflets claiming they'd been raped" (Anne Garrels, National Public Radio, 4 May 2004). A woman from Baghdad University working for Amnesty International has described her own sexual abuse at a check point and what she knows from others. "He pointed the laser sight directly in the middle of my chest, then he pointed to his penis. He told me, 'Come here, bitch, I'm going to fuck you.' . . . According to Prof. Huda Shaker several women in Abu Ghraib jail were sexually abused, including one who was raped by an American military policeman and became pregnant" (London Guardian 12 May). Other sources have confirmed this.

The horrendous prison conditions to which women have been subjected have been mentioned as an aside. Iraq's human rights minister, Abdel Bassat Turki, who resigned a month ago, said he spoke to US chief administrator Paul Bremer last November about the treatment of women in Abu Ghraib: "They had been denied medical treatment. They had no proper toilet. They had only been given one blanket, even though it was winter. And their families had not been allowed to visit them" (London Guardian 10 May 2004).

The International Committee of the Red Cross report hardly mentions women, and their reporter interviewed only men. (There has been no mention either that the ICRC reports there were riots against the prison conditions and Iraqis were shot dead.)

Why are these attacks on women largely invisible? Have you or others asked questions about this? How many men will ask if women do not? If you did ask, what answers have you received? Why are they not yet known to the public?

2. Most women and girls cannot speak out

Organisations like Black Women's Action Project and Women Against Rape which have been demanding justice and protection for women for decades and which work with asylum seekers from all over the world who have fled rape, know only too well that most rape survivors anywhere in the world find it almost impossible to speak about their ordeal. They feel degraded and ashamed, especially since society and the criminal justice system usually blame the woman for what happened to her. In both the UK and the US, women often call the trial of their attacker "a second rape" as it is the woman's mental state and sexual history which are publicly examined to destroy her credibility and get the rapist off. In other countries, hostility to the victim can be even more extreme. Rape survivors may be unmarriageable, ostracised and even killed. We have read that girls as young as nine who were raped under Saddam Hussein were refused hospital treatment and that this practice continues under the occupation.

An Iraqi lawyer said that her client, an ex–Abu Ghraib prisoner, "fainted before providing further details of being raped and knifed by U.S. soldiers." Another lawyer representing five former detainees described to their lawyers having been beaten. But they did not say they had been raped. "They are very ashamed." "They say, 'We can't tell you. We have families. We cannot speak about what happened'" (Los Angeles Times, 12 May 2004). "A female colleague of mine was arrested and taken [to Abu Ghraib]. When I asked her after she was released what happened there she started crying. It is very difficult to talk about rape. But I think it happened." Prof. Huda said the woman made pregnant as a result of rape by a US soldier has now disappeared and may have been killed. "When I went to her house . . . the neighbours said she and her family had moved away" (London Guardian 10 May 2004).

How convenient for the troops that the women and girls they rape should be too vulnerable to tell the truth.

3. Photos of women's torture have not hit the front pages
Given that women and girls who are rape survivors risk being ostracised and even killed, we must protect their anonymity. Yet unless there is incriminating photo proof, those in power seem unwilling to acknowledge what is going on. There has been no statement and no apology regarding the rape and other torture of women and girls.

We attach photos which have been sent to us of women being raped by soldiers, which have already appeared on some websites. We have disguised the women's identity and will not circulate any photo where women are identifiable. While we cannot verify the authenticity of these photos, it is clear from all the other information now circulating that these or similar rapes have taken place. We have heard that thousands of photos like these have circulated like baseball cards among the troops and even used as computer screensavers. The Pentagon is quoted as saying that it knows of at least two CDs of photos containing several hundred images of US troops "abusing" prisoners, including "beating an Iraqi inmate to the point of unconsciousness, having sex with a female prisoner, and gloating over a corpse" (London Guardian 10 May 2004).

It is not new for rape or other sexual torture to serve as pornography. Women Against Rape (WAR) has complained that in Britain in "normal" times photos and witness statements where the victim describes her rape are often circulated for their pornographic value in prisons by convicted rapists as well as among the police.

4. We want to know
We want to know what is happening to women and girls in Iraq, in prison and elsewhere, at the hands of British and US troops, beginning with the women

already mentioned. We want to know what is happening to women in Afghanistan at the hands of occupying forces there. We understand that much of the brutality and murder may be perpetrated by or on the orders of the CIA and private military contractors—a euphemism for mercenaries. We want to know about any mercenaries guilty of any of these crimes against women and children, and how much they were paid to perform and/or oversee these atrocities.

Despite international precedents to the contrary, it is common for the US and the UK to consider rape by agents of the State not to be torture and therefore grounds for political asylum. As a result, women are consistently denied the international protection to which we are entitled. For example, the UK asylum claim of a mother of five who fled Uganda after being raped by soldiers who were interrogating her, was repeatedly rejected by the authorities. The rape, they said, was merely "sexual gratification" and "simple dreadful lust," not torture or persecution. Only after she decided to give up her anonymity so that we could make her case public, and after we called on prominent women to support her, did she finally win the right to asylum in 2003. We have examples of many such cases in our files.

While rape is not limited to war, everyone acknowledges that in war rape is inevitable. In order to make war, men, and now women (since we have been urged to be more like men as the only route to equality), are trained to kill. Once killing is acceptable, rape is hardly a moral problem. And during a period of mass slaughter, rape is even less likely to be taken seriously. When Iraqi casualties are treated as irrelevant as they have been (the body counts are for US and UK troops not for Iraqi or Afghani military or even civilians), are we not also expected to dismiss or ignore the rape and other torture of Iraqis or Afghanis?

So why is the rape of women and children treated as a surprise result of war now? Why were no questions asked about rape during the debate about whether to go to war?

Defence secretary Geoff Hoon, commenting on the photos of torture by US and UK troops, said: "I do not see that it is torture: it is abuse. I do not see any evidence of systematic torture in terms of interrogation" (London Guardian 7 May). Donald Rumsfeld has said publicly that photos and videos depicting worse atrocities are still to come; these are rumoured to contain scenes of the rape of women and children.

How will such rape be viewed if what we have seen so far is not considered torture? How do you plan to deal with further information on rape that is bound to emerge? Will you excuse it as Ann Clwyd, the UK government's special envoy for human rights, initially did, saying that it was not as bad as what Saddam Hussein had done? She now says that she was never shown the International Committee of the Red Cross report. Will she resign?

5. Rape of women soldiers and within soldiers' families

What are the implications for the families of officers, soldiers and mercenaries who are trained to rape, murder and torture with impunity in this way? How often do they face rape and other violence at the hands of these same men? How often do they get justice?

The effects of army training and war on women soldiers and the families of military men is dealt with in an extensive letter by our colleague, former air force captain Dorothy Mackey. Rev. Mackey was herself raped within the US army, and has been in touch with many other women (and some men) survivors of such violence, either within the military or as partners of military men. She makes clear that rape of women within the army is condoned by the hierarchy. Soldiers' rape of women is treated as a component of soldiers' pay, a cost not to governments but to women. We enclose excerpts from Rev. Mackey's expose. More comprehensive documentation is available on request. Rev. Mackey has forwarded to us the preposterous "McDowell's scoring" system used by the US military for assessing the veracity of rape allegations. Investigating themselves and accountable to no one, they employ every prejudice against women to dismiss the victims as liars.

We now hear that 100 US women soldiers are claiming to have been raped by their colleagues while serving in Iraq.

Will this or similar sexist measures be used to "weed out" women who manage to come forward with allegations of rape in Iraq or Afghanistan? What will you do to ensure that these cases are investigated by people truly independent of the authorities that are accused of the assaults?

6. We demand accountability from women in Congress and Parliament

We do not accept that those in authority merely "turned a blind eye." There is mounting evidence that orders to torture, including rape, came from the highest levels. Neither do we accept that the UK government bears no responsibility for the actions of US troops and vice versa. The Coalition of the Willing must mean joint responsibility.

Why are women soldiers who took part in the outrages we all know about apparently the first ones to be named and prosecuted? Why has no one in a position of authority resigned? Will you ask that they do now and face prosecution?

We are asking, urging, in fact demanding, that on the issue of the rape of women and children which took place as a direct result of the war and occupation that your governments perpetrated in Iraq and Afghanistan, that the women in Congress and in Parliament are accountable to women generally. We need the full information and we need to know what you propose to do about it, individually and collectively.

We must point out that even in "normal" times, the forces of law and order have always found ways of protecting the rapist.

In the UK, Soham murderer Ian Huntley, convicted in 2003, was reported nine times for rape and sexual assault over years before killing schoolgirls Holly Chapman and Jessica Wells. This is typical of . . . the sexism of the criminal justice system when dealing with rape. Nationally, just 5% of recorded cases of domestic violence and less than 6% of reported rapes end in conviction. Incompetence and carelessness permeate the gathering of evidence (beginning with the woman's statement to the police), and the decision on whether to prosecute. In court, in the 23% of cases that get that far, the woman or girl is "put on trial," and is left undefended by the prosecuting barrister and by the judge. Victims who are Black, immigrant, working class, single mothers, children, older, lesbian, have disabilities or a mental health history, who were attacked by their partner or ex-partner, are sex workers or have a criminal record, stand even less chance of getting justice or protection, especially if their attacker has higher social status. Rape and sexual abuse by police officers, soldiers and prison guards are notoriously difficult to get the police to investigate and the Crown Prosecution Service to prosecute, even when the victim is a fellow (woman) officer. We can document this from our files.

Notes

1 Black Women's Rape Action Project and Women Against Rape, "To Women Legislators of the Coalition of the Willing: Neither Blood nor Rape for Oil," May 12, 2004. Women Against Rape and Black Women's Rape Action Project website, www.womenagainstrape.net.
2 "Petition: End the Rape of Justice." Women Against Rape and Black Women's Rape Action Project website, accessed Aug. 2017, www.womenagainstrape.net/resources.

91

Women's Global Charter for Humanity *and* Conditions to Make This World Possible
Fifth International Meeting of the World March of Women
Kigali, Rwanda
December 10, 2004

World March of Women logo.

This *Women's Global Charter for Humanity* calls on women and men and all oppressed peoples and groups of the planet to proclaim, individually and collectively, their power to transform the world.

This document went through many drafts as women's groups from about sixty countries had a chance to look at it before a final version was adopted by delegates to the World March of Women Fifth International Meeting. Between March 8 (International Women's Day) and October 17, 2005 (International Day for the Eradication of Poverty), the Charter was taken on a "world relay," with actions organized all along the way to discuss its content and build solidarity.

The Charter[1] is among the most "utopian" documents in this collection. Although the World March of Women (WMW) has as its objectives the less-than-utopian tasks of fighting poverty and violence against women, the focus in this particular piece is entirely on a world that feminists want to construct. The thirty-one affirmations are based on five values: equality, liberty, solidarity, justice, and peace. The vision is positive and collective, and leaves room for local differences alongside its global dimension.

The WMW was inspired by the 1995 Women's March Against Poverty in Québec, which mobilized thousands. In October 1998 about 140 people from 65 countries met in Montréal, where the WMW's seventeen international demands (available on their website) were developed. The organization dates its official launch to 2000. It describe itself as "an international feminist action movement connecting grass-roots groups and organizations working to eliminate the causes at the root of poverty and violence against women." The WMW employs the "tried and true recipe of providing women with the opportunity to talk together, tell our stories and find the common thread that unites us in action."[2] In this description, the organization means to differentiate itself from transnational feminist networks "heavily shaped by their socialization within the UN processes, resulting in the 'NGO-ization,' strong focus on policy advocacy, and its resulting cultures of expertise. Resisting this trend toward professionalization and institutional reformism, the March has built a global network of place-based, grass-roots feminist groups, privileging the agency of poor and working-class women."[3]

Proposing alternatives is risky business. But envisioning a different world is essential to social change. Like its own documents, that vision keeps evolving. The Conditions statement[4] following the Charter connects the vision into what may be more familiar practical terms.

Women's Global Charter for Humanity

Preamble

We women have been marching a long time to denounce and demand an end to the oppression of women and to the domination, exploitation, egotism and unbridled quest for profit breeding injustice, war, conquest and violence.

Our feminist struggles and those of our foremothers on every continent have forged new freedoms for us, our daughters and sons, and all the young girls and boys who will walk the earth after us.

We are building a world where diversity is considered an asset and individuality a source of richness; where dialogue flourishes and where writing, song and dreams can flower. In this world, human beings are considered one of the most precious sources of wealth. Equality, freedom, solidarity, justice and peace are its driving force. We have the power to create this world.

We represent over half of humanity. We give life, we work, love, create, struggle and have fun. We currently accomplish most of the work essential to life and the continued survival of humankind. Yet our place in society continues to be undervalued.

The World March of Women, of which we are a part, views patriarchy as the system oppressing women and capitalism as the system that enables a minority to exploit the vast majority of women and men.

These systems reinforce one another. They are rooted in, and work hand in hand with, racism, sexism, misogyny, xenophobia, homophobia, colonialism, imperialism, slavery and forced labor. They breed manifold forms of fundamentalism that prevent women and men from being free. They generate poverty and exclusion, violate the rights of human beings, particularly women's rights, and imperil humanity and the planet.

We reject this world!

We propose to build another world where exploitation, oppression, intolerance and exclusion no longer exist, and where integrity, diversity and the rights and freedoms of all are respected.

This Charter is based on the values of equality, freedom, solidarity, justice and peace.

Equality
Affirmation 1. All human beings and peoples are equal in all domains and all societies. They have equal access to wealth, land, decent employment, means of production, adequate housing, quality education, occupational training, justice, a healthy, nutritious and sufficient diet, physical and mental health services, old age security, a healthy environment, property, political and decision-making functions, energy, drinking water, clean air, means of transportation, technical knowledge and skills, information, means of communication, recreation, culture, rest, technology and the fruit of scientific progress.

Affirmation 2. No human condition or condition of life justifies discrimination.

Affirmation 3. No custom, tradition, religion, ideology, economic system or policy justifies the inferiorization of any person or authorizes actions that undermine human dignity and physical and psychological integrity.

Affirmation 4. Women are full-fledged human beings and citizens before being spouses, companions, wives, mothers and workers.

Affirmation 5. All unpaid, so-called feminine tasks related to supporting life and social maintenance (household labour, education, caring of children and intimates, etc.) are economic activities that create wealth and that should be valued and shared.

Affirmation 6. Trade among countries is equitable and does not harm peoples' development.

Affirmation 7. Every person has access to a job with fair remuneration, in safe and sanitary conditions, and in which their dignity is respected.

Freedom
Affirmation 1. All human beings live free of all forms of violence. No human being is the property of another. No person may be held in slavery, forced to marry, subjected to forced labor, trafficked, sexually exploited.

Affirmation 2. All individuals enjoy collective and individual freedoms that guarantee their dignity, in particular: freedom of thought, conscience, belief and religion;

freedom of expression and opinion; to express one's sexuality in a free and responsible manner and choose the person with whom to share one's life; freedom to vote, be elected and participate in political life; freedom to associate, meet, unionize and demonstrate; freedom to choose one's residence and civil status; freedom to choose one's courses of study and to choose and exercise one's profession; freedom to move and to be in charge of one's person and goods; freedom to choose one's language of communication while respecting minority languages and a society's choices concerning the language spoken at home and in the workplace, and to be informed, learn, discuss and gain access to information technologies.

Affirmation 3. Freedoms are exercised with tolerance and mutual respect and within a democratic and participatory framework, democratically determined by the society. They involve responsibilities and obligations towards the community.

Affirmation 4. Women are free to make decisions about their body, fertility and sexuality. They have the choice about whether they will have children.

Affirmation 5. Democracy is rooted in freedom and equality.

Solidarity

Affirmation 1. International solidarity among individuals and peoples is promoted free of any form of manipulation or influence.

Affirmation 2. All human beings are interdependent. They share the responsibility and the intention to live together and build a society that is generous, just and egalitarian, based on human rights; a society free of oppression, exclusion, discrimination, intolerance and violence.

Affirmation 3. Natural resources and the goods and services necessary for all persons to live are quality public goods and services to which every individual has equal and fair access.

Affirmation 4. Natural resources are administrated by the peoples living in the area, in a manner that is respectful of the environment and promotes its preservation and sustainability.

Affirmation 5. A society's economy serves the women and men comprising that society. It is based on the production and exchange of socially useful wealth distributed among all people, the priority of satisfying the collective needs, eliminating poverty and ensuring the balance of collective and individual interests. It ensures food sovereignty. It opposes the exclusive quest for profit to the detriment of social usefulness, and the private accumulation of the means of production, wealth, capital, land and decision-making power by a few groups and individuals.

Affirmation 6. The contribution of every person to society is acknowledged and paves the way to social rights, regardless of the function held by that person.

Affirmation 7. Genetic modification is controlled. There are no patents on life or the human genome. Human cloning is prohibited.

Justice

Affirmation 1. All human beings regardless of their country of origin, nationality and place of residence are considered to be full-fledged citizens, with fair and equal entitlement to human rights (social, economic, political, civil, cultural, sexual, reproductive and environmental rights) within an egalitarian, fair and genuinely democratic framework.

Affirmation 2. Social justice is based on the equitable redistribution of wealth to eliminate poverty, limit wealth acquisition and satisfy essential needs to improve the well-being of all people.

Affirmation 3. The physical and moral integrity of every person is protected. Torture and humiliating and degrading treatment are forbidden. Sexual violence, rape, female genital mutilation, violence against women, sex trafficking and trafficking of human beings in general are considered crimes against the person and crimes against humanity.

Affirmation 4. An accessible, egalitarian, effective and independent judiciary is put in place.

Affirmation 5. Every individual benefits from social protection guaranteeing her or him access to care, decent housing, education, information and security in old age. Every individual has sufficient income to live in dignity.

Affirmation 6. Health and social services are public, accessible, quality and free of charge; this includes all treatments, and services for all pandemic diseases, particularly HIV.

Peace

Affirmation 1. All human beings live in a peaceful world. Peace is achieved principally as a result of: equality between women and men, social, economic, political, legal and cultural equality, rights protection, and eradication of poverty, ensuring that all people live in dignity and free of violence, and that everyone has employment, enough resources to feed, house, clothe and educate themselves, is protected in old age and has access to health care.

Affirmation 2. Tolerance, dialogue and respect for diversity are foundations of peace.

Affirmation 3. All forms of domination, exploitation and exclusion, of one person over another, one group over another, a minority over a majority, a majority over a minority, or one nation over another are excluded.

Affirmation 4. All human beings have the right to live in a world free of war and armed conflict, foreign occupation and military bases. No one has the right to decide on the life or death of individuals and peoples.

Affirmation 5. No custom, tradition, ideology, religion, political or economic system justifies the use of violence.

Affirmation 6. Armed and unarmed conflicts between countries, communities and peoples are resolved through negotiations, which bring about peaceful, just and fair solutions at the national, regional and international levels.

Call

This *Women's Global Charter for Humanity* calls on women and men and all oppressed peoples and groups of the planet to proclaim, individually and collectively, their power to transform the world and radically change social structures with a view to developing relationships based on equality, peace, freedom, solidarity and justice.

It calls on all social movements and all forces in society to take action so that the values promoted in this Charter can be effectively implemented and political decision-makers adopt the measures necessary for their implementation.

It is a call to action to change the world. The need is urgent!

No aspect of this Charter may be interpreted or utilized to express opinions or conduct activities that contravene the Charter's spirit. The values defended in it form a whole. They are of equal importance, interdependent and indivisible, and the order they appear in the Charter is interchangeable.

Conditions to Make This World Possible

The Women's Global Charter sets out, in the form of five values and 31 affirmations, the world women want to build. These affirmations might appear utopian to some. We know that many conditions must be put in place for these affirmations to become a reality. So we added this document, which contains the conditions on which women participating in the March were consulted during the drafting of the Charter. The list is far from complete and every woman must adapt it to the situation in her country.

This text continues in the same vein as the 17 world demands that served as the political platform of the World March of Women in 2000 and enriched discussions about the conditions necessary to enable construction of the world the Charter describes. The 17 demands follow the conditions in this document.

1. For identical or equivalent work, women receive remuneration equal to that of men and enjoy similar rights and benefits.
2. Measures are adopted to eliminate gender inequality among children and adults.
3. Household labour, education, and caring of children and intimates is shared equally among women and men. Those who carry out this work benefit from social rights.
4. Spouses are equal within the couple and the family, regardless of the form of union. No family model has more value than any other.
5. Women possess their own identity papers.
6. Women have equal access to property, land and credit, regardless of their civil status.
7. Women and men are responsible for contraception. They have access to reliable and impartial information about contraception and how to protect

themselves from sexually transmitted diseases, and to a free, safe and quality health system.

8. Women have the right and power not to comply with patriarchal social and cultural imperatives that impose a model of behaviour requiring them to be pretty, submissive, silent and industrious.

9. A constitutional, non-denominational and democratic State is created within the framework of a truly representative, participative, gender-representative, non-discriminatory, peaceful democracy, characterized by cooperation, freedom and public control of the common wealth.

10. Biological and cultural diversity is maintained as a social good. Traditional medicine is recognized and valued in every society. The knowledge in this domain of women of all ages, peasant women and indigenous peoples, and of all other communities and populations is recognized and valued.

11. Measures are adopted enabling women and men to balance their paid work with family, social, political and cultural responsibilities. The principle of equal opportunity is a foundation stone.

12. Workers have the right to associate, organize and unionize.

13. Provisions are established to eliminate tax evasion, tax havens and fraud.

14. Every individual has access to social security through universal public programs.

15. When rights are violated, every measure is taken to expose rights violations and effectively ensure reparation and compensation for the wrongs inflicted on individuals or communities.

16. Persons who violate others' rights are responsible for their actions. No one benefits from impunity.

17. Effective means for combating corruption and arbitrary actions are established.

18. Individuals escaping from persecutions and violence, especially women escaping sexual violence and any other form of violence, have the right to asylum in a safe country.

19. Social movements organize, express their views and take action with complete freedom and without fear of repression.

20. Legislation is passed and effectively implemented prohibiting and condemning all forms of violence, particularly violence that specifically targets women, whether it is private or public in character, or occurs in peacetime or wartime. Rape is recognized as a weapon and a war crime.

21. All women and men benefit from educational and training programs that promote a culture of peace, non-violence and conflict prevention and challenge the legitimacy of attitudes that are warlike, male supremacist, dominating, exploitive or competitive in nature. Hateful and degrading representations of women and men are excluded from all means of communication.

22. Military research is abandoned in favour of civilian-oriented research. The arms industry is dismantled and converted for use in health, employment and educational programs. When there are signs of impending war or armed conflict, peaceful methods are employed to prevent them. If a war or armed conflict is already underway, peaceful methods are used to resolve it. Women are actively involved in this process, in social reconstruction, and in creating a State that will ensure peace.

23. Women have equal representation in a global democratic system where people are represented in an egalitarian manner, which genuinely defends

everyone's interests, establishes peace and eradicates poverty and violence. This body guarantees peoples' sovereignty and their self-determination; it protects their territories from occupation and safeguards their natural wealth. This system operates with transparency and its activities are controlled by the members of the societies that created it.

Notes

1 "Women Envision Another Possible World," Feb. 2005. *Envío* online, www.envio.org.ni.
2 "Goals of the World March of Women," Sept. 20, 2006. World March of Women website, www .marchemondiale.org.
3 Ruth Reitan, ed., *Global Movement* (London: Routledge, 2013).
4 World March of Women, "Demands to Make This World Possible," March 1, 2005. *International Viewpoint* online, www.internationalviewpoint.org.

92

Widow's Charter
Widows for Peace through Democracy
London, England
February 2005

 Widows for Peace through Democracy logo.

To ensure widows of all ages, irrespective of their religion, ethnicity, caste, class, or nationality, are protected from discrimination and violence, and can enjoy their full human rights as equal and valuable members of society.
—Widows for Peace through Democracy's Mission[1]

Widows are historically among the most powerless in any society, especially so in patriarchal societies where a man's assets and belongings pass to his brothers instead of his wife and children in the event of his death. In many countries across the world today, cultural practices still leave widows and their children, especially their daughters, destitute. The death of a husband and father, in some cases, is equivalent to a social death: the widow has no social, judicial, or political voice without her husband. In fact, in many countries, "the vernacular translation of widow means whore, sorceress or witch."[2] As the needs of many other groups of women have been addressed by the United Nations and many other human rights groups, the needs of widows are still often ignored or neglected. The Widows for Peace through Democracy organization is an umbrella administration for widows' organizations throughout the world, but especially in parts of the world where becoming a widow means becoming the poorest of the poor.

Margaret Owen, a British lawyer and human rights activist, helped start the organization soon after she herself became a widow. After meeting a widow from Malawi and attempting to find research on widows in the early 1990s, Owen "held the first international workshop on widowhood . . . at the fourth World Women's Conference . . . in Beijing in 1995."[3] From there, organizations for widows across the world were able unite under the Widows for Peace through Democracy umbrella. The most important local organization that continued to inspire Owen to do her work was the Women for Human Rights–Single Women Group, started by Lily Thapa in Nepal during the Gulf War. Thapa helped gather stories and data on over eighty-four thousand widows throughout Nepal, organizing information that she later used to "persuade the Nepalese to include the treatment of widows as one of the indicators for monitoring the implementation of UN Security Council Resolution 1325. She has helped 11 widows attain seats in the Nepalese Parliament; worked to change the law on pension rights, and convinced the Government to develop a national action plan on 1325."[4] Twenty-three local organizations spanning Africa, Asia, and Europe are currently under the Widows for Peace through Democracy's umbrella, and they hope to have similar success.

The Charter[5] below emphasizes the steps that must be taken to ensure widows' human rights across the world. One of the most important steps is to gather data on how many women are widows in different areas of the world so that larger amounts of resources, both monetary and judicial, can be allocated to them. The Charter also emphasizes the importance of protecting widows from relatives, especially the male relatives of their husbands, who traditionally have inherited or taken the husband's possessions and even the widow and children as new, lesser family members. The Charter articulates specifically, "Widows may not be 'inherited' as wives or concubines to their husband's brother, nor forcibly placed in a 'levirate' relationship, nor forcibly made pregnant by a relative in order to continue producing children in her dead husband's name." Many of the Charter's provisions protect widows' sexuality and their right to retain custody of their children and possessions, even protecting widows who consent to abuse because it is customary. The Charter also emphasizes the importance of giving widows equal opportunities to work and support their children and other dependents since they have become the sole provider for those dependents. The Charter ends with a section on the special needs of widows in postconflict areas and a call to action to gather more information so widows can get the support they need from local, national, and international organizations.

Widow's Charter

Noting That: All women are equal before the law and that the human rights of women are inalienable, universal and non-transferable;

Noting That: in many countries widows suffer from low status, discrimination, violence and lack of legal rights;

Noting That: in many communities widows are stereotyped as evil, bringing bad luck, and that social attitudes to widowhood obstruct them from fully participating in civil society;

Noting That: in spite of international and domestic laws guaranteeing equality in inheritance, land ownership, and criminalising violence to women widows are often banned from inheriting, evicted from their homes, deprived of all their property, and left in destitution;

Noting That: widows are often victims of degrading and life-threatening traditional practices in the context of funeral and burial practices;

Noting That: there is no special reference to discrimination and abuse of widows in the Beijing Platform for Action;

Noting That: widows are key social and economic players in development;

Reaffirming the important role that widows do and may play in the resolution and prevention of conflicts;

Expressing Concern that the impact of this treatment of widows has severe and negative implications for the whole of society in particular because the poverty of widows deprives their children of their human rights to shelter, food, education and the rights of the child;

Recognising the urgent need to mainstream a widow's perspective in all policy developments and decisions;

Reaffirming the need to implement fully all international human rights and humanitarian law that protects the rights of women and girls during and after conflict as well as in times of peace;

Requires all governments to use all measures possible to eliminate this discrimination, and to work with widows' groups to assess their numbers and their situation so as to develop policies and laws to alleviate their isolation and poverty, and acknowledge their valuable social capital.

ARTICLE 1

Widows shall enjoy equality with all women and men, irrespective of their age or marital status.

Any treatment of a widow which differs from the treatment, legally, socially, economically, of a widower shall be deemed to be discriminatory and therefore illegal.

Widows shall not be discriminated against, in word or deed, either in family and private life, or in community and public life.

The State is guilty, by omission, of breach of the law, if it implicitly condones discrimination and abuse of the widow by non-state actors, such as family members.

ARTICLE 2

a) Widows shall have the right to inherit from their husband's estate, whether or not the deceased spouse left a will.

b) Widows may not be disinherited.

c) Widows may not be "inherited" as wives or concubines to their husband's brother, nor forcibly placed in a "levirate" relationship, nor forcibly made pregnant by a relative in order to continue producing children in her dead husband's name.

d) A widow has the right to remarry.

e) A widow must be free to marry someone of her own choice.

f) Polygamy and temporary marriage is forbidden.

g) "Honour Killings" are murder.

h) Daughters shall inherit equally with sons.

i) "Property-Grabbing" and "chasing-off" are criminal offences, punishable as the most serious category of crime.

j) Anyone who attempts or manages to deprive a widow of any of her property, take custody of her children, without an order of a judge or magistrate shall be guilty of the most serious category of crime.

k) Anyone, whether a relative or a stranger, who seeks or manages to gain control of the dead husband's bank account, insurance policy, accident compensation claims, without the order of the Court is guilty of the most serious category of crime.

l) Free Legal Aid shall be given to widows in all inheritance, property and personal status disputes.

ARTICLE 3

a) Anyone who arranges or coerces a widow to participate in harmful traditional practices in the context of funeral and burial rites shall be guilty of the most serious category of crime (for example: ritual cleansing through sex; scarification; isolation; restrictions on diet and dress endangering mental and physical health).

b) Anyone who has sexual relations with a widow in the context of funeral and burial rites shall be guilty of Rape, and subject to the maximum penalty.

c) Anyone who forcibly deprives the widow of custody of her children shall be guilty of a serious offence.

d) Anyone who physically, mentally or sexually abuses a widow is guilty of the most serious category of crime.

e) Anyone who verbally abuses a widow by calling her insulting names shall be guilty of an offence.

ARTICLE 4

Any restrictions on a widow's mobility, even where based on "custom," which continues after the 14th day after the death of the spouse are unlawful and anyone responsible for restraining the widow is guilty of a criminal offence.

a) Any restrictions, due to her marital status, on a widow's freedom to access social, health and education services are unlawful.

b) Any restrictions concerning domicile, diet, clothing, life-style imposed on a widow against [her] will are unlawful.

c) All restrictions on widows accessing health care, including family planning services, are unlawful.

d) Any restriction on a widow's right to citizenship, a passport and freedom to travel is unlawful.

ARTICLE 5

All appropriate measures shall be taken to eliminate discrimination against widows in the field of employment, in particular:

a) The right to the same employment opportunities and remuneration as other men and women.

b) It is an offence under the Employment Acts for anyone to dismiss a woman from her employment because she has become a widow and must take some reasonable time off work for the funeral rites. . . .

c) It is an offence to refuse to employ a widow because she is wearing mourning clothes.

d) Suitable child-care and elderly care support shall be provided to widows who work outside the home.

ARTICLE 6

a) The term "violence against women" includes any act of gender-based violence against a widow that results in or is likely to result in physical, sexual or psychological harm or suffering to her, including threats of such acts, coercion, or deprivation of liberty.

b) No widow-abuse may be justified by citing custom, tradition or religion.

c) All appropriate measures shall be taken, through, for example, public education and training of opinion leaders, to change the negative stereotyping of widows.

d) No relative shall detain a widow in his or her household as an unpaid domestic worker without registering before the court and being subject to regular monitoring and inspection by the social services.

e) All appropriate measures shall be taken to protect widows and their children from sexual exploitation, prostitution and trafficking of women and girls.

f) It is no defence to this law that the widow consented to be [the] victim of the alleged violence.

ARTICLE 7

a) All appropriate measures shall be taken to ensure that those dependent on widows—children, other orphans, the old, sick and frail people—are identified [so] that gaps in assistance are filled.

b) Where appropriate, widows should receive financial support to balance opportunity costs in sending children to school.

c) Appropriate measures shall be taken to eliminate discrimination against widows in areas of economic and civil life. In particular:
 (i) The right to a pension and family benefits.
 (ii) Elimination of delaying bureaucratic barriers to widows accessing pensions.
 (iii) Elimination of corruption in the dispensing of pensions to widows.
 (iv) Special measures to assist illiterate widows [to] access their economic and legal rights.

d) Widows' children should have priority in assessment for education scholarships.

ARTICLE 8

WIDOWS OF CONFLICT AND POST CONFLICT

a) Recalling SCR Resolution 1325, and recognising the huge increase in the numbers of widows and wives of the missing as a consequence of armed conflict;

b) Recognizing that many widows of war have also been victims of rape and sexual violence;

c) Recognising also the extreme vulnerability of widows and daughters of widows in the instability of societies in the aftermath of war;

d) Noting the unique role widows play as custodians of the social fabric of communities;

e) Noting also widows' unique roles as peace builders and peacemakers, through their ability to link hands with widows across ethnic, religious and national divides;

f) Recognising that years after Peace Accords are signed widows of war continue to struggle to survive in refugee and IDP camps and are unable to return to their original homes;

g) Concerned with the problems arising for wives of the "missing", unable to rebuild their lives because of uncertainty about their status;

h) Recognising the particular individual security issues for women without male protectors;

i) Noting the alarming rise in domestic violence as well as sexual violence in the community in the post conflict situation;

j) Expressing concern at the vulnerability of widows and their children to rape, forced prostitution and trafficking by criminals, occupying troops, so-called peace-keeper forces;

k) Noting the many numbers of orphans, sick, old, wounded and traumatized people dependent on widows for their survival;

CALLS all actors involved in negotiating and implementing peace agreements to address the special needs of widows and wives of the missing and ensure the protection and respect for their human rights.

CALLS on all actors to ensure that widows are represented in these negotiations so that their particular concerns, for example:

Rights of safe return of displaced widows to former homes

Repair and rebuilding of homesteads

Land allocation and ownership

Clarification of the legal rights and social needs of the wives of "the missing"

Personal status guarantees in Constitutional and Law reform

Protection of widow witnesses at national and international courts and tribunals, before, during and after trials

Addressing needs of refugees and IDPs and widow asylum seekers.

ARTICLE 9

Government will support the establishment of a National Federation of WIDOWS, with clusters and sub-groups in every town and sets of villages so that information on the needs of widows is available and can inform policy making at the national and local level.

a) All appropriate measures shall be taken to support widows organising themselves into self-help and empowerment groups.

b) These groups shall be acknowledged as being decisive components of civil society, to be involved as participants in the development of social, [and] economic policies affecting their situation.

c) Support shall be given to the establishment of a National Federation of Widows' Groups with an advisory status to government.

d) Widows' shelters and legal aid centres for widows shall be established.

e) Statistics and Data shall be collected and a situational analysis undertaken to ascertain the true numbers, needs and roles of widows in society.

f) In recognition of the gap in knowledge, Governments will explore alternative methods of collecting such information, such as participatory poverty and demographic assessment studies involving the widows' groups themselves.

ARTICLE 10

a) Governments shall address the situation of widows in their work programmes to achieve the Millennium Development Goals.

b) Governments shall bear in mind the special situation of widows when identifying measures to implement the CEDAW, the BPFA, the Declaration Eliminating Violence against Women, the Convention against Torture, SCR Resolution 1325 and all other human rights conventions and charters.

c) All human rights training of all actors in the justice system, community and opinion leaders, shall incorporate widows' rights law.

d) Governments shall consult with widows' organisations when reporting to the human rights committees on their implementation of the ratified charters and agreed declarations and programmes.

Notes

1 "What Is WPD?" Widows for Peace through Democracy website, accessed 2016, www .widowsforpeace.org.

2 Kathryn Hovington, "'On the Run' with Margaret Owen OBE," May 9, 2012. International Criminal Law Bureau, www.internationallawbureau.com.

3 Ibid.

4 Ibid.

5 "Widow's Charter," February 2005. Widows for Peace through Democracy website, accessed 2017, http://www.widowsforpeace.org. The original was issued as a draft document, and different versions are available online, presumably in response to suggested additions. See, for example, http://wunrn.com/2015/06.

93

Nunavik Inuit Women's Manifesto: Stop the Violence
Saturviit Inuit Women's Association
Qilalugaq Camp, Quebec, Canada
August 1–4, 2005

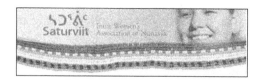

Saturviit Inuit Women's Association logo.

About twelve thousand people, 90 percent of them Inuit, live in fourteen communities in mineral-rich Nunavik, the northernmost part of Quebec. In the summer of 2005, Inuit women came from each community to reflect on their political and social situation, come up with recommendations to bring attention to their needs, and draft a manifesto. The gathering led to the reestablishment of the Staurviit Inuit Women's Association of Nunavik. ("*Saturviit*" comes from the root "*satuq,*" meaning "regaining what one had lost." The name symbolizes hope for restoring peace.)

An overwhelming theme of the meeting was violence in their communities. According to a 2007 report, "Prevalence and Nature of Sexual Violence in Nunavik," these are the key issues:[1]

- One adult in three experienced sexual abuse during childhood and one in five during adulthood.
- About one woman out of two reported having been forced or having faced attempts made to force them to perform a sexual act while a minor. One out of four stated that they faced the same problem in adulthood.
- One man out of five reported sexual abuse during childhood and one in eight reported having been forced or having faced attempts made to force them to perform a sexual act during adulthood.
- Sexual violence within the family is very common. Sexual abuse by a family member affects one third of men and women who reported having been victims of sexual abuse during childhood or adulthood.
- Domestic violence expressed through sexual abuse from a current or previous spouse or partner is of concern. One third of women who were sexually assaulted reported having been sexually abused by their partner or ex-partner. One male victim out of six had experienced sexual abuse by his partner.

- Sexual abuse is not limited to the family or to the marital or dating context. Many adults are confronted by sexual abuse from friends, colleagues, or strangers during childhood or adulthood.
- The Inuit community wants to establish a tradition of prevention and intervention to address sexual abuse. Nunavik residents have suggested a variety of solutions, which can be categorized into four main themes: (1) the value of the community collectively addressing the problem of sexual abuse, (2) the necessity that the victim talk about the abuse, (3) the merits of sanctions, as a preventive tool, following sexual abuse, and (4) the necessity that parents assume a guiding and protective role in their children's lives.

The report asserts that these numbers are much greater than in both non-Native communities and other Inuit communities, such as one in Greenland.

Northern communities, like other Aboriginal reserves, are in Canada among the ones most affected by all kinds of social problems. For decades, they have shown the highest rates of suicide, dropout, family violence, alcoholism, and so on. . . . Unfortunately, too many Canadians are unaware that the current situation is directly connected to still very recent colonial history; nor do they understand how it has impacted individuals and families. Doubtless, rapid changes in lifestyle and the disconnect between generations, caused especially by residential schools in the 1950s and 1960s, still affect all Inuit adversely. . . . The ongoing colonial relationship must also be overcome.[2]

The Manifesto[3] is a call to end the silence about violence, and to take action to stop the epidemic. Inaction and immunity can no longer prevail. Individuals, leaders, and organizations can work together to establish social justice. The women who gathered at the Qilalugaq Camp also developed an action plan. "The goals of this Action plan included: women becoming more involved in decision-making for their communities, in regional organizations, and in the Nunavik government; finding better ways to counter violence, abuse and suicide; finding ways to promote healing, positive parenting, nurturing families and healthy communities; and helping Nunavik women to access programs, resources and services available to them."[4]

Due to climate change, northern waters will be more navigable, and there are already signs of conflict over sovereignty of a Northwest Passage between Canada, the United States, and Europe. What will this mean for the well-being of Inuit communities?

Nunavik Inuit Women's Manifesto: Stop the Violence

For too long now we have been witnessing the rise of violence and its impact on us, our children and our society in general.

We can no longer watch from the sidelines as violent acts continue to permeate our society. We wish to break the walls of silence surrounding violence!

The future of Nunavik lies with our children. We wish to assert the right for our children to grow in peace and security, and only in this way will the cycle of violence be put to an end.

We, Inuit women of Nunavik, demand that violence directed against women and children must stop. Child sexual abuse is absolutely intolerable and must end. All types of violence, whether physical or psychological, against women and children, must cease to occur.

If we continue to not act against this violence, we and our children will continue to bear the scars, for inaction perpetuates the cycle of violence.

When a violent perpetrator is being forgiven, the forgiveness must not translate into immunity for abusers.

Authorities must act against violence and end the impunity.

The women of Nunavik demand social justice for their communities.

Our organizations—Nunavik local and regional authorities as well as the federal and provincial governments—must deal with the epidemic of violence.

All Nunavimmiut are invited to reflect on this manifesto, adopt it and act against the violence that affects our communities, so that our hearts, our souls and our lives may focus on creating a better life for all Nunavimmiut.

Notes

1 Francine Lavoie, Sarah Fraser, Olivier Boucher, and Gina Muckle, "Prevalence and Nature of Sexual Violence in Nunavik" (Nunavik Regional Board of Health and Social Services, Government of Quebec, 2007), pp. 8–9, *Institut National de Santé Publique Québec*, accessed Sept. 30, 2017, www.inspq.qc.ca.

2 Ibid., p. 1.

3 Saturviit, "Nunavik Inuit Women's Manifesto," Aug. 24, 2012. Saturviit website, www.saturviit.ca.

4 Saturviit, "Membership." Saturviit website, accessed 2016, www.saturviit.ca.

94

Final Declaration
Women in Black Thirteenth International Conference
Jerusalem, Israel
August 12–16, 2005

Women in Black logo.

According to their website, Women in Black "is a world-wide network of women committed to peace with justice and actively opposed to injustice, war, militarism and other forms of violence." Their activism is nonviolent and nonaggressive, often manifested in vigils where women wear black, hold placards, and hand out leaflets about their cause. They explain the symbolism of wearing black thus: "Wearing black in some cultures signifies mourning, and feminist actions dressed in black convert women's traditional passive mourning for the dead in war into a powerful refusal of the logic of war." Women in Black has branches and groups across the world, and they estimate that over ten thousand women have participated in Women in Black activism.[1]

Women in Black does not have an official constitution or manifesto, but the Declaration written at the Thirteenth International Conference illustrates the kind of work this group does to create peace in some of the most conflict-ridden areas of our world. According to Gila Svirsky's meticulous notes on the conference, over seven hundred women from thirty-nine countries attended this conference, including many women from regions of conflict, "five women who had been nominees for the Nobel Peace Prize, a member of the European Parliament, a Minister in the Palestinian Authority, three former members of the Israeli Knesset, a Buddhist monk working in Cambodia, three nuns from India, and a liberation theology Catholic pastor from Canada."[2] During the conference, the women held deliberations on the Israel-Palestine conflict and on conflicts across the globe. They also held a peace vigil in Jewish Jerusalem, held a demonstration opposing the Separation Wall at Bil'in, and formed a human chain across the Kalandia checkpoint, which separates Jerusalem from Ramallah.[3] These discussions and actions were very risky: the women had tear gas fired at them, and one woman was arrested. As their Final Declaration states, however, these risks were worth taking to truly live the freedom, peace, and justice the group advocates.

The Declaration[4] specifically advocates for women to be "full partners" in the fight for peace, especially women who are usually denied a voice in public issues like women living in conflict-ridden and poverty-stricken areas of the world. They especially protest occupation of Palestine by Israel and of Iraq by the United States, and they delineate steps to create peace between Israel and Palestine. Their ultimate goal is to engage all men and women, regardless of differences, in the struggle to make "freedom, peace, and justice a reality."

Final Declaration

We, Palestinian, Israeli, and international women, gathered this week in Jerusalem for the "Women in Black 13th International Conference":

1. Affirm our commitment to work together as a worldwide network of women dedicated to freedom, equality, justice, peace, women's rights, and a world free of violence. Agree to meet again to continue our struggle and reaffirm our commitment to the work and goals of our network, in the next Women in Black International Conference to be held in the Spanish state.

2. Insist on the participation of women as full partners in the prevention and resolution of conflicts, and in the negotiation and implementation of peace agreements according to UN Resolution 1325. The active and equal participation of women of diverse backgrounds in decision making is crucial to ensure that issues related to women's economic, social, national, ethnic and cultural rights, freedom of choices and security are raised and effectively addressed.

3. Demand social and economic justice and condemn the exploitative system and structure of multinational corporations' globalization that drive into poverty millions of people all over the world, and that thrive at the cost of social justice and human development.

4. Work for a world where difference does not mean inequality, oppression or exclusion, as we struggle against all causes of oppression and discrimination based on gender, race, sexual preference, age, national and ethnic identity, and religion.

5. Challenge the militaristic policies of our governments, call for disarmament, and condemn the interference of the US and its allies in the political affairs of other sovereign nations.

6. Commit ourselves to promote education and a language of truth and hope that reflect our right to justice, to remedy and to reparation, which are the basis for the creation of a world based on the values of equality, justice, cooperation, and solidarity.

7. Condemn feminicide and all forms of violence—sexual, physical or psychological—to which women are subject in areas of conflict, in militarized zones, and in their daily lives.

8. Demand an immediate end to the war and United States occupation of Iraq, and stand in solidarity with Iraqi women in their struggle for their legal and human rights.

9. Call for a just and sustainable peace between Israel and Palestine based on international law and human rights, to be achieved by
   - An end to the Israeli occupation;
   - Immediate cessation of all actions against civilians, assassinations, closures, house demolitions, land confiscation, settlement building, construction of the Apartheid Wall, water deprivation, denial of access to schools, hospitals and places of work and worship;
   - The immediate release of all political prisoners;
   - Dismantlement of all Israeli settlements in the Palestinian territories occupied in 1967;
   - Immediate final status negotiations leading to a viable sovereign Palestinian state alongside Israel on the June 4th, 1967 borders. Peace and a resolution of the conflict will not be achieved by unilateral actions such as disengagement;
   - The recognition of Jerusalem as two capitals for two states, and the immediate ending of all unilateral actions leading to the ethnic cleansing of Jerusalem;
   - Israel's recognition of responsibility for the plight of Palestinian refugees as a pre-requisite to finding a just and lasting resolution of the refugee question in accordance with the relevant UN resolutions;
   - Recognition of the national and civil rights of the Palestinian minority in Israel.

Though not the same yardstick can be used for occupied and occupiers, we recognize the lack of security, fear, and emotional anxiety experienced by Palestinians and Israelis affected by the ongoing conflict and violence, and by being civilian victims to the conflict itself. We believe that international community intervention is critically needed to make sure Israel is held accountable for its actions in the occupied territories and to build a just peace between Israel and Palestine. We support the call upon the international community to impose non-violent and effective measures such as divestment and sanctions on Israel, for as long as Israel continues to violate international law, and continues the occupation and the oppression of the Palestinian people.

WE CALL ON ALL WOMEN AND MEN IN THE WORLD TO JOIN US IN OUR QUEST TO PRESERVE LIFE, HUMAN DIGNITY AND FREEDOM IN THE WORLD, MAKING OUR VISION OF FREEDOM, PEACE, AND JUSTICE A REALITY.

Notes

1 "About Women in Black." Women in Black website, accessed 2016, www.womeninblack.org.
2 Gila Svirsky, "Who Was There: Conference 2005," August 2005. *Gila Svirsky: A Personal Website*, www.gilasvirsky.com.
3 Ibid.
4 Women in Black, "Final Declaration: Conference 2005," August 2005. *Gila Svirsky: A Personal Website*, www.gilasvirsky.com.

95

Survivors of Prostitution and Trafficking Manifesto: Who Represents Women in Prostitution?
Coalition Against Trafficking in Women
October 17, 2005

Coalition Against Trafficking in Women logo.

Prostitution is sexual exploitation, one of the worst forms of women's inequality, and a violation of any person's human rights.

Like the 1985 World Charter for Prostitutes' Rights, this document is informed by the experiences of those who have been in the sex trade. Unlike the earlier document, however, this Manifesto defines prostitution and trafficking as violence against women and opposes all efforts at regulation.

The Coalition Against Trafficking in Women (CATW) was founded in 1988, the first organization to fight human trafficking internationally. It tries to change the terms of the debate about prostitution and trafficking, and to stop policies aimed at legalizing what it refuses to call "sex work." It views trafficking as inherently harmful to women, and does not see these harms as mitigated by legalization. Despite all the propaganda saying otherwise, it contests the idea that prostitution is simply an individual choice, or associated with sexual freedom, or glamorous, or a way out of poverty, or inevitable; on the contrary, it is a form of women's inequality marked by exploitation and oppression. "When prostitution is understood as violence ... unionizing prostituted women makes as little sense as unionizing battered women."[1] The harms trafficked women suffer are the norm, CATW claims, experienced by the majority, and include physical assault, sexually transmitted diseases, chronic health problems, and sexual violence, from johns, pimps, and law enforcement.

In the document and in CATW's work, what is advocated includes support for victims of sexual exploitation, educational programs about the harms of human trafficking aimed at diverse publics (law enforcement, male youth, etc.), and legislation that punishes those who profit from trafficking rather than those exploited by it. The group works in Asia, Africa, Latin America, Europe, and North America. "CATW supports the Nordic Model, the world's first law to recognize prostitution as violence against women and a violation of human rights. It criminalizes the purchase of commercial sex and offers women and children an exit strategy. The Nordic Model originated in Sweden (1999) and has been passed in the Republic of Korea (South Korea, 2004), Norway (2009) and Iceland (2009)."[2]

Survivors of Prostitution and Trafficking Manifesto

We, the survivors of prostitution and trafficking gathered at this press conference today, declare that prostitution is violence against women.

Women in prostitution do not wake up one day and "choose" to be prostitutes. It is chosen for us by poverty, past sexual abuse, the pimps who take advantage of our vulnerabilities, and the men who buy us for the sex of prostitution.

Prostitution is sexual exploitation, one of the worst forms of women's inequality, and a violation of any person's human rights.

Many women in prostitution have been severely injured, some have died, and some have been murdered by their pimps and customers.

Physical violence, rape and degradation are often inflicted on us by customers, pimps, recruiters, police and others who gain from prostitution. The public either judges us as "whores" or thinks we make a lot of money.

The condition of women in prostitution is worsened by laws and policies that treat us as criminals and the scum of society, while customers, pimps, managers and sex business owners are not made accountable. Our condition is also made worse by giving licenses to prostitution enterprises and legal protection to pimps, customers and the sex industry.

Most women are drawn into prostitution at a young age. The average age of entrance into prostitution worldwide is 13. Victims of prostitution and trafficking have almost no resources to help them exit. Programs that provide alternatives for women in prostitution are very few.

Women in prostitution dream of a life free from oppression, a life that is safe, and a life where we can participate as citizens, and where we can exercise our rights as human beings, not as "sex workers."

We, survivors from Belgium, Denmark, Korea, the UK and the United States declare:

1. Prostitution must be eliminated. Thus, it should not be legalized or promoted.

2. Trafficked and prostituted women need services to help them create a future outside of prostitution, including legal and fiscal amnesty, financial assistance, job training, employment, housing, health services, legal advocacy, residency permits, and cultural mediators and language training for victims of international trafficking.

3. Women in prostitution need governments to punish traffickers, pimps and men who buy women for prostitution and to provide safety and security from those who would harm them.

4. Stop arresting women and arrest the perpetrators of trafficking and prostitution.

5. Stop police harassment of women in prostitution and deportation of trafficked women.

6. Prostitution is not "sex work," and sex trafficking is not "migration for sex work." Governments should stop legalizing and decriminalizing the sex industry and giving pimps and buyers legal permission to abuse women in prostitution.

As survivors of prostitution and trafficking, we will continue to strengthen and broaden our unity, help any woman out of prostitution, and work with our allies to promote the human rights of victims of trafficking and prostitution.

Notes

1 Melissa Farley, "'Bad for the Body, Bad for the Heart': Prostitution Harms Women Even if Legalized or Decriminalized." *Violence Against Women*, Oct. 2004, p. 1089.

2 "Projects and Campaigns." Coalition Against Trafficking in Women website, accessed Aug. 2017, www.catwinternational.org.

96

Political Platform
Women's Network of Croatia
Zagreb, Croatia
2006

51%♀ *Ženska mreža Hrvatske* Women's Network Croatia

Women's Network of Croatia logo.

The feminist principles to which the Women's Network of Croatia (ŽMH, from Ženska mreža Hrvatske) commits itself include both such familiar issues as nondiscrimination, feminist networking, and reproductive justice and more distinctive ones such as female solidarity, antimilitarism, and ecological awareness. All groups who want to be part of the network agree to respect and act in accordance with these principles. Currently, around thirty women's organizations across the country are part of this political advocacy network committed to feminist approaches to democratization. The group was recently (January 2016) in the news for asking Croatian prime minister-designate Tihomir Orešković "to take into account the issues of gender equality and women's rights when choosing ministers for the new government."[1] Apparently, this request arose amidst rumors of rollbacks in both women's rights (regarding reproduction and prostitution, for example) and the number of females holding ministerial posts, at the hands of conservative, right-wing politicians and Catholic fundamentalists.[2]

As of 2011, statistics reveal that the general participation rate of women in the Croatian labor market is 47.0 percent, below the EU average of 58.5 percent; that 9.6 percent of Croatian women work part-time, below the EU average of 20.2 percent; and that only 1.3 percent of Croatian women are college educated, again significantly below the EU average of 24.8 percent. Further, fields of study and employment are very gendered.[3] There has also been concern that women's shelters are substandard and closing due to lack of funding.[4]

The 2006 Political Platform[5] sets up goals for women of participation, safety, and respect. It suggests quotas in decision-making positions, in part on the grounds that women better represent the interests of other women. It recommends switching budgetary priorities from the military to social services. A great deal of emphasis is put on sexual and reproductive healthcare and education, as well as on financial security.

Political Platform

In UN documents, women are recognized as a political, economic and status minority, and the Republic of Croatia, by signing the Convention on the Elimination of All Forms of Discrimination Against Women, not only agreed to create a legal frame that guarantees gender equality, but to administer the measures for eliminating all forms of discrimination from routine practices and customs.

Since women are 51 percent of the population, we deem it necessary for them to exit the endless cycle of political, economical and status minority and gain an equal place in all social processes.

Therefore, the Women's Network of Croatia sets as their primary goals:
- participation of women in politics and political decision making
- realization of the right to education, labour, income, and full employment
- social security
- arresting violence against women
- tolerance and equality policy

Women's participation in politics and political decision making
Since they are 51 percent of the population and, when given the opportunity, they represent female interests far better, it is therefore very important to have at least 30 percent of women in positions of decision-making. *Therefore . . .*
    . . . we request:
- shared responsibility in the home and in administration of the state
- women's quotas in the executive bodies of the political parties, and candidate lists where the genders alternate on all administrative levels
- measures for complete and realistic portrayal of women in public, and cessation and sanctioning of sexism, prejudices and stereotypes
- realization of educational, labour and full-time job rights

Since the work of women and illegal laborers is undervalued, women are forced to have more than one job, in addition to their unpaid work at home, all jobs that contribute to the national economy. *Therefore . . .*
    . . . we request:
- introduction of employment stimulation measures for women [is] jobs in accordance with their education
- grants for self-employment under favourable conditions, with low interest and deferment of debt payoff
- a tax rate reduction in order to stimulate the economy, whose crises affect the poor and middle classes, the majority of whom are women
- organised training of women for work with modern technology

- measures to prevent age discrimination
- respecting the specific problems of women living in the countryside, their contribution to the family income and, in accordance with that, valorisation of their unpaid work
- active legislation which protects women from sexual blackmailing, intimidation, and sexual harassment

Social security

Croatian gender policy provides no quality answers for the actual crisis in the country. Unemployed women, single-mothers, women-farmers, women of the third age and women with special needs do not enjoy welfare such as they need. Working-able, though not employed, women's social welfare is limited, and women in the countryside de facto cannot even gain social protection. *Therefore . . .*

. . . we request:

- reducing state budget assignments for the army, secret services and police and its redirection to the social and health purposes, education, and the improvement of women's social status
- social state and politics that fulfill the specific needs of women
- a clear definition of legal boundaries for assisting women
- instead of narrowing, exercising and efficiently conducting legal social rights
- parliamentary control of assigned and spent means for social protection
- social security for women in the countryside, their right to appropriate, earned, pension
- making possible having additional work whose expenses follow the expenses of life without additional tax fees, contributions to the state budget or freezing gained rights for retired women
- accessible creche and kindergartens for all, during two work-shifts and, for the children of self-sustained mothers and those from poor families, services free of charge
- children's allowance that follows their life expenses, paid regularly; also equal allowance for unemployed women
- transparent information about social rights
- accessible abortion and contraception and safe healthcare for women

The level of health protection is falling and, accordingly, there is a shortage of preventative care, and expert examinations, while hospitalisation and medicines are more often denied. Such a situation especially affects women, in their work and private life. The first health services that Social Security stopped co-financing are contraception and abortion which, due to that fact, are now commercialised, and often unavailable. Since women have the right to decide whether or not she wants to have children, when, and with whom, contraception and abortion must be legal, safe, geographically and financially available to all women. State policy and the Church advocate prohibition of these methods, which leads to unacceptable pressure on gynaecologists and women themselves. *Therefore . . .*

. . . we request:

- medically approved and free abortions at all County hospitals, and severe, easily imposed sanctions for those refusing to perform abortions upon a woman's request
- accessible and free contraception according to the woman's choice
- easily accessible sterilisation and artificial insemination

- a public campaign about the importance of contraception and protection from sexual diseases
- free contraceptive counselling
- liberal sexual education in kindergartens, primary and secondary schools
- gynaecologists who respect women's needs and do not impose their own attitudes, or moral and religious beliefs
- increased state financing for preventative care (i.e. tests for early detection of uterine cancer, mammography, breast ultrasound, etc.), general and reproductive women's health care, and comprehensive health education
- consistent implementation of existing laws/bills regarding health care and its improvements in order to achieve a higher level of health security

Prevention of gender-based violence

Since the last war, there has been an atmosphere of increasing violence against women. One of many counselling helplines gets more than 260 calls a month. There are no legal protections in Croatia for women from domestic violence. The only shelter in Croatia faces an uncertain financial future. *Therefore . . .*

. . . we request:

- protection of women victims from violence by independent, autonomous state financed counselling offices, SOS-lines, shelters and self-help groups
- free medical examinations, treatment and psychological support for women who have experienced domestic violence
- legislative support and protection for women exposed to domestic violence, creation of a bill on domestic violence, and establishment of a special Family Court
- education of those employed at state administration (social care centres, police, Court, educational institutions, and health departments) about problems of violence against women
- establishment of special police units for cases of violence against women in which women will be employed
- a public campaign against gender-based violence financed by the state
- having official statistics on violence against women (Croatian Bureau of Statistics, police, health institutions, Courts, State prosecution) by gender and relation to the violator

Politics of equality and tolerance

Society, particularly in its educational system, supports traditional gender roles and stereotypes. Even more, stereotyping of male-female relationships is growing, and liberal sexual education has vanished from the curriculum. At the same time, society's tolerance decreases and violence increases. *Therefore . . .*

. . . we request:

- abatement of gender stereotypes in manuals and education, and adequate valorisation of women's roles in history and the present
- introducing the principles of non-violent communication and non-violent conflict resolution in primary school education
- abatement of religious education in schools and its return to religious communities
- demilitarisation of society and its politics
- supporting and financing for the non-governmental sector

Notes

1 Vedran Pavlic, "Women's Network of Croatia Asks PM-Designate Orešković to Protect Women's Rights." *Total News Croatia,* Jan. 10, 2016, www.total-croatia-news.com.

2 Kralja Držislava, "Women's Rights in Croatia under Threat after Parliamentary Elections in November 2015." *Split/Zagreb*, Dec. 31, 2015. Women's Network of Croatia/Iniative Féministe Euroméditerranéenne website, www.efi-ife.org.

3 "The Current Situation of Gender Equality in Croatia—Country Profile." Roland Berger Strategy Consultants GmbH Report for the European Commission, Directorate-General Justice, Unit D2, "Gender Equality," 2012, p. 4. European Commission website, ec.europa.eu.

4 "Saving Croatian Autonomous Women's Shelters," 2013. Women Against Violence Europe website, www.wave-network.org.

5 Women's Network Croatia, "Political Platform of Women's Network Croatia," 2006. Women's Network Croatia website, www.zenska-mreza.hr. Grammar in the translation amended by editor.

97

Action Plan
Women's Network of Disability Organisations
Finland
March 8, 2006

A screen shot of the Action Plan of the Women's Network of Disability Organisations.

As numerous international studies have found, women and girls with disabilities are more vulnerable to violence; almost 80 percent of women with disabilities are victims of violence and they are four times more likely than other women to suffer sexual violence.[1]

Globally, women with disabilities face challenges ranging from having a right to vote to having a right to reproduce, and then gaining access to voting and health-care facilities. They confront staggering rates of unemployment, violence, and poverty. Multiple groups and documents address gender and disability,[2] and the Finnish document reproduced here is fairly representative in its understanding of the problems. Finnish law defines a disabled person as "someone who, due to a disability or illness, has long-term difficulties in managing matters of everyday life," and prohibits discrimination based on disability.[3]

The Action Plan asserts a right to womanhood and personhood, and to both autonomy and the support services that make it possible. It is the interests and capacities of individuals with disabilities that should determine the contours of their sexual life and their leisure activities. In many cases, disabled women fight for the rights other women also struggle for: a violence-free existence, a real choice about whether to reproduce, and respect for their sexuality; despite such common ground, however, they face greater obstacles to gathering information and community, and greater vulnerability to violence and economic dependence.

While poverty affects women disproportionately more than men in the developing world (due to patriarchal property ownership structures), gender patterns in relation to disability indicate that poverty also hits women and girls with disabilities harder than other women. Women with disabilities are much further removed from the centres of power, and have very little influence on economic decisions. In addition, aid is less likely to reach women and girls who are less able to compete in situations of scarcity. Disability often leads to limited access to education and good jobs, thus perpetuating situations of poverty and dependence, especially for women and girls with disabilities.[4]

This situation calls for an intersectional approach to gender and disability.

Action Plan

Human rights
Disabled women must have and enjoy the same human rights as non-disabled women.
- Disabled women have the right to womanhood.
- A disabled woman must not be discriminated against on the ground of sex, age, origin, language, conviction, opinion, health, disability or other ground related to her person.

Participation in society and community affairs
- Disabled women shall receive encouragement and necessary prerequisites shall be created for her participation and visible involvement in the decision-making of her society.
- Full participation shall be enabled through appropriate support services.

Control of one's own life
- A disabled woman is entitled to receive information, guidance and support to manage activities of daily life.
- A disabled woman may also need external assistance. In the analysis of support needs, she must be considered as an active individual, rather than as an object to be cared for.

Access to information
- Disabled women and girls have a right to information about growing up into womanhood, as well as information about female sexuality and reproductive health.
- Disabled girls and their parents should receive realistic information about growing up into womanhood. Also, it is necessary to provide guidance on disability-related services, rehabilitation, and opportunities for training, leisure, study and work opportunities in view of the adult life.
- A woman who becomes disabled shall be offered information on services and assistance on how to continue her life as an independent woman in the changed circumstances.
- Access to information shall be ensured through necessary disability-specific methods. Material shall be available in easy-to-read format, in sign language,

in support signage, and signed speech formats, velotype, supportive communication methods, large print and Braille as well as in electronic and audio tape format.

- Professional personnel need education and materials on issues related to disability and womanhood.
- A disabled woman's own voice must be seen and heard in the media.

Rehabilitation, education and training, income support, and employment
- In rehabilitation, the female perspective must be fully taken into account, as well as individual needs that come over the course of a lifetime.
- In education and training, disabled women shall be guaranteed opportunities that are equal to those open to non-disabled women.
- While choosing a training course, the primary consideration must be the capacities and interests of the disabled woman or girl.
- A disabled woman shall have adequate income to enable her to lead an independent life.
- Equal opportunities to employment and equal pay shall be ensured.

Sexuality
- A disabled woman is entitled to her sexuality.
- Sexuality-related health services shall be accessible.
- A disabled woman shall be ensured an equal right to choose her sexual orientation.

Family life and parenthood
- A disabled woman has the right to family and experience parenthood.
- A disabled woman shall not be coerced to an abortion or sterilisation.
- A disabled mother has the right to disability-specific services and assistance in support of her motherhood.
- In divorce and separation situations, disability must not be a factor in a refusal of guardianship.
- Existence of a disability shall not be a factor preventing adoption.
- Taking children into foster care must not be caused by lack of necessary support services.

Violence and abuse
- A disabled woman has the right to personal integrity.
- The society must be made aware of the heightened threat of abuse, mental, economical and physical, towards disabled women.
- Shelters shall be accessible.
- Organizations of disabled people must empower the identity of disabled women and girls, and must support them so that they can be able to pre-empt and recognise the signs of sexual harassment and abuse.
- Disabled women and girls need self-defence courses that are specifically designed to meet their needs.

Networks and peer support
- Disabled women shall be offered an opportunity to empowerment within a peer support group.
- Peer support networks of disabled women shall be a part of the women's movement.

Research and statistics

- Research about disability and womanhood shall be increased by offering topics to undergraduate, postgraduate and doctoral students.
- Research and statistics should take account of disabled women, too.

Notes

1 European Disability Forum, "Joint DPO Submission on Finland," Feb. 2014, p. 7.
2 See, for example, "Our Mission and Vision," DisAbled Women's Network of Ontario, accessed 2017, http://www.dawncanada.net; and the 1997 Manifesto on the Rights of Women with Disabilities, EU Disability Forum, accessed 2017, http//.edf-feph.org.
3 "Disabled Persons." Living in Finland, Infopankki.Fi website, accessed 2017, www.infopankki.fi.
4 Agness Chindimba, "The Place of Women with Disabilities in Feminist Movements." *BUWA! A Journal on African Women's Experiences*, n.d,, p. 98.

98

The Charter of Feminist Principles for African Feminists
African Feminist Forum
Accra, Ghana
November 15–19, 2006

AFF logo.

As we invoke the memory of those women whose names are hardly ever recorded in any history books, we insist that it is a profound insult to claim that feminism was imported into Africa from the West. We reclaim and assert the long and rich tradition of African women's resistance to patriarchy in Africa. We henceforth claim the right to theorize for ourselves, write for ourselves, strategise for ourselves and speak for ourselves as African feminists.

African feminists usually get together across the continent under the auspices of international organizations. But this gathering of some 120 invited people at the African Feminist Forum was an independent event hosted by the African Women's Development Fund. The Charter they created collectively has been used as a movement-building tool by Feminist Forums in several African countries. It has been disseminated as far afield as Latin America and South East Asia in addition to Africa and has been translated into Spanish, Kiswahili (spoken in East Africa) and Wolof (spoken in West Africa). It has been used as a resource for training, awareness raising, mobilisation and constituency building, advocacy, organisational monitoring and review as well as education and policy development. It has been instrumental in shaping attitudes and practice especially within the women's movement in Africa.[1]

Its power is indisputable.

Muthoni Wanyeki describes the Charter's purposes: "The aim really is to provide a set of principles by which self-defined African feminists signing onto the Charter can be held accountable—both personally as well as in relation to the institutions they work in."[2] Josephine Ahikire adds, "[T]he Charter is an audacious positioning of African feminism as an ideological entity in the African body politic. . . . In many ways, the Charter set out to reverse the conservative dynamics that work to undermine the critical edge of African feminism, creating a sense of urgency about the need for the feminist movement to re-assert and re-energise itself."[3] The Charter addresses contentious issues within the African women's movement today, including reproductive freedom and nondiscrimination on the basis of sexual orientation. It also addresses institutional concerns such as ethics in governance, financial management, and human resource management. Putting these two sets of concerns together amounts to a challenge to African feminists regarding their internal practices and their external stands. The Charter is rooted in a commitment to end patriarchy and to grow the feminist movement.

While all the documents in this book appeal to feminist principles, this one, perhaps like that of the World March of Women, very explicitly lays down what those principles are. It celebrates feminist identity, and clarifies the character of patriarchy as an always-evolving system of male authority that enables and legitimizes the oppression of women; because it interacts with relationships based on class, race, ethnicity, religion, and global imperialism, "to challenge patriarchy effectively also requires challenging other systems of oppression and exploitation, which frequently mutually support each other." The document recognizes the role African women played in colonial struggles, and the more recent accomplishments of African feminists, who continue to play a part in the development of postcolonial states and in global feminist movements.

The list of "feminist principles" in the Charter,[4] divided into "individual ethics" and "feminist leadership," is novel and inspiring. Included on the first list are commitments to nonviolence and to difficult dialogue, and to the satisfaction of women's basic needs as well as to their possession of bodily integrity and to spiritual lives of their choosing. Included as guidelines for feminist organizations are

Participants in the AFF conference.

responsible use of power and authority; transparency and accountability; and the importance of growing a multigenerational group of leaders.

The Charter of Feminist Principles for African Feminists

Preamble: Naming Ourselves as Feminists

We define and name ourselves publicly as Feminists because we celebrate our feminist identities and politics. We recognize that the work of fighting for women's rights is deeply political, and the process of naming is political too. Choosing to name ourselves Feminist places us in a clear ideological position. By naming ourselves as Feminists we politicise the struggle for women's rights, we question the legitimacy of the structures that keep women subjugated, and we develop tools for transformatory analysis and action. We have multiple and varied identities as African Feminists. We are African women; we live here in Africa and even when we live elsewhere, our focus is on the lives of African women on the continent. Our feminist identity is not qualified with "Ifs," "Buts," or "Howevers": We are Feminists. Full stop.

Our Understanding of Feminism and Patriarchy

As African feminists our understanding of feminism places patriarchal social relations[,] structures[,] and systems which are embedded in other oppressive and exploitative structures at the center of our analysis. Patriarchy is a system of male authority which legitimizes the oppression of women through political, social, economic, legal, cultural, religious and military institutions. Men's access to, and control over, resources and rewards within the private and public sphere derives its legitimacy from the patriarchal ideology of male dominance. Patriarchy varies in time and space, meaning that it changes over time, and varies according to class, race, ethnic, religious and global-imperial relationships and structures. Furthermore, in the current conjunctures, patriarchy does not simply change according to these factors, but is inter-related with and informs relationships of class, race, ethnic, religious, and global-imperialism. Thus to challenge patriarchy effectively also requires challenging other systems of oppression and exploitation, which frequently mutually support each other.

Our understanding of Patriarchy is crucial because it provides for us, as feminists, a framework within which to express the totality of oppressive and exploitative relations which affect African women. Patriarchal ideology enables and legitimizes the structuring of every aspect of our lives by establishing the framework within which society defines and views men and women and constructs male supremacy. Our ideological task as feminists is to understand this system and our political task is to end it. Our focus is fighting against patriarchy as a system rather than fighting individual men or women. Therefore, as feminists, we define our work as investing individual and institutional energies in the struggle against all forms of patriarchal oppression and exploitation.

Our Identity as African Feminists

As Feminists who come from/work/live in Africa, we claim the right and the space to be Feminist and African. We recognize that we do not have a homogenous identity as feminists—we acknowledge and celebrate our diversities and our shared commitment to a transformatory agenda for African societies and African women in particular. This is what gives us our common feminist identity.

Our current struggles as African Feminists are inextricably linked to our past as a continent—diverse pre-colonial contexts, slavery, colonization, liberation struggles, neocolonialism, globalization, etc. Modern African States were built off the backs of African Feminists who fought alongside men for the liberation of the continent. As we craft new African States in this new millennium, we also craft new identities for African women, identities as full citizens, free from patriarchal oppression, with rights of access, ownership and control over resources and our own bodies and utilizing positive aspects of our cultures in liberating and nurturing ways. We also recognize that our pre-colonial, colonial and post-colonial histories and herstories require special measures to be taken in favour of particular African women in different contexts.

We acknowledge the historical and significant gains that have been made by the African Women's Movement over the past forty years, and we make bold to lay claim to these gains as African feminists: they happened because African Feminists led the way, from the grassroots level and up; they strategised, organized, networked, went on strike and marched in protest, and did the research, analysis, lobbying, institution building and all that it took for States, employers and institutions to acknowledge women's personhood.

As African feminists, we are also part of a global feminist movement against patriarchal oppression in all its manifestations. Our experiences are linked to that of women in other parts of the world with whom we have shared solidarity and support over the years. As we assert our space as African feminists, we also draw inspiration from our feminist ancestors who blazed the trail and made it possible to affirm the rights of African women. As we invoke the memory of those women whose names are hardly ever recorded in any history books, we insist that it is a profound insult to claim that feminism was imported into Africa from the West. We reclaim and assert the long and rich tradition of African women's resistance to patriarchy in Africa. We henceforth claim the right to theorize for ourselves, write for ourselves, strategise for ourselves and speak for ourselves as African feminists.

Individual Ethics
As individual feminists, we are committed to and believe in gender equality based on feminist principles which are:
- The indivisibility, inalienability and universality of women's human rights.
- The effective participation in building and strengthening progressive African feminist organizing and networking to bring about transformatory change.
- A spirit of feminist solidarity and mutual respect based on frank, honest and open discussion of difference with each other.
- The support, nurture, and care of other African feminists, along with the care for our own well-being.
- The practice of non-violence and the achievement of non-violent societies.
- The right of all women to live free of patriarchal oppression, discrimination and violence.
- The right of all women to have access to sustainable and just livelihoods as well as welfare provision, including quality health care, education, water and sanitation.

- Freedom of choice and autonomy regarding bodily integrity issues, including reproductive rights, abortion, sexual identity and sexual orientation.
- A critical engagement with discourses of religion, culture, tradition and domesticity with a focus on the centrality of women's rights.
- The recognition and presentation of African women as the subjects not the objects of our work, and as agents in their lives and societies.
- The right to healthy, mutually respectful and fulfilling personal relationships.
- The right to express our spirituality within or outside of organized religions.
- The acknowledgment of the feminist agency of African women which has a rich Herstory that has been largely undocumented and ignored.

Institutional Ethics

As feminist organisations we commit to the following:
- Advocating for openness, transparency, equality and accountability in feminist-led institutions and organisations.
- Affirming that being a feminist institution is not incompatible with being professional, efficient, disciplined and accountable.
- Insisting on and supporting African women's labour rights, including egalitarian governance, fair and equal remuneration and maternity policies.
- Using power and authority responsibly, and managing institutional hierarchies with respect for all concerned. We believe that feminist spaces are created to empower and uplift women. At no time should we allow our institutional spaces to degenerate into sites of oppression and undermining of other women.
- Exercising responsible leadership and management of organisations whether in a paid or unpaid capacity and striving to uphold critical feminist values and principles at all times.
- Exercising accountable leadership in feminist organisations taking into consideration the needs of others for self-fulfillment and professional development. This includes creating spaces for powersharing across-generations.
- Creating and sustaining feminist organisations to foster women's leadership. Women's organizations and networks should be led and managed by women. It is a contradiction of feminist leadership principles to have men leading, managing and being spokespersons for women's organizations.
- Feminist organisations as models of good practice in the community of civil society organizations, ensuring that the financial and material resources mobilised in the name of African women are put to the service of African women and not diverted to serve personal interests. Systems and structures with appropriate Codes of Conduct to prevent corruption and fraud, and to manage disputes and complaints fairly, are the means of ensuring institutionalized [transparency] within our organizations.
- Striving to inform our activism with theoretical analysis and to connect the practice of activism to our theoretical understanding of African feminism.
- Being open to critically assessing our impact as feminist organizations, and being honest and proactive with regards to our role in the movement.
- Opposing the subversion and/or hijacking of autonomous feminist spaces to serve right wing, conservative agendas.
- Ensuring that feminist non-governmental or mass organisations are created in response to real needs expressed by women that need to be met, and not to serve selfish interests, and unaccountable income generating.

Feminist Leadership

As leaders in the feminist movement, we recognize that feminist agency has popularized the notion of women as leaders. As feminist leaders we are committed to making a critical difference in leadership, based on the understanding that the quality of women's leadership is even more important than the numbers of women in leadership. We believe in and commit ourselves to the following:

- Disciplined work ethics guided by integrity and accountability at all times.
- Expanding and strengthening a multi-generational network and pool of feminist leaders across the continent.
- Ensuring that the feminist movement is recognised as a legitimate constituency for women in leadership positions.
- Building and expanding our knowledge and information base on an ongoing basis, as the foundation for shaping our analysis and strategies and for championing a culture of learning beginning with ourselves within the feminist movement.
- Nurturing, mentoring and providing opportunities for young feminists in a non-matronising manner.
- Crediting African women's labour, intellectual and otherwise in our work.
- Creating time to respond in a competent, credible and reliable manner to other feminists in need of solidarity and support whether political, practical or emotional.
- Being open to giving and receiving peer reviews and constructive feedback from other feminists.

Notes

1 Josephine Ahikire, "African Feminism in Context: Reflections on the Legitimation Battles, Victories, and Reversals." *Feminist Africa* 19 (Sept. 2014): 7.
2 L. Muthoni Wanyeki, "The African Feminist Forum: Beginnings." Isis International website, accessed 2017, www.isiswomen.org.
3 Ahikire, p. 7.
4 African Feminist Forum, "Feminist Charter," 2006. African Feminist Forum website, www .africanfeministforum.com.

99

Dalit Women's Charter
Feminist Dalit Organization
Kathmandu, Nepal
2007

Feminist Dalit Organization logo.

For centuries, democracy and human rights have been looked at and understood based on the views and experiences of men and, as a result, they have been defined in a discriminatory manner.

Dalit women established the Feminist Dalit Organization (FEDO) to create a movement to "fight against caste and gender discrimination and to construct a just and equitable society." It is part of the women's movement that arose after the people's movement for democracy in 1990. FEDO has grown from literacy and awareness classes to become the coordinating force of the national Dalit women's movement. It fights for the Nepalese Dalit community in general, and women in particular, as do most organizations working with women from marginalized groups. It identifies itself as a feminist movement–based organization that employs an international human rights approach while working through its fifty-six chapters to assess local needs and to invite community members to empower themselves and build their skills. Because of the numerous challenges Dalit women confront, FEDO builds coalitions nationally and internationally, and employs strategies ranging from rallies and media campaigns to lobbying and workshops. In 2011 it organized a national conference.

Despite a 1963 legal decree against caste-based discrimination, Dalits continue to be considered the lowest, or "untouchables," in Nepal's centuries-old caste system (and there are over twenty Dalit caste groups).[1] While Nepal is one of the poorest countries in Asia, Dalits, like many oppressed groups, have a higher poverty rate (around 90 percent) and a shorter lifespan (about fifty-one years) than other groups. Dalit women and girls experience "widespread, deep rooted, and hidden" violence, estimated to touch the lives of 75 percent of the female population; they are the most illiterate (around 80 percent), undereducated, politically underrepresented group in the country. FEDO focuses especially on poor, rural Dalit women, but is reaching out to young urban women and girls, as well. Their core issues are gender-based violence, services and opportunities, caste-based discrimination, and political representation.

In some ways the Charter below[2] is reminiscent of documents from a century and a half ago, inasmuch as it is demanding such fundamental rights as the right to own property, to have custody of one's children, to be educated, to have political representation, to be free from forced labor, and to have employment opportunities. But it is also distinctly modern, in that it recommends such things as quotas on representation and appeals to international human rights law, has to reckon with the commercialization of education and healthcare, and employs an intersectional approach. It follows both older and newer manifestos in its understanding that equality for Dalit women requires a restructuring of society socially, legally, culturally, and economically.

Dalit feminist issues have global resonance, as evidenced by this poster advertising a Dalit feminist support event in Los Angeles, California, in 2015.

During a ten-year civil war in Nepal that ended in 2007, Dalit women suffered much violence. The Peace Agreement opened the door for a new constitution, which explains some of the references in the Charter below. In 2015 Nepal experienced an earthquake that killed some nine thousand people and left hundreds of thousands homeless. Like most disasters in poor and politically weak countries, this worsened the conditions of the worst off. Traffickers, for example, preyed on vulnerable women and girls. FEDO established a Rapid Earthquake Relief Support Project to assess the needs of Dalit households and provide support.

Dalit Women's Charter

[Preamble omitted]

The Condition of Dalit Women

We believe that Nepal can be transformed into a fully democratic republic state only by ensuring the representation of Dalit women, who are the most backward in social, economic, political and education sectors, in all aspects of state restructuring. Therefore, we request that (restructuring) be conducted in this manner (through representation of Dalit women). Nepal has been left behind politically and economically because of the feudalistic and patriarchal structure that has existed in the country for centuries, and also because of Brahminic control over means of production. Since only non-Dalit women have access to the facilities and opportunities that are made available by the government for women, Dalit women have been further isolated from the state structure. Nepal is one of the poorest countries in the world because of the state's discriminatory policies towards Dalits from time immemorial.

We, Nepali Dalit women, condemn the various types of ethnic and gender-based discrimination and we demand that our rights be guaranteed by utilising this historical opportunity that the current political changes in the country have offered.

The Dalits, who comprise 25 percent of the total population, have been isolated because of the practice of untouchability, which exists even in the 21st century as the remains of the feudal system. A crime is being committed against Dalits. As a result of such practices of untouchability, Dalit women have been further marginalised. Therefore, they are forced to endure violence, exploitation and risks. We allege that the patriarchal values that dominate the country, society, political parties, civil society and households are core elements that lead to the backwardness of women. The patriarchal system has limited women to the household, within the boundaries of domestic and social work, and only men have taken the responsibility for social and political work and leadership. For centuries, democracy and human rights have been looked at and understood based on the views and experiences of men and, as a result, they have been defined in a discriminatory manner. The structures of community, society and state have been organized and brought into use in a manner such that it is easy for men to (adopt) leadership role[s] and benefit from them (the structures).

We, Dalit women, have the right to make decisions to control our own lives and bodies. We have an important responsibility towards society, home, family and the state. However, we have been deprived of the opportunity to make decisions and we have been isolated from decision-making roles. We want to be partners in all decision-making levels, within the household as well as the state. We demand that proportional participation of Dalit women in all social, economic and political decision-making processes and levels be made mandatory.

The future changes in the social, economic, legal and political systems of Nepal should be based on the experiences of Dalit women, who represent Dalit women from different districts of the country and have been working for Dalit women's issues.

All Dalit women strongly demand that in order to end the existing discriminatory values, behaviours, policies/rules, that impact all aspects of our life, including health, education, communication, traditions, family and married life, culture, religion, and finance, that they be analysed from social, economic and cultural rights as well as political and civil rights standpoint, and that they (the rights) be guaranteed from the human rights perspective.

1. Political and Civil Life

Traditionally, Dalit women were isolated from political, civil and community-level decision-making processes. To ensure inclusive democracy, Dalit women's participation is necessary in all political activities. For this purpose, we demand that the following tasks be accomplished and implemented.

- 13 percent of the seats in the constituent assembly election should be reserved for Dalit women.
- Equal access and opportunities should be ensured for Dalit women at all levels of policy-making and leadership, existing as well as those that will be created. Political parties are the foundation of a democratic republic. Democracy can be upheld in a country only if they (the political parties) are democratic, inclusive and transparent. Since the objective of the democratic system is to make backward communities equally capable as other citizens, we demand proportional representation of Dalit women in each sector.
- Inclusive proportional participation of Dalit women should be made mandatory at all levels within the political parties, from decision making to village levels. Legal provisions should be made to deny national party recognition to the parties that do not have participation of Dalit women at all levels.
- 20 percent of seats reserved for the Dalit community and 10 percent of the seats reserved for women at all levels of the state should be reserved for Dalit women.
- Traditional institutions should be restructured as per the principle of democracy.
- The state should build special mechanisms to support full political participation of Dalit women.
- Dalit women should be free of political fear and threat.

2. Equality

Equality is the main principle of our Charter. All our rights are based on the principle of equality. We believe that there should be equality between men and women and also between Dalit women and non-Dalit women. During the upcoming restructuring of [the] state, disparities between different women should be identified and a special system should be implemented to eliminate the problems of ethnic discrimination, gender discrimination and sexual exploitation that Dalit women have been facing. The demands put forward in the course of our struggle for equality are based on the fact that Dalit women are behind in all spheres of life and are discriminated against. We believe that in the present economic and political context, only superficial equal behaviour towards Dalit women, other women and men cannot (actually) maintain equality. Therefore, in order to promote equality in the real sense, special provisions are necessary for Dalit women for the time being.

Equality is essential in every aspect of life. We demand that we are treated equally in every aspect of life, from family and workplace to state affairs, and an atmosphere be created to ensure equality. Therefore, we demand that the following legal provisions be made to provide directives, so that all the policies, regulations and legal provisions made by the government reflect equality.

- Public places are still not accessible to Dalits. To end this, it should be defined as a crime, which might even lead to invalidation of citizenships of those who engage in discriminatory behaviour in public places.
- Special legal provisions should be made to establish the rights of Dalit women in the future restructured state. We demand that special arrangements be made to ensure their equal proportional participation in the decision-making levels of state restructuring. Apart from this, there should be just participation of Dalit women in social, economic, political, cultural and civil life. Special arrangements should be made so that everyone is able to equally reap the benefits of development.
- By focusing on the provisions of the convention regarding uprooting all kinds of violence against Dalit women, the Civil Act should be amended to allocate a 20 percent quota for proportional participation of Dalit women in government services. There should be provisions for positive discrimination, to increase Dalit women's participation at the decision-making level.
- The participation of Dalit women in nation's security agencies, such as Nepal Police and Nepali Army, is important. This is not possible without making special arrangements for Dalit women and without the amendment of Acts regarding Nepal Police and Nepali Army. Therefore, the Acts pertaining to the Nepali Army and Nepal Police should be changed, and a 20 percent quota should be allocated for Dalit women.
- A separate high level commission should be formed to provide suggestions to the government to ensure and promote participation of Dalit women at all levels of the nation, to investigate as necessary and to monitor whether or not provisions for equal participation exist within government agencies.
- From within the 33 percent, which is reserved for women, proportional participation should be ensured for Dalit women on the basis of population.
- Everyone should strictly follow national laws, based on general conventions, to uproot discrimination based on caste, gender and other criteria. A commission should be formed for its implementation.

3. Rehabilitation/Reunion

Dalit women who were part of the agitating army have been affected in various ways by the 12 years of armed movement in the country. Some are mutilated, some were raped, some are living the lives of a displaced (person) and some have been forced to spend their lives as a widow. Similarly, the children of hundreds of

Dalit women have run away because of the conflict, they were forced to embrace various risky jobs and were made to disappear. Focusing on this, we demand that the current government prioritise and carry out the following activities.

- A countrywide investigation should be carried out to gather accurate information about war-affected Dalit women.
- Proper medical treatment, counselling and suitable compensation should be provided, as needed, to Dalit women, who were mutilated, raped and sexually exploited.
- Appropriate investigation of disappeared Dalits should be carried out and their status should be made public. Appropriate compensation and help should be provided to the families of the disappeared and an environment should be created, where internally displaced people can return home with dignity.
- All Dalit children below the age of 18, who were forced to engage in risky jobs, inside and outside of the country, should be rescued and proper arrangements should be made to improve their lives.
- Rehabilitation/reunion is not possible without justice. Therefore, suitable investigations should be conducted about the crimes that were committed during the conflict and appropriate actions should be taken against perpetrators.
- Special legal provisions should be implemented to end impunity.

4. Law and Justice

We have all accepted the fact that law guided by feudal and patriarchal thinking has not been able to provide necessary justice to Dalit women. Therefore, we demand that the following provisions be made for the development, usage and explanation of laws, based on the principles of equality.

- Appropriate training should be organized to explain gender and ethnic perspectives to all legal practitioners and judges and the restructuring of the judicial administration is absolutely necessary.
- Special policy, incorporating special legal provisions, should be formulated for participation of Dalit women in judicial services. For this, the social, economic and political conditions of Dalit women should be analysed while formulating, using and interpreting policies and making laws.
- Dalit women's rights for legal assistance should be ensured through the creation of family courts and close court system.
- Equality for Dalit women should be guaranteed in every aspect of law.
- Legal provisions should be made to ensure the rights of Dalit women to own property, buy and sell (property), their land rights, ancestral rights and equal rights over paternal property.
- Legal provisions should be made to guarantee participation of Dalit women in the decision-making levels of public, government and non government sectors.
- Necessary new laws should be created, through a human rights perspective, to end different types of violence that are done to or could be done to women because of their status as Dalits and women, due to the weak structure of the country.
- Laws against rape should be promulgated and an implementation mechanism should be immediately built.
- Provisions should be immediately made for a victim-oriented justice system. Policy framework has to be prepared for capacity building of all sectors that are required for this.

- Laws should be created to ensure participation of Dalit women at all levels, from members to employees, in high level independent commissions like the Human Rights Commission, Women's Commission and Dalit Commission.
- Laws should be formed to guarantee proportional participation of Dalit women at all levels, from members to employee, in constitutional commissions like the Election Commission, Commission for the Investigation of Abuse of Authority and Public Service Commission.
- Laws should be created to guarantee participation of Dalit women in all commissions and committees, which are formed by the government to serve any purpose.
- Laws should be formed to ensure participation of Dalit women in judicial services, from the Supreme Court to the Appellate Court, district courts and special courts. Along with this, laws with special arrangements should be created to provide access to Dalit women to every level of judicial services.
- If any Dalit woman is found to be a criminal, provisions should be made to punish her equally, based on the nature of the crime.

5. Economic System

The economic rights of women are of great importance for empowerment and equality of Dalit women. The prevailing economic system and economic policies have not assessed women's work. There is a stronghold of men and non-Dalit women in strategic places of the economic sector. Participation of Dalit women is limited due to different social, economic and ideological impediments prevailing in the economic structure. Similarly, Dalit women don't have social security in workplaces. Even minimum facilities, such as child care, treatment and special arrangements during menstruation are not available. The working environment is not safe for them. Dalit women are exploited in different offices, compelled to leave their job or take risks because of these reasons. Therefore, we would like to put forth the following demands for equal participation of Dalit women in the economic sector.

- The state should implement special programme packages to modernise indigenous occupations and skills of the Dalits.
- The practice of classifying work based on gender and ethnicity should be immediately stopped. To discourage the trend of such classification, division of work on the basis of gender should be made punishable by law.
- Policy based arrangement should be made for (providing) pension, safe accommodation, and medical services at places where Dalit women work. In addition, perpetrators of ethnic discrimination should be punished by the law and arrangements should be made to dismiss registration of such offices and make them pay penalty.
- Statistics of single women, widows and Dalit women who are sole bread earners should be collected and arrangements should be made for (providing) special employment and facilities to them. The government should make provisions for special concession cards for Dalit women who are sole bread earners of the family.
- Health facilities (should be made available) and safe environment should be created for Dalit women working in the informal sector. Their jobs should be evaluated and employment should be guaranteed for them.
- The trend of arbitrarily providing minimum wages to Dalit women in the informal sector, practicing different forms of exploitation and compelling them

to work against their will should be ended. Necessary legal and administrative provisions should be made to end exploitation in the informal sector and to maintain justice.

- Provisions should be made to allow women, working in the informal sector, to form trade unions.
- The state should play a supportive role in providing collateral-free loans to Dalit women, in identifying businesses and in market management, so that they (Dalit women) can initiate new economic enterprises.
- Mechanisms should be developed to ensure participation of Dalit women at all levels, from the Ministry of Finance to policy formulation for economic transactions, discussions for economic development of country, plan formulation and development of implementation mechanisms.

6. Education and Training

Education is a basic human right. Education is the most essential element for the 21st century human being. However, [the] majority of the Dalits in Nepal are deprived of education. The education provided by the current education system especially schools, colleges and vocational training (institutions) does not incorporate the experiences and needs of Dalit women. Thus, we put forth the following demands.

- The current education (system) in Nepal is patriarchal and everyone does not have access to it. Further, it is unpractical and discriminatory. Thus, people-oriented and practical education policy should be implemented.
- Compulsory education with (full) scholarship should be provided to Dalit women from primary to higher level education, in both technical and non-technical fields.
- Rapidly increasing commercialisation of the education sector should be stopped and discriminatory education should be abolished.
- Education institutions with special facilities and materials should be organized for child care centres and for differently-abled people.
- The materials that are in the curriculum and portray ethnic discrimination should be immediately removed and the curriculum should be reformed in a way such that it respects the ancestral occupations of Dalits.
- Educational materials that eliminate ethnic and gender discrimination and raise awareness should be included in the curriculum from primary to higher level education.
- The needs of the working, rural, differently-abled, single and adult Dalit women should be identified and provisions should be made to provide accessible quality education to them.
- Compulsory provisions should be made to include one female Dalit teacher in each school.

7. Development, Physical Infrastructure, and Environment

Women take major responsibility in the community and the household. Despite this, majority of Dalit women are deprived of essential basic facilities that are required for management of household, family and society. We are still deprived of an environment for healthy and productive life. Dalit women have not even been able to enjoy the fruits of basic development, which is essential for life. Slowly increasing encroachment of land, forest and water at the community level and privatisation has made the lives of landless settlers, squatters, and farmer Dalit women, residing in rural communities, more difficult. Realising these facts, we demand that the following tasks be accomplished for (the establishment of) new Nepal. The following task needs to be accomplished to make legal provisions for physical development environment and its implementation.

- Commitments should be made and implementation mechanisms should be developed to execute each development programme from the perspective of Dalit rights.
- While implementing the development projects, it should be ensured that Dalit women also benefit from possible employment opportunities at such projects.
- Policies should be formulated and budget should be allocated for providing safe drinking water and latrines in all places, including Dalit villages and settlements.
- Arrangements should be made to render electricity and telephone available in Dalit settlements and villages through prioritisation.
- Safe shelter is the right of all Dalit women. Understanding that women are exposed to different types of violence in the absence of safe houses, arrangements should be made to develop rural shelters for Dalit women and arrangements should be made to provide loan to Dalit women for safe shelters in an easy manner.
- Dalit squatters should be guaranteed safe shelters.
- Special health, education, entertainment and social welfare facilities should be made available to Dalit women.
- Policies and programmes for conservation and utilisation of natural resources should be implemented in a way such that it ensures Dalit women's rights and the benefits from it should be equally distributed.
- Dalit women play a vital role in management and conservation of natural resources. Therefore, Dalit women's right of participation at the decision-making level should be ensured while making decisions on management and mobilisation of natural resources at the community level.

8. Social Services
Social service is a right, not a facility. The following provisions should be made to provide social services in a manner accessible to Dalit women.

- The state and private sector should provide social welfare services to Dalit women as per the principle of social justice, equality and access.
- Social service should specifically incorporate the needs of differently-abled, single and widowed Dalit women residing in rural and geographically remote areas.
- Provisions for economic and social security should be guaranteed for Dalit women, on the basis of equality.
- All social services should be made easily available and accessible to Dalit women.

9. Family and Conjugal Life
There are many families in our society who have not been able to utilise equal rights or responsibilities and reap the benefits. Dalit women have unequal responsibilities in household chores. They have very limited rights to make decisions. To change this, the current democratic government should guarantee the following provisions and rights for Dalit women.

- All types of families should be entitled to equal recognition and treatment.
- Dalit women should have equality in family matters, marriage and cordial relationships.

- Dalit women should get equal property rights as husbands and brothers.
- During the process of marriage and divorce, Dalit women should be guaranteed the right to equal participation.
- Arrangements should be made to ensure Dalit women's equal access and control over economic resources of the family.
- There should be provisions for Dalit women to receive guardianship of their children.
- Inter-caste marriage should be legally recognised and the state should initiate programmes to further encourage it.

10. Customs, Culture, and Religion

Hindu customs, culture, and religion, which prevail in our society and are followed by the majority, discriminate against and look down upon Dalit women. Gender biased activities and roles are imposed upon Dalit women. The burden of untouchability, on the ground of ethnicity, has been imposed on Dalit women by women themselves. Dalit women have been side-lined from the decision making process and leadership and participation in various religious and cultural traditions and customs. This type of discriminatory tradition and behaviour should be ended. The following provisions are necessary for this.

- Dalit women should be established in society in a respectful manner by ending traditional superstitions and age-old negative traditions, including untouchability, *chhaupadi* , dowry, treasure digging, *balighare* [*tr.* exchanging skill for harvest] and sexual exploitation of Badi women, and by providing security to couples of inter-caste marriage.
- In laws regarding human rights, custom, culture and religion should be incorporated under the glossary of equality.
- All Dalit women should be allowed to freely practice their religion, culture and customs, without any kind of discrimination.
- The cultures, traditions, and customs that adversely affect, discriminate against and harm Dalit women in some way or other, should be changed.
- An action plan should be formed to guarantee elimination of all kinds of systems and traditions that harm Dalit women, keep them in isolation and abuse their human rights under the guise of religion, custom and culture.

11. Violence against Dalit Women

Violence against Dalit women is being practiced in Nepali society on the basis of discriminatory social, cultural, economic, religious and political tradition and beliefs. The following provisions are necessary to end such violence.

- Dalit women should be guaranteed security at home, in the community, workplace and public places, and their rights to be free from all kinds of violence should be ensured.
- The state should take responsibility for enforcing issues like dignity, morality and equality of human beings in the form of public education.
- There should be appropriate provisions for protecting Dalit women from sexual misconduct, violence and exploitation.
- Centres where Dalit women can register their complaints against rape, beatings and sexual misconduct, and get necessary treatment and counselling services, including medical tests, should be established and they should be staffed with trained personnel.

- Necessary education and training should be provided to police, doctors, surgeons, lawyers and judges to register, inquire about and investigate cases like rape, beatings and sexual misconduct.
- Efforts should be made to form laws that provide full justice to victims, and the capacity of implementation mechanism for such laws should be increased, so that they can work from a human rights perspective.
- The state should immediately organize shelters and counselling centres for Dalit women who have been victims of rape, beatings and sexual misconduct. Such counselling centres should be established in all districts. The state should allocate separate budgets for safe shelters, counselling centres, and institutions, which are sensitive towards the rights of Dalit women, [who] should be responsible for managing such centres.
- A high level commission should be formed to end violence and discrimination against Dalit women.

12. Health

Health services and consultation have become a dream for rural Dalit women. Most Dalit women have lost their lives in the absence of basic health services. The mortality rate in Nepal is highest among Dalit women. Along with this, Dalit women are plagued with more health-related problems than people of other castes. Dalit women are even unaware of the fact that health care is their right, thus they are unable to raise their voices to demand it. That is why, to establish health as a human right, the following provisions or tasks need to be immediately implemented.

- Because of increasing privatisation and commercialisation of health services, such services are beyond the reach of Dalit women. Thus, such privatisation and commercialisation should be discouraged and health service should be made easily accessible.
- The special health needs of Dalit women should be addressed through easily accessible and free health service.
- Standard health service and benefits should be ensured for Dalit women from the village level to the national level.
- Family planning related education, information and material should be made available to Dalit women and men free of charge.
- The state should make arrangements to ensure sufficient nourishment for Dalit women.
- The problem of uterine prolapse is predominant among Dalit women. The main reason for this is; they face violence from birth, unequal behaviour toward them, their work load and lack of proper support during child birth and immediately after child birth. These facts should be thought about and policies should be formed, implemented and budget should be allocated to solve problems related to uterine prolapse and treatment should be provided to those suffering from it.

13. Media

The reach of Dalits in media, such as newspapers, television and computers is not currently ensured. Through the following provisions, opportunities should be provided for Dalit women to be well-informed and well-educated.
- Participation of Dalit women should be ensured in all media.
- Policies should be formulated for broadcasting and publishing, in all forms of media, the contributions of Dalit women in public as well as private sectors.

- With the goal of solving the current caste-based and gender-based discrimination, the media should advance activities that encourage equality.
- Participation of Dalit women should be ensured in both government and private media sectors.

14. Dalit Women and Agriculture

Nepal is a country where most depend on agriculture. More than 75 percent of those in the agriculture sector are women. Among them, the participation of Dalit women is highest. Many Dalit farmers in Nepal are landless because of the patriarchal and feudal land-ownership rights system. Dalit women are not even defined as farmers because they don't have land rights. Similarly, hundreds of thousands of Dalit women in the country are surviving by working as agricultural labourers. Thus, we put forward the following demands.

- The right to eat is interlinked with the right to live. Both these rights have to be ensured and implemented by the constitution as the fundamental rights of women.
- Revolutionary land-reform programmes should be immediately implemented and necessary land should be made available to Dalit women.
- Legal provisions should be enforced to grant women equal land rights as men.
- Access and control of local communities, especially Dalit women, to local seeds and saplings, biological diversity and natural resources should be guaranteed.
- Food security should be guaranteed for Dalit women.
- The widespread disparity in daily wages paid to women and men should be immediately brought to an end and an equal wage system should be implemented.
- Infant care should be organized and toilets should be made available for the children of women working as agricultural labourers.

15. Conclusion

This Charter reflects the experiences, perspectives, and expectations of common Dalit women. We are ending our silence, and through this Charter we request that the expected changes and state restructuring be implemented for respect of human values, to end discrimination and for social, economic, cultural and political equality. During the restructuring of the state, special provisions should be guaranteed for ensuring the reproductive role and related rights of Dalit women and the principles of international documents on human rights should also be fully guaranteed. Dalit women are marginalised by the state because of various reasons. They are compelled to endure different types of violence, discrimination and harassments. Bearing this in mind, legal provisions should be made to include women in the decision making levels and to end differences between Dalit and non-Dalit women. New Nepal should guarantee proportional representation of Dalit women, who have for centuries been left behind from all levels of the state. Reiterating that such atmosphere is impossible as long as the unitary regime prevails in the country, we demand a fully democratic republic state.

   We would like to remind, [that] the establishment of sustainable peace in the country is not possible until these demands are fulfilled. We also declare that our struggle will continue until our demands are met.

Notes

1 Much information is taken from FEDOs 2013–2017 Strategic Plan, found on the FEDO website, www.fedonepal.org.

2 "Dalit Women's Charter," 2007. Feminist Dalit Organization website, www.fedonepal.org. Small grammatical changes to translation by author.

100

Women's Declaration on Food Sovereignty
Nyéléni: Forum for Food Sovereignty
Sélingué, Mali
February 23–27, 2007

An illustration of the Nyéléni figure, for whom the forum was named. Art by Anna Loveday-Brown.

In Mali there is a powerful symbol which could serve as the symbol of food sovereignty. It's a woman who left her mark in the history of Mali, as a woman and as a great farmer. When you mention her name everyone knows what this name represents. She is the mother who brings food, the mother who farms, who fought for her recognition as a woman in an environment which wasn't favourable to her. This woman was called Nyéléni. If we use this symbol everyone in Mali will know that it's a struggle for food, a struggle for food sovereignty.[1]

This forum in Mali helped to establish an international agenda for food sovereignty. The general Declaration that emerged was signed by over five hundred people from some eighty countries, representing "organizations of peasants/family farmers, artisanal fisher-folk, indigenous peoples, landless peoples, rural workers, migrants, pastoralists, forest communities, women, youth, consumers, environmental and urban movements." The goals of the gathering were epistemological ("to deepen our collective understanding of food sovereignty, to learn from one another the specific challenges and struggles in which we are engaged"), political ("to broaden our capacity for common action and solidarity, to think together strategically and tactically in terms of both local and international arenas of struggle"), and inclusive ("to root our work in the diversity of peoples, cultures, and struggles we represent").[2]

Site of the 2007 Nyéléni Forum.

The Women's Declaration[3] is an argument that food sovereignty is a feminist issue. What, exactly, are the links between feminism and food sovereignty?

- The document claims that it is "the capitalist and patriarchal world which puts the interests of the market before the rights of people." Food production and consumption are tied to larger political systems that feminism challenges. This "struggle [is] part of the fight for equality between the sexes," the document asserts.
- The goals are consistent with feminist values. As stated in the Declaration, "We want to seize this opportunity to leave behind all sexist prejudice and build a new vision of the world based on respect, equality, justice, solidarity, peace and freedom."
- As producers of "up to 80% of the food in the world's poorest countries," women are particularly affected by neoliberal and sexist policies.
- Women's autonomy is considered a necessary condition for food sovereignty; for example, the goal cannot be reached if women do not have access to land or credit.
- Agricultural chemicals and genetic modification negatively impact women's reproductive lives.

The movement for food sovereignty seems to be one in which women's diverse voices are heard and impactful. At this forum, for example, women both held a "preforum" women's assembly and integrated their perspectives into all the sectors (peasants, Indigenous, etc.). Too, it seems to respect and use women's knowledge of food production and preparation, including women's experiences with collective use of land. Interestingly, food sovereignty is considered a "new right." Feminist analysis of human rights has revealed that rights have not historically been understood in ways that include the diversity of human situations, including most women's lives, so food sovereignty is familiar territory where women can make important contributions.

Women's Declaration on Food Sovereignty

We, women from more than 40 countries, from different indigenous peoples of Africa, the Americas, Europe, Asia and Oceania and from different sectors and social movements, have gathered together in Sélingué (Mali) at Nyéléni 2007 to participate in the creation of a new right: the right to food sovereignty. We reaffirm our will to act to change the capitalist and patriarchal world which puts the interests of the market before the rights of people.

Women, who throughout history have been the creators of knowledge about food and agriculture, who still produce up to 80% of the food in the world's poorest countries and are today the principal guardians of biodiversity and agricultural seeds, are particularly affected by neo-liberal and sexist policies.

We suffer the dramatic consequences of these policies: poverty, inadequate access to resources, patents on living organisms, rural exodus and forced migration, war and all forms of physical and sexual violence. Monocultures, including those dedicated to agrofuels, and the widespread use of chemicals and genetically-modified organisms have a harmful effect on the environment and on human health, particularly reproductive health.

The industrial model and the transnationals threaten the very existence of peasant agriculture, small-scale fishing and herding, as well as the small-scale preparation and sale of food in both urban and rural environments, all sectors where women play a major role.

We want to see food and agriculture taken out of the WTO and out of free trade agreements. What is more, we reject the capitalist and patriarchal institutions that see food, water, land and traditional knowledge, as well as women's bodies, as mere commodities.

Seeing our struggle as part of the fight for equality between the sexes, we are no longer prepared to submit to the oppression of traditional or modern society, nor to the oppression of the market. We want to seize this opportunity to leave behind all sexist prejudice and build a new vision of the world based on respect, equality, justice, solidarity, peace and freedom.

We are mobilized. We are fighting for access to land, to territory, to water and to seeds. We are fighting for access to finance and to agricultural tools. We are fighting for good working conditions. We are fighting for access to training and to information. We are fighting for our independence and for the right to decide for ourselves, and for our full participation in decision-making.

Under the watchful eye of Nyéléni, an African woman who defied discriminatory rules, who shone through her creativity and agricultural prowess, we will find the energy to give effect to food sovereignty and, thereby, the hope of building a different world. We will find this energy in our solidarity. We will take this message to women all over the world.

Notes

1   "Nyéléni was a woman . . ." Speeches from the Nyéléni 2007 Forum for Food Sovereignty. Nyéléni website, www.nyeleni.org.
2   "The Declaration of Nyéléni," 2007. Nyéléni Forum for Food Sovereignty website, www .nyeleni.org.
3   Nyéléni, "Women's Declaration on Food Sovereignty," 2007. World Rainforest Movement website, wrm.org.uy.

101

Nairobi Declaration on Women's and Girls' Right to a Remedy and Reparation
Coalition for Women's Human Rights in Conflict Situations
Nairobi, Kenya
March 19–21, 2007

> Victims of serious violations of international human rights law and international humanitarian law have a clearly established right to remedy and reparation. . . . The concepts of explicitly gender-just, gender-equitable and gender-sensitive repair for serious violations and crimes have only begun to be explored in theory and practice within the last several years.[1]

At the International Meeting on Women's and Girls' Right to a Remedy and Reparation, women's rights advocates and activists, and survivors of sexual violence, met to discuss the relatively new topic of reparations for gender-based violence in conflict areas. Attendees were from Africa, Asia, Europe, and Central, North, and South America. Thirty-four organizations authored and signed the Declaration, including Kenya's Urgent Action Fund, Canada's Rights and Democracy, Sudan's Community Development Centre, Guatemala's Alianza de Mujeres Rurales por la Vida, Tierra y Dignidad, South Africa's Khulumani Support Group, and Peru's Comité de América Latina y El Caribe para la Defensa de la Derechos de la Mujer.

In general, demands for reparations are based on an understanding of the deep, multifaceted, and devastating consequences of armed conflict for both individuals and communities. They are also based on a legal concept of proportional remedies for victims as an aspect of justice, and favor bringing the victim in on determinations of just remedy. Reparations come in a variety of forms, with a variety of related ends, depending on the situation: restitution, rehabilitation, compensation, and/or satisfaction and guarantees of non-repetition.

Concretely, reparations can look like

- medical and psychological care,
- legal and social services,
- monetary compensation,
- public acknowledgment of the facts and acceptance of responsibility,
- prosecution of the perpetrators,
- search for the disappeared and identification of remains,
- remembrance, commemoration, and education aimed at preventing future crimes,
- rebuilding/repairing critical infrastructure.[2]

The Nairobi Declaration moves from a general framework of reparation and "helps inform the principles, processes and outcomes of gender-just reparation in Uganda."[3] The document recognizes a gender difference in the impact of conflict, which can be explained as follows:

> Men, boys, women and girls experience many of the same phenomena during armed conflict, including loss of livelihoods and assets, displacement, physical and mental injury, torture, the death and injury of loved ones, sexual assault and enforced

disappearance. Yet how they experience these phenomena during and after conflict is influenced by different aspects of gender relations. In particular, men, boys, women and girls: are differently embodied; symbolise different things to their communities and those that attack them; are targeted differently and their injuries have different social and livelihood impacts; have different responsibilities in their families and communities and thus end up differently in harm's way; and have differing livelihoods, access to the cash economy, and ability to own and inherit property, all of which impact the resources they can access to aid their recovery. We know enough about the violence of conflict in the Greater North of Uganda and its gendered dimensions to predict women's and girls' vulnerability to particular kinds of loss, violence and harms suffered during war. We can also predict trends in women's and girls' reduced access to resources, livelihood inputs and basic services; increased family and social responsibilities; restricted mobility; unequal access to protective services and legal mechanisms; and inadequate political power at local and national levels.[4]

The Declaration[5] asserts that females should have a role in determining what remedies are appropriate, even in societies that do not regularly encourage their participation in civil procedures, and in the face of obstacles to it. It addresses how female victims can be involved in designing, implementing, and evaluating reparations. It stresses that "the decision-making processes should be participatory, transparent and involve local CSOs, victims groups and the international community."[6]

The document begins by recognizing the "alarming proportions" and "unimaginable brutality" of violations against women and girls in war, including the physical, psychological, spiritual, economic, and social consequences of such violence; such acts, however, often go unnamed and unrecognized. These violations both follow from and perpetuate gender-based inequality. Reparations, in contrast, are based on respect for the personhood of women and girls and for their social contributions; in that sense, remedies have the potential to bring about social change. All guilty parties must take responsibility, "including state actors, foreign governments and inter-governmental bodies, non-governmental actors, such as armed groups, multinational companies and individual prospectors and investors." Done well, meaning "crafted with gender-aware forethought and care," the Declaration concludes, such processes "could have reparative effects, namely reinsertion, satisfaction and the guarantee of non-recurrence."

Nairobi Declaration on Women's and Girls' Right to a Remedy and Reparation

PREAMBLE

DEEPLY CONCERNED that gender-based violence, and particularly sexual violence and violations against women and girls, are weapons of war, assuming unacceptably alarming proportions as wars, genocide and communal violence have taken their toll inside and between countries the world over within the last two decades;

BEARING IN MIND the terrible destruction brought by armed conflict, including forced participation in armed conflict, to people's physical integrity, psychological and spiritual well-being, economic security, social status, social fabric, and the gender differentiated impact on the lives and livelihoods of women and girls;

TAKING INTO CONSIDERATION the unimaginable brutality of crimes and violations committed against women and girls in conflict situations, and the disproportionate effects of these crimes and violations on women and girls, their families and their communities;

ACKNOWLEDGING that gender-based violence committed during conflict situations is the result of inequalities between women and men, girls and boys, that predated the conflict, and that this violence continues to aggravate the discrimination of women and girls in post-conflict situations;

TAKING INTO CONSIDERATION the discriminatory interpretations of culture and religion that impact negatively on the economic and political status of women and girls;

TAKING INTO CONSIDERATION that girls specifically suffer both from physical and sexual violence directed at them and from human rights violations against their parents, siblings and caregivers;

BEARING IN MIND that girls respond differently than women to grave rights violations because of less developed physical, mental and emotional responses to these experiences. Noting also that girls are victims of double discrimination based on their gender and age.

TAKING INTO CONSIDERATION the roles and contributions of women and girls in repairing the social fabric of families, communities and societies, and the potential of reparation programs to acknowledge these roles;

BEARING IN MIND advances in international criminal law that confirm gender-based crimes may amount to genocide, crimes against humanity and war crimes;

RECALLING the adoption by the UN General Assembly in October 2005 of the Basic Principles and Guidelines on the Right to a Remedy and Reparation for Victims of Gross Violations of International Human Rights Law and Serious Violations of International Humanitarian Law;

TAKING COGNIZANCE of the existence of international, regional and national judicial and non-judicial mechanisms for individual and collective, symbolic and material reparation, and the enormous challenges of [caring] for all victims and survivors, individually and/or collectively;

CONCERNED that initiatives and strategies at the local, national, regional and international levels to ensure justice have not been effective from the perspectives of victims and survivors of these crimes and violations in a holistic manner;

DECLARE AS FOLLOWS:

1. That women's and girls' rights are human rights.
2. That reparation is an integral part of processes that assist societies recover from armed conflict and that ensure history will not repeat itself; that comprehensive programmes must be established to achieve truth-telling, other forms of transitional justice, and an end to the culture of impunity.
3. That reparation must drive post-conflict transformation of socio-cultural injustices, and political and structural inequalities that shape the lives of women and girls; that reintegration and restitution by themselves are not sufficient goals of reparation, since the origins of violations of women's and girls' human rights predate the conflict situation.
4. That, in order to accurately reflect and incorporate the perspectives of victims and their advocates, the notion of "victim" must be broadly defined within the context of women's and girls' experiences and their right to reparation.

5. That the fundamental nature of the struggle against impunity demands that all reparation programmes must address the responsibility of all actors, including state actors, foreign governments and inter-governmental bodies, non-governmental actors, such as armed groups, multinational companies and individual prospectors and investors.

6. That national governments bear primary responsibility to provide remedy and reparation within an environment that guarantees safety and human security, and that the international community shares responsibility in that process.

7. That the particular circumstances in which women and girls are made victims of crimes and human rights violations in situations of conflict require approaches specially adapted to their needs, interests and priorities, as defined by them; and that measures of access to equality (positive discrimination) are required in order to take into account the reasons and consequences of the crimes and violations committed, and in order to ensure that they are not repeated.

FURTHER ADOPT THE FOLLOWING GENERAL PRINCIPLES

And recommend that appropriate bodies at national, regional and international levels take steps to promote their widespread dissemination, acceptance and implementation.

1—BASIC PRINCIPLES RELATING TO WOMEN'S AND GIRLS' RIGHT TO A REMEDY AND REPARATION

A. Non-discrimination on the basis of sex, gender, ethnicity, race, age, political affiliation, class, marital status, sexual orientation, nationality, religion and disability.

B. All policies and measures relating to reparation must explicitly be based on the principle of non-discrimination on the basis of sex, gender, ethnicity, race, age, political affiliation, class, marital status, sexual orientation, nationality, religion and disability and affirmative measures to redress inequalities.

C. Compliance with international and regional standards on the right to a remedy and reparation, as well as with women's and girls' human rights.

D. Support of women's and girls' empowerment by taking into consideration their autonomy and participation in decision-making. Processes must empower women and girls, or those acting in the best interests of girls, to determine for themselves what forms of reparation are best suited to their situation. Processes must also overcome those aspects of customary and religious laws and practices that prevent women and girls from being in a position to make, and act on, decisions about their own lives.

E. Civil society should drive policies and practices on reparation, with governments striving for genuine partnership with civil society groups. Measures are necessary to guarantee civil society autonomy and space for the representation of women's and girls' voices in all their diversity.

F. Access to Justice. Ending impunity through legal proceedings for crimes against women and girls is a crucial component of reparation policies and a requirement under international law.

2—ACCESS TO REPARATION

A. In order to achieve reparation measures sensitive to gender, age, cultural diversity and human rights, decision-making about reparation must include victims as full participants, while ensuring just representation of women and girls in all their diversity. Governments and other actors must ensure that women and girls are adequately informed of their rights.

B. Full participation of women and girls victims should be guaranteed in every stage of the reparation process, i.e. design, implementation, evaluation, and decision-making.

C. Structural and administrative obstacles in all forms of justice, which impede or deny women's and girls' access to effective and enforceable remedies, must be addressed to ensure gender-just reparation programmes.

D. Male and female staff who are sensitive to specific issues related to gender, age, cultural diversity and human rights, and who are committed to international and regional human rights standards must be involved at every stage of the reparation process.

E. Practices and procedures for obtaining reparation must be sensitive to gender, age, cultural diversity and human rights, and must take into account women's and girls' specific circumstances, as well as their dignity, privacy and safety.

F. Indicators that are sensitive to gender, age, cultural diversity and human rights must be used to monitor and evaluate the implementation of reparation measures.

3—KEY ASPECTS OF REPARATION FOR WOMEN AND GIRLS

A. Women and girls have a right to a remedy and reparation under international law. They have a right to benefit from reparation programs designed to directly benefit the victims, by providing restitution, compensation, reintegration, and other key measures and initiatives under transitional justice that, if crafted with gender-aware forethought and care, could have reparative effects, namely reinsertion, satisfaction and the guarantee of non-recurrence.

B. Governments should not undertake development instead of reparation. All post-conflict societies need both reconstruction and development, of which reparation programmes are an integral part. Victims, especially women and girls, face particular obstacles in seizing the opportunities provided by development, thus risking their continued exclusion. In reparation, reconstruction, and development programmes, affirmative action measures are necessary to respond to the needs and experiences of women and girls victims.

C. Truth-telling requires the identification of gross and systematic crimes and human rights violations committed against women and girls. It is critical that such abuses are named and recognized in order to raise awareness about these crimes and violations, to positively influence a more holistic strategy for reparation and measures that support reparation, and to help build a shared memory and history. Currently, there is a significant lack of naming and addressing such abuses in past reparation programs and efforts, much to the detriment of surviving victims.

D. Reconciliation is an important goal of peace and reparation processes, which can only be achieved with women and girls victims' full participation, while respecting their right to dignity, privacy, safety and security.

E. Just, effective and prompt reparation measures should be proportional to the gravity of the crimes, violations and harm suffered. In the case of victims of sexual violence and other gender-based crimes, governments should take into account the multi-dimensional and long-term consequences of these crimes to women and girls, their families and their communities, requiring specialized, integrated, and multidisciplinary approaches.

F. Governments must consider all forms of reparation available at individual and community levels. These include, but are not limited to, restitution, compensation and reintegration. Invariably, a combination of these forms of reparation will be required to adequately address violations of women's and girls' human rights.

G. Reparation processes must allow women and girls to come forward when they are ready. They should not be excluded if they fail to do so within a prescribed time period. Support structures are needed to assist women and girls in the process of speaking out and claiming reparation.

H. Reparation must go above and beyond the immediate reasons and consequences of the crimes and violations; they must aim to address the political and structural inequalities that negatively shape women's and girls' lives.

Notes

1 "Making Gender-Just Remedy and Reparation Possible: Upholding the Rights of Women and Girls in the Greater North of Uganda" (Isis Women's International Cross Cultural Exchange/ Feinstein International Center, Tufts University, 2013), pp. 2–3.

2 Demanding the Right to Heal, "Factsheet: The Right to Reparations," 2013. Demanding the Right to Heal website, www.righttoheal.org.

3 "Making Gender-Just Remedy and Reparation Possible," p. 23.

4 "Making Gender-Just Remedy and Reparation Possible," pp. 25–26.

5 "Nairobi Declaration on Women's and Girls' Right to a Remedy and Reparation," 2013. International Federation for Human Rights website, FIDH.org, accessed Oct. 28, 2013.

6 "Making Gender-Just Remedy and Reparation Possible," p. 23.

102

Declaration of Principles *and* GABRIELA's Principles
Gabriela Women's Party and GABRIELA
Manila, Philippines
March 20, 2007, and 2004

Gabriela Women's Party logo.

We believe that the freedom women seek will be brought about by the resolution of the problems of foreign domination, landlessness and political repression and in the changing of patriarchal value systems and structures in Philippine society.[1]

On the twentieth anniversary of the 1986 overthrow of the dictatorial Marcos regime, tens of thousands of Filipinos marched in Manila, despite a police ban on rallies and assemblies and declaration of a state of emergency.

Arrests were made, one newspaper, the *Daily Tribune*, was closed down, a television station, ABS-CBN, was threatened with sedition charges, Congressman Crispin Beltran of the Anakpawis Party was imprisoned and five others marked for arrest. Among them was Representative Liza Largoza Maza of the Gabriela Women's Party, Asia's only all-women political party and one of only a half-dozen of its kind in the world. Rep. Maza was the main author and sponsor of the Philippines' Anti-Trafficking Law and the Violence Against Women Act. Last year, she filed a divorce bill.[2]

GABRIELA (all caps), which links some two hundred women's organizations, was founded in 1984. The umbrella group was named for Gabriela Silang, an eighteenth-century Filipino revolutionary in the battle for independence from Spain, but it also uses its name as an acronym for General Assembly Binding Women for Reforms, Integrity, Equality, Leadership, and Action. The Gabriela Women's Party, backed by the larger coalition, was founded in 2003. In 2004 the party, "promoting the rights and welfare of marginalized and under-represented Filipino women through participation in the country's electoral system and organs of governance,"[3] won a seat in the House of Representatives, and in 2007 gained a second. "The Gabriela Women's Party is known for its unflinching advocacy of women's rights and freedoms."[4] It remains active today.

The party's Declaration of Principles[5] pays homage to the history of women's political activism in the Philippines. Although GABRIELA's principles, also included below, come across as broader and more radical than those of the Gabriela Women's Party, both stand against imperialism and for democracy, both address the most marginalized, and both understand that forces from general cultural values to individual family decision-making processes affect the status of women.

Declaration of Principles

We, members of the Gabriela Women's Party, in the spirit of the Filipina's unbroken legacy of political participation—from the Babaylan of pre-Hispanic times to the Gabriela Silang of today; committed to uphold the interest of the broad masses of Filipino women and their families; dedicated to advancing the rights and promoting the well-being of women, especially of the more marginalized and under-represented; determined to encourage, develop and harness women's full potential, leadership and collective creativity, hereby declare that:

1. Women have the right to a society where all forms of discrimination and violence against women have been banished;
2. Women have the right equal to men to the land they work on; as well as the right to full and gainful employment and living wages;
3. Women have the right to participate freely in all aspects of political debates, action, and decision-making processes in the family, the community and the nation at large; as well as the right to fair and non-sexist representation in all social, political, economic and cultural spheres;
4. Women have the right to fight for basic health care and services for all, especially reproductive and maternal health care;
5. Women have the right to a marriage founded on mutual consent and respect, with equality and dignity, and to adequate support for the rearing and caring of children;

6. Women have the right to fight for children's basic needs like proper care, nutrition, health, safety and play, protection from abuse and exploitation; access to a national, scientific and mass education which is non-sexist as well;
7. Women have the right to advocate for lesbian and gay rights and to insist that society not discriminate on the basis of sexual preference;
8. Women have the right to assert and protect their country's sovereignty and national patrimony;
9. Women have the right to a foreign policy that is independent and beneficial to our economy and security as a nation;
10. Women have the right to a government that is truly democratic and representative of the majority.

GABRIELA's Principles

We seek to forge women's unity within and among classes and constituencies to wage a struggle for the liberation of women and the rest of the Filipino people. This force will work for:

- genuine national sovereignty in Philippine socio-cultural, economic and political life and freedom from all foreign intervention especially that of the United States;
- a truly democratic government, representative of and participated in by grassroot women and women from all sectors and classes of society, that recognizes the cultural communities' struggle for self-determination and preservation of their cultural life and traditions;
- a government that provides support systems for women, initiates programs and policies in consultation with women and promotes equality between women and men;
- an armed forces that truly protect the people, serve their interests and respect the supremacy of the civilian government;
- an end to militarization that has intensified the sufferings of the Filipino people, especially the women;
- a fair, just and independent legal and judicial system that does not discriminate against women and which upholds their rights and welfare;
- genuine land reform, recognition of women's participation in agricultural production, recognition of land rights of cultural minorities;
- a self-reliant economy that is geared primarily towards domestic consumption and nationalist industrialization, gives equal value to the participation of women in production and responds to specific needs of women at work;
- a quality educational system that is nationalist, pro-people, non-sexist and liberating;
- a socio-cultural system that does not demean women;
- the development of basic sciences and technology that serve Filipinos and [consider] the particular needs of women; and,
- the strengthening of solidarity with women's groups in other countries against sexism, imperialism and militarism in the world.

Notes

1 This statement is from the umbrella GABRIELA organization. "History." GABRIELA website, accessed Sept. 2017, gabriela_p.tripod.com.

2 Ninotchka Rosca, "Reign of Terror in the Philippines: Women's Movement Criminalized," March 23, 2006. *Rad Geek People's Daily*, www.radgeek.com.

3 Gabriela Women's Party, "About GWP." *Gabriela Women's Party* blog, accessed Sept. 2017, gabrielanews.wordpress.com.

4 Rosca.

5 Gabriela Women's Party, "Our Declaration of Principles." Gabriela Women's Party website, accessed Sept. 2017, www.gabrielawomensparty.net.

103

Declaration against Sexual Apartheid
Equal Rights Now: Organisation Against Women's Discrimination in Iran
Iran
2008

Women's role in protests and the struggle against misogyny and Islamism in Iran, the Middle East and North Africa is now the standardbearer of any progressive liberation struggle.[1]

Art depicting "sexual apartheid" in Iran from Equal Rights Now.

Iranian women's political activism has a long history. As Ali Akbar Mahdi explains, during the Constitutional Revolution of 1905–1911, "women organized street riots, participated in some fights, joined underground activities against foreign forces, boycotted the import of foreign goods, participated in the demolition of a Russian bank, and raised funds for the establishment of the National Bank." Then, as is often the case,

> In the course of this national struggle, some enlightened women realized the potential of women for organized political activities and used the momentum provided by the revolution as a venue for bringing women's causes into the open. Becoming increasingly conscious of the oppressive conditions of women, these pioneering feminists established secret societies (*anjomans* and *dowrehs*), commonly held by Constitutionalists at the time in order to discuss the situation of women by sharing their personal problems, experiences, and feelings.[2]

The contemporary secular women's movement took shape after Ayatollah Khomeni instituted Sharia law, female dress codes, and gender segregation. "The first major demonstration in Iran was organised by women activists and organisations on 8 March 1979, only a few days after Ayatollah Khomeini's Fatwa for compulsory veiling."[3] Secular and opposition groups, including women's organizations, were banned. Greater activity occurred under the Khatemi regime, addressing a wide range of issues, including education, veiling, political representation, interpretations of Islam, and stoning. The movement remains vibrant.

On International Women's Day in 2008, the Worker-Communist Party of Iran introduced the slogan "No to sexual apartheid." They chose it first because of its ability to describe the status quo. As Hamid Taqvaee explains,

> Subjugation and degradation of women is part and parcel of this Islamic state's judicial system, as well as an ideological pillar of it. It is a state that separates women from men in social life, in assemblies, in group activities, and even in private parties and gatherings, in schools and university classes, buses, sport fields, swimming pools, parks, on public routes, on the beach, at recreational places, mourning ceremonies, wedding parties; in short, in the social life as a whole, men and women must legally, that is, as far as the state is concerned, be kept apart.[4]

However, the choice of slogan was also a very political one. As Taqvee puts it,

> There is another point, another policy, . . . that we have always insisted on, and that is making every effort to get the Islamic Republic of Iran isolated and banned from the rest of the world as a regime of Sexual apartheid. The phrase "Sexual apartheid" expresses, almost comprehensively, the fact that it deprives women of their inalienable rights, and reveals its misogynist character to the people across the world; particularly as the world still vividly remembers the racial apartheid system in South Africa and its reactionary nature. One of the things that at last caused the fall of the racist regime was that progressive people of the world rose up against it, and even forced other states to boycott and break their relations with it. . . . This background, this historical parallel, will also help us call on the people of the world to mobilise and raise their voice of protest against the regime of Sexual apartheid in Iran. This regime is in no way less anti-human and anti-humanity than the former racist regime in South Africa. That is one of the reasons we believe we must focus on "Sexual apartheid," and expose the Islamic state in Iran as a gender-apartheid state.[5]

In 2010 Iran Solidarity issued a "Manifesto of Liberation of Women in Iran."[6] The document clearly has its roots in those reprinted below.[7] The later one, however, adds the following to the earlier list of demands:[8] prosecution of the leaders and officials of the Islamic Republic for crimes against humanity, including for thirty years of the vilest abuse, discrimination, and violence against women in Iran; prohibition of *sighe* (Islamic "rent-a-wife") and polygamy; unconditional right of separation (divorce) for women and men; abolition of all laws that make women's civil rights (such as the right to travel, social intercourse, participation in social activities, etc.) conditional on obtaining the permission of the husband, father, or other male members of the family; complete equality of women's and men's rights and duties in the custody and care of children following separation; abolition of all the barbaric laws of stoning, execution, retribution (*qesas*), and other Islamic punishments; unconditional freedom of expression, protest, strike, assembly, organization, and party formation; immediate release of all political prisoners and prisoners of conscience; and freedom of religion and atheism and freedom to criticize religion. As is obvious in the contents of these documents, and their contrast with others in this collection, there remains a divide between secular and religious approaches to liberation.

Declaration against Sexual Apartheid (or Gender Apartheid)

Sexual Apartheid is the outrage of our century. In Iran, Iraq, Afghanistan, and countries ruled by Islamic laws, millions of women and girls are segregated, degraded and relegated to second class citizenship. Keeping women and girls separate and unequal are important pillars of Islamic rule, affecting every aspect of people's lives. Just as a mass movement rejected Racial Apartheid in South Africa, so too must it reject segregation based on sex in Iran and everywhere.

8 March 2009 will be the 30th anniversary of the mass demonstrations against veiling and sexual apartheid that took place in Iran after Khomeini proclaimed the day before that women were to be veiled in workplaces. The protests were suppressed and the Islamic regime in Iran went on to impose compulsory veiling for girls and women and segregate the society at large.

The women's liberation movement in Iran, however, continued to mobilise and grow in strength and numbers. Today, it is a resolute movement against sexual apartheid and discrimination against women and for freedom and equality.

Equal Rights Now—Organisation against Women's Discrimination in Iran is calling on people everywhere to pay tribute to this movement by recognising 8 March (International Women's Day) as the International Day against Sexual Apartheid.

We also call on individuals, unions, parties and organisations to condemn sexual apartheid and the political Islamic movement that perpetrates it by continuing to sign on to the below declaration.

Declaration Against Sexual Apartheid

We, the undersigned, unequivocally oppose sexual apartheid and the subjugation of millions of women living under Islamic rules and laws.

We condemn regimes and the political Islamic movement that perpetrate sexual apartheid, including in Iran.

We support the legitimate struggle of millions of women and men for freedom, equality and universal rights.

Sexual apartheid, like racial apartheid, has no place in the 21st century.

Principles

1. Unconditional elimination of all types of discrimination and oppression against women and the achievement of full equality between women and men in society.
2. Absolute separation of religion from the state and educational system.
3. Freedom of choice in clothing and the elimination of compulsory veiling and sexual apartheid.
4. Opposition to patriarchy and all misogynist national-Islamic traditions.
5. Uniting the women's liberation movement around secular, radical and egalitarian demands.
6. Organising the women's liberation movement and uniting its activists to establish a strong leadership and far-reaching organisation.

7. Promoting the women's liberation movement in Iran internationally and mobilising support for it amongst supporters of women's rights, secular, left and progressive organisations and individuals.

Notes

1 Worker-Communist Party of Iran, "Women's Liberation Movement: Greatest Threat to Islamism," March 8, 2015. Worker-Communist Part of Iran website, www.wpiran.org.

2 "The Iranian Women's Movement: A Century-Long Struggle." *Muslim World* 94 (Oct. 2004): 428.

3 Sohaila Sharifi, "Women's Liberation in Iran: The Struggle against Sexual Apartheid," March 7, 2008. Equal Rights Now website, www.equal-rights-now.com.

4 Maryam Namazie, "Under Sexual Apartheid the Society Is Defined as a Man's Society," March 7, 2008. Blog post, maryamnamazie.blogspot.com.

5 Ibid.

6 "Manifesto of Liberation of Women in Iran," Jan. 25, 2010. Iran Solidarity website, iransolidarity.blogspot.com.

7 Sohaila Sharifi, "Thirty Years of Struggle for Freedom and Equality." *Unveiled*, vol. 2—Join the Struggle against Sexual Apartheid and Sharia, Jan. 31, 2009. Posted on *MaryamNamazie. Com*, www.maryamnamazie.com.

8 Equal Rights Now website, accessed Sept. 2017, www.equal-rights-now.com.

104

Rural Women's Declaration: Rights, Empowerment, and Liberation
First Asian Rural Women's Conference
Arakkonam, Tamil Nadu, India
March 6–8, 2008

Asian Rural Women's Coalition logo.

The process of neo-liberal globalisation is abusing Mother Nature, destroying the symbiotic relationship between nature and human beings. . . . Rural women are disproportionately and negatively affected, suffering increased gender based violence, hunger and malnutrition, forced evictions and trafficking.

Many women's coalitions present alternatives to the current functioning of globalized systems of power. Women are often the first to face the consequences of global crises, including the financial crisis of 2007–2008, climate change, global food crises, perpetual military conflict, and human displacement. Thus, groups like the Asian Rural Women's Coalition (ARWC) form regional and international networks that respond to these global problems while resisting prior versions of "imperialist globalization."

Rural Women's Parade in Arakkonam.

Over seven hundred people from around twenty-one countries of Asia and the Pacific attended this gathering, which, together with a much smaller one (fifty-two women from fourteen Asian countries) held in the Philippines in 2007 (Asian Rural Women's Regional Consultation), led to the formation of the ARWC. The conference was hosted by the Tamil Nadu Women's Forum, the Tamil Nadu Dalit Women's Movement, and the Society for Rural Education and Development.

The ARWC notes, perhaps surprisingly, given their "invisibility," that "Asian rural women comprise the majority of the women's population worldwide and thus, play critical roles in the fight against imperialist globalization." Further, they assert that "the intensifying crisis brought by globalization warrants an intensified resistance." In fact, such resistance is not new or singular, as these women have long been working "to defend their economic, social and cultural rights—from rights to food, land, water, territories, and other productive resources, health and nutrition, education, traditional knowledge to decent income and jobs as well as civil political rights including right to self-determination."[1]

This Declaration documents the numerous and wide-ranging forms of economic and governmental interference and control exerted over rural women, in all their diversity—"peasants, agricultural workers, indigenous women, Dalit women, nomads, fisherfolk, informal and formal workers, [and] migrants." It names three enemies of rural women's freedom: "neo-liberal globalisation, fundamentalisms and militarisation." Each of these forces is broken down into particular institutions and practices, and the dire consequences of each are laid bare, from displacement to trafficking. The way of life of various cultures and ethnic groups is clearly at stake. This document tracks the interactions and effects of quite disparate policies, from the "war on terror" to micro-financing, from the privatization of healthcare to the corporate control of food production, and from caste discrimination to the precaritization of labor. Their demands, consequently, range from growing local food to reclaiming local knowledge.

The ARWC advances the rights of rural women in Asia by convening local, national, and international dialogues on the following issues: "Corporate control over land and productive resources; Climate change; War and militarisation; Workers and migration; Sexual and reproductive health rights; Ethnic and caste conflicts." The ARWC cosponsored the Conference on Women Resisting Crisis and War in July 2010, which addressed the "impacts and women's responses to the economic and climate crises and war of the Asia Pacific Research Network (APRN)." Since then, the ARWC has engaged in advocacy through the Civil Society Forum of the United Nations' Food and Agriculture Organization's (FAO) Committee on Food Security.[2]

Rural Women's Declaration: Rights, Empowerment and Liberation

We, 716 women from 21 countries representing peasants, agricultural workers, indigenous women, Dalit women, nomads, fisherfolk, informal and formal workers, migrants and supportive activists met for the First Asian Rural Women's Conference in Arakkonam, Tamil Nadu, India from 6th March to 8th March to call for the *Rights, Empowerment and Liberation* of rural women.

Rural women in Asia continue to face exploitation, oppression, multiple forms of discrimination and violence in all forms from the impact of neo-liberal globalisation, fundamentalisms and militarisation.

The process of neo-liberal globalisation is abusing Mother Nature, destroying the symbiotic relationship between nature and human beings; and has disempowered rural women and exacerbated human and labour rights violation and economic injustices. This process driven by G8 countries, perpetuated by the WTO, bilateral and regional trade agreements, sustained by International Financial Institutions such as World Bank, IMF and ADB benefits the landlords, elites and TNCs.

This present imperialist-dominated economic and political processes promote corporate control over all aspects of food and fibre production and have created monopoly control over land, seas and marine resources, water, livelihoods, seeds and genetic biodiversity. Corporate farming and contract farming, intensive industrial aquaculture, expansion of agro-fuel projects, setting up of Special Economic Zones (SEZ), and massive land conversion are displacing thousands of women peasants, agricultural workers and fisherfolk; worsening the loss of livelihoods and productive resources; increasingly poisoning the environment; accelerating poverty and disintegrating the rural economy. Rural women are disproportionately and negatively affected, suffering increased gender based violence, hunger and malnutrition, forced evictions and trafficking.

Industries like mining, logging, energy projects, bio-fuel production and agro-industries are taking away the ancestral lands of indigenous women and their communities. Commercialisation and monopoly control are destroying the traditional knowledge and practices that have kept indigenous women self-sufficient. Displaced from their economic base, indigenous women are forced to migrate and lose the protection provided by their communities and alienate them from their culture and value systems. It is in this way that imperialist globalisation is causing ethnocide among indigenous women, their children and their communities.

Life and livelihood of the small-scale fisherfolk have been destroyed by liberalised policies of globalisation processes, privatization of the sea and marine resources and the push for exports have increased the use of modern fishing techniques including trawler fishing and push nets, thus decreasing fish production. At the same time mega-projects, SEZs, tourism and intensive industrial aquaculture are decreasing the access of women fisherfolk to the sea and marine resources. Women fisherfolk and fish workers are most affected and have to work longer hours for lower incomes and the quality of food and health is affected.

Globalisation processes have caused the greatest destruction of formal and regular work worldwide. The strategy of flexibilisation of labour has pushed more women workers into informal work where they are not covered by labour laws and are therefore subject to greater exploitation and abuse. In many Asian countries, women constitute majority of the informal economy.

The IFI/Micro Finance Institution–led micro credit as a form of women's self-employment and Self Help Groups (SHG) is a myth and misnomer. In reality, this disempowers women and leads to a vicious cycle of debt and poverty.

Rural women forced to cross borders due to state repression and in search of livelihood have had to bear huge social costs, are subjected to increased violence, abuse, exploitation, discrimination and criminalisation, and denied their rights as women and as migrant workers and when they return home, face alienation. The remittances of migrant women workers have sustained the bankrupt economies of Asian countries.

Rising religious fundamentalisms with the support of imperialist forces and the collusion of state and non-state actors, have made rural women more invisible, further restricted women's decision making and mobility, legitimated violence on rural women, revived religious sanctioned prostitution, perpetuated discrimination and denied women's inherent right to control their lives, their sexuality and resources.

Fundamentalisms and globalisation processes are interacting with caste discrimination in further denying Dalit women the right to land, political and equal status and the very right to life. Thus Dalit women daily face increased untouchability, sexual exploitation and the violent atrocities and harassment by the dominant caste. Dalit women face loss of livelihoods, displacement and migration and trafficking due to the onslaught of new economic policies and the destructive globalisation processes.

The U.S.-led global "War on Terror" being used to push globalisation policies, the economic interest of U.S and other big capitalist countries is providing Asian government[s] with the rationale to increase militarisation and state terrorism and is fanning ethnic conflicts in Asia. This has led to killings, detention and harassment of more rural women. In the guise of security, repressive governments like that of Burma, Sri Lanka, Pakistan and the Philippines are carrying out extra-judicial killings and forced disappearances of women, men and children. Ethnic conflicts and civil wars are causing forced displacement of thousands of people; and caste riots are resulting in massive violence against Dalit women. Women in conflict areas are raped as a tool of war, killed, and forced to "service" the armed forces and in extreme circumstances become victims of genocide.

Within the context of War on Terror the top nuclear powers continue nuclear explosions testing. Radiation is the most horrible yet invisible weapon of war. It can kill the environment and lead to the annihilation of mankind. It affects primarily women of fertile age and their children. It causes cancer particularly of the uterus, breast and blood. Women from Kazakhstan, Tajikistan, Uzbekistan, India and Pakistan are suffering and dying from exposure to radiation.

The privatisation of public hospitals, a dictate of globalisation, has worsened the negligence of governments of social services and increased inaccessibility of rural women to accurate and appropriate health information and comprehensive and affordable health services. More rural women suffer from pregnancy and childbirth-related deaths and disabilities, unsafe abortion, HIV/AIDS, reproductive cancers, physical and sexual violence and from limited access to nutritious food and safe drinking water. They are forced to endure dangerous labor conditions all of which leave them ill, injured and malnourished. Pesticide exposure increases vulnerability of women to infertility, reproductive cancers and miscarriage.

Thus, we, the participants to the First Asian Rural Women's Conference is sending a call for rural women to defy injustices and raise our voices against all forms of discrimination and violence on women. We, the rural women and supportive activists resolve to continue to challenge and resist neo-liberal globalisation, imperialist and fundamentalist forces and militarisation.

We call for genuine agrarian reform and rural women's ownership and access to land and productive resources which include access to credit and training; we demand for food sovereignty, to healthy and local foods and healthy agriculture and to reclaim rural women's knowledge and skills.

We demand direct access and control of coastal and marine resources with meaningful participation and decision-making of fisherfolk in all policies related to our livelihoods and marine resources.

We demand for the end of development aggression in indigenous peoples' ancestral lands, state and corporate plunder of our resources and demand for the right to self-determination.

We demand a ban on hazardous agro-chemicals and technologies including pesticides, inorganic fertilisers and genetic engineering in food and agriculture, in favor of ecological and biodiversity-based agriculture.

We condemn the land alienation, state oppression and violations of human rights of Dalit Women; and we say that Dalit women's rights are human rights. We demand for the end of caste system and untouchability practices. We collectively demand the state to protect our right to land, right to expression, right to decision making, right to political spaces and right to life with dignity for Dalit women and that the state is held accountable if these rights are not upheld.

We demand an end to trade liberalisation and privatisation and for livelihood security and decent work for all women. We, the Asian Women workers movement, demand fair living wages, safe and decent working conditions, job security, and the right to freedom of association.

We absolutely repudiate the emphasis of all Asian governments to push micro credit as a tool of development and empowerment of rural women. We demand that governments provide a system to enable rural women access to credit on their own terms.

We demand an end to forced migration kept in place by the agenda of corporations and governments. For migrant workers, we demand protection of all rights including the right to stay or move and work with dignity.

We condemn the revival of fundamentalist and communal forces that are unleashing violence on society, particularly women and children. We demand that all states/governments ensure the representation at all policy levels of peoples of different religions, diverse ethnic groups and the most marginalised sections, particularly women, so that women's rights are protected.

War of aggression has no place in our society and we demand an end to all state-led and state-supported wars; and we demand justice for all human rights defenders and affected communities. We call for the removal of all US bases in Asia, the prioritisation of budget allocations for food production, education and health, social services and empowerment of women over military budgets. We demand the repeal of repressive laws such as the security and anti-terrorism legislation and an end to all extra-judicial killings and enforced disappearances.

Participation of women in the democratic movements and in the political process is necessary to push for pro-people and democratic societies in Asia. We should learn from the successful experiences of Asian countries, express our solidarity with the democratic movements all over Asia and ensure the participation of women in the peace process.

Rural women demand the right to control their bodies, to assert their sexual and reproductive health rights, and choose on issues of contraception, marriage, pregnancy and child birth. We also call for the end of exploitative sex selection and other reproductive technologies.

Now is the time for rural women to come together, create a visible force, consolidate gains and strengthen the global women's movement. To strengthen the rural women's movement, we, participants of the first Asian Rural Women's Conference, are forming ourselves into an *Asian Rural Women's Coalition* for rural women's rights, empowerment and liberation. Our voices will be heard.

Long Live Rural Women's Solidarity!!!

Notes

1 "Asian Rural Women's Campaign," Oct. 15, 2012. Foro Internacional Democracia y Cooperacion website, http://www.democraciaycooperacion.net.

2 "Our Story." Asian Rural Women's Coalition website, accessed 2014, http://asianruralwomen.net.

105

A Women's Declaration to the G8: Support Real Solutions to the Global Food Crisis
MADRE
New York, New York
July 8, 2008

MADRE logo.

"MADRE is an internationally recognized women's human rights organization situated at a crossroads of the movements for women's equality, peace and justice and international human rights, reflecting the understanding that women's rights are human rights, that US foreign policy is a 'women's issue' and that human rights everywhere are inherently political."[1] The organization has an unusual origin story. Nicaraguan women who had endured the attacks of the U.S.-backed contra movement brought suit against the United States in the International Court of Justice. In 1983, a U.S. poet-activist, Kathy Engel, found their testimony so moving that she produced a dramatic public reading of the transcript, and three of the Nicaraguan plaintiffs joined her for the performance. In turn, the Nicaraguans invited the event's organizers to their country, "to understand the lunacy of their government's claim that our Revolution was a threat to the United States . . . [and to see] the misery that their government was causing." Upon their return they established MADRE, which they hoped would "respond to the needs of women and families threatened by US foreign policy and give people in the United States the means to demand alternatives to unjust policies. . . . They came together across differences of culture, class and community, recognizing one another by their shared commitment to linking the struggles against sexism, racism, war, homophobia and economic exploitation in which they were active."[2] MADRE continues to bring attention to the diverse but linked consequences of U.S. policies around the globe, as is evident in this Declaration.

The Group of 8 (G8) is an annual meeting of the wealthiest nations that addresses global challenges such as economic crises, climate change, and poverty. Their agenda for their 2008 summit in Tokyo, Japan, included the global food crisis. The World Bank estimates that in the three years prior to this meeting, global food prices increased by 83 percent,[3] leading to mass protests, political instability, and significant increases in the number suffering from poverty, hunger, and malnutrition, primarily in the Global South. Further,

> The impact of the food crisis is likely to be much more severe among women and children. Because of gender discrimination and various cultural practices that influence intrahousehold resource allocation, these groups tend to be more vulnerable to chronic and transitory food insecurity. Furthermore, the crisis may undermine efforts to reduce maternal and infant deaths as the food and nutrition deficits facing pregnant and lactating women worsen in already adversely affected regions. Lack of social protection for female workers in the informal sector compounds their vulnerability to such external shocks.[4]

This document contests the causes of the global food crisis. The authors contend that the cause is not scarcity but the economic policies of wealthy nations that treat food as a commodity—which primarily benefits multinational corporations—rather than as a right, which would mean fighting poverty and supporting smaller-scale, sustainable agriculture (and most small farms are run by women, it is important to note). It is current financial priorities, then, that perpetuate the food crisis, as well as the linked problems of climate change, social inequities, and resource depletion. A better approach includes tackling gender discrimination (including discrimination against women farmers and disregard for women's agricultural knowledge). Groups like the G8, however, continue to focus on trade liberalization and industrial agriculture. As the Declaration says,

> The G8, through the World Bank and International Monetary Fund, has required developing countries to reduce support to small farmers, cut investment in food production, slash tariffs that protected domestic agriculture, dismantle the marketing boards that once stabilized food prices, and shift land use from food production to export agriculture. Developing countries were forced to accept these demands as conditions for loans needed to repay their debts to the financial institutions, development banks, and governments of the North. Yet, it is the G8 itself which is largely responsible for the debt crisis, brought on by massive lending to illegitimate regimes and decades of costly, ill-conceived development projects.

Given their commitment to working with local organizations, MADRE's letter is cosigned by women's groups from Nicaragua, Colombia, Guatemala, and Haiti.

A Women's Declaration to the G8: Support Real Solutions to the Global Food Crisis

To: Prime Minister Yasuo Fukuda (Japan) Prime Minister Stephen Harper (Canada) President Nicolas Sarkozy (France) Chancellor Angela Merkel (Germany)

Prime Minister Silvio Berlusconi (Italy) President Dmitry Medvedev (Russia) Prime Minister Gordon Brown (United Kingdom) President George Bush (United States)

This year, the world's eight richest governments (the G8) meet against the backdrop of a global food crisis. With prices for all major food commodities at a 50-year-high, world leaders are discussing pervasive "food shortages" that threaten to destabilize dozens of countries. But worsening hunger is the result of cost inflation, not any absolute food shortage. In fact, the world produces more food than the global population can consume. The root cause of the food crisis is not scarcity, but the failed economic policies long championed by the G8, namely, trade liberalization and industrial agriculture. These policies, which treat food as a commodity rather than a human right, have induced chaotic climate change, oil dependency, and the depletion of the Earth's land and water resources as well as today's food crisis.

Yet, in the search for solutions, the G8 is considering expanded support for the very measures that caused this web of problems. Calls for more tariff reductions, biofuel plantations, genetically modified crops, and wider use of petroleum-based fertilizers and chemical pesticides are at the forefront of discussions in Japan.

These measures cannot resolve the global food crisis. They may, however, further boost this year's record profits for agricultural corporations. There are viable solutions to the food crisis, but they will not emerge from a narrow pursuit of the financial interests of multinational corporations.

For nearly 30 years, the G8 has insisted that corporations replace governments in shaping and implementing national agriculture policies in the world's poorest countries. This demand has not maximized efficiency or reduced poverty, as promised. In fact, it has ushered in a sharp rise in hunger and malnutrition. As the World Bank itself acknowledged in its 2008 *World Development Report*, the private sector has failed as a substitute for government when it comes to agriculture.

In fact, corporations have no legal duty to reduce poverty or fight world hunger. Governments, including the G8—and not the private sector—are the ones mandated to resolve the global food crisis. The international human rights framework, which governments are obligated to uphold, is the starting point for a global New Deal on agriculture. In particular, the human rights of small farmers—the majority of whom are women—and rural and Indigenous Peoples must be protected in order to meet the twin challenges of feeding people and protecting the planet.

As women's human rights advocates working with communities on the front-lines of the global food crisis, we call on the G8 to promote a worldwide shift from industrial to sustainable agriculture and to enact the economic policies needed to support this transition.

The Imperative of Sustainable Agriculture
In April 2008, the International Assessment of Agricultural Science and Technology (IAASTD) released an independent, four-year study conducted by over 400 experts. The study was co-sponsored by the World Bank and multiple agencies of

the United Nations and endorsed by over 60 governments. It confirms that large-scale, chemical-intensive agriculture is a major contributor to pollution, climate change, deforestation, social inequity, and the destruction of diversity, both biological and cultural. The study urges a fundamental overhaul of agricultural policy towards sustainable farming, including small-scale and organic agriculture.

The IAASTD report follows numerous other credible studies demonstrating that small-holder organic farms can produce enough food for the global population and avoid the environmental destruction associated with industrial agriculture.

We emphasize that support for small farmers must include a focus on women, who produce most of the world's food. Indeed, in much of Africa, where the food crisis is at its worst, women grow and process 80 percent of all food.

However, the capacity of these farmers is badly undermined by laws and customs that discriminate against women. In many countries, women who grow the food that sustains the majority of the population are not even recognized as farmers. They are denied the right to own land and excluded from government programs that facilitate access to credit, seeds, tools, and training.

We call on the G8 to:
- Recognize gender discrimination as a threat to global food security;
- Uphold the rights of agricultural workers under the International Labor Organization's Conventions;
- Support national policies that provide small-scale farmers with access to land, seeds, water, credit and other inputs and that uphold the rights of farmers to make informed decisions about land use and food production.

The Imperative of Sustainable Economic Policies

A global New Deal on agriculture requires not only different modes of farming, but a new policy environment for food production and agricultural trade. National policies, including investment, funding, and research, as well as international trade rules, must be redirected in support of small farmers and sustainable agriculture. Towards that end, the G8 should:

1. End Food Dependency

The G8, through the World Bank and International Monetary Fund, has required developing countries to reduce support to small farmers, cut investment in food production, slash tariffs that protected domestic agriculture, dismantle the marketing boards that once stabilized food prices, and shift land use from food production to export agriculture.

Developing countries were forced to accept these demands as conditions for loans needed to repay their debts to the financial institutions, development banks, and governments of the North. Yet, it is the G8 itself which is largely responsible for the debt crisis, brought on by massive lending to illegitimate regimes and decades of costly, ill-conceived development projects.

The economic policies demanded by the G8 have destroyed the livelihoods of small farmers in the Global South, leaving millions of people at the mercy of international commodity markets to be able to buy food. The shift from food to cash crops has meant that women, who are responsible for growing food, have lost access to valuable farm land. As a result, rural families have lost a main source of food and nutrition.

Economic policies driven by the G8 eventually transformed food-producing countries in the Global South into net food importers. In the 1960's, developing countries enjoyed an agricultural trade surplus of US $7 billion a year. Today, almost three out of four developing countries are net food importers, although they have the capacity to feed themselves.

We call on the G8 to:

- Move beyond the partial commitment it made to debt cancellation at the 2005 G8 summit in Scotland and enact immediate and unconditional debt cancellation for all developing countries;
- Allow governments to determine their own agricultural policies in consultation with citizens;
- Institute international mechanisms for market stabilization that protect the livelihoods of farmers and guarantee affordable food for all people;
- Endorse the call of Jacques Diouf, Secretary General of the United Nations Food and Agriculture Organization, for developing countries to be enabled to achieve food self-sufficiency.

2. Change Trade Rules

Trade rules demanded by the G8 and administered by the World Trade Organization have bankrupted millions of farmers in poor countries, undermined the role of women in agriculture, and contributed to the current food crisis.

The World Trade Organization's Agreement on Agriculture forbids governments in the Global South from providing farmers with subsidies or low-cost seeds and other inputs. These farmers have been turned into a "market" for international agribusiness companies selling seeds, pesticides and fertilizers.

Women, who are traditionally responsible for conserving, exchanging, and breeding agricultural seeds, are threatened by the WTO's Trade Related Intellectual Property Rights agreement. By granting patents to corporations, the WTO transfers ownership of seeds—the basis of all agriculture—from women farmers to multinational corporations.

The WTO has allowed wealthy countries to subsidize corporate farming by $1 billion a day. The subsidies enable companies based in the Global North to sell food internationally at a price below the cost of production. Recently, British International Development Secretary Douglas Alexander estimated that subsidies to Northern agribusiness cost farmers in the Global South $100 billion a year in lost income because small farmers cannot compete with the subsidized cost of imported food.

We call on the G8 to:

- Recognize that food is first and foremost a human right and only secondarily a tradable commodity;
- Support a process for an international Convention to replace the WTO's Agreement on Agriculture. Such a Convention must uphold the full range of human rights standards and should implement the concept of food sovereignty, whereby communities control their own food systems;
- Respect the rights of small farmers to save and exchange seeds between communities and internationally;

- Initiate a conversion of national agricultural subsidies from support for agribusiness to incentives for sustainable farming, including small-scale and organic farms.

These demands reflect the rights and priorities of the world's food producers, in particular, rural women, who are directly responsible for feeding most of the world's people.

Central to our policy proposals is the understanding that global challenges regarding food, climate change and natural resource depletion are interrelated and must be resolved together. Policies that seek to solve one aspect of the problem by deepening another will only worsen the crisis as a whole. We see this dynamic in the US and European Union decision to subsidize the conversion of food crops into biofuels: the move to address energy demands at the expense of food needs has greatly exacerbated the current food crisis.

We urge the G8 to ground integrated solutions to the food crisis in the framework of human rights. That framework, rather than further pursuit of corporate profits, has the strongest potential to yield policies that can resolve the global food crisis in tandem with the other urgent issues of climate change and development being addressed by the G8.

Notes

1 MADRE website, accessed 2014, www.madre.org. The history provided here is from this site.
2 Ibid.
3 Anup Shah, "Global Food Crisis 2008." Global Issues website, updated Aug. 20, 2008, www.globalissues.org.
4 *The Global Social Crisis* (Herndon, VA: UN Publications, 2011), p. 63, www.un.org.

106

Guatemalan Feminist Declaration
Third Americas Social Forum
Guatemala City, Guatemala
October 7–12, 2008

Third Americas Social Forum poster.

The University of San Carlos hosted over seven thousand social justice and human rights advocates for the Third Americas Social Forum (ASF), part of the broader

Social Forum process first held in 2001 in Brazil. The gathering, ASF's first in Central America, "had more of a female face than previous meetings" and "was an overwhelmingly indigenous event," given that "about 80 percent of the [Guatemalan] population belong[s] to one of 25 different Maya groups."[1] Impressively, "of the more than 200 workshops, panels and other activities at the Forum, 72 were organized by feminist and women's organizations or were centered around women's issues. The majority of women's panels and workshops were filled to capacity and beyond, which is indicative of the organizing power and solidarity among women's groups in the region, as well as the thirst for more knowledge and to build deeper connections amongst us."[2] Among the women's organizations present were Guatemala's Sector de Mujeres, El Salvador's Las Dignas, Mesoamericanas en Resistencia, the World March of Women, and Health Network of Women in Latin America and the Caribbean.[3] At a gathering spot at the forum called the Women's Tent, participants reviewed the day's events and collected their thoughts to put into the Feminist Declaration, which was read during the closing ceremony.

During the forum, news arrived that police had raided the offices of the Autonomous Women's Movement in Managua, Nicaragua. While the Declaration condemns this, and speaks to "smear campaigns" against feminism in general, the act generated some debate. There was obviously condemnation of repression of feminism by Ortega's government (including a ban on therapeutic abortions as a 2006 election tactic), but the fact that his was a "leftist" government caused some to hold back, at least initially.

Since the foes in the Declaration are neoliberalism and "a patriarchal capitalist system," the feminism it supports addresses "control over our sexuality, reproductive rights and economic labor"; that is, feminist struggles encompass work against capitalism, racism, patriarchy, and homophobia, in the public and private spheres. Feminist theory is rooted in such "everyday realities" as exploitation, privatization, criminalization, impoverishment, and forced migration. Resistance includes recognizing women's economic, political, and reproductive contributions, and forming certain kinds of alliances, the nature of which perhaps get more attention in this document than in any other. The goal is "a just and equal distribution of power" and "the right to make decisions freely over our lives, bodies, sexuality and the lands in which we live, with their natural and cultural riches." The Declaration[4] concludes with examples of feminism's own commitments to coalition.

Women gather for the forum in Guatemala City, Guatemala.

Guatemalan Feminist Declaration

As feminists, we know that our everyday realities are marked by the oppressive mandates of a patriarchal capitalist system that reinforces inequality as a natural and inevitable fact of life and institutionalizes control over our sexuality, reproductive rights and economic labor. This system excludes women from decision-making in both public and private spheres, and responds to any challenge with the use of violence against our bodies, criminalization, smear campaigns, and repression against our movements.

In its neo-liberal stage, this system of unchecked wealth positions the market and financial interests as regulators of our lives and our social relations, exploiting natural resources, privatizing and destroying our sources of life, putting millions of people at risk and pushing women into forced migrations, condemning them to further exploitation and poverty.

As feminists, we propose deep and radical transformations in the way that human beings relate to each other and to nature, and by so doing ensure a good quality of life for all. A meaningful quality of life recognizes our contributions in the economic and reproductive dimensions as well as our political participation both in civil society and as part of the state. A Good Life, Ütz k'aslemal, must be based on a just and equal distribution of power.

These transformations are made by developing agreements and alliances that respect our autonomy and diversity within the framework of a democracy that encompasses all spheres of life, from the intimate and domestic spaces to workplace, political and public spaces. As women, we demand the right to make decisions freely over our lives, bodies, sexuality and the lands in which we live, with their natural and cultural riches.

We believe that in order to make these transformation real, we can build alliances only with those movements, actors and individuals
- Who include respect for the individual and collective autonomy of women in their political agendas, as well as possibilities for the full exercise of our rights—especially those most at risk such as sexual and reproductive rights—and will not compromise those rights in order to gain or solidify their own power.
- Who define socioeconomic reorganization in such a way that society's sustainability and reproduction no longer rests on the over-exploitation of women. That they reject slavery and servitude, for example, in factory assembly plants, in household work in particular and in situations where women are trafficked internally and across borders.
- Who refuse to tolerate racist, sexist and macho practices that are part of daily life, or that occur within their organizations; that they commit to a pact of non-violence and equality.
- Who are willing to critically examine their own thinking and transform their ideas and challenge fundamentalisms of all kinds, questioning hetero-reality and the imposition of norms and stereotypes that subordinate women.
- Who fight for a secular state that will guarantee and uphold all rights, protect sovereignties, cover basic necessities and ensure a good quality of life for the entire population.

- Who will recognize and integrate our proposals—proposals made by indigenous women and peoples, youth, black women, lesbians and transgender persons, women with disabilities, women who live with HIV/AIDS, elder women and children. Who will not favor one group or struggle over another because they recognize that all individuals and all struggles for freedom are interdependent in this process of building another world.

We reject all acts of violence against women and oppose the criminalization of abortion and the penalization of all of us who fight for its legalization.

We stand in solidarity with our feminist sisters in Nicaragua who are being harassed and politically persecuted. In condemning these acts, we declare that a government cannot consider itself to represent the left if it holds power due to political pacts made with Somoza's heirs, if it criminalizes feminist actions while treating with impunity cases of sexual abuse in which its government officials have been implicated, and if it condemns hundreds of women to death by eliminating the right to therapeutic abortion.

We also affirm our support and solidarity with our sisters who stand in resistance against mining companies and mega-projects, who are being persecuted for their involvement in local level consultation and community participation efforts and for their legitimate and legal opposition to the exploitation of their natural resources.

We demand the release and safe return to their families of all of the disappeared, as well as the liberation of all political prisoners held by the current regime governing Mexico.

We stand in solidarity with the women of Haiti and we reject the violence provoked by the military forces occupying the country, such as the Kaibil Elite Brigade, well known for its role in the genocide that occurred during the armed conflict in Guatemala.

We recognize and honor the history and contributions of a diversity of feminist activists, particularly of indigenous women activists through their cultural, linguistic, social and political resistance and action.

We believe that when people refuse to discuss the inconsistencies between the discourse and practice of those who claim to be on the left, the transformations that are urgently needed in our societies are only further delayed. The political struggle must be ethical. For this reason, we will continue supporting the development of social movements, providing critical input and analysis, and defending the autonomy and further strengthening of the feminist movement.

FEMINISTS AGAINST THE WAR, FEMINISTS AGAINST INEQUALITY, FEMINISTS AGAINST RACISM, AGAINST NEO-LIBERAL TERRORISM

Notes

1 Marc Becker, "Social Forum of the Americas." *Z Magazine*, Dec. 6, 2008, www.zcomm.org.
2 JASS, "JASS at the III Americas Social Forum, Guatemala City, Guatemala, October 7–12, 2008," report, p. 10. Just Associates website, www.justassociates.org.

3   Michael Leon Guerrero and Cindy Wiesner, "Reflections on the III Americas Social Forum, Guatemala." Grassroots Global Justice Alliance website, accessed Sept. 2017, www.ggjalliance.org.

4   JASS, "JASS at the III Americas Social Forum," 1–27.

107

Manifesto of the First Pan-Canadian Young Feminist Gathering
Waves of Resistance Conference
Montreal, Canada
October 10–13, 2008

Waves of Resistance emblem.

The "Manifesto of the Pan-Canadian Young Feminist Gathering" is our political tool. For us, it is an instrument of identification as well as mobilization and raising consciousness. The Manifesto describes us as young feminists as well as what we are fighting against, what we are struggling for, the world and communities we dream of building together and the gestures we will make to get there. We hope that the Manifesto will be used across Canada, in our feminist networks, as well as in grassroots organisations and national unions: at feminist actions or to educate our friends, colleagues, mothers, brothers, etc. about feminism.[1]

Over five hundred young women gathered to "energize, firmly establish, mobilize and promote networking among the young feminists' movement in Quebec and Canada." They described how they would accomplish these ends:

- By gathering together the most diverse group possible of young women and feminists from different sectors and regions in Canada so that we can meet and get to know each other. By ensuring the representation of a broad range of visions and struggles led by young feminists in Canada.
- By sharing and developing our analysis of different issues that affect us as young women and feminists.
- By collectivizing our feminist struggles and discussing our action priorities as young feminists.
- By thinking together about how to resist and fight against the rising economic, moral and political Right in Canada.
- By creating links of solidarity among young feminists throughout Quebec and Canada.
- And also, by celebrating our struggles and solidarity![2]

The stress here, as in the document the gathering produced, is on having a diversity of voices, developing distinctly feminist analyses of both conservative and liberatory trends, and engaging in continuous collective action. The organizing committee shows how broad collectives continue to build on more local efforts, as it included representatives from the Youth Committee of the Federation des Femmes du Quebec, Groupe F.E.M.M.E.S. Sororitaires, Young Feminists Committee of the Y des Femmes de Montreal, Centre des Femmes de Verdun, Young Women of the Consil Central du Montreal Metropolitain, Power Camp Nation/Filles d'Action, Carrefour de Participation, Ressourcement et Formation, and Women's Committee of the Association pour une Solidarite Syndicale Etudiante.

Procedurally, preparatory groups met in regions, picked representatives for the gathering, and sent in answers to questions about what they wanted the gathering to discuss and how. The three-day program that developed from this input covered a broad diversity of themes, including Indigenous feminism, eco-feminism, antifeminism, neoliberalism, motherhood, the intersection of sexism and racism, hypersexualization of youth, women's health, sexism and the media, poverty, and militarism. Theory and practice were united, as "creative resistance workshops" and "resistance actions" were part of the gathering. As one participant wrote, "Every workshop was followed by a creative resistance workshop, in which the participants planned—and undertook—a public direct action. The actions ranged from street theatre to sidewalk chalk denouncing lack of access to abortion to radical cheerleading. The streets of Montreal crackled that evening with the energy of feminist action."[3]

Like so many manifestos, this declaration[4] begins with evidence of ongoing problems in our supposedly postfeminist age, from violence against women to lack of reproductive and sexual health. Past gains have proved insufficient; for example, "We have gained the right to vote, yet gender-based discrimination keeps women virtually unrepresented in political office." Familiar themes such as the effects of war on women and the threat of growing conservative forces reappear here. The list of grievances continues into the "down with" section of the document. Both the "rise against" and "we will" lists contain calls for action. Colonialism, racism, capitalism, and patriarchy are the targets, and a hopeful vision of nonviolent egalitarianism is proposed, with many suggested means for social transformation.

The moniker 'rebELLEs' lives on in art commemorating the gathering and the movement.

Manifesto of the First Pan-Canadian Young Feminist Gathering

We are the young RebELLEs who have answered a feminist call and we are proud to call ourselves feminists. We recognize that there are multiple interpretations of feminism and we celebrate and integrate this diversity. We are committed to the continual expansion of the plurality of our voices. We are committed to an ongoing process of critical self-reflection to inform and transform our movement. We acknowledge the historical exclusion of "Othered" women by the majority Western feminist movement. We strive to learn from the past, honour the struggles of our foremothers and continue to dream for the future. We value the allies of feminism who support us in our fight for equity and justice.

We are women of diverse abilities, ethnicities, origins, sexualities, identities, class backgrounds, ages and races. Among us are employed, underemployed and unemployed women, mothers, students, dropouts, artists, musicians and women in the sex trade. We state that transfolks, two-spirited and intersexed people are integral to our movement and recognize and respect gender fluidity and support the right to self-identify. Our women-only spaces include everyone who self-identifies and lives as a woman in society.

We are told that feminism is over and outdated. If this were true then we wouldn't need to denounce the fact that:

In reality, many of the demands of our feminist mothers and grandmothers remain unmet. Women continue to be the victims of sexual violence. Our communities are haunted by the silence that follows these assaults. Throughout Canada, in spite of our right to it, access to abortion services remains insufficient. Across Canada as well, colonized, marginalized, racialized and disabled women are coerced and/or forced to undergo unwanted or uninformed abortions, forced to use contraception and are subjected to forced sterilization. The hyper-sexualization of women in the media has taught us to view women as sexual objects rather than complete human beings. Getting off, lesbianism and being queer are taboo and a woman's choice to seek sexual pleasure is seen as negative. Our identities are eroded as we are taught, from the time we are children, and through television and magazines, that how we should look, dress, and act is determined by our sex. Violence is normalized, sexual abuse eroticized. Our sexual health education is inadequate and our reproductive rights are disrespected. Our needs are not being met.

In reality, women still represent the majority of the underprivileged. Our government steals children from poor and Aboriginal women. Capitalism exploits working-class women and confines middle- and upper-class women to "consumer" roles. We are told that equality has been achieved, but still the wage gap persists. Immigrant women are denied acknowledgment of their academic credentials and are forced to endure intolerable work environments in order to stay on Canadian soil. We lack affordable and accessible childcare. Women remain underpaid, underappreciated, and undervalued in the work force. We have gained the right to vote, yet gender-based discrimination keeps women virtually unrepresented in political office.

In this globalized world, we must construct international feminist solidarity. The actions of Canadian political and economic elites harm women around the world, and in a way that is specifically gender-related. War, genocide and militarization are characterized by the use of rape as a war weapon, femicide, and the sexual exploitation of thousands of our sisters. Free trade contributes to women's increasing social, economic and cultural insecurity. In response to Canadian imperialism, we will globalize our feminist solidarity.

In this so-called post-feminist world, our roles in society are still defined by traditional views on gender. Religious and political forces aimed at maintaining the pillars of power in our society silence us from voicing our rights. We denounce the current rise of right-wing ideology in Canadian society and the steps backward in women's rights that this has caused. We are being stripped of rights for which those who came before us fought hard. Geography marginalizes women, with remote, northern and rural women lacking access to basic services. Showing solidarity with our sisters means trying to understand all of the issues we face—including race, class and gender—and standing together against oppression.

Finally, we denounce the dismissal of the feminist movement as redundant. Our struggle is not over. We will be post-feminists when we have post-patriarchy.

Feminists Unite!

DOWN WITH the colonial legacy of genocide and assimilation of Aboriginal peoples, particularly of Aboriginal women

DOWN WITH the sexism and racism of the Indian Act

DOWN WITH dishonoured treaties

DOWN WITH assimilation

DOWN WITH racial profiling

DOWN WITH Canada's fake multicultural policy

DOWN WITH warmongers & military power

DOWN WITH racist child welfare policies

DOWN WITH stereotypes in the media

DOWN WITH genocide and femicide

DOWN WITH stealing women and children

DOWN WITH COLONIALISM

RebELLEs AGAINST banks for hijacking the world

RebELLEs AGAINST drug companies for institutionalizing women's health

RebELLEs AGAINST public spaces that don't accommodate all bodies

RebELLEs AGAINST development that destroys nature

RebELLEs AGAINST the class system that keeps us impoverished and deprives us of safe, affordable housing

RebELLEs AGAINST the state that forces other countries to adopt the capitalist system

RebELLEs AGAINST the devaluation of women's paid and unpaid work

RebELLEs AGAINST corporations for making money off our backs

RebELLEs AGAINST the advertisers who destroy our self-esteem and then sell it back to us

RebELLEs AGAINST CAPITALISM

RISE AGAINST the industries that cause us to hate our bodies and our sexuality

RISE AGAINST heterosexism that makes it seem that there is only one way of living, loving and being sexual

RISE AGAINST the socialization of children in gender binaries, race categories and colonial erasures

RISE AGAINST the education that reinforces the heteronormative nuclear family

RISE AGAINST the religious Right and its influence on State policy and legislation

RISE AGAINST rape and violence against women

RISE AGAINST the objectification and control of women's bodies

RISE AGAINST all anti-choice bills, laws and strategies

RISE AGAINST the sexual division of labour

RISE AGAINST poverty and women's economic disadvantage and dependency

RISE AGAINST income support programs based on family status instead of individual status

RISE AGAINST masculinists, their false claims and demagogic arguments

RISE AGAINST sexual exploitation

RISE AGAINST PATRIARCHY

We envision communities committed to:

- Eradicating all forms of violence—including sexual, institutional, emotional, economic, physical, cultural, racial, colonial, ageist and ableist
- Challenging all forms of oppression, power and privilege
- Recognizing that others' struggles against oppression cannot be separated from one's own, because all people are intrinsically linked; and being conscious of how one fits into the different structures of oppression while fighting to eliminate them all
- Freeing our children and ourselves from the gender binary
- Building institutions and structures that promote the principles of Justice, Peace & Equality
- Eliminating economic inequality
- Funding and supporting affordable, accessible childcare, and the economic freedom to mother in the way we choose
- Learning and teaching true herstory and histories of our victories and struggles, especially those of women of colour and Aboriginal women
- Fighting the stigma and shame of mental health and psychiatric survivors and supporting their struggles

We will: Change our attitude: get pissed off, refuse, resist, walk out, speak up!

We will: Transform our daily lives and relationships: actions can take place in small interactions

We will: Encourage people to learn about, care for and love themselves and their bodies

We will: Support safe and accessible space for individuals to define and express themselves without fear of judgement

We will: Create alternatives, write poetry, articles, letters, make art

We will: Join with others, find common ground, build community, create feminist spaces and gatherings, raise awareness, educate, spread the word

We will: Believe that a better world is possible and work to achieve it

We will: Organize and struggle: build alliances with existing feminist groups and create new ones, fight together in solidarity, be seen and be heard, disrupt, trouble, destabilize established powers, become culture jammers

We will: Build solidarity based on the commonality of our diverse struggles and perspectives

We will: Value people rather than profits

We will: Demand massive State reinvestment in social programs and the end of privatization

We will: Organize pan-Canadian decentralized days of feminist action against the rise of the Right

We will: Protest and resist sexist bills and laws that threaten our reproductive rights, racist immigration laws, war, free trade, repression, the criminalization of political movements, corporate exploitation and plunder of the earth, and violence against women

We will: Champion safety, respect, justice, freedom, equality and SOLIDARITY!

Notes

1 "Manifesto of the Pan-Canadian Young Feminist Gathering," Sept. 21, 2009. *Ottawa RebELLEs* blog, ottawarebelles.blogspot.com/2009.

2 This list is from the program, available at http://files.meetup.com/517311/Toujours%20 Rebelles%20-%20Waves%20of%20Resistance.pdf, accessed September 30, 2017.

3 Maysie (user), "Call Out: Waves of Resistance: Pan-Canadian Young Feminist Gathering," March 12, 2008. Rabble.Ca Babble discussion board, rabble.ca/babble/feminism/ call-out-waves-resistance-pan-canadian-young-feminist-gathering.

4 "Manifesto of the First Pan-Canadian Young Feminist Gathering," *Socialist Voice,* Nov. 2, 2009, www.socialistvoice.ca.

108

Declaration against Violent Extremism
First SAVE (Sisters Against Violent Extremism) Conference
Vienna, Austria
November 28–December 1, 2008

SAVE logo.

SAVE's approach to counterterrorism is unique in that it focuses on women and their ability to combat violent extremism and radicalization on the front lines—at home and in civil society. SAVE believes in empowering women to be sought-after agents of change at all levels of international counterterrorism efforts, from grassroots activists to policy makers.[1]

SAVE is headquartered in the Women without Borders offices, the organization that launched it in 2008. SAVE believes in the power of storytelling and of courageous dialogue as ways to understand "others" and to bring communities together. It is committed to developing alternative strategies for resisting terrorism and extremism, and to strengthening women's skills as peacemakers. It has drawn on women's knowledge as victims and as survivors of terrorist attacks, as mothers, and as community activists. It has created "Mothers Schools," where the "curriculum emphasizes the distinctive role women can play in the security sphere by facilitating constructive communication and thoughtful authority in their families."[2] This innovation is based on an understanding that women often influence their families and communities in distinctive ways, and that counterterrorism efforts need to learn from and draw on women. SAVE is part of a growing effort to utilize a "gendered approach to preventing recruitment and radicalization to violence."[3]

SAVE Conference participants, 2008.

This conference was attended by thirty-three people who, like those at subsequent meetings, focus on sharing their experiences with extremism and strategizing how to combat it. The first group developed the SAVE Declaration.[4] Its tone is different from most in this collection, as it asks each individual to make certain commitments that nurture nonviolence. But the content is familiar now to readers of this book, in its sense of the urgency presented by violence, the need it expresses for new, feminist approaches to peace, and its commitment to women playing a role at every level in diminishing violence.

Declaration against Violent Extremism

Each participant of the first *SAVE*—Sisters Against Violent Extremism—conference declares:
1. I, as a woman, will use the local and global networks of women to stop the killing.
2. I will inspire a new response to prevent terror, violence and discrimination.
3. I will create awareness for not stigmatizing the families of the extremists/terrorists.
4. I will support the young generation with non-violent alternatives in their search for a better life.
5. I will engage all forms of media for spreading the message of non-violence.
6. I will insist on peaceful resolutions to prevent escalation of conflict and violence.
7. I will promote a global dialogue for a future without fear.
8. I will raise my voice against all hostile states and politics that cause suffering.
9. I recognise the urgency to create "SAVE" spaces for a peaceful coexistence.
10. I will always remember those affected by violent extremism.

Notes
1   *Security in Safe Hands: Women Make the Difference!* Second Global SAVE Conference, conference program, Feb. 2010, p. 12. Women without Borders website, www.women-without-borders.org.
2   "Underway: Support Our Projects," 2010. Women without Borders website, www.women-without-borders.org.
3   Krista Couture, "A Gendered Approach to Countering Violent Extremism: Lessons Learned from Women in Peacebuilding and Conflict Prevention Applied Successfully in Bangladesh

and Morocco," July 30, 2014. Policy paper for the Center for 21st Century Security and Intelligence, Brookings Institute, p. 9. Brookings Institute website, www.brookings.edu.

4 "The First SAVE Conference/SAVE Declaration," Dec. 2, 2009. Women without Borders website, www.women-without-borders.org.

109

Women's Assembly Declaration
World Social Forum
Belém do Para, Brazil
January 27–February 1, 2009

We cannot accept that attempts to maintain this system are made at the expense of women.

World Social Forum in Belem, Brazil, 2009. Photo by Marc Becker.

The World Social Forum is an assembly of civil society organizations that sees itself addressing global justice in the era of global capitalist exploitation. It has met since 2001, timed annually to compete with the World Economic Forum, with which it disagrees vehemently. The first article of its original charter reads,

> The World Social Forum is an open meeting place for reflective thinking, democratic debate of ideas, formulation of proposals, free exchange of experiences and interlinking for effective action, by groups and movements of civil society that are opposed to neo-liberalism and to domination of the world by capital and any form of imperialism, and are committed to building a planetary society directed towards fruitful relationships among Mankind and between it and the Earth.[1]

The ninth forum was attended by "about 1,900 indigenous people, representing 190 ethnic groups."[2] This representation is clear in the opening of the Declaration[3] below, which "reaffirm[s] the contribution of indigenous women and women from all forest peoples as political subjects that enriches feminism . . . and strengthens the feminist struggle against the patriarchal capitalist global system." Reminiscent of earlier documents such as the one by the Association of Women in El Salvador (Costa Rica 1981), this one deeply unites opposition to patriarchy with opposition to globalization and assertion of the rights of local peoples. Similarly, then, it links problems that can seem disconnected, such as "financial, food, climate and energetic crises." Consequently, it is deeply committed to more "alternative" answers than found in many other sources: "We, feminist women, demand a change in the production and consumption model." This means, for example, food sovereignty versus transgenic foods, and living wages versus financial rescue of banks.

Unlike many ideologically similar documents, this points out the distinct costs to women of globalization, including control of women's bodies and sexualities. In that context, it recognizes the need "to resist fundamentalist and conservative attacks." Too, it expresses solidarity with women's struggles and resistance around the globe, especially in warring and occupied territories. Both despite and because of its powerful and diverse opponents, this Declaration affirms its commitment "to the construction of the feminist movement as . . . an instrument for women to achieve the transformation of their lives and our societies."

Women's Assembly Declaration

In the year in which the WSF joins with the population of the Pan-Amazon, we, women from different parts of the world gathered in Belém, reaffirm the contribution of indigenous women and women from all forest peoples as political subjects that enriches feminism in the framework of the cultural diversity of our societies and strengthens the feminist struggle against the patriarchal capitalist global system.

The world is currently experiencing various crises that demonstrate that this system is not viable. Financial, food, climate and energetic crises are not isolated phenomena, but represent a crisis of the model itself, driven by the super exploitation of work and the environment, and financial speculation of the economy.

We are not interested in palliative answers based on market logic in response to these crises; this can only lead to perpetuation of the same system. We need to advance in the construction of alternatives. We are against the use of agro-fuels and carbon credit markets as "solutions" to the climate and energy crises. *We, feminist women, demand a change in the production and consumption model.*

In relation to the food crisis, we affirm that transgenic foodstuffs do not represent a solution. Our alternatives are food sovereignty and the development of agro-ecological production.

With respect to the financial and economic crisis, we are against the withdrawal of millions from public funds to rescue banks and businesses. We, feminist women, demand employment protection and the right to a decent income.

We cannot accept that attempts to maintain this system are made at the expense of women. The mass layoffs, cuts in public spending in social fields, and reaffirmation of this production model increase the work involved in reproduction and sustainability of life, and thus directly affect our lives as women.

To impose its domain worldwide, the system resorts to militarization and arms; genocidal confrontations are fabricated that reduce women to spoils of war and use sexual violence as a weapon of war in armed conflict. Entire populations are forcibly displaced, forcing them to live as political refugees. Violence against women, feminicide and other crimes against humanity are committed on a daily basis in armed conflicts, while perpetrators enjoy total impunity.

We, feminist women, propose radical and profound changes in relations among human beings and with the environment, the end of lesbophobia, of hetero-normative and racist patriarchy.

We demand the end of control over our bodies and sexuality. We claim the right to make free decisions in relation to our lives and the territories we inhabit. We are against the reproduction of society through the super-exploitation of women.

We express our solidarity with women in regions of armed conflict and war. We add our voices to those of our sisters in Haiti and reject the violence perpetrated by the military occupation forces. We support the Colombian, Congolese and countless other women who resist—on a daily basis—the violence of military and militia groups in conflict in their countries. We stand together with Iraqi women facing the violence of the US military occupation.

At this current time, we express our particular solidarity with Palestinian women in the Gaza Strip under military attack from Israel, and we join the struggles for the end of war in the Middle East.

In peace, as in war, we support the victims of patriarchal and racist violence against black and [young] women.

Equally, we express our support and solidarity to all sisters in their resistance struggles against hydroelectric dams, timber and mining companies and mega-projects in the Amazon and around the world, as well as those who are persecuted as a result of their legitimate opposition to this exploitation. We unite with those struggling for the right to water.

We stand with all women criminalized for the practice of abortion and defend this right. We strengthen our commitment and join together in actions to resist fundamentalist and conservative attacks, in order to guarantee that all those women who need to, are entitled to safe and legal abortion.

We support the struggle for accessibility for disabled women and for the right of migrant women to freely "come and go."

On behalf of all these women, and of ourselves, we continue committed to the construction of the feminist movement as a counter-hegemonic political force and an instrument for women to achieve the transformation of their lives and our societies, by supporting and strengthening the self-organisation of women, dialogue, and networking between social movements' struggles.

On 8th March and during the Global Week of Action 2010, as women around the world we will unite in our confrontation of the capitalist and patriarchal system that oppresses and exploits us. In the streets and in our homes, in forests and the countryside, in our struggles and in the spaces of our daily lives, we will maintain our rebellion and mobilisation.

Notes

1 "World Social Forum," last edited Aug. 28, 2017. *Wikipedia*, www.wikipedia.org.

2 Ibid.

3 Women's Assembly of the World Social Forum, "Women's Assembly Declaration," Feb. 9, 2009. Committee for the Abolition of Illegitimate Debt website, www.cadtm.org.

110

Framework for Action
Global Meeting of Musawah: For Equality in the Muslim Family
Kuala Lumpur, Malaysia
February 13–17, 2009

Musawah logo.

By the early 1990s, "Islamic feminism" had emerged as a broad movement, feminist in its aspirations yet Islamic in its language and sources of legitimacy. It was nurtured by feminist scholars who were uncovering a hidden history of Muslim women, and re-reading the textual sources to unveil an egalitarian interpretation of the Shari'a.[1]

Many aspects of our family laws, as defined by classical jurists and as reproduced in modern legal codes, are neither tenable in contemporary circumstances nor defensible on Islamic grounds.

This gathering of Musawah (Arabic for "equality") was hosted by the Malaysian group Sisters in Islam. A committee of activists and scholars from eleven countries worked for over two years on the Framework for Action. Over 250 people from forty-seven countries attended the first global meeting in Kuala Lumpur.

The document below[2] contrasts importantly with those such as the Declaration against Sexual Apartheid (2008) and the Declaration of the Rights of Women in Islamic Societies (1997). Those others see Islam as a barrier to equality, while this declaration is much more interested in working within the traditions of Islam, based on the view that Islam is fully compatible with gender equality. This does not mean that Musawah is uncritical of laws and practices in Muslim countries—quite the contrary. Instead, their position is based on a feminist rethinking of male authority in the Muslim legal tradition, and a commitment to reforming male dominance from within. As one member of Musawah wrote, "When the Islamists brought the classical jurisprudential texts out of the closet in order to promote a 'return to Shari'a,' they unintentionally exposed them to public scrutiny and debate and opened a space in which an internal critique of patriarchal interpretations of the Shari'a could be articulated to an extent unprecedented in Muslim history."[3] Such a project fits well with Musawah's description of itself as "a knowledge building movement [that] facilitates access to existing knowledge and creates new knowledge about women's rights in Islam."[4]

The symbol used for Islamic feminism incorporates both feminist iconography and the traditional crescent and star symbol used for Islam.

Led by Muslim women, Musawah is "a global movement for equality and justice in the Muslim family, which advances human rights for women in Muslim contexts, in both their public and private lives."[5] The principles they advocate include equality in the family, and full and equal citizenship for all. They battle to counter the widespread use of Islam to resist women's demands for equality and justice. They offer a "toolkit" online to empower people to talk about and advocate for equal rights and practices. "Musawah contributes to building a public voice of women leaders demanding for an alternative understanding of Islam, one that recognises equality and justice in the context of changing times and circumstances."[6]

Framework for Action

We hold the principles of Islam to be a source of justice, equality, fairness and dignity for all human beings. We declare that equality and justice are necessary and possible in family laws and practices in Muslim countries and communities.

Recognising that:
- The teachings of the Qur'an, the objectives of the Shari'ah, universal human rights standards, fundamental rights and constitutional guarantees, and the realities of our lives in the twenty-first century, all demand that relations between Muslim women and men in both the private and public spheres be governed by principles and practices that uphold equality, fairness and justice;
- All Muslims have an equal right and duty to read the religious texts, engage in understanding God's message, and act for justice, equality and the betterment of humankind within their families, communities and countries;
- Many laws and practices in Muslim countries are unjust, and the lives of all family members, especially women, are impaired by these injustices on a daily basis;
- Human affairs constantly change and evolve, as do the laws and social practices that shape relations within the Muslim family;
- Islam embodies equality, justice, love, compassion and mutual respect between all human beings, and these values provide us with a path towards change;

- The reform of laws and practices for the benefit of society and the public interest (maslahah) has always been part of the Muslim legal tradition; and
- International human rights standards require dignity, substantive equality and non-discrimination for all human beings;

We, as Muslims and as citizens of modern nations, declare that equality and justice in the family are both necessary and possible. The time for realising these values in our laws and practices is now.

I. Equality and Justice in the Family Are Necessary

Most family laws and practices in today's Muslim countries and communities are based on theories and concepts that were developed by classical jurists (fuqaha) in vastly different historical, social and economic contexts. In interpreting the Qur'an and the Sunnah, classical jurists were guided by the social and political realities of their age and a set of assumptions about law, society and gender that reflected the state of knowledge, normative values and patriarchal institutions of their time. The idea of gender equality had no place in, and little relevance to, their conceptions of justice. It was not part of their social experience. The concept of marriage itself was one of domination by the husband and submission by the wife. Men were deemed to be protectors of women and the sole providers for the household, such that their wives were not obliged to do housework or even suckle their babies. Women, in turn, were required to obey their husbands completely.

By the early twentieth century, the idea that equality is intrinsic to conceptions of justice began to take root. The world inhabited by the authors of classical jurisprudential texts (fiqh) had begun to disappear. But the unequal construction of gender rights formulated in their texts lingered—reproduced, in a modified way, in colonial and post-colonial family laws that merged classical juristic concepts with colonial influences and negative aspects of local customs. Most of the current Muslim family laws were created through this process, and are therefore based on assumptions and concepts that have become irrelevant to the needs, experiences and values of Muslims today. The administration of these hybrid statutes shifted from classical scholars, who became increasingly out of touch with changing political and social realities, to executive and legislative bodies that had neither the legitimacy nor the inclination to challenge premodern interpretations of the Shari'ah. Even in Muslim communities where classical juristic concepts have not been codified into law, the centuries-old fiqh rules and colonial and local norms have, in many cases, been invoked to sustain inequality between women and men within the family and wider society.

Injustices resulting from this disconnect between outdated laws and customs and present-day realities are numerous and can be found in many Muslim countries and communities. Such injustices and discrimination were also common in secular laws throughout the world until changes were made in the twentieth century to bring these laws progressively in line with new universal norms of equality. Because family laws and practices are interconnected with all other aspects of society, injustices within the family affect women in many other areas, including dignity, personal security, mobility, property, citizenship, nationality, labour rights, criminal laws and political participation.

In our time and contexts, there cannot be justice without equality. Many aspects of our family laws, as defined by classical jurists and as reproduced in modern legal codes, are neither tenable in contemporary circumstances nor defensible on Islamic grounds. Not only do they fail to fulfil the Shari'ah requirement of justice, but they are now being used to deny women dignified choices in life. These elements lie at the root of marital disharmony and the breakdown of the family.

II. Equality and Justice in the Family Are Possible

Qur'anic teachings encompass the principles of justice ('adl), equality (musawah), equity (insaf), human dignity (karamah), love and compassion (mawaddah wa rahmah). These principles reflect universal norms and are consistent with contemporary human rights standards. These key Qur'anic values can guide further development of family laws and practices in line with the contemporary notion of justice, which includes equality between the sexes and before the law. Several basic concepts in Islamic legal theory lay the foundation for the claim that family laws and practices can be changed to reflect equality and justice and the lived realities of Muslims today:

- There is a distinction between Shari'ah, the revealed way, and fiqh, the science of Islamic jurisprudence. In Islamic theology, Shari'ah (lit. the way, the path to a water source) is the sum total of religious values and principles as revealed to the Prophet Muhammad to direct human life. Fiqh (lit. understanding) is the Musawah Framework for Action process by which humans attempt to derive concrete legal rules from the two primary sources of Islamic thought and practice: the Qur'an and the Sunnah of the Prophet. As a concept, Shari'ah cannot be reduced to a set of laws—it is closer to ethics than law. It embodies ethical values and principles that guide humans in the direction of justice and correct conduct. What many commonly assert to be Shari'ah laws are, in fact, often the result of fiqh, juristic activity, hence human, fallible and changeable.

- There are two main categories of legal rulings: 'ibadat (devotional/spiritual acts) and mu'amalat (transactional/contractual acts). Rulings in the 'ibadat category regulate relations between God and the believer, and therefore offer limited scope for change. Rulings in the mu'amalat category, however, regulate relations between humans, and therefore remain open to change. Since human affairs constantly evolve, there is always a need for new rulings that use new interpretations of the religious texts to bring outdated laws in line with the changing realities of time and place (zaman wa makan). This is the rationale for ijtihad (lit. endeavour, self-exertion), which is the jurist's method for finding solutions to new issues in light of the guidance of revelation. Rulings concerning the family and gender relations belong to the realm of mu'amalat, which means that Muslim jurists have always considered them as social and contractual matters that are open to rational consideration and change.

- Laws or amendments introduced in the name of Shari'ah and Islam should also reflect the values of equality, justice, love, compassion and mutual respect among all human beings. These are values and principles on which Muslims agree and which Muslim jurists hold to be among the indisputable objectives of the Shari'ah. In the words of Ibn Qayyim al-Jawziyyah, the 7th (AH)/14th (CE) century jurist, "The fundamentals of the Shari'ah are rooted in wisdom and promotion of the welfare of human beings in this life and the Hereafter. Shari'ah embraces Justice, Kindness, the Common Good and Wisdom. Any rule that departs from justice to injustice, from kindness to harshness, from the common good to harm, or from rationality to absurdity cannot be part of Shari'ah, even if it is arrived at through individual interpretation."

- Diversity of opinion (ikhtilaf) is a basic concept that has always been a part of fiqh, even after the formal establishment of schools of law. There is not now, nor has there ever been, a single, unitary "Islamic law." The very existence of multiple schools of law, let alone the dozens of Muslim family laws in different countries today, attests to the fact that no one person, group or country can claim there is a unified, monolithic, divine Islamic law over which they have ownership. Within the context of the modern state, we must recognise and engage with this diversity of opinions to determine how best to serve the public interest (maslahah) and meet the demands of equality and justice.

Thus, contemporary family laws, whether codified or uncodified, are not divine, but are based on centuries-old, human-made fiqh interpretations that were enacted into law by colonial powers and national governments. Since these interpretations and laws are human-made and concern relations between humans, they can change within the Musawah Framework for Action framework of Islamic principles and in accordance with the changing realities of time and place. Recent positive reforms in Muslim family laws and evolutions in practices provide support for this possibility of change.

The principles and ideals within the Qur'an lay out a path toward equality and justice in family laws and practices, as they did in ending the institution of slavery. As the injustices of slavery became increasingly recognised and the conditions emerged for its abolishment, laws and practices related to slavery were reconsidered and the classical fiqh rulings became obsolete. Similarly, our family laws—as well as practices that have not been codified into law—must evolve to reflect the Islamic values of equality and justice, reinforce universal human rights standards and address the lived realities of families in the twenty-first century. Likewise, laws or amendments introduced in the name of Islam in the future should also reflect the values of equality, justice, love, compassion and mutual respect among all human beings.

III. Principles on Equality and Justice in the Family
Principle 1: The universal and Islamic values of equality, nondiscrimination, justice and dignity are the basis of all human relations.

Islam mandates justice ('adl), equality (musawah), human dignity (karamah), and love and compassion (mawaddah wa rahmah) in relations among humans and in the family. These principles are also recognised as universal values and enshrined as rights in many national constitutions and international instruments.

In the Qur'an, men and women are equal in creation and in the afterlife. Surah an-Nisa' 4:1 states that men and women are created from a single soul (nafs wahidah). One person does not come before the other, one is not superior to the other, and one is not the derivative of the other. A woman is not created for the purpose of a man. Rather, they are both created for the mutual benefit of each other.

The Qur'an teaches "love and tenderness" (Ar-Rum 30:21) between women and men; that men and women are like each other's garments (Al-Baqarah 2:187); that "be it man or woman: each of you is an issue of the other" (Al-'Imran 3:195); and that "both men and women—they are close unto one another, they [all] enjoin the doing of what is right and forbid the doing of what is wrong" (At-Tawbah 9:71). The four Qur'anic verses that apparently speak of men's authority over women in the family and inequality between them in society (AlBaqarah 2:222, 228 and An-Nisa 4:2, 34) must be understood in light of the broader Islamic principles and the objectives of the Shar'iah, and not in isolation.

Understandings of justice and injustice change over time. Within the context of the Qur'anic worldview of justice and equality, there are many verses that can provide a model for relations within the family and between all human beings that is in line with contemporary notions of justice. To have justice in our time and to remain true to the spirit of Islam and its teachings, equality must be embodied in our laws and practices. Inequality in family relations and human relations must be replaced by mutual respect, affection and partnership.

Principle 2: Full and equal citizenship, including full participation in all aspects of society, is the right of every individual.

Islam teaches that all human beings are born equal in worth and dignity, which is echoed in universal human rights principles. The Qur'an promotes absolute equality of "all men and women" in key aspects of their lives, promising "for [all of] them has God readied forgiveness of sins and a mighty reward" (Al-Ahzab 33:35).

As human beings of equal worth and dignity before God, and as citizens of modern states, all individuals are entitled to exercise equal rights to political participation and leadership, equal access to economic resources, equality before the law, and equal autonomy in the economic, social, cultural and political spheres. The Qur'an notes that all human beings, men and women, are agents (khalifah) of God, charged with realising God's will on earth. In countries where Islam is a source of law and policy, as well as communities in which Islam influences customs and traditions, it is the right and duty of all Muslims—and all people—to openly contribute to laws, policies and practices in order to achieve justice and equality within their families, communities and societies.

Principle 3: Equality between men and women requires equality in the family.

Islam calls for equality, justice, compassion and dignity between all people. Family laws and practices must therefore fulfil this call by promoting these principles and responding to the lived realities of Muslim women and men today.

Women and men alike are entitled to equality and justice within the family, as well as respect and recognition for their contributions. The acknowledgement of joint responsibilities within the family must be accompanied by equal rights, equal decision-making practices, equal access to justice, equal property ownership, and equal division of assets upon divorce or death. Islamic principles, universal human rights standards, constitutional and legal guarantees, and the lived realities of women and men today together provide a path for our communities to ensure equality and justice in family laws and practices. In the twenty-first century, the provisions of the Convention on the Elimination of All Forms of Discrimination against Women (CEDAW)—which stands for justice and equality for women in the family and society—are more in line with the Shari'ah than family law provisions in many Muslim countries and communities.

Realisation of these principles entails laws and practices that ensure:
- The family as a place of security, harmony, support and personal growth for all its members;
- Marriage as a partnership of equals, with mutual respect, affection, communication and decision-making authority between the partners;
- The equal right to choose a spouse or choose not to marry, and to enter into marriage only with free and full consent; and the equal right to dissolve the marriage, as well as equal rights upon its dissolution;

- Equal rights and responsibilities with respect to property, including acquisition, ownership, enjoyment, management, administration, disposition and inheritance, bearing in mind the need to ensure the financial security of all members of the family; and
- Equal rights and responsibilities of parents in matters relating to their children.

We, as women and men who embrace the Islamic and universal values of equality and justice, call for a renewal of these values within the Muslim family. We urge our governments and political leaders, international institutions, religious leaders, and our sisters and brothers to come together to ensure that our family laws and practices uphold these values.

Equality, justice, fairness and dignity are necessary and possible in Muslim families in the twenty-first century. The time for integrating these values into our laws and realising them in our daily lives is now.

Notes

1 Ziba Mir-Hosseini, "In Search of Equality: From London to Kuala Lumpur." *Middle East in London*, July/Aug. 2009, p. 2.
2 Musawah, "Musawah Framework for Action" (Sisters in Islam, 2009). Musawah website, www.musawah.org.
3 Mir-Hosseini, p. 2.
4 Musawah, "What We Do." Musawah website, accessed 2014, www.musawah.org.
5 Ibid.
6 Ibid.

111

The Rio Declaration
Global Symposium on Engaging Men and Boys in Achieving Gender Equality
Rio de Janeiro, Brazil
March 29–April 3, 2009

The MenEngage logo.

In the introduction to the Declaration, the 450 attendees at the symposium, like those at many other gatherings, describe the diversity of the participants. The prefatory note begins its analysis with "outrage at the injustices that continue to plague the lives of women and girls, and the self-destructive demands we put on boys and men" but also with "a powerful sense of hope." What is distinctive in this document is the extent to which the concerns addressed include the many costs to men of sexism, and how the hopefulness centers around "the potential of men's and boys' capacity to change, to care, to cherish, to love passionately, and to work for social and gender justice." The participants "believe that men and women must work together in speaking out against discrimination and violence" and recognize the work men and boys are already doing to dismantle patriarchy, work that "stems from and honours the pioneering work and ongoing leadership of the women's movement." The MenEngage website discusses the definition of masculinity, a theme that is pervasive in the Rio Declaration. The group rejects definitions of manhood linked to numbers of sexual partners, use of violence, or power held over others, for example, and advocates associating it with sustaining respectful relationships and taking a stance against violence.

The Rio Declaration[1] sees men as allies in the quest for gender equality. Men's participation can itself be an act of redefining masculinity, inasmuch as participation requires challenging gender-based violence (including one's own), demonstrates caring for others, mandates nondiscrimination and inclusion as a strategy and principle, and teaches listening and cooperation.

At a later symposium held in 2014, this group passed the Delhi Declaration and Call to Action.[2]

The Rio Declaration

PART 1: INTRODUCTION

We come from eighty countries. We are men and women, young and old, representing the world's cultural and linguistic diversity, working side by side with respect and with the shared goals of social and gender justice. We are active in community organizations, faith-based and educational institutions; we are representatives of governments, NGOs and the United Nations.

What unites us is our outrage at the injustices that continue to plague the lives of women and girls, and the self-destructive demands we put on boys and men. But even more so, what brings us together is a powerful sense of hope, expectation, and the potential of men's and boys' capacity to change, to care, to cherish, to love passionately, and to work for social and gender justice. We know and affirm that men are capable of caring for their partners, themselves and their children.

We are outraged by the pandemic of violence women face at the hands of men, by the relegation of women to second class status, and the continued domination by specific groups of men of our economies, of our politics, of our social and cultural institutions. We know that among women and men there are those who fare even worse because of social class, religion, language, physical differences, ancestry and sexual orientation. We also know that many men are victims of violence at the hands of other men.

As we acknowledge the harm done to too many women and girls at the hands of men, we also recognize the costs to boys and men from the ways our societies have defined men's power and raised boys to be men. Too many young men and boys are sacrificed in wars and conflicts for those men of political, economic, and religious power who demand conquest and domination at any cost. Many men cause terrible harm to themselves because they deny their own needs for physical and mental care or lack health and social services.

Too many men suffer because our male-dominated world is not only one of power men have over women, but of some groups of men over others. Too many men, like too many women, live in terrible poverty and degradation, and/or are forced to work in hazardous and inhumane conditions. Too many men carry deep scars of trying to live up to the impossible demands of manhood and find solace in risk-taking, violence, self-destruction or alcohol and drug use. Too many men are stigmatized and punished simply because they love, desire and have sex with other men.

In the face of these global realities, we affirm our commitment to end injustices for women and men, and boys and girls, and provide them with the means and opportunities to create a better world. We are here because we believe that men and women must work together in speaking out against discrimination and violence.

We also affirm that engaging men and boys to promote gender justice is possible and is already happening. NGOs, campaigns and increasingly governments are directly involving hundreds of thousands of men around the world. We hear men and boys joining women and girls in speaking out against violence, practicing safer sex, and supporting women's and girls' sexual and reproductive rights. We see men involved in caregiving and nurturing others, including those men who assume the daily challenges of looking after babies and children.

We also affirm that the work with men and boys stems from and honours the pioneering work and ongoing leadership of the women's movement. We stand in solidarity with the ongoing struggles for women's empowerment and rights. By working in collaboration with women's rights organizations, we aim to change individual men's attitudes and practices, and transform the imbalance of power between men and women in relationships, families, communities, institutions and nations. Furthermore, we acknowledge the importance of the women's movement for the possibilities offered to men to be more caring and just human beings.

For the past decade, the daily work of many of the 450 delegates to the First Global Symposium on Engaging Men and Boys in Achieving Gender Equality has been to engage boys and men to question violent and inequitable versions of manhood. This work does not promote a spirit of collective guilt nor collective blame. Instead we invite men and boys to embrace healthier and non-violent models of manhood and to take responsibility to work alongside girls and women to achieve gender justice.

We also appeal to parents, teachers, community leaders, coaches, the media and businesses, along with governments, NGOs, religious institutions, and the United Nations, to mobilize the political will and economic resources required to increase the scale and impact of work with men and boys to promote gender justice.

The Evidence Base Exists: New initiatives and programs to engage men and boys in gender justice provide a growing body of evidence that confirms it is possible to change men's gender-related attitudes and practices. Effective programs and processes have led men and boys to stand up against violence and for gender justice in both their personal lives and their communities. These initiatives not only help deconstruct harmful masculinities, but reconstruct more gender-equitable ones. Global research makes it increasingly clear that working with men and boys can reduce violence against women and girls and between men; improve relationships; strengthen the work of the women's rights movement; improve health outcomes of women and men, girls and boys; and that it is possible to accelerate this change through deliberate program and policy-level interventions.

Resources: Resources allocated to achieving gender justice must be increased. We believe that the evidence is clear that investing in integrated program and policy approaches that transform underlying gender inequalities—and engage women, girls, boys and men—is effective. We urge governments to allocate increased funding for mitigating the harm caused to women and men by gender injustice, and to allocate increased resources to actions that transform gender inequalities that lead to such harmful outcomes. We acknowledge that engaging men and boys in activities that have traditionally focused on women and girls requires additional resources, not taking away resources that are already limited.

International and UN Commitments [omitted]

PART 2: SPECIFIC THEMES AND AREAS OF ACTION

Furthermore, we call for action on the following dimensions of working with men and boys to achieve gender justice:

Violence against Women: Women and girls suffer from a pandemic of violence at the hands of some men: physical violence by husbands and male partners, sexual assault (including rape in the context of marriage), trafficking of women and girls, femicide, rape as a weapon of war, sexual harassment at work, and genital mutilation. For too long, all forms of violence (including physical, psychological and sexual violence) against women and girls have been seen primarily as a "women's issue" and have been invisible, regarded as a private matter and been the concern of the women's movement. Patriarchal structures sustain this impunity. Men's and boys' accountability and engagement for social transformation is essential to ensure violence-free lives for women and girls.

Violence against Children: Girls and boys suffer from large-scale abuse and violence (including corporal and other forms of humiliating and degrading punishment) in the home, community, school and institutions that are charged with protecting them. This violence often follows gendered patterns; in some contexts boys are more likely to suffer physical violence from parents while girls are more likely to suffer emotional and sexual violence. Witnessing and suffering violence as children is one of the factors that leads boys and men to repeat violence against intimate partners later in life. This implies the need for a life cycle approach to reducing violence and to engaging with boys, and girls, to break cycles of family violence.

Violence Among Men and Boys: Although violence against women is a priority in our agenda, we also must address different forms of violence among men and boys. These include armed conflict, gang violence, school bullying and homophobia-related violence. Men and boys face higher homicide rates than women and girls worldwide. These deaths—the vast majority gun-related—are highly preventable and are also directly linked to boys' socialization around risk-taking, fighting and the dominance of some groups of men and boys over others. Questioning cultures of violence and gun cultures requires engaging men and boys with an understanding of how salient versions of manhood are too often defined in relation to violence.

Violence in Armed Conflict: In countries that practice sex-specific conscription or demand longer military service from men than women, young men are treated as socially expendable and sent to their deaths in large numbers. Militaries that refuse to enforce international laws on the treatment of civilians in conflict explicitly condone and sometimes encourage the use of sexual violence as a method of warfare, explicitly privileging militarized models of masculinity and ensuring that those men who do refuse violence are belittled and subject to stigma including homophobic violence. Girls and boys are increasingly drawn into armed conflict, both as victims and perpetrators. We call on national governments, to uphold Security Council Resolutions including 1308, 1325, 1612 and 1820 and to proactively contribute to the elimination of all forms of gendered violence, including in times of armed conflict.

Gender and the Global Political Economy: Gender identities are strongly influenced by current trends in the global political economy. The values of competition, consumption, aggressive accumulation and assertion of power reinforce practices of domination and violence. The dominant economic models have led to increasing economic vulnerability as livelihood opportunities have been lost on a large scale. While women have entered the workforce outside the home in large numbers in the past 20 years, men are still primarily defined by being breadwinners and providers. Many men who are not able to live up to this social expectation to be providers experience stress and mental health issues, including substance and alcohol use. Economic stress is also associated with men's use of violence against women and children. We need a better understanding of these phenomena, and we need to advocate for the inclusion of these issues in international economic fora.

Men and Boys as Caregivers: Across the world gender norms reinforce the expectation that women and girls have to take responsibility for care work, including domestic tasks, raising children and taking care of the sick and the elderly. This frequently prevents women and girls from accessing their fundamental human rights to health, education, employment and full political participation. Correcting this requires that National Governments, civil society organisations, UN agencies and donor organisations put in place strategies that shift gender norms and encourage men to share the joys and burdens of caring for others with women, including in their capacity as fathers and providers of child care. It will also require significant investments in public sector services to reduce the total care burden, especially in the context of HIV and AIDS and other chronic diseases.

Sexual and Gender Diversities and Sexual Rights: There are tremendous diversities among men and boys in their sexual and gender identities and relations. Too many men are stigmatized for the fact that they love, desire and/or enjoy sex with men, and those that have non-normative gender identities. Formal and informal patterns of sexual injustice, discrimination, social exclusion and oppression throughout the world shape men's and boys' access to civil rights, health care, personal safety, and the recognition and affirmation of their intimate relations. Constructions of masculinity in many contexts are based on hostility toward sexual behaviours that contradict dominant patriarchal norms, and are policed through heterosexist violence. Programming and policy engaging men and boys must recognize and affirm sexual diversity among men and boys, and support the positive rights of men of all sexualities to sexual pleasure and well-being.

Men's and Boys' Gender Related Vulnerabilities and Health Needs: In most of the world, men and boys die earlier than women and girls from preventable diseases, accidents and violence. Most men have higher death rates from the same illnesses that affect women. We need to work with boys and young men to promote health-seeking and help-seeking behaviours for themselves and their families. Additionally, the emotional and personal experiences of men and boys have to be addressed to better understand the root problems of violence, suicide, substance use, accidents and limited health-seeking behaviour. Gender-responsive and socio-culturally sensitive mental health programs and services are needed to address and prevent these issues at the community level, working to achieve gender-appropriate health services and promotion for women, girls, men and boys.

Sexual Exploitation: Men's use of sexual violence results from social norms that condone the exploitation of women and girls, boys and men. The objectification and commoditisation of women and girls and boys and men normalizes violent and coercive sexual behaviours. Ending sexual violence and exploitation requires holistic strategies from the global to local level to engage men and boys in challenging attitudes that give men dominance, and treating all human beings with dignity and respect. We must also include in this discussion the use of the Internet in sexual exploitation and explore ways that men and boys can be engaged in questioning this new form of exploitation.

Sexual and Reproductive Health and Rights: Sexual and reproductive health and rights (SRHR) are largely considered a women's domain, leaving women and girls responsible for their own sexual health. Men often do not have access to sexual and reproductive health services, do not use such services and/or behave in ways that put themselves and their partners at risk. It is essential that we work with men and boys to fully support and promote the SRHR of women, girls, boys and other men, and that health services address issues of power and proactively promote gender justice. Such services should help men to identify and address their own sexual and reproductive health needs and rights. This requires us to advance sexual rights, including access to safe abortion, and to adopt [a] positive, human-rights based approach to sexuality.

HIV and AIDS: HIV and AIDS continue to devastate communities across the world. Gender inequalities and rigid gender roles exacerbate the spread and the impact of the epidemic, making it difficult for women and girls to negotiate sexual relations and leaving women and girls with the burden of caring for those with AIDS-related illnesses. Definitions of masculinity that equate manhood with dominance over sexual partners, the pursuit of multiple partners and a willingness to take risks while simultaneously depicting health-seeking behaviour as a sign of weakness, increase the likelihood that men will contract and pass on the virus. In line with commitments made at [the] UN General Assembly Special Sessions on HIV and AIDS and in many national AIDS plans, governments, UN agencies and civil society must take urgent action to implement evidence-based prevention, treatment, care and support strategies that address the gendered dimensions of HIV and AIDS, meet the needs of people living with HIV and AIDS, ensure access to treatment, challenge stigma and discrimination and support men to reduce their risk taking behaviours and improve their access to and use of HIV services.

Youth and the Education Sector: The young men and women who participated in the Symposium affirm that early and active involvement in programs that promote gender equitable behaviour at all levels will systematically create an environment where girls and boys are viewed as equals, will promote their awareness of their rights as human beings and instil the capacity to realize these rights in every aspect of their lives, from access to education to the prevention of early marriage, the right to dignified labour, the right to live in equitable relationships and the right to live lives free from violence. Gender justice issues must be included in the school curricula from the earliest ages with a focus on promoting a critical reflection about gender norms.

Recognition of Diversity: We stress that debate, action and policies on gender relations and gender inequities will be more effective and have more impact when they include an understanding and celebration of differences based on race, ethnicity, age, sexual and gender diversities, religion, physical ability and class.

Environment: One foundation of male-dominated societies has been the attempt by some men to dominate nature. With catastrophic climate change and environmental degradation, these actions have had disastrous outcomes. Our goal goes beyond gender justice to say that a world made in the image of violent, careless men is self-destructive. All levels of our societies must urgently act to stop this most dramatic expression of unjust social and economic power.

Strengthening the Evidence Base: It is vital to continue to build the evidence base for gender transformative programs through research and program evaluation, to determine which strategies are most successful in different cultural contexts. Indicators of success should include a specific examination of whether gender norms and behaviours have changed. Furthermore, program and policy evaluation should examine the effects of gender-focused programs and policies on both men and women.

PART 3: THE CALL TO ACTION

1. Individuals should take forward this call to action within their communities and be agents of change to promote gender justice. Individuals and groups need to hold and keep their governments and leaders accountable.
2. Community based organizations should continue their groundbreaking work to challenge the status quo of gender and other inequalities and actively model social change.
3. Non-governmental organizations, including faith-based organizations, should develop and build on programs, interventions and services that are based on the needs, rights and aspirations of their communities, are accountable and reflect the principles in this document. They should develop synergies with other relevant social movements, and establish mechanisms for monitoring and reporting on government commitments.
4. International non-governmental organizations working in the field of gender based violence, gender equity or issues of violence against boys and girls should engage boys and men together with women and girls; should support involved national organizations through facilitating networks, providing capacity building, technical support and should collaborate with governments to develop policies and strategies that promote gender equity and non-violent behaviours for proper implementation and follow-up of international and UN commitments.
5. Governments should act on their existing international and UN obligations and commitments, prioritize and allocate resources to gender transformative interventions, and develop policies, frameworks and concrete implementation plans that advance this agenda, including through working with other governments and adherence to the Paris Principles.

6. The private sector should promote workplaces that are gender-equitable and free from violence and exploitation, and direct corporate social responsibility towards inclusive social change.

7. The role of media and entertainment industries in maintaining and reinforcing traditional and inequitable gender norms has to be addressed and confronted and alternatives must be supported.

8. Bilateral donors should redirect their resources towards the promotion of inclusive programming for gender justice and inclusive social justice, including changes to laws and policies, and develop synergies amongst donors.

9. The United Nations must show leadership in these areas, innovatively and proactively supporting member states to promote gender equitable and socially transformative law, policy and program development, including through interagency coordination as articulated in the One UN approach.

10. We, gathered at the Symposium, pledge to answer the call of the Secretary-General's Campaign UNite to End Violence against Women 2008–2015, to galvanize our energies, networks and partnerships in support of world mobilization of men and boys, and their communities, to stop and prevent this pandemic.

We call on governments, the UN, NGOs, individuals and the private sector to devote increased commitment and resources to engaging men and boys in questioning and overcoming inequitable and violent versions of masculinities and to recognize the positive role of men and boys—and their own personal stake—in overcoming gender injustices.

Notes

1 MenEngage, "Rio Declaration," 2009. MenEngage website, www.menengage.org.

2 MenEngage, "Delhi Declaration and Call to Action," 2014. MenEngage website, www.men engage.org.

112

Manifesto
First Continental Summit of Indigenous Women
Puno, Peru
May 27–28, 2009

Emblem of the Continental Summit of Indigenous Peoples.

We, indigenous women, have had a direct input into the historical process of transformation of our peoples through our proposals and actions in the various struggles taking place and engendered from the indigenous movements.

At the Third Continental Summit of Indigenous Peoples held in Guatemala in 2007, women decided to hold their own gathering preceding the fourth summit in Peru. Over two thousand Indigenous women came together in Puno, Peru, on May 27, 2009. They began with a march, held opening ceremonies, and sponsored three panels, on Cosmology and Identity: Model of Development; Rights of Women: Violence and Racism; and Women in the Construction of Power and Democracy. The panels were followed by sixteen workshops, and then sessions for drafting proposals for the final plenary session, a four-hour meeting at which the document below was discussed. Regarding the general summit following the women's gathering, one reporter noted, "Some observers were concerned that women's issues were not among those listed as topics of discussion at the Indigenous summit. Launching the activities with the women's meeting, however, effectively influenced subsequent discussions in the main summit. Women had a much more visible and active presence in presentations and discussions than in previous events. That is not to say that complete gender equality was achieved, but it was an important step in the right direction."[1]

The Manifesto[2] begins with a reminder of Indigenous women's past and current contributions to the well-being of their peoples and the planet. The status quo for the Indigenous in the Americas is generally one of impoverishment and exploitation due to greed and neoliberalism. With "rebellious hearts," the authors look back to "our ways of mutual respect and a life of harmony with the planet" as they seek "alternatives to eliminate injustice, discrimination, machismo and violence against women." The document makes a commitment to greater economic, political, cultural, and social networking and coalition building, and insists that Indigenous policies affirm the rights of women. It addresses violence within their communities and toward the Indigenous, including repression of social activism. It supports food sovereignty, and demands respect for native cultures and lands.

Manifesto

We, indigenous women gathered in the sacred lands of Lake Titicaca, after two days of discussions and deliberation raise our voices in these times when Abya Yala's[1] womb is once more with childbirth pains, to give birth to the new Pachakutik[2] for a better life on our planet. We, indigenous women, have had a direct input into the historical process of transformation of our peoples through our proposals and actions in the various struggles taking place and engendered from the indigenous movements.

We are the carriers, conduits of our cultural and genetic make-up; we gestate and brood life; together with men, we are the axis of the family unit and society. We join our wombs to our mother earth's womb to give birth to new times in this Latin American continent where in many countries millions of people, impoverished by the neoliberal system, raise their voices to say ENOUGH to oppression, exploitation and the looting of our wealth. We therefore join in the liberation struggles taking place throughout our continent.

We gather here at this summit, with our hearts, minds, hands and wombs, for the purpose of seeking alternatives to eliminate injustice, discrimination, machismo and violence against women, and to return to our ways of mutual respect and a life of harmony with the planet. Whereas women are part of nature and the macrocosm, we are called to defend and take care of our mother earth, because from her comes our ancient history and culture, that make us what we are: indigenous peoples under the protection and spiritual guidance of our parents and grandparents who gave life to all the human beings that now inhabit this wonderful planet, even though a few oligarchs and imperialists seek to plague it with death in their quest for their god called greed. Therefore, before the memory of our martyrs, heroes, leaders, we present to our extended families (Ayllus)[3], communities, peoples and nations of the world the conclusions of our rebellious hearts.

Resolutions and agreements:
- Build a continental agenda that reflects the defence of collective rights and the human rights of indigenous women and which follows up the mandates of the First Continental Summit of Indigenous Women.
- Form the Continental Coordinator of Abya Yala Indigenous Women to defend our mother earth; strengthen our organisations; promote policy and training proposals; and create spaces for sharing experiences in various fields: economic, political, social, and cultural amongst others. Furthermore, this will be the representative and referential body for Abya Yala women before national and international entities.
- We urge on international entities the reform of international instruments, related to indigenous peoples, so as to incorporate the rights of women and submit alternative reports on progress and compliance.
- We are in solidarity with and support the struggles of peoples of Amazonian Peru and demand the government of Peru immediately repeal all laws and decrees which violate the territorial rights of indigenous peoples in the Amazon. At the same time, we demand the government of Peru repeal the state of emergency in the departments where it has been decreed.
- We express full solidarity and support for the government of President Evo Morales.
- We support the Minga[4] resistance undertaken by the indigenous peoples of Colombia and condemn acts of genocide and extermination against the indigenous movement in Colombia and other countries.
- We strongly reject the persecution of social protest and government repression of demonstrations and actions in defence of land rights and the life of indigenous peoples.
- We demand from national governments a real and wholistic [sic] agrarian reform that safeguards land to preserve food sovereignty.
- We demand that governments create institutions and policies for the care and protection of migrants, taking into account their cultural diversity.
- We demand that the state declares our lands and territories inviolable, inalienable and unable to be expropriated, requiring respective titles.
- We support the founding of the Climate Justice Court so as to demand developed countries and transnationals repair and not damage the biodiversity of the Pachamama[5].

- We reject biofuels because they impoverish the land and place at risk food sovereignty and the life of natural ecosystems.
- We demand decriminalisation of the cultivation of the sacred coca leaf.
- We demand an end to genocide and ethnocide, which especially affects our indigenous peoples, carried out by the army, paramilitaries and others, which injure, intimidate and violate the rights of people in every country. We, the women of the First Continental Summit of Indigenous Women, do not want to see more widows, more orphans. We struggle for peace, for life and for world dignity.
- We struggle to end violence committed by: the army, multinationals, transnationals and some NGOs; that engender division in our communities, particularly among women. This brings about all kinds of violence: physical, psychological, sexual, political, financial, institutional, and symbolic among others.
- We struggle for the freedom of men and women who are imprisoned in army and public jails for their fight in defence of Mother Earth and territories, and in defence of the collective rights of indigenous peoples—as it is the case of Leonard Peltier who has been condemned to life in prison in the US.
- We demand the immediate withdrawal of the foreign multinational companies in our territories which are exploiting our mother earth and damaging the environment.
- We, the women of Abya Yala, demand that the government of Alan Garcia stops granting political asylum to individuals who have violated human rights, as in the case of the ex-ministers of Bolivia's Gonzalo Sanchez de Losada.
- The First Continental Summit of Indigenous Women has decided that the Second Continental Summit will take place in Bolivia together with the Fifth Continental Summit of Indigenous Peoples and Nations.
- To follow up the implementation of the UN declaration of the rights of the indigenous peoples, in various countries, in particular on themes related to indigenous women.
- To promote a continental mobilisation in defence of Mother Earth, to be held on October 12.

"I have walked everywhere, but never negotiated with the blood of my people." —Tránsito Amaguaña

Notes:
1. "Abya Yala" means "Continent of Life" in the language of the Kuna peoples of Panama and Colombia (http://abyayala.nativeweb.org).
2. Pachakutik is a Quechua word which signifies change, rebirth, transformation, and the coming of a new era.
3. Ayllu is a word in both the Quechua and Aymara languages referring to a network of families in a given area.
4. "La Minga" means a gathering of all the peoples, and indigenous leadership only call for it when something very important needs to be addressed (http://dallaspeacecenter.org/node/3881).
5. Pachamama means Mother Earth, a goddess revered by indigenous peoples of the Andes.

Notes

1 The report on this meeting can be found at Marc Becker, "Moving Forward: The Fourth Continental Summit of Indigenous Peoples," June 9, 2009. Upside Down World: Covering Activism and Politics in Latin America, www.upsidedownworld.org.

2 "Manifesto of the First Continental Summit of Indigenous Women," *Llapa Runaq Hatariynin*, 34–Inti Raymi 2009. Translation by Marlene Obeid and Tim Anderson, Sydney, June 15, 2009, qtd. in *Links: International Journal of Socialist Renewal*, www.links.org.au. 2009.

113

"Juba Declaration"
Conference for Southern Sudan Women in Political Parties to Develop a Common Agenda for the Elections
Juba, South Sudan
July 17–19, 2009

A banner announcing the Conference for Southern Sudan Women in Political Parties.

As we have seen, elections are one of those "moments" that open the door for rethinking women's participation. At the time of this conference, both the 2010 general elections and the 2011 self-determination referendum were approaching. They posed particular challenges for women, as voters and representatives, for women were new voters (during the last election in 1983 women were neither voters nor candidates), the reservation of 25 percent of seats for women was also new (a result of the 2005 Comprehensive Peace Agreement), and Southern Sudan was a new, struggling, postconflict democracy. Yet in the Declaration[1] women remind readers that they "are renowned for their active participation in the pursuit of peace and good governance." About fifty Southern Sudanese women attended the conference to discuss how to remove obstacles, enable effective political participation, and support "transformational leadership."

The conference and the document it produced are themselves parts of the political education of women. But the manifesto shows some of what it takes to maximize women's participation, since the barriers are cultural, social, economic, and educational. Elaborating on the obstacles, Kwaje Lasuba included

- Stereotypical traditions that prevent the girl child from going to school, which has resulted in high illiteracy among women compared to men.
- Early marriages involving girls between 10–14 years deny them the chance to complete schooling and acquire skills necessary for developing careers.
- Comparing women who are in politics to prostitutes discourages many women from getting involved or participating in politics and developing their full potential.
- Discrimination against women prevents them from participating on equal terms with men not only in politics but also in social-economic development.[2]

The issues touched upon in the Declaration range from women having an influence on party agendas to being educated on campaigning (fundraising, public speaking, media relations). Those with the power to effect change, as named in the Declaration, include political parties, the media, women voters and candidates, the government, the National Electoral Commission, police, village leaders, election observers, political donors, and civil society organizations. It takes a community to build political participation.

The Carter Center observed and analyzed the electoral process, and made recommendations on how to continue improving it.[3] South Sudan did vote for independence.

The Juba Declaration

We, the women from the political parties in Southern Sudan, participating in the Conference for Southern Sudan Women in Political Parties to Develop a Women's Common Agenda for the Elections, which took place in Juba from July 17 to 19, 2009, comprising representatives of the Government, Political Parties and Parliamentarians:

Strongly believe in women working together across party lines;

Affirm that unity of purpose is the foundation of equity and equality;

Also affirm that the women of Southern Sudan are renowned for their active participation in the pursuit of peace and good governance;

Further affirm that gender issues cannot be divorced from the political, social, cultural, developmental, economic and security considerations in Southern Sudan.

Note that women in Southern Sudan have limited access to political party leadership and decision-making, the media, education, economic empowerment, law, security, [and] health, which has compromised women's effective participation in national leadership,

Concerned about the rights and dignity of women, insecurity and the rule of law in Southern Sudan, and the environment in which the General Election will be held,

State that it is in this context that women now seek greater representation and participation in party politics and national leadership,

Affirm our support for all the outcomes of this conference with a view to strengthening democracy through women's greater participation at all levels of leadership as stated in the 25 percent principle,

Appreciate the role played by the Government of Southern Sudan and the international community in supporting efforts to boost the role of women in politics and transformational leadership and drawing attention to the need to involve women in all stages of the election process and in the implementation of the National Elections Act 2008,

NOW WISH to call upon the National Electoral Commission, Political Parties Affairs Council, Political Parties in Southern Sudan and the media to address the following recommendations:

1.0 EFFECTIVE PARTICIPATION OF WOMEN IN POLITICAL PARTIES

1. Raise women's image and visibility within their parties by:
   - Increasing the number of women in political parties through intensive women recruitment campaigns;

- Developing their political knowledge and leadership skills;
- Provision of financial support to women's leagues and groups

2. Build the capacity of all party membership to understand and appreciate gender issues;

3. Prepare and conduct democratic and transparent candidate selection processes through:
- including women in the selection teams and allowing the women leagues to monitor the candidate selection processes;
- widely disseminating candidate selection rules;
- instituting a mechanism whereby at least 10% of the candidates on the party list are women and nomination of candidates for geographical constituency seats;
- committing and promoting fair competition during internal elections;
- establishing an independent monitoring system for internal elections;

4. Party should [provide] support to women candidates through:
- Provision of material and financial support;
  ◊ Visibly support women candidates
  ◊ Set up a women election basket

2.0 DEVELOPMENT OF GENDER-SENSITIVE MANIFESTOS

Political parties should ensure that the following gender specific issues are addressed in their manifestos:

1. Zero-tolerance for corruption
2. Universal primary health care with emphasis on reproductive health
3. Continuous HIV/AIDS awareness campaigns coupled with accessible VCT (Voluntary Counseling and Testing) Centers for the youth and married couples throughout Southern Sudan
4. Mass adult literacy campaign up to the community level
5. Free education for girls and construction of at least one girls' only secondary boarding school in each state in Southern Sudan;
6. Clean and safe water at community level;
7. Micro enterprises and a micro enterprise fund for economic empowerment of women at the grassroots/community level;
8. A policy to address gender based violence by:
- Institutionalizing special protection units at the police stations;
- Providing support and medical care to survivors;
- Giving rehabilitation and/or stiff penalty to perpetrators
9. Establish equal opportunities body to monitor:
- Implementation of the Bill of rights in the Interim Constitution of Southern Sudan;
- Ratification of the international conventions that protect the rights of women;
- Implementation of gender and related policies
- Implementation of the land policy
10. Establish schools for children with disabilities at county level
11. Establish mental health centers for treatment and rehabilitation
12. Inclusive and transparent government

3.0 GENDER SENSITIVE MEDIA

1. Work with women leagues and candidates to promote their visibility through:
   - Provision of media space in electronic and print media;
   - Organizing media listening groups
   - Including gender sensitive training skills in the media training curricula
2. Support dissemination of gender sensitive messages and materials through:
   - Creating awareness and appreciation among voters on the importance and benefits of women candidates;
3. Give media space to women candidates during election campaigns to gain visibility among voters;
4. Institute a monitoring mechanism to ensure that all candidates and political parties have equal access to media;
5. Media should be neutral, not biased towards any party or any candidate.

4.0 PREVENTION OF ELECTION VIOLENCE

1. Political party leaders should commit to any code of conduct that is developed to prevent election related violence
2. Political Parties Affairs Council (PPAC) should be in position to withdraw registration of any party [involved] in election violence
3. Political parties should include discussion on prevention of campaign and election related violence in their South–South dialogues
4. All political parties should issue statements on how they are to conduct transparent campaigns
5. Media should refrain from fueling violence through:
   - not disseminating hate speech and inflammatory remarks
   - not engaging in sensational reporting of contentious issues
6. All political party leaders should encourage party members not to engage in violent activities
7. Women candidates should be united and present themselves to have peaceful elections and should come out with a statement on violence-free elections
8. Women should commit themselves to respecting and abiding by election guidelines and the electoral law
9. Women commit themselves to influencing their respective parties to commit themselves to a violence-free election
10. Media should sensitize the public on free and fair elections and how to prevent and report election violence
11. Media should also play a monitoring role to bring to attention of concerned authorities about potential for violence and malpractices
12. NEC [National Electoral Commission] should raise awareness of the public to prevent corruption, illegal practices and election offences
13. NEC should create awareness among all political party leaders on their obligations under the electoral law and the penalty for non adherence
14. NEC should conduct its affairs in an impartial, transparent and neutral manner
15. Government must take the responsibility of providing security during elections, especially for women candidates, and a special police unit should be trained to deal with election violence.

5.0 GENDER-SENSITIVE ELECTIONS GUIDELINES

1. NEC should provide an easy mechanism for identifying voters in rural areas for registration by involving Chiefs or the village chairpersons.

2. Voter registration centers should be within easy reach and easily identifiable areas.

3. NEC should make it clear that although women have 25% seats, they are also eligible to be nominated for other positions such as President, Governor, party list, and the constituency seats.

4. NEC should set-up a gender responsive voter education and disseminate information concerning elections.

5. NEC should issue strong guidelines against violence in all election processes

6. NEC should invite foreign and local observers during the registration, campaign, voting and counting of votes and announcing of results processes

7. In case government funding, NEC should ensure equal financial support for both male and female at all the levels.

8. PPAC should reject any party list or constituency candidate lists which do not include women

9. NEC should commit to provide financial support for women candidates competing for constituency seats

6.0 CAPACITY BUILDING FOR FEMALE CANDIDATES

Capacity building for women candidates is imperative to their participation and success. The following areas have been identified as critical action areas for women, donors, government and civil society organizations:

1. Training areas:
   - Elections Act provisions and electoral procedures
   - confidence building
   - public speaking
   - communication skills and public relations
   - local administration structure and native administration
   - proposal writing
   - fund raising for women candidates
   - campaign and message development skills
   - political skills
   - networking skills

2. Institute a fund to train women candidates

3. Women should work at increasing their visibility within their political parties and among voters

4. Women should sensitize other women and encourage women at the lower levels to join political parties

5. Women should develop networking skills so as to appreciate the benefits of networking with women groups and civil society organizations within the community

6. Formation of a "Women in Political Parties forum" as a learning platform for political, voter and civic education

7. Develop a relationship with the media by understanding how it works and being pro-active by taking advantage of media houses

8. Establish networks and regular dialogue with association of media women in Sudan

9. Learn the workings and take advantage of media outlets and utilize alternative media such as email, SMS, radio listening groups for women, etc

10. Develop a communication strategy to address election related issues using the media

Notes

1   "Juba Declaration by South Sudan Women." GEM South Sudan Women's Agenda, http://www.awcfs.org. Accessed October 2017. Minor grammatical corrections by editor.
2   Cited in Ruth Omukhango, "Opportunities and Challenges on the Ground." *South Sudan Women's Agenda*, no. 1 (August 2009). African Women and Children Feature Service website, www.awcfs.org.
3   Carter Center, "Observing Sudan's 2010 National Elections, April 11–18, 2010, Final Report." Carter Center website, www.cartercenter.org.

114

Pro-Porn Principles
Our Porn, Ourselves
Online Community

2010

Our Porn, Ourselves: For women who are pro-porn and all those who support us. WE are the answer to anti-porn feminists. All genders welcome. The name is a tribute to the legendary feminist book that helped women take back control of their sexual health and sexual pleasure, *Our Bodies, Our Selves.*[1]

Our Porn, Ourselves is an online resource that wants to stimulate constructive conversation on the use of pornography by women and to "balance" what it calls "the anti-porn feminist agenda."[2] A great deal of difference of opinion exists among feminists about the nature of pornography, its consequences, feminism's role in the sex-positive movement, and whether such a thing as feminist porn exists. This recent debate follows "the sex wars" of the 1970s.

The group began when "Violet Blue found out about [an] upcoming anti-porn feminist conference being held in Boston . . . and decided she'd had enough. So did a lot of other women, and men, and people of all genders and orientations who are pro-porn and support a woman's right to choose, explore and enjoy porn."

The feminist aspects of the Pro-Porn Principles include the demand for an autonomous "self-defined, healthy" sexuality, a critique of paternalism, and agreement with the goal of empowerment. The authors place themselves in the feminist tradition, too, of the famous *Our Bodies, Ourselves*, the women's health movement, and even manifesto writing. They put weight on the fact that some women experience porn positively, they contest its inherent harmfulness, they encourage us to reserve judging others, especially regarding what is sexually "normal," and they want women to have a greater voice in creating pornography. Anti-porn feminists, in contrast, argue that the porn industry commodifies sex (and women), that the content is overwhelmingly misogynist, and that porn plays a role in violence against women.

Pro-Porn Principles

We women are tired of people trying to control our sexuality by telling us what we should or shouldn't like sexually (porn) based on what someone else thinks is best for us. It's like keeping women in a perpetual state of being children about sex. And women who say they are feminists make it worse by discounting all the women who find porn to be an empowering sex toy. Or if not, to at least give us the benefit of the doubt that we can make that decision for ourselves, thank you very much.

In the proud tradition of feminists everywhere, the Our Porn, Ourselves group has already come up with a manifesto:

WE who declare that organizations such as Feminists Against Pornography do not speak for us.

WE who want the world to know that organizations such as Feminists Against Pornography do not represent feminists as a group.

WE who believe that every woman has the right and power to enjoy her sexuality as she decides.

WE who believe that to tell a woman how she may or may not enjoy her sexuality in any way is to deny that woman of her rights over her sexuality.

WE who state that any woman who attempts to control the way another woman enjoys, explores or expresses her sexuality is in fact creating a world that is harmful for all women.

WE who state that we are women, and we like pornography.

WE who state that as women, we are not harmed or threatened by the creation or viewing of pornography, and we wholly support the rights of any gender to view, create and enjoy pornography without judgment.

WE who want a world in which pornography is simply a sex toy enjoyed by all genders and sexual orientations, where women and men view porn within their own self-defined healthy sexuality, without being considered sick, twisted, wrong or mentally ill, and that men who enjoy pornography are no more likely to beat their wives, rape women or become paedophiles than anyone else in society.

WE hereby declare ourselves as adult women capable of making our own choices about our bodies and enjoyment of explicit visual stimulation for our sexual health and well-being.

WE hereby demand that our voices be heard.

Notes

1 Our Porn, Ourselves, "Origins." Our Porn, Ourselves website, accessed 2016, www.ourpornourselves.org.
2 Our Porn, Ourselves website, accessed 2016, www.ourpornourselves.org.

115

Declaration of Romani Women Networks
Second International Conference of Roma Women
Athens, Greece
January 11–12, 2010

The logo of the Romani Women Network Italy, one of the groups participating in the conference.

Prior to this gathering in Athens, numerous conferences on Romani women took place, including in Strasbourg in 1995, Bucharest in 2006, and Stockholm in 2007. This conference, attended by about 150 participants and observers from thirty Council of Europe member states and international organizations, was organized by the Council of Europe; the Greek Ministry of Interior, Decentralisation and E-Government; the Greek Inter-Municipal Roma Network; and the International Roma Women's Network. The conference theme was "I Am a European Roma Woman." The International Roma Women's Network was founded on World Roma Day (April 8) 2003. It includes Roma, Sinti, Gypsies, and Travellers, and is the first group to bring Roma women's groups from Eastern and Western Europe together. The Declaration below was adopted at the conference.

Behind these conferences, as the document states, is "the increased and alarming human rights violations occurring against Romani women," including "trafficking, racially-motivated violence, hate crimes and coercive sterilisation." But also motivating them is the determination to take "joint action to achiev[e] the full enjoyment of Romani women's human rights." Like so many groups speaking in this collection, Romani women confront multiple forms of discrimination, based on their ethnicity and their gender, and violence against them often occurs with impunity.

The situation has not yet improved. According to the European Roma Rights Centre, the Roma are overrepresented among trafficked persons in Bulgaria, the Czech Republic, Hungary, Romania, and Slovakia; Romani children are overrepresented among youth in state care; anti-Romani rhetoric by extremist political parties and politicians has increased; the discriminatory practice of repatriating the Roma continues, as does forced eviction and segregated housing; and educational segregation of Romani children is the norm in several European countries.[1] Alexandra Opia adds that Romani women's unemployment rate is higher than that of men, and Romani women face barriers in reporting domestic violence due to fear of police brutality against the Roma and fear of reinforcing stereotypes of Roma men as violent. And in a familiar story, she says, "The limited feminist and

Poster advertising one of the issues discussed at the conference.

antiracist politics in Europe systematically ignore Romani women. Romani non-governmental organisations (NGOs), at the forefront of the antiracist struggle in Europe, address racism but fail to address the role of patriarchy . . . in the oppression of Romani women. Feminist organisations in Europe, in turn, focus on gender subordination but neglect racism, a crucial barrier for Romani women."[2]

The document below[3] shows that states play a central role in the violation of Romani women's human rights. NGOs, local officials, and the media are also criticized. Change cannot come quickly when poor educational options plague all the children, and especially the girls, who are often pulled out of school to help at home or be married off when young. The gathering suggests many remedies, including recognition of and compensation for forced sterilizations, and putting the problems faced by Roma women on national agendas. Many groups are working to challenge centuries-old stereotypes that still haunt the Roma, and to replace them with more complete pictures of Roma histories and cultures that can be a source of pride and self-esteem. Roma women are creating the organizations and networks and developing the skills necessary to advocate successfully for changed social conditions.

Declaration of Romani Women Networks

Following the international conferences on Romani women in Bucharest 2006 and Stockholm 2007, Romani women and their supporters gathered in Athens at the "I am a European Roma Woman" Conference on 11–12 January 2010 to take stock of the increased and alarming human rights violations occurring against Romani women and to agree on taking joint action to achieving the full enjoyment of Romani women's human rights.

Romani women in Europe face multiple discrimination, based on their ethnicity and their gender. This negatively impacts all areas of their daily life, including housing, healthcare, employment, education, political or civic participation and family relationships. Furthermore, they have often been victims of atrocious human rights violations: trafficking, racially-motivated violence, hate crimes and coercive sterilisation.

While the situation of Romani women has been brought to the attention of international organisations, this has not initiated a functional political process able to effect a concrete, measurable improvement on the lives of Romani women.

To the contrary, the occurrences of discrimination, violence and abuse often go unpunished and the motivations behind them remain unchallenged. This climate of impunity often has a lasting and a dehumanizing impact on the Romani women who are victims.

After reviewing the human rights situation of Romani women, participants in this conference underline the following findings:

- The continuous failure of states to afford human dignity to Romani women and acknowledge them as full citizens. Serious concerns remain about the climate of impunity and states' failure to bring justice and provide remedies to Romani women victims.
- The failure of the governments of the Czech Republic, Slovakia and Hungary to adequately acknowledge and compensate the victims of coercive sterilisation.
- The ongoing school segregation and systematic placement of Romani children in schools for the mentally disabled throughout Europe.
- The high rate of school drop outs among Romani girls and boys during compulsory [education], compounded by the failure of the Ministries of Education to adequately address this and to promote a diverse school environment.
- The failure of state and non-state actors to seriously discuss and address the practice of early marriages in the context of patriarchal dominance and poverty, with a view towards prioritizing the rights of Romani children.
- The lack of action and involvement of local authorities and local actors to address problems and concerns of Romani women.
- The . . . negative and stereotypical portrayal of Romani women by the media and the failure to objectively present situations involving Romani women and Romani communities. Their approach often heightens ethnic division and further stigmatizes Roma communities.
- The lack of specific policies and programmes aimed at improving the situation of Romani women.
- The lack of data disaggregated by ethnicity, gender and other grounds across Europe, which allows the plight of Romani women to remain hidden.

In light of these findings, the participants propose the following recommendations:

- Governments should uphold their obligations under international and European treaties and ensure that Romani women can enjoy and exercise their fundamental rights. Governments must take unequivocal measures with respect to rights violations of Romani women, by convicting and punishing perpetrators and compensating victims.
- While limited compensation and recognition has been awarded in Hungary and the Czech Republic to victims of coercive sterilisation, Hungary, the Czech Republic and Slovakia must acknowledge the past and ongoing occurrences of coercive sterilisation and take active measures to compensate the victims, sanction perpetrators and initiate medical reform in the area of patients' rights.
- The government of the Czech Republic is obliged to take active measures to end segregation and placement of Romani children in special schooling, in accordance with the 2007 ECHR decision, D.H. and Others vs. the Czech Republic.

- All European countries should take measures to prevent all forms of segregation in housing and education, while promoting the principles of equality and integration.
- School personnel and Ministries of Education should facilitate the completion of mandatory education for Romani children, take active measures to encourage their participation in higher education and combat discrimination in education. Governments should develop a specific approach to the education of Romani girls with the participation of the Roma community, based on national examples such as the Romanian model of Roma teaching assistants and school mediators.
- Roma activists should work with Romani communities to raise awareness of their children's rights and their parental responsibilities.
- Local authorities should engage in developing local action plans and allocate budgets to address issues concerning Romani women and girls.
- Roma activists and human rights organisations should actively engage with Roma communities to raise awareness about their human rights and facilitate access to public services and law enforcement mechanisms.
- International organisations should support Roma journalism in order to facilitate a learning process with mainstream journalists about the situation of Romani women and to promote objective journalism.
- Governments should organise hearings in the national parliament about the situation of Romani women. This would help to prioritise issues facing Roma women on the national agendae, raise awareness about the reality of their situation and change the tone of the national debate about Romani women among politicians, the general public and representatives of the media.
- Governments should take steps to monitor and evaluate the situation of Romani women at the national level through the development and use of methodologies for data collection, disaggregated by ethnicity, gender and other grounds, as a basis for targeted and comprehensive measures which impact all areas of life.
- Governments should encourage economic empowerment through supporting small scale business programmes for Romani women.

Romani women activists and networks participating in this conference stand ready to support and advise international organisations, national governments and local authorities in the development and implementation of these recommendations, or other efforts to improve the situation of Romani women in Europe. Participants look forward to efforts to improve the situation of Romani women and facilitate further dialogue on the situation of Romani women, particularly welcoming the follow up conferences proposed by the governments of Finland and Spain.

Notes

1 European Roma Rights Centre, "Factsheet: Roma Rights in Jeopardy," Feb. 16, 2012. European Roma Rights Centre website, www.errc.org.

2 Alexandra Oprea, "The Erasure of Romani Women in Statistical Data: Limits of the Race-versus-Gender Approach," 2009. Open Society Institute report, www.opensocietyfoundations.org.

3 Romani Women Networks, "Declaration," Jan. 11–12, 2010. Council of Europe website, www.coe.int.

116

We, the Women of the World, Declaration to Stop Sex Trafficking
Ways Women Lead Collaborative and Human Rights–Step by Step Association
Varna, Bulgaria
March 28, 2010

Imagine women and girls everywhere, stepping forward to make positive changes in their families, communities, organizations and governments. Imagine women and girls exchanging their diverse perspectives and wisdom to bring new systemic solutions to old intractable problems. Imagine the collective power when women and girls gather and work together to initiate community projects, grow partnerships, and catalyze collaboration. Imagine this feminine influence moving toward a true unity of nations.[1]

Ways Women Lead is a group led more by ideas of feminine power and spiritual activism than are other organizations we have encountered. As they explain,

> The road to discovery and illumination is both an inner and outer journey. It begins within ourselves, continues in conversations with other women and girls, reaches out with the arts and with the technology of our times, and grows into the kinds of leadership that will co-create a just, prosperous, and sustainable world. Using this model of introspection and empowerment, we become the change we want to see happen.
>
> The dream of Ways Women Lead is: to engage and connect as many women and girls as possible on this journey of self-discovery and empowerment for self and others; to implement this vision so simply and inexpensively that everyone has the opportunity to become a good leader, locally and globally.[2]

Women of the World speaks from "a global sisterhood of empathy" for the dignity, safety, and freedom of women and children, regularly violated through practices such as sex trafficking. Like some of our earliest documents, this Declaration[3] asks us to reconceive the trafficking of women—to see it not as a private matter or one of custom or religious ritual, but as a crime to which all public institutions should respond. Practical aspects range from prevention to reintegration of the formerly trafficked, and include addressing the social support of trafficking found in business practices, ideologies, economic policies, and educational institutions.

We, the Women of the World, Declaration to Stop Sex Trafficking

We, the Women of the World,
   Representing the great diversity of humankind, united in a global sisterhood of empathy,
   Stand together for the dignity, respect and equality of each woman, girl child, and boy child in the world.
   We, mothers, grandmothers, daughters, sisters, wives, and girlfriends, with fathers, grandfathers, sons, brothers, husbands, and boyfriends; from different

countries, religions and beliefs declare our commitment to work together to bring safety and freedom to every woman and child.

Violence against women and their children is a gross breach of human rights. It prevents women and the children they raise from exercising their basic freedoms. Sex trafficking and slavery, still widely spread, are the most repulsive forms of violence, threatening women and children's inherent integrity of being.

Sex trafficking of women and children is not a private or family or religious matter, but rather a crime and its prevention and judgment is the responsibility of all public institutions.

Therefore, as givers of human life, as daughters of the earth, we stand firm as:

We invite the support of people worldwide; our families, friends, colleagues, our religious, institutional and government leaders, for the common goal of women and their organizations; to eliminate sex trafficking of women and children and all forms of enslavement, and to promote the dignity of womankind throughout the world.

We require that all UN member states sign and ratify all relevant conventions and documents which will increase public awareness of this issue.

We require that all governments and local authorities develop adequate mechanisms and policies to prevent sex trafficking of women and children, and implement measures to protect and support victims of these crimes and their successful reintegration into society.

We require new economic and educational measures so that families will stop selling and trading their daughters and sisters. The damage done by these deeds to all concerned and to society is immeasurable. Life is sacred, and its trafficking can never be justified either as tradition, custom, morality or as religious ritual.

We require that the basic societal influences that support systems of trafficking be addressed: the business of gaining profit from exploitation, the attitudes that are expressed when relationships are established by force, extreme poverty, and the erosion of human rights. All the efforts of society must be directed towards diminishing the influences of these factors over people's lives.

We commit to working together to do whatever is needed to prevent sex trafficking and all forms of enslavement, to change the attitudes which promote these behaviors, and to build new systems of health and well-being for the women and children of the world.

We further commit to our common values: to the value of each woman, each girl and boy child, each human being, that each of us may live safely, freely, creatively, with equal opportunity, and with equal responsibility to our whole human family.

Notes

1 Ways Women Lead website, accessed 2015, sites.google.com/a/wayswomenlead.net/www.

2 "About Ways Women Lead," Ways Women Lead LightPages, accessed 2015, www.lightpages .net.

3 Ways Women Lead Collaborative, "We, the Women of the World, Declaration." Online petition, accessed Sept. 30, 2017, www.thepetitionsite.com.

117

African LGBTI Manifesto

Nairobi, Kenya
April 2010

As long as African LGBTI people are oppressed, the whole of Africa
is oppressed.

This African LGBTI Manifesto emerged from a roundtable session held in Nairobi
in April 2010. It links the LGBTI movement to Pan-African struggles for liberation,
and challenges certain assumptions about the lack of resistance to homophobia
on the continent. There are, in fact, what Adriaan van Klinken calls "counter-
discourses and -practices" that challenge both homophobia and the local religious
narratives that support it.[1] LGBTI movements are not distinctly "Western," this is
to say, and not unique to Kenya, either, as there are other "example[s] of African
agency, courage, creativity and authority in the struggle for sexual diversity and
gay rights in contemporary Africa" (66). Contemporary groups addressing the
range of LGBTI issues include Integrity Uganda, the Coalition of African Lesbians,
the Gay and Lesbian Equality Project, Triangle, and Gender Dynamix.

In what by now is hopefully a familiar pattern, this document[2] links oppression
to intertwined systems of oppression, especially colonialism, racism, sexism, and
homophobia. It begins with an assertion of the authority and creativity of the oppressed to reimagine structures and systems, lays out a broad set of goals related
to multiple forms of justice, and ends by suggesting coalition building as the only
reasonable strategy for changing intersectional domination.

African LGBTI Manifesto

As Africans, we all have infinite potential. We stand for an African revolution
which encompasses the demand for a re-imagination of our lives outside neocolonial categories of identity and power. For centuries, we have faced control
through structures, systems and individuals who disappear our existence as people with agency, courage, creativity, and economic and political authority.

As Africans, we stand for the celebration of our complexities and we are committed to ways of being which allow for self-determination at all levels of our
sexual, social, political and economic lives. The possibilities are endless. We need
economic justice; we need to claim and redistribute power; we need to eradicate
violence; we need to redistribute land; we need gender justice; we need environmental justice; we need erotic justice; we need racial and ethnic justice; we
need rightful access to affirming and responsive institutions, services and spaces;
overall we need total liberation.

We are specifically committed to the transformation of the politics of sexuality
in our contexts. As long as African LGBTI people are oppressed, the whole of
Africa is oppressed.

This vision demands that we commit ourselves to:
    Reclaiming and sharing our stories (past and present), our lived realities, our
        contributions to society and our hopes for the future;

Strengthening ourselves and our organizations, deepening our links and understanding of our communities, building principled alliances, and actively contributing towards the revolution.

Challenging all legal systems and practices which either currently criminalize or seek to reinforce the criminalization of LGBTI people, organizations, knowledge creation, sexual self expression, and movement building.

Challenging state support for oppressive sexual, gendered, discriminatory norms, legal and political structures and cultural systems.

Strengthening the bonds of respect, cooperation, passion, and solidarity between LGBTI people, in our complexities, differences and diverse contexts. This includes respecting and celebrating our multiple ways of being, self expression, and languages.

Contributing to the social and political recognition that sexuality, pleasure, and the erotic are part of our common humanity.

Placing ourselves proactively within all movement building supportive of our vision.

Notes

1 "A Kenyan Queer Prophet: Binyavanga Wainaina's Public Contestation of Pentecostalism and Homophobia," in *Christianity and Controversies over Homosexuality in Contemporary Africa*, ed. Ezra Chitando and Adrianna van Klinken (London: Routledge, 2016), p. 66.

2 "African LGBTI Manifesto/Declaration," 2010. *Black Looks* blog, May 17, 2011, www.black looks.org.

118

Our Vision Statement *and* Action Agenda
RESURJ: Realizing Sexual and Reproductive Justice
Online Community
November 5, 2010, and 2014

RESURJ logo.

Sexual and reproductive rights and health are integral to building a world where all people are able to live empowered lives free of poverty and violence.

Testifying to the growing links among groups and movements, RESURJ grew out of the International Women's Health Coalition (IWHC) and is committed to the reproductive- and health-rights agenda adopted at the International Conference on Population and Development.[1] It is distinctive in being a global alliance of younger feminists—under forty—from the Global South, working primarily on issues of sexual and reproductive justice. Coordinating with organizations from a variety of movements (HIV, feminist, and youth, for example) in diverse locales (Mexico, Brazil, Pakistan, India, Nigeria, Ireland, and Poland), it tackles issues from sex education to accessible services to reproductive technology, and it especially emphasizes the processes by which decisions are made. All of its work is done in the name of "gender, economic, social, and environmental justice." Using an intersectional approach, it speaks simultaneously of the rights of women and of young people, and attends to differences (such as of ability, gender identity, and sexual orientation) in discussing sexual and reproductive healthcare. Its website includes the blog *Feminist Voices*, and the Sexual and Reproductive Justice Resource Center, which provides country- and region-specific resources.

The status quo against which RESURJ works includes the following:

Today, there are 1.8 billion young people between the ages of 10–24 who do not have access to the comprehensive sexual and reproductive health services and sexuality education that they need for a safe and healthy life. More than 215 million women who are married or living in unions do not want to be pregnant but lack access to modern contraception, and even more lack access to other vital sexual and reproductive health services and information. The prevalence of anemia due to poor nutrition, continuing lack of safe water and sanitation, and the health impacts of rising global and national inequality place the sexual and reproductive health of girls and women at grave risk. Too many women and girls continue to face gender inequality, violence, and other violations of human rights.[2]

RESURJ has been a participant in numerous important meetings and actions around the world related to gender equality and reproductive and sexual justice. The group helped host the African Feminist Dialogue in 2015 to mobilize young feminist activists, cosponsored (with FRIDA, Flexibility Resources Inclusivity Diversity Action) a discussion on the challenges facing young women, and engaged (with IWHC, among others) in intergovernmental negotiations surrounding the UN Conference on Sustainable Development. RESURJ was one of the critics of the UN's Post-2015 Development Agenda. It called for greater recognition of the role of feminist and women's groups in transformative change, for example, and argued for a central place for the rights of women and girls on the agenda.[3] It continues to insist that there is no possibility of sustainable development without equality.

Our Vision Statement

We envision a world where every person's human rights are affirmed and upheld. A world guided by equality and equity, where women, girls, adolescents and young people in all their diversity are empowered. We believe that in order to achieve gender, economic, social, and environmental justice, women and young people must have the ability to live with dignity and autonomy through the different stages of their lives.

Sexual and reproductive rights and health are integral to building a world where all people are able to live empowered lives free of poverty and violence. Every woman, adolescent and young person must have full citizenship and access to an enabling environment in order to realize their sexual and reproductive rights and health. Women and young people should be at the forefront of decision-making in policy and programme processes.

We recognize that women's particular contexts, identities and historic and continued marginalization disproportionately affect their ability to enjoy their sexual and reproductive rights and health, including but not limited to women living with HIV and women with disabilities.

We believe in women's agency. Exercising personal agency is crucial to individuals living happier and more fulfilled lives, and recognizing people's agency [is] an essential precondition for a just harmonious world. No woman is free till all women are free.

We undertake our work within a feminist intersectional analysis which recognizes historic[4] and systemic unequal gender power relations. We believe in meaningfully inclusive, participatory and democratic processes and commit to accountability and transparency within our own movements.

We are a group of feminists who commit to sharing power, building trust and nurturing solidarity. We believe in fostering equal partnership including intergenerational dialogue, and are committed to a culture of activism that integrates pleasure and joy, and understands that without assuring [the] protection, safety and well-being of individual activists we cannot have sustainable organizations and movements.

10-Point Action Agenda
"RESURJ by 2015" is a 10-point action agenda[5] that places women's and young people's human rights, particularly sexual and reproductive rights, participation in decision-making, and accountability at the center of health programs and development efforts. RESURJ calls on all decision-makers to:

1. Expand decision-making opportunities for women and young people by ensuring their meaningful participation in all stages of design, monitoring and implementation of sexual and reproductive rights policies and programs at national, regional and international levels.

2. Prioritize sexual and reproductive rights in health systems by strengthening development programs so that integrated, high-quality services are available, accessible, and acceptable to all women and young people, particularly those most underserved. These services include comprehensive information on sexuality and contraception services and supplies (including emergency contraception, post exposure prophylaxis, male and female condoms); pregnancy care (antenatal and postnatal care, skilled birth attendance, referral systems, and emergency obstetric care); safe abortion services and post-abortion care; access to assisted reproductive technologies; prevention, treatment, and care of sexually transmitted infections and HIV; [and] prevention, treatment and care of reproductive cancers.

3. Guarantee universal access to this package of essential sexual and reproductive health services by providing sufficient and sustainable financing to achieve the training, deployment, and retention of necessary health workers; ensure

equitable access and good quality services; free or subsidized care for those in need; and monitoring of potential disparities through regular collection and analysis of sex- and age- disaggregated data.

4. Protect women's and young people's human rights in sexual and reproductive health programs by guaranteeing that services are designed to respond to individuals' health needs and overcome barriers faced by marginalized groups, including through service provision that is free from stigma, coercion, discrimination and violence, based on full and informed consent, and that affirms the right to pleasure. Programs must ensure respect for women's and adolescents' privacy and confidentiality in accessing services, and their capacity to make free and informed choices regarding their sexual and reproductive lives from childhood to old age in all their diversity; and pay special attention to marginalized groups of women and adolescents, including those with disabilities, living with HIV and AIDS, and of all sexual orientations and gender identities.

5. Create and sustain comprehensive, objective, and accurate sexuality education and information that is accessible and affirming for all children and youth in and out of schools. Comprehensive sexuality education programs promote sexual and reproductive rights, gender equality, self-empowerment, knowledge of the body, bodily integrity and autonomy, and relationship skills development; are free of gender stereotypes, discrimination, and stigma; and are respectful of children's and adolescents' evolving capacities to make choices about their sexual and reproductive lives.

6. Allocate funds targeted to HIV that protect and empower women and young people. In particular, guarantee funding for the provision of comprehensive sexual and reproductive health services that include comprehensive sexuality education; prevention, counseling, voluntary testing, treatment and care of HIV, as well as other sexually transmitted infections and reproductive cancers; and universal access to female and male condoms, microbicides and other women-initiated prevention technologies and vaccines.

7. Ensure that intellectual property agreements support states' obligations to uphold the human rights of women and young people. Governments must make use of all trade-related intellectual property rights (TRIPS) flexibilities to ensure that intellectual property rights rules do not adversely affect individuals' access to medicines, and generic medicines in particular, as well as other prevention technologies.

8. Foster an enabling environment for the realization of women's and young people's sexual and reproductive rights by guaranteeing women's and young people's economic, social, cultural, civil, and political rights; removing all structural, legal, and social barriers to the enjoyment of these rights; guaranteeing other underlying determinants of health (such as good nutrition, and access to clean water and sanitation); and achieving gender equality.

9. Strengthen transparency and ensure the establishment of effective monitoring and accountability mechanisms for health and education programs at the local, national, regional and international levels that are supported politically and financially. Monitoring and accountability mechanisms must adopt a systemic and sustained human rights approach, provide effective remedies and redress to rights holders when sexual and reproductive rights are violated, and lead to the constant improvement of existing programs and policies.

10. Guarantee that financing for development is sustainable and harmonized among donors and multilateral agencies and that sexual and reproductive rights and health programs are prioritized.

Notes

1 RESURJ, "Our Vision Statement," Nov. 5, 2010. RESURJ website, www.resurj.org.
2 RESURJ, "Cairo Call to Action." RESURJ website, accessed September 2017, www.resurj.org.
3 Grace Wilentz, "No Sustainable Development without Equality." June 26, 2015. *RESURJ* blog, www.resurj.org.
4 Footnote in document: "As Feminists, we question and challenge systems of power and oppression both internally (personal) and externally (political), that marginalize women in all their diversity."
5 RESURJ, "10-Point Action Agenda." RESURJ website, accessed September 2017, www .resurj.org.

119

Mandaluyong Declaration
Global Conference on Indigenous Women, Climate Change, and REDD Plus
Mandaluyong City, Philippines
November 18–19, 2010

 Asian Indigenous Women's Network

Asian Indigenous Women's Network logo.

The Global Conference on Indigenous Women, Climate Change, and REDD[1] Plus, sponsored by the Asian Indigenous Women's Network (AIWN), involved eighty women from sixty indigenous peoples from twenty-nine countries. It was also the Third Asian Indigenous Women's Conference, and the subtheme was "Securing Rights and Enhancing Capacities for Adaptation and Mitigation." The mission of AIWN is "to support, sustain and help consolidate the various efforts of indigenous women in Asia to critically understand the roots of their marginalized situation and to empower themselves by becoming aware of their rights as women and as indigenous peoples, and by developing their own organizations or structures for empowerment."[2] Its steering committee is composed of people from Bangladesh, India, China, Vietnam, Philippines, Taiwan, Nepal, Mongolia, Malaysia, Burma, Thailand, and Indonesia.

The Declaration details the "disruptions to Indigenous women's very identities" and to "the overall webs of relationships and responsibilities that matter to their communities" caused by climate change.[3] Its creators hope their communities will adapt and continue, in part by using their existing values and sustainable practices, and by passing on indigenous women's traditional knowledge on such matters as forest management and sustainable agriculture. The Mandaluyong Declaration captures how Indigenous women shared stories on the adverse impacts of climate change, on how they are adapting, and on how they are contributing to the mitigation of climate change. The Declaration also spells out priority areas of work and activities that they, as indigenous women—collectively or individually—can do within their networks, organizations, and communities.

Participants at the meeting.

The publication "Indigenous Women, Climate Change & Forests" includes the Mandaluyong Declaration,[4] and also reports on efforts of indigenous women to confront these issues globally, including in Kenya, China, Vietnam, Nepal, and Cameroon. Rich, industrialized countries are seen as the major source of the problem, with their excessive use of fossil fuels and the driving forces of capitalist development. Problematic experiences include more incidence of disease coupled with inadequate healthcare services (meaning greater burdens on women caregivers), and water and food insecurity exacerbated by the salinization of water aquifers in low-lying coastal areas and by droughts (endangering traditional ways of living). The extent of what is threatened, from traditional rituals to the very existence of sacred lands, is mind-boggling. But AIWN is responding with a vast range of survival tactics, including crop diversification and "strengthening our mutual labour exchange systems which embed the values of reciprocity, solidarity and self-help."

Mandaluyong Declaration

"We must search through our past to understand the ways of our ancestors for thousands of years when they lived in unity with the spirits of the land and mother earth."

We 80 indigenous women coming from 60 indigenous nations and peoples and representing our communities and organizations from 29 countries[5] gathered together on 18–21 November 2010 in Manila, Philippines for the "Global Conference on Indigenous Women, Climate Change and REDD Plus." We came to tell our stories on how we are differentially affected by the impacts of climate change because we are women and because we are indigenous peoples. We shared how we are coping or adapting to climate change. We also examined our distinct contributions in mitigating climate change or reducing the amount of greenhouse gas emissions in the atmosphere. On the last day, we agreed on priority areas of work and activities which we can collectively or individually do within our own organizations and networks.

While we have least contributed to the problem of climate change, we have to carry the burdens of adapting to its adverse impacts. This is because of the unwillingness of rich, industrialized countries to change their unsustainable production and consumption patterns and pay their environmental debt for causing this ecological disaster. Modernity and capitalist development which is based on the use of fossil fuels and which promote[s] unsustainable and excessive production and consumption of unnecessary goods and services, individualism, patriarchy, and incessant profit-seeking have caused climate change.

Extreme and variable weather conditions brought about by climate change have undermined our traditional livelihoods such as rotational agriculture, hunting and gathering, pastoralism, high montane agriculture, lowland agriculture, agroforestry, marine and coastal livelihoods, and handicraft production, among others. These ecosystem-based livelihoods have ensured food and water security and the well-being of our families, communities and nations for centuries. Unfortunately, these are grossly undermined not just by climate change but by the dominant economic paradigm which is highly extractive and destructive of nature. We have experienced and continue to suffer from unprecedented disasters brought about by super-typhoons and hurricanes causing massive floods and landslides. Aside from the loss of lives, some of us have lost our homes and even our ancestral territories. With prolonged droughts, high temperatures and widespread bush and forest fires, some of our peoples suffer from hunger, disease and misery.

Diseases caused by the lack of food and potable water and by extreme hot and cold temperatures have been worsened many times over. Widespread outbreaks of vector-borne and water-borne diseases such as malaria, dengue fever, cholera and other gastro-intestinal diseases, and leptospirosis, among others, continue to happen. Yet health services to address these are sorely inadequate. Thus, our burdens as caregivers and nurturers of our families and communities increased to a point where our capacity to adapt is now seriously weakened.

Water and food insecurity is exacerbated by the salinization of water aquifers in the low lying coastal areas in the islands of the Philippines, Indonesia and the Pacific; the deforestation and degradation of our tropical and temperate forests which are the watersheds; and the melting of glaciers in the high montane areas in the Andes in South America, the Himalayas in Asia and Mt. Kilimanjaro in Africa. Prolonged droughts have resulted in the drying up of our springs and rivers. All these have grossly affected our traditional livelihoods and well-being which are intricately linked with the integrity of our ecosystems. These also led to conflicts over water which are further worsened by the privatization of common water sources by foreign and domestic water corporations and the pollution of these by extractive industries like mining and oil extraction. As the main water providers, we have to search and fight for access to the few remaining water sources.

Rising sea levels are drowning or have already drowned our islands. Those of us from the small islands, such as from Carteret Islands in Bougainville in Papua New Guinea, are forced to leave our ancestral islands and are now refugees on lands located on higher ground. In this particular case, what is at stake are questions of territorial and political sovereignty and identity of the peoples of Carteret. What does sovereignty mean when your ancestral territory is lost? Many other low lying coastal areas are under the same threat.

Cultural norms and values that guide customary sustainable resource use and management associated with food production and consumption are weakened. Miskito women shared: "We now live in a hurry and daughters do not cook as grandmothers . . . We do not catch fish as before, do not cook as before; we cannot store food and seeds as before; the land no longer produces the same; small rivers are drying up . . . I think that along with the death of our rivers, our culture also dies. . . ."[6] In Cameroon, the continuing disappearance of the fish called nwahka has affected the performance of the traditional ritual for Baka girls entering womanhood. The inability to perform this rite not only deprives young women the pride and honor of being initiated into adulthood. It also leads to the continuing erosion of the culture, knowledge and values associated with the ritual. With food scarcity, the health and wellbeing of the new generation are at risk.

Complicating these are the situations of multiple discrimination based on gender and ethnic identity. These are manifested in the lack of gender- and culturally-sensitive basic social services such as education and health and our lack of access to basic utility services such as water and energy. The systematic discrimination [against] and non-recognition of our sustainable resource management, and customary governance systems and their access, control and ownership of their lands, territories and resources, persists.

Out of the two billion people in the world today who do not have access to energy resources, a significant number of these are us, indigenous peoples, because we live in the most remote and isolated areas. Some of us, whose territories are used for mega-hydroelectric dams, still do not have energy in our communities. We spend between two to nine hours to collect firewood and biomass for cooking. The worsening conflicts over ownership and access to our land and resources brought about by past and present discriminatory legal, political and economic systems, some conservation regimes and some climate change responses, as well as the unregulated behavior of corporations, are taking a serious toll on us. We have to continue nurturing our families and communities under such difficult situations. The Bagua Massacre in Peru in June 2009 where the military fired upon indigenous peoples protesting against discriminatory laws which favored mining corporations over them represents what is happening to many indigenous peoples in Africa, Latin America and Asia.

Pastoralism, which is nomadic or semi-nomadic in character, is the main livelihood of our indigenous sisters and brothers in West, East and the Horn of Africa, Mongolia, in the Himalayas, Russia, some parts of India and in Samiland. While scores of cattle die due to prolonged droughts in Africa, pastoralism still contributes significantly to the national revenues of governments. We, indigenous women who belong to pastoralist communities, suffer discrimination from the State which considers pastoralism as backward and, as a result, systematically marginalizes us in many aspects. We have a high rate of illiteracy because we keep on moving, we hardly have access to basic social services like health and education.

We suffer from violence committed against us in the forms of rape, sexual harassment and bigotry.

Amidst all these, we have and continue to struggle against institutionalized discrimination and inequality. Because we live in the most fragile ecosystems, we are highly vulnerable to the adverse impacts of climate change. Those of us from Ecuador, Guyana, India, Indonesia, Papua, Peru, Philippines, and Suriname shared how we stood in the forefront of the struggles against mining, deforestation, oil and gas extraction, and dam-building, which have led to the destruction of our forests and waters and traditional livelihood sources. In New Mexico, USA, our indigenous sisters are engaged in documenting the environmental and health impacts of uranium mining and pressuring government to implement the 1990 Radiation Exposure Compensation Act. Our Baka and Batwa sisters from the Democratic Republic of Congo and Burundi and our indigenous sisters from Thailand are not even considered as citizens in the States where they live; so they are struggling to get their citizenship. In the Central Belt of India, Adivasi women such as the Jharkand and Oraon women continue to fight against the attempts of the State to further exploit their forests and open these up to mineral extraction.

We shared how we are addressing the issues of food, water and energy insecurity. How we are sustaining and transmitting our traditional knowledge to the younger generations. How we are continuing our traditional land, water and forest resource management systems. How we are exerting our best to ensure the overall health and well-being of our families and communities. Our efforts to recover, strengthen, use, and adapt our traditional knowledge and our ecosystems to climate change and to transmit these to our youth are bearing some good results. We recognize the imperative to enhance our capacities for disaster preparedness, management and rehabilitation but we should be provided the necessary financial and technical support. We shared our indigenous ways of predicting and coping with climate change–related disasters and we hope to further strengthen [our] knowledge and practices.

To address food insecurity, we are diversifying our crops and using and developing further our viable traditional plant and livestock species that are more tolerant of extreme weather conditions. We continue to use and adapt our traditional knowledge and land, water, forest and natural resource management systems to climate change. We, who belong to hunting and gathering communities, are getting more into crop cultivation including domestication of fruit trees, and food substitution as we continue to protect our forests from drivers of deforestation such as logging, mining, large-scale chemical-based agriculture and monocrop plantations. Realizing the adverse impacts of industrialized chemical-based agriculture, those of us engaged in rotational agriculture and small-scale cash crop production are reviving and strengthening traditional land, water and pest management systems, recycling of biodegradable wastes, among others.

We are also strengthening our mutual labour exchange systems which embed the values of reciprocity, solidarity and self-help as well as our traditional forest management practices. Examples of these are the ug-ugbo of the Kankana-ey Igorot and muyong of the Ifugao in the Philippines, the bakahnu among the Miskito of Nicaragua, dahas of the Dayak in Indonesia, engelehe of the Maasai in Africa, among others. Our spirituality which link[s] humans and nature, the seen and the unseen, the past, present and future, and the living and non-living has been and remains as the foundation of our sustainable resource management and use. We believe that if we continue to live by our values and still use our sustainable systems and practices for meeting our basic needs, we can adapt better to climate change.

We assert that before we take part in designing, implementing, monitoring and evaluating climate change mitigation and adaptation policies, programmes and activities, we need to learn more profoundly what the risks and opportunities are for us. All adaptation and mitigation plans and activities implemented in our territories, including initiatives such as REDD Plus (Reducing Emissions from Deforestation and Forest Degradation, Conservation, Sustainable Management of Forests, Enhancement of Forest Carbon Stocks), should be adequately understood by our communities before they make their decisions on how to deal with these. Our free, prior and informed consent should be obtained for any climate change project brought into our communities. Most of the world's remaining tropical forests which are those targeted for REDD Plus are our traditional territories.

We are therefore keen to see that the UN Declaration on the Rights of Indigenous Peoples (UNDRIP) be integrally included as the main instrument to protect us against the potential risks from REDD Plus. These risks include our possible displacement from our forests, elite capture of benefits, gross commodification of our forests and all resources found therein, among others. At the same time, we can see some opportunities for us to occupy decision making spaces, reform forest and land laws to recognize indigenous peoples' rights, abatement of deforestation, and possible real and sustained efforts to address land tenure issues and the drivers of deforestation. As indigenous women who are dependent and who live in forests, we continue to play significant roles in protecting the biodiversity and other ecosystem services provided by our forests. We still gather wild food plants and medicinal plants as well as fuel, fodder and fiber. We protect the forest because of its multiple function[s] and roles in our economic, environment[al], social-cultural and spiritual lives. We cannot see forests, therefore, as just timber or carbon. Our holistic regard and our reciprocal relationship with our forest and our rights to these forests and resources should be the defining elements to consider in any initiative around forests and climate change.

We agreed on the following priority areas of work and actions which we will seek to implement in our communities and organizations, jointly with our partners and supporters.

1. AWARENESS RAISING, SKILLS TRAINING WORKSHOPS, INFORMATION DISSEMINATION

1.1. Awareness-raising and training seminars to increase our basic knowledge on:

- Climate change, policies and programmes on climate change adaptation and mitigation of States and NGOs at the national and global levels, which include, among others, the UNFCCC and Kyoto Protocol, REDD Plus, disaster preparedness and risk management;

- Human rights-based, ecosystem approach and knowledge-based framework to climate change adaptation and mitigation;
- Understanding the UNDRIP and CEDAW (Convention on the Elimination of Discrimination Against Women);
- Gender analysis of policies and approaches for mitigation and adaptation.

1.2. Skills training workshops on how to develop popular education materials; effective and culturally- and gender-sensitive methods and approaches to teaching and learning; project proposal development and fund-raising, as well as organizational and finance management.

1.3. More effective and wider dissemination of relevant information and sharing of knowledge on climate change, adaptation and mitigation with the grassroots women's organizations:

- Develop and use diverse methodologies and technologies for information sharing and awareness raising, e.g., community radio, video documentation, community theatre, community newspapers and wall posters, etc.;
- Translation of materials into languages understood by community women;
- Setting up of multiple communications networks at the national, regional and global level for faster dissemination of information;
- Use of multimedia.

2. RESEARCH, DOCUMENTATION AND PUBLICATION

2.1. Research and documentation on climate change impacts on indigenous women and on climate change adaptation and mitigation:

- Undertake training-workshops on participatory and policy research for indigenous women who are interested to do research work that can be used for education and awareness raising and for policy advocacy. Research themes and agenda can cover the following areas:
    - ◊ Food security and climate change—impacts and roles of women;
    - ◊ Traditional knowledge and community forest management practices and the roles of indigenous women;
    - ◊ Monitoring of climate change mitigation measures such as REDD Plus;
    - ◊ Traditional livelihoods of indigenous women and climate change;
    - ◊ Renewable energy development, energy security and indigenous women;
    - ◊ Gender dimensions of adaptation and mitigation policies and measures;
    - ◊ Use of multimedia to disseminate widely research results to the communities, to policy and decision makers and to the media.

2.2. Publish the studies prepared by the indigenous women for this Conference and launch this publication during the 10th Session of the UN Permanent Forum on Indigenous Issues.

3. ENHANCE CAPACITIES OF OUR COMMUNITIES TO ADAPT TO AND MITIGATE CLIMATE CHANGE

3.1. Enhance adaptive capacities and livelihoods including enhancement of our traditional agricultural practices and systems, agro-forestry and the development and promotion of ecological agricultural practices adapted to climate change impacts, including development of and access to diverse seed varieties for food, fiber.

3.2. Facilitate direct access to adaptation funds and technologies for climate change adaptation at the local, national, regional and global levels: Gather and disseminate widely information on existing funds and resources which indigenous women's organizations and networks can tap:

- FIMI (International Indigenous Women's Forum)—Indigenous Women's Fund: www.fimi-iiwg.org, Tebtebba: www.tebtebba.org, AIWN: www.asiaindigenous women.org;
- Indigenous Peoples Assistance Facility (IPAF)—IFAD (International Fund for Agricultural Development): www.tebtebba.org;
- UN Voluntary Fund for the Second Decade of the World's Indigenous People: www.un.org/esa/socdev/unpfii.

3.3. Enhance access of indigenous women to disaster and relief funds from governments and donor agencies and organize disaster and relief task forces of indigenous women.

3.4. Reinforce indigenous women's traditional knowledge on mitigation and adaptation and facilitate the transfer of this knowledge to the younger generations. This includes knowledge on traditional forest management, sustainable agriculture, pastoralism, disaster preparedness and rehabilitation, etc.

3.5. Enhance traditional community sharing and self-help systems like the ug-ugbo, engelehe, binnadang, and bakahnu, among others.

3.6. Facilitate exchange visits between indigenous women from different countries and communities for learning and sharing of experiences.

3.7. Document in multimedia, successful adaptation and mitigation practices of indigenous women.

4. INCREASE POLITICAL PARTICIPATION AND POLICY ADVOCACY

4.1. Ensure full and effective participation of indigenous women in political and decision-making bodies and processes and in the formulation, implementation and evaluation of climate change adaptation and mitigation policies, programmes and projects at the local, national, regional and global levels:

- Undertake training-workshops for indigenous women on political participation and policy advocacy and on leadership development.

4.2. Develop statements and interventions of indigenous women to be presented to relevant bodies and processes at various levels.

5. NETWORKING

5.1. Participate actively in the Indigenous Peoples' Global Network on Climate Change and Sustainable Development (IPCCSD).

5.2. Facilitate participation of indigenous women [in] relevant national and global processes related to climate change and human rights and encourage them to join or play active roles in national, regional and global climate change multistakeholder formations such as National Climate Change Networks, National REDD Plus Formations, etc.

5.3. Facilitate linkages of indigenous women with existing civil society and women's NGOs and organizations that are doing work on climate change.

5.4. Facilitate participation of indigenous women in campaigns and mass actions that are related to women, climate change and human rights.

5.5. Support indigenous women parliamentarians or those in the bureaucracies of official bodies to promote indigenous women's agenda on climate change and human rights.

6. WORK WITH STATES, THE UN, OTHER INTERGOVERNMENTAL ORGANIZATIONS AND MULTILATERAL FINANCING INSTITUTIONS, NGOS AND OTHER INDIGENOUS PEOPLES' FORMATIONS TO ENSURE THE RECOGNITION AND EFFECTIVE IMPLEMENTATION OF THE UNITED NATIONS DECLARATION ON THE RIGHTS OF INDIGENOUS PEOPLES IN ALL CLIMATE CHANGE MITIGATION AND ADAPTATION PROGRAMMES AND ACTIVITIES.

7. DEVELOP WITH OTHERS A HOLISTIC FRAMEWORK FOR A GENDER-SENSITIVE, ECOSYSTEM, HUMAN RIGHTS–BASED, AND KNOWLEDGE-BASED APPROACH TO CLIMATE CHANGE ADAPTATION AND MITIGATION EFFORTS.

Notes

1 REDD stands for "reducing emissions from deforestation and forest degradation."
2 "About AIWN." Asian Indigenous Women's Network website, accessed 2017, www.asianindigenouswomen.org.
3 "Indigenous Women, Climate Change Impacts, and Collective Action," unpublished report, 2014, p. 15. Northwest Climate Science Center website, www.nwclimatescience.org.
4 "Mandaluyong Declaration of the Global Conference on Indigenous Women, Climate Change, and REDD Plus," Nov. 2010. Asian Indigenous Women's Network website, www.asianindigenouswomen.org.
5 Aotearoa (New Zealand), Bangladesh, Burma, Burundi, Cambodia, Cameroon, China, Democratic Republic of Congo, Ecuador, Guyana, India, Indonesia, Kenya, Laos, Micronesia, Mongolia, Nepal, Nicaragua, Pakistan, Papua New Guinea, Peru, Philippines, Taiwan, Thailand, Tanzania, Suriname, the United States, and Viet Nam.
6 Interviews with M. Bobb, Smith Otilla Escobar Duarte, Albita Solis, Lydia Wilson, Clarence Tummy Cleophas, and Thomas Prudilia in a paper presented by Rose Cunningham, Wangki Tangni, and CADPI, Nicaragua. In *Indigenous Women, Climate Change, and Forests* (Baguo, Benguet, Philippines: Tebtebba Foundation, 2011).

120

Manifesto: Men against Gender Violence
Peruvian Masculinity Network
Lima, Peru
November 25, 2010

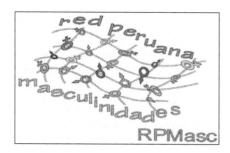

Peruvian Masculinity Network

Like the documents by SAVE and Ways Women Lead, the Manifesto of the Peruvian Masculinity Network (RPM) encourages participants and readers to take a personal pledge, in this case to stop gender-based violence, including its extreme, femicide. In this instance, however, it is particularly men who are being asked by

The "wheel of men" graphic used by the Network conceptualizes the solidarity of the men involved.

other men to take a stand for nonviolence in their personal, social, and professional lives. This Manifesto[1] was issued on November 25, the UN's International Day for the Elimination of Violence Against Women. The group has also written one about equitable parenting. It often takes a health approach to gender issues.

According to RPM's website, Peru had eighty cases of femicide and twenty-nine attempted murders of women in 2010. There, as everywhere, the overwhelming majority of intimate partner violence is also against women, leading to almost one hundred thousand injuries in Peru in 2009, as well as to psychological harm and sexual violation. RPM takes such statistics as their starting point, and works toward a conception and practice of masculinity that values the feminine and female.

Peru is yet another postconflict society, having endured a civil war between the government and the Shining Path guerrilla group that led to about seventy thousand deaths, a devastated Indigenous population, and wide-ranging sexual violence used as a tool of terror. "One long-term effect of this has been the significant rise in incidents of physical and sexual violence perpetrated against women by an intimate partner in peacetime. . . . Peru has one of the highest levels of violence against women in the world."[2] All the more need exists, then, for men to commit themselves to eliminating gender-based violence.

Manifesto: Men against Gender Violence

I, as a man, aware now of the magnitude and seriousness of the problem of male violence against women, willing to adopt a philosophy of respect for a dignified life, free from all forms of violence for women and men, promise to:
- Promote the fight to eradicate gender violence, through an active stance in my personal, professional and social life.
- Exercise zero tolerance for physical, psychological, emotional or any kind of violence, against women and men.
- Not be a silent accomplice, or justify such violence.
- Publicly denounce the problem and those who exercise violence.
- Suggest serious discussion on violence in all areas of my daily life.
- Challenge the traditional male model that I learned and that has taught us that being a man gives us authority over women, and that the only emotion [that] can be manifested without shame is aggressiveness.

- Combat the sexism that causes damage to women and also prevents men from expressing their feelings and emotions and neglecting their safety and that of the people around them.
- Reflect on my own behavior, and be alert and be critical of multiple [means] used by other men to control and dominate women.
- Not take advantage of my strength, whether physical, social or personal, to impose my wishes or benefits on women, or allow other men to do so.

A MAN SILENT ABOUT VIOLENCE
AGAINST WOMEN AND MEN,
IS PART OF THE PROBLEM
INTERNATIONAL DAY FOR THE ELIMINATION
OF VIOLENCE AGAINST WOMEN

Notes

1 "Taller de Introducción al Enfoque de Género y Masculinidades para la promoción de la equidad y la erradicación de la violencia de género." Red Peruana Masculinidades (RPMasc) website, accessed 2015, rpmasc.blogspot.com. Very minor grammar adjustments made to translation by editor.
2 "Katharina Jens on Domestic Violence in Post-conflict Peru," *UNA-UK Magazine* 1 (2015), www.una.org.uk.

121

Every Woman's Right to Learn: The Manifesto
National Institute of Adult Continuing Education
Leicester, England
March 8, 2011

National Institute of Adult Continuing Education logo.

Adult learning should be planned to take account of potential barriers to women learning such as caring and domestic responsibilities, costs and travel distance. It must recognise the ways that gender, class, ethnicity, disability and sexuality can combine and challenge any oppression and discrimination that is an obstacle to women entering learning.

The National Institute of Adult Continuing Education (NIACE) began in 1921 as an educational charity advocating for adult learning. Nearly a century later, in 2016, it merged with the Centre for Economic and Social Inclusion, and is now called the Learning and Work Institute. Education, of course, forms part of most feminist agendas, and is the main issue of documents dating back to the 1848 Paris Manifesto and the 1927 Resolutions from India. Lifelong learning, in particular, is attractive to feminists, especially as it reaches women who may have been forced to leave school early for a number of reasons.

Making use of noteworthy dates, this Manifesto[1] was issued on International Women's Day in 2011, traveled to the three main British party conferences, and was published in final form again on International Women's Day one year later. NIACE links women's education with equality and opportunity, and the ten-point Manifesto encourages all partners in adult education to keep gender equality on the agenda. Gender equality should be a topic in the classroom, a program for decision makers to implement, a goal for employers, and an inspiration for advisors.

Every Woman's Right to Learn: The Manifesto

The Manifesto is for all involved in adult learning.
    The purpose of the manifesto is to:
- regenerate existing knowledge and stimulate some new thinking about women in adult learning;
- encourage decision makers at all levels to address women's equality;
- encourage and support educators to address women's inequality through all aspects of their work; and
- support women who want to learn to aspire and achieve.

1. Lead a debate on women and learning
Adult learning should become a place where gender equality is raised, debated and at the heart of new thinking, decision making and practice.

2. Inspire women to widen their horizons and achieve their dreams
Adult learning should build on the culture that inspires and encourages women to aim high and enables them to achieve their hopes and dreams.

3. Involve more and different women in learning
Creative recruitment and outreach approaches must be used to attract women from different backgrounds and circumstances to take part in learning.

4. Make sure that adult learning promotes gender equality
Adult learning should actively promote gender equality through policy, practice, curriculum content and support.

5. Make sure that learning is affordable and accessible to all women
Adult learning should be planned to take account of potential barriers to women learning such as caring and domestic responsibilities, costs and travel distance. It must recognise the ways that gender, class, ethnicity, disability and sexuality can combine and challenge any oppression and discrimination that is an obstacle to women entering learning.

6. Make sure that work related learning expands opportunities for women
Adult learning should debate and offer alternatives to learning for traditional gender occupations in apprenticeships and other programmes.

7. Make sure that Information, Advice and Guidance opens up the full range of possibilities for women
IAG should actively challenge gender stereotypes and promote a wide range of options. It should recognise the priorities and demands of different life stages to support women to make choices and decisions.

8. Train all members of the workforce to understand and advance gender equality

Adult learning managers, staff and volunteers must be trained and supported to understand gender equality and promote this in their practice.

9. Demand equal participation in adult learning decision making

Adult learning must review its practices and structures to make sure that women participate equally in decision making, planning and evaluation.

10. Campaign for gender equality across all adult learning providers and partners

Adult learning should raise awareness of gender equality and provide the resources to support adult learning partners.

Note

1   "Every Woman's Right to Learn," 2011. Learning and Work Institute website, www.learnin gandwork.org.uk.

122

Manifesto of Young Feminists of Europe
European Camp of Young Feminists
Paris, France
July 2011

European Camp of Young Feminists logo.

This Manifesto was collectively written by about seventy young feminists at a week-long, self-managed camp. The participants came from Basque Country, Belgium, Galicia, Romania, Macedonia, Armenia, Poland, Portugal, and Switzerland. The camp (as conferences, etc., so often do) led to the founding of an ongoing group, the Network of Young Feminists of Europe. The group held camps in Romania in 2012 and Portugal in 2013. It has written another manifesto on immigration and done work on abortion.

While the camp was organized by the Youth Group of Paris of the French Coordination of the World March of Women, WMW did not run it. In fact, the announcement about the conference is interesting in its invitation to autonomy and attention to inclusion:

We would like to organize an autonomous camp of young feminists, in France next summer. For about 10 days, it would be about knowing each other, exchang[ing] our political visions at local, national, European and international levels, and express[ing] new wishes and projects. We would like to tackle topics [such] as political repression of feminist and lesbian movements, merchandisation of bodies, religious integrisms, growth of destitution and poverty, militarization . . . We want to organize this event with you! The project needs your proposal and motivation to come true! We'll have to work together on topics we want to tackle. We'll have to find money to allow a lot of young feminist[s] among Europe to join the camp. We'll have to contact groups of young feminist[s] in countries where the march is not organized yet. We'll have to work closely, learn to know each other to make an event like [this for] us.[1]

The Manifesto[2] offers useful guidelines on the ends and means of political solidarity, and throughout addresses an unusually broad list of groups experiencing multiple forms of oppression. It skillfully raises a number of related issues under the topics of economics, environment, violence, health, sexuality, and promoting feminism. It understands feminism "as a vision of society as a whole" and favors building coalitions among peoples rather than institutions.

Manifesto of Young Feminists of Europe

Women in Europe and in the world today face specific difficulties brought on by a patriarchal system and sexist cultures. We believe new developments in the post-crisis world today have worsened, and continue to worsen, the situation of women, endangering their hard-won rights. We, young feminists of Europe, have gathered together in the Young Feminists of Europe Camp in July 2011 to debate and discuss the current situation of women and how to improve it. The present Manifesto is not meant to be an exhaustive list of all the problems that women face today or to prioritize a feminist agenda, but rather to offer guidelines and a starting point towards a common Young European Feminist Agenda.

The topics we chose to address were: Solidarity, Multiple Discriminations, the Economy, the Environment, Violence, Health, Sexuality and the Promotion of Feminism. We will continue to work together to build a world free of patriarchal oppression and domination and to maintain and strengthen our bonds. We commit to sharing information and experience about our struggles in a European feminist network.

SOLIDARITY
Together, we stand by the following:
1. Solidarity must be a tool for fighting together against patriarchal societies and any kind of oppression of women. International solidarity gives strength to activist women.
2. Solidarity should avoid any kind of racism, imperialism or classism in our struggles.
3. Solidarity should be based on the analyses and demands of women in grassroots communities, including their identification with a specific territory, culture and background.
4. Solidarity among women in countries involved in armed conflicts is a tool of resistance against militarization, war and conflict.

Here and now, we stand in solidarity with all young feminists across Europe and we aim to increase solidarity with women worldwide.

MULTIPLE FORMS OF DISCRIMINATION

We wish to address the situation of women who face multiple forms of discrimination, which render them more vulnerable. In particular, this concerns migrant women, asylum-seekers, exiled women, incarcerated women, women belonging to a cultural minority (religious, ethnic, linguistic or other), women who are victims of human trafficking, and women facing sexual exploitation. All these women share the fact that, apart from belonging to a discriminated group, they face additional pressure due to their status as women. Economic difficulties, racism, disdain and current legislation are all factors that further aggravate their situations.

Few measures have been taken in Europe to protect these women from violence. Sometimes States actually legitimize aggressive measures against these women and enact hypocritical legislation to criminalize them. They often live in a state of isolation and are rendered invisible, which reinforces their dependence on people and institutions that take advantage of their situation (poor knowledge of the official language, difficult economic and social position, etc.). Mainstream political values and actions are Eurocentric and based on a colonialist ideology which tends to present immigrants coming to Europe as parasites and European emigrants as contributing to the development of countries considered inferior.

With this context in mind, we will work to:
1. Deconstruct prejudices and fight against the racist, capitalist, patriarchal system that reinforces different forms of oppression.
2. Build a European network of solidarity to fight the discriminatory inter-State networks that control migration.
3. Study and take account of the heterogeneity of groups and individual uniqueness (e.g. situations of culture shock), and to bring an end to the perception of immigrants and asylum-seekers as single, homogenous groups.
4. Put an end to isolation and to open up venues for self-expression and to highlight the interests of discriminated women.
5. Reinforce solidarity between countries affected by human trafficking (destination and supply).
6. Provide counseling for prostitutes, working towards increasing the visibility of their rights and ensuring support for those who want a way out of this situation.

ECONOMY

The current oppressive, globalized socioeconomic system gives rise to gender inequalities, unequal access to rights and gender-based income gaps. Different women, groups and countries face their own unique challenges, and we believe that a broad approach to this global struggle is needed. The concepts of work and poverty need to be questioned if we are to understand the difficulties facing us as women. Poverty has become feminized and has many facets that lead to exclusion and cumulative deprivation. Poor women have lesser access to community services and culture, as well as less mobility and autonomy. Certain groups of women face additional obstacles and discrimination in the labor market and in earning a decent income: lesbians, bisexuals, transsexuals, queers, intersexes, Roma women, migrant women, undocumented women, poor women, older women, women with disabilities, single mothers, women from ethnic minorities, women who are victims of violence, etc.

1. Care: People's lives are interdependent, and societies depend on the care provided by women. This work needs to be recognized, since so many people depend on it: children, the elderly, people with disabilities, and more. In fact, other people, such as husbands, fathers and male partners also depend on women's care. Although we recognize this interdependence, it cannot be allowed to keep women from being autonomous, and care must be fairly divided between the genders (for example, through State-funded care facilities and by encouraging men to take care of people in need).

2. Labor market: In the labor market, women work in low-paid sectors, part-time work and in lower positions, but also in the invisible and informal markets. Women's working rights should be respected and enforced, and women should be encouraged and supported in reclaiming their work rights, for visible or invisible, formal or informal work. It is also vital that women's invisible work be made visible. Women face discrimination and harassment in the labor market. Women are still paid less than men for the same work. Women who work in traditional, male-dominated well-paid sectors should be supported, and men should be encouraged to work in traditionally female sectors.

3. Social rights: Poverty and social exclusion are closely linked to the cumulative deprivation of various resources, services and rights: education, healthcare, unemployment benefits, pensions, etc. Through feminist struggles, women have gained social rights that are now increasingly endangered, under the pretext of resolving the economic crisis. All women should have access to resources, services and rights. All of this needs to be ensured so that poor women can escape the cycle of poverty, rather than sinking ever deeper into it. Developing women's economic cooperation as an alternative model is an important step in this direction.

Our demands are crucial if women are to be able to freely determine their lives and live them well.

ENVIRONMENT

Today we are facing an international food, energy, climate and environmental crisis created by the globalized capitalist production system in place. This system privatizes and commodifies our land, common goods and biodiversity, destroying and exploiting our environment.

Women are often the first to be affected by this situation. We know that women in the countryside are frequently responsible for food production, in contrast to the large-scale monoculture that is the dominant production model today. In many countries, women are the first to suffer from environmental damage since they are responsible for cooking, household economics and domestic work and have less access to information, land and services. Women and our peoples are not responsible and should not pay for and suffer the consequences of this crisis. We do reject laws that destroy peasant agriculture and our environment, like the European CAP, and false solutions that continue to give priority to an out-dated development model and to profit large corporations that impoverish the lives of women and our peoples.

1. We want to promote solidarity and the exchange of information between our peoples, to create a Europe by and for the people and to fight against the Europe of institutions and big business.

2. We want to promote independent agriculture that is respectful of the environment, to produce food for our peoples and to promote food sovereignty.

3. We want to build alternative modes of consumption based on local production, respect for our environment, biodiversity and the seasons and that prioritize native products, and to provide visibility and information to the public about the food production chain.

4. We want justice instead of the impunity enjoyed by States and corporations that destroy and exploit our environment and local agriculture.

5. We want a new energy model that is sustainable and respectful of the environment and accessible to the population

HEALTH

In the context of women's access to health services and products, we believe the following points are essential:

1. All women should have free access to quality public healthcare; we oppose the increasing commodification of health services and products.

2. Women must have absolute sovereignty over their bodies, and this should always be respected. We must have the freedom to make choices concerning our bodies (in terms of motherhood, abortion, contraception, etc.). We must fight for free access to abortion and to maintain this right in places where it is under attack.

3. The development of sex and health education programs is fundamental.

4. All healthcare systems should ensure that specific women's health issues receive full attention, support and resources for treatment, prevention and research (e.g. breast cancer).

VIOLENCE

Women continue to be subjected to the most diverse forms of violence, as a direct result of the patriarchal system. This system of domination is structured in three axes of oppression—sex/gender, ethnicity/race/culture and class—and is embedded into all domains of collective and individual life, representing in and of itself a form of violence against all women. The imposition of gender roles and stereotypes is at the root of structural, economic, sexual, psychological, verbal and physical violence against women.

Violence against women varies in degree, from body-image-related self-violence, the negative representation of women in the media, discrimination, harassment, anti-lesbian hate crimes, economic dependence, forced marriage, domestic violence, genital mutilation, rape and feminicide, putting women in a situation of constant fear and affecting all of society. This situation is seriously aggravated for women living in situations of armed conflict. Even when women try to free themselves from violence, they continue to suffer new and different forms at every step of the process.

We, young feminists of Europe, propose the following points of action to end violence against women:

1. Awareness-raising and education
   - Raising the awareness of the general population and also of the people involved in the legal process (police, judges, etc.)

- Educational programs about heterosexism, masculinity and feminist self-defense
2. Prevention and total support for victims
   - Open spaces for interaction and dialogue
   - Women-only spaces for support and self-expression—without fear of discrimination
   - Counseling for victims
   - Shelters (based on need) and social housing
   - Economic and welfare subsidies for economically-dependent women subject to violence
   - Raising awareness among women about their rights (peer-to-peer education, formal and informal education)
3. Institutional lobbying
   - Campaigning for legislation covering all women's specific problems related to violence (such as restraining orders against aggressors) and for proper enforcement of the law
   - Legislation criminalizing domestic rape and feminicide

SEXUALITY, LGBTQI and SEXUAL EDUCATION

Regarding issues relating to women's sexuality, LGBTQI and sex education, we propose the following points as guidelines for our future work:
1. Feminist points of view on sexuality, to break with the patriarchal, heterosexist system that creates sex- and gender-based inequalities.
2. Reappropriation of our bodies as women, to control our sexuality.
3. Freedom to choose our sexual identity (lesbian, transsexual, queer, intersex, etc.).
4. Promotion of women's right to pleasure and freedom of choice in all of their sexual experiences: women must always be able to choose when, how and with whom they engage in sexual activities.
5. Fight against lesbo-, homo- and transphobia.
6. Emancipation of women from religious institutions as patriarchal oppressors of our sexuality.
7. Fight for equal rights for everyone, no matter their sexual orientation or identity.
8. Provision of sex education (in schools, through popular education, the media, etc.).
9. Break with the media image of the hypersexualized woman used as an instrument of pleasure for heterosexual men.
10. Reappropriation of pornography from a feminist perspective.
11. Creation of networks to share our experiences and good practices in terms of feminist sexuality (actions, projects, programs, videos and so on).

PROMOTION OF FEMINISM

We believe that the following points are important to the promotion of feminism:
1. Building a world without stereotypes about feminism or gender and, especially, portraying feminism in a positive light (to end anti-feminism).
2. Promoting feminism as a vision of society as a whole, to be included in different domains: economics, environment, law, etc.
3. Promoting and facilitating active citizenship and feminist activism.

4. Promoting and facilitating access to women's contributions, particularly in the creative, artistic and scientific realms.

5. Creating spaces for women to share their experiences, keeping in mind feminist practices such as non-judgment, solidarity, and increased wellbeing for women.

6. Promoting a form of feminism that is inclusive and open to every culture, class and generation.

7. Encouraging a feminist reappropriation of culture by eliminating its omnipresent sexist dimensions.

The objectives presented above can be categorized into three different dimensions in which actions will be proposed: media, culture and education. Naturally [this] is not an exhaustive list; they are merely working guidelines. We believe promoting feminism must be part of an ongoing effort, in all aspects of our collective and individual lives.

Notes

1 "Summer Camp of Young Feminists of Europe!" Call to action, Kofemina website, accessed September 2017, http://www.umarfeminismos.org/.

2 European Camp of Young Feminists, "Manifesto of Young Feminists of Europe," July 2011. http://caravanafeminista.net/.

123

Manifesto—Women's Socio Economic Rights and Gender Equality from a Life-Cycle Perspective
European Women's Lobby
Budapest, Hungary
May 11, 2012

European Women's Lobby logo.

How gender discrimination and inequality manifest themselves at different stages of the life cycle varies. Young girls, young women, middle-aged women and older women may have different experiences of gender discrimination and inequality, yet at all stages of life, gender discrimination and inequality are present and persistent factors in the lives of women and girls. No country has yet succeeded in closing the gender gap in all aspects of economic and social life.[1]

We demand that women's rights and gender equality irrespective of age be placed at the heart of all policies and addressed at the highest political level.

This is the first document that explicitly takes a "life-cycle" approach to gender equality. Such a perspective has been endorsed and employed by groups such as the International Labor Organization and the United Nations, as well as the European Women's Lobby. It emphasizes the impact of gender inequality at every stage of life, an impact that varies and also has cumulative aspects (earning less while employed means a lower pension when retired, for example). It demands an approach to equality that is "long-term and holistic."

This document was written during a time of national economic crises in many locales. It claims that many proposed and enacted solutions hurt women in the short- and long-term, because they are profit-driven and because, frighteningly, "women's rights and gender equality are slipping off the political agenda," again. It emphasizes what policies and practices, in the nation-state, the workplace, and the home, support women's economic independence.

In 1987, 120 women representing eighty-five organizations called for the "creation of a structure for influence, open to all interested women's organisations, to exert pressure on European and national institutions to ensure better defence and representation of women's interest." The European Commission supported the establishment of the European Women's Lobby in 1990, which has a Secretariat based in Brussels. The EWL lobbies and informs policymakers, and promotes the participation of other women's groups. The issues on which it has been most active include violence against women, women's political participation and representation, women's economic independence, and gender aspects of migration. The vision statement of the European Women's Lobby, which was adopted in 2015, reads as follows:

> We believe in a Feminist Europe. We want a holistic, transformational socioeconomic vision, based on well-being, equality, social justice, and a powerful voice against women's poverty. We envision a culture in which women enjoy equal rights and participation in reimagined power and decision-making structures, in which all forms of violence against women [have] been eliminated, and women have been liberated from all forms of oppression. We envision a society in which women's contribution to all aspects of life is recognised, rewarded and celebrated—in leadership, in care and in production; all women have freedom of choice, self-confidence, and freedom from exploitation; and no woman has been left behind.

Manifesto—Women's Socio Economic Rights and Gender Equality from a Life-Cycle Perspective

We, members of the European Women's Lobby, reaffirm that a sustainable future for the European Union and the world is possible only if all women, men, girls and boys are free to contribute equally to society regardless of where they are situated in the "circle of life."

We affirm that gender relations strongly impact the entire life cycle from birth to old age, influencing access to resources and opportunities and shaping life strategies at every stage and that there cannot be wellbeing, growth or prosperity without gender equality.

We affirm that the many pressing challenges facing Europe demand long term and holistic consideration of people's different needs across the life-cycle. Only from a life-cycle perspective can we generate truly sustainable solutions. The EWL therefore calls for a gendered life-cycle approach in all political and economic decisions shaping Europe's future. A gendered life-cycle approach makes the links between how decisions taken at different stages of life impact on each other. Such an approach allows for the identification of the necessary political measures in various phases and at transitional points in women's lives. An example of this are the links between the gender pay and pension gaps which disadvantage women throughout their lives as they earn less and subsequently have lower pensions.

We are concerned that economic policies are increasingly disconnected from the real lives of women and men in the EU. Many of the current austerity measures are not based on long term societal considerations but on short term budgetary restrictions due to private intervention (notably by rating agencies). Such policies are neither democratic nor sustainable for the present generation or for the future generations of women and men.

We recall that such non-sustainable solutions to the economic, social and demographic crisis hit women particularly hard as witnessed by a number of studies. We are outraged by the economic policies that are leading the world. We condemn the way in which the constant search for profit is destroying the planet and human beings. Human beings have lost their place in the hierarchy of values. It is urgent to remedy this and to stop this disastrous spiral.

We are concerned that women's rights and gender equality are slipping off the political agenda and we oppose any backlash or loss of the freedoms, rights and opportunities generated by women and women-friendly societies in the past. The EU cannot afford it; the women of Europe will not accept it.

We demand that women's rights and gender equality irrespective of age be placed at the heart of all policies and addressed at the highest political level. Gender inequalities are costly; equality between women and men must be considered as an investment.

We recall that women constitute more than half of the European population and will represent a growing majority as Europe ages. Over the past few decades, women have contributed more to the expansion of the world economy than either new technologies or the emerging markets of China and India combined.

We call for change in the way women are perceived in policy-making which characterises women as a "group" and in particular a "vulnerable" or discriminated "minority" group. Women also represent the majority in many "minority groups" (older people, people with disability etc.). Women's equal rights and participation in all areas of life must be secured to all women irrespective of their different age, circumstances and backgrounds.

We affirm that women's economic independence throughout the life-cycle is a cornerstone in reaching gender equality. The independence of women and their fullest contribution to society can be achieved only if men and women work together to ensure equal access to paid and unpaid work, education and share burdens, responsibilities and power, benefits and freedoms, equally throughout the life-cycle.

The European Women's Lobby therefore makes the following recommendations:

Policy-makers should engage with women of all ages and backgrounds and their representative organisations in the design, implementation and evaluation of all policies and measures that seek to achieve women's economic independence and active participation in all areas on an equal footing with men throughout their life-cycle.

Economic and Social Policies

Ensure commitments related to equality between women and men in the EU 2020 Strategy and the goals set forth herein for smart, sustainable and inclusive growth: A dignified violence-free life for all, equal access to quality education opportunities, decent and equal wages and income. This should be mirrored in all of the processes of the EU2020 Strategy: The Annual Growth Survey, National Reform Programmes, National Stability and Convergence Programmes, Country-Specific Recommendations, Joint Employment Report, Joint Report on Social Protection and Social Inclusion.

Adopt binding legislation for the equal representation of women and men in decision-making, including on corporate boards as proposed by European Commission Vice-president Reding. Work towards the equal representation of women and men in view of the elections for the European Parliament and nomination of the new European Commission in 2014 as well as in the subsequent allocations of EU "Top Jobs." In line with the EU's Treaty commitments to democracy and fundamental rights, parity in decision-making in all spheres and at all levels is an issue of democratic representation, legitimacy and of social progress at both EU and national levels. Account should also be taken of age, ethnicity and social origins.

Apply alternative economic models which are sustainable for the people and the planet. Such models should introduce new ways of valuing the "care economy," the contributions of which have so far been disregarded in economic decision making. Care work, paid or unpaid, formal or informal must be reassessed and re-prioritised politically so that investments in the sector reflect the fundamental economic and social contributions this sector brings to society. The focus on the care economy is a prerequisite for the economy as a whole: women and men can contribute equally to society while raising future generations only when proper care infrastructures are in place. As the population ages, caring needs of the elderly and dependents are also rising. To ensure sustainability, care must therefore increasingly be addressed politically and economically as a common societal responsibility.

Care and Employment Policies

Place the care sector on an equal footing with other "job rich" growth sectors of the economy, namely the "green economy" and "ICT" in the EU2020 Strategy.

These sectors should seek to create a gender inclusive labour market which focuses on job creation policies.

Ensure fully paid maternity, paternity, parental, carer's and educational leave for both women and men to avoid economic sanctions later in life, such as insufficient pensions (mostly affecting women), due to caring responsibilities. Governments must move forward in negotiating with the European Parliament on the revised Maternity Leave Directive. In particular they must ensure full pay for the entire duration of maternity and paternity leave and the full protection of women returning to work after childbirth. Finally, the issue of pay during maternity leave cannot be dissociated from the gender pay gap. Maternity leave should be promoted politically as one of the factors to closing the gender pay gap which women experience throughout their lives.

Guarantee women's full participation on the labour-market regardless of their level of education and in particular young women. Women of child bearing age continue to be perceived as "risky" due to their potential child birth/child care, and this results in direct discrimination against women in accessing and remaining in the labour-market.

Guarantee women's full access to life-long learning, regardless of their level of education, to enable women to acquire new skills to facilitate their upgrading in a changing work environment and/or reorientation towards professional careers.

Ensure quality employment policies for women of all ages, in particular women over 50, so that they are considered as a valued work force.

Ensure that equality between women and men is promoted through the flexicurity strategy applied in the current re-designing of the labour-market. "Security" can have different meanings for men and women in general and throughout different stages of life: Security as a prerequisite for free choices, security not to be discriminated against, security to find quality employment, security that dependents are being taken care of, security that someone takes care of you, security to have equal wages and pensions and take-home pay and decent adequate income in the periods out of the labour market. Make binding gender equality objectives and practical outcomes of flexicurity, including: realising and strengthening the Barcelona childcare targets, going "beyond Barcelona" towards increasing the provision, quality, affordability and accessibility of care services including quality care for the elderly.

Pay and Pensions

We affirm that the gender pay and pension gaps are the two sides of the same coin. The gender pension gap mirrors gender inequalities accumulated throughout women's lives, which increases women's risk of poverty and social exclusion as they age.

We call for "zero tolerance" of the gender pay gap and demand urgent measures to address all the elements that maintain women's income at a lower level than men's throughout their lives including a binding European target to reduce the gender pay gap by minimum 5% per year in each Member State. This requires inter alia: valuing pay and working conditions and strengthening women's bargaining power in sectors of the economy where women are the majority (primarily care, health, education, and retail, public and social services); addressing the highly gender segregated labour market, particularly in the green and ICT sectors and making the care sector attractive to men; guaranteeing transparency in the composition of wages.

We call for an EU gender pension gap indicator, as one of the means to track and address the gender impact of reforms in pension systems that are currently underway in most EU Member States.

Social Security and Taxation Policies

We deplore that women continue to be considered as "dependents" or "second earners" in taxation and social security systems and ask that such concepts should stop being used in policy documents.

Ensure individualisation of rights with regards to social security and taxation to establish a balance between women and men with regards to social security benefits and individual taxation.

Make closing the gender pay gap a macro-economic priority. This will have a positive impact on social security systems as women's contribution to these systems will increase when women's earnings [rise] and moreover make women less reliant on social benefits to cover shortfalls in income gained through paid work.

Redefine outdated concepts in relation to household composition and family models and provide gender disaggregated data and measures to address the feminisation of poverty throughout the life cycle. The nuclear family/male-breadwinner model is less and less dominant in European societies. This change requires a redefinition of women's status within families and new ways of defining social security and taxation. This redefinition has significant implications for the way we measure poverty, for instance: both "single parents" and "cohabitants" are at increased risk of poverty and women make up the majority of both groups. This insight requires a gendered breakdown of data which is not currently common practice.

Note

1 Mayra Gómez, "Women in Economic and Social Life," n.d., p. 38. United Nations Human Rights, Office of the High Commissioner, accessed Oct. 1, 2017, www.ohchr.org.

124

A Declaration of Rights for Future Generations and a Bill of Responsibilities for Those Present
Women's Congress for Future Generations
Moab, Utah
September 2012

WOMEN'S CONGRESS
FOR
FUTURE GENERATIONS

Women's Congress for Future Generations emblem.

The authors of this document claim "authority and responsibility" to speak on the subject as those who provide "the first environment for Future Generations." Ideas in the preamble seem especially feminist: that we need "new institutions, ideas, and laws," that "humanity is capable of critical and mass change," and that one strategy for change involves "withdraw[ing] our consent" from current practices and institutions. While the UN has also issued a "Declaration on the Rights of Future Generations," this one differs in its challenges to the economic practices and political treatment of corporations, its emphasis on community in several places, and its treatment of multiple environments as "biologically diverse ecosystems with their vital integral cycles." The tone, too, is a little more humble in this one, as in its references to cautionary approaches and recognition of mistakes.

Its creators being committed to "the collaborative articulation of ideas," a working draft of the preamble and principles was written collaboratively before the Moab gathering to facilitate group discussion, and the rights and responsibilities were distilled from discussions held at the Moab Congress. The planners included "writers, dreamers, public speakers, organizers, lawyers, academics, grandmothers, mothers, sisters, filmmakers, and artists."[1] The questions they asked include the following: "What does reclaiming power as women look like? How might women organize on behalf of Future Generations in ways that transcend traditional strategies of action/resistance, and that honor, embody, and translate the sacred feminine spirit into the realm of direct political and social action?"[2] Nearly two hundred people attended the gathering.

The Second Women's Congress in 2014 in Minneapolis, Minnesota, added another document, "A Declaration of the Rights of All Waters, and a Bill of Responsibilities for Those Present." A group called Future First was established in January 2014 as the new place for the work initiated at the first Women's Congress for Future Generations. The 2015 gathering was called "Women's Congress for Future Generations and Future First: Re-Aligning the Law with Justice."

A Declaration of Rights for Future Generations and a Bill of Responsibilities for those Present

Preamble

We seek to galvanize a civil rights movement for future generations through the collaborative articulation of ideas and to influence policy.

We call for new institutions, ideas and laws that recognize the rights of nature and Future Generations, and legal guardians for nature and future generations. Many cultures, particularly indigenous cultures have practiced these principles for millennia. It is time to bring them back. Humanity is capable of critical and mass change. The time for exercising that capability is upon us.

We withdraw our consent from the institutions and practices that have put the world in peril. Therefore, we women, speaking from our authority and responsibility as the first environment for Future Generations, honor and uphold all relationships in the Earth community so that we may leave a healthy, humane and beautiful world to Future Generations. We adopt and give our consent to the following Bill of Rights for Future Generations, Present Generations Bill of Responsibilities and Guiding Principles.

Bill of Rights for Future Generations

The right of individuals, communities and future generations to a clean and healthy environment. This right cannot be bought or sold. It is unalienable.

The right of nature to exist, whole and intact, to persist and to continue the vital cycles, structures, functions and processes that sustain all human beings. Biologically diverse ecosystems with their vital integral cycles and systems intact, must be respected, and not wasted, degraded, polluted, devalued, excluded or cast aside. This right cannot be bought or sold and will require the restoration of ecosystems to their naturally dynamic and healthy equilibrium.

The right of communities to self-representation and self-determination, including the right to Free, Prior, and Informed Consent to activities that could harm present or Future Generations, nature, or the commons.

The right to return or remain in place of origin, heritage or ancestors.

The right to environmentally sustainable economies that [includes] work practice, commerce and economic system and that [does] not sacrifice ecosystems nor [put] them in jeopardy to fulfill single interest goals.

The [rights] of all communities, human and ecological, animate and inanimate are superior to the rights of corporations. Corporations are not people and do not have inherent rights. They exist because people through their states grant them limited privileges and require certain responsibilities based upon needs of the community and governments. Corporate privileges are revocable when there is a violation of their charter, if they break laws or no longer serve the general welfare, or violate the rights of individuals or communities.

The right to peace which includes the opportunity to live in community and generate meaningful relationships or [partnerships] based on respect, trust and humility with fellow members and natural systems.

The right not to be coerced into or implicated in harm.

Present Generation[']s Bill of Responsibilities

Responsibility to honor the continuity of life and Earth's systems, to hold reverence for life, respect and protect the integral limits, boundaries, relationships and natural organization of the Earth and its natural systems, rhythms and cycles.

Responsibility to act as guardians for Future Generations. Present Generation will take active responsibility to speak and openly discuss matters that affect Future Generation. Present Generations carry the responsibility to educate Present Generations, decision-makers and children.

Responsibility to uphold the right of communities human and non-human, animate and inanimate, *to self-representation and self-determination.*

Responsibility of economic practices aligned with the balance of life, and to not denigrate the environment by wasteful practices, polluting beyond its means to regenerate, and by eliminating practices that cause harm to the Present and Future Generation. Present Generations carry the responsibility to align economic, governance and social systems with the balance of life.

Responsibility to prevent harm, assess and predict impacts of social, ecological, political and technical systems on Future Generations, and to apply this knowledge to prevent harm. *Responsibility to heed early warnings* of sentinel species, and of beings and systems that face threats to dignity, survival and integrity.

Responsibility to listen to indigenous communities, and to act on and learn from their wisdom.

Responsibility to warn Future Generations in instances where our actions or decisions have already compromised the health and well-being of Future Generations.

Responsibility to uphold United Nations treaties on Human Rights, Indigenous Rights, Rights of Nature, Rights of Future Generations, and the Rights of the Child.

Responsibility to restore and regenerate ecological systems.

Responsibility to admit mistakes, recognize incomplete knowledge and to course correct upon early indication of harm.

Responsibility to replace, re-imagine, and create systems that heal rather than harm.

Responsibility to treat all beings, systems and communities with respect and to not exploit.

Guiding Principles that Inform the Covenant between Present and Future Generations

Health and well-being is a function of ecological relationships. Without whole, intact and healthy systems, the capacity for Future Generations to live full and healthy lives is diminished.

Rights held in common to the commons, that which is shared among all and that is necessary for life and community integrity. Our commons include our air, water, seeds, climate, belonging and beauty. Rights create responsibilities, [and] responsibilities for protecting rights must be located in specific bodies that can be held accountable, such as government commissions and agencies.

Governments hold two responsibilities: protect rights and care for the commons and they are derived from the rights of the governed.

Precautionary principle is key to fulfilling responsibilities. It is a key method for governments, communities or corporations to fulfill their responsibilities to protect the rights of Present and Future Generations of nature and of communities.

Economies must not destroy ecosystems. Since an economy is situated within ecosystems, economic activities are dependent on intact ecological systems. Economies must honor ecological principles, and be regenerative. For example, economic activities must not take things from the Earth faster than the Earth can regenerate them nor put things into the Earth faster than it can assimilate. Economic activity can't destroy the very basis of economy and life itself.

Ecocide is a violation of the rights of individuals, communities and nature. It is the extensive damage to, destruction of or loss of ecosystem(s) of a given territory, whether by human agency or by other causes, to such an extent that peaceful enjoyment by the inhabitants of that territory has been or will be severely diminished. This includes the large-scale destruction of the environment by war, mining, discharge of nuclear or hazardous materials or other acts. Ecocide is a crime against nature and humanity and will not stand.

Inter and intra generational justice are inseparable. Some places, and the communities that inhabit them, bear a disproportionate burden of harm and threats to common wealth and common health. True justice for Future Generations is predicated on justice within this generation. Inter and intra generational justice are inseparable.

Restorative justice views criminal offenses as an injury to the community as well as the individual and as injuries that must be repaired. Restorative justice is an effective form of justice to address current environmental destruction, to prevent it from being repeated and to restore relationships among people and between people and the natural world.

Notes

1 "About," 2012. Women's Congress for Future Generations website, www.wcffg.org.
2 Ibid.

125

All Are Alike unto God *and* What Mormon Women Know
What Women Know Collective
Online Community
September 2012 and 2007

An image that a Mormon feminist website (www.mormonfeminist.org) advocates supporters use on social media in alliance with the movement.

Here is how the authors of these documents describe themselves:

We are women who differ in age, income, race/ethnicity, and marital status. Many of us are mothers, some with exceptionally large families. Some of us are grandmothers and great-grandmothers many times over. Some are young mothers, with infants and elementary-age children. Others of us—for reasons of biology, opportunity, or choice—do not have children. Some of us have never married. Some of us are single because of divorce, widowhood, choice, or limited opportunity. A few of us have been with the same partner more than 50 years. We all work—paid or unpaid, both inside and outside our homes. We share many decades of church service among us. In fact, our LDS background is our common denominator.[1]

What they do not mention in this description, however, is that the group "included participants and former participants in *Exponent II*, Mormons for ERA, Mormon Women's Forum, and VOICE at BYU."[2] It is unclear whether this omission is a tactic chosen to establish greater common ground with Mormon readers, or a sign of fear left from the excommunication of several Mormon feminists (including Sonia Johnson, Maxine Hanks, Margaret Toscano, and Kate Kelly). Either way, the authors clearly identify as feminists and speak out for respect for the diversity of women's lives.

"What Women Know"[3] was inspired by a speech given in October 2007 by Julie B. Beck, president of the Latter-day Saints women's organization, the Relief Society. Beck claimed that "mothers who know" prioritize childrearing above all else, mother with vigilance, and "are never off duty." Further, they "desire to bear children. . . . honor sacred ordinances and covenants. . . . [and] are nurturers."[4] "What Women Know" contests most of Beck's claims. The authors insist that men must share in childrearing and housework, for example, and that women should determine whether and when they have children. The difference in the way demands upon women are portrayed in the two pieces is palpable. The source of the difference is in the document's assertion, "We have discovered that healthy relationships are equitable relationships."

"All Are Alike unto God,"[5] like "What Women Know," was a petition signable online. The authors object to, and see a connection between, the restriction of the priesthood to men and male authority in the home. The list of recommendations, however, suggests "simple changes in institutional policy" that can be implemented even without resolving the issue of women's ordination. It thus reveals the many ways gender (in)equality can infiltrate and manifest in an organization. Some of the recommended changes have become standard practice.

In "working from within" their religion, these women's documents recall some from Muslim and Jewish women in this collection.

These women were on the staff of *The Women Exponent*. Early Mormon women were part of the effort for suffrage (as well as women's education and equal pay). Women in Utah won the right to vote early, in 1870. Photo from the Utah Historical Society and AspiringMormon Women.org.

What Women Know

Fathers as well as mothers, men as well as women, are called to nurture. Nurturing is not confined to mothering or housekeeping, but is a universal attribute that communicates patience, peacefulness, and care.

Individuals and relationships flourish when we are able to share not only our strengths but also our mutual imperfections and needs. It is difficult to be compassionate with ourselves and others when we internalize injunctions to perform (e.g., "the highest-performing sister missionary," "the best homemaker in the world," "the most patient and loving mother"). Motherhood and sisterhood cannot be reduced to the performance of narrowly-prescribed tasks, but emerge from who we know ourselves to be.

Cleanliness depends upon access to resources and has more to do with priorities than purity of heart. We do not place the additional burden of "outward appearances" on our sisters who are hauling fuel and water long distances; who are struggling with poverty, isolation, or ill health; or who choose values that take precedence over orderly living quarters and polished looks.

Housework is something that grownups do and that children learn by example and instruction. Unfortunately, women and girls still perform the bulk of the world's low-paid and unpaid labor, including housework—often at the expense of their own education, leadership, creativity, health, and well-being. Men and boys who share care-work and household responsibilities make it possible for all family members to live happier, more fulfilling lives.

We reverence the responsibility to choose how, when, and whether we become parents. Many of us have adoptive and foster children and grandchildren from diverse ethnicities and cultures. We have given birth to children who range widely on every dimension—from personality, appearance, and sexual identity to physical, social, and mental ability. No matter what their differences, we care for them all.

Effective parenting is a learned behavior, and, as parents, we learn and grow with each child. Children come with their own gifts, challenges, and freedom of choice. We reject teachings that encourage women to shoulder ultimate responsibility for every aspect of child-rearing and family life, and to take on shame and guilt when things do not go according to plan.

The choice to have children does not rule out other avenues of influence and power. By valuing ourselves as lifelong achievers, apart from our roles as mothers, friends, partners, sisters, aunts, and grandmothers, we stand for creativity, public service, competence, and growth. We take joy in the collective contributions we make in the fields of government, medicine, academia, law, journalism, human services, business, art, health care advocacy, music, technology, child development, and science.

When it comes to employment, most women prefer the luxury of choice to the limitations of necessity. Women-friendly policies such as flex-time and comparable pay for women and men, access to health care, family leave for births and care-work, and affordable, high-quality childcare give all of us—single or partnered, impoverished or privileged—greater choice in how to support ourselves and our families.

We work because we want to; because we need to; and because we have no other choice. We know that "children are more important than possessions, position, and prestige." Some of us have been thrust into the position of sole economic support of our children through desertion, divorce, domestic violence, or death. Indeed, too many of us have learned that we are just one fully-employed male away from poverty.

Men are our fathers, sons, brothers, partners, lovers, and friends. Many of them also struggle within a system that equates leadership with hierarchy and domination. We distrust separate-but-equal rhetoric; anyone who is regularly reminded that she is "equally important" is probably not. Partnership is illusory without equal decision-making power.

We have discovered that healthy relationships are equitable relationships. A relationship that is balanced in terms of economic and emotional power is safer and more resilient than a relationship in which one partner holds most or all of the power. Women with active support networks and marketable skills have greater options, not only in relationships, but in life.

We claim the life-affirming powers of spirit and wisdom, and reject the glorification of violence in all its forms. We are filled with unutterable sadness by the Book of Mormon story of more than 2,000 young soldiers whose mothers teach them that faith in God will preserve them in battles in which they kill other mothers' children. This is not a success story. It is a story of the failure of human relationships and the horrors of war. In a world that has grown increasingly violent, we believe that one of the most important passages in LDS scripture is D&C 98:16: "Therefore, renounce war and proclaim peace. . . ."

Our roles as mothers, sisters, daughters, partners, and friends are just a few of the many parts we will play in the course of our lives. We may influence hundreds, perhaps thousands of lives. But we are not our roles. We are created in the image of the divine—people of worth in our own right, in our choices, in our individuality, and in our belief that the life story we are ultimately responsible for is our own.

All Are Alike unto God

As Mormon women, we call upon the First Presidency, Quorum of the Twelve Apostles, and Relief Society General Presidency of the Church of Jesus Christ of Latter-day Saints to thoughtfully consider and earnestly pray about the full integration of women into the decision-making structure of the Church and the question of women's ordination.

In the interim, we join many others in suggesting some simple changes in institutional policy that will foster a more equitable religious community:

- Encourage partnership in marriage and eliminate the idea that husbands preside over their wives.
- Create parity in the Young Women and Young Men organizations through equivalent budgets, educational programs (leadership, career, and spiritual training) and activities (sports, service, and outdoor events).

- Balance the stories and images of boys and men in church publications, talks, and other media with stories and images of girls and women.
- Invite women in Church leadership positions to speak and pray during General Conference in numbers equal to the participation of men.
- Encourage leaders to use gender-inclusive language whenever possible.
- Recognize that girls and boys, women and men are equally responsible for appropriate sexual behavior, and avoid reducing morality to sexuality, and modesty to a preoccupation with women's and girls' clothing.
- Instruct bishops to refrain from asking Church members probing questions about sexual practices and experiences.
- Call women to perform pastoral counseling, particularly for women and girls who have been sexually abused.
- Choose a General Relief Society Presidency and General Board that reflect the diversity of viewpoint and circumstance in the Church, and establish frequent meetings between the First Presidency and the General Relief Society Presidency.
- Include the Stake Relief Society President in Stake Presidency meetings, and appoint women to meet with the High Council.
- Delegate more expansive supervisory authority to the Stake and Ward Relief Society, Young Women, and Primary presidencies, including approval of personnel, programs, and activities.
- Include women among stake and ward leaders who hear evidence and offer judgment in Church disciplinary councils.
- Include the local Relief Society president in all bishopric meetings, and rotate the planning of Sacrament services among the Relief Society president and members of the bishopric.
- Examine all Church positions to determine whether they can be filled without regard to gender.
- Appoint women as presidents of Church universities and heads of administrative departments.
- Expand hiring practices in the Seminaries and Institutes of Religion and within the religion departments at Church universities to provide women the same placement, advancement, and tenure opportunities as men.
- Call young women as well as young men to serve missions at the same age and for the same length of time, and afford women the same opportunity as men to function as district leaders, zone leaders, and assistants to the president.
- Lift the prohibition on women's participation in the blessing of their children.
- Change temple marriage policies so that men and women have equal opportunity to be sealed to their second spouses after they are widowed or divorced.
- Consider further wording changes to temple ceremonies and ordinances such that both men and women make the same covenants and enjoy the same promises.
- Recognize women as witnesses for baptisms and marriage sealings.
- Restore the former institutionally-accepted practice of women giving blessings of healing and comfort.

Notes

1   What Women Know website, www.whatwomenknow.org. Page updated June 18, 2017.
2   Joanna Brooks and Rachel Steenblik, *Mormon Feminism: Essential Writings* (New York: Oxford University Press, 2015), p. 240.

3 What Women Know website, www.whatwomenknow.org.
4 Beck's 2007 speech, "Mothers Who Know," is available at www.lds.org.
5 "All Are Alike unto God." What Women Know website, www.whatwomenknow.org.

126

Declaration by Burundian Women's Rights Organisations
Conference of Burundi Development Partners
Geneva, Switzerland
October 29–30, 2012

A large segment of the population affected by the conflict is made up of women, 22% of whom are widows and 60% of whom are war victims.

At the time of this conference, over 80 percent of the population of Burundi lived in poverty, and both food insecurity and illiteracy were widespread. Women have made gains in political and workforce participation,[1] but, as this document shows, still have many basic human needs unmet. Ninety percent of the population live in rural areas. Free primary education was introduced in 2005, yet gender-based disparities in education persist.

The Declaration was written at a preconference gathering facilitated by International Alert. Although the Declaration was brought to the main conference, "there was little mention of gender issues throughout the conference and members of the delegation expressed concerns that gender would end up being side-lined if not enough funds were raised to implement" their poverty reduction policies and practices.[2] Nonetheless both the preconference and the conference gave Burundian women's organizations the opportunity to participate in an international development forum, and they were able to present some of their recommendations indirectly through working groups.

The Declaration argues that development and poverty are connected to gendered issues from land ownership and literacy to sexist ideology and transitional justice. It starts with certain daily realities faced by women in Burundi, including their trauma from war and the time they must dedicate to gathering water. From there, it suggests reeducating multiple parties, increasing women's participation in political processes, and establishing regular communication between state actors and nonstate bodies such as the groups behind this Declaration.

Declaration by Burundian Women's Rights Organisations

We,

The members of the Delegation of Burundian women's rights organisations, working for peacebuilding, reconciliation and greater economic empowerment for women;

Recognising the major steps taken by the Government of Burundi towards the country's socio-economic reconstruction;

In keeping with the spirit of the Paris Declaration, which highlights the importance of the partnership between Governments and Non-State Actors, and in respect of the role that we must play alongside the Burundian Government;

Noting the ongoing relevance of UN Security Council Resolution 1325, which calls on all member States to promote the participation of women in decision-making processes, decision-making bodies and the planning of peacebuilding programmes and development policies;

Welcoming the inclusive and participative approach adopted by the Government of Burundi in the development and implementation of the Second Poverty Reduction Strategy Paper (PRSP II);

Recognising that the commitments made by the Government in the first pillar of the PRSP II3 constitute a welcome response to the concerns and priorities outlined by Burundian women;

Reiterating our support for the Government, which by 2015 hopes to have achieved the objectives set out for the implementation of the PRSP II, and calling on it to take all measures necessary to reflect women's priorities in the budget allocated thereto;

Declare the following:

A. In relation to the rule of law, good governance and the promotion of gender equality

The inferior status of women and girls in Burundian society is created by the weight of prevailing mentalities and attitudes. Furthermore, the rights of women and girls, and the national and international instruments established to promote these rights, remain poorly understood by decision-makers and the beneficiaries of development. It should also be noted that the majority of Burundian women (61.7%) are illiterate. This limits their access to information, education and their active participation in the public sphere.

In order to reach the objectives of the PRSP II, concrete actions, achievable through a budget that is gender-sensitive, are required:

1. Support the implementation of capacity-building programmes involving the creation of community centres and community radios across the country, in an effort to stimulate community development and a gradual change in mentalities. This would allow Burundian women in general, and especially those in rural areas, to access information about their rights, civic education, transformative leadership, and conflict transformation.

B. In relation to peacebuilding

Transitional justice is one of the key aspects of peacebuilding identified in the PRSP II. A large segment of the population affected by the conflict is made up of women, 22% of whom are widows and 60% of whom are war victims. This category faces extreme vulnerability and is in need of reparation, resettlement and socio-economic reintegration. This requires the following:

2. Establish a rehabilitation and social cohesion fund to meet the specific needs of the victims of the conflict, including women and girls. Such a fund would be able to support the implementation and smooth functioning of transitional justice mechanisms.

3. Create an early warning system that is open to participation by women's organisations in order to prevent the resurgence of violence and to combat impunity for crimes.

C. In relation to the transformation of the economy, sustained growth and job creation

We note that more than 55.2% of farmers are women and that economic growth in Burundi depends on the agricultural sector. Nonetheless, women have very limited access to the means of production, such as land and credit. Furthermore, of the 80.2% of Burundians who own land, 62.5% are men and just 17.7% are women. The almost insignificant presence of women in growth sectors, such as formal trade, banking and industry, limits their opportunity for greater economic independence. As a result, 90% of Burundian women face both monetary and non-monetary poverty.

The following actions are essential:

4. Establish and finance a venture capital fund and micro-credit schemes to promote small projects initiated by women and young girls from rural communities;

5. Offer financial and technical support to a functional literacy programme based around income-generating activities (IGAs) that favour women and youths from rural communities;

6. Improve the skills of youths so they can be competitive on the labour market in the context of Burundi's integration in the East African Community. To this end, it is necessary to provide secondary schools with IT equipment and to initiate a training programme to enable young Burundians to make use of Information and Communications Technology (ICT).

D. Access to basic services and social welfare

One of the priorities for Burundian women is access to drinking water. There is a deplorable shortage of water standpipes in rural areas, with women spending two hours each day fetching water.

It is therefore necessary to:

7. Support rural development programmes that improve access to drinking water near households through the construction and responsible management of standpipes.

In order to support the efforts made by the Government and women's organisations in the fight against sexual and domestic violence, there is an urgent need to:

8. Finance the creation and running of centres that can fully meet the needs of victims of sexual and domestic violence.

E. Concerning the monitoring of the implementation of the PRSP II

Burundian women's rights organisations believe that the successful implementation of the PRSP II will require:

- gender-sensitive financing of the PRSP II;
- capacity-building in terms of the human, financial and organisational resources of all actors generally, and women and girls in particular. This is essential for development to be equitable, conflict-sensitive and gender-sensitive.

The following actions are indispensable:

9. Support the creation of a mechanism to ensure coordinated interventions and, for greater efficiency, enable this mechanism to plan, monitor and evaluate the implementation of the PRSP II;

10. Reinforce the expertise of women's organisations so that they can carry out efficient monitoring of the implementation of the PRSP II at all levels;

11. Support the creation of a "Gender" observatory to collect all gender-related data and ensure that gender issues are properly taken into account throughout the implementation of the PRSP II.

Notes

1 "Burundian Women Make Their Voices Heard," Nov. 29, 2012. International Alert website, www.international-alert.org.

2 Ibid.

127

Decidir Nos Hace Libres (Deciding Makes Us Free)
Madrid, Spain
February 2013

A poster supporting legal abortion in Spain and the "Decidir Nos Hace Libres" platform.

An astonishing number of Spanish groups—over three hundred—joined the "Deciding Makes Us Free"[1] Platform, including trade unions, women's organizations, and health associations. The Spanish government drafted legislation that would replace the more liberal abortion law passed in 2010 with one of the world's most restrictive abortion laws. *Women's* right to decide would be replaced with *professionals'* right to decide about terminating a pregnancy, and the time and conditions under which anyone had choice would be diminished. (The law would make abortion illegal except in the case of rape, or when there is grave risk to the physical and mental health of the pregnant woman; any woman wanting a termination would need two doctors to vouch for her independently.)

Document after document in this collection addresses how important it is that no one have the power to force women to become mothers, or to deny

The Decidir Nos Hace Libre logo.

women that option. Yet reproductive issues from birth control and abortion to involuntary sterilization and parental leave remain contested political matters, seemingly resolved but challenged again and again. Spain was the first EU country to try to make legal abortion more restricted (Ireland's and Malta's are the most restrictive). In the end, President Mariano Rajoy announced "that the reforms to the 2010 abortion law, sponsored by the Minister for Justice Ruis Gallardón, had been withdrawn for 'lack of consensus,'"[2] and Gallardón resigned. Even members of the Spanish governing party, the Partido Popular, were divided on the issue.

The campaign against the proposed reform was varied, widespread, and creative. Tens of thousands marched. Some women tried to register, as they would register a car, as government "property." Some sought symbolic asylum at the French embassy.[3] A celebrity video campaign explained "Who are the women who have abortions?" and "Who will be affected by the hardening of the current law announced by the Government?"

> Each character says a phrase or a word about women who have abortions: "They are teenagers. They are adults. They used contraception. Or didn't use. They are married. They are girls. They are widows. They are alone. They are accompanied. They had sex education. Or they never talked about sex with anyone, etc." An original way to show, in little more than two minutes, that there is no typical profile of the women who voluntarily interrupt their pregnancy.[4]

The declaration clearly links women's freedom and autonomy with their reproductive and sexual rights. It names the Church and political ultraconservatives as putting women's health and liberty at risk and subscribing to limiting gender stereotypes. Like many other declarations, this one links women's equal status to having a secular, democratic society.

Deciding Makes Us Free

Responding to the announcement of the People's Party of Spain regarding the reformation [amendment] of the Organic Law 2/2010—which deals with sexual health, reproduction, and the voluntary interruption of pregnancy [abortion]—women's organizations undertook the responsibility of signing the following document. WE DECLARE:

• Our total indignation at the degradation of women's sexual and reproductive rights that the reformation of this law represents.

• Our absolute refusal to limit the liberty and autonomy of women in relation to their sexuality and decision making about motherhood. If we cannot decide, we cannot be free.

• Our disagreement with the arguments presented to support the reformation, which are backwards, manipulative and ideologically subjective.

• Our revulsion at running the risk of having women's rights predetermined by the PP [which purports a conservative image of women].

Because of this
• WE DENOUNCE that the loss of sexual health and reproductive rights exposes a major risk to women's health and overall quality of life. WE AFFIRM, on the other hand, that the government is obliged to act in accordance with the European and international regulations and endorse the protection of judicial security in all matters referring to sexual and reproductive rights.

• WE DENOUNCE that "institutionalized gender violence" constrains and limits individual liberties. WE AFFIRM, on the contrary, the unbreakable will of women to live life free from violence and duress.

• WE DENOUNCE the reduction of women's liberties, which is due to the pressure from the ecclesiastical hierarchy and ultraconservative groups. WE AFFIRM, on the other hand, the need for a secular and democratic society free from religious impositions.

• WE DENOUNCE the unfortunate nineteenth century argument that emphasizes that the only right women have is not having freedom of choice. WE AFFIRM, on the contrary, our right to decide about our bodies and our lives instead of following a prototype of femininity [or a feminine stereotype] that discriminates against women.

• WE DENOUNCE the arbitrary use of the concept of "rights" and assuming that women's rights are not human rights incompatible with penal code regulation. WE AFFIRM, on the other hand, that where there are "rights" there are not "assumptions" and that exercising rights should not be punishable under the law.

• WE DENOUNCE the rejection of women's sexual and reproductive rights, resulting in setbacks in sexual education, greater access to contraception, and the availability of emergency contraception. WE AFFIRM, on the contrary, that there ARE specific rights that can be granted to women and, therefore, the National Office must provide specific measures for their sexual and reproductive health.

BECAUSE DECIDING MAKES US FREE
SIGN! GIVE YOUR SUPPORT!

Notes

1 As indicated in the preface, this is an original translation.
2 Liz Cooper, "Abortion Rights: Victory for Women in Spain," Sept. 29, 2014. *50.50: Inclusive Democracy* blog, openDemocracy, www.opendemocracy.net.
3 ANSAmed, "Abortion: Spain, 300 Associations Seek 'Asylum' in France," Jan. 23, 2015. *ANSAmed* online, www.ansamed.info.
4 CELEM, "Spain: 'Deciding Makes Us Free' Campaign for Women's Sexual and Reproductive Rights." European Women's Lobby website, accessed September 2017, www.womenlobby. org. The video is available at www.celem.org.

128

Honduran Feminist Manifesto
Center for Women's Rights
Tegucigalpa, Honduras
March 8, 2013

Center for Women's Rights logo.

From the earliest days of the coup, feminist organizations and groups from the broader women's movement met to discuss the situation in the country and to plan future actions. For the first time in a long time we managed to sit down and talk, and to discuss issues long neglected in our agenda.[1]

Like feminists in other repressive states, those in Honduras must simultaneously fight for a return to constitutional order and for a feminist agenda. Groups such as Feminists in Resistance use slogans such as "No blows against democracy or against women." Other groups opposing the militarized, oppressive regime (the Resistance) are often reluctant to back feminist proposals, including those on reproductive and sexual rights. The story of sexism within liberatory movements is an old one. Nonetheless, the coup reenergized Honduran feminists, as violence against women and the LGBT community escalated.[2] They have worked with human rights advocates to make these violations better known and to coordinate advocacy of democracy.

The document below[3] critiques the political system and notes that a small class benefits from the status quo, with international support. It asserts that women suffer in distinct ways and disproportionately as a result of internal violence, as they do from conflicts between states. The authors link their current problems with global phenomena such as colonialism and neoliberalism. They call for re-establishment of a National Institute of Women not beholden to the most conservative elements. Women suffer from the corruption of political institutions (rapes, beatings, murders, harassment, etc.), and thus are working for their reform.[4] Feminists are demanding to be heard while the government is trying to silence the feminist movement, as it does others who speak out.

As in most locales, feminism has a long history in Honduras.

Women's organizations have been in existence since the 1920s, when the Women's Cultural Society (Sociedad Cultural Feminina Hondureña) was formed and began to fight for women's rights. One leader, Visitación Padilla, actively opposed U.S. intervention in Honduras in 1924. Women also played important roles in the development of the labor movement, which became particularly active in the 1950s. According to Gladys Lanza, a trade union activist, women were extremely active in the 1954 national banana workers strike. They controlled entrances to towns and markets,

The CDM has initiated a campaign, "Femicide is the highest expression of violence against women," citing the "chilling fact that in Honduras every 16 hours a woman is murdered." Source: Redacción Central/*El Libertador*, November 17, 2015, www.web.ellibertador.hn.

closed the bars so men could not get drunk, and ran collective kitchens. . . . In the 1950s women also became active in the fight for women's suffrage, which was obtained in 1955.[5]

The Centro de Derechos de Mujeres (CDM) works to empower women and to urge a greater and wider social commitment to gender justice. It builds on the concept and practice of inclusive democracy. "A social and feminist institution, CDM is committed to defending and promoting women's human rights in Honduras through legal aid, legal education, advocacy and community-organizing. Their objective is to contribute to the construction of an inclusive democracy committed to women's human rights and to end violence against women."[6] Addressing such issues as sexual harassment and domestic violence, the organization offers a series of pamphlets entitled, "What to Do?"

Honduran Feminist Manifesto

We, feminists convened in the month of February, calling together more than 20 organizations, and joined by independent feminists from our first meeting in 2013, worried and aware of the profound crisis signaled by our reality in Honduras, raise our voices regarding the following:

1. That women in all of the corners of the country have historically carried a disproportionate amount of the burdens caused by inequality, poverty, marginalization, and exclusion at the hands of the patriarchy, which, in turn, deteriorates daily as the crisis of neoliberal capitalism grows. We protest against the fact that, in this country, the government's only response is to use violence, repression, corruption, and the militarization of minds as well as of public and private social spaces.

2. That all Honduran women, without exception, share the consequences of generalized violence that bleeds us to death and that leaves our country in a state of undeclared war. In this state, women are cannon fodder, objects of barter, use and abuse, and of buying and selling. Women are the perfect targets for the settlement of accounts between criminal men. In the end, according to this logic, we are the most vulnerable link, even though this reality is supposed to be being neutralized with legal reforms. These reforms are merely palliative and do not address our real problems.

3. We are conscious that in this undeclared war, where the excuse is the war against drugs, the country is being militarized by national and foreign armies in

order to take away our common goods and our territories, just as historically they have tried to take away our bodies and our lives.

4. That this war, that is bringing us feminists together to meet, is an indirect war, implanted as a new, renovated, and more subtle (or sometimes very grim) form of colonialism. In this form of colonialism, a handful of Honduran families receive benefits, and a "blessing" from other national and transnational powers.

5. That corruption in this country is not just corrupt police; it is also in the military barracks, in the operations of justice, in public institutions, in political institutions, in the large media outlets, and in the pulpits. The cosmetic measures that are taken to address corruption are a lie. They do not produce results. Their real objective is to create conflict, to make us confront each other and to lead us into a chaos that, in turn, justifies violence and promotes looting the less fortunate for the economic benefit of a very few.

6. That we do not raise assassins. Assassins are a product of this system and this greedy and devastating culture that is on the road toward the destruction of our lives as well as the life of our land and its resources.

7. That the politicians of this country, along with the legal governing bodies, the military and the paramilitaries, fill us with shame and indignation. The security policies established by these governing bodies do not serve us. Those governing bodies serve neither women nor the general population who dream and work for a different Honduras.

8. That we will continue to defend the Honduran secular state because, as fundamentalist groups are strengthened within the power of the State, there arise more threatening circumstances which imperil our sexual and reproductive rights as well as our rights as citizens. Such threatening circumstances work against the social and cultural advances that the feminist movement has inspired. We will continue to challenge fundamentalisms that want to set themselves up in our lives. We will not give up on our zeal to orchestrate liberty, dignity, the good life, happiness, sisterhood, and justice.

9. That we oppose the approval of the Law of Special Development Regions and the Mining Law, because they will cause an aggressive process of dispossession of common properties, a displacement of large parts of the population, and a greater presence of US military bases that dangerously bleed our national sovereignty.

10. That we are vigilant regarding the actions, the institutions, and the representatives of the State. Especially vigilant is the National Institute of Women (INAM). It and we denounce corruption and the growing utilization of women as instruments within political campaigns.

We, feminists, based in our ethical, aesthetic, and political pact, will continue to be protagonists in the political transformation of this country. We will contribute to the creation, beauty, liberty, dignity, peace, and collective justice. We will continue walking in a feminist spirit, which is no other than to take on, as humans, the maintenance of hope and happiness in the face of a culture of death and suffering. Our feminist spirit flowers in our fight with the Honduran people. Here we are and here we will be.

The revolution will be feminist or it will not be at all.
Honduras, March 8, 2013

Notes

1 JASS, "How Honduras's Military Coup Gave Birth to Feminist Resistance," July 23, 2010. *JASS Blog*, www.justassociates.org.

2 Ibid.

3 Centro de Derechos de Mujeres, "Manifesto Feminista a la Sociedad Hondureña," March 8, 2013. Centro de Derechos de Mujeres website, www.derechosdelamujer.org.

4 "Report on Women's Human Rights Violations Shows Systematic Attack on Women under Honduran Coup," Nov. 5, 2009. *MexicoBlog*, the CIP Americas program, americasmexico. blogspot.com.

5 "Gender Inequality in Honduras," last edited May 25, 2017. *Wikipedia*, www.wikipedia.org.

6 "Center for Women's Rights (CDM)." JASS website, accessed September 2017, www.justasso ciates.org.

129

Final Resolution
Middle East Women's Conference: Jin-Jiyan-Azadi (Women-Life-Freedom)
Free Democratic Women's Movement (DÖKH)
Amed (Diyarbakir), Turkey
May 31–June 2, 2013

Free Democratic Women's Movement (DÖKH) logo.

Women are very much affected by the changes taking place in the Middle East and North Africa. They are actively participating in the ongoing struggle. But with every change of government, the rights of women are further dismantled.

Kurdish women face several layers of oppression as members of a stateless nation in a largely patriarchal feudal-Islamic context, and hence struggle on multiple fronts. While the four different states over which Kurdistan is divided display strong patriarchal characteristics, which oppress all women in their respective populations, Kurdish women are further ethnically discriminated against as Kurds and are usually members of the lowest socioeconomic class.[1]

Some 250 women from twenty-six Middle Eastern and North African countries attended the first Middle East Women's Conference, which was dedicated to three Kurdish women activists murdered in Paris in January of the same year: Sakine Cansiz, Fidan Doğan, and Leyla Şaylemez. The participants see their tasks as confronting both "radical religion" and "monolithic nation-states" through a renewed feminist movement. The feminist fight explicitly against fascism dates back to the 1940s. The conference organizers describe their objectives:

- Elicit a perspective of common stance and struggle based on the comprehensive evaluation of the lived political and social developments in the region from the viewpoint of women,
- Arrive at a perspective of effective struggle against racist nation-state structures, the hegemonic capitalist system, and problematic approaches to women by religions and political Islam which are instrumentalized by tyrannical powers,
- Weave the lines of a common democratic women's struggle and enhance the existing organizational capabilities by extending women's will and struggle for freedom from local to the regional level,
- Create a common ground for discussion, acquaintance and sharing of mutual experiences in the current process of regional reshaping, with a view to take part in this newly emerging system as Middle Eastern women, with the rights, color, will and identity, as well as justice, of our own.[2]

This ambitious agenda is matched by the complex range of issues brought together in the Resolution[3] in order to understand and resist the forces oppressing women in the Middle East. The Resolution proclaims the participants' commitment to nondiscrimination on all grounds, and to ending occupation. Attention ranges from the specifics of stoning to the generalities of neoliberalism. They affirm that peace cannot happen without equality.

Turkey is in the midst of political turmoil, with an overreaching, divisive president, a huge refugee population, and a Kurdish independence movement. During the second day of the conference a statement was read speaking to police violence in Istanbul: "Taksim Square belongs to everyone. The attacks are directed against the democratic rights of the population, like the right to protest. We support

The women's conference in Diyarbakir.

all people who fight for the natural environment and the right to breathe."[4] The Free Democratic Women's Movement is an autonomous, democratic organization founded by Kurdish women. There are branches in twenty-five cities. It has established

> 3 shelters for battered women, 17 women cooperatives, 6 women associations, 3 women academies, the peace mothers' initiative in 12 cities, a women press agency called JINHA, women council organizations within the Peace and Democracy Party and Democratic Society Organization. It publishes a women's journal and runs women academic programs in 3 academic centers. In all other mixed organizations, it supports formation of women's authentic and autonomous councils. All women candidates of national and local elections are determined by DÖKH women council and activists.[5]

Final Resolution

Together we will build a network of communication between all participants in this conference. In order to strengthen our collaboration, a rotating coordination group will guarantee the communication until the second conference takes place. We will put together a group of observers who will be working in the refugee camps where women from Syria are based.

Women are very much affected by the changes taking place in the Middle East and North Africa. They are actively participating in the ongoing struggle. But with every change of government, the rights of women are further dismantled. In collaboration with the patriarchal power system, violence, attacks and rape are used as weapons to force women out of political and public space and out of decision-making bodies. Our understanding of history and our personal experiences have proven that radical religion and dogmas of monolithic nation-states—based on "laicism"—are the main dangers for women's freedom. One of the most important actions is therefore to intensify the struggle against those two models and to transform the current process of change into a women's revolution.

No ideology, religion or belief system shall be used to pressure women. The choices women make with regards to their way of life or their way of dressing shall not be allowed to lead to any form of discrimination or restrict their social and political rights or their rights to an education and work.

We declare that we will fight against rape, stoning sentences, genital mutilation, the killing of women, state or patriarchal violence against women, as well as against the neoliberal politics, which are designed to force women into poor working conditions. We also announce that we will initiate joint activities to gain support from the international community for women who are facing the death sentence. Together we will fight against torture and ill treatment in custody.

We are opposing any form of discrimination based on ethnicity, ideology, religious convictions, sexual identity and orientation. Also the rights of those without religious beliefs need to be protected. All peoples have the right to use and defend their native language. The right to education and usage of your mother tongue are integral parts of our demands.

We are against all forms of occupation and foreign intervention. We believe that national and social forces cannot be separated from the fight for women's rights and that these two struggles need to be aligned.

We denounce the mono-nationalist model and support a democratic-pluralistic state model. We fight against imperialistic politics and for the friendship of nations. The fight against fascism and any form of dictatorship is one of our basic principles.

We declare that we will continue our fight until all women who are imprisoned for political reasons will be released. These women are championing our rights, freedom and democracy on a political, legal and democratic level. We call on the governments to free these prisoners immediately.

In remembrance of all women who have lost their lives while fighting for freedom, we hereby declare that 9 January—the day when Sakine Cansiz, Fidan Doğan and Leyla Şaylemez were murdered—to be a day of action against political killings.

As women we believe that peace negotiations cannot lead to true peace building measures unless gender equality is guaranteed. This is why we invite all women to increase their struggle for more female representation in the peace negotiations. We support the peace talks that are taking place between Abdullah Öcalan—representative of the Kurdish people—and the Turkish state. We declare that we will campaign for these negotiations to have positive results, which will benefit the Kurdish population. We demand freedom for Abdullah Öcalan. We support the struggle for rights and freedom for Kurdistan, which has been colonised by four states at the beginning of the 20th century.

We view the question of liberation of the Kurdish and Palestinian people and refugees as the main issues in the Middle East. Without freeing these two peoples there can be no peace in the region. We support the fight for freedom of the Palestinian and Kurdish people and all other peoples. We refer to the right of self-determination of people.

We support the fight of the Palestinian people, the right of return and the liberation of the Palestinian territory.

We demand the release of the political prisoner Zeynep Celaliyan; the Tunisian activist Amina, who was arrested because she said, "my body belongs to me"; the Palestinian activist Ahmat Saadat and Marwan Barguti, as well as the Bahraini human rights activist Abdulhadi Al Khawaja.

We denounce political, ideological and ethnically motivated discrimination and the restrictions on women's freedom. We declare that we will fight together against the problems we face as women, no matter our political leanings and ideological convictions.

This is why we will start a campaign against state and patriarchal violence, to draw attention to the violence women face in both the public and private sphere.

We nominate the 25 November as a "day of activism" to oppose violence against women.

We will also campaign against the destruction of nature, our cultural history and the occupation through war.

This conference offers us women a platform to coordinate our joint international struggle against those in power, the dictators and the patriarchal power system. It depends on us to strengthen these foundations. We have faith in ourselves and are convinced that it will be women who will bring peace to the Middle East.

Notes

1 "Stateless Democracy: How the Kurdish Women's Movement Liberated Democracy from the State," Oct. 22, 2014. *Revolutionary Strategic Studies* blog, revolutionarystrategicstudies .wordpress.com.
2 "Call for Participation: DÖKH's 1st Middle East Women's Conference, Amed (Diyarbakir), Turkey, 31 May–2 June 2013," March 3, 2013. *Middle East Women's Conference* blog, middlee asternwomenconference.wordpress.com.
3 "Final Resolution," Middle East Women's Conference final resolution. *Peace in Kurdistan Campaign* blog, accessed September 2017, www.peaceinkurdistancampaign.com.
4 Ibid.
5 "Democratic Freewoman Movement." *Middle East Women's Conference* blog, accessed September 2017, middleeasternwomenconference.wordpress.com.

130

Manifesto
Fourth Women's Assembly
International Women's Commission of Vía Campesina
Jakarta, Indonesia
June 6–7, 2013

Via Campesina logo.

Women produce 70% of the food on earth but they are marginalized and oppressed by neoliberalism and patriarchy.[1]

"*La vía campesina*" translates as "the peasant's way." In 2013, Christophe Golay wrote,

[T]he vulnerability of peasants and other people working in rural areas, including herders, pastoralists and fisherfolk, remains of particular concern. They represent

70 per cent of the people living in extreme poverty and 80 per cent of the world hungry. Hundreds of millions of them are victims of multiple discrimination and violations of human rights and most of them are not effectively protected by the International Labour Organization (ILO) conventions because they are not engaged in the formal sector.[2]

La Vía Campesina was established in 1993 by farmers from five continents. All the attendees at the first gathering were male, and gender was not raised as an issue. Over time, however, women became more involved, and organized the Women's Commission. Gender equity also informs the structure of the organization, as each region is represented by one man and one woman, representation that also speaks to the group's commitment to democracy. As the Commission's Statement on International Women's Day puts it, "For Nettie Wiebe of the Via Campesina North America, 'the work, the perspectives, the energy, the leadership, and the presence of women in the Via Campesina have transformed and strengthened our movement.' Not only does the model of peasant and small-scale agriculture espoused by the Via Campesina International include women, but it also insists upon their rights and allows them to be fully equal as women peasants and small-scale farmers."[3]

La Vía Campesina may be most noted for introducing the notion of food sovereignty:

> La Vía Campesina introduced the idea of food sovereignty at the World Food Summit in 1996 as "the right of peoples to healthy and culturally appropriate food produced through sustainable methods and their right to define their own food and agriculture systems." The phrase "culturally appropriate" signifies that the food that is available and accessible for the population should fit with the cultural background of the people consuming it. . . . Food sovereignty differs from food security, which . . . is more centrally focused on the provision of food for all by whatever means necessary. . . . [including] production through industrial farming and corporate food companies that can produce a greater amount of food at a lower price.[4]

The Via Campesina Women's Commission Assembly took place for two days before the general Via Campesina Fourth International Conference. Among the topics that speakers addressed were unequal housework, violence against rural women, the ravages of mining and extractive industries, the informal work sector, and the connections between capitalist and patriarchal oppression.[5] They passed the Manifesto[6] and renamed themselves the International Women's Articulation, a change they intended to reflect that "[w]omen are not just a small part of, or a 'topic' in, the movement, We are the totality."[7]

The Manifesto is written "with the ethical and political imperative of protecting the right to food, defending peasant agriculture, biodiversity, our natural resources and . . . struggling to end violence in every form." It is a response to neoliberal practices, also uniquely called "entrepreneurial and colonial capitalism," systems "far from representing the views and aspirations of indigenous and peasant women" and actually in conflict with the values and ways of peasant agriculture. Neoliberal practices affect peasant agriculture in ways that include people losing their jobs and being forced to migrate and leave their lands; for women, these changes mean greater poverty and gender-based violence, and taking on a greater role as economic providers. Among the demands are equal land rights for

This poster advertised the conference where this Manifesto was drafted.

the sexes, land redistribution (with women's input into the process), protection for peasant agriculture, respect for women's historical and contemporary contributions to agriculture, food sovereignty, demilitarization and decriminalization of social movements, and a greater voice for rural women in public policy.

Manifesto

We are peasant women of the world that in the course of these 20 years of Via Campesina have worked tenaciously to build a universal, broadly based democratic, politically and socially engaged movement in the defense of peasant agriculture, food sovereignty and the struggle for the land, territories, justice, equality and the dignity of peasant women and men.

We are women from various continents and cultures, with common histories and struggles for life, our emancipation and that of our peoples, coupled with the ethical and political imperative of protecting the right to food, defending peasant agriculture, biodiversity, our natural resources and . . . struggling to end violence in every form, sharpened before this capitalist and patriarchal economical system.

"Via Campesina is a movement that recognizes the full equality and value of both men and women."

This is clearly established in the conclusions of our III International Conference in Bangalore. Via Campesina, through a structural change, guarantees that peasant women and men in the movement share responsibilities equally seeking to strengthen open and democratic processes in our international structure.

We deliver this Manifesto and its political statement, to the women of the world and to the VI Via Campesina International Conference, as input for the deliberations, for the work, the action and the struggles that we continue to develop around the world. Going forward in the unity and the action for the full incorporation of women on equal terms in the political, economic, social and cultural aspects, eliminating the discrimination that affects us in our daily lives, in agricultural areas and indigenous communities, is a task of all of us, both men and women.

In these two decades of life, struggle and hope of Via Campesina, we women have had a key role in pushing forward the political/organizational strategies for the future, fighting day by day for the defense of Mother Earth, our territories, against the looting, the devastation, the death and oppression caused by entrepreneurial and colonial capitalism.

In these two decades deep changes in the life conditions of rural women around the world were made; capitalist invasion in the fields and the appropriation of food systems by the multinational companies have led millions of peasants to incorporate themselves into paid labor, causing severe migration processes, forced displacements and land losses, precipitating many changes inside families where women must assume the greatest responsibilities for the economic support of the family. The emigration of women from the countryside is closely related to the impoverishment and the levels of violence that women and girls suffer, and this situation is more severe because of the discrimination they also suffer in the recipient countries. Despite this situation women that have migrated have [become] important to the support of their families since in many cases remittances constitute the principal income of their families.

Confronting this reality is one of the fundamental objectives of [the] struggle of women and the entire Via Campesina. Our biggest step towards ending injustice in the world is taken by breaking the poverty cycle and granting the rightful place that we peasants have to provide and guarantee sufficient and balanced food for the peoples, recognizing the central role of women in food production.

However, tragically, far from decreasing, poverty has increased in recent years in most countries. Studies of United Nations agencies and the World Bank, indicate that this situation is worsening and the gap of wealth distribution has expanded, presenting to the agricultural sectors the grim picture of increased poverty, where women continue to suffer the more dramatic effects. Ending these shameful inequalities of class, gender and ethnicity that affect millions of women worldwide and eliminating the scourge of hunger and violence is a constant struggle that governments and parliaments of the world need to take into account when legislating and approving laws searching to guarantee the comprehensive development of dignified lives of rural women and their communities in the whole world.

Access to land, a key right

"To us, the peasant and indigenous women, the land is more than a means of production. It is a space of life, culture, identity, an emotional and spiritual environment. Because of that, it's not a commodity, but a fundamental component of life, which is accessed by rights that are inalienable and only allocated through property and access systems defined by each people or nation."

Equal access to land for men and women is a fundamental component of overcoming poverty and discrimination. The assumption that fair access to land can be achieved through market mechanisms and individual property is far from representing the views and aspirations of indigenous and peasant women.

We women demand a comprehensive Agrarian Reform to redistribute land with our full participation and integration throughout the process, ensuring not only access to land, but to all the instruments and mechanisms on an equal footing, with a just appreciation of our productive and reproductive work, where rural areas guarantee a dignified and fair life for us.

To protect and enhance our ways of doing and improving agriculture, our seeds, markets, foods, using our knowledge, our science and our technology.

To encourage and generate appropriate public policies and programs for our cultures and ways of life, with resources that make viable peasant production, ensuring food sovereignty and the rights of peasant men and women with social justice.

In this way the access to land for us rests on a comprehensive Agrarian Reform that promotes the development of a management model that places at the center of the process the social function of land and the peasants' and the indigenous peoples' practices of land use and production, ensuring the human needs to food as a fundamental right for life.

Food sovereignty with Gender Justice
"To maintain dignity and the land, to keep alive and strengthened our own food production, to recover food self-sufficiency to the greatest extent possible, to protect the water, to exercise in practice Food Sovereignty, it's time for us to value, in all its dimensions, the role of women in the development of our agricultures."

Our struggle and action for Food Sovereignty has given us women the opportunity to make visible our historical participation in the development of the food systems in the world and the role we have played since the invention of agriculture, in collection and propagation of the seeds, in the protection and preservation of biodiversity and genetic resources, placing us as primary emotional, ethical and social pillars.

The dominant model "is the food processing industry and the large supermarket chains that standardize production and concentrate much of the wealth created by the sector. The resistance and the alternative to this standardization of consumption is in food diversification and other forms of relation and consumption where the producers have their work valued, and the consumer [receives] decent wages to purchase food of their choice." (Nyeleni Miriam Nobre)

Under the slogan "the food is not an issue of market, but of sovereignty," we have been defining our sovereign rights to decide and organize the distribution, exchange and consumption of food in quantity and quality according to our possibilities and needs, prioritizing solidarity, cultural, social, health and welfare factors for the benefit of our families and our rural and indigenous communities.

We can affirm that we have taken up the fight and the exercise of Food Sovereignty. In order to reach this objective we have worked hard "to summon all our knowledge, to recover our seeds, multiplying them, care for them, swap them and let them walk again, grow and multiply by our fields without hindrance or aggression." This has put us in an opposition to intellectual property, certification rules, GMOs and Pesticides.

Women's work and power within families and in movements must be recognized, including the economic and productive value of seed selection and food production by women, which requires personal and collective processes, of us and our partners. The economic contribution that our work represents to agriculture, the household economy and macro economic indicators of the nations must be appreciated.

We are convinced that the most significant and revolutionary proposal of Via Campesina has been to initiate Food Sovereignty as distinct from the food security proposals of the FAO and the Governments[;]seeking a solution to hunger through food security, understood as the availability of food and the financial capacity to purchase, leaves food in the hands of the market forces that are resulting in a global scourge of hunger, and suffering for a billion human beings in the world.

We are fighting for our rights, against neo-liberalism and patriarchy.

"Women, historical creators of knowledge in agriculture and food, continue to produce 80% of food in the poorest countries, are currently the main guardians of biodiversity and crop seeds, being the more affected by neo-liberal and sexist policies." (Nyeleni women statement)

Neoliberal adjustment policies have deepened the conditions of oppression, discrimination and increased violence against women and girls in rural areas, insecurity and instability in the work of women, and the lack of social protection, allowing for further exploitation with increased working hours becoming common, and a climate of violence undermines our dignity. Anti-capitalist and anti-patriarchal struggle go hand in hand with the struggle for gender equality and against oppression of traditional societies and sexist, individualist and consumerist modern societies, based on market dominance. Our political project is to move toward a new vision of the world, built on the principles of respect, equality, justice, solidarity, peace and freedom, waging battles to take forward the fight jointly by:

Initiating immediate actions and measures in order to eradicate violent and sexist practices and physical, verbal and psychological aggressions in our organizations, in our families and in society;

Ensuring equality of gender and no discrimination;

Fighting without compromise against all forms of violence in rural areas, against the increasing militarization and criminalization of the movements and social struggles in most countries in the world, adding to this the introduction of antiterrorist laws that are used against peasants and indigenous people, the main victims of the worst attacks and abuses committed in the name of law. We express our firm decision to struggle and mobilize for justice, equality and peace in our territories and in the world;

Building proposals and lines of action that our movement [needs] to advance the socio-political processes and technical training with teaching methods aimed at raising awareness in communities to political views and cultural barriers to advance gender equality;

Strengthening mechanisms for participation of rural women in the formulation of public policy proposals and programs both internally and externally, to ensure resources for development, both locally and globally, and the management of these, expanding access to education and technology.

Confronting patriarchy means recognizing privileges and myths of male superiority, re-socialize and sensitize leaders studying the history of women, in order to evaluate it. Until now, women have taken the lead, but it requires equal involvement to move forward from declarations to concrete practices. The organized peasant women are convinced that the future is promising, as there is no possibility of moving back in the progress and triumphs achieved, and even less so in the minds of women. Fighting for the "sovereignty of the land, the territory and the body" saying no to violence against women in all its forms.

Because of this and inspired by the debates of the women of Latin America and their process of constructing a political proposal for the construction of a base for "Popular Peasant Feminism" our Assembly has taken on the challenge to also expand this debate within the organizations of La Via Campesina at an international level.

SOWING HOPE AND STRUGGLES

FOR FEMINISM AND FOOD SOVEREIGNTY

Notes

1 Via Campesina, "Organisation," Feb. 9, 2011. Via Campesina website, www.viacampesina.org, p. 1.
2 Christophe Golay, "Legal Reflections on the Rights of Peasants and Other People Working in Rural Areas," 2013. Background paper, Geneva Academy of International Humanitarian Law and Human Rights. Office of the High Commissioner of Human Rights, United Nations, www.ohchr.org.
3 La Via Campesina, "Women's Struggle: For Food Sovereignty; Against Violence and Agribusiness," March 4, 2015. La Via Campesina website, www.viacampesina.org.
4 "Via Campesina" last edited Aug. 15, 2017. *Wikipedia*, www.wikipedia.org.
5 Nikhil Aziz, "Report from the Women's Assembly of the Via Campesina," June 10, 2013. *Grassroots International* blog, www.grassrootsonline.org.
6 La Via Campesina, "Women of Via Campesina International Manifesto," July 16, 2013. La Via Campesina website, www.viacampesina.org.
7 Aziz.

131

Women's Climate Declaration
International Women's Earth and Climate Action Network
New York, New York
September 20–23, 2013

The logo of the Women's Earth and Climate Action Network, which developed out of this summit.

We are gathering to raise our voices to advocate for an Earth-respecting cultural narrative, one of "restore, respect, replenish," and to replace the narrative of "domination, depletion and destruction" of nature.

Feminist attention to environmental issues is again central in this document, and it, too, is informed by a sense that while "natural systems upon which all living things depend are in jeopardy," governmental responses to the danger have been inadequate. The document especially speaks to the then-upcoming (December 2015) Paris summit of global national leaders on climate change (UN COP21), which led to an international climate treaty. As with other documents that seize such moments of opportunity to give voice to marginalized groups, this one contains hope that women will be major actors addressing the climate crisis, but also fears that climate policy and programs, like many others, could fail to be gender responsive, or might fail to "embrace the internationally agreed principles on gender equality, non-discrimination, human rights and women's empowerment."

The Declaration claims that "[a]mong the most severely vulnerable to climate change are women, Indigenous Peoples, and those who live in extreme poverty." But it states that "while women are among the most negatively impacted by climate disruption, we are also key to creating climate solutions." It appeals to women as environmental activists given their roles globally as voters, peacemakers, food producers, food preparers, keepers of seed banks, water collectors, consumers, recyclers, social activists, and caretakers of families. The group challenges practices from fossil fuel development to high-risk technologies, and supports reforestation and protection of the oceans. At the root of the problem are patterns of unsustainable consumption and production; addressing "crises" always threatens the most recent gains of the more vulnerable, but this document holds that this crisis *requires* gender-responsive climate-change policy and programs that in fact benefit all.

This gathering of about one hundred women leaders (by invitation only) from thirty-five countries led to the transformation of the Women's Earth and Climate Caucus (WECC), which had been established in 2011, into the Women's Earth and Climate Action Network (WECAN), which has a long-term agenda. The founding goals of WECC included the following:

- Advocate for women (especially those that are under-represented from developing countries and Indigenous communities) to be positioned at the decision-making table on conversations pertaining to climate change mitigation, adaptation and sustainability solutions. This includes forest protection and fossil fuel resistance campaigns.
- Convene women leaders from various backgrounds and areas of expertise (including grassroots organizations, policy-making agencies, as well as the business and scientific communities) to ensure interdisciplinary collaboration on policies regarding water, food, energy, climate change and community resilience.
- Provide trainings in bioregional knowledge, skills and resilient community development. This includes addressing long-term cultural and societal narratives, values, lifestyles, the status quo and designing a different, alternative path forward.
- Promote Rights of Nature policies and offer programs that foster Rights of Nature. Advocating for "Rights of Nature" as a strategic legislative tool to address climate change, promote international advocacy, and to offer educational events about Rights of Nature, community rights and new economic structures.
- Educate and support women and men in building equitable, resilient communities from encouraging local and ecological food and energy models to advocating for rights of nature and sustainable policies. Trainings include reconnecting with the nature and understanding the vital importance of living within the earth's carrying capacity.[1]

Both groups speak to the presence of what the Declaration calls a "global women's movement for climate action and sustainable solutions." Another summit was held in Washington, D.C., in 2015.

A Declaration: Women of the World Call for Urgent Action on Climate Change & Sustainability Solutions

We are the mothers and the grandmothers, sisters and daughters, nieces and aunts, who stand together to care for all generations across our professions, affiliations and national identities.

We are teachers and scientists, farmers and fishers, healers and helpers, workers and business peoples, writers and artists, decision-makers and activists, leaders and thinkers. We work in the halls of power, the halls of faith and the halls of our homes.

We are gathering to raise our voices to advocate for an Earth-respecting cultural narrative, one of "restore, respect, replenish" and to replace the narrative of "domination, depletion and destruction" of nature.

We are committed to a transition from a future of peril to a future of promise, to rally the women around the world to join together in action at all levels until the climate crisis is solved.

PREAMBLE
Climate change threatens life as we know it on our one and only home planet. Our children, our grandchildren and all future generations are in danger. Natural systems upon which all living things depend are in jeopardy.

The world's governments have committed to avoiding a global temperature rise of 2.0 C degrees. But emissions of Greenhouse Gases (GhGs) are setting us on a course toward a likely 4.0 C (7.2 degrees F) temperature rise. Scientists repeatedly warn this will cause unprecedented, large-scale disruptions of human and natural systems, food and water insecurity, and untold loss of life.

We are experiencing more frequent, extreme weather events, droughts, floods and displacement of millions around the world.

International commitments and national responses of governments have not been equivalent to the escalating urgency and local communities are bearing the brunt.

Humanity is in a crisis—a dangerous, carbon fueled, urgent climate crisis. This crisis is not only a scientific reality, but also demands the moral imperative to act. Future generations depend upon our capacity to solve climate change before it is too late.

The time is now to usher in a sustainable future.

Among the most severely vulnerable to climate change are women, Indigenous Peoples, and those who live in extreme poverty. Climate disruption, including disasters and their enduring effects, is jeopardizing livelihoods and well-being around the world.

Unsustainable consumption and production reverses development gains in the global North and the global South: Women and men of industrialized nations have a responsibility to educate themselves, examine their worldviews, commit to action, and lead by example.

No one person, organization, community, province, region, or nation is capable of solving the challenge of climate change alone. This is a time for collaboration at a global level as never before required.

We are coming together to demand a just and necessary transition from fossil fuels to renewable energy, to reduce consumption by our families and communities and to actively embrace a high quality–low footprint lifestyle.

We are coming together to embrace a new way of living with each other and the Earth.

We have a choice: between a path of continued peril and a path towards climate justice and a safe and clean energy future. We can and must join together as women to take action with common but differentiated responsibilities for achieving sustainability.

We must act now for ourselves, for future generations, for all living things on Mother Earth.

DECLARATION

We are gathering from diverse cultures and backgrounds.

We are gathering from diverse nationalities, faiths, families and professions.

We are gathering in defense of our children, grandchildren, and the generations beyond.

We are gathering in defense of the animals, plants and natural systems that are under siege.

We are gathering and uniting in solidarity to grow the global women's movement for climate action and sustainable solutions.

We are gathering to put the world on notice that women will take action at all levels to avert the trajectory of a 4 degrees C (7.2 degrees F) rise in global temperatures.

We are gathering to ensure that the sovereignty of communities to design and determine their own destinies into a thriving future is respected.

We are gathering to take action and chart a new course.

The science is clear. There is no more debate. The time for action is *NOW.*

We will answer humanity's increased vulnerability with our increased commitment.

We know that while women are among the most negatively impacted by climate disruption, we are also key to creating climate solutions.

We stand together to accelerate a Global Women's Climate Action Movement.

We, the undersigned, call on ourselves, our communities, and our governments to:

Cancel plans for future carbon developments and deforestation and bring atmospheric CO_2 concentrations back below 350 ppm;

Divest from dangerous and dirty fossil fuel developments—coal fired power plants, oil shale fracking, deep-water oil drilling and Tar Sands and rapidly phase out fossil fuel subsidies;

Put a price on carbon and implement carbon-fees and Financial Transaction Taxes;

Call for urgent action prior to 2020, in order to accelerate the phase-out of greenhouse gas pollution and to close the gap between the science and national pledges; action is needed at all levels, from the grassroots to the United Nations;

Negotiate and ratify a binding, international climate treaty of the United Nations Framework Convention on Climate Change (UNFCCC) to reduce carbon emissions;

Prioritize adaptation funding to build community resilience for those most affected by climate change in existing climate funds under the UNFCCC;

Increase available funding for adaptation and ensure that community-based groups, including women's groups, have direct access to those adaptation funds;

Invest in an energy revolution with massive and swift expansion of conservation, energy efficiency, and safe energy by

- implementing radically increased efficiency standards and
- generating 100% of all new electricity from renewables
- incentivizing conservation and reduction of consumption, especially in the Global North;

Recognize that the transition to renewable energy does not justify or require a massive increase in mega hydro dams, biofuels and major monoculture biomass plantations that cause displacement, food insecurity, human rights abuses and deforestation;

Prioritize natural forest protection and increase funding for natural reforestation;

Reject Greenhouse Gas emissions reductions schemes that come from high-risk technologies which create irreversible damage to human and planetary health including tar sands, shale gas, nuclear energy, and geo-engineering;

Embrace and implement common but differentiated responsibilities to solve the climate crisis between the global North and global South;

Implement new economic indicators and structures that encourage sustainability, Buen Vivir (living well), and abandon models for limitless economic growth;

Recognize that the planet's freshwater heritage is under threat and that abuse, over-extraction and displacement of water is a major cause of climate chaos. Essential to the recovery of climate stability is a strong plan to conserve, protect and restore the world's watersheds and rebuild the health of aquatic ecosystems;

Take action to protect one of our essential life support systems—the world's wild oceans—as a start, protect 20% of the world's oceans by 2020 and 40% by 2040 in marine preserves and sanctuaries;

Fulfill existing international agreements on women's equality and climate change by

- ensuring implementation of gender-responsive climate change policy and programs
- ensuring all climate financial mechanisms embrace the internationally agreed principles on gender equality, non-discrimination, human rights and women's empowerment;
- recognizing that gender-sensitive climate policy benefits men, women, children and the planet;

Respect and learn from the Traditional Ecological Knowledge, wisdom and experience of the world's Indigenous Peoples;

Respect and implement the Rights of Women, the Rights of Indigenous Peoples, the Rights of Nature and the Rights of Future Generations;

Take individual action on a daily basis to avert climate chaos and to implement solutions at all levels.

This is the clarion call to the women and men of the world.

Please join us by sharing this Declaration and by taking urgent action for climate change and sustainability solutions.

Note

1 "About the Women's Earth & Climate Action Network (WECAN) International." WECAN International website, accessed September 2017, www.wecaninternational.org.

132

Public Statement
Third International Intersex Forum
Valletta, Malta
November 29–December 1, 2013

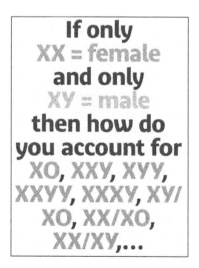

Supporters of intersex rights, as declared in this statement, share graphics like this one online to spread awareness.

[E]nd discrimination against intersex people and [. . .] ensure the right of bodily integrity, physical autonomy and self-determination.

Current research shows that as much as 2 percent of the world's population is intersex, defined by the UN Office of Human Rights as people "born with sex characteristics (including genitals, gonads and chromosome patterns) that do not fit typical binary notions of male or female bodies. Intersex is an umbrella term used to describe a wide range of natural bodily variations. In some cases, intersex traits are visible at birth while in others, they are not apparent until puberty. Some chromosomal intersex variations may not be physically apparent at all."[1] The intersex movement for understanding and equality is connected to the feminist movement because both work to recognize the inherent human dignity of all persons, no matter their sex, gender, race, class, or any other discriminating feature. The intersex movement is also a direct challenge to the concept of gender binaries because intersex people's bodies cannot be assigned to a wholly male or wholly female category. Instead, they, like many other people across the gender spectrum, fall somewhere between male and female.

Since 2011, scholars and activists have been meeting in an international forum to develop a movement that will support intersex people's legal, political, and social rights. At the third forum, held in Malta in 2013, thirty-four activists representing thirty intersex organizations from across the continents met. The first two gatherings, in Brussels in 2011 and Stockholm in 2012, resulted in shorter public statements consistent with this lengthier one. The group was originally supported mainly by ILGA-Europe, which is the European Region of the International Lesbian, Gay, Bisexual, Trans, and Intersex Association.[2] By the third conference, it was also supported by GATE (Global Action for Trans* Equality) and OII (Organization Intersex International). The gathering in Malta was significant for reaching beyond Western Europe into a country that "has now adopted onto its statutes the most comprehensive protections for intersex people that can be found anywhere in the world."[3] This legislation includes making the nonconsensual medical alteration of sexual anatomy illegal.

The Public Statement below[4] aims to make such legislation widespread in order to allow intersex people to choose where they would like to fall on the gender spectrum. Instead of having doctors or parents choose a binary gender for infants and children and treat intersexuality as a disease, the Intersex Forum advocates "self-determination" for intersex people to ensure they get to live in the body and gender with which they identify. For those who have already suffered surgery or other nonconsensual treatments, the Statement demands justice, transparency of medical records, and reparations. The Statement also demands the normalization of nonbinary gender by not including gender on birth certificates and making it easy to change one's gender on other identificatory documents. It considers other important aspects of social life, including the ability to play sports and create a family, as rights that should be protected for intersex people, too. Finally, the Statement calls on organizations and supporters at all levels to work together to make these demands a reality so intersex people can live safely, freely, and autonomously in every society across the world.

Public Statement by the Third International Intersex Forum

Preamble:

We affirm that intersex people are real, and we exist in all regions and all countries around the world. Thus, intersex people must be supported to be the drivers of social, political and legislative changes that concern them.

We reaffirm the principles of the *First* and *Second International Intersex Fora* and extend the demands aiming to end discrimination against intersex people and to ensure the right of bodily integrity, physical autonomy and self-determination.

Demands:

- To put an end to mutilating and "normalising" practices such as genital surgeries, psychological and other medical treatments through legislative and other means. Intersex people must be empowered to make their own decisions affecting [their] own bodily integrity, physical autonomy and self-determination.
- To put an end to preimplantation genetic diagnosis, pre-natal screening and treatment, and selective abortion of intersex foetuses.
- To put an end to infanticide and killings of intersex people.
- To put an end to non-consensual sterilisation of intersex people.
- To depathologise variations in sex characteristics in medical guidelines, protocols and classifications, such as the World Health Organization's *International Classification of Diseases*.
- To register intersex children as females or males, with the awareness that, like all people, they may grow up to identify with a different sex or gender.
- To ensure that sex or gender classifications are amendable through a simple administrative procedure at the request of the individuals concerned. All adults and capable minors should be able to choose between female (F), male (M), non-binary or multiple options. In the future, as with race or religion, sex or gender should not be a category on birth certificates or identification documents for anybody.
- To raise awareness around intersex issues and the rights of intersex people in society at large.
- To create and facilitate supportive, safe and celebratory environments for intersex people, their families and surroundings.
- To ensure that intersex people have the right to full information and access to their own medical records and history.
- To ensure that all professionals and healthcare providers that have a specific role to play in intersex people's well-being are adequately trained to provide quality services.
- To provide adequate acknowledgement of the suffering and injustice caused to intersex people in the past, and provide adequate redress, reparation, access to justice and the right to truth.
- To build intersex anti-discrimination legislation in addition to other grounds, and to ensure protection against intersectional discrimination.
- To ensure the provision of all human rights and citizenship rights to intersex people, including the right to marry and form a family.
- To ensure that intersex people are able to participate in competitive sport, at all levels, in accordance with their legal sex. Intersex athletes who have been humiliated or stripped of their titles should receive reparation and reinstatement.

- Recognition that medicalization and stigmatisation of intersex people result in significant trauma and mental health concerns.
- In view of ensuring the bodily integrity and well-being of intersex people, autonomous non-pathologising psycho-social and peer support be available to intersex people throughout their life (as self-required), as well as to parents and/or care providers.

In view of the above the Forum calls on:

1. International, regional and national human rights institutions to take on board, and provide visibility to intersex issues in their work.
2. National governments to address the concerns raised by the Intersex Forum and draw adequate solutions in direct collaboration with intersex representatives and organisations.
3. Media agencies and sources to ensure intersex people's right to privacy, dignity, accurate and ethical representation.
4. Funders to engage with intersex organisations and support them in the struggle for visibility, increase their capacity, the building of knowledge and the affirmation of their human rights.
5. Human rights organisations to contribute to build bridges with intersex organisations and build a basis for mutual support. This should be done in a spirit of collaboration and no-one should instrumentalise intersex issues as a means for other ends.

Notes

1 "Fact Sheet: Intersex." Free & Equal: United Nations for LGBT Equality, accessed September 2017, www.unfe.org.
2 ILGA-Europe, "What Is ILGA-Europe?" ILGA-Europe website, www.ilga-europe.org.
3 Organisation Intersex International UK, "The Third International Intersex Forum—Malta 2013." OII-UK website, accessed April 20, 2015, www.oiiuk.org.
4 ILGA-Europe, "3rd International Intersex Forum Concluded." ILGA-Europe website, accessed Dec. 2, 2013, www.ilga-europe.org.

133

Election Platform
Feminist Initiative (Feministiskt Initiativ)
Sweden
2014

Feministiskt Initiativ logo.

A broad and inclusive anti-racist feminism is the answer to the ecological, economic, social and security-related political challenges we are facing.

"Replace the racists with feminists!" In a Europe where racist, right-wing, nationalist, and anti-immigrant parties are proliferating, this is the rallying cry of Sweden's Feminist Initiative, a political party now represented in the European Parliament.

> We challenge the image of Sweden and Europe as the paradise of gender equality. . . . It is an image that is used by nationalists wanting to portray women's oppression as a foreign problem that originates in other parts of the world. Women's rights are thus hijacked in racist rhetoric that aims to close borders. At the same time, nationalist and racist parties are the ones peddling the most misogynistic policies. Culture is in focus for these parties, described as something that is nationally homogenous, and is used to construct boundaries between people.[1]

The status quo described by the Feminist Initiative includes the growing forces of fascism and consequent threats to democracy. Such threats, it says, always endanger women, whose status is already insecure:

> The value of women's work is less than that of men's, women shoulder more of the unpaid domestic, reproductive and care work, are more likely to be working part-time involuntarily, and are overrepresented among those having precarious forms of employment. Women born outside the country have the lowest salaries, more precarious forms of employment and inferior working conditions. The gender related income inequalities are entrenched since decades, despite official rhetoric of gender equality. The gap between men's and women's wages is widening and gender- and social inequality is increasing.[2]

Instead of endlessly lobbying other parties to please keep gender issues on the agenda, feminists in Sweden (and then Norway and Finland) started their own party in 2005. The Feminist Initiative wants to remedy unequal pay, end gender-based violence, and increase access to abortion, as well as rethink defense organizations, keep EU borders open, and support sustainable agriculture. "Our political platform is built on equality, human rights and freedom from all forms of discrimination. We want to reallocate resources by investing in welfare, sustainability, accessibility and human security."[3]

The Election Platform[4] is a dramatic departure from the platforms of most traditional political parties. It challenges ideas about work and welfare, and offers a very full definition of equality. It disagrees with aspects of both liberalism and socialism, all moves that show how many ideas and practices do not accommodate feminism. The party has used distinctive, innovative tactics, too, from informal

This political cartoon, by Janna Lundius for *SheRa* magazine in 2014, illustrates the bold, energetic tactics that have given the F! party its momentum.

groups called "homeparties" to electoral slogans such as "Put feminists in their place" (meaning political office) to leaving painted pink chairs on the street to symbolize seats in Parliament.[5] F! as the party is known, embodies pragmatic feminist political goals and actions. And along the way, it is changing the debate about gender and racial equality.

Election Platform

Everyone's right to travel well through life is the point of departure for Feministiskt initiativ.

Freedom from violence and discrimination, and everyone's right to welfare and culture are corner stones in a democratic society. This view on welfare opposes the idea that work is an end in itself and that people need to be disciplined into working—regardless of the content, meaning and usefulness of the work performed. Our idea of welfare aims, conversely, to enable participation and solidarity and to create the space needed to allow us to grow as human beings, through culture and meaningful interaction. The education system has an important democratic role to play in terms of fostering equality, by leveling the playing field and thus compensating for the unequal life chances created by our belonging to different social classes. Welfare should be viewed not as a safety net, but rather as a tool, with which a democratic society can be built. Human rights, ecological and social sustainability should take precedence over economic interests.

Equality is not just about economics. It also involves being able to participate and feel reflected in the cultural, political and economic spheres. Every person should have the right to make decisions about their own body. Society needs to be accessible to all, regardless of ability. Equality is also about freedom from violence, being able to love who you love, to present yourself in the way that you choose and to believe in what you want, without fear of threats and discrimination.

A broad and inclusive anti-racist feminism is the answer to the ecological, economic, social and security-related political challenges we are facing. We strive to be a force that can channel visions of a different development trajectory—in Sweden as well as globally. Bringing more feminists into the halls of power will lead to greater political responsibility with regards to the role that Sweden plays in a global order characterized by rich countries profiting on poor ones and where there is overconsumption of natural resources.

We need a new political force in parliament, which challenges existing ideologies. Discrimination, sexism and racism are not derived from class oppression and capitalism. These social ills can be enhanced by these structures, but will not necessarily disappear in a socialist society. Neither can liberalism, with its focus on individual rights, sufficiently address structural inequality. Wage discrimination exists in all wage categories. Men's violence against women, other men, and LGBTQ persons, exists in all social classes. Compared to other countries, Sweden is notable for having a larger proportion of people born outside of Europe as well as their children being excluded from the labour market and living in poverty.

Discrimination of people with different abilities is a barrier to participation and influence. Children, youth and the elderly are marginalized based on ageism where society's norms are centered on middle-age.

For all of these reasons, an ideologically independent feminist party is needed.

The political landscape 2014

Fascism and nationalism are always accompanied by limitations of the rights of women and LGBTQ persons. With growing fascism we are also seeing a strengthening of the anti-racist and feminist movement. While a political path leading to increasing inequality had been charted prior to the current government, eight years of bourgeois politics by the current four party alliance has made it clear that a different development trajectory is urgently needed. People who have steady jobs, whose health is good, who do not live with disabilities, who have stable housing and who do not risk having their Swedish identity questioned may not have noticed the changes brought about by the current politics and the entry of a fascist party into the halls of power. What we see is how all of us who do not fit into the very narrow norm are being negatively affected.

The parties in parliament have united around national goals for gender equality, but the political direction needed to reach them is lacking. The value of women's work is less than that of men's, women shoulder more of the unpaid domestic, reproductive and care work, are more likely to be working part-time involuntarily, and are overrepresented among those having precarious forms of employment. Women born outside the country have the lowest salaries, more precarious forms of employment and inferior working conditions. The gender related income inequalities are entrenched since decades, despite official rhetoric of gender equality. The gap between men's and women's wages is widening and gender- and social inequality is increasing.

We are seeing how the government is unable to prioritize for the good of the whole society and for future generations. We are seeing a welfare system being exploited by private profit motives, and an increasingly segregated school system, accelerating the development towards growing inequality. We are also seeing that society is failing children who are faring poorly, with galloping youth unemployment, and an acute unmet housing need. We are seeing inadequate maintenance of the railroads, Sweden is failing to take responsibility for reaching climate mitigation goals, and meat consumption is increasing. Moreover we are seeing maltreatment of the elderly and every second woman in today's Sweden retires into poverty. We are concerned about the limitations of the rights to support and service for people with different abilities, increasing racism and hate crimes, and women's shelters having to close down due to increasing demand in combination with shrinking resources.

Ours is a world characterized by profound injustice. People fleeing their homes are dying as they strive for a life in dignity. Among those who do make it to Sweden, many are deported, others are hiding without identification documents, facing police persecution and imprisonment in holding cells, despite having committed no crime. What we need is a view of security that is freed from nationalism. Men's violence against women is a global pandemic and the real security threat facing Sweden. LGBTQ persons are facing discrimination and hate crimes. We are raising the level of ambition in the struggle against violence and for every person's right to protection.

Sweden can afford it. As a developed democracy that has not seen war on its territory during the last two centuries and that, in international comparisons, still has a robust welfare system coupled with a relatively high degree of interpersonal trust, the necessary preconditions exist to tackle the challenges we are facing. While we are standing for elections based on our own political program, we see opportunities for cooperation with several others. Alongside feminists in other parties we intend to pursue politics that stand for gender equality and the equal rights of all persons regardless of sex, skin colour, ethnicity, sexuality, ability, gender identity, or religious belief. *Feministiskt initiativ* challenges the existing parties and through our politics we will push for a change of direction of Swedish politics in a truly feminist and anti-racist direction, with the goal of freeing Sweden and the world from discrimination.

Prioritized issues 2014
WORK AND THE ECONOMY
An accessible labour market free from discrimination and political action for wage equality. Your name, sex or appearance should play no part in whether or not you are hired for a job. All public procurement should be undertaken in a way that actively counters discrimination. Systems for imposing sanctions against discriminatory employers will be developed and opportunities for affirmative action in the labour market with regards to people with different abilities and racialized persons will be instituted. *Medlingsinstitutet* (the Swedish National Mediation Office) will be given new directives to take action for wage equality, rather than continuing the current system wherein the industrial sector sets the standard for the wage structure, with other sectors trailing behind. A gender equality fund will be instituted, with the purpose of financing necessary wage increases in sectors and vocations dominated by women.

Individualized parental leave insurance schemes. The right of the child to care and participation should be the guiding principle for all political decisions concerning children. Being a parent is an individual responsibility. Children with two parents have the right to both of them. All other public insurance schemes are individual in nature and there is no reason for the parental leave insurance scheme to deviate from this principle. Gender equality is also at stake here. Women's larger responsibility for reproductive care work and for unpaid domestic work, weakens their position in the labour market as well as their opportunities for economic independence. The right of the child to their parents and women's rights to equality in the labour market both speak to the urgent need for individualizing the parental leave insurance scheme.

Reduced working hours. Sharing jobs is beneficial for public health, gender equality as well as the climate. Increasing economic productivity has historically led to wage increases as well as a reduction in working hours. While many people lack jobs, others are working themselves into ill health and premature retirement.

Feministiskt initiativ seeks to build a society where people have regained power over their time and we will work towards a generalized reduction of working hours to a six-hour work day. In addition to allowing for recuperation, preventing stress and illness, we believe that a reduction of working hours will enable a more equal sharing of unpaid domestic work, increased social engagement, reduced unemployment, energy consumption and emissions.

Other prioritized issues concerning work and the economy are to:
- Combine the unemployment benefits, medical benefits and social security benefits into one single combined social insurance scheme with guaranteed minimum levels of remuneration. No one should fall through the net in the social security systems.
- Increase minimum pension rates and reform the pension system with the aim of making it more just and no longer punishing those who have performed unpaid care work.

WELFARE

A more robust welfare system that is not hollowed by the return of profit. We seek to nurture diversity and a range of alternative forms of operations in the organization of the welfare system. However, we see that any surplus generated should be re-invested in the enterprise or organization or be refunded to the state or municipality. Any enterprise, regardless of type, that operates within the welfare system, and which derives at least 50 percent of its budget from public finances, should transparently account for its finances. Tax funds are meant to finance education and health care and should be used for these purposes—not to increase the wealth of venture capitalists and private shareholders.

Critical pedagogy in schools and pre-schools. Every child and young person should be aware of their rights and to have somewhere to turn to, should these rights be violated. The democratic mission of the education system needs to be strengthened through a long term strategy centering on critical thinking and a deepened knowledge of human rights and non-discrimination. Schools need resources to achieve this mission, including increased human resources for school health, salary increases and professional development for teachers, as well as smaller group sizes. A safe learning environment is foundational for the school system to succeed in its mission. Critical pedagogy needs to be mainstreamed into all educational settings including pre-school, school and extra-curricular activities. Racism, sexism and discrimination against people with different abilities and LGBTQ persons needs to be addressed through knowledge and concrete politics.

The education system plays a critical role in this mission.

Other prioritized welfare issues are to:
- Ensure education equality and recall education as a responsibility of the state.
- Develop legislation for the right to full time employment and access to child care during irregular working hours
- Strengthen the right to *LSS* (the act concerning support and service for people with certain disabilities) and put a stop to cutbacks of financial and service support.

- Roll-back *RUT* (the opportunity for tax deduction when purchasing household services) since it functions as a targeted support to people who are better off at the expense of investments in the general welfare system.

SECURITY AND HUMAN RIGHTS

New legislation on sexual crime—criminalize sex without consent. The right to bodily integrity is a fundamental democratic issue. Young women and LGBTQ persons are the primary victims of sexual harassment, forced sex and sexual violence. Current legislation as well as jurisprudence places responsibility for human rights violations on the victims. This practice is unacceptable. *Feministiskt initiativ* has long since been advocating for new legislation concerning rape of which the main element is the criminalization of sex without consent. Contrary to the rulings of several courts we believe that men are capable of taking responsibility for their actions and respect their fellow human beings. While reformed legislation is needed, this is not enough. Obligatory training is needed within the justice system on central issues such as violence, sexism, racism and human rights. In addition, sex education in schools needs to be improved and youth centers and clinics need to be made more accessible.

Open borders and amnesty for refugees. Grant stay permits to all persons in Sweden who are lacking identification documents. A study needs to be commissioned in preparation for the opening of Sweden's borders. Let the resources that are currently spent on controlling people's movements, be used to strengthen people's opportunities for participation in and influence over societal affairs. Rewrite the directives to *Migrationsverket* (the Migration Board) from its current focus on assessing people's rights to live in Sweden, to supporting those who are newly immigrated with regards to issues such as labour rights, the tax system, housing, education and health care—for a more open and equal Sweden.

Other prioritized issues with regards to security and rights are to:
- Found an independent institute for human rights tasked with promoting, protecting and monitoring progress on human rights in Sweden
- Incorporate the Convention on the Rights of the Child (CRC) into Swedish law
- Remove the existing exemptions in the legislation concerning accessibility and start implementing the provisions included in the UN Convention on the Rights of Persons with Disabilities (CRPD)
- Ensure government core funding for women's shelters
- Develop a new co-habitation code that includes all types of families
- Discontinue the export of weapons
- Cut military spending and instead direct substantial resources to violence preventive work

SUSTAINABILITY AND PLANNING

Build away the lack of housing. Housing is a right that needs to be ensured politically. We want to grant state subsidies to the development of environmentally friendly, cheap public housing of several varieties to benefit different types of families and constellations. The ROT-subsidy (the opportunity to deduct 50% of labour costs when purchasing services by craftsmen in the household) should be discontinued. Instead the public housing projects from the 1950's and 60's (the so called "miljonprogrammen") should be renovated in order that accessibility and quality of social services in those areas are improved.

Taxing greenhouse gas (GHG) emissions. The climate issue is primarily one about justice. Women living in poverty in the global south are the ones hardest hit by climate change. Sweden should be pushing for the institution of a global tax on greenhouse gas emissions. The revenue should be managed by the UN and be used to support poor communities as they face natural disasters, and to support sustainable rehabilitation and rebuilding. We see a need for Sweden to take responsibility, through levying a tax on the GHG emissions emanating from food production. The aim of this tax is to reduce meat-consumption, which is responsible for a large share of the GHG emissions and which impacts the environment negatively. The proposed tax should take into account the GHG emissions resulting from the entire lifecycle of the products.

Other prioritized issues with regards to sustainable development are to:
- Invest in accessible public transport and free public transport, primarily in bigger cities
- Remove VAT on rail-road and bus travel, increasing the resources of SJ (the Swedish National Railways) and Trafikverket (the National Transport Administration) and providing those entities with new directives such that ticket prices are reduced
- Reinstate Djurskyddsmyndigheten (the Authority for Animal Protection) and raise ambitions with regards to animal rights
- Actively push for a reduction in our dependence on fossil fuels, so that Sweden will have a fully renewable energy system no later than 2040.

Out with the racists—in with the feminists!

The feminist breakthrough is happening now. A feminist politics that is based on anti-racism, human rights and sustainability is the best alternative for those of us who want to consign fascism to history once and for all. We seek to build an equal society free from discrimination—for a dignified life and participation of all.

Notes

1 Feminist Initiative, "The Tide Is High! Replace the Racists with Feminists!" Feminist Initiative website, accessed September 2017, www.feministisktinitiativ.se.
2 Feminist Initiative, "Election Platform." Feminist Initiative website, accessed September 2017, www.feministisktinitiativ.se.
3 Feminist Initiative, "The Tide Is High!"
4 Feminist Initiative, "Election Platform."
5 Dominic Hinde, "The Feminist Parties Redefining Scandinavian Politics," May 7, 2015. *50.50: Inclusive Democracy* blog, openDemocracy, www.opendemocracy.net.

134

Womanifesto *and* Women's Charter for the Sixteenth Lok Sabha Elections
India
2014

Indian feminists gather.

The participation of women in politics and decision making is influenced by the actions of political parties and the extent to which parties are committed to the promotion of women's involvement in politics.[1]

On behalf of scores of women from diverse sections of society from rural and urban areas, across the length and breadth of our country, we wish to draw public attention to the issues that have affected women in recent times. The concerns highlighted here need to become part of the mainstream political agenda in the forthcoming elections and in future government policy to ensure equality and dignity for the women of this country across social groups.

These manifestos[2] are calls from civil-society activists from multiple NGOs to political candidates, urging them to adopt a platform to improve conditions for women and girls and other marginalized groups. The authors use the opportunity of national elections to press their case, as well as ongoing outrage over brutal and highly publicized incidents of sexual violence. Sadly, women are still struggling to put issues such as violence against women on the political agenda. The Women's Charter contains a long list of grievances that remain priorities for Indian feminist activists: increasing violence against women; crimes in the name of honor; piecemeal legislation that does not fully address the various dimensions of violence against women; a conservative backlash that blames women themselves for the violence against them; laws enacted due to the protracted struggles of the women's movement rendered ineffective due to grossly inadequate finances, personnel, and infrastructure; decline in child sex ratios and gross neglect of the girl child; unrelenting rise in prices of food and other essential commodities; privatization of public services like health and education increasing family burdens; unequal property rights; increasing unemployment among women; plunder of natural resources; and the singular pursuit of high economic growth accompanied by chronic food deficiency and hunger.

These documents build on a long Indian tradition of feminist organizing, and come at a time when a national poll revealed that safety from gender-based violence ranks second among voter priorities, only behind corruption. "Over 90% of

Protests of Indian women, like this one pictured here, have drawn on the ideas in the documents featured in this chapter and help support successful campaigns of women politicians and increased turnout of women in recent Indian elections.

Indians want tackling sexual violence treated as a priority, and 75% are not satisfied with the promises made by politicians on the issue so far."[3]

What is the minimum program a government can institute to contribute to the safety, welfare, and freedom of women and girls? What does a feminist agenda for government look like? These documents point to classic solutions such as increased access to education and greater political representation, and add others like public service campaigns and ending discrimination against women on the basis of religion, caste, sexuality, age, economic status, or disability. The Women's Charter[4] contains a greater breadth of issues, but both documents break each issue down into practical actions, many based on specific grievances such as inadequate police response to sexual violence, and moral policing of women in the name of "protection." They cover life-cycle matters from the creche to old-age pensions.

The 2014 Lok Sabha (Parliament) elections—the object of the second document—included several victories for women. There were 668 female candidates and, consequently, the Sixteenth Lok Sabha will have the most women MPs (sixty-one, or 11.3 percent) since the first 1952 election. The turnout of female voters was another record: 65.63 percent of women and 67.09 percent of men voted in India's 2014 parliamentary general elections. "In 16 out of 29 states of India, more women voted than men. A total of 260.6 million women exercised their right to vote in April–May 2014 elections for India's parliament."[5] Narendra Modi of the Hindu right Bharatiya Janata Party was elected prime minister, and his party won decisively in Parliament.

Speaking of the first document below, Javati Ghosh remarks,

This can serve as the beginning to opening up a wider—and louder—debate on gender concerns in the political process generally. Women actually hold up more than half the sky in India, through myriad and often unrecognised contributions to society and the economy, but the false eulogies that seek to put them on a pedestal while denying them true equality simply will not work anymore. It is time for women themselves to demand their rights, and the democratic electoral process is a good place to start.[6]

Womanifesto

A freedom movement for women has caught fire. Citizens across the country are demanding an end to the generations-deep violence and suppression faced by hundreds of millions of Indian women and girls. Voters are calling on elected officials to commit the resources and political will for change now. This Indian Womanifesto is a 6-point plan critical to the freedom and safety, equality and flourishing of India's women and girls:

1. EDUCATE FOR EQUALITY

We will implement comprehensive, well-funded and long-term public education programmes to end the culture of gender-based discrimination and violence. These will include: SMS, radio and TV public service campaigns, accessible lesson plans for schools, modules for training teachers and to train professionals such as doctors and lawyers. To this end we will reach men, women, boys and girls in both urban and rural areas.

2. MAKE LAWS COUNT

We will ensure each government agency produces a detailed action-plan to implement laws to end violence against women, and we will fund it. We will work with state governments to provide comprehensive services to women who are victims of violent crimes, helping them to fund and set up one-stop, 24-hour crisis centres and safe shelters in each police district, and to give financial compensation. We will create and fund a comprehensive scheme to prevent sexual abuse of children, including safe childcare for children in villages and urban jhuggis, and awareness campaigns among children and parents. We will work with state governments to establish responsive and fair fast track courts for crimes of violence against women and raise the number of judges to 40 per 1,000,000 population. We will also ensure increased access to accountable legal aid, ensure that money damages are rapidly paid by the State in cases of sexual violence, and create robust witness protection programmes.

3. PUT WOMEN IN POWER

We will support the Women's Reservation Bill in the Lok Sabha, and ensure that women will be represented in all councils, committees and task forces related to policy and practice across the board. We will support the adoption of a Code of Conduct to disqualify electoral candidates who have committed offences of gender-related violence and end misogynist comments and behaviour in the Lok Sabha. We will strengthen the autonomous functioning of the National and State Commissions for Women, with experienced professionals being selected through a transparent process.

4. POLICE FOR THE PEOPLE

We will establish and enforce a comprehensive response protocol for crimes against women, and publicise it. We will work with state governments to change service rules and ensure police and prosecutorial recruitment, promotion and penalties are made on attitudes and performances based on gender. We commit to implementing police reforms and to ensure that police personnel who breach the new procedures are investigated and disciplined accordingly. We will also establish rape crisis response teams, with rural and urban pilot projects. There will be zero tolerance of moral policing by State and non-State actors.

5. SWIFT, CERTAIN JUSTICE

We will support amendments to laws that perpetuate violence and discrimination against women and sexual minorities, and those that directly/indirectly sanction discrimination against women on the basis of religion, caste, sexuality, age, economic status or disability. We will stringently implement the Pre-Conception and Pre-Natal Diagnostics Technique Act. We will support the amendment of existing laws, to remove the marital rape exemption, repeal Section 377 IPC and make sure that the rape of any person is criminal. We will change the law so that consenting couples aged 16 and 17 do not fall foul of rape laws. We will remove the impunity to perpetrators of custodial rape under the Armed Forces Special Powers Act and will appoint special commissioners in conflict areas to monitor and prosecute sexual offences. We will enact the Prevention of Atrocities (Amendment) Bill to stop crimes against dalit and adivasi women and commit to a strong law against communal violence that holds state and non-state actors accountable. We will take strong action against racial discrimination and violence against women from the North-East. We will push to enact a special law to combat honour crimes. We will take steps to bring speedy justice in long-pending cases of communal and caste massacres, as well as custodial rapes.

6. ECONOMIC FLOURISHING

We will ensure secure, dignified, remunerative employment for women. Action plans will be created to secure equal pay for equal work in all sectors; provide creches and other critical support to MNREGA workers; rights, dignity and minimum wage to all women workers in the organised and unorganised sectors. We will grant government employee status to ASHA and anganwadi workers in "voluntary" schemes where women work with informal honorariums. We will push to amend the law to address the range of unfair discrimination at work, including in the unorganised sector, and we commit to implementing the Central Government mandate under the sexual harassment law. We will bring universal, non-contributory old age pensions for women. We will create action plans to accelerate quality education for girls. We will devise a scheme to ensure that women achieve equal property rights in natal families and fair shares through marriage. Public toilets shall be set up, especially in the poorest areas, and all women will have access to regular, safe public transport. We will ensure development justice for women and respect community rights to resources. All action plans will include infrastructure, personnel, training, monitoring and evaluation, supported by central finances.

Women's Charter for the 2014 Lok Sabha Elections
TOWARDS A SECULAR GOVERNMENT THAT
PROMOTES WOMEN'S INTERESTS

Part I—Preamble

As India once again goes into another general election for the 16th Lok Sabha, we, the women of India consider it a crucial battle, coming as it does in the wake of increasing sexual violence, honour crimes, atrocities against dalit, adivasi and minority women, together with rising unemployment, hunger, and relentless price rise. The aggressive pursuit of pro-corporate neoliberal policies by the Congress-led United Progressive Alliance II (UPA II), with its huge loot of public resources on the one hand, and inadequate expenditures on economic and social development on the other, has resulted in severe miseries for the people. The Bharatiya Janata Party is seeking to utilise this rising discontent to its political advantage. Backed by a willing corporate media, it is projecting itself as the alternative. However, as we have experienced earlier, its economic policies are no different from that of the Congress. The BJP's record in the states where it is in government on socio-economic development, equity, social justice and corruption is far from satisfactory. Along with other constituents of the Sangh Parivar, it has launched an extremely vicious and communal electoral campaign in order to polarise the people and consolidate its votes. It is projecting, as its Prime Ministerial candidate, the very person who as Chief Minister oversaw the 2002 Gujarat pogrom. The BJP and its parent Rashtriya Swayamsevak Sangh ideology stands for divisiveness, disunity and a highly conservative patriarchal attitude towards women.

We, the women of India, feel that the outcome of these elections will greatly impact women's struggles for safety, equality and progress. On behalf of scores of women from diverse sections of society from rural and urban areas, across the length and breadth of our country, we wish to draw public attention to the issues that have affected women in recent times. The concerns highlighted here need to become part of the mainstream political agenda in the forthcoming elections and in future government policy to ensure equality and dignity for the women of this country across social groups.

Violence against women has increased manifold in the last five years. The crimes against women statistics reveal 68 rapes (3 rapes every hour) and 23 dowry deaths per day (almost 1 every hour). Over 2.5 lakh cases of crimes against women have been recorded every year. The conviction rates on the other hand continue to remain very low—at 24% for rape cases, 32% for dowry deaths and a paltry 21.3% for all crimes against women. This is a severe indictment of the failure of the criminal justice system to address the issue of crimes against women.

Women from Dalit and Adivasi communities face structural violence and rape from those who wield enormous social and economic power. The demand to amend the Prevention of Atrocities Act to include certain acts like parading, denying entry to public places, etc. was not acceded by the UPA II government despite repeated demands. [. . .] The untouchability still prevents them to have access in the society and all economic development activities of the nation. The attacks against women from the north east are on the rise and have raised the serious issue of racial discrimination and violence.

The spate of crimes in the name of honour continue, the most recent being a gruesome incident of gang rape of [an] adivasi girl in West Bengal and the beheading of the couple in Rohtak, Haryana. More and more such crimes are being reported from Uttar Pradesh, Rajasthan, Maharashtra, West Bengal and Tamil Nadu. The government has failed to take action against khaps and other such extra constitutional bodies who encourage such criminal acts, for fear of losing political support. There has been a singular failure on part of the UPA-II government to enact a special law to deal with crimes of honour, despite recommendations from the Planning Commission's Working Group on Women's Empowerment. The Empowered Group of Ministers that was set up to look into the matter has been quietly withdrawn.

The horrific gang rape and murder of a young medical intern in the capital city in December 2012 saw unprecedented outrage and anger flowing into the streets all over the country. It resulted in the preparation of a comprehensive report by the Verma Committee, whose recommendations constituted a big step forward in the struggle for women's rights. Unfortunately, the Criminal Law Amendment Bill, 2013 passed by the UPA Government was a piece meal legislation that does not fully address the various dimensions of violence against women. It failed to address the important issues of marital rape exception, does not acknowledge the social, economic and political power of those who rape with impunity women from the most vulnerable sections of our society, does not protect young boys and girls who are in a consensual relationship between the ages of 16 and 18 years from the criminal consequences of statutory rape; does not accept the recognition of command responsibility, excludes Armed Forces Special Powers Act from its purview and retains the death penalty.

The recent demands by young women for personal freedom and choice and an equal right to public spaces and the rising protests against crimes against women have led to a sharp conservative and patriarchal backlash that blames women themselves for the violence against them. Their clothes, their very presence in public spaces, "modern values of freedom," "free association of young women and men" are conceived as the causes of rising sexual crimes. For the Sangh Parivar, this presents an opportunity to reinforce the myth that "Hindu" women were safe and secure in a "glorious India" of the past. The attacks on young women sitting in a pub in Bangalore or questioning young couples in public spaces and opposing inter community relationships are examples of such moral policing. The Islamist fundamentalist forces are no less conservative, with attempts to impose dress codes, ban the use of mobile phones by young women and prohibit co-education. There are attempts to reinforce control over women in the name of safety through the creation of extra-constitutional bodies and "women's safety neighbourhood groups." It is unfortunate that such views are shared by a large number of people, including government officials and members of the judiciary, whose opinions influence policy.

For women, one of the biggest betrayals has been the utter failure of the UPA II to pass the 33% Women's Reservation Bill, despite its majority in the Parliament. With the exception of the Left parties, not a single opposition party seriously pressed for its passage, and some openly opposed it. Along with the failure to have more women in decision making bodies, it means that women are unable to exercise an effective role in policy making.

Several laws such as the Protection of Women from Domestic Violence, anti-dowry laws etc. have been enacted due to the protracted struggles of the women's movement [but] have been rendered ineffective due to grossly inadequate provision of finances, personnel and infrastructure. An additional allocation for the Nirbhaya Fund, of 1000 crores this year carries little meaning if the survivors and victims of sexual violence are unable to access the funds for rehabilitation and relief purposes. A similar allocation made grandiosely in the last budget has been spent only partially, and in a non transparent manner.

The 2011 Census figures have brought to the fore the further and steep decline in child sex ratios (CSR) from 927 to 914 between 2001 and 2011 and spread across 27 states and UTs. Recently released data from the 2011 Census shows a sex ratio of 919 for the age group 1–6 years, and even lower at 911 for 7–15 years, showing a gross neglect of the girl child. This is a damning indictment of the policies of the Central and some State governments and an exposure of the utter failure to implement the Pre-Conception and Pre-Natal Diagnostic Techniques Act. The government has taken virtually no action against those doctors and medical technologists who are out to make profits, without whose collusion sex selective abortion cannot occur. The PcPNDT Act continues to be violated with impunity. The monitoring and supervisory bodies are dysfunctional.

Despite a Constitution that mandates equality, women still do not have the right to property on the same terms as men. It varies according to personal and community laws that are patriarchal and deny women equal right to inherited and matrimonial property. Due to women's struggles, the government was forced to incorporate changes in the Hindu Succession Act in 2005. Even where law has given a right, conventions and practices do not recognise them. Women are still compelled to make relinquishment deeds since there is no bar on doing so.

One of the most striking failures of the UPA government has been its inability to check the unrelenting rise in prices of food and other essential commodities. For seven long years since 2007, India has lived with persistent double-digit food inflation. Prices of potatoes have doubled and even quadrupled over this 5 year period, onion prices have at an average doubled from already high levels, and the increase in rice, wheat and groundnut oil too is between 50 to 100% per cent. LPG and kerosene prices have increased enormously causing huge strains on family budgets. The privatization of public services like health, education, transport, etc. is also increasing family burdens.

The singular pursuit of high economic growth has been accompanied with chronic food deficiency and hunger. As per the 2013 UNDP Human Development Index, India ranks 94th out of 199 countries in the Global Hunger Index. According to the World Food Programme, each minute, five Indians die of hunger which makes 7000 each day and 2.5 million people dying of hunger in India every year. The NSS reports falling average consumption of calories from 2246 per capita per day in rural areas in 1972–73 to 2020 in 2009–10, and from 2107 calories to 1946 in urban areas. The high growth states of BJP-ruled Gujarat and Congress-ruled Maharashtra are amongst the worst where malnutrition is especially pronounced for children and women. Almost half of India's children under age five years (48%) are chronically malnourished while seven out of every 10 children age 6–59 months in India are anaemic. 36% of women are undernourished, with a BMI less than 18.5, indicating a high prevalence of nutritional deficiency. Over half of women (55%) are anaemic.

Food security has been severely impaired by the weakening of the PDS, the continuation of the hopelessly flawed targeted system and the exclusion of large sections of the poor in the name of their being APL. Four years after the expiry of the "100 day" promise, the National Food Security Act was finally passed by both Houses of Parliament, at a time when 70 million tonnes of foodgrains were being held as stock by the government, four times in excess of the buffer norms. Far from being universal, the Act guarantees only 5 kg of food grain per month to 67% of Indian households, 75% in rural and 50% in urban areas. This is well below the ICMR's 14 kg requirement. It does not ensure availability of sugar, pulses, oil and other essential items. This is resulting in irrational exclusions of many people.

UID-enabled Direct Benefit Transfer and Direct cash transfer schemes are being projected as an efficient means of transferring subsidies. In reality, once cash transfers are introduced, the prices of food and other commodities and services will be deregulated and left entirely to the market forces and further push up prices. The UID biometric technology is unproven and the infrastructure costs huge. There is no guarantee that DBT cash will actually be used for buying the commodity for which the cash is given. The implementation of schemes that are based on cash transfers to bank accounts like MNREGA, old age pension, widow pension, etc show that the problems of corruption and undue delays continue. At present the LPG Cash Transfer Scheme has been suspended but has caused great hardship to women while it was being implemented.

Government's own surveys show that women are increasingly out of work. Even those who are working are doing lowly paid work under highly exploitative and insecure conditions. More and more women are being pushed into unpaid domestic and outside work. Despite several cases of inhuman torture and sexual exploitation there is yet no law to protect domestic workers. Mechanization has led to a huge decline in availability of agricultural workers. Many poor women are being pushed into unsafe and exploitative migration and trafficking.

The Unorganised Sector Workers Act of 2008 cruelly excludes most poor women workers by limiting beneficiaries to the BPL category. There is a need for a single window system which caters to workers from all occupations and industries especially when women are simultaneously in multiple occupations.

The MNREGA has been an important instrument for addressing rural unemployment and distress. It witnessed a high participation of women which rose from 41% in 2006–07 to 52% in 2012–13. But the average days of work per household has fallen from the 54 days per annum peak in 2009–10 to 45 days in 2012–13. The fall is entirely due to the cut in fund allocation by the centre, which has not kept pace with the wages in the programme. High productivity norms, difficult working conditions, long delays in payment and the unequal wages received by women have continued thereby sabotaging a good Act.

The agrarian distress is unabated. It is reflected in the high and continuing rate of farmers' suicides and distress migration. As per NCRB data, a total of 2,70,940 Indian farmers have committed suicide; the yearly average between 2001 and 2011 is 16,743, or 46 suicides a day. Women are still not recognised or registered as farmers, they are left out of the credit ratings, and excluded from the debt waiver schemes. The recommendations made by the Swaminathan Commission, which included specific measures for women, have been ignored.

Public expenditure for the provision of universal, affordable or free services like food security, health, water & sanitation, child care, etc. has sharply declined even as taxes foregone on account of concessions to the corporate sector and other elites have remained as high as 6–8% percent of GDP. As per the CAG reports, lakhs of crores of rupees have been lost on account of corruption in high places which could have been used for development of the common people.

The open plunder of natural resources by corporates with government facilitation has had adverse implications for women, who have the primary responsibility to collect fodder, fuel, water, minor forest produce, etc. The encroachment and annexation of natural resources and the widespread displacement on account of land acquisition and large projects has meant that these resources have become less accessible and more expensive, increasing women's work and drudgery. The absence of adequate rehabilitation and resettlement takes a heavy toll off women.

The Government has been swift to safeguard corporate interests with concessionary loans, but has denied women's self help groups lower rates of interest as part of priority sector lending. The Micro Finance Institutions (Development And Regulation) Bill, 2011 came in the wake of demands to effectively regulate and control the highly unfair and exploitative practices of microfinance lenders which drove some borrowers to suicide. However, UPA's draft Bill was totally inadequate and pro-MFI with no interest caps or ban on for-profit MFIs and was rightly rejected by the Parliamentary Standing Committee.

Secularism has been under siege. The communal forces, led by the Sangh Parivar, have been unleashing communal violence against minorities in states like Uttar Pradesh. Caste and community identity are being used to polarise society. But the government has refused to intervene and take stringent action to safeguard those affected by communal violence. Regional and ethnic chauvinism is raising its ugly head in many states. It is a matter of deep concern that the mainstream political parties are not just unwilling to stand up boldly against divisive hate politics but are actually using it for narrow political gain.

Successive governments have failed to address the needs of minorities. The UPA government failed to act in a substantive manner on the plight of the Muslim minorities highlighted by the Sachar Committee report. It has ignored the claims of Dalit Christians to reservation under the SC category, as recommended by the Justice Ranganath Misra committee. It has betrayed the cause of social justice by hastily passing a Bill in the Rajya Sabha that keeps 47 Institutes of excellence outside the purview of reservations for SCs and STs.

It is time for women to stand up to protect the secular pluralist heritage of our country, push for alternative policies that will effectively deal with the agrarian crisis and the recession, for a government that is conscious of the need to protect the rights of the economically and socially oppressed sections and will work for their upliftment, a Government that will recognize the rights of women and will work towards gender equality and justice.

On behalf of the undersigned women's organisations, we call upon all political parties national, and regional, to include our following demands in their election manifesto for the 16th Lok Sabha elections. We will conduct a widespread campaign amongst the electorate on the basis of this Women's Charter.

Part II: Charter of Demands
Political Reservation
- Enact the 33% Women's Reservation Bill to reserve one-third seats in Parliament and State Assemblies for women.
- Legislation for at least 50% reservation for women in all decision-making bodies;
- Enact the Constitution (One Hundred and Tenth Amendment) Bill, 2009 after necessary amendments to enhance reservation for women from one-third to one-half of the total seats in the Panchayats and Municipalities; provide similar reservation for the offices of Chairpersons.

Food Security and Price Rise:
- Remove the cap on "Priority" households in the National Food Security Act and universalise the PDS to exclude only tax payers. Ensure a minimum entitlement of 35kgs or 7 kgs per person, whichever is higher, of foodgrains per household. Special drives to ensure ration cards to all, especially single women, unorganized sector workers, disabled, migrants and street dwellers.
- Strengthen the PDS and provide pulses, sugar, tea, edible oil, salt, milk and vegetables at controlled prices through ration shops. Take strict action against hoarders and blackmarketeers under the Essential Commodities Act. Ban futures trading in essential commodities.
- Remove the cap on number of domestic LPG cylinders available at administered prices. Ensure a minimum quota of at least 5 litres of kerosene per person at controlled prices through the PDS shops. Provide subsidized LPG for cooking Mid Day Meals and ICDS Centres.

- Reduce the prices of petrol and diesel by cutting excise and customs duties.
- No to cash transfers and linkage of Aadhar for availing of essential commodities especially food and fuel through the PDS.
- Universalise the ICDS. Ensure hot cooked meals in ICDS, MDMS and other nutrition programs.
- Control the price of all essential drugs.
- Stop the export and auction of foodstocks and instead provide them to the states.
- Extend procurement of all food crops at remunerative prices in all areas of the country.

Employment and Wages:
- Remove the 100 workdays cap in the MNREGS. Revise work norms and ensure payment of minimum wages to women. Ensure implementation of crèches at worksites.
- Enact an Urban Employment Guarantee Act.
- Regularise ICDS, ASHA, Mid Day Meal and other scheme workers with minimum wages pensions and social security benefits.
- Implement the Unorganised Workers Social Security Act of 2008 by universalizing its provisions for all workers irrespective of all occupations and industry. Provide adequate budgetary support to implement various social security schemes in a single window system.
- Implement a special protective legislation for agricultural workers for minimum and equal wages, maternity benefit and pensions and other social security for them.
- Recognise working women in the organized and unorganized sector as independent economic units.
- Ensure equal and index linked minimum wages of at least Rs 10000 per month.
- Implement a universal and mandatory child care scheme. Set up Committees and ensure implementation of the Sexual Harassment of Women at the Workplace (Prevention, Prohibition and Redressal) Act. Amend the Act to expand the definition of workplaces to including homes and farms and remove the penalty clause.
- Ban FDI and control the entry of big business houses in retail trade.
- Include women's Self Help Groups as part of priority . . . credit sector and provide them with loans at 4%. Ensure adequate training and marketing support for their products. Pass a law to stringently regulate MFIs.

Social Development:
- A minimum universal non-contributory publicly funded pension [of] Rs 2000 per month for all women above the age of 55 years, all widows and all disabled women irrespective of age.
- Increase public spending on Education to 6% and on Health to 5% of the GDP.
- Regulate and bring social control on private educational and health services. Promote public funding of education and health systems.
- Universal and free public health care for all. Control prices of essential drugs and provide them free of cost in public facilities.
- Regulate and monitor clinical trials.
- Enact a Central law to provide free and compulsory education in the age group 0–18 years, with special emphasis on the girl child.

- Universalise ICDS and extend it to all habitations. Increase expenditure on supplementary nutrition schemes including Mid Day Meals.
- Universalise all health, welfare and educational schemes without any conditionalities. Remove the two child norm. Give priority to single women, SC, ST, minority women headed households and disabled women.
- Implement special packages for the rehabilitation of women and children in households affected by suicides of farmers, handloom workers, agricultural workers, etc.
- Implement the recommendations of the Sachar Committee and the Rangnath Mishra Committee for reservations for Muslims in educational institutions and jobs.

Land, Water, Natural Resources
- Distribute surplus ceiling land to landless households with joint pattas to women.
- Ensure land for house sites for all homeless, with priority to single women in rural and urban areas in the joint names of women and men.
- Prevent the diversion, acquisition, encroachment and takeover of common lands like pastures, community forests, scrublands, etc and ensure user rights for women over them, especially for those from SC, ST, migrant and nomadic communities.
- Treat women as Project Affected Persons in all relief and rehabilitation measures, minimize displacement, no displacement without prior informed consent; and ensure alternative means of employment and livelihood for women displaced due to infrastructure, urbanization and industrial projects.
- Stop privatization of water resources and drinking water schemes in rural and urban areas. Give priority to water for agricultural and drinking water purposes.

Resource Mobilisation and Budgetary Allocations:
- Increase substantially public expenditure on economic and social development programmes for the people, maintain integrity and ensure full utilization of allocated resources, stop budget cuts on pro-people works.
- Provide central budgetary support for the effective implementation of the PWDV Act, anti-Sexual Harassment Act, Prevention of Atrocities Act and for schemes to support survivors of crimes against women, particularly sexual assault, acid attack, honour crimes and sectarian violence.
- Discard privatization and the failed PPP model which subsidizes the corporate sector, worsens service delivery and raises costs/user charges/fees for the consumers.
- Stop proliferation of liquor vends as a source of revenue mobilization.
- Ensure that all Ministries and Departments effectively allocate at least one third allocations for women. Ensure a minimum of 30% allocations for women within schemes for SC, ST, Denotified Tribes, Minorities and other socially deprived groups. Ensure that allocations for sub-plans for dalits and tribals are not diverted.
- Stop giving tax concessions to the rich and corporate sector. Raise taxes on the wealthy and the corporate sector and unearth black money in order to increase the expenditures on public infrastructure, health, education, welfare schemes, etc.

- Make available data of beneficiaries of different welfare schemes disaggregated on the basis of sex, caste and community groups in order to enable a proper assessment of their outcomes on different social groups of women.

Protection of Civil Rights
- Enact a comprehensive law against communal violence. Ensure speedy justice and adequate compensation to the victims of communal violence, particularly rape survivors and children.
- Amend the SC and ST (Prevention of Atrocities) Act to include obstructing the use of common resources such as wells, ground, social and economic boycotting, prevention of participation in elections, etc. Fill up the backlog in all SC, ST and other reserved posts in a time bound manner. Give reservations to Dalit Muslims and Dalit Christians.
- Provide for the reparation and compensation of families of wrongfully confined minority and tribal youth.
- Take stringent action against army, para-military and security personnel indulging in human rights violations in disturbed areas. Repeal the AFSPA.
- Enact an anti-racist law to ensure greater security of people from the North-East.

Violence against Women and Legal Issues:
- Implement all the recommendations of the Justice Verma Committee Report. Include sexual violence against women from SC, ST and minority communities as aggravated sexual assault. Make marital rape an offence. Safeguard S498A of the Indian Penal Code.
- Fast track all cases of violence against women within a legally bound period of time.
- Stringent implementation of the PcPNDT Act. Safeguard women's right to safe abortion.
- Protect young couples in a relationship and their right to choose a partner. Enact a comprehensive stand alone law to deal with crimes in the name of "Honour" and khap panchayats.
- Amend the criminal law so that the statutory rape provision does not apply in consensual sexual relations between young couples when the girl is 16 years or more and the age difference is 3 years or less.
- Enact a comprehensive law to prevent trafficking of women and children for labour and sexual exploitation. Oppose the proposal to delink prostitution and trafficking.
- Enact a law for equal rights in marital and inherited property for all women. Strengthen laws relating to maintenance for women and children. All family laws should give equal rights to women in marital and inherited property.
- Ensure equal rights and equal laws for women from all communities. Make registration of marriages compulsory.
- Introduce and enforce a stringent liquor policy to control production and sale of liquor. Delegate powers to women gram sabhas and ward sabhas to permit opening liquor vends in the area.
- Re-orient the educational syllabus to inculcate values of gender equality and conduct multi-level campaigns against regressive anti-women practices such as dowry, [witch] hunting, etc.

- Repeal Section 377 of the Indian Penal Code (IPC) and decriminalise same sex adult consensual relationships.
- Enact a comprehensive law against superstitions and irrational practices.

Others
- Institute and implement a Code of Conduct for the prevention of anti-women derogatory statements by persons in public office.
- Draft and implement a gender-sensitive Media Code.
- Strengthen the autonomous functioning of the National and State Commissions for Women, the selection and composition of the members must be made through an institutionalized, independent and transparent process and Members should be not be political appointees but should be experienced professionals and women's rights activists.
- Promote and financially support Women's Studies Centres in all Universities.
- Ensure minimum 10% of Plan fund for gender budget. Gender auditing should be strengthened.

Notes

1 The Women in Public Service Project, "Women Leading Public Service and Political Participation in South Asia: New and Emerging Developments," 2014, p. 43. Report, Woodrow Wilson Center for Scholars, www.womeninpublicservice.wilsoncenter.org.
2 "The India Womanifesto." AVAAZ, accessed September 2017, www.avaaz.org.
3 Preethi Nallu, "Gender Issues Could Be a Game Changer in India's Elections." *Time*, April 14, 2014, www.time.com.
4 "Women's Charter for the 16th Lok Sabha Elections—2014." *Economic & Political Weekly*, March 15, 2014, www.epw.in.
5 "Women's Political Participation in India." *Wikipedia*, accessed September 2017, www.wikipedia.org.
6 Jayati Ghosh, "A Manifesto for Women." *Frontline*, April 4, 2014, p. 3, www.frontline.in.

135

Manifesto
Estonian Sixth Women's Congress
Estonian Women's Union
Tallinn, Estonia
March 7, 2014

Estonian Women's Union logo.

We will not accept that Estonia still holds on to outdated gender stereotypes and beliefs, since this is a major cause for many important problems concerning women and the entire society that have, up to now, remained unsolved.

The Estonian Women's Union (ENL) existed from 1920 to 1940, and was reestablished in May 1989. The Manifesto was written at the Sixth Women's Congress in Tallinn. Its simultaneous support for the independence of a peaceful, democratic Estonia and greater sexual equality is reminiscent of many groups represented in this collection, both older and newer. This group's ethical principles include commitments to participatory democracy, respect for diversity, sustainability, transparency, civil courage, and popular education.[1]

Throughout its history, Estonia has experienced being ruled by Denmark, Sweden, and, most recently, Russia. Estonia redeclared its independence in 1991, and joined the EU in 2004. "Traditionally, Estonia has been seen as an area of rivalry between western and eastern Europe on many levels."[2] Women's literacy is nearly universal there today, and the state asserts that "[w]omen's rights, gender equality, and the empowerment of women are some of the main priorities of Estonia's foreign policy."

Nonetheless, a report on gender equality in Estonia begins by noting a "low awareness of gender equality issues and a lack of interest among different stakeholders (eg employers, employees, legal professionals, civil servants)."[3] Other problems discussed include a lack of services for (and prejudices against) victims of sexual violence (6), inadequate spending for gender equality (7, 10), higher poverty and lower employment rates for women than for men (14), and an estimation that "33% of Estonian women have experienced physical and/or sexual violence since the age of 15" (19).

The Manifesto[4] begins with the existing state commitment to equality and recognition that women and men are equally responsible for the welfare of the republic. However, women, and whatever is associated with them, is devalued, it continues. It takes decisive stances on more active fathering and equal pay, and connects abuse and trafficking of women to their economic vulnerability and second-class status. It asks for both equal rights and recognition of situational differences. Its demands focus especially on the role of the state in furthering gender equality.

Manifesto of Estonian VI Women's Congress

This Manifesto is based on the principle of equality of men and women and the prohibition of gender discrimination, as established by international law, European Union treaties and the constitution of the Republic of Estonia. It recognizes the equal responsibility of men and women for the current situation in our society and [for the] future of the Estonian nation. It also is inspired by the historical experience of [the] Estonian women's movement, witnessing that gender inequality causes demographic, social and economic problems and critically assesses the activity of the Estonian state in promoting the gender equality. For all of these reasons, the *Estonian VI Women Congress has adopted the following declaration:*

> We find that a woman, her thoughts, words, actions, knowledge, work and creation, is less valued in Estonian society than those of a man. The biggest gender pay gap in Europe as well as the current situation in politics and [the] economy, where[in] mainly men hold the leading positions, demonstrates this.

We wish that Estonian economic and financial policy would consider primarily the unity of the people and the interests of different groups in society. The resources of the state ought to be divided fairly, taking into account the equal rights of men and women as well as [the] different needs of men and women due to their different situations.

We want the many jobs that are mainly held by women (such as museum workers, teachers, librarians, social workers etc.) to be valued and fairly rewarded and that the birth of a child would not hinder a woman's career opportunities.

We are of the opinion that both parents should participate equally in raising children, [and that] this [practice] should be supported by valuing fatherhood and the respective laws. The right of the child to receive monthly alimony from the parent living apart should be guaranteed.

We decisively denounce domestic abuse, human trafficking as well as [the] humiliation of woman's human dignity and [the] violation of [her] bodily integrity. We see the reason for all this [abuse] in women's economic vulnerability and lower status in society.

We find that the Estonian Gender Equality Act, which has been effective for ten years already, and international promises, have been ignored in Estonia both due to ignorance as well as due to lack of clear political will. Unlike other European democratic states, Estonia has not set national goals for decreasing gender inequality nor has it defined specific methods to encourage equality.

We will not accept that Estonia still holds on to outdated gender stereotypes and beliefs, since this is a major cause for many important problems concerning women and the entire society that have, up to now, remained unsolved.

Estonian VI Women's Congress demands:

1. The Parliament election law must include regulations to ensure equal opportunities to be elected for both men and women and these regulations [must] be actively enforced. It is necessary to establish [the "zipper system"] electoral lists for all parties, in which women and men candidates are presented alternatively on the list. This new requirement must be established by the 2015 parliament elections;

2. In all public administration collegial bodies, including state-owned companies, and foundations, the governing bodies must include both men and women, with no less than 40% women; furthermore, gender balance must also be guaranteed while forming Governments;

3. In order to fully apply the Gender Equality Act, the Government together with civil society organisations must prepare a strategic plan for gender equality based on expert knowledge and taking into account the best practices of other countries; the plan must set specific aims and means to decrease gender inequality in all key areas of social life.

4. To achieve equal pay for equal work done by men and women, the state must immediately establish a state-wide supervision of wage conditions and wage agreements, create transparency in pay systems and prosecute employers who violate the equal pay principle for men and women.

5. To counterbalance parents' work and family life responsibilities, and to improve women's situation in the labour market, parental leave, and parental benefits conditions must be made more flexible, and supportive of fatherhood. Fathers' individual right to receive parental benefit covered with parental leave must be legitimized.

The social and political inequality and poverty of women are passed on to our children, diminishing their well-being and development possibilities. Our daughters and sons are the future of Estonia and deserve better.

We turn to all women and progressive men, asking them to show support for the aspirations expressed in this Manifesto.

Notes

1 "Eetikakoodeks." Eesti Naisliit website, accessed September 2017, www.naisliit.ee. Code of Ethics adopted April 7, 2002.

2 "Culture of Estonia." *Wikipedia*, accessed September 2017, www.wikipedia.org.

3 "Women's Rights, Women Empowerment, and Gender Equality," Statement by the Ministry of Foreign Affairs, Estonia, May 6, 2014. Republic of Estonia Ministry of Foreign Affairs website, www.vm.ee; "Estonia National Review," UN Women report, p. 6, *UN Women*, accessed September 2017, www2.unwomen.org. Subsequent page references are to this text.

4 I put together and tweaked two available translations: "Manifesto of Estonian VI Women's Congress," Naised website, www.naised.net; and "Kongressi Manifesto," March 24, 2014. Eesti Naisliit website, www.naisliit.ee.

136

Manifesto
Indigenous Women Against the Sex Industry
Canada
March 28, 2014

Indigenous Women Against the Sex Industry logo.

The sex industry has no interest in challenging patriarchy, racism, colonialism, or capitalism. We need to remember that men, both as individuals and collectively, control and benefit from a billion dollar sex industry that negatively impacts all women and girls.[1]

Indigenous Women Against the Sex Industry is a group of Indigenous women, some of whom were formerly prostituted, who work for the prevention and abolition of prostitution. They understand the sex industry as created by the intersecting systems of racism, sexism, and colonialism; consequently, it does disproportionate damage to Aboriginal girls and women, and to women of color. The group works to end all three systems of domination, and its Manifesto clearly explains the overlapping relationships of each to the sex trade. Further, it "recognizes the leadership, knowledge, and wisdom of Indigenous women and girls" as resources in the "fight for our lives, our lands and traditions, and our right to live free from male violence."

The members of Indigenous Women Against the Sex Industry (IWASI) describe themselves as radical feminists from many nations. They emphasize the numerous forms and impacts of male violence against women. Rather than stopping with legal change, they want "true social change that improves the lives of all women and girls and recognizes our rights to safety, security, and freedom." Their challenge to "harm reduction" strategies in favor of real safety is especially noteworthy, as is their refutation of many myths about prostitution. They call for a new vision of male sexuality that recognizes women's humanity and sexual autonomy.

The Native Women's Association of Canada takes a position similar to that of IWASI. The association states, for example, "Aboriginal women are grossly overrepresented in prostitution and among the women who have been murdered in prostitution. It is not helpful to divide women in prostitution into those who 'choose' and those who are 'forced' into prostitution. In most cases, Aboriginal women are recruited for prostitution as girls and/or feel they have no other option due to poverty and abuse. It is the sex industry that encourages women to view prostitution as their chosen identity."[2] Meghan Murphy suggests that in Vancouver, "70 per cent of prostitutes are First Nations women. Considering that First Nations people make up about 2 per cent of the total population in Vancouver and 10% of the population on the Downtown Eastside, this number is significant."[3] Murphy also explains how the feminist abolitionist approach to prostitution is wrongly characterized by progressives and leftists as moralistic.

December 6, 2014, brought about new legislation in Canada regarding prostitution, and Aboriginal women's groups were among its supporters. As recommended in the Manifesto below, the legislation decriminalizes most prostituted women, and criminalizes johns, pimps, and advertising for sexual services.

Manifesto

Indigenous Women Against the Sex Industry (IWASI) is an unfunded group of radical feminists from many nations committed to ending patriarchy, colonialism, racism, and capitalism.

IWASI sees prostitution and pornography as forms of male violence against women. The misogyny inherent in these systems of women's oppression is compounded by colonialism and racism, disproportionately harming Indigenous women and girls and our sisters of colour.

We are committed to abolishing prostitution and pornography, using public education and advocating for the decriminalization of prostituted women and girls, and the criminalization of johns, pimps, and sex industrialists. We are committed to not only advocating for legal change, but for true social change that improves the lives of all women and girls and recognizes our rights to safety, security, and freedom.

Indigenous Women Against the Sex Industry (IWASI) is a group of Indigenous feminists that stand with women and girls affected by prostitution and pornography. We stand firm in our opposition to the sex industry: johns, pimps, and sex industrialists. IWASI works toward freedom and equality for all women and girls.

INDIGENOUS WOMEN AGAINST THE SEX INDUSTRY RECOGNIZES:

- The system of prostitution as a continued source of colonialism that has grave, if not lethal, consequences for Indigenous women and girls worldwide. The institution of prostitution is fundamentally opposed to our traditional ways of life where women and girls were valued, loved, and treated with the respect we deserve.
- Prostitution as a colonial system, an extension of the reserve system, the residential school system, and other colonial institutions that target Indigenous women and girls.
- The system of prostitution as an inherently patriarchal system that exists on a continuum of male violence that includes rape, incest, wife battery, emotional, sexual and physical assault. The system of prostitution requires the existence of inequality between women and men in order to exist. It relies and thrives on the unchallenged male demand for sexual access to the bodies of women and girls.
- The sex industry relies on capitalism and greed to justify its existence. We have seen and continue to see our homelands stolen from us and bought and sold to the highest bidder as "product." We have seen and continue to see this colonial process applied to not only our precious homelands, but to the very bodies of our sisters and little sisters.
- The sex industry treats all women and girls as hated objects, and that hatred is amplified by racism. Overt racism is not only acceptable, but is sanctioned and encouraged by the sex industry. This industry, hierarchal in nature, places Indigenous women and girls and our sisters of colour on the bottom rungs, where we are subjected to the worst and most degrading forms of male violence.

INDIGENOUS WOMEN AGAINST THE SEX INDUSTRY STANDS AGAINST:

- The total decriminalization, legalization, or normalization of prostitution.
- The deceitful assumption that prostitution has always existed and that it will exist forever. We know from our Elders and Ancestors that there were times and places among Indigenous peoples where the sexual exploitation of women and girls did not exist.
- The misguided rhetoric of harm reduction. We assert our right to be safe, not safer. We assert our right to live full and meaningful lives and we reject the limitations placed on us by the harm reduction industry.
- Divisions among women created by the patriarchy in attempts to subdue the global women's liberation movement.
- The colonial, patriarchal, capitalist, and racist institution of prostitution in all forms and we pledge to fight against this system for the benefit of women and girls everywhere and for our generations to come.

INDIGENOUS WOMEN AGAINST THE SEX INDUSTRY STANDS FOR:

- An immediate end to the male demand for paid sexual access to the bodies of women and girls worldwide.
- A global sisterhood that recognizes the leadership, knowledge, and wisdom of Indigenous women and girls in a fight for our lives, our lands and traditions, and our right to live free from male violence.
- The recognition of prostitution as a form of male violence against women and the implementation of the Nordic model of state policy as a way to advance women's equality, especially benefiting Indigenous women and girls.

- The abolition of prostitution and a recognition of the rights of Indigenous women and girls to food, safe housing, lands, traditions, culture, language, health, spirituality, education and safety.
- A social re-construction of male sexuality based upon the recognition of women's human rights, especially in regard to women's sexual autonomy.

Notes

1 Cherry Smiley, "In Support of Meghan Murphy, in Support of Feminism." *Feminist Current*, May 15, 2015, www.feministcurrent.com.
2 This resolution is cited in Megan Murphy, "There Is No Feminist War on Sex Workers," Feb. 4, 2013. *Rabble* blogs, www.rabble.ca.
3 Ibid.

137

Feminist Principles of the Internet
Gender, Sexuality, and the Internet Meeting
Association for Progressive Communications
Port Dickson, Malaysia
April 13–15, 2014

Emblem for the Gender, Sexuality, and Internet Meeting.

One can argue that we should not be online if we don't want to also accept the consequences, such as its inequality and misogynistic nature. But we can answer that with a question: Why are human rights principles so important in the offline world and then become so unimportant in the online world?[1]

GenderIT began in 2006 to provide a place for feminist monitoring and discussion of Internet culture and policy. "Many years later, GenderIT.org remains a unique space for its focus on the global South, its focus on those working at the grassroots level (grounded in the experience of the women in the society in which they live), and its emphasis on both advocacy and social justice."[2] It is part of the Women's Rights Programme of the Association for Progressive Communications, the organization that sponsored the 2014 meeting at which Feminist Principles of the Internet was developed.

The fifty participants who debated the principles at the gathering in Port Dickson, Malaysia, came from about thirty countries on six continents and included

gender and women's rights activists, LGBTQI (lesbian, gay, bisexual, trans* and intersex) movements, internet and technology rights organizations, and human rights advocates. The goal of the meeting was to bridge the gap between feminist movements and internet rights movements and look at intersections and strategic opportunities to work together as allies and partners. The existing discourse around gender and the internet tends to focus on gender components lacking in policies that govern the internet, violations that take place as a result, and the need for increased women's participation in decision-making forums. In a bid to reframe the conversation, the Global Meeting used a collaborative process to ask the question: "As feminists, what kind of internet do we want, and what will it take for us to achieve it?"[3]

Created as an "evolving document," about which one can comment online, Feminist Principles treats the Internet as a public space where, as in other such spaces, gender, sexuality, and global politics intersect. It views the Internet as a site for movement building to end patriarchy. The problems it confronts range from unequal Internet access and state surveillance to "misogynistic attacks, threats, intimidation, and policing experienced by women and queers LGBTQI people" and the silencing of feminist voices. Included as feminist principles, applicable beyond the Internet, are empowering women and queer people, democratization, respect for diverse sexualities, and both individual autonomy and collective responsibility.

This document clearly addresses issues whose time has come: "Debates in preparation for the meeting were accompanied by Twitter discussions, which can be followed with the #ImagineaFeministInternet hashtag. Hundreds participated and the hashtag garnered over 2 million views in one week."[4] The APC took the document to the Sexual Rights Pre-Event of the 2014 Internet Governance Forum in Istanbul, Turkey. A second global conference was held the next year in Malaysia to continue the conversation.

Feminist Principles of the Internet

1. A feminist internet starts with and works towards empowering more women and queer persons—in all our diversities—to dismantle patriarchy. This includes universal, affordable, unfettered, unconditional and equal *access* to the internet.

2. A feminist internet is an extension, reflection and continuum of our movements and *resistance* in other spaces, public and private. Our agency lies in us deciding as individuals and collectives what aspects of our lives to politicize and/or publicize on the internet.

3. The internet is a *transformative* public and political space. It facilitates new forms of citizenship that enable individuals to claim, construct, and express our selves, genders, sexualities. This includes connecting across territories, demanding accountability and transparency, and significant opportunities for feminist movement-building.

4. *Violence* online and tech-related violence are part of the continuum of gender-based violence. The misogynistic attacks, threats, intimidation, and policing experienced by women and queers LGBTQI people are real, harmful, and alarming. It

is our collective responsibility as different internet stakeholders to prevent, respond to, and resist this violence.

5. There is a need to resist the religious right, along with other extremist forces, and the state, in monopolizing their claim over morality in silencing feminist voices at national and international levels. We must claim the power of the internet to *amplify* alternative and diverse narratives of women's lived realities.

6. As feminist activists, we believe in challenging the patriarchal spaces that currently control the internet and putting more feminists and queers LGBTQI people at the *decision-making* tables. We believe in democratizing the legislation and regulation of the internet as well as diffusing ownership and power of global and local networks.

7. Feminist interrogation of the neoliberal capitalist logic that drives the internet is critical to destabilize, dismantle, and create alternative forms of *economic power* that are grounded on principles of the collective, solidarity, and openness.

8. As feminist activists, we are politically committed to creating and experimenting with technology utilizing *open source* tools and platforms. Promoting, disseminating, and sharing knowledge about the use of such tools is central to our praxis.

9. The internet's role in enabling access to critical *information*—including on health, pleasure, and risks—to communities, cultural expression, and conversation is essential, and must be supported and protected.

10. Surveillance by default is the tool of patriarchy to control and restrict rights both online and offline. The right to *privacy* and to exercise full control over our own data is a critical principle for a safer, open internet for all. Equal attention needs to be paid to surveillance practices by individuals against each other, as well as the private sector and non-state actors, in addition to the state.

11. Everyone has the right to be forgotten on the internet. This includes being able to access all our personal *data* and information online, and to be able to exercise control over [them], including knowing who has access to them and under what conditions, and being able to delete them forever. However, this right needs to be balanced against the right to access public information, transparency and accountability.

12. It is our inalienable right to choose, express, and experiment with our diverse sexualities on the internet. *Anonymity* enables this.

13. We strongly object to the efforts of state and non-state actors to control, *regulate* and restrict the sexual lives of consenting people and how this is expressed and practiced on the internet. We recognize this as part of the larger political project of moral policing, censorship and hierarchization of citizenship and rights.

14. We recognize our role as feminists and internet rights advocates in securing a safe, healthy, and informative internet for *children* and young people. This includes promoting digital and social safety practices. At the same time, we acknowledge children's rights to healthy development, which includes access to positive information about sexuality at critical times in their development. We believe in including the voices and experiences of young people in the decisions made about harmful content.

15. We recognize that the issue of *pornography* online is a human rights and labor issue, and has to do with agency, consent, autonomy and choice. We reject simple causal linkages made between consumption of pornographic content and violence against women. We also reject the umbrella term of pornographic content labeled to any sexuality content such as educational material, SOGIE (sexual

orientation, gender identity and expression) content, and expression related to women's sexuality.

Notes

1 Dhyta Caturani, "Why Do the Feminist Principles of the Internet Matter?" Sept. 16, 2014. *Engage Media* blog, www.engagemedia.org.
2 "About GenderIT.Org," GenderIT.Org website, accessed September 2017, www.genderit.org.
3 APC, "Feminist Principles of the Internet," Aug. 20, 2014. GenderIT.Org website, www.genderit.org.
4 "APC Launches 'Feminist Principles of the Internet' at the 2014 Internet Governance Forum," Sept. 3, 2014. Press release, APC website, www.apc.org.

138

Declaration: LBT Women in Fiji, for Gender Equality, Human Rights, and Democracy
Diverse Voices and Action for Equality
Suva, Fiji
April 30, 2014

Diverse Voices and Action for Equality emblem.

The Republic of Fiji in the South Pacific contains over three hundred islands, 110 of them inhabited; some 85 percent of the population lives on the two largest islands. Fiji was first settled by Austronesians. Europeans arrived in the 1600s, and it was a British colony from 1874 (when thousands of indentured Indian laborers were brought over) until 1970. While it became a republic in 1987, political turmoil continued for many years. The 2014 elections were democratic.

The history of colonialism, and the segregation of Indigenous Fijians from Indians and of both from Europeans, helped shaped early feminisms there. The first women's group was probably the Indian Women's Committee of the early 1900s, while the largest early group was an association of Indigenous Fijian women, Qele ni Ruve, that started in 1924. "In the late 1960s, women began to assert that despite social, cultural and geographical differences, Pacific Island societies were predominantly patriarchal and women were often seen as secondary to men. Their struggle for equality was located within experiences of colonialism, questions concerning land rights, environmental concerns and other political and social factors."[1] Thus, over time, "the postindependence feminist and women's rights movement in Fiji has by necessity been a 'multiracial,' 'multiethnic,' multicultural project."[2] More recent groups include the Fiji Women's Rights Movement, the Fiji Women's Crisis Centre, and Diverse Voices and Action for Equality (DIVA).

As the group describes itself,

> DIVA for Equality network creates diverse opportunities and safe spaces for lesbian, bisexual, trans* masculine people and marginalized women (including FTM/trans* masculine people, young LBT, unemployed women, women in informal settlements, and women in non-traditional sports and employment), to fully participate in all areas of life and community in Fiji. We use a south lesbian feminist framework to work toward gender equality, universal human rights, and social, ecological, and economic justice for all.[3]

The authors of this Declaration[4] represent a different population group than the authors of any other document: people living on small, remote islands threatened by climate change, who face high levels of economic, social, and environmental injustice. The coalition of "lesbians, bisexuals and transmen" is also distinctive. Unlike some trans* declarations, this one links sexual and gender equality.

The authors speak first to the government, since they view government as the entity responsible for guaranteeing "the right to life and to sustainable development, freedom from violence and torture, and to all our civil, political, economic, social and cultural rights." In addition, they appeal to international and regional declarations and platforms that defend sexual and reproductive rights and the right to bodily integrity. (The attention to such documents may be the result of a great deal of publicity given to CEDAW in Fiji around 2008.) Nonetheless, the document addresses a broad range of issues, including the satisfaction of basic needs, sustainable development, equal political participation, and positive attention to diversity in education, all of which are prerequisites for democracy.

Declaration: LBT Women in Fiji, for Gender Equality, Human Rights and Democracy

We, Diverse Voices and Action (DIVA) for Equality, are a group of active and committed lesbians, bisexuals and transmen (LBT) including young LBT from around the Central and Eastern division of Fiji, who have gathered in Suva, Fiji to discuss issues of gender equality, human rights, elections and democracies.

Therefore, in recognition of the Government of Fiji as primary duty bearer for our human rights as LBT women, the existing recognition of our human rights under the current Fiji Constitution, and in order to realise our inherent human rights, including the right to life and to sustainable development, freedom from violence and torture, and to all our civil, political, economic, social and cultural rights, [we] strongly call for the following:

1. The promotion of substantive equality in Fiji that protects the rights of all lesbian, bisexual and trans* people (LBT), including the right to sexual and reproductive health and rights, [and] recognition of all rights linked to sexual orientation and gender identities and expressions, without fear or discrimination;

2. Recognition and utilisation of internationally recognised Yogyakarta principles, in line with the Universal Declaration of Human Rights (UDHR) and other international and regional gender equality normative frameworks including the Pacific Leaders Gender Equality Declaration, Moana Declaration, Beijing Platform for Action and Reviews, CEDAW, ICPD and POAs, etc, in order to uphold and sustain the rights to bodily integrity and freedom of LBT women of Fiji;

3. We call for a demonstration of accountability and transparency by all duty holders including the Fiji Government, Security forces, Fiji Police Force, political parties, NGOs, other civil society and the wider community, for an inclusivity of all sexual orientations whilst addressing gender equality and human rights, and to recognise that lesbian, bisexual and trans* rights are women's rights and human rights, and these rights need to be fulfilled.

4. Freedom from all forms of violence, torture, discrimination and neglect of LBT women and all people of Fiji, and for safe counselling services and professionalism in schools, work places and organisations;

5. Implementation of legal standards through legislation and policies that comply [with] international human rights standards and universal, comprehensive, integrated and quality access to medical, health and education services, food, water and adequate land and housing;

6. Commitment to the review of the Fiji education system with particular emphasis on [the] girl child and young LBT women. Diverse Voices and Action for Equality calls for affirmative action programs directed at the enhancement of young LBT women's formal and informal education, and other development opportunities;

7. Elimination of all forms of civil and political, social, economic and cultural discrimination directed at LBT women including in the homes, workforce, sports and recreation, and demand fair treatment, equality and representation in public and private sectors. CEDAW means the convention on the elimination of ALL forms of discrimination against women, which includes LBT women;

8. To recognise our rights as LBT women to sustainable development, which is not possible without the equal participation of LBT women in democracy, elections and voting, among all other rights. As young LBT women of all ages, including young women advocates, we further pledge to continue to work with each other, and state and non-state allies, to:

9. Build strong, supportive and adequately resourced LBT and other SOGIE groups including Diverse Voices and Action for Equality, to carry forward our work for gender equality, sexual rights, and for universal human rights in Fiji, and in the Pacific. We cannot take forward this work without resources. LBT women will self-organise for positive change in Fiji, with support of allies, as there must be no human rights and development work that takes place without our direct and informed input, and our free, prior and informed consent. "Nothing about us, without us" is our constant call.

10. We will focus on self-care, wellbeing and mental health, as issues of great importance to LBT women and others from marginalised and discriminated groups in our society. This requires work on systems of mental health, and also public education campaigns, training and awareness workshops, and more. When self-esteem is damaged by others, information and communications must also be part of the human rights and social justice response.

11. We highlight the importance of the role of the media, in a just and sustainable democracy. We call on media and political leaders to commit to the principle of free media, with a strong emphasis on human rights, social justice, balanced reporting and responsible journalism.

12. Schools and other educational institutions in Fiji are powerful social and cultural institutions in constructing gender identity, as they have a major influence on how children and young people view each other, and on their acceptance and enjoyment of diversity. On the issues of informal and formal education and right to decent work, DIVA will prioritise rights-based and sustainable development programmes that recognise that bodily freedom, health and wellbeing, safe spaces, and non-discrimination are essential to all advances in education and employment for young LBT women. This includes content on comprehensive sexuality education, SRHR, human rights and sustainable development. We demand the promotion of high-quality gender identity and relations teaching and learning, at all educational levels, including early years settings.

13. On the right to decent work, we reaffirm that the International Labor Organization (ILO) identifies four aspects of decent work: creating jobs, guaranteeing rights at work, social protection, and social dialogue, with gender equality as a cross-cutting objective. Lack of access to recognised national qualifications, decent work and living wage undermines lesbian, bisexual and trans* people's rights, perpetuates gender inequalities in societies and dampens the prospects for sustainable development and inclusive rights-based economic progress.

14. We call for young LBT women to be supported to pursue education and employment in male-dominated fields. This includes attention to workplace safety for women entering such fields. The State must commit to the advancement of LBT young women in self-employment initiatives and small businesses, by providing necessary support and services including financial assistance, training and development, and access to markets regardless of young women's age, ethnicity, status, location, social standing, and other variables.

15. In closing, we especially recognise that lesbian women, trans people and those LGBTQI with non-conforming gender identity and gender expression face even greater, intersectional forms of violence, marginalisation and discrimination. We call for an immediate end to all violence and torture of LGBTQI people around the world including the Pacific, and including implementation of enabling legislation, policies and practices in Fiji.

We stand in solidarity with all LGBTQI people.
   We are not free till all are free!
   All women, all people, all rights!

Notes

1 Margaret C. Mishra, "A History of Fijian Women's Activism (1900–2010)." *Journal of Women's History* 24.2 (2012): 115–43.

2 Teresia Teaiwa, "Women and Indians," in *Security Disarmed: Critical Perspectives on Gender, Race, and Militarization*, ed. Sandra Morgen, Barbara Sutton, and Julie Novkov (New Brunswick, NJ: Rutgers University Press, 2008), p. 127.

3 Diverse Voices and Action for Equality Fiji, "About." DIVA Fiji website, accessed September 2017, www.divafiji.com.

4 DIVA Fiji, "Declaration: LBT Women in Fiji, for Gender Equality, Human Rights, and Democracy!" May 4, 2014. *DIVA Fiji* blog, www.divafiji.com.

139

Position Statement: Femicide
Canadian Council of Muslim Women
Ontario, Canada
August 19, 2014

Canadian Council of Muslim Women
Le conseil canadien des femmes musulmanes
CCMW

Canadian Council of Muslim Women logo.

Our argument is that no murder of a woman should be categorized by the rationale provided by the murderer, or by society itself, whether it be so called honour killing or crimes of passion. . . . The focus on cultures and the naming of murders as "honour killings" ignores the fundamental issues of patriarchy, tribalism, control and power over women. These are the issues we need to address.

The issue of femicide has been drawing increased attention in recent years. Held in 2012 in Vienna, the first UN-sponsored symposium on the issue resulted in the Vienna Declaration on Femicide. The Declaration includes the following definition, which most discussions generally accept:

> [F]emicide is the killing of women and girls because of their gender, which can take the form of, inter alia: 1) the murder of women as a result of domestic violence/intimate partner violence; 2) the torture and misogynist slaying of women; 3) killing of women and girls in the name of "honour"; 4) targeted killing of women and girls in the context of armed conflict; 5) dowry-related killings of women and girls; 6) killing of women and girls because of their sexual orientation and gender identity; 7) the killing of aboriginal and indigenous women and girls because of their gender; 8) female infanticide and gender-based sex selection foeticide; 9) genital mutilation related femicide; 10) accusations of witchcraft and 11) other femicides connected with gangs, organized crime, drug dealers, human trafficking, and the proliferation of small arms.[1]

The Canadian Council of Muslim Women (CCMW) employs a shorter version: "Femicide is defined as the intentional killing of females by males, and sometimes by other females in the interest of men." The council's statement below[2] specifically addresses item 3, "killing of women and girls in the name of 'honour.'" The council believes that this label diminishes women's deaths, feeds into racism, and masks the extent of femicide. It insists that femicide be understood as one end of a continuum of forms of violence against women and girls, all rooted in misogyny and patriarchy. It is concerned that those who refuse to challenge "honor killings" on the grounds that they are "cultural" are as problematic as those who name culture as the cause of gender-based violence only when it happens to "outsiders," leaving their own practices unquestioned. A global concern regarding femicide is that "these murders continue to be accepted, tolerated or justified—with impunity as the norm."[3]

CCMW began in 1982, with a gathering in Winnipeg, Manitoba. The group is equally committed to improving the status of women and to empowering Muslim Women to remain true to both their Islamic heritage and their Canadian identity. CCMW's goals are:

- To promote Muslim women's identity in the Canadian context.
- To assist Muslim women to gain an understanding of their rights, responsibilities and roles in Canadian society.
- To promote and encourage understanding and interfaith dialogue between Muslims and other faith communities.
- To contribute to Canadian society the knowledge, life experiences and ideas of Muslim women for the benefit of all.
- To strengthen the bonds of sisterhood among the Muslim communities and among Muslim individuals.
- To stimulate Islamic thinking and action among Muslim women in the Canadian setting.
- To acknowledge and respect the cultural differences among Canadian Muslim women, and to recognize and develop our common cultural heritage.
- To promote a better understanding of Islam and the Islamic way of life in the North American setting.
- To represent Canadian Muslim women at national and international forums.
- To encourage the organization and coordination of Muslim women's organizations across Canada.[4]

The group has also issued statements on female genital mutilation and forced marriage.

Position Statement: Femicide

The Canadian Council of Muslim Women is strongly opposed to the use of the terms "honour killing" and honour-based violence to identify the murder of women and girls. Our argument is that no murder of a woman should be categorized by the rationale provided by the murderer, or by society itself, whether it be so called honour killing or crimes of passion. CCMW is opposed to such categories, as all murders and violence should be within the comprehensive definition of the UN Declaration on Elimination of Violence Against Women.

We hold that all forms of violence against women are regressive because they are rooted in misogyny and patriarchal norms, which devalue the lives of women and girls. Defining the murder by the rationale for the killing diminishes the death of the woman, as it shifts the focus from the woman to the perpetrator.

We urge that all murders/killings be identified as femicide, as this term does not separate women and girls into distinct groups based on race, culture or religion, and murders are the crimes committed against any woman or girl.

Femicide is defined as the intentional killing of females by males, and sometimes by other females in the interest of men. When other women have been involved in murders, it is important to remember that they have absorbed the patriarchal model of family honour. An example of femicide is the killing of infant girls simply because they are females, and both males and females of a family are involved in these murders.

Femicide avoids inferences about the motives of the killers, and clearly states that violence is used as a tool against females and murders are the extreme end of the same continuum of violence against women and girls.

Recently in Canada, some organizations and individuals, such as some media, academics and professionals, are trying to build a list of so called honour killings, using their own criteria of characteristics. This is plain dangerous and incorrect, as Canada does not keep distinct statistics under the label of honour killing. It is dangerous to surmise that there have been 13 or 15 honour killings in Canada, when no such statistics have been kept.

What is the motivation to name these specific killings? How does this help the women as victims? Besides being racist, what is the purpose in separating these murders from other murders? Who is defining them? Is it the perpetrators who seek to legitimize or dignify the murder, or is it done for racial or religious discrimination to separate some women from the sisterhood of all women?

It is important to remember that Canada is a signatory of the Declaration on Elimination of Violence against Women, and accepts the definition which includes any intentional use of physical force with potential for causing death, injury or harm. The definition includes all forms of violence including spousal violence and violence against children.

The Declaration states: *"Recognizing that Violence Against Women is a manifestation of historically unequal power relations between men and women, which have led to domination over and discrimination against women by men . . . VAW is one of the crucial social mechanisms by which women are forced into a subordinate position compared with men."*

The Declaration recommends that a state not allow any justification of VAW by anyone invoking "custom, tradition or religious considerations."

For Muslims, the Quran has no mention of any kind of death for adultery or unchaste behavior. It has the punishment of lashing for both men and women, bad enough but no reference to stoning and murdering.

For us Canadians to label these murders as "honour killings" is both divisive and dangerous.

In the West, gender violence is assumed to be the work of a "deviant individual" while immigrant women suffer from "death by culture." We acknowledge that if culture and traditions are involved, then these must be identified and addressed, but only as part of the problem.

The focus on cultures and the naming of murders as "honour killings" ignores the fundamental issues of patriarchy, tribalism, control and power over women. These are the issues we need to address.

Naming some murders as honour-based, makes these murders exotic, foreign, and alien to Western culture as if the West is free from all forms of patriarchy. It encourages blatant racism for some, as it gives them permission to blame "those people" and demand their ousting from Canada. It makes others defensive or apologetic about their culture or religion, and blocks any acknowledgement that these murders do irreparable harm to religion and culture.

There are those who view femicide in racist and stereotypical terms, blaming culture or religion, while others in "false" sympathy are ready to accept the practice as part of a culture or religion and therefore not to be judged as a terrible injustice against women.

As women of minority communities, we are dismayed by both perspectives. To those who use cultural relativist arguments and bend backwards to accommodate all practices, we inform them that they end up hindering our struggle for our gender equality.

Are there limits to cultural tolerance, without reference to discrimination and prejudice? The yardstick to measure the limits are fairly clear if we link these to human rights and the rights of citizenship, and acknowledge that these must take precedence over membership of communities.

This will not eliminate the contest between defending human rights versus the cultural or religious rights of communities, but we must try.

Femicide will not disappear, but we cannot separate murders of women and girls by race, ethnicity, culture or race. In Canada, we should address the issue according to our values and our laws as articulated in the Charter of Rights and Freedoms as well as various policies.

Our hope is for Canada to abandon the terms—honour killing and honour based violence—and join the U.N., several countries in South America and southern Africa to condemn these forms of violence.

CCMW maintains that VAW conflicts with human rights as well as contradicting Islamic principles of social justice, equality and compassion. These practices must be denounced and actively resisted by religious leaders, Canadian Muslims and the wider Canadian society. It is our hope that any collective opposition to VAW reflects a spirit of collaboration and dialogue which will lead to action to eradicate all violence against women.

Notes

1 Academic Council on the United Nations System (ACUNS), *Femicide: A Global Issue That Demands Action*, 2013. Geneva Declaration on Armed Violence and Development website, www.genevadeclaration.org.
2 Canadian Council of Muslim Women, "Position Statement: Femicide" Aug. 19, 2014. CCMW website, www.ccmw.com.
3 ACUNS, *Femicide*.
4 Canadian Council of Muslim Women, "Objectives." CCMW website, accessed September 2017, www.ccmw.com.

140

A Political Manifesto for the Emancipation of Our Bodies
Latin American and Caribbean Thirteenth Feminist Encounter for Latin America (EFLAC XIII)
Lima, Peru
November 22–25, 2014

Logo for the 2014 conference.

It is on our bodies, as the primary territory, that multiple mechanisms
of domination operate; but this is also where our resistance, defiance,
and emancipatory activity takes place.

Since the first *encuentro feminista* (feminist meeting) in Bogotá in 1981, thousands of feminists from all over Latin America and the Caribbean have been meeting every two–three years to talk feminist theory and practice.[1] Occasionally, as in 2014, they have left a manifesto.

As Virginia Vargas says, "Latin American feminisms have been built through the Encuentros, and have given us all a perspective that transcends the national. They have stimulated an internationalist perspective on feminism and several networks have been born out of the interactions that have taken place at the Encuentros."

Alvarez et al. add that the gatherings "have served as critical transnational sites in which local activists have refashioned and renegotiated identities, discourses, and practices distinctive of the region's feminisms."[2] The effects have been both regional and local. "Indeed, a key product of these dialogues has been the formation of numerous intraregional issue-specific and identity networks as well as advocacy coalitions on a range of issues such as women's health and sexual and reproductive rights, violence against women, and women's political representation" (5). Over the years, *encuentros* have tackled issues including relations between feminism and the Left, the "NGO-ization" of the women's movement, the importance of working for democratic states, racism within the movement, and trans-inclusion.

The EFLAC XIII manifesto emerges from "capitalist-neoliberal, colonial, patriarchal, heteronormative and racist societies" but tries to speak "from a critical intercultural and intersectional perspective." It considers bodies as both produced by such oppressive societies and also the sources of resistance to them. It celebrates the multiple progressive social movements active in Latin America while highlighting the challenges inequality and diversity present for feminism. It considers feminism's promotion of democracy its "historic contribution." It critiques capitalism and reassesses affective labor, and "challenges us to think about our individual and collective bodies as part of a community and constituent part of territories."

For the Liberation of Our Bodies

We as feminists affirm that our bodies are produced and transformed by the social relations in which we are immersed. Thus, in capitalist-neoliberal, colonial, patriarchal, heteronormative and racist societies, where relations of domination and exploitation prevail, our bodies are affected by all relations of exploitation, subordination, repression, racism and discrimination. It is on our bodies, as the primary territory, that multiple mechanisms of domination operate; but this is also where our resistance, defiance, and emancipatory activity takes place, leading to transformations in the direction of justice and the acceptance of pleasure and creativity. Today, the bodies of women—as carriers of rights—have become a disputed territory. This is what we mean when we say that "the body is a political category" and that as such it embodies feminist discourses. In the struggle for the defence of democracy and the expansion of rights, we feminists have always contributed from our understanding of the body as a political category; but we have not always done it from a critical intercultural and intersectional perspective. This is the challenge we face today, and on which we will reflect and dialogue in this 13th Feminist Encounter in Latin America and the Caribbean.

I. THE LATIN AMERICAN AND CARIBBEAN CONTEXT AND THE CHALLENGES THAT FEMINIST MOVEMENTS FACE

In the early twenty-first century, we live at an exceptional historical moment both in the Latin America/Caribbean region and globally. We are experiencing the beginning of a profound crisis that puts into question the very foundations of the dominant system. This historical moment is exceptional because of the active presence of thousands of women and men who through their bodies resist and carry out struggles to end hunger, exploitation, sexual violence, homophobia, silencing—among other mechanisms of domination. These are part of the diverse social movements that now dispute imaginaries, territories and resources in our Latin-Caribbean continent. These racial/ethnic, generational, transgender, lesbian, disabilities movements enrich feminisms with new perspectives and reasons for struggle, but also pose major challenges. The diversities that characterize our societies are imbued with inequality and violence, reflecting severe power imbalances, which have implications for our movements. It seems that diversity has not been given its full value, not understood in its possibility of confronting discrimination in all its forms. "Low-intensity" democracies in our region display the unresolved tension between democracy and development. These tensions are expressed in the fact that we have never achieved full economic, social and cultural rights. On the contrary, the conservatism and the weakening of the secular character of the state encourage policies that ignore the human rights of women. Sexual and reproductive rights have now become a strategic issue for the democratization of our Latin-Caribbean societies. The promotion of democracy in the country—at home and in bed; in the neighbourhood and social organizations; at local and global level—is a historic contribution of feminism for all humanity, not just for women, and in the present context we must reassess it and defend it. More than the ability to mobilize masses, the power of the feminist movement has been its ability to contest and achieve changes in democratic imaginaries and in transformative horizons. Our energy and capacity for change is based on a political-cultural argument, enriching it with the voices of new actors whose presence regenerates and deepens democracy. Our feminisms are becoming de-normalizing, becoming black, indigenous, transgender, lesbian, and queer. Feminism in its various streams has made profound criticism of the current oppressive system. Feminisms have challenged modern capitalist values that exacerbate violence against territories and bodies. Feminisms have identified the extractive development model that threatens life and nature, the logic of accumulation that commodifies all livelihoods, and subordinates and exploits working people—particularly care and reproductive work which is primarily performed by women. In the current crisis of civilization, Latin and Caribbean feminisms come together in our commitment to confront and fight to change the multiple systems of domination that impact—simultaneously and powerfully— on all women, in their undervalued, exploited and hijacked bodies.

II. NEW HORIZONS AND A NEW DIRECTION FOR OUR STRUGGLES
1) Critical interculturality from an intersectional perspective
The recognition of sexual and gender diversity within the multicultural and multi-ethnic situation of Latin America and the Caribbean has not been an easy process. Both coloniality and a monocultural gaze have marked the relationships between the populations that today inhabit the sub-continent. The places from which "talking," feeling, desiring, doing, producing wealth, culture and knowledge, are loaded with unequal power relations that invisibilise and degrade forms of life, knowledge and societies, considering them as subaltern and subordinating them to Western hegemony. This realization compels us to look at diversity as an expression not only of difference but also as a source of inequalities that, depending on their origins, intersect and differentially impact women. Moreover, this challenge demands that we recognize the urgency of redistributing power among

women in both society in general and social movements in particular, thereby empowering them. To socialize power is the key challenge for the creation of radical democracy. This requires that we learn to accept and manage conflicts, disagreements and dissenting views.

Critical interculturality allows us to retrieve other voices, knowledges and ways of thinking, and to appreciate diverse worldviews that speak of the complexity of reality and the multiple ways of living and being a woman. This is not a call to "celebrate" or "tolerate" diversity, but a call to recognize the incompleteness of any political proposal that does not incorporate dialogue with diversity, building identities and producing knowledge. This demands that we take on an ethical-political commitment to incorporate diversity in our ways of living, thinking and coming together.

2) The sustainability of life as priority

Feminist economics demonstrates how, for centuries, the way of sustaining life has been through the sexual division of labour with a consequently excess workload for women. The capitalist system imposes discourses as "truths" that legitimize it as a hegemonic mode of production. Among these "truths," it produces a series of false dichotomies, such as production/reproduction, public/private, nature/culture, normal/abnormal. It also reduces the notion of work to the production of goods and services with exchange value in the market. The systemic devaluation of social reproduction by nation states reflects the deep biases of [the] socio-economic-cultural system as a whole, which avoids its responsibility and increases the burden of survival on people and, in particular, on women in Latin America and the Caribbean. This advanced stage of an extractive and predatory capitalism threatens the sustainability of life on the planet and urgently calls into question the prevailing ways of life and production. As feminists—and like other social movements—we condemn this form of social organization and its values, and demand dignified living conditions for all people. This implies not only new forms of sustainable economic production but also relationships of care and affection. Feminist movements strive for a radical change in the current capital-centric logic of the economy and for a new balance between production and reproduction, in which the state stops seeing the carework of women as a resource to be tapped freely in order for the state to cover its obligations to protect and care for life. Human life and its sustainability should be the first and only priority of state economic and social policy.

3) Body and territory: safeguarding community life

A territory is much more than a plot of land: it is a cultural, symbolic and historical living space. Understanding the body as a territory—as a whole complex and living system, consisting of multiple relationships in which all living beings and natural resources like water, land, mountains are involved—challenges us to think about our individual and collective bodies as part of a community and constituent part of territories. Ecofeminism, communitarian feminisms, indigenous and Afro feminisms, lesbian and transgender feminisms, invite us to question the anthropocentric and androcentric vision of our society, which has put white/individual/rational/man/straight at the epicentre of the universe, the centre of power, whose purpose is to dominate nature in the same way as women are dominated. These various feminisms invite us to reassess our relationship with nature, our ancestry, our social community.

III. THE APPROPRIATION OF OUR BODIES BY PATRIARCHAL, RACIST AND HETERONORMATIVE CAPITALISM

Our bodies have been turned by patriarchal capitalism into territories on which discourses that restrict our freedoms are constructed. Open and hidden violations of women's bodies oppress us at work, on the street, in intimate daily life, in sexual life, in emotional and in the subjective spheres of life. Heternormativity, racism, sexual and social division of labour, economic exploitation, the devaluation of bodies and their energies, their reduction to mere carriers of working forces or of invisible work (reproductive or carework, without economic and social recognition), the repudiation of disability—these are all expressions of bodies seen as territories for others, alien and distant, putting in question whether our bodies are our own.

Let's see how they operate:

"Standardized" bodies: the rejection of difference in performance

Latin American and Caribbean feminisms condemn the hegemonic culture that considers bodily differences and variations in performance as subjects of oppression and discrimination, whether using medical, religious or aesthetic arguments, or via suggestions of lower productivity in the labour force. Feminists condemn the discrimination by a medicalized and normalized model of the body that does not pay attention to the obstacles that determine disability in people. We seek to problematize what is "normal" and to display the inability of modern society to accept functional diversity.

Bodies as "workforce" and "objects of consumption"

Under patriarchal capitalism, control over the body, reproduction and sexuality is directly related to the needs of the reproduction of capitalism as a system. The body is seen primarily as a labour force, as a condition for the creation of material wealth. The sexual division of labour, which is based on the separation between production as men's work and reproduction as women's work, is central to capitalist accumulation. Our bodies generate demand in the capitalist market: this is through rampant consumerism, which promotes an ideal of beauty that causes anorexia and bulimia and self-harm, leading ultimately to death as women compete in the struggle for a place to be seen, identified and "consumed" by the male gaze.

Sexual bodies that are denied desire and joy

Heternormativity has been a constituent of the ruling order since the capitalist mode of production restructured the patriarchal system. Under capitalism the relationship between the body/sex/reproduction became a central dimension of social (economic) relations. It is here that the church hierarchy and conservative groups have concentrated their efforts to control the bodies of women as a strategy to maintain and expand their political power. And while bodies contain the possibility of self-determination, beyond the binary sex/gender framework, the challenge of this freedom implies high costs because it is perceived as threatening and hence stigmatized as something that should be expelled or pathologized.

IV. OUR BODIES IN MOTION

By recovering body politics we recover other powerful and transgressive political dimensions as we engage in various forms of struggle. We need to overcome a modern sense of self that imposes separation from the body, reason from subjectivity and emotion, and the individual body from the social context. As the body is the carrier of rights, our bodies are the source of new political struggles, reclaiming new forms of autonomous struggle around production, reproduction and sexuality.

The denial of sexual and reproductive rights has generated a countercultural struggle, reaffirming the right to decide about our own bodies, the right to pleasure, to a diverse eroticism, to a non-normative/non-heteronormative sexuality, to a sovereign gender identity, to self-determination. Our struggle for reproductive health and rights require[s] not only adequate services, but also the retrieval of non-Western healing practices. These struggles also include the fight against AIDS and the monopoly of the big transnational drugs industry.

Compulsory heterosexuality and the compulsive determination of our gender, are confronted by the movements of sexual-gender dissent and by feminisms condemning the biological approach and the binary framework of gender and sexuality, advocating the right to self-determination over our desires and our gender identity

The impacts of neoliberal reforms of extractive economic policies and commercialisation, which produce hunger and poverty, have led to struggles against free trade, in defence of the land and territory, against the damage and privatization of our commons—such as water and land—which are fundamental for survival.

Similarly, the struggles against racism and ethnic discrimination, and their intersection with other forms of discrimination, have caused in the case primarily of women, of African descent and indigenous, special impacts on their sexual bodies. Today, their powerful resistance has managed to include the fight against ethnic and racial discrimination in the agendas of all feminist and democratic social movements.

Meanwhile, movements of women with disabilities confront: the way in which normality and beauty have been defined; and the disempowering role of society in limiting the opportunities of women with disabilities to exercise their rights, which are exactly the same rights as all citizens.

Moreover, immigrants, whether of their own choice or as a result of repressive political and economic processes within the sub-region, have been forced to seek new destinations, are questioning—as part of the globalization of feminist struggles—the unfair, racist and colonial global system.

In all of these processes, feminisms have produced feminist theory, knowledge and new categories that question the limitations of reproductive work and put forward the "care economy" as an ethical, economic, legal and political dimension. This requires the responsibility of men, society and the state in the function of care.

In recovering all these aspects of body politics, Latin-Caribbean feminists have taken a political, conceptual and imaginative leap. Today they rebel, transgress, transcend borders and transform the political and cultural landscape of our times.

Notes

1 The meetings were held in Colombia (1981), Peru (1983), Brazil (1985), Mexico (1987), Argentina (1990), El Salvador (1993), Chile (1996), Dominican Republic (1999), Costa Rica (2002), Brazil (2005), Mexico (2009), and Colombia (2011).

2 Sonia E. Alvarez, Elisabeth Jay Friedman, Ericka Beckman, Maylei Blackwell, Norma Chinchilla, Nathalie Lebon, Marysa Navarro, and Marcela Ríos Tobar, "Encountering Latin American and Caribbean Feminisms." Havens Center for Social Justice, accessed September 2017, www.havenscenter.org. Subsequent page references are to this source.

141

Charter of Female Comics Creators Against Sexism
Collective of Female Comics Creators Against Sexism (Collectif des créatrices de bande dessinés contre le sexisme)
France
2015

This cartoon, based on the iconic Olive Oyl from the Popeye comics, serves as the de facto mascot for the collective that issued this manifesto.

The purpose of our collective remains to aid our partners in creating more inclusive projects.[1]

A collective of over one hundred female comics creators wrote this Charter. It could have been written by women in a great number of fields.

The origins of the Charter lay in a sequence of events. First, female comics (again, like those in many fields) are regularly asked gendered questions, while their male peers are not ("What's it like to be a female comic artist?" "How often do you encounter sexism when applying for a job?" "Will boys like your work?" etc.). Comic writer Lisa Mandel organized a satirical "Les Hommes Du BD" (Men of Comics) panel at a 2014 convention, where the males were asked the same, now-ridiculous-because-reversed gendered questions, and the audience was made aware of the women's professional situation. The next event was an invitation from the Centre Belge de la Bande Dessine to Julie Maroh inviting her to participate in an exhibition called "Le BD des filles" (Comics for Girls) that was "an expo for all comics aimed at girls aged 7 to 77 including graphic novels for little girls, young adult titles, feminist comics, romance comics for single women, and shopping addicts."[2] Maroh's discomfort with this framing, and a complaint to the expo organizers that went nowhere, led to online exchanges and meetings with other female creators, and eventually to the collective and the Charter. When the Charter was published, the expo project was cancelled, and growing support for the Charter led to the creation of a website.

The Charter[3] has two components. The first element is against the ghettoizing of women and women's work, stereotyping only females and what they produce by their gender. It also opposes stereotyping the fans of comics by assuming that all their interests are determined by biology. And, they claim, there's nothing "neutral" about this, as labeling something "female" (girly, etc.) labels it as "inferior," removes it from the "universal," and "leads to nothing but negative effects on women's self-perception, self-confidence and performance." The second element of the Charter is a call to the industry ("institutions, publishers, authors, booksellers, librarians and journalists") to take responsibility for growing equality and diversity. It is a distinctly feminist cry against discrimination, including racism, homophobia, sexism, and transphobia.

Charter of Female Comics Creators Against Sexism

Given that "masculine comics" have never been narrowly defined or limited, it is degrading for women authors to be typecast as creating "female comics." If such a tag stereotypes our work or thought process, then we, female comics creators, don't recognize ourselves in it. Indeed, as much as our male peers are not obliged to refer to their "masculinity" when they design something, we aren't obliged to refer to our "femininity."

"Female comics" is not a genre of storytelling. Adventure, science-fiction, thriller, romance, autobiography, humor, history, tragedy are genres of storytelling and women authors master them without having to be reduced to their sex.

To define someone's taste and ability by their biological sex is a prejudice that isn't based on reality. Studies in neurobiology and experimental psychology prove that cognitive development is the same for both sexes.

The word "girly" only reinforces sexist clichés. We refute the idea that talking[,] baking cupcakes[,] or Sales is a "feminine" prerogative. To love shopping and/or soccer is not a sexed feature. Given that "girly" is mostly defined by the futility and/or "sentimentality" of a theme addressed, to decide that such features are "feminine" is misogynistic.

To publish "for-women" collections is misogynistic. It creates polarization and hierarchy within literature, implying that everything that isn't "for-women" is "for men." Why should the feminine be outside the scope of what is universal? This sort of distinction, based on stereotypes, leads to nothing but negative effects on women's self-perception, self-confidence and performance. This also holds true for men, especially if they feel attracted to what the authorities classify as "feminine." As long as we maintain masculine as the norm and feminine as an inferior aside, children will continue to use terms like "girl" and "homosexual" as pejoratives in schoolyards.

IN SUPPORT OF A FEMINIST PROGRESS FOR COMICS FIELD

"Feminist" is not an insult. Feminism struggles for women's equality with men in our societies, being therefore anti-sexism, and we wish to promote literature that is more egalitarian.

We encourage diversity of representation in comics. Authors and protagonist[s] in the book industry ought to give more visibility to women, to diverse family structure, gay parenting, people of color, and socio-ethnic diversity.

We expect institutions, publishers, authors, booksellers, librarians and journalists to assert moral responsibility in the diffusion of narrative material with sexist and, generally speaking, discriminative (homophobic, transphobic, racist, etc) features. We hope to see them promote literature that frees itself from ideology based on gender stereotypes.

We encourage booksellers and librarians not to segregate so-called "for-women" books and books by female authors while organizing displays. The fact that female characters are more present or active than male characters in a book doesn't mean that boys and men cannot identify with them or enjoy their story.

We hope for authors, publishers and institutions to be attentive to the inner wealth that we all hold in ourselves. There is no hermetic divide inside us between masculine and feminine, except for what society and religions impose. There is inside everyone an endless supply between, around, and beyond these notions of masculine and feminine. This is our strength, and the literature shouldn't be afraid of it.

Notes

1 "The BCSC Turned a Deaf Ear!" Sept. 17, 2015. Collectif des créatrices de dande dessinée contre le sexism website, www.bdegalite.org.
2 Emma Houxbois, "Blue Is the Warmest Color: Creator Julie Maroh Discusses Anti Sexist Charter," Sept. 12, 2015. *Rainbow Hub*, www.therainbowhub.com.
3 "Charter of Female Comics Creators Against Sexism." Collectif des créatrices de dande dessinée contre le sexism website, www.bdegalite.org.

142

State of the Black Union
Black Lives Matter
January 22, 2015

The Black Lives Matter logo.

For ten years (2000–2009), the State of the Black Union was a one-day conference hosted by Tavis Smiley during February, Black History Month, to discuss "the current status and future hopes of African America." This conference attracted "black academics, civic, political, labor, religious and business leaders" by the thousands and was broadcast on C-SPAN. In 2010, the conference was canceled because a Black president was elected and "we no longer have to wait for one day a year in February to discuss issues that matter to us on TV."[1] The name of this event resurfaced in 2015 after President Obama gave his sixth State of the Union address, in order to enumerate the concerns of the African American community that were not addressed by the president.

The Black Lives Matter movement, endorsed by many other progressive organizations, created this message in an attempt to show why they felt left out of the president's address, especially after a year of many violent and widely publicized Black deaths at the hands of police. The statement[2] "presents a sweeping indictment of what it asserts is the systemic and institutionalized subjugation of, and violence towards, Black Americans."[3] The document accuses businesses, police, the military, and the government of targeting Blacks and the areas where Black people live for their own profit, and it delineates the many inequalities that Black people still experience in America today. It speaks out against the Obama administration's racial initiative, My Brother's Keeper, saying that it is too narrow to help many who need the most help in Black communities. There is a refusal here to accept that the only problem is police violence against Black men, though that is certainly a core issue. Importantly, the statement declares, "None of us are free until all of us are free." The central focus of this document—its call for inclusivity—speaks to the heart of the movement launched by Alicia Garza, Patrisse Cullors, and Opal Tometi, and to the continuing need for progressives to be reflective about internal politics.

State of the Black Union

The Shadow of Crisis has NOT Passed.

2014 was a year that saw profound injustice, and extraordinary resilience. Homicides at the hands of police sparked massive protests, meaning that America could no longer ignore bitter truths of the Black experience. Gabriella Naverez, a queer Black woman was killed at 22 years old, unarmed. 37 year old Tanisha Anderson's family dialed 911 for medical assistance. Instead, Cleveland police officers took her life. Anyia Parker, a Black trans woman, was gunned down in East Hollywood. This brutal attack was caught on camera, yet her murder, like so many murders of Black trans women, ha[s] gone unanswered. This country must abandon the lie that the deep psychological wounds of slavery, racism and structural oppression are figments of the Black imagination. The time to address these wounds is now.

Freedom Rider Diane Nash, once unapologetically declared, "We will not stop. There is only one outcome." Black lives—men and women, queer and trans, immigrant and first-generation—will be valued, protected, and free.

In the face of the tragic killing of Mike Brown, Black youth in Ferguson said no more, sparking resistance against state violence that spread across the nation. For over 160 days we have been marching, shutting down streets, stopping trains and occupying police stations in pursuit of justice. We have stood united in demanding a new system of policing and a vision for Black lives, lived fully and with dignity. Gains have been made, but we who believe in freedom know we cannot rest until justice is won.

The current state of Black America is anything but just. For Black people in the U.S., the shadow of crisis has not passed.
- The median wealth for single White women is $42,600. For Black women, it's $5,001.
- The infant mortality rate for Black mothers is more than double that of White mothers, due to factors like poverty, lack of access to health care, and the physiological effects of stress caused by living under structural oppression.
- 22 states have passed new voter restrictions since 2010, disenfranchising as many as 34 million Americans, most of them Black.

- In cities across the country, profit-driven policies fuel displacement and gentrification, leading to the destruction of entire Black communities.
- Blacks and Latinos are about 31 percent of the US population, but 60 percent of the prison population.
- In our country 1 in 3 black men will be incarcerated in his lifetime, and Black women are the fastest growing prison population.
- The life expectancy of a Black trans woman is 35 years. The average income of a Black trans person is less than 10K. Trans people are denied jobs, housing and healthcare just for living in their truths.
- It is legal in many jurisdictions to fire LBGT people from employment and deny them access to healthcare and housing.
- Since 1976, the United States has executed thirteen times more black defendants with white victims than white defendants with black victims.
- Black U.S. political prisoners have collectively served over 800 years in prison and have consistently been denied parole despite good behavior and time served.
- Increasingly, students in white areas are nourished and taught while Black children are criminalized and judged.
- Black neighborhoods lack access to affordable healthy food resulting in disproportionate levels of obesity and other chronic illnesses.

Our schools are designed to funnel our children into prisons. Our police departments have declared war against our community. Black people are exploited, caged, and killed to profit both the state and big business. This is a true State of Emergency. There is no place for apathy in this crisis. The US government has consistently violated the inalienable rights our humanity affords.

We say no more.
- We demand an end to all forms of discrimination and the full recognition of our human rights.
- We demand an immediate end to police brutality and the murder of Black people and all oppressed people.
- We demand full, living wage employment for our people.
- We demand decent housing fit for the shelter of human beings and an end to gentrification.
- We demand an end to the school to prison pipeline & quality education for all.
- We demand freedom from mass incarceration and an end to the prison industrial complex.
- We demand a racial justice agenda from the White House that is inclusive of our shared fate as Black men, women, trans and gender-nonconforming people. Not My Brother's Keeper, but Our Children's Keeper.
- We demand access to affordable healthy food for our neighborhoods.
- We demand an aggressive attack against all laws, policies, and entities that disenfranchise any community from expressing themselves at the ballot.
- We demand a public education system that teaches the rich history of Black people and celebrates the contributions we have made to this country and the world.
- We demand the release of all U.S. political prisoners.
- We demand an end to the military industrial complex that incentivizes private corporations to profit off of the death and destruction of Black and Brown communities across the globe.

This country owes Black citizens nothing less than full recognition of our human rights. The White House's current racial justice initiative, My Brother's Keeper, ignores too many members of our communities. It does not address the inhumane conditions we collectively experience living in a white supremacist system. The issues facing Black women, immigrants, trans and queer people must be included and we demand a full expansion of My Brother's Keeper to do so.

We demand the same inclusion from our movement.

None of us are free until all of us are free. Our collective efforts have exposed the ugly American traditions of patriarchy, classism, racism, and militarism. These combined have bred a violent culture rife with transphobia, and other forms of illogical hatred.

This corrupt democracy was built on Indigenous genocide and chattel slavery. And continues to thrive on the brutal exploitation of people of color. We recognize that not even a Black President will pronounce our truths. We must continue the task of making America uncomfortable about institutional racism. Together, we will re-imagine what is possible and build a system that is designed for Blackness to thrive.

We fight in the name of Aiyana Stanley-Jones, killed by Detroit Police at the age of 7 years old, who never got to graduate from elementary school. We fight in the name of Mike Brown, who was killed by officer Darren Wilson, weeks before starting college. We fight in the name of Islan Nettles, a 21 year old Black trans woman who was pummeled to death outside a NYC police station in Harlem. We fight in the name of Tarika Wilson, who was killed by an Ohio police officer while holding one of her babies, and will never get to embrace any of her six children again.

2015 is the year of resistance. We the People, committed to the declaration that Black lives matter, will fight to end the structural oppression that prevents so many from realizing their dreams. We cannot, and will not stop until America recognizes the value of Black life.

Notes

1 Bruce A. Dixon, "Tavis Smiley Ends State of Black American Union Show, Continues Media Lockdown of Obama's Black Left Critics," Jan. 13, 2010. *Black Agenda Report*, www.blackagendareport.com.

2 "Black Lives Matter Declaration—State of the Black Union (2015)." *Declaration Project*, www.declarationproject.org.

3 Ibid.

143

International Women's Day Statement
Union of Palestinian Women's Committees
Palestine
March 8, 2015

Union of Palestinian Women's Committees emblem.

From its founding in 1980, the Union of Palestinian Women's Committees has fought on two fronts: for equality between men and women, and for an independent Palestinian state. As usual in documents by women from groups oppressed by class, religion, race, etc., the UPWC sees the two as connected—as parts of a progressive and democratic struggle for self-determination and against all forms of discrimination.

The Statement below[1] expresses Palestinian solidarity with others "who are confronting the forces of colonialism, exploitation, occupation, discrimination, and racism" and working for their alternatives: "freedom, equality, justice and dignity; . . . self-determination of peoples, sovereignty over their resources and capabilities, and liberation from all forms of oppression." When it comes to naming the sources of violations of women's rights around the world, it first lists "wars and armed conflicts. . . . the power and oppression of racism . . . [and] reactionary forces in many regions, including in the Arab world" before later adding "discrimination against them in the legal and social fields." This is consistent with the historical tendency of Palestinian women's groups to prioritize the freedom of Palestine over the equality of women, even as they link the two.

Palestinian women live in a particularly vulnerable state of fear and horror. Writing in 2015, Ebru Buyukgul reports that

> [a]ccording to the Palestinian women's group "Women against Violence," since 1991, 162 Palestinian women have been murdered by a family relative in the Green Line area alone. A study by the Palestinian Central Bureau of Statistics in 2012 highlights that 37 percent of married women in the occupied territories have been subjected to some form of domestic violence by their husbands. And the Middle East focused publication, "The Tower," also notes that "honour killings" doubled in 2013 in the West Bank and Gaza. As things stand today the future looks grim for Palestinian women who find themselves victims of both Zionism and patriarchy.[2]

The Union of Palestinian Women's Committees was founded in 1980. Its vision is of "a civil, democratic, progressive community free of all forms of discrimination [that] respects women's rights as part of human rights in general."[3] It addresses inequality based on sex and class. On its list of objectives, establishing an independent Palestinian state is first, followed by several items including empowering women socially, politically, economically, and culturally; motivating women to participate in decision making; and defending the rights of refugee and imprisoned women.[4] The Palestine Poster Project has a stunning collection of pieces produced by Palestinians to commemorate International Women's Day.

Statement from the Union of Palestinian Women's Committees

On March 8, International Women's Day, the Union of Palestinian Women's Committees extend our solidarity and commitment to joint struggle to all activists and campaigners for freedom around the world who are confronting the forces of colonialism, exploitation, occupation, discrimination and racism and struggling for freedom, equality, justice and dignity; to those who defend self-determination of peoples, sovereignty over their resources and capabilities, and liberation from all forms of oppression; and to those who seek true peace with justice.

On this International Women's Day, the rights of women around the world are violated in numerous ways: through wars and armed conflicts, through the power and oppression of racism; through reactionary forces in many regions, including in the Arab world, where such forces carry the support of imperialism to benefit its clear colonial objectives for control of peoples and their resources. Imperialism in our region has resulted in an increasing number of victims of its policies and ever more risk to the lives of people, especially women and children.

In Palestine, which is still under the yoke of Zionist settler colonialism, the Zionist movement seeks to proclaim its "democracy" and "progressiveness," but in reality is committed to a mission of racism, murder, destruction and criminality. Palestinian women are struggling for the freedom of their people, and their message is one of insistence on freedom and refusal to compromise our rights, whether national or social, and thus continue their legitimate struggle for the inalienable national rights of the Palestinian people, the right of return of Palestinian refugees, the right of self-determination, of full sovereignty, and the right to Jerusalem as capital of an independent Palestinian state. At the same time, Palestinian women struggle for full equality in all economic and social fields, ending all forms of discrimination against them in the legal and social fields and the development of laws in line with international conventions upholding the rights of women.

March 8, 2015 comes not long after months of barbaric aggression launched by "Israel" in the Gaza Strip, killing more than 2260 martyrs including many women and children, destroying tens of thousands of homes and displacing hundreds of thousands. Nearly 100,000 are still living without proper shelter, while the siege on Gaza has tightened, leading to further aggravation of the health, social and economic conditions of our people. In the West Bank, the occupation practices its strategy for control over all of Palestine through the brutal repression of our people, through ongoing land confiscation, home demolitions, military invasions, the targeting of our people for arrest, killing and wounding. The number of Palestinian prisoners in Israeli jails has increased to 6500, including 22 women and about 200 children, suffering from harsh conditions of detention and many abuses committed against prisoners, especially as Israel refuses to recognize them as prisoners of war under the Geneva Conventions. Simultaneously, the project to Judaize Jerusalem continues, as do the racist assaults on our people in the occupied lands of 1948 and the intensification of discrimination and oppression, and the apartheid wall continues to be built, intensifying racism and apartheid in Palestine.

In Diaspora, more than half of the Palestinian people are suffering as refugees, especially those displaced from the camps in Syria and especially the besieged Yarmouk camp. Palestinian refugees in Lebanon are facing extremely difficult conditions that have only become more severe after tens of thousands of Palestinians and Syrians fleeing Syria have come to the overcrowded camps in Lebanon.

All of the above only confirms that the Palestinian people are confronting a criminal strategy of colonialism and demand that the world act to stop these crimes, applying international law and holding the Zionist state and its war criminals accountable for their crimes against the Palestinian people.

The Union of Palestinian Women's Committees salutes March 8 this year and emphasizes the following:
- The continuation of the struggle of Palestinian women for freedom and self-determination until we achieve our national rights;
- The need to confront all crimes and violations by the occupation forces against Palestinian women;
- The escalation of the boycott of Israel, divestment, and sanctions;
- The struggle for unity with a real national strategy to confront the occupation and support the steadfastness of the Palestinian people;
- The urgency of lifting the siege on the Gaza Strip and of reconstruction;
- The necessity to release Palestinian prisoners and force Israel to apply international conventions to their treatment, in particular the Geneva Conventions;
- The importance of developing the Palestinian social and economic structures to protect the rights of women and children and defend the equality of women, in line with international conventions signed by Palestinian officials, and to end all forms of discrimination against women;
- The need to confront the reactionary forces that practice terror against the people, especially women, through the use of religion, and the promotion of the progressive, democratic political trend.

Notes

1 "International Women's Day: Statement from the Union of Palestinian Women's Committees," March 14, 2015. *Fight Back! News*, www.fightbacknews.org.
2 Ebru Buyukgul, "The Women of Palestine: Caught between the Occupation and Patriarchy," June 8, 2015. *Your Middle East*, www.yourmiddleeast.com.
3 Union of Palestinian Women Committees website, accessed September 2017, www.upwc.org.ps.
4 Ibid.

144

Resolutions
2015 Women's Congress about Women and Media
National House of Vinohrady, Czech Republic
June 20, 2015

The logo of the Women's Congress about Women and Media.

We believe women are often being portrayed in the media with use of sexism and prejudice, and that this has a significant impact on women's status in society as a whole, and not just the Czech Republic. We focused on the cause and effect of media portrayal of women, and its connection to the underrepresentation of women in the highest decision-making positions in media worldwide.[1]

About a thousand people from a range of nations, professions, ages, and political backgrounds attended the Second Czech Women's Congress, on the topic of Women and Media. Presentations covered "sexism in media; women and social media; [and] women in decision making in media. Creative workshops were focused on soft-skills development: coaching; mentoring; rhetoric; presentation skills or presentation in media."[2] The First Women's Congress took place in Prague, and so the second intended to move outside the capital. Preparatory meetings, using the World Café method,[3] took place in Prague and Brno, and additional roundtables with media representatives followed before the Congress.

The group's website provides some statistics to accompany the manifesto, and they help explain some of the manifesto's contents.

Women represent

51% of the total population (men 49%)
61% of university graduates (men 39%)
8.9% of the unemployed between the ages of 30 and 34 (men 4.3%)
61% of those in judicial roles (men 39%)
19% of those in judicial roles in the highest court of the Czech Republic (men 81%)
0% of members in 85 percent of the boards of directors of the 60 biggest organisations in the Czech Republic
18.8% of members of Czech government
26% of municipal representatives in Czech towns and villages
(sources: Czech Statistical Office, McKinsey & Company)

Facts about women in the labour market in the Czech Republic

Between the ages of 15–64, only 56% of women are in paid work (Norway 73%, Germany 66%, Estonia 61%, Poland 53%).

In the Czech Republic, there are fewer employed women with small children between the ages of 0 and 6 than in all other EU states.

Less than 40% of women, compared to nearly 95% of men, with two children are
employed (across the EU the ratio is 65:91). Compared to all other EU countries,
only a small percentage of the Czech Republic's working population are employed
part time (2% of employed men, 9% of employed women).

At the same time, just over 30% of all employed women in the EU are engaged in part
time work (approximately 8% of employed men).

Women earn an average of a quarter less than men (the average monthly wage
paid to women is 22 666 CZK, to men 30 192 CZK), and they are minimally represented in managerial roles and in the business world.

Research done by McKinsey & Company evaluating the potential of women
in the Czech economy shows that on the management boards of the sixty biggest
companies in the Czech Republic, women represent only 4 percent on boards of
directors, and in 85 percent of these companies there is no woman on directory
boards at all. For these and other related reasons, women are generally more at
risk of poverty than men.[4]

As described by Monika McGarrell Klimentová, one of the organizers of the
congress, media issues in the Czech Republic are familiar: "Women are usually
reporting about local political issues, they rarely report on international affairs
and business. They usually report about lifestyle, buildings, design, health and
science. Also, if you look at the TV presenters, they are disproportionately good-
looking and usually under 35."[5]

The Resolutions read as advice to those producing and broadcasting on
the media, as well as consumers. The media is treated as a workplace and a social institution, and practices from sexist advertising to treatment of feminism
are mentioned, topics of concern in repeated declarations. The next Women's
Congress was scheduled for 2017 and will be dedicated to gender and public
space.

2015 Women's Congress Resolutions

1. LANGUAGE IS POWERFUL, LET'S USE IT IN A GENDER SENSITIVE
MANNER
Generic masculine . . . Why [use it] when speaking about women?
2. LET'S FIGHT STEREOTYPES
It's simple: If I were a man, would you ask me the same question? Try some-
thing different!
3. LET'S DEMAND BALANCED REPRESENTATION OF WOMEN AND
MEN IN DISCUSSION PROGRAMMES
Are you organizing a debate, writing an article, inviting guests for a programme?
Balance = diversity.
4. LET'S INSIST ON GENDER BALANCE IN REGULATORY BODIES
Quotas, quotas, quotas . . . they do work, actually.
5. WIN MORE LEADERSHIP POSITIONS FOR WOMEN IN THE MEDIA
Society consists of 50% women and 50% men; so why are there almost no
women in leadership positions in the media?

6. LET'S CREATE FAMILY FRIENDLY WORK ENVIRONMENTS

Shared work positions, part-time work, homeworking . . . Why should it not work in the media?

7. SAY NO TO PRODUCTS SOLD THROUGH SEXIST ADVERTISING

Sexist advertising? No, thanks.

8. LET'S SUPPORT DIVERSITY ON SCREEN AND ON AIR

Age, sex, orientation, ethnicity, race . . . Diversity belongs on screen as well as in everyday life.

9. LET'S NOT DIVIDE THE WORLD INTO MEN'S AND WOMEN'S WORLDS, THERE'S JUST ONE

There is only one common world. Let's behave that way.

10. WOMEN, LET'S COOPERATE!

Feminism isn't a swearword!

Notes

1 Women's Congress website, accessed September 2017, www.kongreszen.cz/womens-congress.
2 Ibid.
3 "The World Café Method." *World Café*, accessed September 2017, www.theworldcafe.com.
4 "Czech Women's Congress about Women and Media in 2015." NKC Gender & Science website, accessed September 2017, www.genderaveda.cz.
5 Ruth Fraňková, "Czech Media Foster Gender Stereotypes, Says Equal Rights Campaigner," June 18, 2015. Radio Praha online, www.radio.cz.

145

Statement and Action Agenda
The Girls in Emergencies Collaborative
Annals of Global Health
September 2015

Despite a plethora of gender guidelines and litany of "duty bearers," adolescent girls are left behind in emergencies, just as they have been left behind in conventional development. This must change.

In this document[1] from late 2015 we can see how institutions and practices are still shaped and implemented on the basis of female invisibility and silence about their own needs. It lists a number of ways emergency response organizations fail to "see" adolescent girls, to provide them with the resources—from identification cards to community—they need, or to structure services with an eye to their safety and participation. Thus, the collaborative sadly concludes, the adolescent girl "not only faces a multiplicity of risks during a crisis, but also . . . remains invisible, unprotected, and unengaged, particularly in the crucial first 45 days of a crisis."

Importantly, this document links the dire situation of girls in immediate crisis to a general state of crisis that "the poorest girls in the poorest communities" live in "normally." The implication is that we cannot address emergency situations without tackling the everyday vulnerabilities to which adolescent females are subject, and without answering the question of why emergencies are becoming increasingly common and longer lasting. Only then can we grasp how "[g]irls are controlled under the guise of protection while their rights are violated and their goodwill and capacities are drawn on to mitigate scarcities and family trauma," and how what "begins as an 'event' . . . transforms into a lifetime" for them. Human rights commitments are clearly not enough. We need to act pre-emptively to empower girls in the places where they are subject to both human rights abuses and climate challenges, making them more able to survive sudden displacements, and also to increase their knowledge and ability to assist in the delivery of services for health promotion, human development, and climate mitigation.[2]

The Girls in Emergencies Collaborative came together as a working group in 2013, growing out of the Girls in Emergencies workshop of the Adolescent Girls Learning Circle led by the Population Council. The members of the GIE Collaborative Statement drafting group are experienced in working with diverse populations in emergency situations, and clearly speak from frustration and despair about the situation of adolescent girls. They represent some of the largest organizations responding to emergencies, and their determination and ability to improve things also comes through. The drafting group includes Omar Robles and Dale Buscher, with the Women's Refugee Commission; Judith Bruce, of the Population Council; Holly G. Atkinson, from the Human Rights Program, Arnhold Institute for Global Health, Mount Sinai; Karen Scriven, of Mercy Corps; Kristin Kim Bart and Shelby French, from the International Rescue Committee; and Judithe Registre and Audrey Anderson, of Plan USA. While not a "grassroots" collective, it is a group with ground-level knowledge and a feminist commitment to basing change on the knowledge and voices of the girls they hope to assist, who are displaced within and across national boundaries. Numerous agencies have signed the statement.

Statement and Action Agenda

Many adolescent girls—the poorest girls in the poorest communities—already live in an "emergency." Humanitarian crises only amplify the call on their coping and caring capacities, while exacerbating their vulnerabilities. The frequency and intensity of emergencies, including natural disasters, conflicts, and infectious disease outbreaks such as Ebola, appear to be growing.[3] These emergencies threaten entire communities and whole countries, often with global implications. Many become virtually permanent. Although news coverage is short-lived, the average length of displacement for refugees is almost 20 years. For too many girls worldwide, an emergency begins as an "event" and transforms into a lifetime. The Girls in Emergencies (GIE) Collaborative—a group representing several major emergency response organizations—focuses on the adolescent girl because evidence reveals that she not only faces a multiplicity of risks during a crisis, but also because she remains invisible, unprotected, and unengaged, particularly in the crucial first 45 days of a crisis. Current practice lags behind field realities. To the extent that we identified "good practices," these are small in scale and implemented too late. We need on-the-ground engagement with girls and purposeful field-testing of strategies and tools. Despite a plethora of gender guidelines and litany of "duty bearers," adolescent girls are left behind in emergencies, just as they have been left behind in conventional development. This must change.

Why This Matters

The adolescent girl is already at a triple disadvantage pre-emergency: her age, her sex, and her economic status all put her at risk. Her thin (or absent) friendship network, fragile access to safe public space, and tenuous claim on schooling are further strained or erased by displacement. Girls are maltreated and exploited, even before childbearing age; puberty dramatically elevates their risk for sexual violence, pregnancy, and HIV infection. Many bear or inherit children while still children themselves. Social norms travel with the girl, generating a paradox: Girls are controlled under the guise of protection while their rights are violated and their goodwill and capacities are drawn on to mitigate scarcities and family trauma.

In the severest moments of an emergency, adolescent girls function as a default safety net or virtual credit card. A girl's assets—labor, time, integrity, and safety— can be deployed to underwrite the risks and to "smooth" others' material needs. She is the last to access survival resources, but the first expected to provide; she actively seeks out food, fuel, and water for her family. She may be encouraged or driven by circumstances to trade sex for goods or money; she may be forced into child marriages or short-term sexual liaisons for which her family (and intermediaries) receives money. Her lack of education undermines her own ability to obtain accurate information, discern dangers, or define realistic choices. Without a place to meet other girls and develop her voice and agency, she may doubt her abilities or blame herself for her circumstances. Sexual access to girls, promoted or simply not prevented, is not only a human rights abuse but an injustice that extends her crisis, whether through life-crippling pregnancies or disease (HIV, other sexually transmitted infections, and now, Ebola).

Who We Are and What We Intend to Do

Humanitarian protocols are siloed in content and marked in time—rigidly defined clusters responding during "phases of an emergency." To support the humanitarian community and its collective effort to reach adolescent girls (ages 10–19), the GIE Collaborative has united around 3 urgent and doable actions:

1. To identify and gather critical information about girls in the earliest days of an emergency when risks may be the highest. We need to "see" girls—early and often. At registration, we have to provide girls the documentation they need to independently access services, such as identification cards. Although humanitarian actors may collect age- and sex-disaggregated data on displaced persons, this basic information often is not analyzed, not acted on, or insufficient. The GIE Collaborative aims to develop, test, and deploy acute-phase rapid field enumeration tools that identify the least visible, "offtrack" girls and connect them to survival resources, to other like-situated girls, and to tailored programs and mentorship support.
2. To develop specific and visible mechanisms that connect girls to basic human needs services and logistical support. We will explore explicit girl-branded mechanisms (eg, vouchers, color-coding) that link girls to resources and also build places (formal and informal) where we build their skills and assets.

Because of the fluid, unpredictable nature of emergencies and intense siloing, basic infrastructures often are inconveniently timed and dangerously located. For example, decisions about the location of permanent water points, the timing of food distributions and the weight of prepackaged humanitarian kits are made with nominal consideration to young, female users. We need girls' early input on service design and delivery in concert with the creation of girl-centered safe places and delivery platforms. The GIE Collaborative will experiment with explicit ways to connect adolescent girls to the humanitarian resources that measurably benefit them, with an emphasis on priorities during different phases of an emergency (eg, day 1, days 2–14, days 15–45, days 46–180, and after day 180).

3. To engage girls in the relief and recovery process. We recognize that meaningful engagement is a priority. Intentionally seeking girls' input—their self-expressed needs and concerns—and then incorporating their voices into immediate service delivery and programming must become a foundational pillar for relief, recovery, and empowerment. In addition to seeking girls' input, humanitarian operations should not sideline their capacities to safely participate in relief and recovery efforts. Options include participation in community health campaigns (eg, using bed nets and safe water), in social mobilization (eg, community mapping), and in the introduction and management of economic recovery assets (eg, solar lights, green energy sources, and thermal stoves). The GIE Collaborative aims to identify creative and substantive ways that girls can appropriately and safely contribute to the response.

We commit ourselves and call on the humanitarian community to go beyond the rhetoric—to move [the] earth with bold and measurable actions that protect, serve, and engage adolescent girls from the onset of an emergency.

Notes

1 Girls in Emergencies Collaborative, "Statement and Action Agenda from the Girls in Emergencies Collaborative." *Annals of Global Health* 81.3 (2015): 330–32, www.annalsof globalhealth.org.

2 Holly Atkinson and Judith Bruce, "Adolescent Girls, Human Rights, and the Expanding Climate Emergency." *Annals of Global Health* 81.3 (2015): 323–30, www.annalsofglobalhealth .org.

3 Footnote in document: "Original statistic, ie, reference to 17-year average length of displacement, was first featured at the 30th Standing Committee Meeting of the Executive Committee of the UNHCR in New York City on June 10, 2004." Executive Committee of the High Commissioner's Programme, "Protracted Refugee Situations," report, June 10, 2004. Refugee Agency, UNHCR, www.refworld.org.

146

Manifesto for Rural Women
Northern Ireland Rural Women's Network
Dungannon, County Tyrone, Northern Ireland
September 23, 2015

Northern Ireland Rural Women's Network logo.

It is important to note that rural women often develop a sense of self that is inseparable from the context in which they are located. . . . One of the unique facets of Northern Ireland women's experiences is that of the conflict which has been present in the region for many years and has served to heighten the role of women in the affected areas as nurturers and caretakers. . . . There is a markedly noticeable gap in the literature regarding factors that positively influence leadership development. It is possible that this is the result of a conceptualizing of the rural community as a place where change may take place, but is not created.[1]

Especially in policy literature, "rural" is equated with areas that have a relatively small and dispersed population, are characterized by heavy land use, and are distant from many centralized services. Rural women in Northern Ireland share many of the same problems as rural women elsewhere: limited transportation options, lack of adequate childcare facilities, few job opportunities, underrepresentation in local politics, and limited educational and training institutions, all of which coexist with unequal household responsibilities and gender-based violence. Too, as elsewhere, women in rural Northern Ireland tend to feel the impact of conflict and economic austerity first and hardest, but their social isolation can put collective solutions out of reach.

The Northern Ireland Rural Women's Network (NIRWN) was established in 2006 and is administered by the Department of Agriculture and Rural Development. Its objectives are

- To increase the voice of rural women at a policy level
- To advocate and lobby on behalf of rural women
- To provide information and networking opportunities for rural women
- To represent rural women on the Women's Regional Consortium
- To pilot innovative projects to further the vision of rural women
- To hold statutory bodies to account to measure their impact on rural women.[2]

The Rural Women's Manifesto is a collation of NIRWN's key findings from rural women on the issues directly impacting their lives, and the actions decision makers need to take to address them. It was designed by and for women to amplify their voices in policymaking. The Manifesto project began when NIRWN sponsored events for World Rural Women's Day and International Women's Day. These gatherings gave the organization the chance to talk with over two hundred women about the issues and challenges facing them, their groups, and their rural communities. NIRWN then conducted a research survey to put the women's comments into a firm context.

The Manifesto[3] emphasizes that if Northern Ireland is to attain gender equality, and if rural women are to participate fully in society, they need quality, affordable, flexible childcare; local transport services; support for small businesses and other solutions to part-time, minimum-wage work; a role at every level and stage of rural development; a range of local educational and training options; opportunities to develop social networks; and programs that reckon with women's lesser self-confidence and higher rates of domestic violence.

Manifesto for Rural Women

The Rural Women's Manifesto is a collation of NIRWN's key findings from rural women on the issues directly impacting on their lives, and what actions decision makers need to take to address them.

CARING RESPONSIBILITIES

It is part of our rural and cultural tradition that women in families bear most of the caring responsibilities in terms of childcare, elder care and caring for those with a disability. Caring responsibilities often isolate women, particularly those in rural areas who may become excluded from fully participating in social, economic and community-based activities. Flexible, affordable, accessible quality childcare is very difficult to find in rural areas. Distance from work means rural women's childcare starts earlier and ends later, up to 2 hours a day more than their urban counterparts. This can make childcare unaffordable and work/life balance unrealistic. The recent economic downturn has also had an impact on grandmothers, who are increasingly required to shoulder greater childcare responsibilities.

We call on decision makers to:
- Recognise the work of carers
- Provide adequate resources, support and respite for carers
- Agree [to] a Rural-proofed Childcare Strategy that delivers flexible, affordable, accessible childcare options for rural families
- Acknowledge that childcare is both a social and economic issue; encouraging mothers to return to work or training needs to be supported by affordable childcare provision

RURAL TRANSPORT

Women are much less likely to have access to their own private transport than men. This means that women depend much more on public transport, and are at an economic disadvantage to men. The accessibility of education, training, work and childcare provision and the cost of public transport are factors in determining women's participation, especially in rural areas. The economic disadvantages of lack of access to transport are compounded by the impeded ability to access basic services and social isolation. Feedback from NIRWN members clearly indicates that transport provision varies greatly across the region depending upon where you live, and often provision is linked to the school terms, resulting in no service during holidays.

We call on decision makers to:
- Deliver better, more frequent and more affordable public transport, which takes account of women's needs all year long
- Develop more strategic, long term support for local community transport schemes in rural areas geared towards enabling women to access appropriate childcare, work, education and training
- Ensure public and community transport take account of the needs of women with disabilities and women who have children with disabilities

RURAL DEVELOPMENT

Rural women play a vital role in farm families, businesses and as entrepreneurs. Whilst the Rural Development Programme for NI [Northern Ireland] provides a strong platform for women's needs to be articulated, women continue to be an underrepresented group across Programmes to date. The new 2014–2020 Programme needs to be made accessible to rural women. The Rural Development Programme has the potential to be transformative for rural women by engaging them in decision making; supporting entrepreneurship; improving villages and developing rural tourism, but rural women must be recognised as a target group and actively sought to engage in the Programme.

We call on the Managing Authority to:
- Develop a communication strategy that delivers communication of the Programme effectively to rural women specifically
- Consider the particular needs of rural women at each development stage of the Programme
- Ensure that the LAGs have a 50:50 gender balance over the course of the Programme
- Look at innovative approaches of collecting gender disaggregated data on Programme beneficiaries

We call on the Government Departments to:
- Work with the Managing Authority to look at ways of collaborating and maximising the delivery of the Programme e.g. DETI to increase female entrepreneurship

EDUCATION AND TRAINING OF WOMEN

The right to education is one of the most important means to achieve gender equality. Education and training need to be delivered over the course of a lifetime, adapting to changing life circumstances and reflecting rural women's needs at the time. Community based education and training for women is imperative in rural areas. It is a fundamental building block in supporting women to rebuild confidence and capability to enter the work place, and as a means to access lifelong learning in its own right to maintain overall wellbeing. Community based education is generally delivered based on the local community need, and as such takes account of the complexity of women's lives and barriers to education such as childcare, course fees and academic environment.

We call on decision makers to:
- Rural-proof education and training investment
- Address the barriers to rural women's lifelong engagement in training and education and [remove] these barriers
- Provide a range of education and training options, offering both accredited and non-accredited training
- Recognise low confidence as a major barrier to women's participation in education
- Ensure training can be delivered in the rural communities

RURAL WOMEN, POVERTY, AND THE ECONOMY

Household incomes, poverty rates and the labour market have all worsened in the last five years. The farming and the construction industry, which once sustained and extended families through male employment, can no longer do so. This has resulted in the need for rural women to take on extra work or return to the workplace, often in part-time, low paid jobs. Paid work is not equal for women and men. Two thirds of those earning minimum wage or below are women and women's annual earnings are on average 33% below that of men. The poverty rate for pensioners is higher in NI than in other parts of GB [Great Britain] with nearly half a million pensioners in NI living below the poverty line, including fuel poverty.

Women are outliving men in a population which is living longer but lacks the infrastructure to support this emerging demographic. Many rural women have embraced self-employment and entrepreneurship but would like support to achieve sustained business success. They require networking opportunities, mentoring and training and support that is not just focused on extra job creation and export. Rural women would also like embryonic start up business support that is not focused on farm diversification, for those women who are considering self-employment but do not live on a farm. Without a thriving rural economy, rural way of life is under threat.

We call on decision makers to:
- Introduce a dedicated women's employment strategy to address the dominance of women in low paid work
- Take account of the effect of the economy on older women and take measures to mitigate against pensioner poverty
- In consultation with rural business women, create a sustained support structure for small rural business owners
- Address inadequate infrastructure support such as poor mobile telephone coverage, including roaming charges in border areas and lack of Broadband provision to enable rural businesses to flourish

SOCIAL ISOLATION, HEALTH, AND WELL-BEING

Rural life is often portrayed as idyllic, countryside living where life is slower and the beauty of the surroundings compensates for the lack of services that may be available in an urban setting. This can be the case; rural life has a lot to offer many. This image does not however account for the impact of lack of service provision on health and wellbeing. Rural Women's Groups and Rural Community Groups offer a vital link to rural women and their families in reducing social isolation; providing activities; a base for service delivery and often, bespoke support. This work has been historically under resourced, yet has the potential to save the economy by addressing social isolation's inevitable impacts. Rural women experiencing domestic violence are more vulnerable due to their social isolation and distance from service support.

We call on decision makers to:
- Support the call made by the UN's CEDAW Committee in 2008 for increased and sustained funding for women's groups
- Implement the delivery of Health & Wellbeing Programmes in rural areas specifically targeting rural women
- Address the historical underfunding of rural women's provision
- When budgeting, take account of the specific needs and challenges faced by rural women and their children when experiencing domestic abuse

Notes

1 Lori Ann McVay, *Rural Women in Leadership: Positive Factors in Leadership Development* (Oxfordshire, UK: CABI, 2013), pp. 17–18, emphasis added.
2 Northern Ireland rural Women's Network, "About." NIRWN website, accessed September 2017, www.nirwn.org.
3 Northern Ireland Rural Women's Network, "Manifesto for Rural Women." NIRWN website, accessed September 2017, www.nirwn.org.

147

The Mulata Globeleza: A Manifesto
Brazil
February 8, 2016

Brazil has the largest population of people of African descent outside of Africa. This Manifesto comes out of the long history of activism by Black women in Brazil, evident in events from the presentation of a Black Women's Manifesto at the Congress of Brazilian Women in 1975 to the March of Black Women—numbering some ten thousand—in Brasilia in 2015.

The Manifesto[1] links a contemporary event—the selection of a light-skinned Black woman who dances naked to promote Carnival—with the history of enslavement and the current dearth of cultural space for women artists. It challenges "the myth of racial democracy" by making clear the exploitation and exoticization given life by such practices as the *mulata globeleza*. "Brazilian society generally reserves two 'places' for black women: she is either a maid, whose domain is in the household, specifically the kitchen, or she is the sexually alluring 'mulata' whose talents are thought to be suitable only for the bedroom."[2] The issues raised here speak to the reinforcing domains of patriarchal and racist media, capitalism, and sexuality.

The Mulata Globeleza: A Manifesto

The Globeleza Mulata is not a natural cultural event, but a performance that invades the imaginary and the Brazilian televisions during Carnival. A spectac[le] created by art director Hans Donner to be the symbol of the popular party, which exhibited for 13 years his companion Valéria Valenssa in the super-expositional function of "mulata." We're talking about a character that appeared in the nineties and still strictly follows the same script: it is always a black woman that dances the samba as a passista (Carnaval dancer), naked with her body painted with glitter, to the sound of the vignette displayed throughout the daily programming of Rede Globo (TV).

To start the debate on this character, we need to identify the problem contained in the term "mulata." Besides being a word naturalized by Brazilian society, it is a captive presence in the vocabulary of the hosts, journalists and reporters from the Globo broadcasting. The word is of Spanish origin [and] comes from "mula" or "mulo" (the masculine and feminine of "mule"): that is a hybrid originating from a cross between species. Mules are animals born crossing donkeys with mares or horses with donkeys. In another sense, they are the result of the mating of the animal considered noble (equus caballus) with the animal deemed second class (donkey). Therefore, it is a derogatory word indicating mestiçagem (racial mixture or crossbreeding), impurity; an improper mixing that should not exist.

Employed since the colonial period, the term was used to designate lighter skinned blacks, fruits of the rape of slaves by masters. Such a nomenclature has sexist and racist nature and was transferred to the Globeleza character, naturalized. The adjective "mulata" is a sad memory of the 354 years (1534–1888) of escravidão negra (black slavery) in Brazil.

The black woman exposed as Globeleza continues including a standard of an aesthetic selection near to that made by the masters choosing enslaved women that they wanted near. The slaves considered "beautiful" were chosen to work in the casa grande (big house/master's house). Likewise, the future victims of harassment, intimidation and rape were selected. Black women subjected to the yoke "of the owners." It was common [that] lighter-skinned slaves, with features closer to that of branquitude (whiteness)[, who were] judged as beautiful[,] would assume these posts of service. The bodies of the women were not seen as their own property, they would serve only to be exploited in exhaustive menial jobs in addition to serving as a constant deposit of sexual abuse, humiliation, vexation and emotional violence.

Luiza Bairros has a very interesting phrase that explains very well the place that society gives to the black woman, "we carry the mark." No matter where we are, the mark is the exotificization of our bodies and subordination. Since the colonial period, black women have been stereotyped as being "hot," naturally sensual, seducers of men. These classifications, seen through the eyes of the colonizer, [romanticize] the fact that these women were [held] as slaves and thus were raped and abused, in other words, her will did not exist in front of her "masters."

Just look at how true this is: in 2015, Globo swapped the Globeleza Nayara Justino, elected by popular vote in the Fantástico news program, for one with lighter skin, the current Globeleza Érika Moura, chosen internally, as the first "would not have aligned herself to the proposal," according to them. Reaffirming Eurocentric "taste" choosing the black woman fit to be exposed as a sexual object. In other words, guided by racism and sexism (in a roundabout way for some, for us, very clear) they selected which standards of black women they will exploit in their vignettes following a criteria of lighter skin, features considered finer, and a slimmer, but voluptuous and luxurious body "tipo exportação" (of the exportation type). The black woman, in this position, again loses autonomy over herself and the place she should occupy comes to be defined by others.

An example of the stigmas that are placed on the bodies of black women and demonstrating . . . the imposition of the place we occupy is the case of the Venus Hottentot. Her original name is Sarah Baartman. Born in 1789 in the region of South Africa in the early 19th century she was taken to Europe. Sarah Baartman gave a body to racist theory. She was exhibited in cages, halls and arenas because of her anatomy that was considered "grotesque, barbaric, exotic": voluminous buttocks and genitalia with large lips (a characteristic in women of her people, the Khoi-san). Her body was placed between the boundary of what would be an abnormal black woman and a normal white woman, the first considered wild.

Finally, the body of Baartman didn't receive a proper burial. After death, her skeleton, genitals and brain were preserved and put on display in Paris at the Musée de l'Homme (Museu do Homen/Museum of Man). Even after her death she was managed and experienced as a specimen, a collection piece at the service of research and white European scientism. Only in 2002, at the request of Nelson Mandela, were her remains returned to South Africa. And for many, over 200 years later, she was not considered people.

Baartman's story happened centuries ago, but this stigma still rests with us, black women. Currently we see an influential channel like Globo that, for nearly 30 years, has exposed naked black women at any time of day or night during Carnival period, refusing to represent us beyond that place of exploitation of our bodies in the rest of the whole year. How many black women do we see as actresses, hosts, reporters on the ranks of the big broadcasters? And when we see actresses, what are the roles they are playing? Rarely do [we] see black women in the Globo grid hosting programs or being protagonists, but in the period of Carnival, the station promotes "mulata hunts" to elect the new Globeleza, which only appears naked and at this time of year.

It is necessary to understand the reason one criticizes places like Globeleza. It's not the nudity itself, nor . . . [who] performs this role. It's because of the confinement of black women to specific places. We have no problem with the sensuality, the problem is only confin[ing] us to these places denying our humanity, multiplicity and complexity. When we reduce humans only to certain roles and places, we are withdrawing our humanity and turning us into objects.

We are not protagonists of novelas (soap operas)—not the mocinhas (good girls) nor the villains, at the most maids who serve as mere setting, a prop (including apt to abuse) to the story of the white household. Just remember the last part of the great actress Zezé Motta on the station, where she was the maid Sebastiana in the novela Boogie Oogie. In contrast, some actresses like Taís Araujo and Camila Pitanga stand out, but we cannot pretend that this is not because they are young and black women with lighter skin. Women like Ruth de Souza are forgotten in

an environment that values greats such as Fernanda Montenegro. This has nothing to do with talent, since both the first and second have versatility and plenty
of technique, but rather the color of the skin of each and the opportunities they
are given.

What will be the fate of the current black Brazilian actresses?

Or black girls who dream of studying theater and film?

Is there no place for them? If so, what is this place?

Perhaps the same of the older black actresses and Globelezas: disposal and obliv-
ion when their bodies no longer serve. The naked truth is that Globeleza currently only reinforces a fatalist, cast, pre-set place . . . to the black woman [in] a
racist and sexist Brazilian society and this fixed place must be interrupted, broken, starting with the end of that symbol/character.

We don't accept having our identity and humanity denied for those who still believe that our only place is connected to entertainment via the exploitation of our
body. No longer do we accept our body as hostage of preference and at the will
of the third party, to the delight of a male audience and an audience that deprives
itself of hypocritical puritanism only during Carnival. No longer do we accept our
body narrated from the point of view of Eurocentris[t] aesthetic, ethical, cultural,
educational, historical and religious. No longer do we accept the shackles of the
media on our body!

It's necessary to exit from common sense, break the myth of racial democracy
that camouflages the latent racism of this society. We can no longer accept that
black women are relegated to the role of exoticization.

This Manifesto not only calls for the end of Globeleza as born of urgency and
screams ([these] are too stuffy) [but also] for the opening and incorporation of
new roles and spaces for black women in the Brazilian art scene. A new paradigm
needs to dawn on the horizon of the black artists ever so talented, but still without the embrace of recognition.

What is missing for black women, as emphasized by the American Viola Davis
in her speech after winning the Golden Globe, are opportunities. In Brazil, they
need to go beyond ideology propagated by attractions like Sexo e as Negas and
Globeleza (both from the same station, Globo). The question is about the end of
this only place for women who are multiple.

The construction of new spaces has already been made in an arduous way in
real society, in the poor classes, in organized collectives, in peripheral youth,
student[s] and workers where black women are the majority among the devo-
tees of programs such as Prouni, or are already cotistas (quota students) in universities. However, this new place is not yet reflected in the media, at least not
the most reliable and probable possible. It is evident that there is no interest in
representing us as we are. We appear to be a nuisance and the few prominent

black voices are made-up, interrupted or scripted to ease our reality and when they're not, glamorize the favela (slum).

We can no longer naturalize this concealed violence of culture. Culture is constructed, thus its values are also. It's necessary to realize how much the reification of these subaltern and exotificized roles for black women denies opportunities for us to perform other roles and occupy other places. We do not want to star in the gringo imagery that comes in search of sex tourism.

Enough! It's past time!

Notes

1 "A Call for the End of the 'Globeleza Mulata': A Manifesto," Feb. 8, 2016. *Black Women of Brazil* blog, www.blackwomenofbrazil.co; translated from Stephanie Ribeiro and Djamila Ribeiro, "A Mulata Globeleza: Um Manifesto," Jan. 29, 2016. *Agora É Que São Elas* blog, agoraequesaoelas.blogfolha.uol.com.br. Minor adjustments made for readability.

2 "When the Bright Lights Go Dim: Two of Carnaval's Poster Girls Fall into Depression after Losing Their Status," Oct. 20, 2014. *Black Women of Brazil* blog, www.blackwomen ofbrazil.co.

148

Walls and Enclosures: This Is Not the Europe in Which We Want to Live
Spanish Federation of Feminist Organizations
Madrid, Spain
February 26, 2016

Spanish Federation of Feminist Organizations logo.

Changes made by globalization . . . have made it impossible and unacceptable to maintain those barriers and borders that divide humanity into those who have the right to live and those who don't.

How fitting it is that among the closing documents in this collection is a feminist petition on the subject of the current immigration crisis in Europe. It is an apt finale because it leaves us with a lasting reminder of how feminist voices have been raised on virtually every significant event in history, and continue to plead for alternative values and practices. It is apt because so many are still surprised that feminism speaks to issues beyond those most narrowly associated with it in various places.

Inspired by multiple Italian feminist groups (that also signed onto the Manifesto), this document was penned by the Federation of Feminist Organizations of Spain, which was established to coordinate local efforts and bring greater social and political effectiveness to their demands. In the decades since it was founded, in 1978, it has campaigned for the right to divorce, for free abortion, against gender-based violence, for sexual freedom, for equal employment opportunities, and for equal distribution of domestic labor.[1]

The Manifesto shows feminist groups' continued engagement in current events.[2] It calls on both the international community and European countries to change the policies and practices that have resulted in intolerable conditions for many seeking refuge in Europe from devastating wars and disasters. The Manifesto[3] speaks up for the importance of safety, and notes the universality of vulnerability.

What makes this a feminist issue? First, groups that have long opposed violence against women here make visible the violence that women asylum seekers in particular confront, both as they flee and in refugee camps. Second, the Manifesto contains a feminist cry for treating all human beings with basic dignity, and resists tactics that delegitimize them or their claims, including disregarding economic refugees and calling humans "illegals." Third, the document holds responsible for the exodus the neocolonial practices and "penitentiary logic" that are indicted in multiple documents in this collection. Finally, feminisms committed to democracy and working across differences see in the opposition to refugees "fear and the rejection of what is different . . . founded in patriarchal ideology." Calls for rethinking nationality and citizenship follow, as do pleas to build on the knowledge and experience of women as alternatives are carefully considered.

Walls and Enclosures: This Is Not the Europe in Which We Want to Live

To be able to be where we want is the original sign of being free, whereas the limitations of such freedom have been since time immemorial the prelude of slavery.
We cannot choose with whom we live in the world.
—Hannah Arendt

Barbed wires, walls, and enclosures are multiplying in Europe. The roads taken by fleeing migrants, both women and men, are turning into roads of war, and are filled with mines, metaphorical and real. We are also seeing chilling symbolic elements like the numbers drawn on migrants' arms and the welcoming of refugees in the concentration camps of Buchenwald. The routes of exodus are changing. Right now, we are seeing an overland route in the Balkans, although the journeys and deaths on the sea still continue. Some fugitives are dying, electrocuted, in Calais as they try to climb the net that blocks the entrance to the United Kingdom. Other people are seriously injured in the border fences in Ceuta and Melilla.

Together with many other networks of women, we believe it is necessary to highlight a different kind of immigration policy, another type of reception.

1. The international community has the duty to guarantee safe travel routes for every asylum applicant. This duty must be carried out with special care

by humanitarian organizations controlling women's status at refugee camps, for instance the camps in Libya, as well as in other places where women suffer from violence.

2. Every immigrant should be guaranteed asylum, including the so-called "economic immigrants," who risk their lives as they flee unbearable conditions. These unbearable conditions include the unsustainable effects of climate change as well as the negative effects of Western and neocolonialist powers (desertification, drought, land grabbing, resource hoarding, price increase of raw materials . . .).

3. There are no "clandestine people," just people avoiding hunger and war, with no intention of hiding. This language distortion is unacceptable.

4. Following the "safe cities" example, promoted by the Mayor of Barcelona, Ada Colau, it is necessary to guarantee refugees a dignified reception, welcoming them to be a part of communities without segregating them into isolated camps where they would forever remain "foreigners."

Women and men who are seeking refuge enter our societies and become part of our realities. Their bodies could be our bodies. Their children could be our children. We could be the ones feeling the same coldness, the same fear, the same hunger.

What does it mean, then, for us to be European citizens? What do borders represent to us in connection with the right to live? "Primum vivere": it is the challenge many women initiated at the conference in Paestum. A Europe full of penitentiary logic and borders is not the place where we want to live.

We are aware that behind the rejection of immigrants lies the rejection of what is different. This rejection is founded in patriarchal ideology that has created hierarchies among human beings, defining one's superiority in relation to another: white-black, north-south, and above all masculine-feminine . . . In the world of politics only a few seem to understand what is at stake: the deep and unstoppable metamorphosis that immigrants are carrying out, a change that will transform thoughts, practices, rules of coexistence. It is all about overcoming fear and the rejection of what is different . . . Women know very well what this means.

Keeping in mind Hannah Arendt's simple but beautiful words regarding freedom and the right to relocate, we have to take an evolutionary leap in our civilization. Changes made by globalization, especially in the realm of communication, have made it impossible and unacceptable to maintain those barriers and borders that divide humanity into those who have the right to live and those who don't.

Ancient and new powers are trying to keep the system of domination alive by strengthening the tools of patriarchy—weapons, wars, borders—against a fleeing "continent" (almost 60 million people) that is trying to move forward. In contrast, it is increasingly evident that we need to construct an understanding of citizenship that considers the real material conditions of life that are common to all people on this planet. It is also essential to recognize our individual and collective differences as sources of enrichment. This is not an easy path. It requires care. But it is necessary to begin. Women's ways of thinking and their experience can effectively contribute to this project, because historically our gender has learned to confront being ignored and excluded.

Finally, we believe that it is necessary to learn to reflect deeply so that we can overcome the barriers set by patriarchal norms. Such patriarchal barriers are still based on a concept of citizenship that forms an identity by belonging to an "exclusive" nation. Every day we witness the consequences of this patriarchal structure, as the meaning of Europe itself disintegrates.

Notes

1 Federación Estatal de Organizaciones Feministas, "Presentación," Jan. 20, 2014. Coordinadora Feminista website, www.feministas.org.

2 Translated by Madeleine Brink and Violeta Martinez Morones.

3 Federación Estatal de Organizaciones Feministas, "Manifiesto: Murallas y recintos: no es la Europa en la que queremos vivir," Feb. 26, 2016. Coordinadora Feminista website, www.feministas.org.

149

Statement: Do Not Militarize Our Mourning; Orlando and the Ongoing Tragedy against LGBTSTGNC POC

Audre Lorde Project
Brooklyn, New York
June 15, 2016

Logo for the Audre Lorde project.

[W]e are considered disposable by a racist, transmisogynist, Islamophobic, and xenophobic country.

Despite increased visibility and recent legal victories, LGBT communities of color remain economically and socially disadvantaged, as individuals experience "chronic harassment" and are "four times more likely than the general population to report living in extreme poverty."[1] The Audre Lorde Project describes its mission as follows:

The Audre Lorde Project is a Lesbian, Gay, Bisexual, Two Spirit, Trans and Gender Non-Conforming [LGBTSTGNC] People of Color [POC] community organizing center, focusing on the New York City area. Through mobilization, education and capacity-building, we work for community wellness and progressive social and economic justice. Committed to struggling across differences, we seek to responsibly reflect, represent and serve our various communities.[2]

The organization began in 1994 as a multiracial group struggling with HIV in the gay male community, and has expanded to devise culturally specific services that still involve the targeted communities in project identification, design, and implementation. The group is strongly committed to organizational practices that are feminist and antiracist.[3] With inspirational quotations from Audre Lorde in all of its statements, the group today works on issues such as sensitive medical care for and violence against the trans community (like Incite! they prefer to work outside the criminal justice system), prison reform, HIV/AIDS policy, and pro-immigrant activism. Clearly located at the intersections of race, class, sexual orientation, and gender identity, the Audre Lorde Project claims to be "the only intergenerational LGBTSTGNC People of Color Community Organizing Center in New York City, and one of the few in the country."[4]

The Statement below is a passionate response to the recent mass shooting at a nightclub in Orlando, Florida, in which most of the victims were queer and trans people of color. Such events differ only in scale from the sorts of violence the center regularly works to end by building strong communities—"this massacre is not the exception, it is part of the economy of violence against LGBTSTGNC, Black people & People of Color, indigenous people, and immigrants." The Statement links the Orlando murders to U.S. foreign and economic policies, police violence, hate crimes, and discrimination within LGBT communities. Most adamantly, the Statement rejects the solution of increased police presence at gay bars and pride events, and reveals the hypocrisy of such supposed concern with safety given the general, everyday indifference or hostility toward LGBTSTGNC people of color.

Statement: Do Not Militarize Our Mourning; Orlando and the Ongoing Tragedy against LGBTSTGNC POC

We at the Audre Lorde Project are devastated by the massacre at the Pulse nightclub in Orlando which resulted in the murder of 49 queer and trans people (the majority of whom are Black, Latinx, and/or Afrolatinx), including Enrique Rios from Brooklyn. We send our deepest condolences to all of the families, lovers, and friends of the victims and all of the Southern queer and trans organizers who continue to fight for liberation in their name. We are with you in solidarity. We are constantly reminded that there is no separation from our need to heal and our need to organize for our continued survival. We need each other now more than ever.

Our community in New York City is struggling today as we reconcile with the constant reality that we are considered disposable by a racist, transmisogynist, Islamophobic, and xenophobic country. From our experiences on the ground as an organizing center for and by Lesbian, Gay, Bisexual, Trans, Two Spirit, and Gender Non Conforming People of Color (LGBTSTGNC POC) we know that this massacre is not the exception, it is part of the economy of violence against LGBTSTGNC, Black people & People of Color, indigenous people, and immigrants. It makes explicit what the institutions of war, prisons, detention centers, and the police teach our communities every day: that we were never meant to survive.*[5]

Contrary to what the media and mainstream LGBT organizations and publications are depicting: the victims and survivors are Black, Latinx, AfroLatinx, Trans, Gender Non Conforming, undocumented, and working class. These identities matter. They matter because of the US occupation and militarization of Puerto Rico and Latin/South America due to US sanctioned economic violence. They matter because our communities have to make separate Latinx nights at clubs due to racism even within the LGBT community. They matter because Black and Latinx club sanctuaries and safe spaces (like Starlight in Brooklyn, Club Escuelita in Manhattan) are routinely shut down due to rampant gentrification and increased policing of our neighborhoods. They matter because Bayna Lehkiem El-Amin, a Black HIV/AIDS counselor and Ballroom community leader, has been demonized as a homophobe and is currently awaiting sentencing in Rikers for defending himself against an attack by a white gay man. They matter because there is an epidemic of murder of Black and Latinx Trans Women and Gender Non Conforming people and this tragedy is part of this ongoing colonial project.

The fact that only the race of the perpetrator and not the victims is being discussed is telling. Besides erasing the lived reality of Muslim LGBTSTGNC people, Black Muslims, and LGBTSTGNC people of color more generally, this promotes the xenophobic stereotype that Muslim people and immigrants are more "homophobic," and become "radicalized" elsewhere. The culprit becomes the figure of the "Islamic terrorist," and the heroes become the politicians, the police, and the military. We reject this deliberately racist framing. Individual perpetrators are part of a much larger system of militarization and colonization. We recognize that terrorism is not imported, it is home grown in a culture that is deeply anti-Black, anti-immigrant, and anti-queer. It is of a culture where the Christian Right has attempted to pass over 200 pieces of anti-LGBT legislation across the country, it is a culture where 59 year old Mohamed Rasheed Khan was beaten on his way out of a Queens mosque this month, where an immigrant detention center in Santa Ana still detains and assaults many Latinx trans women who came to the US to escape US-backed political violence. In order to do justice to the victims of Orlando we have to address these problems at their root causes, not their symptoms. While the daily violences of settler colonialism (the continued occupation of indigenous land), of Christian supremacy, of anti-Black policing, of Islamophobia, of criminalization of gender non conformity, of immigrant detention and deportation are never elevated to the status of national tragedy, we must commit ourselves to abolishing these systems if we want to prevent Orlando from ever happening again.

Already the NYPD, along with other security forces across the country, has heightened security outside of our bars and Pride events. This has looked like armed cops in riot gear policing our safe spaces—cops who are carrying the same kind of weapon that Omar Mateen used in Orlando. Politicians (both Trump and Clinton alike) are calling for a harsher crackdown on "Islamic extremism." Our allies are pledging to keep us safe as we assemble for Pride this month. But we ask: safety for whom? They call for increased policing, but never for affordable housing. Hate crimes legislation has been shown to fuel mass incarceration and disproportionately criminalize Black and People of Color survivors of violence. The Christopher Street Pier, a sacred space for LGBTSTGNC youth and poor people of color, is barricaded shut by NYPD during Pride. Calls for gun control never seem to include demands for demilitarization of the police.

In order to prevent the violence we witnessed in Orlando, it is more important than ever that LGBTSTGNC POC turn to each other for community safety rather than relying on systems that were never meant for us. It is more important than ever that we reject increased militarization at home and abroad. It is more important than ever that we uplift the experiences, politics, and movements of Black, Indigenous, and Latinx queer and trans people fighting for self-determination of our bodies, homes, neighborhoods, clubs, and lands.

It will be imperative that we look towards each other for our political survival, for our collective well being and safety. We honor the names of those lost in Orlando, as a reminder of the conservative backlash in this country and [a] reminder [that] we must continue to fight, to love, to build power and transform violence and colonization that has always deemed our bodies expendable.

In Solidarity,

Audre Lorde Project Members, Board, Staff

Notes

1 Katy Steinmetz, "Why Transgender People Are Being Murdered at a Historic Rate." *Time*, Aug. 17, 2015. www.time.com.
2 Audre Lorde Project website, accessed September 2017, www.alp.org.
3 "About ALP." Audre Lorde Project website, accessed September 2017, www.alp.org.
4 "The Audre Lorde Project," Nov. 10, 2016. Host Organizations, Civil Liberties, and Public Policy website, clpp.hampshire.edu.
5 On the website, this asterisk leads to Lorde's poem, "Litany for Survival."

150

Manifesto for a Migrant Feminism
Intercultural Women's Center of Trama di Terre
Rome, Italy
December 2016

Women's migration has slowly become part of the story of scattered lives, diasporic and hyphenated existences.[1]

[W]e call to fight for a new Migrant Feminism, taking into account the class/status differences which affect deeply women's possibility of self-determination, and fighting against the rising fundamentalism and fascism.

Women march in solidarity with migrant feminists in Imola, Italy, on February 13, 2016. Photo by Marco Semenzin/Trama di Terre.

Immigration and feminist studies and activism intersect in this document, as they do daily in an era marked by both globalization and massive movements of displaced people. In Italy, where this document was written, over half a million refugees have arrived in the last three years, many "travelling the perilous route from Libya to Italy."[2] The numbers have overwhelmed some older structures built to serve immigrants, and anti-immigrant sentiment is commonly voiced, there as elsewhere. Into this complexity come the women of Trama di Terre (Weave of Lands), who confront some new challenges posed by gender, race, class, and nation, at home now rather than abroad. "The micro-practices by which migrant women endeavor to relocate their lives across manifold symbolic and geographical borders reveal the ambivalent sentiments connected with the lived experiences of migration. Indeed, migrant women's encounter with the Italian nation-state, its material and symbolic borders, sheds light on the multiple forms of exclusion that they experience in their daily lives."[3]

This document[4] details the forms of violence to which women are subjected at various stages of emigration, and confronts the question of how to capture and address the situation of women coming from one set of gendered societies and religions to differently gendered ones with different majority religious traditions—without buying into neoliberalism's versions of "progress" and individualism, and with attention to the added vulnerabilities of being female and an immigrant. The group argues that women's rights should take precedence over "cultural rights" and that the state must stay secular. It recognizes the difficult, "intricate process" of interculturalism and condemns the absence of humanitarian corridors. "Trama di Terre stands in this space of rebellion and struggle for autonomy, in . . . resistance to imposed identities. Identities which are imposed by racism, still deeply rooted in Italian society, and also by anyone who, in the name of tradition, religion or culture, tries to relegate women into roles that limit the full exercise of their rights and freedoms, conquered at such a high price in many parts of the world."[5]

Trama di Terre was founded in 1997 by women of five nationalities (currently twenty-three are represented).[6] The Women's Intercultural Center opened in 2001. It is described as "a permanent laboratory aiming to help foreign women bring out and fully exploit the knowledge they possess, through collective paths of empowerment, autonomy and speak[ing]-out."

Manifesto for a Migrant Feminism

Male violence [against] women has no colour, no religion, no culture—it crosses all patriarchal societies because it needs to maintain the power imbalance between men and women. But there are forms of violence which are imported with migration, and affect mainly migrant women, putting their lives and bodies at stake, when they are not in a position where they can enforce their own rights.

Today we suffer the consequences of "neutral" anti-racist policies which have been favouring cultural rights [over] women's rights, strengthening the patriarchate within some migrant communities. We need to defend secularism not only against Catholic fundamentalists but against every kind of interference in the public sphere and in women's self-determination by every religion in this country.

Interculturalism is an intricate process that has to be built day after day through dialogue and conflict as well. It may fail if we don't have a strong focus on the protection of women's rights and individual liberties. That's why we prefer talking about GENDER INTERCULTURALISM.

For migrant women the current immigration law [entails] a double blackmailing: it makes them more exploitable in labour, and it ties them down to their husbands' documents in case of family reunification. Therefore, for foreign women the residence permit can become an instrument of patriarchal control in the hands of violent employers and family members.

Women asylum-seekers and women refugees have survived many different forms of male violence—gender discrimination, domestic violence, traffic for sexual exploitation, difficult access to education and efficient social services, abuse related to traditional practices such as forced marriage (including early marriage), genital mutilations, corrective rape; situations which are exacerbated by the ever-increasing religious fundamentalism and by war.

Due to the absence of humanitarian corridors, migrants are forced to travel in a total lack of safety. Travelling poses an even greater risk for women, as they are exposed to systematic rape, also used as a blackmail to exploit them economically and sexually.

In transit and arrival countries, women find even more violence. In the absence of gender-sensitive policies, the public-funded so-called "reception" centres (*centri d'accoglienza*) are often the scene of sexist abuse, while outside these centres, in addition to the growing race/gender intersectional discrimination, there is the institutional violence of economic and social policies which are strengthening poverty and inequality and therefore affecting migrant women's lives in a double way.

In the current context of daily episodes of sexist and racist violence, it becomes more important; reporting the abuse suffered by migrant women and women asylum-seekers, and supporting them in the realization of their life projects. Therefore, we call to fight for a new Migrant Feminism, taking into account the class/status differences which affect deeply women's possibility of self-determination, and fighting against the rising fundamentalism and fascism.

Notes

1   Anastasia Christou, "Migrating Gender: Feminist Geographies in Women's Biographies of Return Migration." *Gender and Globalisms* 17 (2003).
2   Zoie O'Brien, " 'Time to Act': Italy Calls for Mass Migrant Deportations as Half a Million Refugees Arrive." *Daily Express*, Jan. 3, 2017, www.express.co.uk.
3   Laura Menin, "Feminist Desires, Multi-culturalist Dilemmas: Migrant Women's Self-organizing in Milan," in *Feminism and Migration: Cross-Cultural Engagements* (New York: Springer, 2012).
4   Trama di Terre, "Towards the 26th November March against Male Violence on Women . . . MANIFESTO FOR A MIGRANT FEMINISM." Trama di Terre website, accessed September 2017, www.tramaditerre.org.
5   Trama di Terre, "Trama di Terre: Who We Are." Trama di Terre website, accessed September 2017, www.tramaditerre.org.
6   Trama di Terre, "Chi siamo." Trama di Terre website, accessed September 2017, www.tramaditerre.org.

APPENDIX
For Further Reading

Note: Subsequent documents by the groups included in this volume are not listed.

"Preamble" and "Constitution," Female Anti-Slavery Society of Chatham Street Chapel. New York, New York; 1834.

"Resolutions," Women's Loyal National League Meeting. New York, New York; May 14, 1863.

"Statutes," General German Women's Association. Leipzig, Germany; October 17, 1865.

"National Convention Resolutions," American Equal Rights Association, Church of the Puritan. New York, New York; May 9, 1867.

"Declaration of Principles" and "Resolutions," New England Woman's Suffrage Association. Boston, Massachusetts; November 18–19, 1868.

"Resolutions," American Equal Rights Association Meeting. New York, New York; May 12–14, 1869.

"Constitution," National Woman Suffrage Association. Washington, D.C.; 1883.

"Constitution and By-Laws," National Consumers League. Washington, D.C.; 1899.

"War and Women: Manifesto of the Women's Group of the Ethical Movement." June 1, 1915.

"Resolutions of the Zurich Conference," Women's International League for Peace and Freedom. Zurich, Switzerland; May 12–17, 1919.

"Aims and Principles," American Birth Control League. New York, New York; Nov. 11–19, 1921.

"Resolutions," Arab Women's Association. Jerusalem, Palestine; October 26, 1929.

"Manifesto," Women's World Committee, 1935.

"Birth Control Pills and Black Children: The Sisters Reply." 1968.

"A Political Organization to Annihilate Sex Roles," The Feminists. 1969.

"Politics of the Ego: A Manifesto," New York Radical Feminists. 1969.

"About Us," A San Diego Women's Collective. 1970.

"Specific Characteristics of Women's Liberation," Women of Youth Against War and Racism. 1970.

"The Male-Feasance of Health," Women's Health Collective. 1970.

"A Statement about Female Liberation," Female Liberation. 1971.

"Statement of Purpose," Westchester Radical Feminists. 1972.

"Resolution," Comisión Femenil Mexicana Nacional, Inc. Goleta, California; October 17, 1973.

"Towards Equality," Committee on the Status of Women in India. Kolkata, India; 1974.

"Principles of Unity," Berkeley-Oakland Women's Union, *Socialist Revolution* 4, no. 1 (Jan–March 1974): 69–82.

"Black Women's Manifesto"/"Manifesto das Mulheres Negres," Congress of Brazilian Women/Congresso das Mulheres Brasileiras. Rio de Janiero, Brazil; July 1975.

"Declaration on the Rights of Women of Pakistan." 1976.

"Mission Statement and Purpose," National Coalition Against Domestic Violence. Denver, Colorado; 1978.

"What We Want," Women's Global Network for Reproductive Rights. Philippines; 1984.

"Our Mission and Vision," DisAbled Women's Network (DAWN). Winnipeg, Ontario; March 26–29, 1987.

"Abuja Declaration on Participatory Development," Regional Conference on the Integration of Women in Development. Abuja, Nigeria; November 6–10, 1989.

"African American Women in Defense of Ourselves." 1991.

"Black Women in Europe," Women's and Equality Units of Camden, Hackney, Haringey, and Islington Councils. London, England; February 24, 1991.

"Statement of Principles," Network of East-West Women. Dubrovnik, Poland; June 1991.

"Mission Statement," Independent Forum of Albanian Women. Tirana, Albania; September 1991.

"Alto da Boa Vista Vision Statement," Women, Procreation, and Environment Conference. Rio de Janeiro, Brazil; September 30–October 7, 1991.

"Sri Lanka Women's Charter." 1993.

"The European Charter for Women in the City," Commission of the European Union Unit (Equal Opportunities Unit). Brussels, Belgium; 1994.

"Inter-American Convention on the Prevention, Punishment, and Eradication of Violence against Women." Convention of Belem do Para at the Twenty-Fourth Regular Session of the General Assembly to the Organization of American States. Belem do Para, Brazil; June 9, 1994.

"The Victoria Falls Declaration of Principles for the Promotion of the Human Rights of Women," African Regional Judicial Colloquium for Senior Judges on the Domestic Application of International laws on Gender Issues. Victoria Falls, Zimbabwe; August 19–20, 1994.

"Resolution Calling on the OAU to Formalize the African Women's Committee on Peace," Ad Hoc Experts Group/Women's Leadership Forum on Peace. Johannesburg, South Africa; November 8, 1996.

"Kigali Declaration on Peace, Gender, and Development." Pan-African Conference on Gender, Peace, and Development in Kigali. Rwanda; March 1–3, 1997.

"The Addis Ababa Declaration," Inter-African Committee on Traditional Practices Affecting the Health of Women and Children. Addis Ababa, Ethiopia; September 12, 1997.

"A Declaration of Women's Rights in Islamic Societies." Amherst, New York; Fall 1997.

"Gender and Human Security," Gender and Human Security Network. 1999.

"Zanzibar Declaration," Women of Africa for a Culture of Peace. Zanzibar, Tanzania; May 17–20, 1999.

"Declaration of Sexual Rights," World Sexology Organization. Hong Kong, China; August 26, 1999.

"Women's Caucus Declaration," Third Seattle Ministerial Meeting of the World Trade Organization. Nov. 30–Dec. 3 1999.

"The Women's Charter." Zimbabwe; 2000.

"The Aachen Declaration on Midwifery for All," First European Congress for Out-of-Hospital Births. Aachen, Aix-la-Chapelle, Germany; September 28–October 1, 2000.

"Women's Charter of Rights." East Timor; 2001.

"Declaration," World Conference against Racism, Racial Discrimination, Xenophobia, and Related Intolerance. Durban, South Africa; August 31–September 8, 2001.

"Afghan Women's Bill of Rights." 2003.

"Charter on Sexual and Reproductive Rights," International Planned Parenthood Foundation. London, England; 2003.

"Kampala Declaration to Prevent Gender-based Violence in Africa," Regional Dialogue organized by Raising Voices and UN-HABITAT's Safer Cities Programme. Kampala, Uganda; September 4–6, 2003.

"Manifesto of the First Feminist Meeting." Paraguay; November 18, 2003.

"Panlyurfa Declaration on Violence against Women," Human Rights Association of Sanliurfa. Panlyurfa, Turkey; November 22–23, 2003.

"Charter for the Rights and Freedoms of Women in the Kurdish Regions and Diaspora." 2004.

"Namibian Women's Manifesto." 2004.

"The Women's Manifesto for Ghana." 2004.

"Statement on the Occasion of International Women's Day," Revolutionary Association of the Women of Afghanistan, March 8, 2004.

"Declaration of the Extended Forum of the Albanian Feminist Movement's Activists and Reconciliation Missionaries." Fier-Shegan Commune, Albania; March 14, 2004.

"Solemn Declaration on Gender Equality in Africa," Assembly of the African Union, Third Ordinary Session. Addis Ababa, Ethiopia; July 6–8, 2004.

"Reproductive Justice: Vision, Analysis, and Action for a Stronger Movement,"Asian Communities for Reproductive Justice. 2005.

"The International Consensus Statement on Women's Mental Health" and the "WPA Consensus Statement on Interpersonal Violence against Women," World Psychiatric Association Section on Women's Mental Health. Cairo, Egypt; September 2005.

"The Declaration of the Rights of Sex Workers in Europe," European Conference on Sex Work, Human Rights, Labour, and Migration. Brussels, Belgium; October 15–17, 2005.

"Demands," First European TransGender Council on Civil and Political Rights. Vienna, Austria; November 3–6, 2005.

"The Africa Declaration on Violence against Girls," Second International Policy Conference on the African Child. Addis Adaba, Ethiopia; May 11–12, 2006.

"Managua Declaration," Afro-Caribbean and Afro Latin-American Women's Network. Managua, Nicaragua, July 14-17, 2006.

"Declaration by Israeli Women in War." Israel; August 16, 2006.

"Manifesto for Gender Equality in Indian Media," EU-India Final Conference on Gender Equity in Media. New Delhi, India; December 9–10, 2006.

"Charte Pour la Promotion des Femmes en Mauritanie." 2007.

"Resolutions," International Conference on Kurdish Women for Peace and Equality, Kurdish National Congress of North America. Southern Kurdistan; March 8, 2007.

"Open Manifesto to the ANC's Fifty-second National Conference from LGBTI People." South Africa; December 5, 2007.

"Charter for Women's Rights—Ensuring Equality through the Constitution in Nepal." 2008.

"Charter of Rights of Women in Aceh." 2008.

"Sexual Rights: An International Planned Parenthood Declaration," International Planned Parenthood Federation. 2008.

"Sudanese Women Declaration on Darfur," First African Consultation on Darfur. Addis Ababa, Ethiopia; January 25, 2008.

"Charter of Demands." India; 2009.

"Iranian Women's Rights Charter." 2009.

"'Together We Must': The Women's Manifesto of Antigua and Barbuda." 2009.

"Kabul Declaration on Women's Rights," Family Law and Women's Rights in Muslim Countries. Kabul, Afghanistan; April 6, 2009.

"Declaration," National Federation of Dalit Women, Eighth National Convention. New Delhi, India; June 29, 2009.

"Conclusions and Recommendations" and "Resolution," First World Women's Conference: Decent Work—Decent Life for Women: Trade Unions Taking the Lead for Economic and Social Justice & Equality, International Trade Union Confederation. Brussels, Belgium; October 19–21, 2009.

"Declaration of the Trans Rights Conference." International Lesbian, Gay, Bisexual, Trans, and Intersex Association of Europe. October 28, 2009; Malta.

"The Addis Ababa Declaration on the Enhancement of Women's Participation and Representation in Decision Making Positions," IGAD Women Parliamentary Conference. Addis Ababa, Ethiopia; December 14–16, 2009.

"Manifesto for the Trans-Feminist Insurrection." 2010.

"Sri Lanka Women's Manifesto." 2010.

"Declaration: State of Women's Rights in Honduras since the Coup d'Etat," Central America Women's Network (CAWN). January 24, 2010.

"Dakar Declaration on Accelerated Girls' Education and Gender Equality," United Nations Girls' Education Initiative. Dakar, Senegal; May 20, 2010.

"Declaration of the European Feminist Gathering of the World March of Women," Third International Action of the World March of Women. Istanbul, Turkey; June 30, 2010.

"Declaration for Health, Life, and Defense of Our Lands, Rights, and Future Generations," International Indigenous Women's Environmental and Reproductive Health Symposium. Alamo, California; June 30–July 1, 2010.

"Declaration of the Federation of Vietnamese Au Co Women," Federation of Vietnamese Au Co Women. United States; September 2010.

"Egyptian Women's Charter: Partners in the Revolution and in Building Democratic Egypt," Egyptian Feminist Union. Egypt; 2011.

"Montevideo Declaration of Young Feminist Activists from Latin America and the Caribbean," DAWN. Montevideo, Uruguay; March 18–21, 2011.

"Undoing Borders: A Queer Manifesto," San Francisco Pride at Work. San Francisco, California; April 2011.

"The Kathmandu Declaration of Indigenous Woman," International Conference on the Evolving Indigenous Woman. Kathmandu, Nepal; April 21, 2011.

"The Kuwait Declaration on Gender Equality," Eighth Forum for the Future/Forum pour l'Avenir. Kuwait City, Kuwait; May 4–5, 2011.

"Afghan Women's Declaration," International Conference on Afghanistan. Bonn, Germany; December 5, 2011.

"Negombo Declaration," Regional Feminist Forum on Women's Economic, Social, and Cultural Rights. Negobomo, Sri Lanka; August 24–26, 2012.

"Charter of Demands," National Conference on Women's Social Security and Protection in India. New Delhi, India; May 6–7, 2013.

"Strengthening Quality Midwifery Care: Making Strides, Addressing Challenges," Second Global Midwifery Symposium. Kuala Lumpur, Malaysia; May 26–27, 2013.

"Manifesto," First National Meeting of Women for Construction of Feminist Socialism. Venezuela; 2014.

"WOLF Statement of Principles," Women's Liberation Front, January 2014.

"Statement." Istanbul Feminist Collective, March 7, 2014.

"Constitution," IDWF, International Domestic Workers Federation. September 30, 2014.

"Statement of the African Women's Groups," Fourth Conference on Climate Change and Development in Africa. Marrakech, Morocco; October 8–10, 2014.

"Declaration: Three Decades of Our Rights, Resistance, Demands, and Proposals," Second Central American Meeting of Women. Tegucigalpa, Honduras; December 11–12, 2014.

"National Woman's Manifesto of Uganda, 2016–2121: Unfinished Business." Uganda; 2015.

"Womanifesto," Ain't I A Woman Collective. 2015.

"Women's Manifesto," Women's Resource and Development Agency. Belfast, Northern Ireland; March 31, 2015.

"Declaration," PEO Central Working Women's Office, Pancyprian Federation of Labour. Nicosia, Cyprus; March 8, 2016.

PERMISSIONS

"Statutes of the Viennese Democratic Women's Association" (1848) and "Appeal of the Married Women and Maidens of Württemberg to the Soldiers of Germany" (1849) are reprinted with permission of German History in Documents and Images, German Historical Institute, Washington, D.C. (www.germanhistorydocs.ghi-dc.org).

The papers of the Federation of South African Women, including the 1954 "Charter and Aims," are held by the Historical Papers Research Archive at University of the Witwatersrand. See www.historicalpapers.wits.ac.za.

Permission to reprint the 1969 "Redstockings Manifesto" and the accompanying photo is granted by Redstockings of the Women's Liberation Movement.

The Radicalesbians' 1970 "Woman-Identified Woman" is part of the Atlanta Lesbian Feminist Alliance (ALFA) archives at the David M. Rubenstein Rare Book & Manuscript Library at Duke University.

Permission to reprint the 1971 Women's Liberation "Manifesto" is granted by Anna Yeatman and Anne Summers. Permission to use the image is granted by the photographer Sandy Turnbull Kilpatrick. Australian National University librarian Roxanne Missingham was incredibly resourceful in tracking down the document and photo.

The 1971 "Workshop Resolutions" from the First National Chicana Conference are reprinted with permission from Pathfinder Press Copyright © 1971.

Chicago Women's Liberation Union's 1972 "Statement of Purpose" and accompanying photo are reprinted with permission of the Chicago Women's Liberation Union Herstory Project.

The image and text of Ezrat Nashim's 1972 "Jewish Women Call for Change" are reprinted with permission of the Jewish Women's Archive.

The 1977 "Working Women's Charter" is used with permission of the New Zealand Council of Trade Unions.

The National Alliance of Black Feminists' 1977 "Workshop Resolutions" and "Everywoman's Bill of Rights" are from the Brenda Eichelberger/National Alliance of Black Feminists Papers (Box 1, Folder 22 and Box 9, Folder 7, respectively), Vivian G. Harsh Research Collection of Afro-American History and Literature, Chicago Public Library.

Permission to publish the 1982 "Anarchafeminist Manifesto" and accompanying logo is granted by the Anarcha-Feminist International.

Permission to reprint the 1985 "Women in Prison Manifesto" is granted by the organization Women in Prison.

FINRRAGE's 1985 "Resolution" and 1989 "Comilla Declaration," along with the group's logo, are reprinted with permission of Feminist International Network of Resistance against the New Reproductive Technologies and Genetic Engineering.

Permission to reprint the 1992 "Joint Resolution" of the First Asian Solidarity Conference on Military Sexual Slavery by Japan is granted by the Korean Council for the Women Drafted for Military Sexual Slavery by Japan.

The group's logo and 1992 "Women's Declaration on Population Policies" are reprinted with permission of the International Women's Health Coalition.

Permission to reprint the 2007 image accompanying the 1994 EZLN Women's Revolutionary Laws is granted by Melanie Cervantes and Jesus Barraza of DignidadRebelde.com.

The 1994 "Dyke Manifesto" and Lesbian Avengers graphic, designed by Carrie Moyer, are reprinted with permission of the Lesbian Avengers Documentary Project.

The logo and 1996 "Platform Papers" of the National Asian Pacific American Women's Forum are reprinted with their permission.

The 1997 International Women's Working Conference's "Final Statement: Women and Children, Militarism, and Human Rights," and images, are reprinted with permission of the International Women's Network Against Militarism.

The image from "Disabled Women on the Web" and the "Priorities for Actions" and "Conclusions" from the 1998 Changing Borders Conference are used with permission of the Disability Social History Project.

Permission to reprint the 2001 "Gender Violence and the Prison Industrial Complex," and the accompanying logo, is granted by INCITE! Women, Gender Non-Conforming, and Trans People of Color* Against Violence.

Permission to reprint the 2001 "Resolutions to Member Organisations" and accompanying image is granted by Women's Ordination Worldwide and We Are Church Ireland.

Permission to reprint "The Manukan Declaration" from 2004, and the accompanying photograph, is granted by the Indigenous Women's Biodiversity Network.

"Letter to Women Legislators of the Coalition of the Willing," from 2004, and the group's logo, are reprinted with permission of Women Against Rape.

Permission to use the logo and 2005 "Manifesto: Stop the Violence" is granted by the Saturviit Inuit Women's Association of Nunavik.

Permission to reprint "Survivors of Prostitution and Trafficking Manifesto: Who Represents Women in Prostitution?" and the accompanying logo is granted by the Coalition Against Trafficking in Women. According to the organization, the document is from a 2005 press conference held at the European Parliament where survivors of prostitution from Belgium, Korea, the United States, and the United Kingdom spoke against legislation normalizing prostitution as "sex work," and was based on a similar 2003 statement issued at the first National Conference of seventy-five Filipina survivors of prostitution calling on governments to resist legalizing or decriminalizing the sex industry.

The Feminist Dalit Organization granted permission to use their logo and reprint their 2007 "Dalit Women's Charter."

Permission to reprint the 2007 "Women's Declaration on Food Sovereignty" and the accompanying image is granted by Nyéléni: Forum for Food Sovereignty.

Permission to use the 2008 "Guatemalan Feminist Declaration" and accompanying image is granted by Sandra Moran.

The 2008 "Declaration against Violent Extremism" and accompanying photo are reprinted with permission of Sisters Against Violent Extremism (office@women-without-borders.org).

The World Social Forum's 2009 "Women's Assembly Declaration" and image are reprinted with permission of the International Lesbian, Gay, Bisexual, Trans, and Intersex Association.

Musawah's 2009 "Framework for Action" and accompanying graphic are reprinted with the group's permission.

The "Rio Declaration" and the group's image are used with the permission of MenEngage.

The First Continental Summit of Indigenous Women's 2009 "Manifesto" and image are reprinted with permission of *Links International Journal of Socialist Renewal*.

The 2011 "Manifesto of Young Feminists of Europe" and accompanying image are reprinted with permission of the Network of Young Feminists of Europe—World March of Women.

The 2012 "Declaration of Rights for Future Generations and Bill of Responsibilities for Those Present," and accompanying image, are reprinted with permission of the Women's Congress for Future Generations.

The European Women's Lobby has granted permission to reprint their logo and their 2012 "Manifesto—Women's Socio Economic Rights and Gender Equality from a Life-Cycle Perspective."

CELEM's 2013 "Deciding Makes Us Free" and accompanying graphic are reprinted with permission of European Women's Lobby.

The Free Democratic Women's Movement's 2013 "Final Resolution" and images are reprinted with permission of Peace in Kurdistan.

The 2013 "Manifesto" of the International Women's Commission of Via Campesina, and accompanying image, are used with permission of Via Campesina, which can be contacted at viacampesina.org.

The 2013 "Women's Climate Declaration" and accompanying graphic are reprinted with permission of artist Lori Waselchuk and the Women's Earth and Climate Action Network (WECAN) International.

The 2014 "Action Agenda" and accompanying graphic are reprinted with permission of RESURJ, Realizing Sexual and Reproductive Justice.

The 2014 "Manifesto" and logo of Indigenous Women Against the Sex Industry are reprinted with the group's permission.

The 2014 "Feminist Principles of the Internet" and accompanying image are reprinted with permission of the Association for Progressive Communications.

The 2014 "Declaration: LBT Women in Fiji, for Gender Equality, Human Rights, and Democracy," and the group's logo, are used with permission of Diverse Voices and Action for Equality.

The 2014 "Position Statement: Femicide" and accompanying logo are reprinted with permission of the Canadian Council of Muslim Women.

The 2015 "Charter of Female Comics Creators against Sexism" is reprinted with permission of the Collectif des créatrices de bande dessinée contre le sexisme. Artist Julie Maroh gave permission to use the group's image.

The 2015 "Rural Women's Manifesto" and accompanying graphic are reprinted with permission of the Northern Ireland Rural Women's Network.

Permission to reprint the 2015 "Statement and Action Agenda" is given by the Girls in Emergencies Collaborative.

For other documents and images, we have records of repeated good faith efforts to get permissions, but were ultimately unable to locate a copyright holder or get a response; for the most part, these involve manifestos from groups that no longer exist. These documents are overwhelmingly in the public domain. We are most appreciative of the good will behind every group's willingness to be included in this volume. No one we asked said "no."

ABOUT THE EDITORS

Penny Weiss is Professor and Chair of Women's and Gender Studies at Saint Louis University. She is the author of *Canon Fodder: Historical Women Political Thinkers, Conversations with Feminism: Political Theory and Practice,* and *Gendered Community: Rousseau, Sex, and Politics.* Dr. Weiss has also coedited *Feminist Reflections on Mary Astell, Feminist Reflections on Emma Goldman,* and *Feminism and Community.* She has three children and is about to become a grandma!

Megan Brueske is a PhD candidate in Saint Louis University's English Department. Her dissertation explores community violence in twentieth-century American novels by women. She currently lives in Dallas, Texas, with her husband and son.

dowry, 42; dowry hunting, 462, 616; dowry-related killings, 312, 609–10, 630. *See also* marriage

dyke, 221–24; Dyke Manifesto, 339–40

economy: care economy, 559, 639; definitions of, 348, 424, 491; and the ecosystem, 564–65; feminist alternative models, 159–60, 317, 328, 475, 601–2, 637; feminist analysis of the, 8, 41, 214, 240, 272, 279–78, 320, 553; improvements to, 325, 442, 459–60, 487–88, 556–71, 572, 658; oppressive/discriminatory effects of economic systems, 152, 231, 233–34, 273, 296–97, 481, 552; women's contributions to, 36–37, 184, 289, 315, 606; women's role in, 120, 122, 261, 321–22, 348, 391, 513, 558, 650

ecosystem: 406, 408, 519, 540, 542–44, 546, 562–564, 593; ecocide, 565

education: access to 367–69, 657–58; adult education, 176, 548–49, 560; for change, 148, 207–8, 210, 427, 607; higher education/college, 72–73,175, 215, 369; impact on Indigenous Peoples, 407–8; inform public, 324; language spoken, 75, 363, 582; moral, 89, 134, 136, 173; parent-teacher conferences, 151; physical, 137, 354–55; primary education, 41–42, 74, 125–26, 150, 174, 570; race, 278–79; reform, 328; religious, 19, 41, 414, 444; secular, 134, 150; sex/reproduction education, 174, 195, 309, 318, 444, 535, 537, 555, 574; in South Africa, 348–49; special needs, 175, 192; to stop violence against women, 335, 351, 444, 554–55; vocational, 15, 135–37, 174, 376; voter, 354, 364; and welfare, 602–3

egalitarian, 3, 15, 226, 359, 424–25, 452, 494, 641

election: on feminist platforms in Sweden, 597–604 and India, 605–17; process for female candidates in Sierra Leone, 396–98; and South Sudan; 520–24

emancipation: "of our bodies," 634–35; "real" emancipation, 332–35; from religious institutions, 555; Society for the Emancipation of Women (Paris), 69–75; in South Africa, 204–5; of women, 122–123, 180; of the working class, 159

England, 29–35, 299–301; Brighton, 352–56; Leicester, 548–50; London, 258–60, 415–21, 428–34

epistemology 14, 100, 465

equal opportunities, 8, 41–42, 87, 167, 243, 258, 522; for communication, 328; in education, 18, 70–73, 81–82, 89, 92–93, 103, 108–9, 112, 134, 159, 178, 193 243; and the EEOC, 216; in employment, 40–43, 71, 73, 79, 89, 95–97, 178, 187, 189–90, 203, 429, 447; 243; in politics, 72–73, 80, 87–88, 92–93, 96, 100, 119–20, 123, 187–88, 216, 323, 333, 350, 545, 619

equal pay, 95, 97, 98–99, 102, 108–9, 131, 159, 178, 190; the Lowell Factory Girls Association Strike for, 53–55; the wage gap, 215, 560–561, 618

equal rights: on basis of sex, 211, 335, 478, 506, 618, 647; between men and women, 104, 105–6, 188, 214, 333, 466–67, 601; concept of, 347, 575; in the family, 298, 461, 508–9; in politics, 307; to protection under the law, 128, 158–59, 189; for women, 86–88, 90–93, 128, 216, 278, 345, 476, 557; for working women, 170, 553. *See also* equal opportunities; equal pay; Equal Rights Amendment; rights

Equal Rights Amendment (ERA), 165–66, 257, 281–82

Estonia, Tallinn, 617–20

eugenics, 305–10

Europe. *See individual countries*: Australia; Austria; Bulgaria; Croatia; Czech Republic; England; Estonia; Finland; France; Germany; Greece; Hungary; Italy; Malta; Netherlands; Northern Ireland; Norway; Romania; Spain; Sweden; Switzerland

European Union, 489, 557, 618, 674

eviction, 479, 481, 527

exploitation: of labor, 53, 72, 159, 167, 323, 588; sexual, 242, 371–72, 423, 457, 497, 514, 612. *See also* capitalism; sweatshops

extremism, 10, 625; anti-Romani rhetoric, 527; opposition to 498–99; religious, 24, 668; violent extremism, 413

family: criticism of marriage/family institution, 239–42, 254, 265, 298; democratization of, 15–16, 238, 300, 317; disabled women and, 447; diversity in family structures, 561, 641; family honor and femicide, 632; family status, freedom from, 335, 497; feminist criticism of, 227–28; in Islam, 505–9; models of, 274, 561, 603; nuclear, 209, 254, 298, 496, 561; proposed equality within, 70, 72, 328, 426–27, 461, 477, 506–7; and religion, 414; sex roles within, 1, 166–68, 181, 498, 517, 567, 588, 616; as source of oppression, 289–90, 312, 315, 333, 343, 350; in Soviet Union, 320–24; in times of conflict, 403, 418, 469–70, 499, 541, 652–53; violence within, 315–16, 419–20, 430, 434–35, 470, 512, 646; women limited to, 224, 232, 252; women's financial role within, 33, 36, 122, 206, 217, 234, 392, 540, 586. *See also* care work; parenting

individualism, 70, 670; and modern society, 588; of rights, 561; in South Asia, 317; and violence, 386

individuality: development of, 120, 328, 422; and the divine image, 568; right to exercise, 119; suppression of, 240, 326

Indonesia, Jakarta, 583–89

industrialization, 64, 160, 307, 409, 475, 539–40, 542, 592

internalization: of different cultures, 311; of domination, 12; of oppression, 4, 23, 87, 224–25, 228, 290, 567; of sexism, 331

International Women's Day, 121, 398–400, 548–49, 647

internet: and disability, 375–76; Feminist Principles, 623–26; manifestos by/from online communities: 402–5, 525–26, 534–38, 565–70; as space for community organizing 368–69, 374

intersectional/ity, 41; analysis, 213, 297; of race and gender, 204–5

intersex: discrimination against, 552; freedom of identity, 495, 555; represented in movement, 594, 624; Third International Intersex Forum, 594–97

Intimate Partner Violence (IPV), 386, 512, 547, 630.

Iran, 476–79

Ireland, Dublin, 388–91

Islam, 312–14, 476–79, 503–9, 579–80, 610, 631, 633, 666–68

Israel, Jerusalem, 436–39

Italy, Rome, 226–30, 669–71

Japan: Naha City (Okinawa), 370–73; Tokyo, 169–71

Judaism, 577; anti-Semitism, 331; "Jewish Women Call for Change," (New York, 1972), 13, 251–53; Jewish Jerusalem, 437; and racial persecution, 198

judiciary, 74, 103, 131, 347, 610; court of justice, 147, 395, 484; independent, 325, 328, 425; "law as obstacle," 207

justice, 425, 533, 627, 667; economic, 54, 364, 473, 481; and food sovereignty, 587; gender, 5, 23, 388, 412, 577; restorative, 565; in the Rio Declaration, 509–16; sex inequality and injustice, 119–20; social, xv, 12, 202, 216, 299, 385–88, 394, 414, 629; transitional, 470, 472, 570–72. See also justice system

justice system, 299, 347, 384–86; failure to address crimes against women, 347, 609; and penalizing rape, 416, 418; separate community response, 387, 667; training for, 603;

victim-oriented, 458, 555. See also judiciary; justice; law

Kenya, Nairobi, 468–73, 533–34

Kurd/ish, 579–83, 674, 675

labor movements, 160–161, 164, 259, 576

Latter Day Saints (LDS), 565, 568

law, the: demand for improvement, 80, 88–89, 206, 347; equality under, 33–35, 92, 166, 189, 291, 347, 429–30, 508, 571; ineffectiveness of, 8, 10, 113, 385, 610–11; and justice, 458, 505, 563; participation in forming, 67–68, 72; as tool for change, 150, 217, 345, 430, 555, 586, 607; as tool for control, 6–7, 20, 34, 78, 102–3, 120, 205, 207, 298, 312, 489, 671; Women's Revolutionary Law, 15, 342–44

leadership: development, 655; feminist approaches to, 449, 452–53, 531, 545; lack of women in, 355, 651; in the military, 344; obstacles to women in, 41, 295, 323; in religious communities, 251–52, 414; transformational, 520–21, 571

lesbians, 265, 280; Avengers, 339–42; Daughters of Bilitis, 209–10; and feminism, 551, 627, 636–37; hate crimes against, 554; lesphobia, 502; Radicalesbians, 221–26; and sexuality, 495

LGBTI: in Africa, 533–34; and the Audre Lorde Project, 666–69; in Fiji, 627–629; sexual identity as rebellion against patriarchy, 221. See also lesbians

literacy programs, 179, 382, 454, 522, 572; near universality of literacy in Estonia, 618

machismo, 231, 255, 518; macho, 223, 237, 331, 343, 491; Young Lords, 230–34. See also male chauvinism; manhood; men; sissy

Malaysia: Kuala Lumpur, 503–509; Manukan (Sabah), 405–12; Port Dickson, 623–26

male chauvinism, 237, 311–14, 316; and machismo, 231, 233

male supremacy, 17, 427; and lesbianism, 223; Redstockings, 219–20; as societal construction, 450

Mali, Selingue, 465–67

malnutrition: in India, 611; international crisis, 485–486; leads to trafficking, 479; maternal mortality rate, 396. See also hunger

Malta, Valletta, 594–97

manhood: defined by capitalism, 231; defined by dominance, 514; defined by violence, 512; and sex roles, 315; and sexual prowess, 234, 510–11. See also boys: as soldiers; masculinity; men marriage: and adultery, 106–7, 158; arguments against, 228, 265; in the Chicana community, 244, 248; choice to enter into, 42, 216, 344, 508; equality between spouses, 168, 197, 350, 426, 568; feminist approach to, 69, 217, 474, 505, 508; forced, 383, 554, 631, 671; in Islamic law 505–9; marital rape, 512, 608, 610, 616; marriage/family institution, 239–42, 254, 265, 298; marrying into slavery 42, 57, 59; nontraditional, 335, 363–64; as patriarchal system, 222, 254; as system of oppression, 72, 78, 101, 105–7, 207, 232, 383; violence within, 343, 434, 632, 646. *See also* divorce

Marx, 157, 222, 229, 236, 261, 273, 298

masculinity: assumed default, 70, 641, 650; definitions of, 510; masculine supremacy, 229; masculinists, 497; masculinized woman, 38; and the military, 371; Peruvian Masculinity Network, 546–48; societal constructs of, 239, 292–93, 642, 665. *See also* boys; men; sissy; tomboy

Massachusetts: Boston, 269–77; Lowell, 53–55, 64–66; Salem, 50–53; Stoneham, 98–99; Worcester, 90–94

maternity: as a dilemma, 228; education about duties, 125, 196; employment benefits, 108, 122, 141, 161–62, 187, 243, 259, 348, 452, 614; and healthcare, 179, 192, 208, 360; as obstacle to employment, 215; maternal mortality rates, 396, 400, 485; as a societal concern, 310. *See also* mothers; parenting

media/press/journalism, 33, 352, 373; antislavery publications, 52, 86–87, 70, 90; critique of, 24–25, 516; diverse representation in, 201–3; media's negative portrayal of women as masculine, 37, 39, 58, 90; publication/preservation of manifesto, 39, 177; as part of the solution, 52, 79–80, 89, 91, 93, 95, 96, 115–16, 139, 328, 341–42, 463–64, 499, 530, 569, 597; publication run by women's groups, 33, 64, 105, 149, 157, 179, 185, 209, 230, 276, 333, 340, 535; women working in, 201–3. *See also* media/press/journalism as tool

media/press/journalism as tool: of abolitionists, 61; of feminism/feminists, 17–18, 24, 313, 330; for oppression, 7–8, 11, 516; of people of color, 114, 280, of Romani people, 527, 529; of women, 17, 495–96

men, 17, 255–56; as allies, 4, 23, 78, 82–83, 63, 205–7, 241, 262, 568; benefit from system they made, 174, 322–23, 346, 455; and care work, 298, 359, 561, 566–67, 639; costs of sexism to men, 223, 334, 386, 509, 548; on engaging men and boys in achieving gender equal-

ity, *v*, 509–16; against gender violence, 388, 546–48; and militarism, 154, 292, 403, 419; as oppressors, 179, 219, 222, 231–32, 247, 289–90, 440, 566, 603, 628, 632; personal responsibility, 358; and sex roles, 238–39, 283; stereotypes of, 527; victims of rape, 417, 420; in women's organizations, 82–83, 100. *See also* fathers; machismo; male chauvinism; male supremacy; manhood; masculinity; sex roles

Mexico: Reidia (Yucatan), 149–151; Chiapas, 342–44

micro-credit, 572

microfinance, 612; criticisms of, 483

Middle East. *See* Iran; Syria; Turkey

migrant labor, 364, 480–83

militarism, 323, 480; in America, 645; in Australia, 152–56; and demilitarisation, 444; effects on rural women, 480–83; in Honduras, 577–78; intersectional system of, 130–31, 370–73; impact on children, 370; and men, 154, 292, 403, 419; militaristic domination, 323; militarization and violence, 313, 370, 492; opposition to, 436, 438, 475; and sexual slavery, 336–39; in South Asia, 312–17

minimum wage, 129–31, 259, 608, 614, 656

mining, 578; damage to environment, 406, 409, 502, 540, 565, 584; and indigenous land, 481, 492, 541–42

mothers: in education, 367–68; education about, 115, 125 139; feminist, 10; freedom to choose motherhood, 234, 266, 394, 414, 554, 573–74; in Judaism, 252–253; moral obligation to take action, 48, 57, 61, 73, 143, 152, 156, 568; and Mormon feminism, 565–68; Mother Nature, 479, 481; "Mothers Schools," 498; parenting rights, 103, 141–42, 291; patriarchal power over, 228, 232, 310; paying, 124–25, 162, 187, 191–92, 194; peace mothers initiative, 581; in prison, 300; rhetoric of, 47, 67, 73; role of, in moral education, 61, 96, 115, 247; social contributions of, 69; working, 248, 259, 656; unwed/single, 133, 138, 140, 248, 349, 443, 552; women are all "natural mothers of all children," 141. *See also* family; fathers; maternity; parenting

Muslim, 503–9; 13, 312, 314, 566, 613, 615–16, 630–33, 668

nationalism, 157–59, 236, 269, 271, 314, 326, 600

neocolonialism, 269, 451, 664–65

neoliberalism, and the body, 635; definition of, 670; economic harm, 8, 343, 608, 639; and food sovereignty, 465–66; and patriarchy, 24, 490

Nepal, Kathmandu, 453–56

Netherlands: Amsterdam, 201–4, 302–4; The Hague, 143–48

New Left, 226, 359

New York, 36–37, 251–53, 260–64, 339–42, 590–94; in 1837, 56–64; in 1969, 218–20; in 1970, 220–26, 230–37, 256–58, 356–61, 484–89; Albany, 66–68; Brooklyn, 666–69; Seneca Falls, 75–81

New Zealand, 267–68

NGOs (non-governmental organizations), 5–6, 17, 412, 422, 519, 635; and climate change, 543, 545–46; in Hungary, 332; protests against, 392; Rio Declaration, 510–11, 516

Nicaragua, Anuncio, 398–401

nonviolence, 66, 127–28, 498–99. *See also* anti-militarism; peace

North America. *See* Canada; Cherokee Lands; Mexico, United States

North Carolina, 37–39

Northern Ireland, Dungannon (County Tyrone), 655–59

Norway, Oslo, 296–99

nuclear war/weapons, 314; environmental impact of, 409, 565; and systemic violence, 387; and War on Terror, 482

Ohio: Akron, 94–97; Salem, 86–90

oligarchy, 293, 295, 518

oppression: in Afghan nations, 382; and apartheid, 345–46; of Black America, 643, 645; Black feminism's definition, 269–70, 272–73; and the body, 635, 638; and capitalism, 231, 233, 265, 270, 272; challenging women's movement's views, 255; in Chicana communities, 244–45, 248; economic, 387, 552; in Europe, 598; in the family, 343; of female role, 222; institutionalized, 363; internalized, 23, 87, 89, 220, 225, 255, 270, 288; intersectional approach to, 14, 17, 270, 296–98, 385, 450, 481, 497, 533, 636, 646; 551; in Latin America, 288, 295, 517; of men, 513; in the Middle East, 579–80, 648; as an obstacle to learning, 549; by patriarchal capitalism, 491, 584, 588; by patriarchy, 316, 364, 422, 449, 451, 528; and prostitution, 23, 234, 440, 621; and religion, 248, 388; resistance, 496; in rural communities, 588; sexual, 271; and slavery, 61; social, 88–89; in South Asia, 315–16; state, 49, 312, 399, 483; systems of, 4, 12, 23–24, 76, 96, 104, 119–20, 218–20, 227, 240, 250, 270; and the Third World, 230–37; world free from, *v*, 423–24, 438, 451, 557; of workers, 94, 154, 290

orphans: and education, 134–36; orphanages, 138, 432; of war, 85, 153, 519

pacifism, 14, 21, 127, 333. *See also* non-violence

Palestine, 198, 437–38, 502, 646–649

parenting: disabled women and parenthood, 446–47; effective, 567; equal legal rights, 141, 158, 168; equal roles in family, 166, 168, 359–60, 509, 619; groups, 300; in the Inuit community, 435; parenting leave, 267–68, 560, 567, 601, 619; positive, 435; single parents, 561; social parenthood, 310; sons preferred over daughters, 42. *See also* fathers; mothers

paternalism, 334, 525

patriarchy: and the body, 638; burdens women disproportionately, 577; cause of climate change, 540; definition of, 76, 449, 622; and female sexuality, 221–26, 338; intersectional analysis of, 7, 24, 296, 325–16, 346, 635; liberation from, 273; men against, 510; and oppression, 77, 257, 528, 579; patriarchal-capitalist system 9, 130–31, 159–60, 206, 490–92, 501, 588; perpetuates violence, 233–34, 581–83, 631, 670; relation to feminism, 450–51, 496, 622, 664; resistance to, 448, 624; source of inequality, 288; systemic, 94, 100, 103, 589

peace, 201, 338, 425; anti-militarism, 124, 143–48, 370; Australian Women's Peace Army, 15, 152–56; feminist approaches to, 499; peace-building, 84–85, 186–88, 396, 427, 436–38, 571, 582; peacekeeping, 131, 371, 432; Peace Council, 412; peacemakers, 187, 403–4, 498, 590; peace with justice, 436–37; permanent peace, 205, 208; right to peace, 563; Statement of Conscience: A Feminist Vision for Peace, 19, 402–4; Widows for Peace Through Democracy, 36, 428–33. *See also* pacifism; non-violence

peasants, 2, 8, 40, 293–94, 315–16, 465–67, 553, 583–89

pedagogy, 134–36, 602

Pennsylvania, Philadelphia, 99–104, 254–55

pension, 259, 348, 350, 365, 443, 459, 553, 557–558, 560–61, 602, 606, 608, 611–14; for widows, 197–98, 429, 432

personhood, 225, 445, 451, 469

Peru: Puno, 516–20; Lima, 546–48, 634–39. *See also* masculinity: Peruvian Masculinity Network

Philippines: Global City, 211–12; Manila, 473–76; Mandaluyong City, 538–46

police: harassment, 209, 254, 490; response to violence against women, 102, 351, 385–87, 416, 420, 440–41, 444, 463, 554, 606–7; systemic corruption, 269, 578, 642–45, 600, 668; violence committed by, *v*, 384–85, 527–80, 667

rural women, 454; and climate change, 589; Dalit women, 460–64; discrimination against, 541; and feminism, 13; and globalization/capitalism, 9, 487–88, 586, 588; oppression against, 315; resources for, 196, 349–50, 572, 659; "Rural Women's Declaration" (Asia), 479–84; "Rural Women's Manifesto" (Ireland), 655–59; and violence, 588

Rwanda, Kigali, 421–28

safety net: for API women, 364–66; and welfare, 599; for widows, 126

scapegoat, 248, 333–34

science, 73; in education, 137, 140; as morally dangerous to women, 43; and patriarchy, 4, 305–10

secular: laws, 505; Indian, 314; schools, 5, 134, 150; society, 574–75; state/government, 399, 491, 578, 608, 613, 636, 670; women's movement, 476

security: climate of insecurity, 413; definitions of, 370–72, 560, 600; economic, 194–95; existential, 334; and the family, 507–8; financial, 442; human, 598, 603; judicial, 575; national, 314, 457, 483; personal/individual, 304, 351, 432; political, 578, 599; in schools, 498; social, 189, 259, 393, 442–43, 561, 602. See also citizen/citizenship; food: (in)security; state violence

segregation, 368, 383, 626; by race, 51, 63, 527, 529–530; by sex, 4, 29, 180, 205, 476, 478

self-care, 629

self-defense: battered women, 385; as justification for war, 143–45, 155, 338; in mass political actions, 294; right to armed self-defense, 236; training, 375, 447

self-esteem/self-confidence, 10, 73, 327, 349, 375–76, 496, 528, 557, 629, 641, 656

separatism, 317; lesbian separatism, 272–73

sex, 618; and discrimination in sports, 354; intellectual difference, 43, 95, 120, 150–51; and power in relationships, 274; and roles in society, 206; as separate from gender, 227

sex roles, 238–43; breaking out of, 150–51, 547–48; challenged by lesbianism, 222–26; equality in, 217–18, 265; fear of deviation from, 29; guide to, 41; in Judaism, 252; for men, 238–39, 505; sex/gender dissent, 639; socialization into, 241; tyranny of men over women, 76, 119

sex work, 391; and adolescent girls, 653; indigenous women against sex industry, 620–23; and intersectionality, 620; safety for workers, 348; sex tourism industry, 336, 663. See also prostitution; trafficking; sexual slavery

sexism, 238; accurate portrayals of sexism in the media, 442; anti-sexism, 195, 272, 641; in the arts, 330; in comics, 641; in criminal justice system, 416, 420; in culture, 556; effects on women, 222, 548; as the foundation of inequality, 220, 227, 250, 484; hierarchy of the sexes, 228; internalization of, 257–58, 331; in the media, 266, 516, 649–51; nonsexist 277, 318, 345; in other movements, 209, 265, 270, 576; and religion, 281, 389–90, 414, 555, 569; "Reverse sexism," 331

sexual assault. See rape

sexual harassment, 603; protection from, 47, 397, 439, 443, 512, 608; in schools, 349; victims of, 542, 603; in the workplace, 348, 386, 614–15

sexual justice, 278, 425, 534–35

sex(ual) object: 219, 223–25, 239, 327, 660; and degradation of human relationships, 334; in the media, 495, 555; physical difference, 95, 135, 150–51, 273, 548; and sexual fascism, 234; and third world women, 231; women withhold sex as tool, 84–85. See also body/bodies

sexual orientation, 223; as basis for discrimination, 213, 449, 475, 552, 607–608; and prejudice, 209–10. See also gay/male homosexuality; gender; heterosexism; heteronormativity; heterosexual(ity); HIV/AIDS; Intersex; lesbians; LGBTI; sexual orientation; trans; two-spirited

sexual politics, 271–72; sexuality awareness education, 282; of widows, 429; of wives, 233; women's right to expression of sexuality, 265, 358, 424, 482, 490–91, 502

sexual slavery, 336–339, 403–4

sexual violence, 385, 416–20, 468–73, 472, 512, 547, 605; and asylum, 427; in Inuit communities, 434–36; and Native women, 318; shelters, 572; in South Africa, 351; sexual abuse, 271, 375; as weapon of war, 501; against women before incarceration, 299; against women with disabilities, 445, 447

sexuality: and the Chicana community, 247; controlled by marriage/family institutions, 240, 254, 316; of disabled women, 447; feminist approach to, 555; and globalization, 501; as immoral, 233; hypersexualization of youth, 494; and the internet, 623–26; laws concerning, 140, 533–34; male sexuality, 621, 623; and morality, 569; non-heteronormative, 639; positive attitudes towards, 229, 247, 283, 412, 525; and the pro-porn movement, 525–26; sexual pleasure, 262, 341; sexual relationships, 242, 358–59. See also virginity

Sharia/Shar'iah, 447

victim/victimization: definitions of, 470; male victimization, 218, 388, 434; prejudice against victims, 418, 420; secondary victimization by the justice system, 101, 351, 416, 434, 603; victim-oriented support, 458, 463, 468–73, 555; victims of economic systems, 242, 246, 279; victims of state violence, 386; victims of systems, 220, 363; victims of war, 81, 147, 247, 370–71, 438, 571–72

Vietnam: resisting invasion, 236–37; U.S. war in, 25, 244, 247

violence, 402–403, 616; backlash against women, 610; and the criminal justice system, 384–88, 607; crisis in Inuit communities, 434–36; election violence, 522–23; in the family, 335; as form of oppression, 297, 414, 554–55; het-erosexist, 513; in Honduras, 577; as human rights violation, 316; in marriage, 158; racist, 502; and militarization, 313, 370, 492; right to be free from, 344, 423, 437, 451, 519, 575; statistics, 318; in times of war, 325, 371. *See also* armed conflict; battered women; femi-cide/feminicide; Intimate Partner Violence; nonviolence; nuclear war/weapons; pacifism; police; rape; security; self-defense; sexual violence; state violence; stoning; terrorism; victim/victimization; violence; violence against women

violence against women, 351, 383, 468–73, 510, 532; against Dalit women, 462–63; against disabled women, 445; against rural women, 481–82; definitions of, 431; in Europe, 552, 554–55; "Men Against Gender Violence" (Peru), 546–48; prevention of, 444; prostitu-tion as, 440; in times of war, 325, 372, 468–70; shelters for women, 572. *See also* battered women; domestic violence; femicide/femini-cide; violence

virginity/chastity: 95, 97,141–42, 227, 232

voices: black voices, 663; of Cherokee women, 47; collective, 51; demand to be heard, 39, 84, 526, 573; diversity of, xvi, 2, 494–95, 625, 627–28, 636–37; of female leaders, 2, 504; feminist voice, 17, 557, 590–91, 663; legitimizing silenced and marginalized voices, 5, 9, 11, 14–15, 23; in public sphere, 76, 100, 153; raising

against hostile states/politics, 499, 502, 517, 577, 590; for rural women in public policy, 585, 655; silencing of, 78, 179, 181, 312, 624–25; women's political voice, 34, 39–41, 56, 59, 67, 87–89, 92; of young women, 653–54

vulnerability: economic, 485, 571, 583, 618–19; of groups facing multiple oppressions, 432, 469; physical, 482; universality of, 664; to violence, 387; the vulnerable have solutions, 590, 593

Washington, D.C.: in 1888, 108–10; in 1896, 110–16; in 1919, 160–65; in 1922, 165–68; in 1966, 212–18; in 1990s, 329–32

welfare, 555; rights, 257, 260, 276, 598–603

whore: First World Whores' Congress, 302–3; survival of prostitution, 440; word as insult, 233–34; word as vernacular translation of widow, 428

widows, 36–37, 126, 519, 566; pursuit of pensions, 197–98, 611; Widow's Charter for peace (London), 428–33

womanhood: American, 102; and anti-colonial nationalism, 315; cultural understanding of, 47; and disability, 446–48; gifts of, 153, 156; personal development of, 92–93; and personhood, 225, 445; rituals for, 541; uplifts, 113, 115

woman-identified, 221–22

Women in Black: joined by Feminist Network in Hungary, 333; Thirteenth International Conference, 436–39

women of color, 52, 161, 230, 620; analysis centering, 387; facing multiple forms of op-pression, 260; violence against, 384–88. *See also* Aboriginal/Aborigines; Black women/Negro women; Chicana

World Bank, 467; criticism of 481–82, 485–88

WTO (World Trade Organization), effect on food and agriculture, 467, 482, 488; and globalization, 481

Xenophobia, 312, 422, and LGBTSTGNC POC, 666–68

Yugoslavia, Belgrade, 325–32